INDUSTRIAL AND ORGANIZATIONAL PSYCHOLOGY

INDUSTRIAL AND ORGANIZATIONAL PSYCHOLOGY

(In Two Volumes)

(Volume - I)

Dr. H.L. Kaila

KALPAZ PUBLICATION

Delhi - 110052

Industrial and Organizational Psychology

Rs. 1500 (Set)

ISBN : 81-7835-525-6 (set)
ISBN : 81-7835-526-4 (vol.1)

Published in 2006 in India by
Kalpaz Publications,
C, 30 Satyawati Nagar,
Delhi-110052
email : kalpaz@hotmail.com

Laser Type Setting by: Mega Graphics, Delhi
Printed at: Salasar Imaging System, Delhi

Contents

Preface

Subjects and specializations dealing with human behaviour are increasingly becoming relevant, popular, and acceptable in the societies across the world. Psychology through its scientific endeavours has contributed adequately in the understanding of human behaviour in various settings and contexts; but still a lot of remains to be achieved, as the human dynamics and complexities are ever changing and increasing.

At the same time, the competitive and globalizing world has added and posed enough challenges to the psychologists and other mental health experts to address issues that have sustained and become integral part of everyday living, be it media, technology, terrorism, politics or religion, which impact human behaviour to a larger extent in our societies.

As far as psychology education and training is concerned, the universities across the world are responding continuously to the needs of mankind by introducing and offering new specializations in psychology to its students, by holding cross-cultural dialogues among the behavioural science professionals, and publishing new researches in order to equip themselves better in the service of humanity.

The applied fields of psychology especially the industrial and organizational psychology has greater responsibilities to serve the organizations with its established theories, principles and researches conducted in the diverse work settings across cultures.

This publication has touched upon the relevant areas of industrial and organizational psychology such as Foundations of Organizational Behaviour, Work Motivation, Group Behaviour, Leadership, Human Resource Management, Resourcing the Organization, Performance Appraisal, Developing Human Resource, Perspectives of Workplace Counselling, Quality of Work Life. Training and Development, Stress in Organizations, Core Competencies, Assessment Centre, Performance Management, Ergonomics, and Absenteeism and Managers as Counsellors, Behavioural Based Safety in Organizations, Counselling in Organizations and Managerial Problems in Indian Organizations.

This book titled **Industrial and Organization Psycholoy** shall be useful for psychology, commerce and management students, teachers and courses. The practicing managers also would find it a good reference material.

Dr H.L. Kalia

Introduction

This book on **Industrial and Organizational Psychology** has been based on the literature review of more than 200 references on the subjects mentioned below keeping in view the topics that usually become part of the syllabus of psychology, commerce and management courses.

Chapter 1. Foundations of Organizational Behaviour discusses classical organization, theory and design, modern organizational theory, information processing view of organizations, contingency, ecological, and learning organization, modern organizational designs, project designs, the virtual organization, international organizational behaviour.

Chapter 2. Theories of Work Motivation reflects on theories of motivation, content theories, process theories, reinforcement theories, Theory X and Theory Y, reinforcement theory, attribution theory, etc.

Chapter 3. Dynamics of Group Behaviour describes groups, formal groups, informal groups, formation of work group, managing conflict among group, group dynamics, teams, special kinds of groups etc.

Chapter 4. Leadership elaborates on leadership characteristics, leadership studies, transformational leadership, transactional leadership, charismatic leadership, leadership styles...

Chapter 5. Introduction to Human Resource Management mentions the concept of human resource, human resource management, characteristics of HRM, HRM versus personnel management, HRM versus HRD, theories of HRM, conditions favourable and unfavourable to HRM, current status of HRM etc.

Chapter 6. Resourcing the Organization describes human resource planning, and recruitment planning.

Chapter 7. Performance Appraisal Mentions Objectives for performance appraisal, legalities of performance appraisal, components of performance appraisal, sources of performance appraisal information, and relevant objectives for performance appraisal.

Chapter 8. Developing Human Resource refers to training and development, training the trainers, post-training environment, evaluation of training, grid training.

Chapter 9. Employee Counselling details about types of employee counselling, directive counselling, non-directive counselling, participative counselling, functions of employee counselling.

Chapter 10. Perspectives of Workplace Counselling discusses performance counselling, counselling orientation models, how counselling works, performance counselling, career counselling.

Chaper 11. Quality of Work Life reflects what is quality of work life (QWL), constitutionalism in the work organization, alternative work schedules, QWL programming, humanization of work.

Chapter 12. Training and Development describes about determining training needs and objective, learning principles underlying industrial training, criteria for training effectiveness, training methods, evaluating training programmes, training trends, team training.

Chapter 13. Stress in Organizations elaborates on work stress, sources of stress, stress consequences, coping with stress and stress vulnerability.

Chapter 14. Core Competencies cites competency profiling, competency mapping, competency management, competency development competency categories and definitions.

Chapter 15. Assessment Centre mentions features, uses and stages of assessment centre, designing the assessment centre programme, assessor-participant-exercises.

Chapter 16. Performance Management discusses performance measurement, performance appraisal, performance-related skills training, performance-related pay, performance indicators, and performance management process.

Chapter 17. Ergonomics refers to designing work environments for maximizing safety and efficiency. It includes time-and-motion study, person-machine systems, design of personal protective equipment for work and hostile environments. Ergonomics focuses on designing workstations, tools and work tasks for safety, efficiency and comfort. Effective ergonomic design reduces discomfort, and injuries and increases job satisfaction and productivity.

Chapter 18. Absenteeism and Managers as Counsellors details about innocent absenteeism, culpable absenteeism, tackling absenteeism, identifying excessive absenteeism, counselling innocent absenteeism, and workplace counselling.

Chapter 19. Behavioural Based Safety in Organizations reflects BBS Concepts, Myths of behaviour-based safety, Implementation problems in BBS, Behavioural Safety observation and Feedback process. It emphasizes that BBS is "safety for each other"; BBS a more than safety regulations; and BBS trained observers monitor safety behaviours.

Chapter 20. Counselling in Organizations elaborates on the service of employee counselling offered by companies to their employees. The ways in which problems affect employees. What should organizations do to help employee's overcome personal/professional problems?

Chapter 21. Managerial Problems in Indian Organizations brings out the problems faced by male and female managers. Some of the problems for managers include communication problems, performance evaluation problems and attrition.

It is hoped that this text would provide the reader an interesting, useful and handy study material for their courses.

1
Foundations of Organizational Behaviour

Organizational Behaviour: an Introduction

Organizational behaviour is concerned with the study of the behaviour and interaction of people in restricted or organized settings. It involves understanding people and predicting their behaviour, and knowledge of the means by which their behaviour is influenced and shaped.

Organizations are bodies or entities created for a stated purpose. They may consist of more than onc or more people. In the case of the sole trader or single operator, he needs to build relationships with suppliers, contractors, customers, clients and the community. For those that consist of more than one person, internal as well as external relationships have to be created and maintained. Organizations therefore consist of individuals; groups; and relationships. Objectives, structures, systems and processes are then created to give direction and order to activities and interactions.

Organizational behaviour is thus of great concern to anyone who organizes, creates, orders, directs, manages or supervises the activities of others. It is also of concern to those who build relationships between individuals, groups of people, different parts of organizations and between different organizations, for all these activities are founded on human interaction.

Organizational behaviour is therefore concerned with:

The purpose for which organizations are created;

The qualities that individuals bring to particular situations;

The creation of groups (collections of people brought together for given purpose);

The background and context within which activities take place;

The relationships and interactions with the wider environment with other organizations and groups;

The management and ordering of the whole and its parts into productive and effective work relationships.

The Relationship to other Fields

Figure1.1 shows in very general terms the relationships between organization behaviour (OB) and the related disciplines of Organization Theory (OT), Organizational Development (OD), and Personnel/Human resources (P/*HR*). Organizational theory tends to be more macro-oriented than OB and is concerned primarily with organizational structures and designs. Organizational Development tends to be both more macro and more applied than OB. Personnel/Human Resources tends to have a more applied focus than OB. The personnel/Human resources functions is a part of practicing organizations as much as the marketing, finance, or productions/operations functions are.

Personnel/Human Resource Managers are hired and found with this title in practicing organizations; Managers who apply and draw from the field of OB (be from marketing, finance, Hospital administration, or academic administration) are called "human resource managers". They are also called so because they all manage people, regardless of their technical functions.

Fig.1.1

OT (Organization Theory)	OB (Organization Behaviour)
OD (Organization Development	P/HR (Personnel Human Resources)

Foundations of OB

The Behavioural Approach to Management

OB represents the behavioural approach to management, not the whole of management. The charge that old wine (applied or Industrial psychology) has merely been poured into a new bottle (organizational behaviour) has proved to be groundless. Although its certainly true that the behavioral sciences make a significant contribution to both the theoretical and the research foundation of organization behaviorist is equally true that applied or industrial psychology should not be equated with organization behaviour. For example, organizational structures and management processes (decision making and communication) play an integral, direct role applied or Industrial psychology. The same is true of many important dynamics and applications of organizational behaviour. Although there will probably never be total agreement on the exact meaning or domains of OB-which is not necessarily bad, because it makes the field more exciting –there is little doubt that OB has come into its own as a field of study, research and application.

Theoretical Frameworks

Although organizational behaviour is extremely complex and includes many inputs and dimensions, the cognitive, behaviouristic, and social learning, theoretical framework can be used to develop an overall model.

Cognitive Framework

The cognitive approach emphasizes the positive and freewill aspects of human behaviour and uses concepts such as expectancy, demand, and incentive. Cognition, which is the basic unit of the cognitive framework, is the act of knowing an item of information. Under this framework, cognitions precede behaviour knowing and constitute input into the person's thinking, perception, problem solving, and information processing.

The classic work of Edward Tolman can be used to represent the cognitive theoretical approach. Although Tolman believed behavior to be the appropriate unit of analysis, he felt that behaviour is purposive, that it is directed toward a goal. In his laboratory experiments he found that animals learned to expect that certain events would follow one another. For example, animals learned to behave as if they expected food when a certain cue appered. Thus, Tolman believed that learning consists of the expectancy that a particular event will lead to particular consequences. This cognitive concept of expectancy implies that the organism is thinking about or is conscious or aware of, the goal. Thus, Tolman and others espousing the cognitive approach felt that behaviour is best explained by these cognitions.

Because of the recent advances from both theory development and research, there has been what some have termed a "cognitive explosion" in the field of psychology. Applied to the field of organizational behavior, cognitive approach has traditionally dominated through units of analysis such as perception, personality and attitudes, motivation, and goal setting. Very recently, there has been renewed interest in the role that cognitions can play in organizational behaviour in terms of advancement in research on how managers make decisions and in the area of social cognition. The behavioural decision-making area is concerned with the cognitions involved in judgment and choice. Social cognition involves the process of understanding or making sense of people's behaviour and is especially relevant to organizational behaviour in terms of social perception.

Behaviouristic Framework

Its roots can be traced to the work of Ivan Pavlov and John B.Watson.These pioneering behaviourists stressed the importance of dealing with observable behaviours instead of the elusive mind that had preoccupied earlier psychologists. They used classical conditioning experiments to formulate the stimulus-response (S-R) explanation of human behaviour. Both Pavlov and Watson felt that behaviour could be best understood in terms of S-R. A stimulus elicits a response. They concentrated mainly on the impact of the stimulus and felt that learning occurred when the S-R connection was made.

Modern behaviorism marks its beginnings with the work of B.F. Skinner; He is widely recognized for his contribution to psychology. He felt that the early behaviorists helped explain respondent behaviours but not the more complex operant behaviour. He found through his operant conditioning experiments that the consequences of a response could better explain most behaviors than eliciting stimuli could. He emphasized the importance of the response-stimulus (R-S) relationship. The organisms have to operate on the environment in order to receive the desirable consequence. The preceding stimulus does not cause the behaviour in operant conditioning; it serves as a cue to emit the behaviour. For Skinner, behaviour is a function of its consequences.

Social Learning Framework

It should be emphasized that the social learning approach is a behavioral approach. It recognizes that behaviour is the appropriate unit of analysis. However, unlike a strict or radical behaviouristic approach; the social learning approach suggests that people are self aware and engage in purposeful behaviour. Under a social learning approach, people are thought to learn about their environment, alter and construct their environment to make reinforcers available, and not the importance of the rules and symbolic processes in learning.

Although a number of psychologists are associated with social learning, the work of Albert Bandura is probably the most representative of this approach. He takes the position that behaviour can best be explained in terms of a continuous reciprocal interaction among cognitive, behavioural, and environmental determinants. The person and the environment situation do not function as independent units but, in conjunction with the behaviour itself, reciprocally interact to determine behaviour. Bandura explains, "It is largely through their actions that people produce the environmental conditions that affect their behaviour in a reciprocal fashion. The experiences generated by behaviour also partly determine what a person becomes and can do, which in turn, affects subsequent behaviour.

Organizational Behaviour Model

Organizational behaviour has the advantage of being a relatively young and growing field of study. It can legitimately borrow, in an eclectic manner, the best from the various established frameworks for human behaviour. Traditionally, most writers on organizational behaviour have taken a humanistic, cognitive approach. For example, Douglas McGregor, who wrote the classic Human Side of Enterprise in 1960,took a humanistic approach, and well-known theorists such as Victor Vroom, Lyman Porter, and Edwin Locke depend mainly on cognitive concepts in their well-known writings on organizational behaviour. In the last few years, the behaviouristic model has begun to be used in theorizing and research on organizational behaviour.

The reason for presenting the cognitive and behaviouristic theoretical frameworks was to be better understand, not evaluate, the complex phenomena collectively called human behaviour. Understanding human behaviour in organizations is also a vital goal for a conceptual model for organizational behaviour. In addition, however because organizational behaviour is not a basic behavioral science such as psychology or sociology, two other especially desirable goals besides understanding are predictions and control. The field of OB serves as the basis for modern human resource managers. Predictions and control of human resources are critical to the goals of the new approach to management that will help solve the problems and meet the environmental challenges. Thus, the goals of a conceptual model of OB are to understand, predict, and effectively manage human behaviour in organizations.

The cognitive approach seems essential to the understanding of OB. The behaviouristic approach contributes to make predictions and control. For example, on the basis of Edward Thorndike's classic law of effect, the behaviouristic approach would say that organizational behaviour followed by a positive or reinforcing consequence will be strengthened and will increase in subsequent frequency and that OB followed by an unpleasant or punishing consequence will be weakened and will decrease in subsequent frequency. Thus, OB can be predicted and controlled on the basis of managing the contingent environment.

If the three goals of understanding, prediction, controls are to be met by a conceptual model for OB, both the cognitive and the behaviouristic approaches become vitally important. Both the internal causal factors, which are cognitively oriented and the external environmental factors, which are behaviouristically oriented, become important.

In a strictly social learning model, the letters in this model would stand for stimulus, Organism, Behaviopur, and consequence. The arrows recognize the interactive, reciprocal nature of the environmental (S and C), cognitive (O) and behavioral (B) variables. The S represents the environmental situation, both contextual and organizational. The O becomes the cognitive understanding of organizational participants as the relevant organism that mediates between the environmental situation and the resulting organizational behaviour. The B is the Organizational Behaviour. The C in this model represents the organizational and group dynamics and consequences that result from the previous interactions among the environmental, personal, and behavioral variables. As shown by the feedback interactions, the consequences also affect and are affected by the other variables.

Environmental situation (S)	↔	Cognitive Mediating Processes of the org.partic- -ipants (O)	↔	Organizational Behavior (B)	↔	Organizational & Behavioural Dynamics & Consequences (C)

Obviously, this S-O-B-C model gives only a bare-bones sketch of organizational behaviour rather than a full-blown explanation. Neverthless, it can serve as a conceptual framework.

Historical Background: The Hawthorne Studies

The early management pioneers, such as Henry Ford, Alfred P. Sloan, Henri Fayol, and even the scientific managers such as Frederick W. Taylor, recognized the behavioral side of management. However, they did not emphasize the human dimension: they let it play only a minor role in comparison with the roles of hierarchical structure, specialization, and the management functions of planning and controlling. Although there were varied and complex reasons for the emergence of the importance of the behavioral approach to management, it is generally recognized that the Hawthorne studies mark the historical roots for the field of organizational behaviour.

The Illumination Studies: A Serendipitous Discovery

In 1924, the studies started at the huge Hawthorne works of the western Electric Company outside of Chicago. The initial illumination studies attempted to examine the relationship between light intensity on the shop floor of manual work sites and employee productivity. A test group and a control group were used. The test group in an early phase showed no increase or decrease in output in proportion to the increase or decrease of illumination. The control group with unchanged illumination increased output by the same amount overall as the test group. Subsequent phases brought the level of light down to moonlight intensity; the workers could barely see what they were doing, but productivity increased. The result was baffling to the researchers. Obviously, some variables in the experiment were not being held constant or under control. Something bedsides the level of illumination was causing the change in productivity. The something of course was the complex human variable. These serendipitous results of the illumination experiments provided the impetus for the further study of human behaviour at work.

Subsequent Phases of the Hawthorne Studies

The illumination studies were followed by a study in the relay room, where operators assembled switches. This phase of the study tried to test specific variables, such as length of workday, rest breaks, and method of payment. The results were basically the same as those of the illumination studies: each test period yielded higher productivity than the previous one. Even when the workers were subjected to the original conditions of the experiment, productivity increased. The conclusion was that the independent variable (rest pauses and so forth) was not by themselves causing the change in the dependent variable (output). As in the illumination experiments, something was still not being controlled.

Still another phase was the bank wiring room study. Unlike the relay room experiments, this study involved no experimental changes once the study had started. Instead, an observer and an interviewer gathered objective data for study. If particular interest was the fact that the department's regular supervisors were used in the bank wiring room. Just as in the department out on the factory floor, their main function was to maintain order and control.

The results of the bank wiring room study were opposite to those of the relay room studies. The bank wiring room there were not the continual increases in productivity that occurred in the relay room. Rather, output was actually restricted by the bank wirers, by scientific management analysis-for example, time and motion study-the industrial engineers had arrived at a standard of 7312 terminal connections per day. This represented 2.5 equipments. The workers had a different brand of rationality. They decided that 2 equipments was a "proper" day's work. Thus, 2.5 equipments represented the management norm for production, but 2 equipments was the informal group norm and the actual output. The researchers determined that the informal group norm of 2 equipments represented restriction of output rather than a lack of ability to produce at the company standard of 2.5 equipments.

Of particular interest from a group dynamics standpoint were the social pressures used to gain compliance with the group norms. The incentive system dictated that the more an individual produced, the more money the individual would earn, also, the best producers would be laid off last, and thus they could be more secure by producing more. Yet in the face of this management rationale, almost all the workers restricted output. Social ostracism, ridicule, and name-calling were the major sanctions used by the group to enforce this restriction. In some instances, actual physical pressure in the form of a game called "binging" was applied. In the game a worker would be hit as hard as possible, with the privilege of restoring one "bing", or hit. Forcing rate-busters to play the game become an effective sanction. These group pressures had s tremendous impact on all the workers. Social ostracism was more effective in gaining compliance with the informal group norm than money and security were in attaining the scientifically derived management norm.

Implications of The Hawthorne Studies

Despite some obvious philosophical, theoretical, and methodological limitations by today's standards of research, the Hawthorne studies did provide some interesting insights that contributed to a better understanding of human behaviour in organizations. For instance, one interesting aspect of theses studies is the contrasting results obtained in the relay room and the bank wiring room. In the relay room, production continually increased throughout the test period, and the relay assemblers were very positive. The opposite was true in the bank wiring room; disgruntled workers practiced blatant restriction of output.

To find out the reason behind the difference in these two phases of the studies one can trace the results of a questionnaire administered to the subjects in the relay room. The original intent of the questions was to determine the health and habits of the workers. Their answers were generally inconclusive except that all the operators indicated they felt "better" in the test room. A follow-up questionnaire then asked about specific items in the test room situation. In discussions of the Hawthorne studies the follow up questionnaire cite the subjects unanimous preference for working in the test room instead of the regular department. Often overlooked, however, are the workers explanations for their choice. In order of prefererence, the workers gave the following reasons:

1. Small group.
2. Type of supervision.
3. Earnings.
4. Novelty of the situation.

5. Interest in the experiment.
6. Attention received in the test room.

It is important to note that novelty, interest, and attention were relegated to the forth, fifth, and sixth positions. These last three areas usually are associated with the famous Hawthorne effect. Many social scientists imply that the increases in the relay room productivity can be attributed solely to the fact that the participants in the study were given special attention and that they were enjoying a novel, interesting experience. This is labeled the Hawthorne effect and is of course a real problem with all human experimental subjects. Variables like experimental design, group dynamics, styles of leadership and supervision, and rewards and much more separate the old human relations movement and the modern approach to the field of organizational behaviour. So do the refinement and fine-tuning of the research methodology used to accumulate meaningful knowledge about organizational behaviour.

Organisational Theory And Design

Organizational structure represents the skeletal framework for organizational behaviour. The organizational structure is the dominant environmental factor that interacts with the person and the behaviour.

Classical Organization Theory And Design

The classical organization is most often associated with bureaucracy. Even though organizations are undergoing dramatic changes, bureaucracies still exist and must be understood to move toward and interpret some of the new theories and designs. For example, even though IBM has undergone a total reorganization and has implemented some of the newest structural designs, a critical analysis concluded, "IBM's stifling corporate bureaucracy remains a barrier to change."

The Bureaucratic Model

Bureaucratic theory and design are attributed to max Weber, one of the pioneers of modern sociology. He formulated this approach to organization in the early 1900s,and his work was first translated from German to English in the 1940s.Weber presented what he thought was an ideal organization structure, which he called a bureaucracy. His concern for the ideal was a natural extension of his interest in the development and change of western society.specifically; Weber believed that rationalization is the most persistent cultural value of western society. On an organizational level, to Weber the bureaucracy represented a completely rational form.

Weber specifies several characteristics of his ideal organization structure. The four major ones are the following:

1. *Specialization and decision of labour.* Weber's bureaucracy contained "a specified sphere of competence. This involves (a) a sphere of obligations to perform functions which has been marked off as part of a systematic division of labour,(b)The provision of the incumbent with the necessary authority...., (c) That the necessary means of compulsion are clearly defined and their use is subject to definite conditions". This statement implies that Weber recognized the importance of having the authority and power to carry out assigned duties. The bureaucrats must also know the precise limit of their sphere of competence so as not to infringe upon those of others.

2. *Positions arranged in a hierarchy.* Weber stated: "the organization of offices follows the principle of hierarchy: that is, each lower office is under the control and supervision of a higher one". This bureaucratic characteristic forces control over every member in the structure. Some organization theorists, such as Herbert Simon, have pointed out that hierarchy is the natural order of things.

3. *A system of abstract rules.* Weber felt a need for "a continuous organization requires a set of formal rules". A rational approach to organization requires a set of formal rules to ensure uniformity and coordination of effort. A well-understood system of regulations also provides the continuity and stability that Weber thought was so important. Whereas personnel may frequently change, rules persist.

They may range from no smoking in certain areas to the need for board approval for multi-thousand-dollar capital expenditures.

4. *Impersonal relationships.* It was Weber's belief that the ideal official should be dominated by "a spirit of formalistic impersonality, without hatred or passion, from the viewpoint of ideal rationality and not of realistic implementation. He felt that in order for bureaucrats to make completely rational decisions, they must avoid emotional attachment to subordinates and clients/customers.

The four characteristics just described are not only ones recognized and discussed by Weber. Another important aspect of the ideal bureaucracy is that employment is based on technical qualifications. The bureaucrat is protected against arbitrary dismissal, and promotions are made according to seniority and/or achievement's sum up, it must be remembered that Weber's bureaucracy was intended to be an ideal construct: no real-world organization exactly follows the Weber model.

It has been pointed out by the organization theorists like Peter M. Blau, that the classical, rational approach to structure is of value to managers of formal work organizations that have no conflict or whose subordinates have no power, but this is the ideal, not reality. In this age of comlex, highly conflicting relationships, advanced information technology, and empowered employees, this bureaucratic model is only the historical starting point of organization analysis.

Bureaucratic Dysfunctions. With the exception of Weber, sociologists and philosophers have been very critical of bureaucracies. For example, Karl Marx believed that the dominant capitalist class to control the other, lower social classes uses bureaucracies. According to Marx, bureaucracies are characterized by strict hierarchy and discipline, veneration of authority, incompetent officials, lack of initiative and imagination, fear of responsibility, and a process of self-aggrandizement. This interpretation of bureaucracy is basically exactly opposite to what Weber proposed. The Weber model can serve equally well in analyzing either the functional or the dysfunctional ramifications of classical organization structure.

The Dysfunctions of specialization. The bureaucratic model emphasizes that specialization enhances productivity and efficiency. The model can be used to point out the dysfunctional qualities of specialization as well. Empirical investigations have uncovered both functional and dysfunctional consequences. Specialization has been shown to lead to increased productivity and efficiency but also to create conflict between specialized units, to the detriment of the overall goals of the organization. For instance, specialization may impede communication between units. The management team of a highly specialized unit has its own terminology and similar interests, attitudes, and personal goals. Because "outsiders are different", the specialized unit tends to withdraw into itself and not fully communicate with units above, below, or horizontal to it. Performing a highly specialized job is also a major cause of employee boredom and burnout-blue-collar blues and white-collar woes.

The Dysfunctions of hierarchy. The functional attributes of a hierarchy are that it maintains unity of command, coordinates activities and personnel, reinforces authority, and serves as a formal system of communication. In theory, the hierarchy has both a downward and an upward orientation, but in practice, it has often turned out to have only a downward emphasis. Thus, individual initiative and participation are often blocked upward communication is impeded and there is no formal recognition of horizontal communication. Personnel who follow only formal hierarchy may waste a great deal of time and energy.

The Dysfunctions of Rules. Contributing to the bureaucratic image of red tape, rules often become the ends in themselves, rather than the means for more effective goal attainment. The famous management consultant Peter Drucker cites the following common misuses of rules that requires reports and procedures:

1. First is the mistaken belief that procedural rules are instruments of morality. They should not determine what is right or wrong conduct.

2. Procedural rules are sometimes mistakenly substituted for judgement. Printed forms should not mesmerize bureaucrats; forms should be used only in cases where judgment is not required.

3. The most common misuse of procedural rules is as a punitive control device from above. Bureaucrat are often required to comply with rules that have nothing to do with their jobs-for example, plant managers who have to accurately fill out numerous forms for staff personnel and corporate management which they cannot use in obtaining their own objectives.

The dysfunctions of Impersonal characteristics: The impersonal quality of the bureaucracy has even more dysfunctional consequences than specialization, hierarchy, and rules. Behaviorally oriented organization theorists and researchers have given a great deal of attention to the behavioural dysfunctions of bureaucratic structures.

The Modern View of Bureaucracies

The acknowledged bureaucratic dysfunctions have led most people to readily accept Parkinson's popular "laws" (for example, bureaucratic staffs increase in inverse proportion to the amount of work done) and the popular "Peter principle" (managers rise to their level of incompetence in bureaucracies). These laws and principles have received wide public acceptance because everyone has observed and experienced what Parkinson and Peter wrote about.

In addition to the popularized criticisms of bureaucracy, a more academic analysis also uncovers many deficiencies. Ennis summarized some of them as follows:

1. Bureaucracy does not adequately allow for personal growth and the development of mature personalities.

2. It develops conformity and groupthink.

3. It does not take into account the informal organization and the emergent and unanticipated problems.

Modifications of Bureaucratic Structuring

The classical bureaucratic model has served as a point

of departure for modified vertical and horizontal structural arrangements.

Vertical analysis. Concentrates on centralization versus decentralization and on flat versus tall structuring. These characteristics represent modifications of the classical principles of delegation of authority and limited span of control. Decentralization expands the principle of delegation to the point of an overall philosophy of organization and management. A tall organization structure means a series of narrow spans of control, and a flat structure incorporates wide spans. The bureaucratic principle of hierarchy is also closely related to the vertical concept.

Horizontal structural. Analysis is concerned with organizing one level of the hierarchy. The concepts of departmentation and of line and staff represent this approach. They are derived chiefly from the bureaucratic doctrine of specialization. Departmentation concentrates on organizing each level to attain optimum benefit from high degrees of specialization. The staff concept attempts to resolve the vertical and horizontal conflicts that appeared in the classical scheme. These concepts are of greater weight to the human element and recognize that simple, mechanistic structural arrangements are not satisfactory for modern organizations.

Centralization and Decentralization. Types and Meaning: There are three basic types of centralization and decentralization. The first type is geographic, or territorial, concentration (centralization) or dispersion (decentralization) of operations. For example, the term "*centralized*" can be used to refer to an organization that has all its operations under one roof or in one geographic region. On the other hand, the dispersion of an organization's operations throughout the country or the world is a form of decentralization. This is particularly relevant as organizations today begin to create international structures.

The second type is functional centralization and decentralization. Say a separate human resources department that performs functions such as selection or training for the other departments is said to be centralized. However, if the various functional departments e.g. marketing, production etc, handle their own HR functions, then HR is considered decentralized.

The third type is the only analytical use of the concept. Here the terms centralization and decentralization refer to the retention or delegation of decision-making prerogatives or command.

Optimum Degree of Decentralization

Conventionally, decentralization is thought to be somewhat better than centralization. But in reality neither concept is ideal or intrinsically good or bad.

Its found that decentralization is much more compatible with the behavioral aspects of management. This relevance is due in part to the lower-level participation in decision-making and the currently popular notion of empowerment of employees that results from decentralization. Increased motivation, through giving more autonomy and personal control over the work, is an extremely important by-product.

Besides the behavioral benefits, more effective decisions are possible because of the speed and first hand knowledge that decentralization provides. It also affords invaluable experience in decision making for lower-level executives. Finally, it allows more time for top management to concentrate on policymaking and creative innovation.

Many organizations are still experiencing success in moving from centralization to decentralization. A good example is Johnson and Johnson, the highly successful pharmaceutical firm, with 165 units worldwide. Each unit has considerable autonomy. Although corporate headquarters in New Jersey sets overall corporate policies on financial and certain administrative matters, the units presidents, many in their late thirties and early forties, have full responsibility for their unit's research and development, manufacturing, marketing, and sales.

Though decentralization has supported and stimulated the behavioral approach to management, there exists a wide discrepancy between its theory and practice. Yet because of its wide acceptance, decentralization has had a definite impact on developing a managerial attitude favoring the implementation of behavioral concepts in organizations.

However, it is now recognized that a third dimension, such as cooperation, may also be structurally needed, in addition to centralization and decentralization. It can be added to create a triangular design so that the organization becomes a function of three variable-autonomy (decentralization), control (centralization), and cooperation (teamwork).

Flat and Tall Structures

In organizational analysis, the terms flat and tall are used to describe the total pattern of spans of control and levels of management. Whereas the classical principle of span of control is concerned with the number of subordinates one superior can effectively manage, the concept of flat and tall is more concerned with the vertical structural arrangements for the entire organization.

The tall structure has very small or narrow spans of control, whereas the flat structure has large or wide spans. In tall structures, the small number of subordinates assigned to each manager allows for tight control and strict disciple. Classical bureaucratic structures are typically very tall.

Advantages and Disadvantages

Tall structures assume a role in assessing the value of flat structures similar to that of centralization in assessing the relative merits of decentralization. Tall structures are often viewed negatively in modern organizational analysis.

Both flat and tall structures could have the same number of personnel. However, the tall structure could have four levels of management, and flat one only two levels. The tall structure has the definite advantage of facilitating closer control over subordinates. The very nature of flat structures implies that managers cannot possibly keep close control over many subordinates. Therefore, they are almost forced to delegate a certain amount of the work. Thus, wide spans structurally encourage decentralization.

Behavioural Implications of Flat Versus Tall Structures

One behavioral implication that is often overlooked in analyzing flat vs. tall structures is the opportunity that tall structure offer for more personal contact between managers and subordinates. This contact is generally assumed to be negative and conflicting, but it need not be. The manager may create a positive rapport with his or her subordinates that may not be possible in a flat structure.

Another consideration besides personal contact is the levels of communication in the two structures. In the flat structure there are few levels, which means that both downward and upward communication are simplified. There should be less distortion and inaccuracy. The red tape and endless communication channels associated with a bureaucratic tall structure are not present in a flat structure. On the other hand, the increased equality that exists between subordinates in a flat structure may lead to communication problems. if no status or authority differentials are structurally created, a heavy burden is placed upon horizontal communications.

Overall, the flat structure, at least from a behavioral standpoint, is generally preferable to the tall structure. It can take advantage of the positive attributes of decentralization and personal satisfaction and growth. Although managers who have wide spans will have to give a great deal of attention to selecting and training subordinates, a flat structure has the advantage of providing a wealth of experience in decision making.

Departmentation

Departmentation is concerned with horizontal organization on any one level of the structure, and it is closely related to the classical bureaucratic principle of specializtion. There are different types of departmentation.

Functional Depatmentation. The most widely used and recognized type of departmentation is functional in nature and may be found in all types of organizations, be it a business firm, hospital, university, government agency and so on.

The greatest single advantage of functional departmentation is that it incorporates the positive aspects of specialization, theoretically; functionalism should lead to the greatest efficiency and the most economical utilization of employees. In practice however, certain dysfunctions may negate its merits. For example, functional empires may be created that conflict to the point of detracting from overall goal attainment.

Product Departmentation. At the primary level, many organizations have chosen to organize along product or unit rather than along functional lines. The product form of departmentation is particularly adaptable to the tremendously large and complex modern organizations. It goes hand in hand with profit-centered decentralization. it allows the giant corporations, such as General Motors, General Electric, and Du Pont, to be broken down into groups of self-contained, smaller product organizations or strategic business units (SBUs). Thus, the advantages of both large and small size can exist in one large organization.

Because of their self-contained nature, product departments are very adaptable to accounting-control techniques and management appraisal. Product department performance, measured according to several different criteria, can usually be objectively determined. Another advantage is that product departments can be readily added or dropped with a minimum of disruption to the rest of the organization.

As a structural form, product departmentation is very compatible with the behavioural approach. Many of the conflicts that exist in the upper level under functional departmentation are generally resolved by product departmentation, however may reappear in the lower levels that are functionalized. Besides reducing the potential for conflict, product division also provides an opportunity for personal development, growth, and self-control.

The Staff Concept of Organization

This concept is borrowed from the military. Under the "pure" military approach, line carries command or decision-making responsibilities, whereas staff gives advice and provides backup and support to the line. Almost every type of organization has attempted to adopt to some degree the military staff concept, but these organizations have not given much attention to operationally defining the difference between line and staff. Unlike military, there develops lack of understanding of the very concept and results in the breakdown of communication and open conflict. One reason could be that managers generally wear more than one hat. Managers are line within their own depts. And become line and staff when dealing with outside depts.

Modern Organizational Theory

Historical roots: The real break with classical thinking on organizational structure is generally recognized to be the work of Chester Bernard. In his significant book, *The Functions of the executive*, he defined a formal organization as a system of consciously coordinated activities of two or more persons. It's interesting to note that the words "system" and "persons" are given major emphsis. People, not boxes on an organization chart, make up a formal organization; Barnard was critical of the existing classical organization theory because it was too descriptive and superficial. He was especially dissatisfied with the classical bureaucratic view that authority should come from the top down. Barnard maintained that authority should come from the bottom up, rather than the top-down bureaucratic approach. From this auspicious beginning, modern organization theory has evolved in several directions. The first major development in organization theory was to view the organization as a system made up of interacting parts.

The Organization as an Open System

Both the closed and open systems approaches are utilized in modern organization theory and practice. The key for viewing organizations as open systems is the recognition of the external environment as a source of significant input. In systems terminology, the boundaries of the organization are permeable to the external environment (social. legal. technical. economic, and political).

The simplest open system consists of an input, a transformation process, and an output, which is depicted thus:

Input → Transformation process → Output

A system cannot survive without continuos input, the transformation process, and output.

There are many types of inputs, transformation processes, and outputs. For example, one kind of input actually enters the open system in the "closed" sense. This type of input has a direct effect on the internal system rather than an outside effect-in systems jargon, it loads the system. Another type of input affects the system in an "open" sense. This input would consist of the entire environmental influence on the system. Still another kind of input takes the form of replacement or recycling. When a component of the system is ejected or leaves, the replacement becomes an input. This recycling process perpetuates the system.

At the heart of the open system are the processes, operations, or channels that transform the inputs into the outputs. Here is where the internal organization design plays an important role. The transformation process consists of a logical network of subsystems, which lead to the output. The subsystems are translated into complex systems networks that transform the inputs into the desired outputs.

The third and final major component of any simple open system is the output. This is represented by the product, result, outcome, or accomplishment of the system. Specific examples of the outputs of a business organization system that correspond to the inputs of monetary, material, and human resources are profit or loss, product sales, and role behaviors.

The simple open-systems concept has universal applicability. Any biological, human, social, economic, or technical phenomenon can be conceptualized in open-systems terms.

From an organizational structure standpoint, the critical factor is the design of the transformation process. Oddly, this transformation design involves a close-systems analysis. In other words, the closed system is a subsystem of the open system. The closed-systems aspects of the transformation process are concerned with the interrelated and interdependent organizational subsystems of structure, processes, and technology. These subsystems must be organized in such a way that they will lead to maximum goal attainment or output.

Although the approach has decreased in popularity in recent years, it has been pointed out that, till date, very little research on organizations has been guided by open-systems thinking. It is not that the open-systems approach has proved to be wrong or lacking in some way but rather that "in order to most fruitfully utilize the systems paradigm of organizations, scholars in the field must re-examine their beliefs about the paradigm and, perhaps, re-educate themselves about how they should think about and study organizations as systems."

Information Processing View of Organizations

The information processing view makes three major assumptions about organizations:

1. Organizations are open systems that face external, environmental uncertainty (for example, technology or the economy) and internal, work-realted task uncertainty. Jay Galbraith defines task uncertainty as "the difference between the amount of information required to perform the task and the amount of information already possessed by the organization."

2. The organization must have mechanisms and be structured such that it can diagnose and cope with this environmental and task uncertainty. In paticular, the organization must be able to gather, interpret, and use the appropriate information to reduce the uncertainty. Thus, the second assumption is as follows: "Given the various sources of uncertainty, a basic function of the organization's structure is to create the most appropriate configuration of work units (as well as the linkages between these units) to facilitate the effective collection, processing, and distribution of information."

3. The final major assumption of this view deals with the importance of the subunits or various departments of an organization. Because the subunits have different degrees of differentiation (i.e, they have different time perspectives, goals, technology, and so on), the important question is not what the overall organization design should be but, rather, "(a) What are the optimal structures for the different subunits within the organization (e.g., R & D, sales, manufacturing);(b) What structural mechanisms will facilitate effective coordination among differentiated yet interdependent subunits?"

Contingency, Ecological, and Learning Organization Theories:

The most recent organization theories focus even more on the environment than do the open systems and information processing views.

Contingency theories are proactive and are analogous to the development of contingency management as a whole; they relate the environment to specific organization structures. More specifically, the contingency models relate to how the organization structure adjusts to fit with both the internal environment, such as work technology, and the external environment, such as the economy or legal regulations.

Some organization theorists feel that contingency theory should be replaced by an ecological view. This new approach is best represented by what is called "population ecology". It can be summarized as follows:

1. It focuses on groups or populations of organizations rather than individual ones.

2. Organizational effectiveness is simply defined as survival.

3. The environment is assumed to be totally determining. At least in the short or intermediate term, management is seen to have little impact on an organization's survival.

4. The carrying capacity of the environment is limited.

Therefore, there is a competitive arena in which some organizations will succeed and others will fail.

This theory represents a much different view of organization than the classical or even modern approaches. A more rational, proactive approach to management that is able to adapt the organization structure to fit the changing demands of the environment is more accepted and practical than environmental determination.

The key to understanding the potential organizational dinosaurs of recent years is not necessarily that they did not change or attempt to adapt to their new environment. But the key is that these firms and most others were in a reactive mode; they did not anticipate change or stay ahead of change. In terms of organizational learning, the potential dinosaurs exhibited only single-loop, or adaptive, learning, not double loop, or generative, learning. In order for today's organizations to gain a competitive advantage and even to survive in the long run, they must be able to learn how to learn (double-loop) and through generative learning be creative and innovative in order to be ahead of and anticipate change.

This double loop, generative learning view has emerged as the latest widely accepted view of organization theory. However, other theories, such as radical humanism and chaos, also have advocates claiming the best understanding of today's organizations. For example, a radical humanist argument would use a neo-Marxist conceptualization to empower workers, or give them significant control over their own environments and working conditions. Chaos theory would argue that prediction and control of systems behaviors is unobtainable, even in extremely simple and deterministic structures, let alone in the increasingly complex and changing organizations of modern times.

Modern Organizational Desingns

Up until a few years ago, most managers attempted only timid modifications of classical structures and balked at daring experimentation and innovation. However, many of today's managers have finally overcome this resistance to making drastic organizational changes. They realize that a simple solutions offered by the classical theories are no longer adequate for many of their complex problems. In particular, the needs for flexibility, adaptability to change, creativity, innovation, as well as the ability to overcome environmental uncertainty, are among the biggest challenges facing a growing number of modern organizations.

Project Designs

Together with the aerospace industry, project designs are becoming widely used in other industrial corporations and also in financial instutions, health care facilities, government agencies, and educational institutions. Projects are of various degrees of importance and magnitudes are always under way in modern organizations. The project structure is created when management decides to focus a great amount of talent and resources for a given period on a specific project goal.

There are different ways in which the project approach can be designed. Fig. 1.2 a shows that the project managers under this design have no activities or personnel reporting directly to them. The project manager, along with the heads of quality control, research and development, contract administration, and scheduling, acts in a staff capacity to the general manager. The project manager must rely on influence and persuasion in performing a monitoring role, with direct line authority exercised only by the general manager.

Another type is shown in Fig. 1.2b, here,project managers have all the personnel necessary for the project. They have staff and functional line personnel reporting directly to them. Fig. 1.2 b shows that the project managers under the aggregate design have full authority over the entire project. In reality, the aggregate project organization is very similar to the traditional product or unit form of departmentation.

There are other possible variations besides the two figures shown, and the project organization almost always coexists with the more traditional functional structure. But project experts stress that even though there are many similarities between project and functional organizations, project managers must take a new approach to their jobs:

1. They must become reoriented away from the purely functional approach to the management of human and nonhuman resources.

2. They must understand that purposeful conflict may very well be a necessary way of life as they manage their project across many vertical organizational lines.

3. They must recognize that project management is a dynamic activity in which major changes are almost the order of the day.

These three statements make it clear that the project concept is a philosophy of management as well as a form of structural organization.

Fig. 1.2 a: Types of Project designs

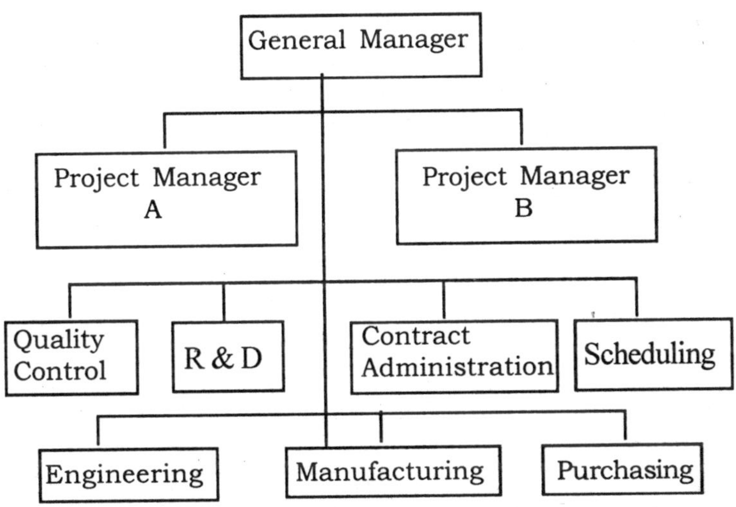

Fig. F1.2b : Type of project Designs.

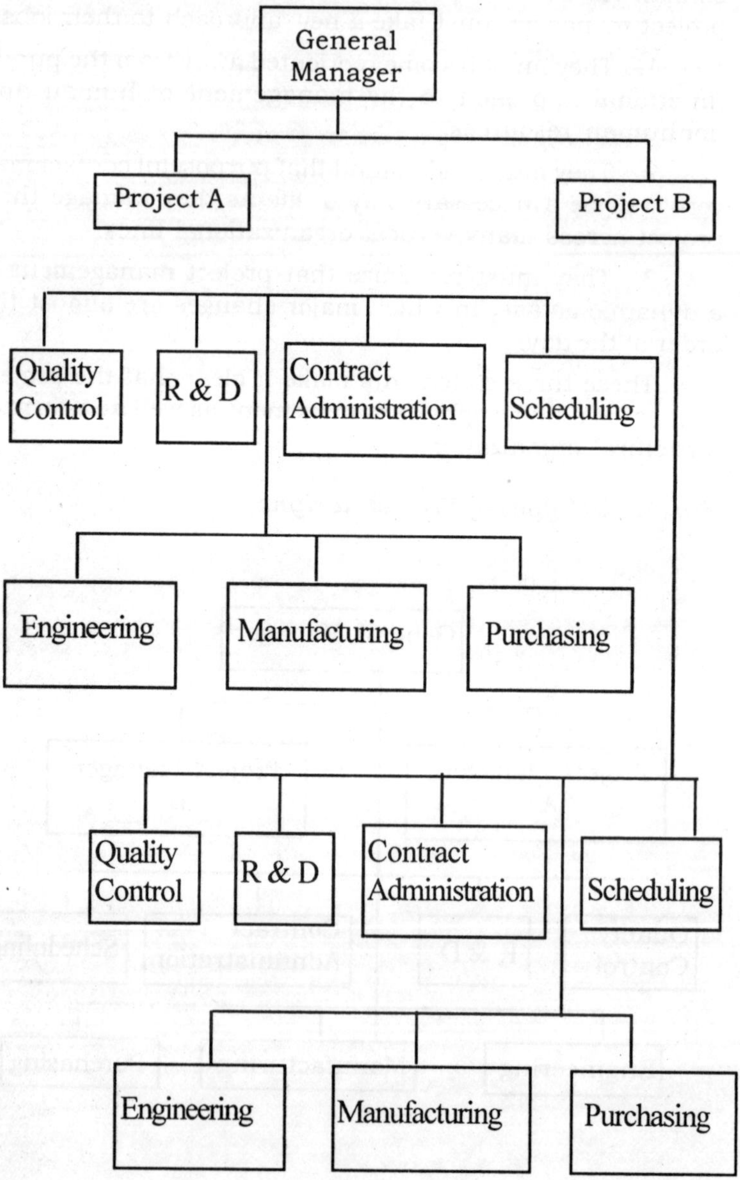

Fig. 1.3 : An Example of a matrix design

General
Manager

R & D   Contract Admn.   Engg.   Manufacturing

Project Manager A   R & D   Contract Admn.   Engg.   Manufacturing

Matrix Designs

When a project structure is superimposed on a functional structure, the result is a matrix. A matrix organization is a project organization plus a functional organization. Fig. 1.3 shows a very simplified matrix organization. Here, the functional department heads have line authority over the specialists in their departments (vertical structure). The functional specialists are then assigned to given projects (horizontal structure). These assignments are usually made at the beginning of each project by collaboration between the appropriate functional and project managers.

Matrix designs directly violate classical principles, such as unity of command (i.e., each employee is responsible to only one boss), and can generate considerable conflict for personnel who have both functional and project responsibilities. But there are advantages too.

1. The matrix design can combine the positive aspects of both the functional and the project designs.

2. The cross-functional arrangement found in the matrix design may outweigh the inherent demerits.

3. Matrix organization tends to have high levels of performance in dealing with complex, creative work products.

4. The matrix organizations usually have greater worker job satisfaction due to the high levels of responsibility they possess and the amount of interaction among the members of the matrix structures.

Horizontal Organization

The project and especially the matrix designs were the first to emphasize the importance of horizontal over traditional vertical structuring of the organization. Frank Ostroff, a McKinsey and company consultant, along with colleague Douglas Smith, is given credit for developing some of the following guiding principles that define horizontal organization design:

1. Organizaion revolves around the process, not the task. Instead of creating a structure around the traditional functions, the organization is built around its three to five core processes. Each process has an "owner" and specific performance goals.

2. The hierarchy is flattened: to reduce levels of supervision, fragmented tasks are combined, work that fails to add value is eliminated, and activities within each process are cut to the minimum.

3. Teams are used to manage everything: Self-managed teams are the building blocks of the organization. The teams have a common purpose and are held accountable for measuring performance goals.

4. Customer drive performance: customer satisfaction, not profits or stock appreciation, is the primary driver and measure of performance.

5. Team performance is rewarded: the reward systems are geared toward team results, not just individual performance. Employees are rewarded for multiple skill development rather than just specialized expertise.

6. Supplier and customer contact is maximized: Employees are brought into direct, regular contact with suppliers and customers. Where relevant, supplier and customer representatives may be brought in as full working members of in-house teams.

7. All employees need to be fully informed and trained: Employees should be provided all data, not just sanitized information on a "need to know" basis. However, they also need to be trained how to analyze and use the data to make effective decisions.

Today, this horizontal structure has become a reality in an increasing number of organizations. For example, AT & T units are doing budgets based not on functions but on processes, such as the maintenance of a worldwide telecommunications networkImportantly, AT & T is also rewarding its people based on customer evaluations of the teams performing these processes, and GE, Motorola, and Xerox, among other leading firms, have moved to the principles of the horizontal design of organization.

Network Designs

Network organizations have been discussed in the academic literature for a number of years. For example, organization theorists Miles and Snow identified what they call the dynamic network. This involves a unique combination of strategy, atructure, and management processes. They more recently have described the network organization as follows: "Dealayered, highly flexible, and controlled by market mechanisms rather than administrative procedures, firms with this new structure arrayed themselves on an industry value chain according to their core competencies, obtaining complementary resources through strategic alliance and outsourcing."

With the advent of teams and outsourcing (concerning on core competencies and forming outside partnerships to perform the peripheral activities and functions of the organization), network designs are actually being used by practicing organizations. Tapscott and Caston note that such networked organizations are "based on cooperative, multidisciplinary teams and businesses networked together across the enterprise. Rather than a rigid structure, it is a modular organizational architecture in which business teams operate as a network of what we call client and serve functions."

Miles and colleagues have recently identified three types of radical redesign of today's organizations:

1. Greenfield redesign. As the term implies, this means starting from just a piece of green field or from a clean slate, breaking completely from the classical structure and establishing a totally different design. Examples include such highly successful firms as Rubbermaid and Southwest Airlines. Rubbermaid's top management concluded that the key to success in their consumer plastic goods industry was constant product innovation and speed to market. They had to create a brand-new structure characterized by flexibility and decentralization to facilitate innovation, quality, and rapid responsiveness across a broad range of consumer markets.

2. Rediscovery redesign. This is a more usual type of redesign, whereby established companies such as general Electric and Chrysler return to a previously successful design by eliminating unproductive structural additions and modifications. For example, Chrysler not only created cross-functional teams but also returned to a more centralized structure that could better coordinate and controls the needed innovations and acquisitions/divestments for its product line.

3. Network design. Firms such as Ford and Harley-Davidson are not just redesigning in the "Greenfield" sense or rediscovering and extending their past. Instead, they are undergoing efforts to disaggregate and partner. In the network approach, the firm concentrates on where it can add the greatest value in the chain, and it outsources to upstream and/or downstream partners who can do a better job. This network of the firm and its upstream and downstream partners can be optimally effective and flexible. Another network approach is to require internal units of the firm to interact at market prices-buy and sell to each other at prices equal to those that can be obtained by outsourcing partners. This "insourcing" approach to the internal network organization can be found in global firms such as the well-known and respected Swiss conglomerate Asea Brown boveri (ABB).

The Virtual Organization

The term virtual organization has emerged not so much because it describes something distinct from network organization but because the term itself represents the new Information Age and the partening and Outsourcing arrangements found in an increasing number of global companies. The word "virtual" has come from from "virtual memory", which has been used to describe a way of making a computer's memory capacity appear to be greater than it really is. The virtual organization is a temporary network of companies that come together quickly to exploit fast-changing opportunities.

Different from traditional mergers and acquisitions, the partners in the virtual organization share costs, skills, and access to international markets. Each partner contributes to the virtual organization what it is best at-its core capabilities. Briefly summarized, here are the key attributes of the virtual organization:

1. *Technology Informational.* Networks will help far-flung companies and entrepreneurs link up and work together from start to finish. The partnerships will be based on electronic contracts to keep the lawyers away and aped the linkups.

2. *Opportunism..* Partnerships will be less permanent, less formal, and more opportunistic. Companies will band together to meet all specific market opportunities and, more often than not, fall apart once the need evaporates.

3. *No borders.* This new organizational model redefines the traditional boundaries of the company. More cooperation among competitors, suppliers and customers makes it harder to determine where one company ends and another begins.

4. *Trust.* these relationships make companies far more reliant on each other and require far more trust than ever before. They share a sense of "co-destiny", meaning that the fate of each partner is dependent on the other.

5. *Excellence.* Because each partner brings its "core-competence" to the effort, it may be possible to create a "best-of-everything" organization. Every function and process could be world-class—something that no single company could achieve.

Since networks and virtual organizations both represent such radically different ways to structure firms, there are many challenges ahead, especially on the human side of these new structural forms.

International Organizational Behaviour

The Impact of Culture on International Organizational Behaviour

Culture per se can be defined, as the acquired knowledge that people use to interpret experience and generate social behaviour. It is important to recognize that culture is learned and helps people in their efforts to interact and communicate with others in the society. When placed in a culture where values and beliefs are different, some people have a great deal of difficulty adjusting. This is particularly true when U.S. business people are assigned to a foreign country. There is considerable evidence that U.S. expatriates have a much greater chance of failure than their European and Japanese counterparts These expatriates quickly learn that the values of U.S. culture are often quite different from those of their host country, and, even though increasing attention is being given to expatriate management, U.S.MNCs are incurring millions of dollars of costs due to expatriate failures. And this phenomenon holds true for the expatriates from pother countries as well.

How do Cultures Vary?

There are several basic dimensions that differentiate cultures. These are as follows:

1. ***How people see themselves.*** In some countries of the world, people are viewed as basically honest and trustworthy. In others, people are regarded with suspicion and distrust. For example, a reason some people around the world regard the United States with suspicion and distrust may result from the way these people view themselves. They assume others are like them, that is, prepared to cut corners if they can get away with it. On the other hand, many other people of these countries are just the opposite. They do not lock their doors and are very trusting and assume that no one will break in. Most people from the U.S. still view others as basically honest but also believe that it is important to be alert for any sign of trouble.

When people travel outside their home country, they carry their values with them, just like their baggage. This sometimes results in their being surprised over the way they are treated.

2. ***People's relationship to their world.*** In some societies people attempt to dominate their environment. In other societies they try to live in harmony with it or are subjugated by it. People from the United States and Canada; for example, attempt to dominate their environment. In agriculture they use fertilizers and insecticides to increase crop yields. Other societies, especially those in Asia, work in harmony with the environment by planting crops in thee right places and at the right time. In still other societies, most notably developing countries, no action is taken regarding the subjugation of nature, so, for example, when the floods come, there are no dams or irrigation systems for dealing with the impending disaster.

3. ***Individualism versus Collectivism.*** Some countries of the world have cultural values that encourage individualism. The United States, Great Britain, and Canada are examples. In other countries collectivism, or group orientation, is important. Japan, China, and the Israeli Kibbutzim emphasize group harmony, unity, commitment,

and loyalty. The differences reflect themselves in many ways, such as in hiring practices. In countries where individualism is important, job applicants are evaluated on the basis of personal, educational, and professional achievements. In group-oriented societies applicants are evaluated on the basis of trustworthiness, loyalty, and compatibility with coworkers. Also in highly collectistic cultures, employees tend to show considerable commitment to their organization, while in highly individualistic cultures, managers tend to be more mobile, going from job to job.

4. The Time Dimension. In some societies people are oriented toward the past. In others they tend to be more focused on the present. Still others are futuristic in their orientation. People from U.S. and Canada are most interested in the present and the near future. Buisness people in these countries are particularly interested in where their companies are today and where they will be in 5 to 10 yrs down the line. In the Indian context, people place more importance on the past. They believe in preserving history and continuing traditions as well as to plan the future, so it's a nice balanced one.

5. Public and Private space. Some cultures promote the use of public space; others favor private space. For example, in Japan bosses often sit together with their employees in the same large room. The heads of some of the biggest Japanese firms may leave their chauffer-driven limousines at home and ride the crowded public subways to work in the morning so that they can be with their workers. In contrats, North Americans prefer private space. The more restricted or confined a manger is, the more important the individual is assumed to be. Anyone coming to see the person must first go past a secretary before being admitted to the manager's presence.

Hofstede's Cultural Dimensions

Till date, the most common way to study and draw conclusions about organizational behaviour across cultures and explain the difference that exist is to use the framework of Geert Hofstede.This well known Dutch researcher conducted what is considered to be the largest organizationally based study ever done. Through a questionnaire measure he found differences in the behaviour and attitudes of 116,000 respondents from seventy countries that worked for subsidiaries of IBM. From this data, published in 1980, he identified four major cultural dimensions: individualism/ collectivism, power distance, uncertainty avoidance, and masculinity/feminity.

There has been some reanalysis and criticism through the years of Hofstede's dimensions. For example, a recent study found that some of the dimensions are highly interrelated, and, because all his data were collected from one company, the study has been criticized for not being representative of the various countries. However, Hofstede has countered such criticism by arguing "samples for cross-national comparison need not be representative, as long as they are functionally equivalent. IBM employees are a narrow sample, but very well matched. The only thing that can account for systematic and consistent between national groups within such a homogenous multinational population is nationality itself- the national environment in which people were brought up before they joined this employer. Comparing IBM subsidiaries therefore shows national cultural differences with unusual clarity.

1. Individualism/Collectivism And Power Distance

Individualism is the tendency to take care of oneself and one's immediate family. A tight social framework in which people distinguish between their own group and other groups characterizes collectivism. Power distance is the extent to which less powerful members of organizations accept the unequal distribution of power, i.e, the degree to which employees accept that their boss has more power than they do.

When Hofstede examined employees from fifty countries in terms of individualism and power distance, he found cultural clusters. For example, United States has high individualism and small power distance. This is in contrast with Mexico, which has high collectivism (tight group) and large power distance (a lot of power granted to the boss).

In general, Hofstede found that wealthy countries have higher individualism scores and poorer countries have higher collectivism scores. An exception would be Japan and countries like India that have manage to come up.

2. Uncertainty Avoidance

Another dimension of cultural difference identified by Hofstede is uncertainty avoidance. It is the extent to which people feel threatened by ambiguous situations and the degree to which they try to avoid these situations by doing such things as:

- Providing greater career stability.
- Establishing more formal rules.
- Rejecting deviant ideas and behaviour.
- Accepting the possibility of absolute truths and the attainment of expertise.

In Japan, for example, where lifetime employment traditionally exists, at least in the large companies, there is high uncertainty avoidance. In US, by contrast, where there traditionally has been relatively high job mobility, there is low uncertainty avoidance.

3. Masculanity/Feminity

Hofstede also measured the impact of masculinity/ feminity. Masculinity is the extent to which the dominant values of a society emphasize assertiveness and the acquisition of money and other material things.feminity is the term used by Hofstede to refer to the extent to which the dominant values in a society emphasize relationships among people, concern for others, and interest in quality of life. In masculine societies with strong uncertainty avoidance, such as Japan, the managers tend to be very assertive and materialistic. In feminine societies, such as Scandinavian countries like Norway, the work force in factories is concerned with quality of work life.

Trompenaars's Cultural Dimensions

A more up-to-date classification scheme for international

organizational behaviour is proposed by another Dutch researcher, Fons Trompenaars.One of the most comprehensive studies (respondents were 15000 managers from twenty-eight countries) has five cultural dimensions from extensive data on how people deal with each other.

1. Universalism Versus Particularism

Trompenaars labeled the cultural dimension of universalism as the belief that ideas and practices can be applied everywhere without modification. While Particularism is the belief that circumstances dictate how ideas and practices should be applied. For example, highly Universalist cultures like US or European countries would emphasize and be guided by strict, formal rules. Highly particularistic cultures, on the other hand, would focus more on personal relationships and trust.

The cross-cultural implication is that the attitudes and style of management would be quite different in these two types of culture. Universalist would tend to have a "let's get down to business" attitude and not deviate from the rules and regulations, while particularists would tend to engage in a lot of small talk to get to know one another and let the situation dictate their actions.

2. Individualism/Collectivism

Although Trompenaar's derived these two dimensions differently than Hofstede, they still have the same basic meaning, but refinements are being made in terms of theory and measurement.

Individualism refers to people regarding themselves as part of a group. The U.S., Czech republic, Argentina, the former Soviet Union, and Mexico, have high individualism.

These findings of Trompenaar's is somewhat different from Hofstede, e.g., Mexico and Argentina are collectivists in Hofstede's findings but individualistic in Trompenaar's research. This points out that the cultural values may be shifting in some countries. For example, with Mexico now part of NAGTA and the global economy, this country may have moved from dominant collectivist cultural values to more individualistic values. The same may be true of the former communist countries of Czechoslovakia and the republic of the former Soviet Union.

The implications that these dimensions have for cross-cultural analysis would be in areas such as reward system, decision-making, and work design. For example, individualistic cultures would respond better to individually base pay-for-performance, individual executive decision-making and traditional work designs. In collectivistic cultures, however, it would be more appropriate to use a gain sharing reward plan, group problem solving, consumer decision-making, and an autonomous teamwork design.

3. Neutral Versus Affective

In a neutral culture, emotions are held in check and not outwardly expressed. The Japanese and British try not to outwardly show their feelings. However, in affective cultures the opposite is true; emotions are openly and naturally expressed. Examples can be Mexicans, the Dutch, and the Swiss, who tend to smile a great deal, talk loudly when they are excited, and greet each other enthusiastically. Thus, in communication and other interpersonal interactions, the nonverbal and verbal cues may have to be read quite differently in both highly neutral and highly affective cultures.

4. Specific Versus Diffuse

By a specific culture, Trompenaars means one in which individuals have a large public space they readily let others enter and share and a small private space they guard closely and share only with close friends and associates. A diffuse culture is one in which both public and private space are similar in size and individuals guard their public space carefully, because entry into public space affords entry into private space as well.

In diffuse cultures, outsiders should respect a person's title, age, and background connections, and should not get impatient when people from the diffuse cultures are being indirect or circuitous. Conversely, when dealing with individuals from specific cultures, outsiders should try to get to the point and be efficient, learn to structure things, and minimize the use of titles and play down achievements or skills that are irrelevant to the situation.

5. Achievement Versus Ascription

An achievement culture is one in which people are accorded status based on how well they perform their functions. An ascription culture is one in which status is attributed based on who or what a person is. Achievement cultures give high status to high achievers, such as the company's number-one salesperson or the manager of the unit with the highest profit. Ascription cultures accord status based on age, gender, or social connections. For example, in such culture, a person who has been with the company the longest may be listened to more carefully because of the respect that others have for the individual's age and longevity with the firm. Also, individuals who have friends in top management may be afforded status because of whom they know. Austria, the US, Switzerland, and UK are achievement cultures, while Venezuela, Indonesia, and China are ascription cultures.

Communication in an International Environment

As Adler notes, "Communicating effectively challenges managers worldwide even when the work force is culturally homogeneous, but when employees speak a variety of languages and come from an array of cultural backgrounds, effective communication becomes considerably more difficult". For example, the people at the home office of an MNC and the nationals in the foreign branch or subsidiary may not have the same meanings for the same words.

Communication Breakdown Across Cultures

There are a number of factors leading to communication breakdown across cultures. Some of them are as follows:

1. Perceptual Problems. People are taught to "see" things in a given way, and this will affect their interpretation (i.e., their perception) of reality. Examples of such interpretation of reality would be Japanese stockbrokers who perceived that the chances of improving their careers are better with U.S. firms, so they have changed jobs. Perception can affect international management, but misperceptions due to cultural differences can also become a barrier to effective communication.

2. Stereotyping Problems. Stereotyping is the tendency to perceive another person as belonging to a single class or category. Stereotyping is a very simple, widely used way of constructing an assumed overall profile of other people, but can be very misleading or unfair.

3. Ethnocentric Problems. Ethnocentrism refers to the sense of superiority that members of a particular culture have. Those from many countries, for example, claim that people in the United States believe they are the best in everything regardless of what area is under discussion. Even the term "American" as used by those in the United States reflects ethnocentrism, because all people in North, south, and Central American countries are Americans.

People are taught the "right" way to do things and, at least for them, it is regarded as the "best" way as well. When people interact with each other on an international basis, ethnocentrism can cause communication problems.

Improving Communication Effectiveness Across Cultures

Communication is very important. Thus firms doing business in other countries, sensitize their employees to the culture of these nations by employing effective ways. Some of them are as follows:

1. One of the most effective ways is by learning about the culture of that country before going there. Some firms have developed "cultural assimilator" training programs. These programmed learning approaches ask the participants to read about a particular situation and then choose one of four course of action or type of language that they would use. After the participants have made the choice, they then immediately learn if it was right or wrong, along with an explanation. By being put through a couple of hundred situations that they are likely to encounter in the foreign

country, they become somewhat sensitized to the culture of that country and are able to communicate more effectively. There is even evidence that speaking the language correctly is not enough. Prononciation and accent are even important.

2. A second, and often complementary, approach is to provide the trainee with educational background material on the country, including social structure, religion, values, language, and history. In particular, these training programs are designed to help managers going to a foreign assignment create the right climate between themselves and those with whom they will be communicating. This type of training is becoming particularly important for women expatriates, whose numbers have been increasing in recent years. A recent suggestion is that MNCs include in their predeparture training for male cxpatriates some suggestions for enhancing the adjustment and success for women colleagues who will be joining them.

3. A more recent training approach called "skill streaming" also seems to hold promise for learning culture-specific behaviours. Originally developed to train people in prosocial behaviors (e.g., thank someone, apologize, ask a favour, or introduce oneself), this approach can be used to train expatriates in culture-specific prosocial benaviours. Techniques such as modeling, role-playing, reinforcing feedback, and transfer of training can be applied in this skill-streaming approach to cultural training.

Motivation Across Cultures

Besides communication, motivation is of central importance in the study and application of international organizational behaviour.

Do Motivation Theories And Approaches Hold Across Cultures?

The major content and process theories and techniques of motivating human resources have been almost solely developed by scholars in the United States about U.S. employees. There are some research findings indicating that these theories and techniques hold across cultures.

For example, one study found that motivational processes such as equity might be found in the U.S., Japan, and Korea. Though Adler concluded "American motivation theories, although too often assumed to reflect universal values, have failed to provide consistently useful explanations of behaviour outside the U.S."

Most of the cross-cultural research on motivation has mainly been limited to date to the content theories such as Maslow's hierarchy of needs, Herzberg's two factor theories and McClelland's achievement theory. The result of this research is that there are definitely variations of these content motivation theories across cultures. For example, since the Chinese stress collective rather than individual needs, it has been suggested that Maslow's hierarchy, from most basic to highest, should be 1. belonging 2. physiological, 3. safety and 4. self-actualization to society.

The same has been suggested for Hertzberg's two factors and McClelland's need for achievement; they need to be recast in light of cultural differences. For example there is little question that individual's sense of responsibility and need for achievement differ greatly by culture. Yet the frameworks of these motivation theories still hold across cultures. That is, the people of all cultures have a hierarchy of needs (Maslow), factors that prevent their dissatisfaction and lead to motivation (Hertzberg), and a level of achievement motivation (McClelland). It not that these theories disappear or are not relevant across cultures. In other words, all cultures have a hierarchy of needs, but the ordering of these needs may differ by culture.

The same is true for the process theories of motivation. As Adler points out: "Expectancy theories are universal to the extent that they do not specify the types of rewards that motivate a given group of workers." The same motivational process holds across cultures, but the content and successful application will be culture-specific. Thus, the key to the understanding in the international context is to explore the basic meaning of work and the cultural dimensions that contribute to the possible differences in motivation of people across cultures.

The Meaning Of Work Across Cultures

In some cultures, work has been equated with economic rewards; e.g, North Americans can be generally characterized as working because they want to earn money with which to buy things. Thus, for most of them, time on the job is money.

Although work is important to most people in the world, and the motivational theories and processes may be the same, there are some similarities, but also some important differences, in how to motivate human resources across cultures. There is even recent research that found a difference in the motivation of employees between East and West Germany since the reunification of their country.

The role of work and the motivation of human resources in given cultures also change over time. For example, in recent years, because of downsizing and increased competitive pressures facing U.S. firms, the number of hours employees must work has increased. By contrast, the average number of hours Japanese employees work has diminished.

Motivational Differences Across Cultures

There are factors contributing to the motivational differences across cultures. Some of them are as follows:

1. The Role of Religion

One answer to motivational differences across cultures may be found in religions and their accompanying values. For instance, some religious values put emphasis on allowing events to develop in their own way, just letting things happen. An example would be the Hindus in India. Most North Americans, on the other hand, follow religions that teach them to try to control events. Some religions teach the importance of caring for others as much as oneself (collectivism); most North Americans believe that the best way to help others is to ensure one's own success (individualism) These differing values may have an indirect and, in some cases, a direct impact on the motivation of the followers.

2. The Role of Uncertainty Avoidance

Another contributing factor to motivational differences may revolve around the cultural value of avoiding ambiguity and uncertainty. If the cultural values of employees make them willing to live with uncertainty, they may be motivated quite differently from those who prefer to know what is going on. For example, those who thrive on uncertainty may not have strong job security needs. Or those with a low tolerance for ambiguity may really respond to objective performance feedback.

A recent analysis concluded: "People who have high uncertainty avoidance prefer to specialize, avoid conflict, want clear instructions, and do not want competition.Some ways to reduce uncertainty about other people are to observe them, try to get information about them, and interact with them."

3. The Role Of Power Distance

Can the people in a particular country accept the fact that others have more power than they, or do they find this difficult to live with? People in U.S., Britain, Canada, and the Scandinavian countries have trouble accepting that others have more power than they do. On the other hand, people in India, Mexico, Japan and South Korea do not. This may explain why empowerment would be more accepted and effective as a motivation strategy in those countries with a small power distance (e.g., the U.S. and the Scandinavian countries) than it would be in countries with a high power distance (e.g., Asian countries).

Managerial Leadership Across Cultures

Leadership is portrayed as the process of influencing others to direct their efforts toward the pursuit of specific goals.

As leadership expert Warren Bennis noted:

"*Given the nature and constancy of change and the transnational challenges facing American business leadership, the key to making the right choices will come from understanding and embodying the leadership qualities necessary to succeed in the volatile and mercurial global economy.*"

In the context of organizational behaviour, leadership is mainly concerned with managerial activities and style. Most of the study of leadership traditionally presented in the field of OB has come from U.S.-based theories and research samples. The leadership/management activities and styles can be the same across cultures, but the way these approaches to and processes of leadership are used and successfully applied may differ greatly from culture to culture.

Research till date has found both similarities and differences when leadership activities and styles have been examined cross-culturally. a study by Luthans called Real Managers Study was replicated in a Russian factory. The Russian managers in this factory were observed to perform, in order, traditional management, communication, human resources, and networking activities. It was found that the relationship between the Russian managers various activities and their effectiveness were similar, but less clear.

Although cross-cultural generalizations cannot be made on the basis of one study, the study can serve as a microcosm for beginning to better understand how Russian and U.S. managers are similar and different. Although some studies do find surprising similarities in leadership styles and approaches, in say, Japan and the U.S. most cross-cultural research finds differences. There are a number of possible contributing factors to the differences in effective managerial leadership across cultures. Some of the more important and those, which have been researched, are as follows:

Personal Values

Manager's personal values help shape their perception of a situation, influence their analysis of alternative solutions to a problem, and have an effect on the ultimate decision. The follower's personal values will also influence their manager. For example, how they accept authority, their power distance, and their loyalty and commitment. Such personal values on the part of both managers and subordinates will differ across cultures.

For example, those from individualistic cultures would have leadership styles driven more by values reflecting self-interest, individual distinction, and notoriety within the group. They would tend to be less participative and to assume personal responsibility. In contrast collectivistic leader would tend to be more team-oriented and to take joint responsibilities.

Manager's backgrounds may also influence the way their subordinates are led. Research shows that U.S. managers come from all economic strata: lower, middle, and upper. Virtually all today are college-educated, but because performance is important to promotion, there is no guarantee that attending a certain school will lead to success. Although graduates of Ivy League schools and those with M.B.A. from prestigious institutions may have an advantage, many U.S. managers from all types and sizes of colleges have made it into the upper ranks. The same pattern may not be as true in other countries. For example, in France managers often are chosen from the graduates of the '*grandes ecoles*'. In Japan, those who gain entrance into the prestigious schools have a much better chance of becoming top managers of the large corporations. In Korea, many of the newly emerging managerial leaders have been educated in the U.S.

Besides educational background, class and family background also make a difference. In U.S. managers come from all the classes. However, in Turkey, many of the top managers come from the upper class.

At the same time family upbringing is also important. For example, in India, it is common to accept the authority of elders. Thus, in superior-subordinate relations there is generally little delegation of authority. Instead, the head of the enterprise exercises a directive leadership style and everyone follows these orders.

Interpersonal Skills

There is research evidence that managers differ across cultures in their interpersonal skills. For example, Bass and Burger conducted a comprehensive study of managers in the U.S., Belgium, Britain, France, Germany-austria, Iberia, India, Japan, Latin America, and Scandinavia. Some of their relevant findings in relation to interpersonal styles and skills include the following:

- Spanish and Portuguese managers were most willing to be aware of other's feelings, to be concerned with their subordinates welfare, and to accept feedback from others. The Germans, Austrians and French were less willing to do these things. The other countries fell between these two extremely different groups

- Managers from India saw themselves as most dependent on higher authority. German and Austrian managers viewed themselves as very independent.

- Managers from India were the most concerned about bureaucratic rules; the Japanese were the last concerned.

- Dutch managers were the most willing to cooperate with others; the French were the least willing.

- Japanese managers had a greater desire to be objective rather than intuitive than did managers from any other country.

- U.S. and Latin American managers demonstrated much greater interpersonal competence than other managers.

The above findings demonstrate that interpersonal approaches differ by culture.

International Joint Ventures (IJVs) also lead to many interpersonal conflicts between members of the same company from vastly different cultures. For example, local managers of IJVs may become frustrated by the lack of promotion opportunities to key jobs if senior positions are reserved for "outsiders" or those whose loyalty lies not with the current IJV but with the parent company. In such instances, conflicts may arise that prevent full cooperation among the staff.

Transnationally Competent Managers

With the coming of the new millennium, it is becoming increasingly clear that traditionally conceived and practiced international management leadership is no longer sufficient.

Adler and Bartholomew. Has identified some of the transnational skills that are needed for the borderless, global economy.

1. Undersatnd the worldwide business environment from a global, rather than a single-country, perspective.

2. Learn about many foreign cultures perspectives, taste, trends, technologies, and approaches to conducting business.

3. Be skillful at working with people from many different cultures simultaneously.

4. Be able to adapt to not only living in other cultures but also using cross-cultural skills on regular multicultural business trips and in daily interaction with foreign colleagues and clients worldwide.

5. Interact with foreign colleagues as equals, rather than from within clearly defined hierarchies of structural or cultural dominance and subordination.

This profile of the transnationally competent manager serves as a point of departure for research and guidelines for the successful practice and application of leadership in the international arena now and in the future.

References

1. Luthans, F. (1998) *Organizational Behaviour* (8th Edition) Irwin/McGraw-Hill. International Edition.

2. Pettinger, R. (1996) *Introduction to Organizational Behaviour,* Macmillan Press Ltd., London.

3. Fincham, R. & Rhodes, P.S. (1999) *Principles of Organizational Behaviour (3rd Edition)* Oxford University Press.

4. Kaila H.L. (2006). *Human Resource Management* (Two volumes). Delhi: Kalpaz Publications.

2

Theories of Work Motivation

1. Motivation – An Introduction
2. Theories of motivation.
3. Content theories of motivation.
   - Theory X and Theory Y
   - Maslow's need hierarchy
   - Herzberg's Two Factor theory
   - Alderfer's ERG Theory
   - McClelland's Theory of Needs
4. Process theories of motivation.
   - Vroom's Expectancy Theory
   - Porter and Lawler
   - Adam's Equity Theory
   - Goal Setting Theory
5. Reinforcement Theory.
6. Attribution Theory.
7. References.

Motivation

Motivation is derived from the word motive. "A motive is an inner state that energizes, activates or moves and directs or channels behavior towards goals." Motivation is not directly observable, it must be inferred. Motivation represents an unsatisfied need, which creates a state of tension, or disequilibrium, causing the individual to move in a goal directed pattern towards restoring a state of equilibrium by satisfying the need. According to the encyclopedia of management, "Motivation refers to the degree of readiness of an organization to pursue some designated goal and implies the determination of the nature and the locus of the forces, including the degree of readiness."

Motivation is a pivotal concept. It is closely related to arousal, attention, anxiety, and feedback/reinforcement. It is a process that starts with a physiological or psychological deficiency or a need that activates a behavior or a drive that is aimed to a goal of incentive. Thus, the process of motivation involves the relationship among needs, drives and incentives.

Need ⟶ Drive ⟶ Goals/ Incentives

Motivational processes can be inferred from an analysis of a continuous stream of behaviors that are determined by both environment and heredity and are observed through their effects on personality, beliefs, knowledge, attitudes and skills.

Many contemporary authors have also defined the concept of motivation. Motivation has been defined as: the psychological process that gives behavior purpose and direction (Kreitner, 1995); a predisposition to behave in a purposive manner to achieve specific, unmet needs (Buford, Bedeian, and Lindner, 1995); an internal drive to satisfy an unsatisfied need (Higgins, 1994); and the will to achieve (Bedeian, 1993). But in general, motivation is operationally defined as the inner force that drives individuals to accomplish personal and organizational goals.

Work motivation refers to the domain of motivational processes directed to the realm of work. Pinder (1998) defined it as: "Work motivation is a set of energetic forces that originate both within as well as beyond an individual's being, to initiate work related behavior, and to determine its form, direction, intensity and duration."

Theories of Motivation

In the past 35 years there has been a profusion of work motivation theories. These theories give markedly different explanations for the same aspect of human behaviour. These theories have been proposed from environmental, social, dispositional and cognitive perspectives. These theories are broadly classified into content theories, process theories and reinforcement theories.

Theories

Content Theories	Process Theories	Reinforcement theories
Theory X & Theory Y	Vroom's Expectancy Theory	
Maslow's need hierarchy	Porter and Lawler	
Herzberg's Two Factor theory	Adam's Equity Theory	
Alderfer's ERG	Cognitive Evaluation	
McClelland's Theory of Needs	Goal Setting	

Content Theories of Motivation

Content theories of motivation deal with identifying the needs of people and how they prioritize them. These needs include wages, salary in order to satisfy physiological drives, incentives, social needs, security, recognition etc.

I. Theory X and Theory Y

Douglas McGregor (1960) proposed two distinct views of human beings: one negative, labeled Theory X and the other positive, labeled Theory Y. After viewing the way managers dealt with employees, McGregor concluded that a manager's view of the human beings is based on a certain grouping of assumptions, and he/she tends to mould his or her behaviour towards subordinates according to these assumptions.

Under theory X, following are the assumptions:

- Employees inherently dislike work and whenever possible will attempt to avoid it.

- Since employees dislike work, they must be coerced, controlled or threatened with punishment to achieve desired goals.

• Employees have little capacity for creativity in solving organizational problems.

• Employees will shrink responsibilities and seek formal direction whenever possible.

• Most workers place security above all other factors associated with work, and will display little ambition.

Managers who accept the assumptions of theory X attempt to structure, control, and closely supervise their employees. These managers feel that external control is clearly appropriate to deal with unreliable and irresponsible people. However McGregor felt that the assumptions of theory X, when applied universally are inaccurate and that the management practices that develop from these assumptions may fail to motivate many people to work towards organizational goals.

McGregor felt that management needed practices based on more accurate understanding of human nature and motivation. As a result of this feeling, in contrast to these negative views (theory X), towards the nature of human beings, McGregor listed other assumptions that he called theory Y:

• Employees can view work as being as natural as rest or play.

• People will exercise self-direction and self-control if they are committed to the objectives.

• The capacity for creativity in solving organizational problems is widely distributed in the population.

• The average person can learn to accept or even seek responsibility.

• The ability to make good decisions is widely dispersed throughout the population, and not necessarily the sole province of those in management positions.

McGregor himself held to the belief that the assumptions of theory Y were more valid than theory X. Therefore he proposed ideas like participation in decision making, responsible and challenging jobs, and good group relations as approaches that would maximize an employees job motivation.

In their book "In Search of Excellence", Peters and Waterman (1982) stated that one of the chief differences between American and Japanese management is that American managers tend to use Theory X and Japanese managers tend to use Theory Y. This difference may be lessening, as evidenced by the practices of the management of the General Motors Saturn plants.

In his book "Theory Z", William Ouchi (1981) described the characteristics of the Japanese companies that produce high employee commitment, motivation, and productivity. Many Japanese employees are guaranteed a position for life, increasing their loyalty to the company. Careful evaluation occurs over a period of time, and the responsibility for success or failure is shared among employees and management. Most employees do not specialize in one skill area, but work at several different tasks, learning more about the company as they develop. And Japanese companies are often concerned about all aspects of their employees' lives, on and off the job. According to Ouchi, Type Z organizations tend to have stable employment, high productivity, and high employee morale and satisfaction. Many of these outcomes are similar to Theory Y.

Evaluating Theory X and Theory Y

The assumptions of theory X and Y are based on social science research which has been carried out, and demonstrate the potential which is present in man and which organizations should recognize in order to become more effective. McGregor sees these two theories as two quite separate attitudes. Theory Y is difficult to put into practice on the shop floor in large mass production operations, but it can be used initially in the managing of managers and professionals.

In "The Human Side of Enterprise" McGregor shows how Theory Y affects the management of promotions and salaries and the development of effective managers. McGregor also sees Theory Y as conducive to participative problem solving. It is part of the manager's job to exercise authority, and there are cases in which this is the only method of achieving the desired results because subordinates do not agree that the ends are desirable.

However, in situations where it is possible to obtain commitment to objectives, it is better to explain the matter fully so that employees grasp the purpose of an action. They will then exert self-direction and control to do better work - quite possibly by better methods - than if they had simply been carrying out an order which they did not fully understand. The situation in which employees can be consulted is one where the individuals are emotionally mature, and positively motivated towards their work where the work is sufficiently responsible to allow for flexibility and where the employee can see his own position in the management hierarchy.

If these conditions are present, managers will find that the participative approach to problem solving leads to more improved results compared with the alternative approach of handing out authoritarian orders. Once management becomes persuaded that it is under estimating the potential of its human resources, and accepts the knowledge given by social science researchers and displayed in Theory Y assumptions, and then it can invest time, money and effort in developing improved applications of the theory.

McGregor realizes that some of the theories he has put forward are unrealizable in practice, but wants managers to put into operation the basic assumption that: Staff will contribute more to the organization if they are treated as responsible and valued employees.

II. Hierarchy Of Needs

The most well known theory of motivation is Abraham Maslow's hierarchy of needs. Most of Maslow's writing was not concerned with work motivation. However later in his career he focused on the applications of the theory. According to Maslow (1987), motivation arises from certain needs. Needs are biological or instinctive, they characterize humans in general and have a genetic base. They often influence behaviour unconsciously. What causes people to behave as they do is the process of satisfying these needs. He hypothesized that within every human being there exists a hierarchy of 5 needs. These are:

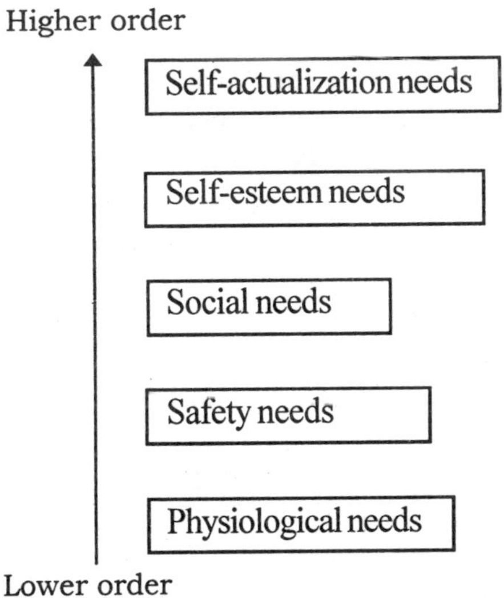

Physiological Needs. They are the most basic; their fulfillment is necessary for survival. They include air, water and food.

Safety Needs. They include freedom from threat, danger and deprivation. They involve self-preservation.

Social Needs. Include the desire for association, belonging and companionship.

Self-Esteem Needs. Include self-confidence, recognition, appreciation and the respect of one's peers.

Self-Actualization. Is the last need. It is realization of one's full potential, in Maslow's words, "to become more and more what one is, to become everything that one is capable of becoming."

Maslow made the following propositions about the need hierarchy:

- Behaviour is dominated and determined by the needs that are unfulfilled.

- An individual will systematically satisfy his or her needs by starting with the most basic and working up the hierarchy.
- Basic needs take precedence over all those higher in the hierarchy.

Thus when these needs are satisfied, a sense of adequacy is experienced. Their thwarting produces feelings of inferiority and helplessness.

Recently there have been additions to the hierarchy of needs. The three new needs are as follows:

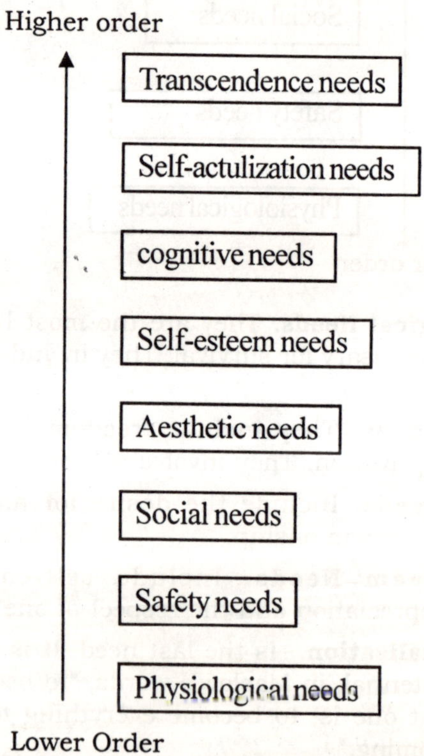

- **Aesthetic Needs.** wherein the luxuries, looks, work in place of beauty and form are considered before self esteem needs.

- **Cognitive Needs.** this refers to the need for challenging jobs, updating one's knowledge and such other needs.

- **Transcendence Needs.** this need is even above the self-actualizing need, which refers to the need to help others become self actualized after the person himself attains self-actualization.

Evaluating the Hierarchy of Needs Theory

Maslow's need theory has received wide recognition, particularly among practicing managers. This can be attributed to the logic and ease with which the theory is intuitively understood. Unfortunately however research does not generally validate the theory. Maslow provided no empirical substantiation and also several studies that sought to validate the theory found no support. However Maslow's theory is not a "theory" in the real sense, he did not propose a testable hypothesis. It is based on logical and clinical insights into human nature rather than on research findings.

Another point would be that Maslow states that we systematically progress from one need to the next. Yet we all need to eat, drink and breathe everyday. Thus we never really have our physiological needs satisfied. We try to fulfill our esteem needs even when our social needs remain unsatisfied. Thus we attempt to satisfy all needs concurrently. Maslow did not deal with this speculation.

Thus Maslow's theory would be regarded as more philosophical than empirical. His notion of self-actualization is well ingrained in the way we think about our mission in life. Though Maslow's theory is deficient in explaining day-to-day behaviour at work; his contributions to the field cannot be ignored.

III. Frederick Herzberg's Motivational Theory

Frederick Herzberg's book 'The Motivation to Work', written with research colleagues B Mausner and B Snyderman in 1959, first established his theories about motivation in the workplace. Herzberg's work, originally on 200 Pittsburgh engineers and accountants, has become one of the most replicated studies in the field of workplace psychology. Herzberg was the first to show that satisfaction and dissatisfaction at work nearly always arose from different factors, and were not simply opposing reactions to the same factors, as had always previously been believed. He showed that certain factors truly motivate ('motivators'), whereas others tended to lead to dissatisfaction ('hygiene factors').

According to Herzberg, Man has two sets of needs one as an animal to avoid pain, and two as a human being to grow psychologically. He illustrated this also through Biblical example: Adam after his expulsion from Eden having the need for food, warmth, shelter, safety, etc., - the 'hygiene' needs; and Abraham, capable and achieving great things through self-development - the 'motivational' needs. Certain parallels can clearly be seen with Abraham Maslow's theory.

Motivator Factors. (The Job itself)

- Sense of achievement
- Recognition for accomplishment
- Challenging work/ job
- Increase in responsibility
- Growth and development.

Hygiene Factors. (The environment)

- Policies and Administration
- Supervision
- Working conditions
- Interpersonal relations
- Money, status, security

Herzberg's research proved that people would strive to achieve hygiene needs because they are unhappy without them, but once satisfied the effect soon wears off - satisfaction is temporary.

But research shows otherwise. Surveys repeatedly

show that other factors motivate more. For example, a survey by Development Dimensions International published in the UK Times newspaper in 2004 interviewed 1,000 staff from companies employing more than 500 workers, and found many to be bored, lacking commitment and looking for a new job. Pay actually came fifth in the reasons people gave for leaving their jobs. The main reasons were lack of stimulus jobs and no opportunity for advancement - classic Herzberg motivators - 43 per cent left for better promotion chances, 28 per cent for more challenging work; 23 per cent for a more exciting place to work; and 21 per cent and more varied work.

Evaluating Herzberg's Theory

According to this theory, hygiene factors when satisfied tend to eliminate dissatisfaction and any work restrictions for the employee. But they can do little to motivate an individual to perform better. Whereas, enhancement of the motivators can help the individual to experience job satisfaction which intern will lead to an increase in his output. Thus hygiene factors affect an individual's willingness to perform while motivators will affect an individual's ability to perform.

In fact a research study concluded that whenever hygiene factors were increased, and motivating factors remained the same, there was satisfaction. When both the factors did not increase, there was no satisfaction. Thus if hygiene factors are increased and motivating factors decreased, then there was demotivation.

IV. Alderfer's ERG Theory

A revised and realigned version of Maslow's Hierarchy of Needs theory is the ERG theory developed by Clayton Alderfer of Yale University. Instead of Maslow's 5 categories of needs, Alderfer suggested that there are three core needs: Existence needs, Relatedness needs, and Growth needs.

Existence Needs. Refers to the material needs namely food, air, water, pay, fringe benefits and working conditions.

Relatedness Needs. Can be satisfied by establishing

and maintaining interpersonal relations with colleagues, superiors, subordinates, friends and family.

Growth Needs. Are expressed by an individual's attempt in seeking ways for individual personal development by making creative contributions at work places.

Thus as can be seen, there is some similarity between Maslow's hierarchy of needs and Alderfer's ERG theory. Alderfer's existence grouping of needs corresponds to Maslow's basic or physiological needs, Relatedness needs corresponds to social needs and growth needs corresponds to esteem and self-actualization needs. The following table shows a comparison of Maslow's and Alderfer's Categories of needs.

Maslow	*Alderfer*
Self –actualization Esteem	Growth
Social	Relatedness
Safety Physiological	Existence

The basic difference between the two theories is in their perceptions of how people attempt to satisfy different sets of needs.

(a) Maslow has stated that unfulfilled needs act as motivators and the next higher level need is not activated until the preceding lower level need is satisfied. ERG theory suggests that in addition to the fulfillment progression process there is also a frustration regression process at work. Which means that if an individual gets frustrated while attempting to satisfy growth needs, and then relatedness needs will re –emerge as a motivating force.

(b) Maslow's theory works on the assumption that only one of the five categories of needs will be predominant at a given time. Whereas the ERG theory allows for more than one need to be operating more or less equally at the same time.

Evaluating the ERG Theory

The ERG theory can help managers to gain an insight into employees' behaviour because of the assumption it holds that individuals are motivated to adopt a behaviour to satisfy one of the three sets of needs. Research evidence indicates that there is more support of ERG theory's three sets of needs rather than the five categories of needs.

Also the proposition that the three needs can be dominant simultaneously and there is no order of the needs in terms of priority seems more plausible than Maslow's hierarchy of needs.

The three needs are simple and easy to understand as compared to Maslow's needs like self- actualization, etc., that Maslow proposes not many people can attain.

V. David McClelland's Achievement Motivation Theory

David McClelland's theory is a content model of motivation, which he believed to be rooted in culture. He opined that every person has three important needs viz. achievement need, an affiliation need and a power need.

- **Achievement need.** McClelland's research led him to believe that human beings distinctly possess the need or desire to achieve something. For this purpose they compete to reach (or achieve) a certain standard of excellence or make a unique contribution which will speak of their achievement.

- **Affiliation need.** Human beings being social animals like to interact with other people and experience the feeling of belongingness and togetherness. McClelland's study led him to accept the fact that individuals with a strong affiliation motive tend to establish and maintain intimate personal relations with other people. Such people are concerned with maintaining pleasant social relations, experience the feeling of intimacy and understanding and also lend their hand to others in trouble.

• **Power need**. The ability to induce or influence other's behaviour is called power. McClelland found that persons with a high power need display a great concern for exercising influence and control. They are also interested in providing status rewards to their followers.

Individuals with a high need to achieve prefer job situations with personal responsibility, feedback, and an intermediate degree of risk. When these characteristics are prevalent, high achievers will be strongly motivated. The evidence consistently demonstrates that high achievers are successful in entrepreneurial activities such as running their own business, managing a self-contained unit within a large organization, and serving in a variety of sales positions. However a high need to achieve does not necessarily lead to being a good manager, especially in large organizations. People with a high achievement need are interested in how well they do personally and not in influencing others to do well. Also the needs for affiliation and power tend to be closely related to managerial success. The best managers are in their need for power and low in their need for affiliation. Employees have been successfully trained to stimulate their achievement need. Thus if the job calls for a high achiever, management can select a person with a high need for achievement or develop its own candidate through achievement training.

Process Theories of Motivation

The content theories of motivation identify what motivates people, while the process theories deal with cognitive antecedents that go into motivation and effort. These theories contribute to the complex processes involved in motivational effort.

1. Vroom's Expectancy Theory

Victor Vroom felt that content models were inadequate explanations of the complex process of work motivation and he developed a relatively new theory of motivation. This theory is a cognitive theory. Thus, each person is assumed to be a rational decision maker who will expend effort on activities that lead to desired rewards. According to this theory, motivation of any individual depends on the desired goal and the strength of his expectations of achieving the goal. Vroom's model (1964) is built on 3 concepts – Valence, instrumentality and expectancy.

Valence. Vroom says that valence is the strength of an individual's preference for a particular outcome. It can be taken as an equivalent of value, incentive, attitude, and expected utility. For the valence to be positive, the person must prefer attaining the outcome to not attaining the outcome. The valence is negative when the individual prefers not attaining outcomes o attaining it.

Instrumentality. Another major input into the valence is the instrumentality of the first level outcome in obtaining desired second level outcomes. For example, if an individual desires promotion and feels that superior performance is a very strong factor in achieving that goal, then his first outcomes are superior, average or poor performance. His second level outcome is promotion. The first level outcome of high performance thus acquired a positive valence by virtue of its expected relationship to the preferred outcome of second level promotion. In this case the person is motivated to achieve superior performance because he has a desire to be promoted. Thus the superior performance is seen as being instrumental in obtaining promotion.

Expectancy. The third major variable in Vroom's theory is expectancy. Though expectancyn and instrumentality appear to be the same, they are quite different. Expectancy is a probability (ranging from 0 to 1) or strength of a belief that a particular action or effort will lead to a particular first level outcome. Whereas instrumentality refers to the degree to which a first level outcome will lead to the second level outcome.

There are two other concepts besides the above three. They are:

Job Outcomes. They are things organizations can provide for its employees, such as pay, promotions, and vacation time. They are usually thought of as rewards. But they need not be always positive. Outcomes can also be negative like being fired, or even intangible like feeling of recognition, acceptance etc.

Force. The amount of effort or pressure within the person to be motivated. The larger the force, the greater the hypothesized motivation.

Vroom says that the sum if these variables leads to motivation.

Evaluating the Expectancy Theory

This theory is highly rational and conscious explanation of motivation. People are assumed to behave in a way that will maximize expected gains from exhibiting certain job behavior and expending certain levels of effort. To the extent that behavior is not directed toward maximizing gains in a rational, systematic way, the theory will not be upheld. Whenever unconscious motives deflect behavior from what a knowledge of conscious processes would predict, expectancy theory will not be predictive.

Also research suggests that people differ in the extent to which their behaviour is motivated by rational processes (Muchinsky, 1977). The general findings are that some people have a very rational basis for their behavior, and thus the theory works well for them, others appear to be motivated more by unconscious factors and for them the theory does not work well (Stahl & Harrell, 1981).

Research by Van Eerde & Thierry (1996) concluded that the individual components of the theory (valence, instrumentality and expectancy, VIE) made as accurate predictions of criteria as did the complete multiplicative model. In other words, the concepts measured by the theory are valid in predicting effort, but the VIE model does not enhance our understanding of motivation. However as Pinder (1998) concluded "At the very least the expectancy theory is probably an accurate representation of how people form work related intentions."

2. Porter and Lawler

All the content theories assume that satisfaction leads to improved performance. However, it was later found that there is a very low positive relationship between satisfaction and performance. Lyman W. Porter and Edward E. Lawler explored the complex relation between motivation, satisfaction and performance. According to them performance is a function of three important factors:

- If an employee wants to perform, he must be motivated.

- Motivation does not alone ensure performance and hence a person must have the necessary abilities and skills as well.

- An employee must have an accurate knowledge of the requirements of the job.

Following are the key variables of the model:

- ***Effort.*** Effort does not directly lead to specific levels of performance. Effort is only the amount of energy exerted by an individual to achieve a specific task. It is only the result of the attractiveness of the reward and how he perceives a relation between effort and pay – off. The individual will exert greater effort if he perceives that there is a greater probability that his effort will lead to the reward. So motivation is seen as a force on the employee to expect effort.

- ***Performance***. Effort alone is not enough, as performance results only when the effort is continued with the ability. Effort and performance cannot be taken to be the same.

- ***Reward***. A person gets intrinsic reward himself by performing the task well. If an individual feels that he should have received more of what he had done, it results in dissatisfaction and vice versa.

- ***Satisfaction***. It depends on the perceived rewards and the actual rewards. If an individual feels that he should have received more for what he had done; it results in dissatisfaction and vice versa.

Thus motivation and achievement result in satisfaction or dissatisfaction of an employee about the job, organization etc. Porter and Lawler say that for employees to perform, effort is required along with positive rewards and satisfaction. But for the person to take effort he/she must have the necessary skills, ability and knowledge about the job in the first place.

3. Adam's Equity Theory

J Stracy Adams drawing from the principle of social comparison developed this theory. Adams suggested that motivation has a social rather than biological origin. This theory argues that a major input into job performance and satisfaction is the degree of equity (or inequity) that people perceive in their work situation. Inequality occurs when a person perceives that the ratio of his or her outcomes to inputs and the ratio of others relevant outcome to inputs are unequal.

Equity theory has four major parts:

(1) Because it is a perceptually based theory, the individual perceives himself in comparison with others. The person who does the perceiving is the PERSON.

(2) It is postulated that the Person compares himself or herself with another individual. This other person is called the OTHER.

(3) All the assets Person brings to the job are the third component, collectively. These assets are referred to as INPUTS. Inputs include Persons education, intelligence, experience skills, seniority, effort level, health, etc. They are anything of perceived value or importance that Person brings to the job.

(4) All benefits Person derives from the job are the fourth component, collectively referred to as OUTCOMES. Outcomes include pay, benefits, working conditions, status symbols, seniority benefits, etc. They are those factors Person perceives as being derived from employment.

The theory states that Person forms a ratio of his/her inputs to outcomes and compares it with perceptions of Other's inputs/ outcomes ratio. Adams assumes that people can quantify both their inputs and outcomes into common scale units.

Schematically this can be represented as follows:

Inequity occurs when

$$\frac{\text{Person's outcomes}}{\text{Person's inputs}} < \frac{\text{Other's outcomes}}{\text{Other's inputs}}$$

OR

$$\frac{\text{Person's outcomes}}{\text{Person's inputs}} > \frac{\text{Other's outcomes}}{\text{Other's inputs}}$$

Equity Occurs When

$$\frac{\text{Person's outcomes}}{\text{Person's inputs}} = \frac{\text{Other's outcomes}}{\text{Other's inputs}}$$

Both the inputs and outputs of persons and others are based upon the person's perceptions. The age, sex, education economic and social status, skill, experience, training, effort, education, past and present performance, level of difficulty, position in the organization etc are examples of perceived input variables. Outcomes consist of rewards like pay, status, promotion and intrinsic interest in the job. If the person's perceived ratio is not equal to others, he or she will strive to restore the ratio to equity. Thus, the work motivation of oneself depends upon other's inputs, output and one's perceived outputs.

Adams felt that people could alter their motivation levels in an attempt to bring feelings of inequity back into line. The drive to reduce the tension caused by the inequity manifests itself in more or less effort being put into the job, which is a form of input.

Evaluating the Equity Theory

To date, research on equity theory has only addressed financial compensation, yet that is only one of many outcomes derived from a job. People feel either underpaid or overpaid, which is intern associated with absenteeism and turnover. However the whole issue of organizations deliberately manipulating their employees to induce feelings of inequity raises moral and ethical questions.

The components of the equity theory have been substantiated from research. It is evident that people do consider the inputs they bring to the job. It is also true that people hold beliefs about the nature and quantity of the consequences or outcomes they receive as a result of doing their work. The process of social comparison is also valid because what we do is in part a product of what others do around us.

However the problem with the theory from a motivational perspective pertains to how people deal with feelings of inequity or unfairness. Inequity need not always be resolved by expending greater effort, which cuts to the core of the theory.

4. Goal Setting Theory

The goal setting theory is a motivation theory whose crux is the relationship among goals, intentions and task performance. The basic premise is that conscious ideas regulate a person's actions. Goals are what the individual is consciously trying to attain, particularly related to future objectives.

According to Locke and Latham (1990) goals have two major functions: They are the basis of motivation and they direct behavior. A goal provides guidelines for a person deciding how much effort to put into the work. However two important conditions must be met before goals can positively influence performance.

First, the individual must be aware of the goal and know what must be accomplished. Second, the individual must accept the goal as something he or she is willing to work for. Thus, goals can be rejected because they are seen as too difficult or too easy or because the person does not know what behaviors are needed to attain them.

Edwin Locke in the late 1960s proposed that intentions to work toward the goal are a major source of work motivation. If we know the goals clearly we can determine what should we do, and how much effort we should put in and in what direction. To be precise, specific goals enhance performance. Difficult goals, when accepted would lead to higher performance than normal goals. Further, feedback contributes to higher performance. Employees do better when they get feedback on how well they are programming towards their goals. And what extra effort they should take.

The specificity of the goal itself acts as an internal stimulus. Specific hard goals produce a higher level of performance and output than the generalized goal. Normally it is expected that the employee is motivated to achieve higher results if he/she is allowed to participate in goal setting. In fact, the concept of MBO suggested by Peter Drucker, assumes that employee involvement in the setting of objectives contributes to higher outputs.

Evaluating the Goal - Setting Theory

The theory is simple and elegant. The theory focuses on the question of why some people perform better on work tasks than others. If they are equal in ability and environmental conditions, then the cause must be motivational. People perform better than others because they have different performance goals. Research shows that different type of people also prefer different types of goals, but it is clear that goal setting elicits better performance.

The theory is extensively generalizable. Its application is not limited to highly rational people, although it does assume that people follow through with their intentions. There is also evidence that goal setting is effective for groups. Thus, a group can set a goal to decrease scrap rate, for e.g. to increase productive outcomes.

Locke, Shaw, Saari, and Latham (1981) reviewed 12 years of goal setting research studies and concluded the following:

(a) 90% of the studies show that specific and challenging goals lead to higher performance than easy goals.

(b) Goal setting was found to improve task performance when

- Subjects have sufficient ability
- Feedback is provided on progress related to goals
- Rewards are given for goal attainment
- Management is supportive
- Individuals accept the assigned goals.

However the principles of goal setting were empirically supported more often in laboratory than in field studies. Nevertheless, the overall verdict on the value of goal setting as a theory of motivation is overwhelmingly positive.

Reinforcement Theory

B.F. Skinner developed this theory of motivation. According to Skinner, behaviour of people is mostly influenced by its consequences. The actions, which result in positive consequences, tend to be repeated more often. In contrast, the actions that result in negative consequence tend to be repeated less often. An action is said to be reinforcing, if the occurrence of the event following some behavior makes the behavior more likely to repeat in the future.

There are four types of reinforcements viz. positive reinforcement, negative reinforcement, punishment and extinction. The different types of reinforcements are the results of either the application or withdrawal of either pleasant or unpleasant events.

Positive Reinforcement. Following the positive behavior, the employee is provided with a pleasant or a desirable event like higher salary, better benefits, praise, recognition and status. This results in the occurrence of the pleasant behavior frequently.

Negative Reinforcement. Following the withdrawal of a negative reinforcement, like strict supervision, strict controls, harassment and threatening etc. the positive behaviour tends to occur more frequently.

Punishment. Some supervisors feel that strict control

and supervision lends to enhance performance. Hence, they impose control. Punishment takes place when an unpleasant or undesirable event occurs following some behaviour and makes the behaviour less likely to occur.

Extinction. here reinforcements, either negative or positive, are given in such a way that the behaviour is eliminated all together. The behaviour ceases to occur in the future.

The theory has three key variables: stimulus, response and reward. A stimulus is any variable or condition that elicits a behavioural response. In an industrial setting, a response is some measure of job performance, like productivity, absenteeism, or accidents. A reward is something of value given to the employee on the basis of the elicited behavioural response; it is meant to reinforce the occurrence of the desired response.

Most attention has been paid to the response-reward connection. Based on animal research, four types of response-reward contingencies have been found to influence the frequency of the response:

(i) Fixed interval. The subject is rewarded at a fixed time interval, such as every hour.

(ii) Fixed ratio. The subject is rewarded for a fixed number of responses.

(iii) Variable interval. The subject is rewarded at some time interval that varies.

(iv) Variable ratio. Reward is based on behavior, but the ratio of reward to response is variable.

Proponents of this theory believe that that the subject's motivation to respond can be shaped by manipulating these reinforcement schedules. Many authors have discussed the potential benefits and liabilities of using reinforcement theory as a basis for motivating employees. The theory entails placing the control of employee motivation in the organization's hands, since organizations can regulate the energy output of employees by manipulating reinforcement schedules.

Evaluating the Reinforcement Theory

Research indicates that the principles of the reinforcement theory do work. But the theory suffers from some limitations in industrial settings. The current applications of reinforcement theory tend to ignore individual differences in what are valued as rewards.

The reinforcement theory has wide applications for problem solving; it can be used for reducing absenteeism, and turnover, enhancing productivity and improving supervisory training.

However detractors of the theory cite possible ethical matters associated with the reinforcement of behaviour. They question, is it ethical for an organization to use a payment system that increases productivity but may cause adverse side effects.

Nevertheless this theory has a history of producing desired changes in work behaviour. Unlike other motivational theories, its focus is not on the individual but on environmental factors that shape or modify behaviour. While implementation problems exist, they address only the theory's applicability rather than its validity.

Attribution Theory

Heider (1958) was the first to propose a psychological theory of attribution, but Weiner and colleagues (e.g., Jones et al, 1972; Weiner, 1974, 1986) developed a theoretical framework that has become a major research paradigm. Attribution theory assumes that people try to determine why people do what they do, i.e., attribute causes to behaviour. A person seeking to understand why another person did something may attribute one or more causes to that behaviour.

Principles

1. Attribution is a three-stage process: (1) behaviour is observed, (2) behaviour is determined to be deliberate, and (3) behaviour is attributed to internal or external causes.

2. Achievement can be attributed to (1) effort, (2) ability, (3) level of task difficulty, or (4) luck.

3. Causal dimensions of behavior are (1) locus of control, (2) stability, and (3) controllability.

Weiner focused his attribution theory on achievement (Weiner, 1974). He identified ability, effort, task difficulty, and luck as the most important factors affecting attributions for achievement. Attributions are classified along three causal dimensions: locus of control, stability, and controllability.

Locus of Control: Internal-External

Causation for events may be placed in a continuum ranging from conditions completely within to those completely outside of the individual's influence. Locus of control refers to the degree to which results are due to factors inside (internal locus of control) or outside (external locus of control) an individual. For instance, factors such as mood and ability are internal causes; luck and teacher bias are external causes.

Stability: Stable-Unstable

Stability refers to an unchanging cause. Consider the following statement: "I'm good at playing guitar because I've practiced for more than a year". In this case, the ability to play guitar is a stable cause for this person. Or this: "I got an A in math this time because the test was very easy. Almost everyone made an A." Such a belief suggests that the successful performance resulted from chance; the easy test is an inconsistent or unstable cause.

Controllability. controllable-uncontrollable

Controllability refers to those factors that can be controlled to influence results. Skill and competence are classified as controllable, while luck and mood are classified as uncontrollable.

Example

Attribution theory has been used to explain the difference in motivation between high and low achievers. According to attribution theory, high achievers will approach rather than avoid tasks related to succeeding because they believe success is due to high ability and effort, which they are confident of.

Failure is thought to be caused by bad luck or a poor exam, i.e., not their fault. Thus, failure doesn't affect their self-esteem but success builds pride and confidence. On the other hand, low achievers avoid success-related chores because they tend to (a) doubt their ability and/or (b) assume success is related to luck or to "whom you know" or to other factors beyond their control. Thus, even when successful, it isn't as rewarding to the low achiever because he/she doesn't feel responsible, i.e., it doesn't increase his/her pride and confidence.

The Attributional Process

From review attributional theories, Pintrich and Schunk (1996) generated a model to present the attributional process. This model provides the effect of attribution on motivational, affective, and behavioral consequences. The incidents can be classified as either environmental or personal factors. An individual will attribute these incidents to the perceived causes and different causal dimensions. These causes will affect an individual's psychological consequences and influence behaviours. The overview of the general attributional model can help in gaining an understanding of the attributional process.

Antecedent Conditions →	**Perceived Causes** →	**Causal Dimensions** →	**Psychological Consequences** →	**Behavioral Consequences**
Environmental factors • Specific information • Social norms • Situational Features				
Personal factors • Causal schemas • Attributional bias • Prior knowledge • Individual differenzes	*Attributions for* Ability Effort Luck Task difficulty Teacher Mood Health Fatigue, etc.	Stability Locus of Control Controllability	Expectancy for success Self-efficacy Affect	Choice Persistence Level of effort Achievement

References

- Hersey, P. (2001). "Management of Organizational Behaviour: Utilizing Human Resources". (7th Ed.); Prentice Hall of India Pvt. Ltd.; New Delhi.
- Luthans, F (2000). "Organizational Behaviour" (8th Ed.); McGraw Hill.
- Muchinsky, P.M., (2001). "Psychology Applied to Work". (6th Ed.); Wadsworth, Thompson Learning. Belmont, U.S.A.
- Saal, F.E., Patrick, A.K., (1988). "Industrial/ Organizational Psychology; Theory & Practice". Wadsworth Inc., California.
- Weiner, B. (1974). "Achievement motivation and attribution theory". Morristown, N.J.: General Learning Press.
- http://www.hbg.psu.edu/faculty/jxr11/glass1sp.html
- Www.coe.uga.edu/epltt/Motivation.htm
- http://www.tvrls.com/dm.htm

3
Dynamics of Group Behaviour

What Is A Group? A Working Definition

Imagine three people waiting in line at the cashier's stand at a supermarket. Now, compare them to the board of directors of a large corporation. Which collection would you consider to be a "group"? Although in our everyday language we may refer to the people waiting in line as a group, they clearly are not a group in the same sense as the members of the board. Obviously, a group is more than simply a collection of people. But what exactly is it that makes a group a group?

Social scientists have formally defined a group as a collection of two or more interacting individuals with a stable pattern of relationships between them who share common goals and who perceive themselves as being a group.

The Four Key Characteristics Of Groups

Social Interaction

One of the most obvious characteristics of groups is that they are composed of two or more people in social interaction. In other words, the members of a group must have some influence on each other. The interaction between the parties may be either verbal (such as sharing strategies for a corporate takeover) or nonverbal (such as exchanging smiles in the hallway), but the parties must have some impact on each other to be considered a group.

Stability

Groups also must posses a stable structure. Although groups can change-and often do – there must be some stable relationships that keep group members together and functioning as a unit. A collection of individuals that constantly changes (e.g., the people inside an office waiting room at any given time) cannot be thought of as a group. To be a group, a greater level of stability would be required.

Common Interests or Goals

A third characteristic of groups is that their members share common interests or goals. For example, members of a stamp collecting club constitute a group that is sustained by the mutual interests of members. Some groups form because members with common interests help each other achieve a mutual goal. For example, the owners and employees of a sporting goods shop constitute a group around a common interest in athletic equipment and the common goal of making money.

Recognition as Being a Group

Finally, to be a group, the individuals involved must perceive themselves as a group. Groups are composed of people who recognize each other as a member of their group and can distinguish these individuals from nonmembers. The members of a corporate finance committee or a chess club, for example, know who is in their group and who is not. In contrast, shoppers in a checkout line probably don't think of each other as being members of a group. Although they stand physically close to each other and may have passing conversations, they have little in common (except, perhaps, a shared interest in reaching the end of the line) and fail to identify themselves with the others in the line.

By defining groups in terms of these four characteristics, we have identified a group as a very special collection of individuals. As we shall see, these characteristics are responsible for the important effects groups have on organizational behavior. To better understand these effects, we will now review the wide variety of groups that operate within organizations.

Types Of Groups

From an organizational behavior point of view, there are basically two types of groups. They are: formal groups and informal groups.

Formal Groups

A group is formal when it is purposely designed to

accomplish an organizational objective or task. It is created via a formal authority for some defined purpose.

A formal group can be command group or functional group which is relatively permanent and is composed of manager and their subordinates who meet regularly to discuss general and specific ideas to improve product or service. In business organization, most employees work in such command groups. A typical command group in an organization chart may be illustrated as follows.

The formal work groups usually work under a single supervisor, even though the structure of these groups may vary. For example, in one form of group such as in production, the members of the work group depend on each other as well as on the supervisor and in other form of group, such as sales force, the member of the group work as fairly independently and their common contact may be the district sales manager.

Other types of formal groups include *task forces* and *committees.* The task forces are temporary in nature and are set up for some special project. The committees can be permanent, such as a planning committee finance committee or a budget committee and may become an integral part of the organizational structure. A committee can also be temporary such as a special task force which is set up for a particular purpose and is then disbanded when the purpose is achieved. For example the committee to re-elect the President is temporary in nature and is disbanded after the election.

Informal Groups

Whereas formal groups are established by organizations to achieve some specific objectives, the informal groups are formed by the members of such groups by themselves. They emerge naturally in response to the common interests of organizational members. They are formed spontaneously, without any formal designation, and with common interests such as self-defense, work assistance and social interaction. They exist outside the formal authority system and without any set rigid rules.

Though officially unrecognized, they exist in the shadow of the formal structure as a network of personal and social relations which must be understood and respected by the management.

The informal work groups are based upon socio-psychological support and reasoning and depend upon member's interaction, communication, personal likings and dislikings and social contacts within as well as outside the organization. How powerful are these informal groups can be seen from the fact that if one member of the group is fired, sometimes all workers go on strike in support if that member of the group. The bonds between members are very strong and these bonds bring in a sense of belonging and togetherness. This togetherness can have a powerful influence on productivity and job satisfaction, since employees motivate each other and share each other's burden by training those who are new and by looking up to old timers for guidance, advice, and assistance.

Informal groups generally result due to personal bonds social interaction among people who work together at the same place and may have similarities as well as differences in their own structure, sometimes parallel to the formal structure with their leaders and followers, group goal, social roles and working patterns. They have their own unwritten rules and a code of conduct which every member implicitly accepts. Members trust and help each other. For example, in a department of a college, the departmental secretary may yield more authority in some areas than even the chairperson as in the case of typing exams and typing course outlines. Thus a professor who has a good rapport with the secretary as a member of the informal group, would have the papers typed sooner than others.

The leadership of the informal group develops from within rather than a formal election. An individual who is working in a group for a long time and has a good rapport with other members, may emerge as a leader due to his technical expertise and his seniority. For any problem within the group, either technical or social, the members would go to this leader rather than the formally assigned supervisor.

Why Do People Join Groups?

We have noted that people often join groups to satisfy their mutual interests and goals. To the extent that getting together with others allows us to achieve ends that would not be possible alone, forming groups makes a great deal of sense. In fact, organizations can be thought of as collections of groups that are focused toward achieving the mutual goal of achieving success for the company. But this is not the only motivation that people have for joining groups. There are also several additional reasons.

Not only do groups form for purposes of mutually achieving goals, they also frequently form for purposes of seeking protection from other groups. If you've ever heard the phrase "there's safety in numbers," you are probably already aware that people join groups because they seek the security of the group membership. Historically, for example, trade unions, such as the AFL/CIO, the UAW, and the Teamsters, have been formed by labor for purposes of seeking protection against abuses by management. Similarly, professional associations, such as American Medical Association and the American Bar Association, were created, in large part, for purposes of protecting people in their respective fields against undesirable governmental legislation.

This is not to say that groups are always designed to promote some instrumental good; indeed, they also exist because they appeal to a basic psychological need to be social. As Maslow's need hierarchy theory says that people are social animals; they have a basic need to interact with others. Groups provide good opportunities for friendships to develop and, hence, for social needs to be fulfilled.

Also as suggested by Maslow, people have a basic desire for their self-esteem to be fulfilled. Group memberships can be a very effective way of nurturing self-esteem. For example, if a group to which one belongs is successful (such as a sales group that meets its quota); the self-esteem of all members (and supporters) may be boosted. Similarly, election to membership in an exclusive group (e.g., a national honor society) surely will raise one's self-esteem.

As we have shown, people are attracted to groups for many different reasons. Despite the fact that people may have different motivations for forming groups, it is interesting to note that once formed, groups develop in remarkably similar ways. We will now turn our attention to this issue.

Formation of Work Group

By going to work for an organisation you are actually joining a group they also join or create informal groups because of common interests and characteristics. These and other reasons (check) for the group formation suggest that common location and attitudes strongly influence people to join or establish informal groups.

A case study on "the relationship between work-team personality composition and the job performance of teams" investigated the relationship between work effectiveness and two distinct aspect of the personality composition of team (a) the average level of a given trait within a team, referred to as team personality elevation (TPE) and (b) the variability or differences in personality diversity (TPD). Across the set of big five traits, TPE and TPD predicted unique variance in ratings of team job performance. For each specific trait of the big five, either TPE or TPD predicted team performance. For the traits of conscientiousness, agreeableness, and openness to experience, TPE was positively related to team performance, TPD of extraversion and emotional stability was positively related to team performance.

1. Location

When people are close in proximity they tend to interact and communicate. Some degree of interaction and communication is necessary for group formation particularly informal groups.

2. Economic Reasons

In some cases work groups form because individuals believe that they can gain economic benefits on their jobs if they bond together.

3. Safety

Work groups can protect member from management pressures such as demands for better quality and quantity of production, for instance employees punch on the clock on time, and recommend for change in individual work area layout by being member of the groups. Individual's employees can openly discuss the management demands with other workers.

Simulated small-group discussion of an industrial safety issue explored the possible influences that work groups have upon their members' safety-related behavior. Subjects made their own private selections of personal protection, contributed to a 4-person group consensus selection, and then made a final private selection. As predicted, subjects preferred self-protective behaviors shifted after group discussion, becoming simultaneously more risky, more homogenous and more confident. However, little support was obtained for a hypothesized polarization of preferences following group interaction.

4. Social

Employees often join work groups because of their need for affiliation. The basis of affiliation ranges from wanting to interact with and enjoy other employees to more complex desires for support of the self- image.

5. Esteem

Employees often join work groups because they gain prestige by being in it. A particular group in the organization may be viewed by employee as a top-notch work groups. Consequently membership in an elite group bestows prestige on the members. Other employees confer this prestige on the members, which leads to more gratification of the esteem needs by sharing in the activities of the high prestige work groups. The individual identifies more closely with the group. This form of identification is valued highly by some employees.

6. Self-Actualization

The desire of individuals to grow and develop psychologically on the job constitutes the self-actualization need. Employees often believe that rigid job requirements prevent them from satisfying this need sufficiently. One reaction is to join a work group which can be a vehicle for communicating among friends about the use of jobs related skill. The jargon used and the skill employed are appreciated by knowledgeable group member. This appreciation can lead to the feeling of accomplishing a worthwhile task. This feeling is similar of being creative and skillful often help satisfy the self-actualization need.

Basic Attributes of Groups

In general, a number of people together at a given place and given time can be considered as a group. People in a bus or the same compartment of a train or students in a class are all known as group. However, for an organizational point of view, a group has a different meaning and definition. According to Marvin Shaw, "A group is two or more persons who are interacting with one another in such a manner that each person influences and is influenced by each other person". There are two keys elements in this definition which are essential. First is the "interaction" among group members. For examples, co-workers may work side by side on related tasks, out if they do not interact with each other, they are not a group in the organizational sense. The second element is the influence of one group member on each other group member. This means that the group members are mutually dependent with respect to the attainment of one or more common goal.

While all individuals in the group are primarily required to direct their efforts towards common organization goal, there may be situation where individuals within the group are more interested in the achievement of their personal goal, thus making the organizational goal secondary. For examples, a member of the high school basketball team may be more interested in highlighting his own performance in order to win a college scholarship irrespective of whether the entire teams wins or not, even though all members of the team interact with each other and influence each other's performance.

It could be noted that in order for the group members to interact with each other effectively, the group size should be reasonably small. It is difficult to interact closely with each other when the group size is very large. In fact, the dynamics of large groups are significantly different than the dynamics of small groups. Accordingly, our concern is primarily with groups of reasonable size.

Reasons for Group Formation

Why do individuals form them into groups? What are the reasons for forming or joining a group and what are the benefits to such individuals who become a part of the group? There are many factors that influence the formation of the group, the most important being the individual need satisfaction. This means that the members expect affiliation with the group to satisfy a need. This means that the members expect affiliation and friendship which is the third level need in Maslow's model of hierarchical needs. But the need could also be economic in nature because of economic group incentives. Also being a member of a union is economically adventurous because union can fight for higher pay and fringe benefits more effectively.

The most basic theory explaining group affiliation is the geographic proximity. For example, individuals working in the same area are more likely to form a group than those who are not physically located together. Similarly, students sitting near each other in a class room are likely to form into a group than students sitting at opposite ends of the class room.

According to George Homans, there are three elements that form the foundation of groups. These are activities, interaction and sentiments. These three elements are inter-related. An improvement in one element will trigger an improvement in others. For example, the more activities persons share, while means improvement in the first element, the more interaction will take place and stronger will be their sentiments.

While there are many reasons why individuals would either form a group, some reason stand out. A sense of belonging and interpersonal attraction may be so strong that some people are willing to pay a high price in joining an exclusive country club, golf club or flying club. Some of the more important reasons are illustrated as follows:

Personal Characteristic

People are more likely to form with others who are similar beliefs, values and attitudes. As the saying goes, "birds of a feather fly together", so the group form around common political and cultural philosophies, ethnic and religious affiliations and such factors as age, sex, intelligence or similar interest and hobbies. For examples, salesman who are high need achiever may want to interact with similar other high achiever salesman. There is also a contradictory saying that, "opposites attract each other" there may be situation where some dominant individuals may seek the company of submissive individuals specially when these grouping leads to achievement of a common goal. For example, if a vice-president and a low level clerk of the same company together.

Interest and Goals

Interest and goals that are common require cooperation with others for achievement of such goals are a powerful force behind such groups' formation. Individuals with common goals tend to work together. For examples, within an organization, the salesman forms a group, so do the production people and the accounting people. Even though, the salesman may have individual goals, their organization goal is common.

Some goals cannot simply be physical activity. For examples, the sky-scrapers cannot be built by one person alone. It requires group efforts in all areas of building. Similarly, there are a number of groups involved in construction and sending a satellite into space. If these individuals in the group with a common group and organizational goal also have similar personal characteristic, then the group cohesion can be strengthened and group effort can be improved. Some groups form because of similar intellectuals and recreational goals and pursuits.

Golf club, chess club and hunting club are some groups with recreational pursuits. Groups are often organized to accomplish some problem solving and decision making tasks such as designing political strategies or designing computers.

The goals can be social and emotional in nature. Thus the groups are formed because of the individuals need and safety and security, sense of belonging and affiliation and self esteem. Safety and security needs of individuals are satisfied through groups. Even from the early days men used to go out hunting for food together in groups to face outside threats from animals and other hostile environments. Group formation is likely when environment becomes hostile and threatening. For examples, in times of flood. One or another natural disasters, neighbors who may not be even speaking with each other form effective groups to help and shelter the people affected by such disasters. In an organizational setting individual worker join unions because the unions have the ability to meet their needs and interests as well as protect them from threats of being fired.

A sense of belonging is the third level need in the Maslow's model of hierarchical needs. It is an emotional need for friendship, love, affection and affiliation with others. Most people have strong need for being with others who can understand, support and help them when they are in need and render them moral and emotional support in time of difficulty. The concept of family and friends fills this need.

Membership in a prestigious group is a source of enhanced self-esteem. The members of the group feel good about themselves by virtue of the group's power, prestige and social standing. For example, being in United States marines or SWAT team can be a source of pride for the members.

Opportunity for Interaction

When people are provided with an opportunity to interact, they may discover that they have a lot in common, thus necessitating the formation of a group. This interaction, for example, leads to friendships and group formation in college dormitories, apartment complexes and sometimes in the same compartment of a train or on cruise ships where people are together and have an opportunity to form informal groups.

In an organizational setting, management generally tries to create a physical as well as psychological environment to induce interaction some times, the office are designed in such a manner so that people who need to interact with each other are assigned work space close to each other. Common cafeterias and coffee breaks given at the same time increases opportunity for interaction.

Influence and Power

There is a saying in India that, "while a single one is just a one, two single ones make it an eleven". We all know that there is strength in unity. Henry Fayol's last of the fourteen principals of effective administration is "Esprit de Corps ", which means the "power of spirit of togetherness". There is another saying supporting the same sentiments as, "united we stand, divided we fall".

Most managers listen to a complaint of employees when the employees approach the manager together. The same manager may not listen to individuals complaints. In the case of one college, that the author knows, there were many individuals' faculty complaints against the president of the college for some of his decision and action, as well as against many aspect of the physical and conceptual academic environment of the college. But the president refused to listen or show sympathy for the needs and desires of "faculty organization "approached the president with their problems and difficulties and the president still refused to listen, he was forced to resign, because of the power of the group.

Groups also provide opportunities for individuals members to become leaders of the group and influence other members of the group with their views and reasoning. As a leader of a group, he may influence people outside the group or other groups. Leaders of certain groups are often called upon to speak to other groups, thus giving them an opportunity to express their own viewpoints and ideologies.

These leaders may also find that their leadership roles give them increased public visibility and may prove to be stepping stones for enhancement of their own careers

How Groups are Formed

Social scientist have long been interested in the question of how people form groups. Although we cannot predict with perfect certainty exactly how all groups will form, two systematic models of group development appear to be most descriptive - the five stage model and the punctuated-equilibrium model.

The Five Stage Model

Just as infants develop in certain ways during their first months of life, groups also show relatively stable signs of maturation and development. One popular theory, the five-stage model identifies five distinct stages through which groups develop. Here is the summary of the five stages shown below:

1. The first stage of group development is known as forming. During this stage of group development, the members get acquainted with each other. They establish the ground rules by trying to find out what behaviors are acceptable with respect to both the job (how Productive they are expected to be) and interpersonal relations (who's really in charge). During the forming stage, people tend to be a bit confused and uncertain about how to act in the group and how beneficial it will be to become a member of the group. Once the individuals come to think of themselves as members of a group, the forming stage is complete.

2. The second stage of group development is referred to as storming. As the name implies, this stage is characterized by a high degree of conflict within the group. Members often resist the control of the group's leaders and show hostility toward each other. If these conflicts are not resolved and group members withdraw, the group may disband. However, as conflicts are resolved and the group's leadership is accepted, the storming stage is complete.

3. The third stage of group development is known as

norming. During this stage, the group becomes more cohesive, and identification as a member of the group becomes greater. Close relationships develop, shared feelings become common, and a keen interest in finding mutually agreeable solutions develops. Feelings of camaraderie and shared responsibility for the group's activities are heightened. The norming stage is complete when the members of the group accept a common set of expectations that constitutes an acceptable way of doing things.

4. The fourth stage is known as performing. During this stage, questions about group relationships and leadership have been resolved and the group is ready to work. Having fully developed, the group may now devote its energy to getting the job done – the group's good relations and acceptance of the leadership help the group -perform well.

Recognizing that not all groups last forever, the final stage is known as adjourning. Groups may cease to exist because they have met their goals and are no longer needed (such as an ad hoc group created to raise money for a charity project), in which case the end is abrupt. Other groups may adjourn gradually, as the group disintegrates, either because members leave or because the norms that have developed are no longer effective for the group.

To illustrate these various stages, imagine that you have just joined several of your colleagues on your company's newly created budget committee. At first, you and your associates feel each other out: you watch to see who comes up with the best ideas, whose suggestions are most widely accepted, who seems to take charge, and the like (the forming stage). Then, as members struggle to gain influence over others, you may see a battle over control of committee (the storming stage). Soon, this will be resolved, and an accepted leader will emerge. At this stage, the group members will become highly cooperative, working together in harmony and doing things together, such as going out to lunch as a group (the norming stage). Now it becomes possible for committee members to work together at doing their best and giving it their all (the performing stage). Then, once the budget is created and approved, the group's task is over and it is disbanded (the adjourning stage).

It is important to keep in mind that groups can be in any one stage of development at any given time. Moreover, the amount of time a group may spend in any given stage is highly variable. In fact, some groups may fail long before they have had a chance to work together. Research has revealed that the boundaries between the various stages may not be distinct and that several stages may be combined, especially as deadline pressures force groups to take action. It is best, then, to think of this five-stage model as a general framework of group formation. Although many of the stages may be followed the dynamic nature of groups makes it unlikely that they will progress through the various stages in a completely predictable order.

The Punctuated - Equilibrium Model

Not all scientists agree that groups develop in the order identified in the five-stage model. In fact, it has been argued that, although there may not be a universal sequence of stages, there are some remarkable consistencies in the ways group form and change. These patterns are described in the punctuated-equilibrium model. This approach to group formation recognizes that group members working to meet a deadline approach their task differently in the first half of their time together than in the second half.

During the first half of time, phase 1, groups define their task, setting a mission that is unlikely to change until the second half of the group's life. Even if group members have new ideas, these are generally not acted on. Interestingly, as soon as groups reach the midpoints of their lives (whether this is just a few hours or several months), something curious happens. Almost as if an alarm goes off, at the midpoint of their lives groups experience a sort of "middle crisis," that is, a time when they recognize that they are going to have to change the way they operate if they are going to meet their goals. This begins phase 2 of their existence – a time when groups drop old ways of thinking and adopt new perspectives. Groups then carry out these missions until they reach the end of phase 2, when they show bursts of activity needed to complete their work.

The Idea is Straight Forward

Groups develop inertia, which keeps them going (i.e., "equilibrium") until the halfway point, when they realize that deadlines loom large. This stimulates them to confront important issues and to initiate changes, beginning (i.e., "punctuating") a new equilibrium phase. This phase lasts until the group kicks into a final push before the deadline. To illustrate the punctuated-equilibrium model, consider what might happen in a group people working to elect a political candidate. When the group first meets in January, the members get to know each other and plan their campaign strategy. They figure out what they have to do in the 10 months that follow to get their candidate into office, and they spring into action. Then, by the following May or June, something happens: it becomes clear that there are problems, and the original plan needs to be changed. People working on the campaign begin taking critical looks at what they've been doing and take active steps to change things. This would continue through October. Then, in the weeks or days right before the November election, the group will meet for a long time and make its final push.

Although the punctuated-equilibrium model is relatively new, studies suggest that it does a good job of describing how groups develop. We think it will make great sense to you if you compare it to your own experience working with others in groups (e.g., on class projects).

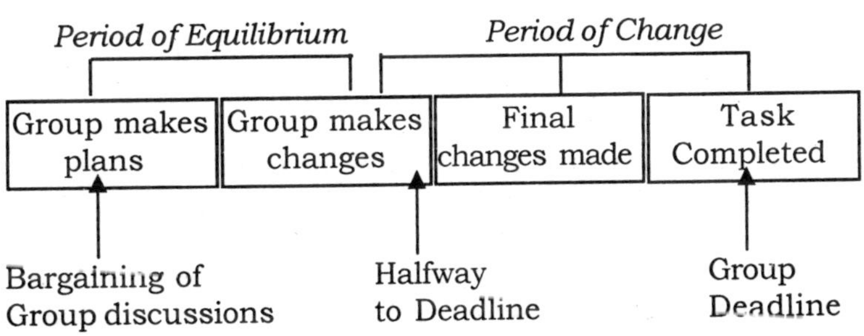

Conflicts In Organizations

Managing of Conflict among Group

(A) To increase understanding of the problem of

suboptimization in organizations, particularly where group goals take precedence over total organizational goals.

(B) To examine strategies for reducing the negative effects of conflict on the effectiveness of inter group relations.

(C) To explore ways of establishing collaborative, as opposed to competitive, intergroup relations.

Nature of Conflict in Organizations

The concept of conflict, being an outcome of behaviours, is an integral part of human life. Wherever there is interaction, there is conflict. Conflict can be defined in many ways and can be consider as an expression of hostility, Negative Attitudes, Antagonism, Aggression, Rivalry and Misunderstanding. It is also associated with situations that involve contradictory or irreconcilable interest between two opposing groups. It can be defined as a disagreement between two or more individuals or groups, with each individual or group trying to gain acceptance of its view or objectives over others.

Conflict must be distinguished from competition, even though sometimes intense competition leads to conflict. Competition is directed towards obtaining a goal and one group does not interfere with the efforts of another group while conflict is directed against another group and actions are taken to frustrate the other group's actions towards goal achievement.

Conflict, according to the opening quote by Tagiuri, "*is inherent to social life.*" Conflict is any situation in which two or more parties feel themselves in opposition. Conflict is an interpersonal process that arises from disagreements over the goals to attain or the methods to be used to accomplish those goals. In the potential arguments reported above, Joyce and Joan differ over both the goal and the method of achieving it. Consequently, the conflict may be even more difficult to resolve, but they must find a way. In organizations everywhere, conflict among different interests is inevitable, and sometimes the amount of conflict is substantial. One survey reported that managers spend an estimated 20 percent of their time dealing with conflict. They may be either direct participants or mediators trying to resolve conflict between two or more of their employees. In either case, knowledge and understanding of conflict and the methods for resolving it are important.

Several research studies overtime have consistently indicated the important role of interpersonal behaviour in the success or failure of managers. One of the prime reasons for derailment of previously successful executives is "insensitivity to others." Some female managers, lauded as exceptionally intelligent and sporting strong track records, later failed because of inability to adapt to a boss. And a composite portrait of failed European managers indicated that they were insensitive, manipulative, abusive, demeaning, overly critical, and incapable of building trusting relationships. Under these conditions, conflict – with peers and employees – inevitably emerges.

Sources Of Conflict

Interpersonal conflict arises from a variety of sources:

Causes of Conflict

- Organization Change
- Personality Clashes
- Different Sets of Values
- Threats to Status
- Contrasting Perceptions
- Lack of Trust

Perceptions of Conflict

- Constructive
- Destructive
- Participant intentions
- Winning
- Losing

Resolution Strategies

- Avoiding
- Smoothing

- Forcing
- Compromising
- Confronting

Conflict Outcomes

- Lose-lose
- Lose-win
- Win-lose
- Win-win

Causes of Conflict

Organizational Change

People hold differing views over the direction to go, the routes to take and their likely success, the resources to be used, and the probable outcomes. With the pace of technological, political, and social change increasing and the marketplace hurtling toward a global economy, organizational changes will be ever-present.

Personality Clashes

Not everyone thinks, feels, looks, or acts alike. Some people simply "rub us the wrong way" and we cannot necessarily explain why. Although personality differences can cause conflict, they are also a rich resource for creative problem solving. Employees need to accept. Respect, and learn how to use these differences when they arise.

Different Sets of Value

People also hold different beliefs and adhere to different value systems. Their philosophies may diverge, or their ethical values may lead them in different directions. The resulting disputes can be difficult to resolve, since they are less objective than disagreements over alternative products, inventory levels, or promotional campaigns.

Threats to Status

Status or the social rank of a person in a group is very

important to many individuals. When one's status is threatened, face saving becomes a powerful driving force as a person struggles to maintain a desired image. Conflict may arise between the defensive person and whoever created a threat to status.

Contrasting Perceptions

People perceive things differently as a result of their prior experiences and expectations. Since their perceptions are very real to them (and they feel that these perceptions must be equally apparent to others), they sometimes fail to realize that others may hold contrasting perceptions of the same object or event. Conflict may arise unless employees learn to see things as others see them and help others do the same.

Lack of Trust

Every continuing relationship requires some degree of trust - the capacity to depend on each other's word and actions. Trust opens up boundaries, provides opportunities in which to act, and enriches the entire social fabric of an organization. It takes time to build, but it can be destroyed in an instant. When someone has a real or perceived reason not to trust another, the potential for conflict rises.

The Causes of Conflict

Addition to the causes mentioned above, the causes of conflict fall into three distinct categories. Accordingly, these causes can be restructured and placed into one of these categories. These categories deal with communicational, behavioural and structural aspects.

Communicational Aspect of Conflict

Poor communication, though not reflecting substantive differences, can have powerful effect in causing conflict. Misunderstood or partial information during the process of communication can make a difference between the success and the failure of a task and such failure for which the responsibility becomes difficult to trace can cause conflict between the sender of the communication and the receiver of the communication. Thus the problems in the communication process-whether these problems relate to too much or too little communication, filtering of communication, semantic problems or noise – act to regard collaboration and stimulate misunderstanding. The filtering process occurs when information is passed through many levels or when it passes through many members. The amount of information is functional up to a point, beyond which it becomes a source of conflict. Semantic difficulties arise due to differences in backgrounds, differences in training, selective perception and inadequate information about others.

As an example, if a manager going on an extended vacation fails to communicate properly with his subordinates as to who would be doing what, he will find these jobs only partially done with subordinates blaming each other for not completing the tasks. Accordingly, adequate, complete, and correctly understood communication is very important in orderly completion of tasks, thus reducing the chances of a conflict.

Behavioural Aspect of Conflict

These conflicts arise out of human thoughts and feelings, emotions and attitudes, values and perceptions and reflect some basic traits of a personality. Thus some people's values or perceptions of situations are particularly likely to generate conflict with others. For example, highly authoritarian and dogmatic persons are more prone to antagonize co-workers by highlighting minor differences that might exist. On the other hand, persons with low self-esteem may feel threatened by others in simple matters and may overreact causing a conflict. This conflict may also be based on personal biases regarding such factors as religion, race or sex. Some men feel poorly about women workers. These conflicts are not about issues but about persons. Some families carry on enmity for generations.

The conflict can also arise due to differing viewpoints about various issues. For example, two Vice-Presidents may differ about their viewpoints regarding which strategic plan to implement. The value based conflict arises due to different values which may be culturally based. For example, one

Vice-President may want to fire some workers to save costs while another Vice-President may have human sensitivity and support other methods of cutting costs. As another example, a professor may value freedom of teaching methods and a close supervision of his teaching technique is likely to induce conflict.

Likert and Likert analyzed some general causes of conflict created by modern society which are behaviourally oriented. These include unrealized expectations and complexity of social and organizational systems. The widening gap between "haves" and "have nots" causes considerable conflict between the two because the unprivileged believe that they are not given the same opportunities as the privileged. Thus the expectations of the underprivileged are unrealized and this causes frustration and conflict.

From an organizational behaviour point of view, there is conflict between the goals of the formal organization and the psychological growth of the individual. While the formal organization demands dependency, passivity and to some degree obedience from its members, the psychologically developed individuals exhibit independence, creativity and a desire to participate in decision making and decision implementing process. The needs of individuals and the formal organization being inconsistent with each other result in behavioural conflict.

Structural Aspects of Conflict

These conflicts arise due to issues related to the structural design of the organization as a whole as well as its sub-units. Some of the structurally related factors are:

Size of the Organization

The larger the size of the organization, the more basis for existence of conflict. It is likely that as the organization becomes larger there is greater impersonal formality, less goal clarity, more supervisory levels and supervision and greater chance of information being diluted or distorted as it is passed along. All these factors are breeding grounds for conflict.

Line Staff Distinction

One of the frequently mentioned and continuous source of conflict is the distinction between the line and staff units within the organization. Line units are involved in operations that are directly related to the core activities of the organization. For example, production department would be a line unit in a manufacturing organization and sales department would be considered a line unit in a customer oriented service organization. Staff units are generally in an advisory capacity and support the line function. Examples of staff departments are legal department, public relations, personnel and research and development. The line usually complains that if things go right then the staff takes the credit and if thing go wrong, then the line gets the blame for it.

Generally the staff people typically think in terms of long-range issues while line people are more involved with short-term or day-to-day concerns. These differing time horizons can become a source of conflict.

Participation

It is assumed that if the subordinates are not allowed to participate in the decision making process then they will show resentment which will induce conflict. On the other hand ironically, if subordinates are provided with greater participation opportunities, the levels of conflict also tend to be higher. This may be due to the fact that increased participation leads to greater awareness of individual differences. This conflict is further enhanced when individuals tend to enforce their points of view on others.

Role Ambiguity

A role reflects a set of activities associated with a certain position in the organization. If these work activities are ill defined, then the person who is carrying out these activities will not perform as others expect him to, because his role is not clearly defined. This will create conflict, specially between this individual and those people who depend upon his activities. A hospital or a medical clinic employing a number of physicians with overlapping specialities might cause conflict due to role ambiguity. Such conflicts can be reduced by redefining and clarifying roles and their interdependence.

Design of Work-flow

These are primarily inter-group problems and conflicts which are outcomes of poorly designed work-flow structure and poorly planned coordination requirements, specially where tasks are interdependent. According to Sashkin and Morris "organization are made up of many different groups that must work together towards the accomplishment of common objectives." For example, in a hospital, the doctors and nurses must work together and their tasks are highly interdependent. If they do not coordinate their activities well, then there will be confusion and conflict. Similarly, in a restaurant, the cook and the waiter depend upon each other for critical information and services. A poorly designed work-flow and uncoordinated activities between the cook and the waiter would create conflicts and problems.

Scarcity of Resources

When individuals and units must share such resources as capital, facilities, staff assistance and so on. And these resources are scare and there is a high competition for them then conflict can become quite intense. This is specially true in declining organizations, where resources become even more scarce due to cutback in personnel and services so that the concerned units become highly competitive for the shrinking pool of resources and this breeds conflict. This scarcity may bring out some of the latent hostility among groups who may have put up a peaceful front at the time of abundance. For example, two research scientists who do not get along very well, may not show their hostility until a reduction in laboratory space provokes each to protect his area.

Effects of Conflict

Conflict is often seen by participants as destructive, but this is a limited view. In fact, if all conflict with coworkers is avoided, each party is likely deprived of useful information about the others preference sand views. Conflict is not all bad, but rather may result in either productive or nonproductive outcomes. A more positive view, then, is to see that conflict is nearly inevitable and to search for ways in which it can result in constructive outcomes.

Advantages

One of the benefits produced by the conflict is that people are stimulated to search for improved approaches that lead to better results. It energizes them to be more creative and to experiment with new ideas. Another benefit is that once-hidden problems are brought to the surface, where they may be confronted and solved. Just as fermentation is necessary in the production of fine wines, a certain amount of ferment can create a deeper understanding among the parties involved in a conflict. And once the conflict is resolved, the individuals may be more committed to the outcome through their involvement in solving it.

Disadvantages

There are also possible disadvantages, especially if the conflict lasts a long period of time, becomes too intense, or is allowed to focus on personal issues. At the interpersonal level, cooperation and teamwork may deteriorate. Distrust may grow among people who need to coordinate their efforts. At the individual level some people may feel defeated, while the self-image of others will decline, and personal stress levels will rise. Predictably, the motivation level of some employees will be reduced. It is important, then, for managers to be aware of the potential for interpersonal and intergroup conflicts, to anticipate their likely outcomes, and to use appropriate conflict resolution strategies.

Resolving Behaviour Conflict

Various researchers have identified five primary strategies for dealing with reducing the impact of behavioural conflict. Even though different authors have given different terminology to describe these strategies, the basic content and approach of these strategies remain the same. These are:

Ignoring the Conflict. In certain situations, it may be advisable to take a passive role and avoid it all together. From the manager's point of view, it may be specially necessary when getting involved in a situation would provoke further controversy or when conflict is so trivial in nature that it would not be worth the managers' time to get involved and try to solve it. It could also be that the conflict is so fundamental to the position of the parties involved that it may be best either to leave it to them to solve it or to let events take their own course. The parties involved in the conflict may themselves prefer to avoid conflict, specially if they are emotionally upset and the tension and frustration created by it, people may intrinsically believe that conflict is fundamentally evil and its final consequences are never good. Thus people may try to get away from conflict causing situations.

Smoothing. Smoothing simply means covering up the conflict by appealing for the need for unity rather than addressing the issue of conflict itself. An individual with internal conflict may try to "count his blessings" and forget about the conflict. If two parties have a conflict within the organization, the supervisor may try to calm things down by being understanding and supportive to both parties and appealing them for cooperation. The supervisor does not ignore or withdraw from the conflict nor does he try to address and solve the conflict but expresses hope that "everything will work out for the best of all." Since the problem is never addressed, the emotions may build up further and suddenly explode. Thus smoothing provides only a temporary solution and conflict may resurface again in the course of time. Smoothing is more sensitive approach than avoiding in that as long as the parties agree that not showing conflict has more benefits than showing conflict then such conflict can be avoided.

Compromising. A compromise in the conflict is reached by balancing the demands of the conflicting parties and bargaining in a give and take position to reach a solution. Each party gives up something and also gains something. The technique of conflict resolution is very common in negotiations between the labor unions and management. It has become custom for the union to ask for more than what they are willing to accept and for management to offer less than what they are willing to give in the initial stages. Then through the process of negotiating and bargaining, mostly in the presence of arbitrators, they reach a solution by compromising. This type of compromise is known as integrative bargaining in which both sides win in a way.

Compromising is a useful technique, particularly when two parties have relatively equal power, thus no party can force its viewpoints on the other and the only solution is to compromise. It is also useful when there are time constraints. If the problems are complex and many faceted, and the time is limited to solve them, it might be in the interest of conflicting parties to reach a compromise.

Forcing. Webber puts it, "the simplest conceivable resolution is the elimination of the other party – to force opponents to flee and give up the fight – or stay them." This is a technique of domination where the dominator has the power and authority to enforce his own views over the apposing conflicting party. This technique is potentially effective in situations such as a president of a company firing a manager because he is considered as a trouble maker and conflict creator. This technique always ends up in one party being a loser and the other party being a clear winner. Many professors in colleges and universities have lost promotions and tenured reappointments because they could not get along well with their respective chairpersons of the departments and had conflicts with them. This approach causes resentment and hostility and can backfire. Accordingly, management must look for better alternatives if these become available.

Problem Solving. This technique involves "confronting the conflict" in order to seek the best solution to the problem. This approach objectively assumes that in all organizations, no matter how well they are managed there will be differences of opinions which must be resolved through discussions and respect for differing viewpoints. In general, this technique is very useful in resolving conflicts arising out of semantic misunderstandings. It is not so effective in resolving non-communicative types of conflicts such as those that are based on differing value systems where it may even intensify differences and disagreements. In the long run, however, it is better to solve conflicts and take such preventive measures that would reduce the likelihood of such conflicts surfacing again.

Types of Conflict Situations

Since conflict has both positive and negative connotations and consequences. It must be looked into and managed for useful purposes. The management must survey the situation to decide whether to stimulate conflict or to resolve it. Thomas and Schmidt have reported that managers spend up to 20 percent of their time in dealing with conflict situations. Hence, it is very important that managers understand the type of conflict that they have to deal with so that they can devise some standardized techniques in dealing with common characteristics of conflicts in each type of category. There are five basic types of conflicts. These are:

Conflict within the Individual

The conflict within individual is usually value related, where the role playing expected of the individual does not conform with the values and beliefs held by the individuals. For example, a secretary may have to lie on instructions that her boss is not in the office to avoid an unwanted visitor or an unwanted telephone call. This may cause a conflict within the mind of the secretary who may have developed an ethic of telling the truth. Similarly many Indians who are vegetarians and come to America and find it very hard to remain vegetarians, may question the necessity of the vegetarian philosophy, thus causing a conflict in their minds.

In addition to these value conflicts, a person may have a role conflict. For example, a telephone operator may be advised and required to be polite to the customers by her supervisor who may also complain that she is spending too much time with her customers. This would cause a role conflict in her mind. Similarly, a policeman may be invited to his brothers wedding where he may find that some guests are using drugs which is against the law. It may cause conflict in his mind as to which role he should play – as of a brother or as a policeman. Conflict within an individual can also arise when a person has to choose between two equally desirable alternatives or between two equally undesirable goals.

Interpersonal Conflict

Interpersonal conflict involves conflict between two or more individuals and is probably the most common and most recognized conflict. This may involve conflict between two managers who are competing for limited capital and manpower resources. For example, interpersonal conflicts can develop when there are three equally deserving professors and they are all up for promotion, but only one of them can be promoted because of budget and positional constraints. This conflict can become further acute when the scarce resources cannot be shared and must be obtained.

Another type of interpersonal conflict can relate to disagreements over goals and objectives of the organization. For example, some members of a board of a school may want to offer courses in sex education while others may find this proposal morally offensive thus causing conflict. Similarly, a college or a university may have a policy of quality education so that only top quality students are admitted while some members of the organizational board may propose "open admissions" policy where all high school graduates should be considered for admission. Such a situation can cause conflicts among members of the governing board. In addition to conflicts over the nature and substance of goals and objectives, the conflicts can also arise over the means to reach these goals. For example, two marketing managers may argue as to which promotional methods would result in higher sales. These conflicts become highlighted when they are based upon opinions rather than facts. Facts are generally indisputable resulting in agreements. Opinions are highly personal and subjective and may provide for criticism and disagreements.

These conflicts are often the results of personality clashes. People with widely differing characteristics and attitudes are bound to have views and aims that are inconsistent with the views and aims of others.

Conflict between the Individual and the Group

As we have discussed before all formal groups as well as informal groups have established certain norms of behavior and operational standards which all members are expected to adhere to. The individual may want to remain within the group for social needs but may disagree with the group methods. For example, in some restaurants all tips are shared by all waiters and waitresses. Some particular waitress who may be overly polite and efficient may feel that she deserves more, thus causing a conflict within the group. Similarly if a group is going on strike for some reason, some members may not agree with these reasons or simply may not be able to afford to go on strike, thus causing conflict with the group.

This conflict may also be between the manager and a group of subordinates or between the leader and the followers. A manager may take a disciplinary action against a member of the group, causing conflict which may result in reduced productivity. "Mutiny on the Bounty" is a classic example of rebellion of the crew of the ship against the leader, based upon the treatment the crew received. The conflict among the armed forces is taken so seriously that the army must obey their commander even if the command is wrong and in conflict with what others believe in.

Intergroup Conflict

An organization is an interlocking network of groups, departments, sections or work teams. These conflicts are not so much personal in nature, as they are due to factors inherent in the organizational structure. For example, there is active and continuous conflict between the union and the management. One of the most common, unfortunate and highlighted conflict is between line and staff. The line managers may resent their dependence on staff for information and recommendations. The staff may resent their inability to implement directly their own decisions and recommendations. This interdependence causes conflict. These conflict which are caused by task interdependencies require that the relationship between interdependent units be redefined, wherever the values of these interdependent factors change, otherwise these conflicts will become further pronounced.

These interunit conflicts can also be caused by inconsistent rewards and differing performance criteria for different units and groups. For example, salesman who depends upon their commission as a reward for their efforts may promise their customers certain quantity of the product and delivery times which the manufacturing department may find it impossible to meet, causing conflict between the two units.

Different functional groups within the organization may come into conflict with each other because of their different specific objectives. There are some fundamental differences among different units of the organization both in the structure and process and thus each unit develops its own organizational sub-culture. These sub-cultures, according to Lawrence and Lorsch differ in terms of (a) goal orientation which can be highly specific for production but highly fluid for Research and Development, (b) time orientation which is short run for sales and long run for research, (c) formality of structure which is highly informal in research and highly formal in production and (d) supervisory style which may be more democratic in one area as compared to another.

A classic example of interunit conflict is between as sales and production, as discussed earlier. The sales department is typically customer oriented and wants to maintain high inventories for filling orders as they are received, which is a costly option as against the production department which is strongly concerned about cost effectiveness requiring as little inventory of finished product at hand as possible.

Similarly, intergroup conflict may arise between day shift workers and night shift workers who might blame each other for anything that goes wrong from missing tools to maintenance problems.

Inter-Organizational Conflict

The conflict also occurs between organizations which in some way are dependent on each other. This conflict may be between buyer organizations and the supplier organizations about quantity, quality and delivery times of raw materials and other policy issues, between unions and organizations employing their members, between government agencies that regulate certain organizations and the organizations that are affected by them. These conflicts must be adequately resolved or managed properly for the benefit of both types of organizations.

Conflict Management

Except in very few situations where the conflict can lead to competition and creativity so that in such situations the conflict can be encouraged, in all other cases where conflict is destructive in nature, it should be resolved as soon after it has developed as possible, but all efforts should be made to prevent it from developing.

Preventing Conflict. Some of the preventive measures that the management can take, according to Schein are:

Goal Structure. Goals should be clearly defined and the role and contribution of each unit towards the organizational goal must be clearly identified. All units and the individuals in these units must be aware of the importance of their role and such importance must be fully recognized.

Reward System. The compensation system should be such that it does not create individual competition or conflict within the unit. It should be appropriate and proportionate to the group effort and reflect the degree of interdependence among units where necessary.

Trust and Communication. The greater the trust among the members of unit, the more honest and open the communication among them would be. Individuals and units should be encouraged to communicate openly with each other so that they can all understand each other, understand each other's problems and help each other when necessary.

Coordination. coordination is the next step to communication. Properly coordinated activities reduce conflict. Wherever there are problems in coordination a special liaison office should be established to assist such co-ordination.

Group Dynamics

Objectives

(A) To increase understanding of interpersonal processes that facilitates or hinders a group's ability to function effectively.

(B) To sharpen ability to observe and diagnose these process factors.

(C) To practice trying to combine the role of a participant in task accomplishment with the role of an observer.

It is not an exaggeration to say that Kurt Lewin had a profound impact on a generation of researchers and thinkers concerned with group dynamics. Brown argues that two key ideas emerged out of field theory that are crucial to an appreciation of group process: interdependence of fate, and task interdependence.

Interdependence of fate: Here the basic line of argument is that groups come into being in a psychological sense 'not because their members necessarily are similar to one another (although they may be); rather, a group exists when people in it realize their fate depends on the fate of the group as a whole. However, Lewin's insight does seem to be applicable to many different group settings. Subsequently, there has been some experimental support for the need for some elementary sense of interdependence (Brown 1989).

Task Interdependence. Interdependence of fate can be a fairly weak form of interdependence in many groups, argued Lewin. A more significant factor is where there is interdependence in the goals of group members. In other words, if the group's task is such that members of the group are dependent on each other for achievement, then a powerful dynamic is created.

These implications can be positive or negative. In the former case one person's success either directly facilitates others' success of, in the strongest case, is actually necessary for those others to succeed also... In negative interdependence - known more usually as competition - one person's success is another's failure.

Kurt Lewin had looked to the nature of group task in an attempt to understand the uniformity of some groups' behaviour. He remained unconvinced of the explanatory power of individual motivational concepts such as those provided by psychoanalytical theory or frustration-aggression theory. He was able to argue that people may come to a group with very different dispositions, but if they share a common objective, they are likely to act together to achieve it. This links back to what is usually described as Lewin's field theory. An intrinsic state of tension within group members stimulates or motivates movement toward the achievement of desired common goals.

Interdependence (of fate and task) also results in the group being a 'dynamic whole'. This means that a change in one member or subgroups impacts upon others. These two elements combined together to provide the basis for Deutch's (1949) deeply influential exploration of the relationship of task to process (and his finding that groups under conditions of positive interdependence were generally more co-operative. Members tended to participate and communicate more in discussion; were less aggressive; liked each other more; and tended to be productive as compared to those working under negative task interdependence).

The Structural Dynamic of Work Group

One of the key characteristics of a group is its stable structure. When social scientists use the term group structure, they are referring to the interrelationships between the individuals constituting the group, the characteristics that make group functioning orderly and predictable. There are describe four different aspects of groups structure, the various parts played by group members (roles), the rules and expectations that develop within groups (norms), the prestige of group membership (status), and the member's sense of belonging (cohesiveness).

Roles: The Hats We Wear

One of the primary structural elements of group is members' tendencies to play one or more specific roles in group interaction. Social scientists use the term role in much the some way as a director of a play would refer to the character that plays a part. Indeed, the part one plays in the overall group structure is what we mean by a role. More formally, we may define a role as the typical behaviors that characterize a person in a social context.

In organizations, many roles are assigned by virtue of an individual's position within an organization. For example, a boss may be expected to give orders, and a teacher may be expected to lecture and to give exams. These are behaviors expected of the individuals in that role. The person holding the role is known as the role incumbent, and the behaviors expected of that persons are known as role expectations. The person holding the office of the president of the United States (role incumbent) has certain role exceptions simply because he or she currently has that post. When a new president takes office, that person assumes the same role and has the same formal powers as the previous president. This is the case although the new president may have very different ideas about key issues facing the nation.

The role incumbents recognition of the expectations of his or her role helps avoid the social disorganization that surely would result if clear role expectation did not exist. Sometimes, however, workers may be confused about the things that are expected of them on the job, such as their level of authority or their responsibility. Such role ambiguity, as it is called, is typically experienced by new members of organizations who have not had much of a change to "learn the ropes" and often results in job dissatisfaction, a lack of commitment to the organization, and an interest in leaving the job.

As work groups and social groups develop, the various groups members come to play different roles in the social structure - a process refers to as role differentiation. The emergence of different roles in groups is a naturally occurring process. Think of committees to which you have belonged. Was there someone who joked and made people feel better and another member who worked hard to get the group to focus on the issue at hand? These examples of differentiated roles and typical of role behaviors that emerge in groups. Organizations, for example, often have their "office comedian" who makes every one laugh, or the "company gossip" who shares others' secrets, or the "grand old man" who tells newcomers the stories about the company's "good old days".

Norms: A Group's Unspoken Rules

One feature of groups that enhances their orderly functioning is the existence of group norms. Norms may be defined as generally agreed upon informal rules that guide group member's behavior. They represent shared ways of viewing the world. Norms differ from organizational rules in that they are not formal and written. In fact, group members may not even be aware of the subtle group norms that exist and regulate their behavior. Yet they have profound effect on behavior. Norms regulate the behavior of groups in important ways, such as by fostering workers' honesty and loyalty to the company, establishing appropriate ways to dress, and dictating when it is acceptable to be late for or absent from work.

If you recall the pressures placed on you by your peers as you grew up to dress or wear your hair in certain styles, you are well aware of the profound normative pressures exerted by groups. Some norms, known as perspective norms, dictate the behaviors that should be performed. Other norms, proscriptive norms, dictate specific behaviors that should be avoided. For example, groups may develop prescriptive norms to follow their leader or to help a group member who needs assistance. They may also develop proscriptive norms to avoid absences or to refrain from telling each other's secrets to the boss.

Sometimes the pressure to conform to norms is subtle, as in the dirty looks given a manager by his peers for going to lunch with one of the assembly-line workers. At other times normative pressures may be quite severe, such as when one production worker sabotages another's work because he is performing at too high a level and making his coworkers look bad. Although our examples emphasize the underlying social dynamics responsible for how groups develop norms, this is only one reason. There are, in fact, several factors responsible for formation of norms.

Status: The Prestige of Group Membership

Have you ever been attracted to a group because of the prestige accorded its members?

You may have wanted to join a certain fraternity or sorority because it is highly regarded by others on campus. No doubt, members of championship-winning football teams proudly sport their Super Bowl rings to identify themselves as members of that highly regarded team. Clearly, one potential reward of group membership is enjoying the status associated with being in that group. Even within social groups, different members are accorded different levels of prestige. Fraternity and sorority officers and committee chairpersons, for example, may be recognized as more important members of their respective groups. This is idea behind status-the relative social position or rank given to groups or group members by others.

Within most organizations, status may be recognized as both formal and informal in nature. Formal status refers to attempts to differentiate between the degrees of formal authority given employees by an organization. This is typically accomplished through the use of status symbols – objects reflecting the position of an individual within an organization's hierarchy. Some examples of status symbols include job titles (e.g., director); perquisites, or perks (e.g. a reserved parking space); the opportunity to do desirable and highly regarded work (e.g., serving on important committees); and luxurious working conditions (e.g., a large, private office that is lavishly decorated).

Status symbols help groups in many ways. For one, such symbols remind organizational members of their relative roles, thereby reducing uncertainty and providing stability to the social order (e.g., your small desk reminds you of your lower organizational rank). In addition, they provide assurance of the various rewards available to those who perform at a superior level (e.g., "maybe one day I'll have a reserved parking spot"). They also provide a sense of identification by reminding members of the group's values (e.g., a gang's jacket may remind its wearer of his expected loyalty and boldness). It is, therefore, not surprising that organizations do much to reinforce formal status through the use of status symbols.

Symbols of informal status within organizations are also widespread. These refer to the prestige accorded individuals with certain characteristics that are not formally recognized by the organization. For example, employees who are older and more experienced may be perceived as higher in status by their coworkers. Those who have certain special skills (such as the home-run hitters on a baseball team) also may be regarded as having higher status than others. In some organizations, the lower value placed on the work of women and members of minority groups by some individual also can be considered an example of informal status in operation.

One of the best-established findings in the study of group dynamics is that higher status people tend to be more influential than lower-status people. This phenomenon may be seen in a classic study of decision making in three-man bomber crews. After the crews had difficulty solving a problem, the experimenter planted clues to the solution with either a low-status group member (the tail gunner) or a high-status group member (the pilot). It was found that the solutions offered by the pilots were far more likely to be adopted than the same solutions presented by the tail gunners. Apparently, the higher status accorded the pilots (because they tended to be more experienced and hold higher military ranks) was responsible for the greater influence they wielded.

Cohesiveness: Getting the Team Spirit

One obvious determinant of any group's structure is its cohesiveness – the strength of group member's desires to remain part of their groups. Highly cohesive work group are ones in which the members are attracted to one another, accept the group's goals, and help work toward meeting them. In very non-cohesive groups, the members dislike each other and may even work at cross-purposes. In essence, cohesiveness refers to we - feeling, an esprit de corps, and a sense of belonging to a group.

Several important factors have been shown to influence the extent to which group members tend to "stick together." One such factor involves the severity of initiation into the group research has shown that the greater the difficulty people overcome to become a member of a group, the more cohesive the group will be. To understand this, consider how highly cohesive certain groups may be that you have worked hard to join. Was it particularly difficult to "make the cut" on your sports team? The rigorous requirements for gaining entry into elite groups, such as the most prestigious medical schools and military training schools, may well be responsible for the high degree of camaraderie found in such groups. Having "passed the test" tends to keep individuals together and separates them from those who are unwilling or unable to "pay the price" of admission.

Group cohesion also tends to be strengthened under conditions of high external threat or competition. When workers face a "common enemy," they tend to draw together such cohesion not only makes workers feel safer and better protected but also aids them by encouraging them to work closely together and coordinate their efforts toward the common enemy. Under such conditions, petty disagreements that may have caused dissension within groups tend to be put aside so that a coordinated attack on the enemy can be mobilized.

Research also has shown that the cohesiveness of groups is established by several additional factors. For one, cohesiveness generally tends to be greater the more time group members spend together. Obviously, limited interaction cannot help but interfere with opportunities to develop bonds between group members. Similarly, cohesiveness tends to be greater in smaller groups. Generally speaking, groups that are too large make it difficult for members to interact and, therefore, for cohesiveness to reach a high level. Finally, because "nothing succeeds like success," groups with a history of success tend to be highly cohesive. It is often said that "everyone loves a winner," and the success of a group tends to help unite its members as they rally around their success. For this reason, employees tend to be loyal to successful companies.

Thus, our discussion has implied that cohesievenss is a positive thing. Indeed, it can be. For example, people are known to enjoy belonging to highly cohesive groups. Members of closely knit work groups participate more fully in their group's activities, more readily accept their group's goals, and are absent from their jobs less often than members of less cohesive groups. Not surprisingly, cohesive groups tend to work together quite well, are sometimes exceptionally productive, and have low levels of voluntary turnover.

However, highly cohesive groups also can be problematic. For example, if a highly cohesive group's goals are contrary to the organization's goals, that group is in a position to inflict a great deal of harm to an organization by working against its interests. Highly cohesive group members who conspire to sabotage their employers are a good example. With this in mind, it's important to recognize that when it comes to performance group cohesiveness is a double-edged sword: its effects can be both helpful and harmful.

Teams

Managing Work Team Effectiveness

Objectives

(A) To learn about the task-related factors that influence team effectiveness.

(B) To sharpen the ability to see the impact of those factors upon team functioning.

(C) To practice using this model to enhance a team's effectiveness.

Defining Teams and Distinguishing Team From Groups

A team may be defined as a group whose members have complementary skills and are committed to a common purpose or set of performance goals for which they hold themselves mutually accountable. At this point, it probably is not entire clear to you exact how a team is different from an ordinary group. This confusion probably stems in part from the fact that people often refer to their groups as team, although they are really not team. Yet, there are several important distinctions between them. In groups, performance typically depends on the work of individual members. The performance of a team, however, depends on both individuals contributions and collective work products—the joint outcome of the team members working in concert.

Typically, members of groups pool their resources to attain a goal, although it is individual performance that is taken into consideration when it comes to issuing rewards. Members of groups usually do not take responsibility for any result other than their own. By contrast, team focus on both individual and mutual accountability that is, they work together to produce an outcome (e.g., a product, service, or decision) that represents their joint contributions, and each team member shares responsibility for that outcome, the key difference is this: in group, the superior holds individual members accountable for their work, whereas in teams, members hold themselves accountable.

Whereas group members may share a common interest in attaining a goal, team members also share a common commitment to purpose. Moreover, these purposes typically are concerned with winning in some way, such as being first or best at something. For example, a work in a manufacturing plant of a financially troubled company may be highly committed to making the company the top one in its industry. Another team, one in a public high school, may be committed to preparing all its graduates for the challenge of the worlds better than any other school in the district. Team members focusing jointly on such lofty purposes, in conjunction with special performance goals, become heavily invested in its activities. In fact, teams are said to establish "ownership" of their purpose and usually spend a great deal of time establishing their purpose. Like groups, teams use goals to monitor their progress. Teams, however, also have a broader purpose that supplies a source of meaning and emotional energy to the activities performed.

Teams differ from groups with respect to the nature of their connection to their management. Work groups are typically required to be responsive to demand regularly placed on them by management. By contrast, once management established the mission for the team and sets the challenge for it to archive, it typically gives the team enough flexibility to do its job without any further interference. Thus, many teams are described as being *autonomous* or *semiautonomous* in nature. This is not to say that team is completely independent of corporate management and supervision. They still must be responsive to demand from higher levels (often higher level teams, known as top management teams).

Groups v/s Teams

Groups and teams are not the same thing. In this section, we want to define and clarify the difference between a work group and a work team.

We defined a group as two or more individuals, interacting and interdependent, who have come together to achieve particular objectives. A work group is a group that interacts primarily to share information and to make decisions to help each member perform within his or her area of responsibility.

Work groups have no need or opportunity to engage in collective work that requires joint effort. So their performance is merely the summation of each groups member's individual contribution. There is no positive synergy that would create an overall level of performance that is greater than the sum of the inputs.

A work team generates positive synergy through coordinated effort. Their individual efforts results in a level of performance that is greater than the sum of those individual inputs.

Team : Special Kinds of Groups

Although each is composed of several individuals working together towards common goal, the connection between the employees at consolidated diesel appears to be much deeper in scope. Although the budget committee members may be interested in what they're doing, the group members of consolidated diesel seem more highly committee to their work and are more highly in the way their jobs are done. This is not to say that, there is necessarily anything wrong with the corporate budget committee; in fact, it would appear to be rather typical group. The groups at consolidated diesel, however, are examples of special kinds of teams.

Creating Teams: A Four-Stage Process

As you might imagine, assembling a team is no easy task. Doing so requires not only having the right combination of skilled people but also having individuals who are wiling to work together with others as a team. Designing a work team is a project that, when done effectively, involves four distinct stages. Making an effort to carefully follow these steps is a useful way of giving groups a head start on the road to success.

Stage 1: Prework. Before teams are created, a decision has to be made about whether or not a team should be formed – a stage known as prework. One of the most important objectivities of this phase is to determine whether a team should be created. A manager may decide to have several individuals working alone answer to him, or a team may be created if it is believed that it may develop the most creative and insightful ways to get.

Things Done. In considering this, it is important to note exactly what work needs to be done. The team's objectives must be established, and an inventory of the skills needed to do the job should be made. In addition, decisions should be made in advance about what authority the team should have. It may just be advisory to the manager, or it may be given full responsibility and authority for executing its task (i.e., self-regulating).

Stage 2: Creating Performance Conditions. Building on the prework, organizational officials ensure that the team has the proper resources needed to carry out its work. This involves both material resources (e.g., tools, equipment, and money). Human resources (e.g., the appropriate blend of skilled professionals), and support from the organization (e.g., willingness to let the team do its own work as it sees fit). Unless managers help create the proper conditions for team success, they are contributing to its failure.

Stage 3: Forming and Building the Team. Three things may be done to help a team get off to a good start. First, managers should form boundaries – clearly establish who is and who is not member of the team. Some teams fail simply because membership in it is left unclear. Reducing such ambiguity can help avoid confusion and frustration. Second, members must accept the team's overall mission and purpose. Unless they do, failure is inevitable. Third, organizational officials should clarify the team's mission and responsibilities – make perfectly clear exactly what it is expected to do (but not necessarily how to do it). Will team members be responsible for monitoring and planning their own work? If so, such expectations should be spelled out explicitly.

Stage 4: Providing Ongoing Assistance. Finally, once a team is functioning, supervisors may be needed to help the team to eliminate problems and perform even better. For example, disruptive team members may be either counseled or replaced. Similarly, material resources may have to be replenished or upgraded. Although it may be unwise for a manager to intervene in the successful affairs of a team that has taken on its own life, it also may be unwise to neglect opportunities to help a team do even better.

As you ponder these suggestions, you will doubtlessly recognize the considerable managerial skill and hard work required to create and manage teams effectively. However, as managers learn these skills, and as individuals gain successful experiences as member of effective work teams, the deliberate steps outlined earlier may become second nature to all concerned. In the words of one expert, "When that stage is reached, the considerable investment required to learn how to use work teams well can pay substantial dividends – in work effectiveness and in the quality of the experience of both managers and (team) members.

In view of their widespread popularity, it should not be surprising to learn that there are many different kinds of teams.

Types of Team

Purpose of Mission

The first dimension has to do with the teams major purpose or mission. In this regards, some teams—known as work teams—are primarily concerned with the work done by the organization, such as developing and manufacturing new products, providing services to customers, and so on. Their principle focus is on using the organizations resources to effectively create its results (be their goods or services). (the teams at consolidated diesel, describes in our preview case, are of this type) other teams known as improvement teams are primarily oriented towards the mission of increasing the effectiveness of the process that are used by the organization. For example, texas instrument has relied on teams to help improve the quality of the operation at its plant in Malaysia.

Time

A second dimension has to do with time. specifically, some teams are only temporary and are established for a specific project with a finite life. For example, a team se up to develop a new product would be considered temporary. As soon as its job is done, it disbands. However other kinds of teams are permanent and stay intact as long as organization is operating. For example, teams focusing on providing effective customer services tend to be permanent part of may organizations.

Degree of Autonomy

A third distinction has to do with the degree to which teams operate autonomously. This reflects the extent to which employees are responsible for making their own decisions (as opposed to having their bosses make them) and the degree to which they (as opposed to their bosses) are accountable for their own work outcomes. Various points along the resulting continuum of autonomy can be conceptualized as different types of groups.

Authority Structure

The Fourth dimension reflects the team's connection to the organization's overall authority structure – that is, the connection between various formal job responsibilities. In some organizations teams remain intact with respect to their organizational functions. For example, at Ralston-Purina projects are structured such that people work together on certain products all the time and do not apply their specialty to a wide range of products. Within such organizations, teams can operate without the ambiguities created by straying from one's area of expertise.

However, with growing frequency, we are seeing teams that cross over various functional units (e.g., marketing, finance, human resources, and so on). Such teams are commonly referred to as cross-functional teams. These are teams composed of employees at identical organizational levels, but from different specialty areas, to work together on a task. Cross-functional teams represent an effective way of bringing people together from throughout the organization to cooperate with each other on the diverse tasks needed to complete large projects. In organizations using cross-functional teams, the boundaries between all teams must be considered permeable. Indeed, people are frequently members of more than one team – a situation often required for organizations to function effectively. For example, members of an organization's manufacturing team must carefully coordinate their activities with members of its marketing team. To the extent that people are involved in several different kinds of teams, they may gain broader perspectives and make more important contributions to their various teams.

For over a decade, many automobile manufacturers – including the major American and Japanese companies – have relied on cross-functional teams to create and manufacture new models. As a case in point, the successful Neon was completely created by cross-functional teams of experts from throughout Chrysler (now, Dailmer-Chrysler). Similarly, in the aircraft industry, Boeing created cross-functional teams that designed and manufactured its latest aircrafts, the 777. In both cases, the use of teams has been credited with both the record speed with which the products came to market and their exceptional quality. As you might imagine, cross-functional teams are difficult to manage. It takes time for specialists in different areas to learn to communicate with each other and to coordinate their efforts. It also takes time to develop the mutual trust and acceptance that are required for people to work closely with each other. However, in view of the great successes of cross-functional teams, the effort required to make them work out appears to be worthwhile.

Physical Presence

The teams we have been describing thus far may be considered physical team insofar as they involve people who physically meet to work together. Although teams have operated this way for many years and will continue to do so, technology has made it possible for teams to exist without ever having their members physically meet. Teams of this sort are known as virtual teams – teams that operate across space, time, and organizational boundaries, communicating wit each other only through electronic technology.

Sometimes virtual teams form quite unintentionally, such as when valued team members begin telecommuting (the practice of working from home but communicating via e-mail). They also may be formed very deliberately such as when it is important to bring together on a project the most talented people in the world. Sun Microsystems did this, for example, when it developed a new electronic customer order system. The virtual team was composed of 15 engineers from three different companies in three different countries. They worked together over a seven month period without ever being together in the same room. Instead, intranets, teleconferencing, conference calls, and e-mails were used to bring the members together.

Today, virtual teams are possible because technology allows them to exist. To the extent that computer-based technology makes possible communication over long distances, that fact that the team members are far away from each other becomes less important. This is known as the law of telecosm – the idea that as computer networks expand, distances become irrelevant. In today's global economy, it is safe to say that virtual teams are not only possible, but they also are a clear necessity.

How to Develop Successful Teams

- Provide Training in Team Skills.
- Compensate Team Performance.
- Provide Support.
- Communicate the Urgency of the Team's Mission.
- Promote Cooperation within and between Teams.
- Select team Members Based on their Skills or Potential Skills.
- A Cautionary Note: Developing Successful Teams Requires Patience.

Team Building

To be effective, team members must have the right blend of skills needed for the team to contribute to the group's mission. Rather than simply putting teams together and hoping they will work, many companies are taking proactive steps to ensure that team members will get along and perform as they should. Formal efforts directed toward making teams effective are referred to as team building. Team building is usually used when established teams are showing signs of trouble, such as when members lose sight of their objectives and when turnover is high. Workers having high degrees of freedom and anonymity require a depth of skills and knowledge that surpasses that of people performing narrower, traditional jobs. For this reason, successful teams are those in which investment are made in developing the skills of teams members and leaders. In the words of one

Biblography

Jit's Chauhan - Organizational Behaviour - Group Behaviour - Pg. No. 226 to 233 ; Inter group relation and conflict - Pg. No. 273 to 282.

HL Kaila - Organizational Behaviour: Group Processes - Pg. No. 139 to 145.

Robins Stephen - Organizational Behaviour: 5th edition. Pg. No. 91 to 122.

Greenberg J. & Baron R. A. - Behavioural Organization: Formation of group - Pg. No. 275 to 284; Conflict in organization - Pg. No. 196 to 200.

Rubins - Organizational Behaviour.

John. W. Newstrom & Keith Davis – Organizational Behaviour – human behaviour at work, 10th edition.

Nicky Hayes – Essential Bus. Psychology: Successful Team Management.

4

Leadership

"Leadership is about having a flexible attitude. It is about matching your styles with the character traits of your subjects. It is also about guiding them on how to follow" - management guru, Mr. Arindam Chaudhuri.

1.1. What is Leadership?

Leadership is an integral part of management and plays a vital role in managerial operations. Dynamic and effective leadership is the factor that helps us differentiate between successful and unsuccessful leaders.

Leadership can be defined as the ability to influence a group toward the achievement of goals. Leadership is the process of influencing people and providing an environment for them to achieve team or organisation objectives. Leaders are supposed to have the art of influencing and inspiring subordinates to perform their duties willingly, competently and enthusiastically for achievement of group objectives.

Leadership is considered as a function of followers, goal, willingness on the part of the subordinates and a situation.

> Leadership (L) is considered as the function *(f)* of-
>
> - Followers (F)
> - Goals (G)
> - Willingness of subordinates (W)
> - Situation (S)
>
> L= *f* (F, G, W, S)

1.2. Leadership Characteristics

A leader has certain inherent qualities and traits that assist him in directing others towards the achievement of the goal. Some of these traits according to Jago are as follows :-

Energy, drive

Appearance, present ability

A sense of Cooperativeness

Enthusiasm

Personality- height and weight

Initiative

Intelligence

Judgement

Self-confidence

Sociability

Tact and diplomacy

Moral courage and integrity

Willpower and flexibility

Emotional stability

Knowledge of human relations

According to Ralph Stogdill, who studied the subject of leadership most extensively, "a person doesn't become a leader by virtue of the possession of some combination of traits, but the pattern of personal characteristics of the leader must bear some relevant relationship to the characteristics, activities and goals of the followers."

Leadership Studies

Leadership has been the topic of interest from more than a century. A number of different theories and approaches have been developed on leadership. Prior to 1945, the most common approach to the study of leadership concentrated on leadership traits. Later on the other views develop.

Classical Theories

2.1.

(1) Great man theory:

The basic assumption of the theory was that the 'leaders are born and not made'.

Early research on leadership was based on the study of people who were already great leaders. These people were often from aristocracy, as few from lower classes had the opportunity to lead. This contributed to the notion that leadership had something to do with breeding.

The idea of the Great Man also strayed into the mythic domain, with notions that in times of need, a great Man would arise, almost by magic. This was easy to verify, by pointing to people such as Jesus, Moses, and Buddha etc.

The great man theory and such other early leadership theories attributed success to the possession of abstract abilities such as energy, intuition and foresight.

2.2.

(2) Trait Theory:

From the great person theory, more realistic approach emerged, which is known as the trait theory of leadership. Trait theory states that leadership traits are not completely inborn but can also be acquired through learning and experience.

The advantage of trait theory was that, the trait research led to a change of focus from abstract personality traits to specific attributes that can be related directly to behaviours required for effective leadership in the particular situation.

By 1950 the traits associated with successful leadership were as follows:

- intelligence
- initiative
- self assurance
- overview
- health
- physique
- social background

2.3.

(3) Behaviour Theory

This theory studies leadership by looking at leaders in terms of what they "do". It emphasises what leaders actually do on the job and the relationship of this behaviour to leader effectiveness. Thus according to behaviour theory, leadership is shown by a person's acts more than by his traits. Research studies conducted by Katz, Maccoby and Morse, suggested that leadership behaviour be defined along employee-centred dimension and production-centred dimension complementing each other so that the employees performance and productivity is enhanced. The leadership effectiveness is determined in terms of leader-subordinate interaction and outcome.

At the end of World War II, the Bureau of business research at Ohio State University initiated studies on leadership. A team of researchers from psychology, sociology and economics developed and used the Leader Behaviour Description Questionnaire (LBDQ) to analyse leadership in numerous types of groups and situations. The extensive research made them isolate two particular factors affecting leadership. The two factors are as follows:

(1) Consideration: it refers to the extent to which there is a rapport between the leader and the group, mutual warmth and trust, a concern for the needs of the members of the work group, an attitude that encourages participative management, two-way communication and respect for the feedback of the followers.

(2) Initiating structure: it refers to the extent to which a leader is task oriented and his ability and concern in utilizing resources and personnel at optimum level. It involves creating a work environment so that the work in the group is organised, coordinated, sequential and organisationally relevant. An important observation made by the Ohio state university studied that the leader doesn't necessarily have to rate high both on consideration and as well as structure element. According to Weissenberg and Kavanaugh, these two elements are considered to be relatively independent dimensions of a leader's behaviour.

Consideration		
High	Low structure and high consideration	High structure and high consideration
Low	Low structure and low consideration	High structure and low consideration

Initiating Structure

Thus a manager with high structure and high consideration rates high on directing and controlling his subordinates and has a high level of consideration and warmth towards employees. Such managers have subordinates who are more satisfied have fewer grievances and stay longer with the organisation.

The advantage of this theory is that these two dimensions of leader's behaviour are tangible and observable and do account for a major part of leader behaviour.

Managerial Grid

The managerial grid/leadership grid was developed over 30 years ago by two behavioural scientists, Dr. Robert R. Blake and Jane S. Mouton. It is quiet popular among managers as a tool for identifying their style. The grid emerged during the late 1960s and is based upon the idea that leadership is function of: concern for people and concern for production.

In the grid structure, the horizontal axis indicates concern for production and vertical axis indicates the concern for people. And the leadership style is assessed with the help of the grid scale from 1 (low) and 9 (high).

Leadership Grid Talks About 5 Styles of the Leaderses

(1) Impoverished Management Style (1, 1)

Managers who focus neither on their people nor on results accomplish little. They simply do what they need to do to 'hang on', and their people appear lazy, apathetic, and indifferent. They are often in conflict and the workplace is essentially in chaos.

(2) Task Management Style (9, 1)

These ego-driven, autocratic managers are focused solely on results, and view people as commodities, essentially machines. Micromanagement is common, driven by their desire for control, mastery and domination. They see their role as being to plan, direct and control their subordinates and they are afraid to be seen as weak or as failures.

(3) Country Club Management Style (1, 9)

These managers put little weight on the results and focus on pleasing everybody and on minimising conflict. They do all they can to be appreciated and approved by their people. They have the fear of rejection. While they may have a peaceful workplace in the short-term, little gets accomplished, and problems inevitably arise in trying to please everybody all of the time.

(4) Middle-of-the-road Management Style (5, 5)

Some managers take what they think is a 'middle-of-the-road' approach. This type of managers wants to be popular and accepted. They push for production but only so far – that they don't go 'all-out' because they fear criticism and censure. Their motto is to be 'fair but firm'.

(5) Team Management Style (9, 9)

Effective leadership of teams and organisations require a balance between the maintenance functions and task functions to produce sustainable results. A maintenance functions involve the people issues and relationships while task functions are focused on delivering results.

Managers with team management style manage this balance.

Researches have shown that the most effective leaders are usually (9, 9) type managers. By addressing the needs of each individual employee, they align the employees with the task at hand and build commitment to results. It takes significant up-front time and effort to understand, develop and focus each individual employee. Once the employee is committed, there is little for the (9, 9) manager to do other than support the employees and ensure that everyone stays focused and aligned.

Contingency Theories

The contingency theories state that an analysis of leadership involves not only the *individual traits and behaviour* but also a *focus on the situation*. Here the focus is on the situation in which leadership is exercised and not upon the leader. Different types of situations demand different characteristics and behaviours because each type of leader faces different situations. A successful leader under one set of circumstances may be a failure under different set of circumstances, for example, Indira Gandhi was considered a successful Prime Minister and an effective leader of India during the war in 1971. However she turned out to be much less successful after the war when the situation changed.

Following are some of the important contingency theories:

4.1.

(1) Life-Cycle Theory / Situational Approach

Paul Hersey and Kenneth Blanchard have developed a leadership model which is known as life-cycle theory or situational leadership theory. This theory focuses on the "maturity" of the followers.

Hersey and Blanchard argue that successful leadership is achieved by selecting the right leadership style which is contingent on the level of followers' readiness. The focus on the leader effectiveness reflects the reality that it is the followers who accept or reject the leader.

Situational leadership uses two leadership dimensions, namely, task and relationship behaviours. Hersey and Blanchard considered each as either high or low and then combining them into four specific leader behaviours:

- Telling (high task- low relationship)

  The leader defines roles and tells people what, how, when and where to do various tasks. It emphasises the directive behaviour.

- Selling (high task- high relationship)

  The leader provides both directive and supportive behaviour.

- Participating (low task- high relationship)

  The leader and the followers both share in decision making, with the main role of the leader being facilitating and communicating.

- Delegating (low task- no relationship)

The leader provides little direction or support.

According to Hersey and Blanchard, readiness/ maturity of the followers is their ability and willingness to accomplish the specific tasks. They defined four stages of followers' readiness:

R(1) People are both unable, and either unwilling or too insecure to take responsibility to do something. They are neither competent nor confident.

R(2) People are unable but willing to do the necessary job. They are motivated but lack the appropriate skills.

R(3) People are able but unwilling or too apprehensive to do what the leader wants.

R(4) People are both, able and willing to do what exactly the leader wants.

As followers reach high levels of readiness, the leader responds by, not only decreasing the control gradually over the activities but also by gradually decreasing the relationship behaviour.

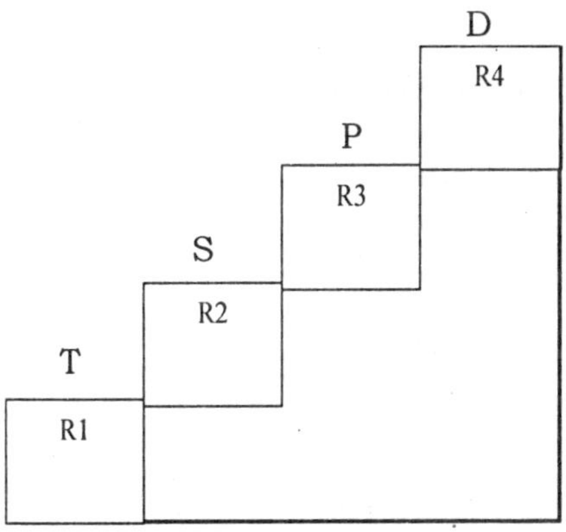

SITUATIONAL THEORY MODEL

4.2.

(2) Fiedler's Contingency Theory

Fred Fiedler was one of the earliest proponents of a leadership model that explicitly accounted for situational factors. In 1967 he proposed a theoretical explanation for interaction of three situational variables which affect the group performance. These three variables are –

(a) Leader- Member Relations

This relationship reflects the extent to which the followers have confidence and trust in their leader as to his leadership ability. A situation in which the leader member relations are relatively good with mutual trust and open communications is much easier to manage than a situation where the relations are strained.

(b) Task Structure

It measures the extent to which the tasks performed by subordinates are specified and structured. It involves clarity of goals, as well as clearly established and defined number of steps required to complete the task. When the tasks are well structured and the rules, procedures and policies clearly mentioned, then there is little ambiguity in the accomplishment of the job.

(c) Position Power

Position power refers to the legitimate power inherent in the leader's organisational position. It refers to the degree to which a leader can make decisions about allocation of resources, rewards and actions. A high position power gives the leader the right to take charge and control the situation as it develops.

The most favourable situation for the leader would be, when the leader group relations are positive, the task is highly structured and the leader has substantial power and authority to exert influence on the subordinates.

Fiedler developed an instrument, which he called the least preferred co-worker (LPC) questionnaire that helps to measure whether a person is task or relationship oriented. It measures the leader's esteem for the unfavourable co-worker as to whether or not the co-worker is viewed in the positive or negative way. A leader with a high LPC score is more relationship oriented and a low LPC score leader is a more task oriented.

4.3.

(3) Path- Goal Theory

The path-goal theory of leadership is proposed by House and Mitchell. According to them the effectiveness of leaders can be measured in terms of their influence on their subordinates' motivation. It states that leaders motivate higher performance in subordinates by acting in ways that influence them to believe that valued outcomes can be attained by making a serious effort.

A leader sets up clear path and clear guidelines through which the subordinates can achieve both personal as well as work related goals.

The theory holds the view that a leader must be able to show four different styles of behaviour:

(I) Directive: the leader provides specific guidelines to subordinates on how to perform their tasks.

(II) Supportive: the leader must demonstrate concern for subordinates' well-being and must be supportive to them as individuals.

(III) Participative: the leader must consider the ideas and suggestions from subordinates and invite their participation in decisions.

(IV) Achievement oriented: a leader must set challenging goals, emphasize improvements and encourage high levels of goal attainment.

4.4.

(4) Vroom- Yetton Model

This leadership model is normative in nature as it simply tells, how leaders should behave in decision-making.

The model indicates three variables that affect the performance of the leader in terms of his capacity as a decision maker. The three variables are as follows:

(I) The Quality of theDecision

It refers to not only the importance of the decision to the performance of the subordinates but also whether such performance is optimal in nature and whether all relative input has been considered during decision-making process.

(II) Decision Acceptance

It refers to the degree of subordinate commitment to the decision. Whether the decision is made by the leader himself or with participation of subordinates, it must be accepted by those who have to implement it.

(III) Time required to make the decision

Many situations develop in the form of crisis where immediate and fast actions have to be taken in order to make quick decisions.

4.5.

(5) Leader-Member Exchange (LMX) Theory

Graen and his associates (Dansereau, Graen, and Haga,1975) Proposed a theory of leadership based upon mutual influence, called leader member exchange theory. The theory says that leaders differentiate their subordinates in terms of - (a) their competence and skills, (b) the extent to which they can be trusted (especially when they are not being watched by the leader) (c) their motivation to assume greater responsibility within the unit.

Subordinates with the greater assumed responsibility become members of what Graen calls the in- group. In group members are those who go beyond their former job duties and take responsibility for completing even the critical tasks.

In return, they receive more attention, support and sensitivity from their leaders.

Subordinates, on the other hand, who don't assume strong responsibilities, are called the out group. They do the routine, mundane tasks and have a more formal relationship with the leader. Leaders influence out group members by using formal authority.

In the review of the theory, Dienesch and Liden (1986) concluded that there are three psychological bases for the "exchange" between the superior and subordinate. (A) Personal contribution: refers to the perception of the amount, direction and quality of work oriented activity each member puts forth. (B) Loyalty: is the expression of public support for the goals and personal character of the other members. (C) Affect: is the degree of liking, members have for each other.

Transformational and Transactional Leadership

Kuhnert and Lewis (1987) developed this model.

5.1.

Transformational Leadership

It refers to the process of influencing major changes in the attitudes and assumptions of organisation members and building commitment for major changes in the organisation's objectives and strategies. Transformational leadership involves influence by a leader on subordinates but the effect of the influence is to empower subordinates who would also become leaders in the process of transforming the organisation.

Bass (1998) defined transformational leadership in terms of leader's effect on followers. Leaders transform followers by making them more aware of the importance and value of the task outcomes, by activating their higher-order needs and by inducing them to transcend self-interest for the sake of the organisation.

There are four different styles of influencing, which are used by the leaders-

(I) Idealised influence: transformational leaders behave in ways that make them role models for their followers. The leaders are admired, respected and trusted. Followers identify with the leaders and want to emulate them.

(II) Inspirational motivation: transformational leaders behave in ways that motivate and inspire those around them by providing meaning and challenge to their followers' work. Leaders get followers involved in envisioning attractive future states; they create clearly communicated expectations that followers want to meet.

(III) Intellectual stimulation: transformational leaders stimulate their followers' efforts to be innovative and creative by questioning assumptions, reframing problems and approaching old situations in new ways.

(IV) Individualised consideration: transformational leaders pay special attention to each individual follower's needs for advancement and growth by acting as a coach or mentor. Followers and colleagues are developed to successively higher levels of potential. Individual differences of needs and desires are recognised and the leader's own behaviour demonstrates acceptance of these differences.

5.2.

Transactional Leadership

These kinds of leaders guide or motivate their followers in the direction of established goals by clarifying role and task requirements. Transactional leadership is "managing"- helping organisations achieve their current objectives more efficiently, such as linking job performance to valued rewards and ensuring that employees have the resources needed to get the job done. This includes the allocation of work, making routine decisions, monitoring performance and interacting with other functions within the organisation.

The transactional leader works through creating clear structures whereby it is clear what is required of their subordinates, and the rewards that they get for following orders. Punishments are not always mentioned, but they are also well-understood and formal systems of discipline are usually in place.

The early stage of Transactional Leadership is in negotiating the contract whereby the subordinate is given a salary and other benefits, and the company (and by implication the subordinate's manager) gets authority over the subordinate.

When the Transactional Leader allocates work to a subordinate, they are considered to be fully responsible for it, whether or not they have the resources or capability to carry it out. When things go wrong, then the subordinate is considered to be personally at fault, and is punished for their failure (just as they are rewarded for succeeding).

6. Charismatic Leadership

Word charisma, is derived from the Greek word meaning 'gift'.

A charismatic person attracts others by some magnetism in their personality and presence.

Charismatic leadership refers to follower perception that a leader possesses a divinely inspired gift and is somehow unique and larger than life. Followers not only trust and respect the leader but also idolize or worship the leader as a superhuman hero or spiritual figure.

House (1977) proposed theory that identifies how charismatic leaders behave and how they differ from other people. The theory specifies some behaviours that are typical of charismatic leaders. There are as follows:

(1) impression management to maintain follower confidence in the leader

(2) articulation of an appealing vision that defines the task in terms of ideological goals in order to build follower commitment

(3) communication of high expectations from the followers

(4) expression of confidence in followers' ability to build their self-confidence

Charismatic leaders are regarded as individuals who give their followers a vision of the future that promises a better and more meaningful life. Conger and Kanungo (1987) believed that charismatic leaders are the "heroes" who exhibit unconventional behaviours and transform people to share the radical changes they advocate. Manz and Sims (1991) added that such leaders should also be viewed as hero makers, and the spotlight should be on the achievements of the followers as well as the leaders. Gardner and Avolio (1998) identified the effective use of "staging" by charismatic leaders. Staging involves attention to the development and manipulation of symbols, including physical appearances, settings, props and other artifactual displays.

Hogan and others (1990) found out the "dark side" to charismatic leaders. According to them many of the charismatic leaders face the psychological problems, for example, adjustment problems, anxiety problems etc, behind the mask of charisma and social life likeability.

7. Leadership Styles

There are three major styles of leadership.

(1) Autocratic or Dictatorial Leadership

Autocratic leaders keep the decision-making authority and control in their own hands and assume full responsibility for all actions. Also, they structure the entire work situation in their own way and expect the workers to follow their orders and tolerate no deviation from their orders. The subordinates are required to implement instructions of their leaders without question. They are entirely dependent on their leader and the output suffers in the absence of the leader.

(2) Participative or Democratic Leadership

In this type of leadership, the subordinates are consulted and the feedback is taken into the decision-making process. The leader's job is primarily of a moderator, even though he makes the final decision and he alone is responsible for the results. The leader recognises that the subordinates are equipped with talents and abilities and that they are capable of bringing new ideas and new methodologies to work setting. This coordination between the leader and the subordinates ensures better management-labour relations, higher morale and greater job satisfaction. This type of leadership is especially effective when the workforce is experienced and able to work independently.

(3) Laissez-Faire or Free-Reign Leadership

In this type of leadership, the leader is just a figure-head and doesn't give any direction but delegates the authority to subordinates so that they must plan, motivate, control and otherwise be responsible for their own actions. The leader acts principally as a mediator between the group and outside elements and supplies necessary materials and information to group members. He lets subordinates develop their own techniques for accomplishing goals within the generalised organisational policies and objectives. This type of leadership is highly effective when the group members are highly intelligent and are fully aware of their roles and responsibilities.

Conclusion

Though all the leadership studies and theories hold different views and explanations, there is unanimity regarding the fact that "Leadership is a vital process in directing work within organisations". Recent thinking about leadership considers leaders as not only heroes but also as hero makers. Thus, leadership need not be a phenomenon only related to upper level positions but rather it is a contagious process that can manifest itself throughout all levels of an organisation.

Reference and Further Reading

Chandan, J. S. (1998). Leadership. *Organisational behaviour (second edition)*, Vikas publishing house Pvt. Ltd., 339-361.

Greenberg, J. and Baron, R. A. (2003). Leadership in organizations. Behaviour in organisations (eighth edition), Prentice hall of India Pvt. Ltd., 469-512.

Muchinsky, P. M. (2001). Leadership. *Psychology applied to work (sixth Edition)*, Thomson learning, 363-388.

http://changingminds.org/disciplines/leadership/styles/transactional_leadership.htm

5
Introduction to Human Resource Management

- HUMAN RESOURCE: THE CONCEPT
- HUMAN RESOURCE MANAGEMENT
- CHARACTERISTICS OF HRM
- HRM VERSUS PERSONNEL MANAGEMENT
- HRM VERSUS HRD
- THEORIES OF HRM
- CONDITIONS FAVOURABLE AND UNFAVOURABLE TO HRM
- CURRENT STATUS OF HRM
- REFERENCES

Human Resources: The Concept

Human Resources Management (HRM) is concerned with the human beings in an organisation. It reflects a new philosophy, a new outlook, approach, and strategy, which views an organisation's manpower as its resources and assets, and not as liabilities or mere hands.

Human resources are human wealth or means that can be drawn on. Human capital or manpower resources of a company can be treated as its human resources.

In generic terms, it can be defined as the total knowledge, skills, creative abilities, talents and aptitudes of an organisation's workforce, as well as the values, attitudes, approaches and beliefs of the individuals involved in the affairs of the organisation.

Human resources approach takes into consideration the potentiality and vitality of the people available for the organisation. Resourcefulness of various categories of people say: managers, scientific and research people, executives, supervisors, workers (skilled, unskilled) and all such people available for the organisation to be drawn on, can be treated as human resources. In fact, without appropriate human resources, no business or organisation can exist and grow. This is, perhaps, the reason why human resources management has become the focus of attention of progressive organisation of today.

Human Resources Management

According to George Terry, "Management is a distinct process consisting of planning, organising, actuating and controlling, performed to determine and accomplish stated goals by the use of human beings and other resources".

Koontz and O'Donnel defines management as, "Managing is defined as the creation and maintenance of an internal environment in an enterprise, where individuals, working together in groups, can perform efficiently and effectively towards the attainment of group goals".

Human resources management is the process of managing the people of an organisation with a humane approach. Human resources approach to manpower enables the manager to view his people as an important, if not the most important, resources. It is benevolent approach to develop and effectively utilise the manpower not only for the benefit of the organisation but for the growth, development and self-satisfaction of the concerned people. Thus, HRM is a system that focuses on human resources development, on the one hand, and effective management of people on the other, so that people will enjoy human dignity in their employment.

The human resources manager must act as a catalyst and exemplar, who directs all the aspects of managing manpower, human resources development, counselling, industrial relations, welfare activities, and so on. HRM is visualised here as a line function or a general management function which actuates, perfects and causes to happen the activities and operations of an organisation to make the best performance toward organisational objectives and goals.

Human resource management (HRM) consists of numerous activities, including: (a) Helping the organisation reach its goals. (b) Equal employment opportunity (EEO) compliance. (c) Job analysis. (d) Human resource planning, i.e., employing the skills and abilities of the workforce efficiently. (e) Employee recruitment, selection, motivation, and orientation. (f) Performance evaluation and compensation. (g) Training and development. (h) Increasing to the fullest the employee's job satisfaction and self-actualization. (i) Labor relations, i.e., communicating HRM policies to all employees. (j) Helping to maintain ethical policies and socially responsible behavior. (k) Managing change to the mutual advantage of individuals, groups, the enterprise, and the public.

Characteristics Giving Key to Understanding of Management

The following are the important features of management that clearly brings out its meaning and nature:

- ***Management is Purposeful***

Management deals with the achievement of something specific, expressed as an objective. Management exists because it is an effective means of getting needed work accomplished. The fact that some executives have a number of subordinates reporting to them does not ipso facto, make them managers. Managers focus their attention and efforts on bringing about successful action. They know where to start, what to do to keep things moving, and how to follow through. Management is acceptable because by its means things are accomplished that people know should be done and that they want done, but they realize probably won't be done if management is absent.

- ***Management is a Process***

Management is a process of planning, organising, directing and controlling. The process of management is necessary in order to attain objectives. For this purpose, managers must: (a) Plan the activities, (b) Organise the resources, (c) Direct the subordinates, and (d) Control the activities.

- ***Management is an Activity, not a Person or a Group of Persons***

The word "managing" is a more precise and descriptive

term than management. Popular usage, however, has made management the widely accepted term. Management is not people, it is an activity like walking, reading, swimming or running. People who perform management can be designated as managers memebers of management, or executive leaders. In addition, management is a distinct activity. It can be studied, knowledge about it obtained, and skilled in its application acquired.

- ***Management is accomplished by, with, and through the efforts of others***

To participate in management necessitates relinquishing the normal tendency to perform all things yourself and get tasks accomplished by, with, and through the efforts of group members. Normally a person acquires ability in a specialized type of work and wins promotions by acquiring increasing knowledge and skill in this given field of specialization. However, the time comes when further promotion requires shifting from the role of a specialist to that of a management member. The prime measure of success now becomes setting or securing agreement on the proper goals and getting others to accomplish these specific goals. How successfully this deliberate shift is made determines the potentialities of this new manager. To sum up management involves getting things done through the people in the organisation. To get the work done, managers need to: (a) Lead the subordinates, (b) Communicate effectively, and (c) Motivate the subordinates.

- ***Management is a Group activity***

Proper management requires teamwork. The combined efforts of all the managers bring success to the organisation. A single manager, however capable, may not be able to attain organisational goals without the support of other managers.

- ***Management is Result Oriented***

Management place emphasis on results. The activities of the managers are focused on the attainment of goals or results. What matters is not just activities but better results. The results can be in the form of: (a) Optimum use of resources, (b) Higher efficiency, etc.

- ***Management is an Art as Well as a science***

There is a considerable debate as to whether management is an art or science. In practice, managing is an art. However, a manager can work better by using the organised knowledge (science). In other words, management has characteristics of both art as well as science.

- ***Management Need To Follow Well Established Principles***

Management follows well established principles in managing their organisation. The principles include (a) Division of work, (b) Authority- responsible balance, (c) Discipline, (d) Unity of command, etc.

- ***Management Need Not be Ownership***

In large organisations, management and ownership need not be one and the same. The owners, i.e. shareholders can hire the service of professional managers. However, in small organisations, owners themselves undertake management activities.

- ***Management is Dynamic in Nature***

Management needs to be creative and innovative. The success and survival of the organisation largely depends upon innovation. Managers must come up with: (a) New and creative ideas, (b) New and better products, (c) Cost-effective processes, etc.

- ***Management Adopts Professional Approach***

Now a days, managers adopt a professional approach in getting the work done from the subordinates. Professional managers: (a) Delegate authority, (b) Encourage initiative, (c) Invite suggestions, (d) Provide training, etc.

- ***Management is Aided but Cannot be Replaced by Computers***

Computers can aid managers in decision-making. Managers can take quick and better decisions with the help of computerised data. It can widen a manager's vision and sharpen insight by supplying information for key decisions. Computers cannot replace managers. However a manager must supply judgment and imagination as well as interpret and evaluate what the data mean in a specific individual case. Thus, the judgment and experience of managers is required to use computerised data. However, computers may reduce the number of managers required.

- ***Management is all Pervasive***

Management is an activity that touches all walks of life. It is applicable not only to business organisations, but also to other organisations such as educational institutions, charitable trusts and even individual activities such as study.

- ***Management is Intangible***

Management as a process or activity is not directly visible. It has been called the unseen force-its presence evidenced by the results of its efforts-orderliness, enthusiastic employees, buoyant spirit, adequate work output, efficiency, and cordial relations in the organisation.

- ***Management is Required at All Levels***

In the organisation, there are various levels of management. Generally, there are three levels of management, i.e., Top Level Management, Middle Level Management, and Lower Level of Management. The managers at all levels need to plan, to organise, to direct and to control their activities.

- ***Management is a Continuous Process***

The process of management, i.e., planning, organising, directing and controlling continues as long as the organisation is in existence. Management process in not a one-time activity.

- ***Other Characteristics***

(a) Management involves delegation of authority.

(b) Management is an important factor of production.

(c) Management is responsible to various parties.

(d) Management ensures optimum use of resources.

(e) Management requires specialized knowledge and skills.

HRM Versus Personnel Management

At least some managers misunderstand that human resources management is a dignified term of personnel management, while some are of the opinion that both the terms represent the same concept or identical function. In this context, one should understand that HRM is not personnel management, though the latter is included in the former. The very outlook of philosophy of HRM is different from that of personnel management.

According to Flippo, "Personnel Management is the planning, organizing, directing, and controlling of the procurement, development, compensation, integration, and maintenance of people for the purpose of contributing to the organizational, individual, and social goals". This highlights that various managerial functions relating to procurement and maintenance of people in an organisation come under personnel management. This may include developing people in a way the organisation wants, for attaining competitive advantage for the organisation. It is that phase of management, which deals with the effective control, and use of manpower as distinguished from other sources of power.

"The management of human resources is viewed as a system in which participants seek to attain both the individual and group goals."

Personnel (or manpower) management involves procedures and practices through which human resources are managed (i.e. organised and directed) towards the attainment of the individual, social and organisational goals. Prof. Thomas G. Spates visualized personnel administration as, "a code of the ways of organising and treating individuals at work so that they will each get the greatest possible realisation of their intrinsic abilities, thus attaining maximum efficiency for themselves and their group, and thereby giving to the enterprise of which they are a part its determining competitive advantage and its optimum results".

In this definition, personnel administration has been regarded as a code which deals with the ways of organising the human resources in such a way that their potentialities are best utilised bringing them satisfaction and efficiency in their work and helping the organisation in attaining its objectives, with minimum of cost, in a competitive market.

Thus the sole purpose of personnel management was to attain competitive advantage and best result for the organisation. The individual's interests, desires and aspirations were submerged into the oraganisational objectives and goals.

Human resources management is viewed in entirely different perspective. Though organisational interest is important in all the management policies, HRM projects the development of individuals in accordance with the individual needs and aspirations so that the individuals would be motivated to make their best contribution towards the accomplishment of common goals. While personnel function was designed to respond to the organisational objectives like profit maximisation, HRM visualised human elements of enterprise as important resources. Hence, HRD is the most crucial aspect of HRM.

Personnel function has been traditionally considered as an independent function responsible for personnel record keeping and rule enforcing. A personnel manager advises the top management about the personnel function. This may, perhaps be the reason why personnel function was viewed as a staff function at least by some writers on management.

But there is no reason why HRM should be reckoned as a staff function. On the contrary, HRM is part and parcel of every line function. HRM must be the job of every operating manager in an oraganisation. Actually speaking, the primary job of every manager is actuating, and HRM cannot be isolated from actuating. As already observed essentials of personnel function are necessarily incorporated in both actuating and HRM functions in its refined form. Hence, one must not be under the impression that the traditional personnel management is replaced by HRM. Rather, HRM has absorbed the personnel function in its refined form.

Manpower planning is incorporated into human resources planning. Recruitment, selection, training, placement, compensation, direction, appraisal, supervision., and such other functions of personnel management form part of HRM, also while other aspects like human resources development, career planning and development, counselling and redemptive measures, constant efforts for appraisal, research and feedback system, data storage and retrieval system, and so on receive greater attention in HRM. A humane approach to the people at work backed by welfare amenities and cordial industrial relations policies must also be an integral part of HRM. In the HRM approach, personnel function is not merely record keeping function. Rather it is a constant endeavour to motivate the people at work to foster a oneness with the organisation and its performance goals. This is achieved neither through pressure tactics nor through conflicts and struggles, but through constant cooperation, team-building and mutual understanding. This is what is meant of HRM. Thus, HRM is not limited to mere personnel management. It is an integrated systems approach to actuating.

HRM Versus HRD

Some writers have used both the terms interchangeably. But these two terms cannot be one and the same nor synonyms. They are used in different contexts and they represent different concepts. At the same time HRD is at the centre of HRM.

As a result of the fundamental changes in attitudes, approaches, outlook, philosophy, perspective and practices emerged in the personnel area of human resources management (HRM) strategy, it has become necessary for every organisation to develop skills, talents, potentialities, capabilities and attitudes of company's own people to meet the emerging challenges. Hence, HRD (Human Resource Development) policies have been adopted by many companies. It is now-a-days spreading to many others. HRD strategies are supposed to bring forth necessary changes in skills, capabilities and attitudes of people who are required to cope with the emerging changes. Thus, HRD has become an integral part of human resources management.

The new HRD approach, that stresses the need for developing the company's own people to suit the updated technology, modernisation of machinery and equipments and the changing trends in attitudes and approaches, necessitates to develop individual employee in accordance with his aspirations and potentialities on the one hand, and the company's requirement on the other. This is what the HRD does. Quite often Organisation Development (OD) programmes are effectively integrated with the HRD programmes. HRD interventionists primarily seek to know what the individuals seek to have, and then try to match it with organisational needs. Training and development programmes form part of OD, while training and development are the most decisive aspects of HRD too.

HRD efforts are now described in terms of the training and educating programmes and the number of people who are exposed to these programmes. Unless a systematic and constant monitoring of these programmes and a systematic appraisal of the actual effects of these programmes, in terms of actual results achieved, can be determined, it may not be possible to understand whether these programmes serve the real purpose. At present, therefore, the end results of both HRD and OD are perceived as synonymous. Of course, no change can be effectively and totally incorporated nor their results achieved, over-night. It needs constant efforts and continuous monitoring for a considerably long period. These efforts must go on simultaneously with the human resources management strategy.

HRM has its various tools like appraisal schemes, feed-back system, Quality Circle and Organisation Development interventions, T-group training, MBO objective setting, consensus in decision making, and so on. All such tools are useful in human resources development also. At present, however, training programmes seem to dominate the HRD scene.

An effective management information system backed by information collecting, storing and retrieval system and research and analysis must be the basis for every HRD programme. This would enable the organisation to motivate its own people to strive to be developed in accordance with the organisational needs. Thus, HRM is the integrated approach to actuating and managing the company's own people, while HRD deals with the process of developing people in accordance with their aspirations and to suit the organisational needs. Both are not synonyms; the latter is at the centre of the former, and both are interdependent and integrated into one system.

Theories of HRM

Huczynski (1996) classifies management concepts into five major groups such as bureaucracy, scientific management, administrative theory, human relations movement, behavioural approach and modern management approaches such as Quantitative approach, Systems approach, and Contingency approach.

I. Bureaucracy

According to Max Weber (1864-1920), bureaucracy represents the most efficient organizational design. For him, bureaucracy was management by the "office" or position rather than by the person or "patrimonial". Weber described bureaucracy as "an administrative body of appointed officials". Bureaucracy is the term used for organizational form, which is based on legal-rational authority. where objectives and rules could lead to efficiency and avoid the evils of personal favouritism It is designed rationally and assumes that individuals are rational in their roles and actions. The model of legal-rational bureaucracy designed by Weber has the following characteristics:

(a) A hierarchy of authority and levels of organization. (b) Specialization of tasks, duties, and responsibilities. (c) Positions designed as "offices". (d) Planned succession to office. (e) Impersonality of officials. (f) A system of abstract rules and standards for discipline and control. (g) Specified qualifications for individuals holding office. (h) Protection of individuals against arbitrary dismissal. (i) Official business is conducted on a continuous basis. (j) Officials do not own the resources necessary for rendering the duties, but they are accountable for use of official resources. (k) Administration is conducted on the basis of written documents.

Weber also described the marks of officials, which are

as follows: (a) He is personally free (and not a servant to anybody personally) and appointed to an official position on the basis of a contract. (b) He exercises the authority delegated to him in accordance to impersonal rules, and his loyalty is expressed through faithful execution of his official duties. (c) His appointment and job placements depend upon his technical (administrative) qualifications. (d) His administrative work is his full-time occupation. (e) His work is rewarded by a regular salary and by prospects of regular advancement in a lifetime career.

In Weberian model of bureaucracy, the main elements can be noted as (I) impersonal order, (ii) rules, (iii) sphere of competence, (iv) hierarchy, (v) personal and public ends, (vi) written documents, and (vii) monocratic type.

Weber thought that it would be most efficient form of organization possible, for in this mechanism, precision, speed, unambiguity, knowledge of the files, continuity, discretion, unity, strict subordination, reduction of friction and of material and personal costs are raised to the optimum point in the strictly bureaucratic administration.

II. Scientific Management

Frederick Winslow Taylor (1856-1915) is regarded as the father of scientific management with his main contribution in the field of production management, i.e., at the plant level or shop floor level. Scientific management means acceptance and application of the principles of science in the field of business management. Taylor believed that decisions in business should be taken on the basis of certain principles and laws derived by scientific investigation and analysis. The basic components of scientific management as propounded by Taylor are as follows: -

- ***Determination of Standards of Performance.*** Each man in the establishment, high or low, should daily have a clearly defined task laid out before him. He believed that there was one best way to do the job i.e., he advocated a systematic job specification and established responsibilities.

• ***Functional Foremanship.*** Taylor introduced the concept of functional specialists. Taylor suggested that the work should be planned by a foreman and not by the worker. Further, he said that there should be as many foremen as there are special functions involved in doing a job and each of these foremen should give orders to the workers on his specialty.

He also fixed the responsibilities of the managers to design work systems.

• ***Differential Payment.*** Taylor introduced a new payment plan called the differential piece-work, in which he linked incentives with production. Under this plan a worker received low piece rate if he produced the standard number of pieces and high piece rate if he surpassed the standard. Taylor thought that the attraction of high piece rate would motivate workers to increase production.

• ***Standardization of tools, equipments and materials.*** A careful analysis of all tasks and functions, followed by analysis of associated routines-production planning, stock control and office procedures will lead to standardization of equipments, methods and procedures.

• ***Time and motion study.*** The real trouble, Taylor thought was that no one knew how much work it was reasonable to expect a man to do. He, therefore, started time and motion study, under which each motion of a job was to be timed with the help of a stopwatch and shorter and fewer motions were to be developed. Thus the best way of doing a job was found. This replaced the old rule-of–thumb knowledge of the workman.

• ***Scientific Recruitment and Training.*** Taylor emphasized the need for scientific selection and development of the worker. He said that the management should develop and train every worker to bring out his best faculties and to enable him to do a higher, more interesting and more profitable class of work than he has done in the past.

• ***Mental Revolution* (The Heart of the Approach).** Taylor said that for above suggestions to succeed, "a complete mental revolution" on the part of management and labour was required. Rather than quarrel over whatever profits there were, they should both try to increase production. By doing so, profits would be increased to such an extent that labour and management would no longer have to compete for them. In short, Taylor believed that management and labour had a common interest in increasing productivity.

The fundamental principles that F.W.Taylor recommended as a part of scientific management are summarised as follows: (a) Replacing rules of thumb with science. (b) Obtaining harmony in group efforts, rather than discord. (c) Cooperation, not individualism. (d) Maximum output rather than restricted output. (e) Development of all the workers to the fullest extent possible in order to enhance efficiency and productivity of the entire business enterprise.

Taylor's principles and concepts were refined and enlarged by several of his followers, notable among them bieng Henry L.Gantt and the Gilbreths.

Gantt saw the importance of the human element in productivity and propounded the concept of motivation, He introduced two new features in Taylor's incentive scheme. First, every worker who finished a day's assigned workload was to win a 50-cent bonus for that day. Second, the foreman too was to earn a bonus for each worker who reached the daily standard, plus an extra bonus if all the workers reached it. This, Gantt reasoned, would spur a foreman to train his workers to do a better job. Gantt also developed the idea of rating an employee's work publicly. Going beyond this, Gantt originated a charting system for production control. It reflects each man's daily performance in relation to a predetermined quota or standard of performance.

Frank and Lillian Gilbreth made motion and fatigue study their lifework. Using motion picture cameras, Frank Gilbreth tried to find the most economical motions for bricklaying. According to Gilbreths, motion and fatigue studies raised workers' morale, not only because of their obvious physical benefits but also because they demonstrated management's concern for the workers.

III. *Administrative Management*

Henri Fayol (1841-1925) is considered the Father of

administrative management theory with focus on the development of broad administrative principles applicable to general and higher managerial levels (He used the word 'administration' for what we call management.) His perspective, extended beyond the shop level and the physical production processes and was of a macro nature, covering the general administrative and managerial functions and processes at the organisational level.

Fayol believed that all activities of business enterprises could be divided into six groups: (1) Technical (production, manufacture) (2) Commercial (buying, selling and exchange (3) Financial (search for and optimum use of capital) (4) Security (protection of property and persons) (5) Accounting (stock-taking, cost, statistics,, balance sheet) (6) Managerial (planning, organising, command, coordination, and control). Fayol's primary focus, was on managerial activity because he felt managerial skills had been the most neglected aspect of business operations. He defined management in terms of five functions: planning, organising, coordinating and controlling.

Fayol also presented 14 principles of management as general guides to the management process and management practice. These are as under:

- ***Division of work.*** Division of work in the management process produces more and better work wth the same effort. Various functions of management like planning, organising, directing and controlling cannot be performed efficiently by a single proprietor or by a group of directors. They must be entrusted to specialists in related fields.

- ***Authority and Responsibility.*** The manager should have the right to give orders and powers to exact obedience (authority). Fayol argued that authority flows from responsibility. 'Authority' is in direct relation to 'responsibility', that implies clearly an obligation to achieve the goals. The acceptance of authority implies acceptance of responsibility for the performance of their given tasks.

- ***Discipline.*** By discipline we mean, the obedience to authority, observance of the rules of service and norms of performance, respect for agreements, sincere efforts for completing the given job, respect for superiors, etc. The best means of maintaining discipline are (a) good supervisors at all levels, (b) clear and fair agreements between the employees and the employer, and (c) judicious application of penalties. In fact, discipline is what leaders make it.

- ***Unity of Command.*** This principle requires that each employee should receive instructions about a particular work from one superior only. Fayol believed that if an employee was to report to more than one superior, he would be confused due to conflict in instructions and also it would be difficult to pinpoint responsibility to him.

- ***Unity of Direction.*** It means that there should be complete identity between individual and organisational goals on the one hand and between departmental goals *inter se* on the other. They should not pull in different directions.

- ***Subordination of individual interest to General Interest.*** In a business concern, an individual is always interested in maximising his own satisfaction through more money, recognition, status, etc. This is very often against the general interest, which lies in maximising production. Hence the need to subordinate the individual interest to general interest.

- ***Remuneration.*** The remuneration paid to the personnel of the firm should be fair. It should be based on general business conditions, cost of living, and productivity of the concerned employees and the capacity of the firm to pay. Fair remuneration increases worker's efficiency and morale and fosters good relations between them and the management.

- ***Centralization.*** The management must decide the degree of centralisation (less role and importance of subordinates in the management) or decentralisation (more role and importance) of authority on the basis of the nature of the circumstances, size of the undertaking, the type of activities and the nature of organisational structure. The objective to pursue should be the optimum utilisation of all the personnel.

- ***Scalar Chain.*** Scalar chain means the hierarchy of authority from the highest executive to the lowest one for the purpose of communication. It states superior-subordinate relationship and the authority of superiors in relation to subordinates at various levels. As per this principle, the orders or communications should pass through the proper channels of authority along the scalar chain. But in case there is need for swift action, the proper channels of authority may be short-circuited by making direct contact (called gang plank) with the concerned authority.

- ***Order.*** Management should obtain orderliness in work through suitable organisation of men and materials. The management should observe the principle of "right place for everything and for every man". To observe this principle, there is need for scientific selection of competent personnel, correct assignment of duties to personnel and good organisation.

- ***Equity.*** Equity means equality of fair treatment resulting from a combination of kindness and justice. It requires managers to be free from all prejudices, personal likes or dislikes. Equity ensures healthy industrial relations between management and labour which is essential for the successful working of the enterprise.

- ***Stability of Tenure of Personnel.*** In order to motivate workers to do more and better work, it is necessary that they should be assured security of job by the management. If they have fear of insecurity of job, their morale will be low and they cannot give more and better work. Further, they will not have any sense of attachment to the firm and they will always be on the outlook for a job elsewhere.

- ***Initiative.*** The zeal and energy of employees are augmented by initiative. According to Fayol, initiative is one of the keenest satisfactions for an intelligent man to experience, and hence, he advises managers to give their employees sufficient scope to show their initiative. Employees should be encouraged to make all kinds of suggestions to conceive and carry out their plans, even when some mistakes result.

- ***Esprit de Corps.*** This means team spirit. Since "union is strength", the management should create team spirit among the employees. Only when all the personnel pull together as a team, there is scope for realising the objectives of the concern. To achieve this, Fayol suggested two things: I) Avoidance of the motto of divide and rule. 2) Verbal communication should be used for removing misunderstandings. Differences grow bitterer when cleared through written communication.

IV. The Human Relations Movement

This movement emerged in part because managers found that Taylor's scientific management and Fayol's administrative management did not quiet achieve complete production efficiency and work place harmony. Thus, there was an increased interest in helping managers deal more effectively with the 'people side' of their organisations. The real inspiration for the movement, however, came from the Hawthorne experiments done by Prof. Elton Mayo and his colleagues at the Western Electric Company, near Chicago, from 1924 to 1933. The Hawthorne study applied socio-psychological techniques to managerial problems and gave impetus to the development of a theory of human bahaviour in organisations. It focused attention upon the importance of social forces and corrected some earlier misconceptions about cooperative behaviour. This study led to the discovery of many new dimensions relating to work, motivation, and organisational and interpersonal relationships. The main contributions of Elton Mayo or Hawthorne studies are as follows:

- ***Human Relations Approach.*** Mayo said that "human beings are complex and influential input into organizational performance". Man is not a machine and his social and psychological needs cannot be ignored. This was one of the most outstanding contributions of Mayo

- ***Non-Economic awards.*** Mayo found that traditional assumptions and techniques of economic incentives were not only inadequate but also unrealistic. Mayo was able to show that humane and respectful treatment, sense of participation, and belonging, recognition, morale, human pride, and social interaction are sometimes more important than pure monetary rewards.

- ***Informal Groups.*** Being social creatures, workers tend to establish informal groups that affect job satisfaction and effectiveness. Mayo studied the worker as part of a group, saw how the group affected each of its members, and how it was related to the formal structure of the company. He concluded that proper understanding of such informal groups is essential for organisational efficiency.

- ***Social Man.*** Mayo developed a concept of 'Social Man' and put a set of assumptions about the nature of man which are quite different from those concerning rational human man: (I) Man is basically motivated by social needs and obtains his basic sense of identity through relationships with others. (ii) As a result of the industrial revolution and the rationalization of work, meaning has gone out of work itself and must, therefore, be sought in the social relationships on the job. (iii) Man is more responsive to the social forces of the peer group than to the incentives and controls of management. (iv) Man is responsive to management to the extent that a supervisor can meet a subordinate's social needs and needs for social acceptance.

- ***Productivity is Social Phenomenon.*** Mayo had discovered that productivity is not only a technical phenomenon. It is also a social concept. It is largely a function of the worker's attitude towards work, their workmates and supervisors that governs their efficiency and morale.

- ***Notion of Irrationality.*** Mayo believed that it was important for managers to take into account the psychology of the worker, especially his irrational behaviour and non-logical response. They may not cause 'breakdown' in the individual but they do cause 'breakdown' in the 'industry". He further said that "the non-logical response, that, which is in strict conformity with a social code, makes for social order and discipline, for effective collaboration in a restricted range of activity, and for happiness and a sense of security in the individual.

- ***Organisation as a Social System.*** Mayo revealed that work places are actually complex social settings. They are social situations of relationships, informal networks and other human variables. Mayo wrote: "An organisation is a social system, a system of cliques, grapevines, informal status systems, rituals and a mixture of logical, non-logical and illogical behavior. Viewing the organization as a social system, Mayo concluded that the managers should maintain an equilibrium between the "logic of efficiency" demanded by the formal organization. He said that people are motivated not only by facts and logic, but are also guided by sentiments and feelings. To handle human situations, Mayo emphasized the need of diagnostic and interpersonal skills for the managers, along with the technical skills.

- ***Disregard of "Rabble Hypothesis".*** According to Mayo, most managers assumed that society consisted of a horde of unorganized individuals whose only concern was self-preservation or self-interest. People were dominated by physiological needs and worked for money. Taylor's theory was based on this assumption. Mayo called this assumption the Rabble Hypothesis. Mayo attempted to refute the rabble hypothesis by: (I) Postulating that it was collaboration with others, not competition among a disorganized horde, that was important; (ii) Stating that all individuals acted to protect their group status and not their self-interest; and (iii) Repeating the Hawthorne findings that thinking was guided more by sentiment than by logic.

- ***Human Collaboration.*** Elton Mayo was very much awakened towards the human, social and political problems of industrial civilization. He deplored the failure of social and political institutions to provide means for effective human cooperation. He said that overemphasis on technical progress and material life to the neglect of human and social life would create the problems in industrial society. In his own words: We do not know how systematically to set out the task of inducing various groups and nations to collaborate in the tasks of civilization. Civilized society can destroy itself, if it fails to understand intelligently and to control the aids and deterrents to cooperation.

- ***Developing New Leadership and New Skills.*** Mayo believed that to overcome anomie, the rabble hypothesis, and social disorganization in society, a new leadership equipped with social and human skills, should emerge. The "new" leader must focus its efforts on the maintenance of group integrity and social solidarity. The new leader must develop his "listening" and counseling skills and must recognize and understand the nonlogical side of human behaviour.

V. Modern Management Approaches

- ***Behavioural Approach.*** This approach is an improved and a more mature version of the human relations approach to management. Douglas McGregor, Abraham Maslow, Kurt Lewin, Chester Bernard, Mary Parker Follett, George Homans, Rensis Likert, Chris Argyris, and Warren Bennis are some of the foremost behavioural scientists. These scientist were more rigorously trained in various social sciences (such as psychology, sociology and anthropology). Thus, these people came to regarded as 'behavioural scientist' rather than members of the 'human relations' school.

The behavioural approach recognizes the practical and situational constraints on human rationality for making optimal decisions. It says that in actual practice, the decision-making is done in a sub-optimal manner. Also, behavioural scientists attach great weightage to participative and group decision-making because it is felt that business problems are so complex that it is neither fair nor feasible to make individuals responsible for solving them.

Behaviourists underline the desirability of humanizing the administration of the control process and encouraging the process of self-direction and control instead of imposed control. They also favour participation in the establishment, measurement and evaluation of standards of performance, prompt information feedback to those performance is off the mark and the need for positive and reformative measures instead of punitive measures.

Behavioural scientists consider organisations as groups of individuals with certain goals. They have, therefore, made wide ranging studies of human groups-big and small. They have studied such issues as why individuals join groups, group size, structure and process, group cohesiveness, and so on.

Behavioural scientists have made extensive studies on leadership. Their view is that while in general, the democratic-participative style is desirable, the autocratic, task-oriented style may also be appropriate in certain situations.

To behavioural scientists, the realistic model of human motivation is complex man. This model suggests that different people react differently to the same situation or react the same way to different situations. No two people are exactly alike, and the manager should tailor his attempts to influence people according to their individual needs.

The behavioural approach to organisational conflict and change is quite pragmatic. It recognizes that conflict is inevitable and sometimes is even desirable and should be faced wit understanding and determination, that every orgainisational change involves technological and social aspects and that it is generally the social aspect of a change with people resist.

- ***Quantitative Approach.*** This approach is also called the management science approach. Today OR works in approximately the following manncr. A mixed team of specialists from relevant disciplines is called in to analyse the problem and to propose a course of action to the management The team constructs a mathematical model to simulate the problem. The model shows, in symbolic terms, all the relevant factors that bear on the problem and how they are interrelated. By changing the values of the variables in the model(such as increasing the cost of raw materials) and analysing the different equations of the model generally with a computer, the team can determine what the effects of each change would be. Eventually, the OR team presents the management with a rational base for making a decision.

It is clear from the above description that the focus of the quantitative approach is on decision-making—to provide quantitative tools and techniques for making objectively rational decisions. Objective rationality implies an ability and willingness to follow a reasoned, unemotional, orderly and scientific approach in relating means with ends and in visualizing the totality of the decision environment.

This approach facilitates disciplined thinking, while defining management problems and establishing relationships among the variables involved. The keynote of this approach is precision and perfection which is achieved by expressing relationships and facts in quantitative terms. The approach has been widely used in planning and control activities where problems can be precisely identified and defined in quantitative terms. But its use is still uncommon in such areas as organising staffing and leading the organisation where the problems are more human than technical in nature.

- ***Systems Approach.*** A common pitfall of the classical, behavioural, and quantitative schools is that they stress one aspect of the organisation at the expense of others. However, it is difficult to know which aspect is most useful_and appropriate in a given situation. What is needed is one broad, detailed, conceptual framework that can help a manager diagnose a problem and decide which tool or combination of tools will best do the job. The systems approach provides him this integrated approach to management problems.

Some important advocates of the systems approach are Chester Barnard, George Homans, Philip Selznick and Herbert Simon. The following are the key concepts of this approach:

A system is a set of interdependent parts which together form a unitary whole that performs some function An organisation is also a system composed of four interdependent parts, namely, task, structure, people and technology.

Central to the systems approach is the concept of 'holism', which means that no part of the system can be accurately analysed and understood apart from the whole system. Conversely, the whole system cannot be accurately perceived without understanding all its parts. Each part bears a relation of interdependence to every other part. This means that rather than dealing separately with the various parts of one organisation, the systems approach tries to give the manager a way of looking at the organisation as a whole.

A system can either be open or closed. A system is considered open if it interacts with its environment and is considered closed if it does not interact with the environment. Traditional organisation theorists regarded organisations as closed systems while according to the modern view organisations are open systems, constantly interacting with their environments.

Each system, including an organisation has its own boundaries which separate it from other systems in the environment. The boundaries for open systems are, however, 'permeable' or penetrable, unlike those of the closed systems.

They are quite flexible and changeable, depending upon its activities. The boundaries for closed systems are rigid. The function of management is to act as a boundary- linking pin among the various subsystems within the organisational system, on the one hand and between the organisation and the external environmental system, on the other. In the context of a business organisation, it has many boundary contacts or 'interfaces' with many external systems like suppliers, creditors, customers, government agencies, etc.

Every system has flows of information, material and energy. These enter the system from the environment as inputs and leave the system as outputs. The inputs of a business organisation are raw materials, equipment, human effort, technology and information. The organisation changes these inputs into outputs of goods, services and satisfactions.

This change process is known as 'throughput'. It should be remembered that the output of a system is always more than the combined output of its parts. This is called 'synergy'. In organisational terms, synergy means that as separate departments within an organisation cooperate and interact, they become more productive than if they had acted in isolation. For example, it is obviously more efficient for each department in a small firm to deal with one financing department than for each department to have a separate financing department of its own.

One important mechanism that enables a system to adapt and adjust to the changing conditions of its environment and to exercise control over its operations is 'feedback'. As operations of the system proceed, information is feedback to the appropriate people so that the work can be assessed and if necessary, corrected.

- ***Contingency Approach.*** According to this approach, there is no one best way of doing things under all conditions. Methods and techniques, which are highly effective in one situation, may not work in other situations. Results differ because situations differ. Accordingly, the contingency approach suggests that the task of managers is to try to identify which technique will, in a particular situation best contribute to the attainment of management goals. Managers have, therefore, to develop a sort of situational sensitivity and practical selectivity.

Contingency views are applicable in designing organisational structure, in deciding the degree of decentralisation in planning information decision systems, in motivational and leadership approaches, in establishing communication and control systems, in resolving conflicts and managing change, in employee development and training programmes and in several areas of organisation and management.

Conditions Favourable and Unfavourable to HRM

Figure below shows that any HRM program or activity in an organization does not operate in a vacuum. It is influenced by and influences the external environment (outside the organization) and internal environment (inside the organization). Lets look at the conditions favorable and unfavorable to the successful working of HRM:

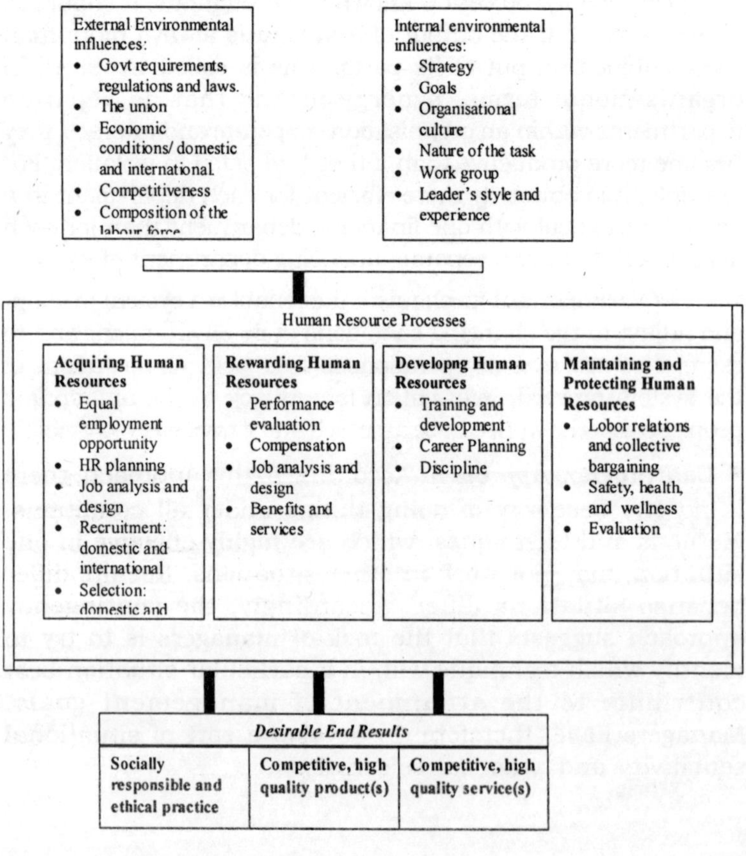

Government Law and Regulations. A powerful external environmental influence is government law and regulations, which affect organizations directly. Federal regulations influence HRM activities, policies, and programs. When an organization makes decisions about hiring, promotion, managing diversity, performance evaluation, downsizing, and discipline, it must weigh the impact of government regulations.

The government regulates and influences some aspects of HRM more directly than others. Major areas of legislation and regulation including: (i) Equal employment opportunity and human rights legislation, which directly affects recruiting, selection, evaluation, and promotion, and indirectly affects employment planning, orientation, career planning, training, and development. (ii) Employment of illegal aliens. (iii) Discrimination based on sex, age, and disability. (iv) Compensation regulation, which affects pay, hours of work, unemployment, and similar conditions. (v) Benefits regulation, which affects pensions and retirement. (vi) Workers compensation and safety laws, which affect health and safety. (vii) Labor relations laws and regulations, which affect the conduct of collective bargaining. (viii) Privacy laws.

John Dunlop lists a number of the problems government regulation imposes on management. All of these make the operating and HR managers' job more difficult: (i) Regulation encourages simplistic thinking on complicated issues. Small enterprises are treated like large ones. Different industries are regulated alike. (ii) Designing and administering regulations is an incredibly complex task, leading to very slow decision making. (iii) Regulation does not encourage mutual accommodation but rather leads to complicated legal maneuvering. (iv) Many regulations are out of date and serve little social purpose, yet they are not eliminated. (v) There is increasing evidence of regulatory overlap and contradictions among different regulatory agencies.

To cope with Increasing governmental control, management has tried to influence the passage of relevant legislation and the way it is administered. Managements have sued to determine the constitutionality of many of the laws When such efforts fail to influence the process as management prefers, it has learned to adapt its HRM policies. In sum, almost no HRM decisions remain unaffected by government.

- ***The Union.*** The presence of a union directly affects most aspects of HRM—recruiting, selection, performance evaluation, promotion, compensation, and benefits, among others.

A union is an organization that represents the interest of employees on such issues as working conditions, wages and salaries, fringe benefits, employees' rights, grievance processes and work hours. Unions differ, just as people and other organizations differ. There are cooperative unions and combative unions. In sum, unions often play a significant role in HRM programs.

- ***Economic Conditions.*** Two aspects of economic conditions affect HRM programmes: productivity and the work sector of the organization.

Productivity Data, empirical evidence, and general opinion indicate that the productivity of employees is an important part of a nation's general economic condition. Managers are concerned with productivity because they feel it is a representative indicator of the overall efficiency of an organization. Before productivity can be effectively managed and improved, it must be measured. This can be done by isolating the outputs—division by division, department by department, work team by work team, individual by individual, or product line by product line. Next, the costs that went into producing the output must be determined, including labor (salaries, bonuses, fringes), heating, lighting, and capital.

Then, using the previous year as a baseline period, the manager must compare the current year's figures with those of the previous year Some period of comparison is needed to make necessary adjustments. While improve productivity is a worthy goal, managers should lay the groundwork for measuring and monitoring productivity before they rush into changes.

Some suggested solutions for increasing productivity include reducing government controls, developing more favorable income tax incentives to invest in new plants and equipment, and reindustrializing the entire business—industrial complex (such as plants and equipment).

On the other hand, the managers can influence productivity by the sound application of HRM programs. Specific activities and practices can improve individual performance and consequently organizational productivity. Managers can through diagnosis, prescription, implementation, and evaluation help employees achieve their optimum level of productivity. Also, recruitment and selection techniques can be used to attract and hire the best performers Motivational and compensation techniques can be used to retain employees and improve job performance. Training and development can improve job performance or rectify deficiencies in skill and competency, in turn increasing performance.

Productivity problems will not be solved without utilizing HRM activities. Every HRM activity in the diagnostic model *(Exhibit 2—l)* can affect productivity. Thus, productivity pressure from the external environment directly and indirectly affects an organization's HRM program.

The work sector of the organization. The diagnostic model in *Exhibit 2—1* does not consider the work sector in which the organization is located. About 60 percent of professional HR specialists work in the private sector while 30 percent of all HR employees in the United States work in the public sector. Many economists define other institutions that are neither governmental nor profit-oriented as the third sector like museums, private schools and colleges, not-for-profit hospitals and nursing homes, and voluntary organizations such as churches. About 10 per cent of HR specialists and employees work in the third sector.

In general, private-sector and third-sector HRM are structured similarly. Hospitals have different internal organization problems from most businesses, though. For example, the presence of three hierarchies—physicians, administrators, and the board of trustees (representing the public)—can lead to conflicts. Pressures from third party payers such as Blue Cross or Medicare can lead to other conflicts. Hospitals employ professional groups that zealously guard their "rights," and this also leads to conflict. Structurally, HRM work in the private and third sectors is similar, but because of organizational differences jobs in HRM vary

HRM in the public sector is fundamentally different from HRM in the other two sectors because it varies structurally The public manager faces a different world; in fact. a manager who moves from the private or third sector to the public sector will find the HRM role much more complicated. HR in the public sector generally is under much more direct outside pressure.

- ***Competitiveness.*** At the organizational level, competitiveness is an important issue. How effectively do the workers produce the product? How good is the quality of the services or goods provided? Can employees handle new technology and produce the product at lower costs? Does the firm have the human resources needed to increase the size of the manufacturing facility to handle global demand? Will the push to work harder and faster raise turnover, absenteeism, and the number of defects? An increasing amount of research suggests that the way organizations implement and modify their HRM activities can provide them with competitive advantages. Sustainable competitive advantage requires a firm to deal effectively with employees, customers, suppliers, and all competitors.

- ***Geographical Location of the Organization.*** The location of the organization influences the kinds of people it hires and the HRM activities it conducts. A hospital, plant, university, or government bureau located in a rural area confronts different conditions than one located in an urban area. For example, the workforce in a rural area might be more willing to accept a bureaucratic organization style. Recruiting and selection in rural areas will be different in that there may be fewer applicants. Yet the organization may find a larger proportion of hirable workers ingrained with the work ethic.

An urban location might be advantageous for recruiting and holding professional workers. Urban locations provide a bigger labor force but generally call for higher wages. Late shifts may be a problem because workers may not feel safe at night in the parking lots or going home.

Geographic location, therefore, influences the kinds of workers available to staff the organization. The location or setting is extremely significant for companies operating in other countries. The employees may speak a different language. practice different religions, have different attitudes toward work, and so on. Lets consider some of the major differences between home-based and multinational organizations:

(I) Educational factors. include the number of skilled employees available, attitude toward education. and literacy level. Educational deficiencies in some countries can lead to a scarcity of qualified employees, as well as a lack of educational facilities to upgrade potential employees.

(ii) Behavioural factors. Societies differ in factors such as attitudes toward wealth and profits, managerial roles, and authority

(iii) Legal-political factors .Laws and political structures differ and can encourage or discourage private enterprises. Nations also differ in degree of political stability. Some countries are very nationalistic in their business practices. Such countries can require local ownership of organizations or, if they are so inclined, expropriate foreign concerns.

(iv) Economic factors. Economies differ in basic structure, inflation rate, constraints on ownership, and the like. In the fully developed countries managers will find fewer differences in educational, behavioural, economic, and legal-political factors than they are likely to encounter in developing or less developing countries The less developed countries are the most difficult to work in because of significant constraints in terms of education, economic system, political structure, and the general infrastructure. To be successful abroad, managers must learn all they can about the countries in which they will be working. Knowledge of differences among nations in (1) educational, (2) behavioural, (3) legal- political, (4) economic factors is essential for managerial success abroad. In sum, the physical location of the organization (rural or urban, at home or abroad) can have a significant impact on how HRM programs are used and which activities are conducted.

- ***Strategy.*** A strategy indicates what an organization's key executives hope to accomplish in the long run. As a plan, a strategy takes the firm into the area of competition in the environment and into alignment with the resources of the firm. There are companies that believe that the long-term success of their firms is linked to helping their employees achieve a work-life balance. These companies have instituted programs designed to help employees feel safe and better about such is sues as childcare, families, and home life.

- ***Goals.*** The goals of organizations differ within and among departments. All departments probably have goals that include employee satisfaction, survival, and adaptability to change. The differences arise in the importance the decision-makers place on the different goals. In some organizations, profit is of such major importance that other goals, such as increased employee satisfaction, are not well developed. In these organizations where profits take precedence, HRM goals involving the human resources are paid only minimal attention. The result of such negligence is typically problems in the effectiveness area of the diagnostic model (e.g., high absenteeism, performance decrements, high grievance rates). In other organizations, HRM related goals are highly regarded by decision makers. Thus, how much the HRM function is valued and how it is implemented are affected by these goals.

- ***Organization Culture.*** The essence of a firm's culture is shown by the firm's way of doing business, the manner in which it treats customers and employees, the extent of autonomy or freedom that exists in the departments or offices, and the degree of loyalty expressed in employees about the firm. Organization culture represents the perceptions held by the organization's employees. Is there a sense of shared value? Is there a common value system held by employees? These are the kinds of questions asked to arrive at a picture of the firm's culture. There is no one "best" culture for the development of human resources. Culture can have an impact on the behavior, productivity, and expectations of employees. It provides a benchmark of the standards of performance among employees. For example, it can provide clear guidelines on attendance, punctuality, concern about quality, and customer service.

- ***Nature of the Task.*** Many experts believe that the task to be performed is one of the two most vital factors affecting HRM. They describe HRM as the effective matching of the nature of the task (job) with the nature of the employee performing the task. There are perhaps unlimited similarities and differences among jobs that attract or repel workers and influence the meaning of work for them. Some of the most significant are the following:

(i) Degree of knowledge and ability to use information technology. Advantages in informational and computer technology have resulted in a need for employees with the skill to use these technologies. Instead of physical lifting and moving as requirements of a task, the use of "knowledge skills" has become significant. "Knowledge workers" are now expected to plan, decide and solve problems using databases, computer programs, and other technology-driven information sources.

(ii) Degree of empowerment. Empowering employees to complete job tasks means that power or authority to make relevant and meaningful decisions is delegated. In fact, the empowered worker can complete his or her job task because he or she has information, knowledge, and power.

(iii) Degree of physical exertion required. In general, most people prefer work involving minimal physical exertion. Some companies, believe that working with the mind is better for curing productivity problems than working with the back.

(iv) Degree of environmental unpleasantness. Contrast the environment of a coal miner with that of a bank teller. People generally prefer physically pleasant and safe conditions.

(v) Physical location of work. Some jobs require outside work; others, inside work. Some jobs require the employee to stay in one place. Others permit moving about. Contrast the job of an employee on an assembly line with that of a traveling sales representative. There are individual differences in preference for physical location.

(vi) Time dimension of work. Some jobs require short periods of intense effort; others require long hours of less taxing work. In some jobs, such as automobile assembly, the work is continuous; in others, such as toll booth operation, it is intermittent.

(vii) Human interaction on the job. Some jobs require interaction with others. Contrast the position of a radar operator in an isolated location who rarely sees anyone else with that of a receptionist in a busy city hall.

(viii) Degree of variety in the task. The amount of freedom and responsibility a person has on the job determines the degree of autonomy provided for in the work. Contrast the autonomy of a college professor with that of an assembly-line worker.

(ix) Task identity. The degree of wholeness in a job-feeling of completing a whole job as opposed to contributing to only a portion of a job—is its task identity. Contrast the job of an auto assembler with that of a tax accountant.

(x) Task differences and job design. Because jobs are not created by nature, engineers and specialists can create jobs with varying attention to the characteristics described here. There are a number of approaches to those aspects of job design that affect variety, autonomy, task identity, and similar job factors.

How do these task factors affect HRM type decisions? They obviously affect recruiting and selection, since employees will probably be more satisfied and productive preferences are met. As we mentioned, few jobs match all preferences exactly. With jobs that are difficult, dirty, or in smoky or hot environments, the manager must provide additional incentives (more pay, shorter hours, or priority in vacations) because few people prefer such jobs. Or the manager may try to find employees who can handle the conditions better.

• ***Work Group.*** Group plays a major role in the life of an individual. Once a person joins an organization, a work group largely influences his or her experiences. In work group people are interdependent with one another for the accomplishment of a purpose, communicate and interact with one another on a more or less continuous basis. In many cases they work next to each other. An effective group is one in which: (i) Members function and act as a team. (ii) Members participate fully in group discussion. (iii) Group goals are clearly developed. (iv) Resources are adequate to accomplish group goals. (v) Members furnish many useful suggestions leading to achievement of goals.

Although the effective group, supports management and the organization's goals, it can also work against them. This is usually the case when the group perceives the organization's goals as being in conflict with its own. If the work group is effective and works with management, the manager's job is easier, and objectives are more likely to be achieved

Work groups are directly related to the success of HRM activities. If a work group opposes HRM programs, it can ruin them. Examples of programs that can be successes or failure depending on the support or resistance they receive from work groups include incentive compensation, profit sharing, safety, and labor relations. Operational and HR managers who desire success in such programs should at least consider permitting work-group participation in designing and implementing HRM.

• ***Leader's Style and Experience.*** The experience and leadership style of the operating manager or leader directly affect HRM activities because many, if not most, programs must be implemented at the work-unit level. Thus, the operating manager or leader is a crucial link in the HRM function. Leaders must orchestrate the distinctive skills, experiences, personalities, and motives of individuals. Leaders also must facilitate the interactions that occur within the work groups. In his or her role, leader provides, directions, encouragement, and authority to evoke desired behaviors. In addition, leaders reinforce desirable behavior so that it is sustained and enhanced. The leader is an important source of knowledge about the tasks, the organization, and the HRM policies, programs, and goals. The experience and operating style of a leader will influence which HRM programs are communicated, implemented, and effective.

Current Status of HRM

A lot has changed over the past few years, including the name that summarizes the activities. The personnel management has become human resources. HRM concerns a broad range of important company functions, including the recruitment, selection, training, development, compensation, retention, evaluation, and promotion of personnel within an organisation.

Responsibilities have expanded and greater prestige is associated with the leading HR positions. The majority of top HRM executives now report directly to the CEO, and half of Fortune 500 firms assigned the top HR professional to a vice president. Many HR executives now serve on major strategy and policy committees for corporations (e.g., Coca-Cola, Microsoft, Sun Microsystems). More importantly, progressive HRM activities are now considered to be major sources of competitive advantage and a growing body of research supports this view.

While there is still plenty of room for improvement, the status of HRM activities has clearly changed and is continuing to improve in the United States. We believe that HR processes such as hiring and maintaining the most effective and efficient workforce are growing in importance relative to other potential sources of competitive advantage of an organisation. We are not alone in this belief. Stanford University scholar, Jeffrey Pfeffer notes, "Traditional sources of success(for e.g., speed to market, financial, technological) can still provide leverage, but to a lesser degree now than in the past, leaving organisational culture and capabilities, derived from how people are managed, as comparatively more vital".

HRM activities are often faddish and disjoint, giving little consideration to the organisation's mission or goals and the ultimate effect on customer satisfaction. Companies often adopt some procedure simply because they learn that some competitor or successful company was using it. Many HR systems and activities are not systematically evaluated. Many organisations do not assess either the short-term or the long-term consequences of their HRM program or activities in terms of meaningful criteria. Many decision makers in HRM are neither qualified nor motivated to properly evaluate the effectiveness of an HRM program. Stanford Professor, Pfeffer considers measurement to be one key to competitive advantage. Yet research indicates a minority of HRM programs or activities are subjected to any systematic evaluation using carefully defined outcomes or criteria. A growing number of organisations look at HRM functions and systems as major contribution to accomplishing the organisation's mission. The 21st century HR roles are that of strategic partner, administrative expert, employee champion, and change agent. The responsibilities are to provide deliverables in all four areas. These deliverables must be responsive to an increasing competitive and global marketplace and must be closely linked to business strategic plans. Ulrich, Pfeffer, and others conclude that the most effective companies are serious about treating their employees as assets-assets to be invested in the real and potential customer base.

A growing body of research shows that progressive HRM activities can have a profound effect on corporate performance. Studies now document the relationship between specific HR practices and critical outcome measures such as productivity, product and service quality, and cost control. Companies are now fully recognizing that their work force can be their greatest strength.

Greater demands are now being made on HRM professionals to respond to contemporary trends in the business environment. Hr professionals should now show that they can make a difference in the company's bottom line. Today HRM professionals are much more concerned with business management functions, government relations, and international issues-issues beyond human resources. Many corporate strategy specialists maintain that the key to sustained competitive advantage is building and sustaining more core competencies within the organisation and maintaining flexibility in order to react quickly to the changing global marketplace and the incredible advances in technology.

A study analyses 1372 on-line responses to a national survey of the membership of the professional body of the Australian Human Resources Institute (AHRI). The study is the latest research in a continuing line of work that has reviewed the changing role of the HR profession in Australia. The major aims of this research are to review changes to the HR role, report on the reactions of HR professionals to strategic role expectations and evaluate measurement attempts of HR's contribution to bottom line outcomes. The results of the research indicate that HR professionals have strengthened their strategic positioning within Australian organizations and this development represents a positive step towards the recognition of a business partnership role for HR professionals. Results also reveal, however, a potential narrowing of the HR professional's career path and the failure to provide HR metric information to management about the impact of HRM programs and practices on organisational performance. Despite the continuing progress being made by HR to become a strategic HR, therefore, the restricted career breadth of HR professionals and inadequate measures of HR's contribution to the bottom line may ultimately impact on the credibility of those involved in the HR function and moderate the successful continuation of the involvement of HR at the senior decision-making level. Effective human resource (HR) management is viewed increasingly as a source of competitive advantage (Wright, Dunford & Snell, 2001). This realisation, coupled with the growing capacity of Australian organisations to deal directly with employee relations at the workplace level, has elevated the status of HR professionals and raised expectation about what they can add to the bottom line. Although this transition has presented people working in the HR function with an opportunity to make a more comprehensive contribution to organisational success, the transition demands a considerable re-configuration of the roles and skills adopted by HR professionals (Beer 1997; Ulrich, 1997).

More recent research indicates that a closer relationship between human resource management (HRM) and organizational strategy continues to develop (Cleland et al., 2000;Khatri & Budhwar, 2002; Michelson & Kramar, 2003; Sheehan, 2005; Teo, 2002). Sheehan (2005), for example, has established evidence of a strategic role for HR managers with broad business backgrounds who provide credible input into senior decision-making processes. The study also establishes however that this strategic role for HR professionals has not been established in all organisations. Michelson & Kramar (2003) similarly have suggested that the complete integration and acceptance of a strategic role for HRM is uneven. First, Dowling and Fisher's 1995 study revealed increasing levels of higher education among HR professionals.

Study provides an important potential source of credibility when these individuals are contributing to strategic discussions (Dowling & Fisher, 1997). In the 1995 study, there was also a reported tendency for younger HR professionals to begin their careers within the HR area. This provides HR professionals with the opportunity to become fully skilled within the function. Concern was expressed in the 1995 research however that although this choice allows strong development in the HR field, the narrowing of the career base may have negative implications for the acquisition of broad based business skills. Recently Sheehan (2005) has noted the importance of a broad career background for HR professionals who are operating within the strategic decision-making processes. HR professionals who begin their career in the HR area are less likely to gain this career breadth and this may pose challenges for HR professionals who are establishing roles in strategic business decision-making partnerships. The research questions associated with the first area of investigation are: 1. Are educational levels of HR professionals continuing to increase? And 2. Where are HR professionals beginning their careers? Second, although there has been some evidence of a shift to a more strategic role for HR professionals there is still some doubt about the extent of the change.

Other commentators of HRM confirm difficulties for the expected strategic HR role change. More recently Michelson & Kramar (2003) have reported evidence of the growing implementation of a HRM approach but suggest that there is considerable variation across organisations. These authors describe perceptions of HR's contribution to strategic outcomes as 'moderate' to 'fair' with evidence of remnants of the view of HRM as an administrative function. There is therefore a lack of consensus on the extent to which HR has actually taken on strategic responsibilities. Finally, in addition to reviewing the strategic positioning of the HR function, the current survey also reports on attempts by HR to measure its contribution to company performance, reflecting the increasing attention given by HR researchers and professionals to the measurement of HRM. A strategic approach to HRM involves the design and implementation of a set of internally consistent policies and practices that ensure that a firm's human capital is enhanced via increasing capacity to learn and apply new knowledge, thus contributing to the achievement of business objectives and sustainable competitive advantage. A strategic approach to HR measurement adopts a broad approach, including the development of system to measure the efficiency, effectiveness and impact (Boudreau & Ramstad, 2002, 2003; Lawler, Levenson & Boudreau, 2004) of HRM.

Three main types of measures, or metrics, may be applied to HRM. First, efficiency metrics focus on the cost of an HRM practice, such as the administrative cost per employee of a training program, to determine the return on investment (ROI). While these measures can be useful, they reveal little about the value added by an HRM practice; they focus only on the cost.

Second, effectiveness measures aim to provide an indication of the fit between HRM programs and the organisation's business strategy. Typical effectiveness metrics include measures of the strategic skills and core competencies in the work force. They assess outcomes such as whether HRM programs and practices have the intended effect on people. Such measures are useful but still have some limitations. For example, measuring employee satisfaction with HRM programs does not reveal whether this has actually had an impact on organisational performance. Employee satisfaction surveys often have no known connection to business results.

The third type of measures focuses on the impact of HRM programs and practices on organizational performance, by measuring the value added to an organisation by an HR M practice. For example, impact measures endeavour to demonstrate a link between training programs and tangible effects on the organization's competitive advantage, such as reduced defects and increased production speed and service quality and retention rates following training programs. It is important to note that there are numerous pitfalls of measurement for HRM (Pfeffer, 1997), such as measuring items that are easily available, or adopting a short-term focus.

A measurement system should enable an organisation to obtain and evaluate evidence about the performance of HR policies and practices, to ensure clear relationships between its goals and outcomes.

HR professionals are taking the opportunity to increasingly improve their educational qualifications. With respect to career entry points younger respondents were more likely to enter the profession through the HR functional area. Although HR professionals may be establishing credibility through improved educational qualifications, their exposure to a broad range of business experiences may be reduced if they restrict their career path to movements within the HR department.

Full HR representation on boards of directors has increased slightly since 1995 and there is greater recognition of HR's role on senior management committees. Overall then results indicate that HR managers are reporting increasing levels of strategic involvement.

There have been major changes to their role and that the HRM role demands a new set of skills. The majority of respondents claim however that this has made their job more rewarding and that there have been no substantial negative implications such as increasing role ambiguity or the marginalization of existing priorities.

References

Human Resource Management- An Experiential Approach by H. John Bernardin, second edition, 1998. p. 1 to 4.

Human Resource Management by John. M. Ivancevich. p. 4 to 50.

Kaila H.L. (2006). *Human Resource Management* (Two Volumes). Delhi: Kalpaz Publications.

Management and Human Resource Development by Kalyani, Iyer and Paranjape, 2001 (revised edition). pp. 3 to 7, 19 to 25.

Management and Human Resource Development by Manan Prakashan, 2003 (revised edition). pp. 2 to 17, 25.

Management Approaches and Theorists by G.S. Sudha, 1998.

Management-20th Century Management Tools and Techniques by S.Shiva Ramu, 2000. Page No, 8 to 14.

Managing Human Resources-Preparing for the 21st Century by John Storey, 1997. pp. 41 to 45, 138 to 219.

Principles of Management by George Terry, pp. 2 to 7.

Principles of Management by Tripathi Reddy, second edition, 2001. pp. 15 to 28.

6

Resourcing The Organisation

1. Resourcing The Organization

2. Human Resource Planning

Introduction

Meaning of Human Resource Planning

Integrated Strategic Planning and Human Resource Planning

Need and Importance of Human Resource Planning

Process of Human Resource Planning

Factors Affecting Human Resource Planning

Organizing Human Resource Planning

Merits of Human Resource Planning

Limitations of Human Resource Planning

Conclusion

3. Recruitment

Introduction

Definition

Objectives & Importance of Recruitment

4. Recruitment Planning

Subsystems of Recruitment

Recruitment Policy

Process of Recruitment

Sources of Recruitment

Merits and Demerits of Internal and External Sources

Techniques and Modern Sources of Recruitment

Types of Recruitment Appeal

5. Managing Recruitment Operations

Recruitment in the Information Age

Evaluation and Control of Recruitment Operations

Factors affecting Recruitment

6. Impact of Recruitment on Productivity

7. Summary

8. Bibliography

Resourcing The Organization

Resourcing can be defined as strengthening the organization with the requisite manpower. In fact, resourcing is a dynamic process: the movement of human resources through an organization.

Resourcing is a major issue for people managers. Even in conditions of high unemployment there are shortages of people with skills, which are in demand. Developed countries such as Australia and Britain, for example, have a long record of failure to provide their young people with appropriate vocational training. If companies are unable to find staff with appropriate skills, their growth prospects and competitiveness are constrained.

Most large organizations employ human resource or personnel specialists to conduct or, at least, coordinate employee resourcing. This is a role that has long been regarded as part of the domain of personnel management and personnel textbooks conventionally describe resourcing as a passive, technical procedure - a matching of available candidates to the requirements of the organization. In fact, successful recruitment must be proactive. Organizations can take one of three actions to fulfill their employee resourcing:

1. Reallocate tasks between employees, so that existing staff takes on more or different work. The emphasis is on flexible working practices, requiring multi-skilled workers and sophisticated assessment and development programmes.

2. Reallocate people within the company. Traditionally, German and Japanese organizations have filled their supervisory and management posts from existing staff.

3. Recruit new staff from the external job market. Countries in the free-market tradition have focused most of their resourcing activities on bringing in people from outside the organization.

Businesses can assign people largely from existing staff

or from the external job market. Companies that focus on internal supply are likely to view people as assets, carrying long-term value, rather than costs.

For resourcing to be successful it must be translated into practical action by formulating effective human resource planning and recruitment planning.

Human Resource Planning

Introduction

Human resource planning is reputed to first been introduced in 1676, when **Samuel Pepys** first became concerned with the provision of careers for officers in the Royal Navy. Planning for human resource is more important than planning for any other resource as demand for the latter depends upon the size and structure of the former whether it is in a country or in an industry. Further, management of human resource hardly begins from human resource planning. In fact it is the basis for most of the other functions.

Meaning Of Human Resource Planning

E.W. Vetter. Viewed human resource planning as " a process by which an organization should move from its current manpower position to its desired manpower position. Through planning management strives to have the right number and right kind of people at the right places at the right time, things which result in both the organization and the individual receiving maximum long-run benefit."

Stainer. Defines manpower planning "as a strategy for the acquisition, utilization, improvement and preservation of an enterprise's human resources."

Human resource planning may be viewed as "foreseeing the human resource requirements of an organization and future supply of human resources in terms of quantity and quality parameters."

Integrated Strategic Planning And Human Resource Planning

Human resource planning like production planning and marketing planning should be an unified, comprehensive and integrated part of the total corporation. Human resource manager provides inputs like key HR areas, HR environmental constraints and internal HR capabilities and HR capability constraints to the corporate strategists. The corporate strategists in turn communicate their needs and impediments to the HR manager. The corporate strategic plan and HR plan, thus incorporates both HR and other functional plans.

Corporations formulate plans to fit four time spans:

(i) **Strategic plans.** That establish company's vision, mission and major long-range objectives. The time plan for strategic plans is usually considered to be five or more years.

(ii) **Intermediate – range plans.** Covering about a three-year period. These are more specific plans in support of strategic plan.

(iii) **Operating plans.** Cover about one year. Plans are prepared month by month in sufficient detail for profit, human resources, budget and cost control.

(iv) **Activity plans.** Are day-by-day and week-by-week plans. These plans may not be documented.

Need And Importance of Human Resource Planning

Recently, organizations are becoming more and more dependent upon people. They are increasingly involved in new complex technologies and are functioning in extreme complex economic, social and political environments. As a result, the organizations face shortages of the right kind of human resources. HRP enables to get the right type of personnel in the organization.

There is a growing importance of HRP, due to the following reasons:

1. Personnel Requirements

HRP involves forecasting of personnel requirements in an organization. In other words, HRP helps management to anticipate personnel shortages and surpluses and develop ways to avoid or correct problems before they become serious.

2. Recruitment and Selection

A proper forecasting of personnel requirements enables

the organization to determine proper sources of recruitment. The required personnel can be selected either from internal or external sources.

The organization can also adopt a proper selection procedure depending upon the needs of the jobs. Proper tests can be designed to select the right candidate for the right job.

3. Placement of Personnel

HRP facilitates proper placement of the employees in the organization. Placement refers to fitting the right person at the right place of work. Proper placement brings job satisfaction to the employees and enhances employees' efficiency.

The selected personnel are placed at the right place of work. Persons are placed in those departments or in those areas where there is a shortage of personnel. If there is a surplus, then that personnel can be shifted to some other areas or departments as the case may be.

4. Performance Appraisal

HRP assists in performance appraisal of the employees in the organization. Performance appraisal refers to identification of strengths and weaknesses of the employees, relating to their jobs.

The performance appraisal is conducted to find out whether the existing work force has the necessary qualifications and qualities as per the job requirements. If there are weaknesses, then additional training or some other measures can be undertaken.

5. Promotions

HRP ensures right promotion of the employees in the organization. Promotion involves higher position, higher powers and higher pay.

HRP involves performance appraisal. Necessary performance reports are prepared. The organization would be in a position to promote the right person depending upon the performance appraisal reports.

6. Training

HRP ensures training of the employees in the organizations. Training involves imparting knowledge and developing attitudes, skills and social behavior of the employees.

HRP identifies the training needs of the personnel. If the personnel lack knowledge and skills, then necessary arrangements can be made by the organization to provide training.

7. Transfers

HRP facilitates proper transfer of the employees in the organization. Transfer involves side-ways movement of the employees in the organization.

There may be a situation where there are surplus personnel in one department and shortage in another department. This situation can be corrected by effecting transfers at the right time.

8. Career Development

HRP facilitates career development of the employees in the organization. Career development refers to developing career of the employees in the organization.

HRP is conducted taking into consideration the long range plans of the organization. The plans are made known to members of the organization. The employees can plans for their careers within the organization once they come to know of the qualifications and qualities that would be required to implement the long range plans.

9. Organizational Development

HRP assists in organizational development. Organizational development takes place when there are better results in the form of higher productivity or efficiency.

10. Motivation of Personnel

HRP is concerned not only with the identification of the personnel in terms of quality and quantity, but it is also concerned with the improvement and motivation of the human resources. The organization would make every possible effort to have dedicated and committed personnel at all levels in the organization.

11. Miscellaneous

In addition, the following factors are quite relevant towards HRP:

(a) The shortage of certain categories of employees due to rapid changes in technology and consequent need for new skills and new categories of employees.

(b) The demographic changes like the changing profile of the workforce in terms of age, sex, education etc.

(c) The government policies and labor laws affecting the demand and supply of labor.

(d) Pressure from trade unions, politicians, sons of soil etc.

Process Of Human Resource Planning

Process of Human Resource Planning consists of the following steps:

(1) Analyzing the Organizational Plan

The process of human resource planning should start with analyzing the organizational plan in to production plan, technological plan, plans for expansion, diversification, marketing plan, sales plan, financial plan. Each plan can be further analyzed into sub-units. Detailed programmes should be formulated on the basis of unit-wise plans. Practicability of each programme should be ensured. Analysis of organizational plans and programmes helps in forecasting the demand for human resources as it provides the quantum of futher work activity.

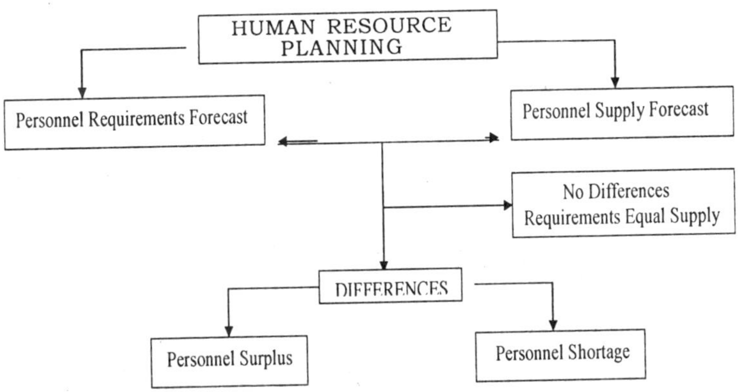

Take Action

- Lay Off
- Terminate
- Voluntary Retirement

Take Action

- Hire
- Overtime
- Sub-contract etc. or Deployment

Exhibit 2.1: Human Resource Planning

(2) Analysis of Human Resource Planning Objectives

Human resource planning is a part of corporate plan. Its objectives are to be fixed in the light of corporate objectives. The emphasis is given on future requirements than the present one. The main purpose of human resource planning is to match the present and future manpower needs of an organization. The human resource department should specify the policy regarding acquisition of human resources. It may recruit them by way of promotion, transfer i.e., from within the organization or from external source. It has also has to clarify the selection criteria and the need for training and development. It has to decide on abolishing or continuing some old and routine jobs or replace them by meaningful jobs to meet challenges thrown by the speedily changing business and in industrial environment. These objectives should be integrated with the objectives of all the functional areas of the organization. The emphasis should also be given on to maximize the return on investment in human resources.

(3) Personnel Requirements Forecast / Demand Forecast

The existing job design and analysis may thoroughly be reviewed keeping in view the future capabilities, knowledge and skills of present employees. Further, the jobs should be redesigned and reanalyzed keeping in view the organizational and unit wise plans and programmes, future work quantum, future activity or task analysis, future skills, values, knowledge and capabilities of present employees and prospective employees. The jobs generally should be designed and analyzed reflecting the future human resources and based on future organizational plans. Job analysis and forecasts about the future components of human resources facilitate demand forecasting. One of the important aspects of demands forecasting of the quality of human resources (skill, knowledge values, capabilities etc) in addition to quantity of human resources. Important foreseeing methods are: (a) Managerial judgment; (b) Statistical techniques; and (c) Work study techniques.

(4) Projecting Personnel Supply Forecast

To make assessment of supply of human resources for the organization it should begin with the current human resource inventory of the organization. It is also known as auditing of the human resource to be undertaken by departments of the organization where complete information regarding skills, abilities, qualifications, capacity for hard work is available and so also the quantity and quality of human resources manning various positions, the probable retirements. On the basis of this information they can determine the supply of manpower that is sufficient enough to meet the departmental need or in excess or in short supply. This can be quantitatively and qualitatively worked out. The sum total of supplies of all departments shall equal the organizations supply of human resources. In this way the current or present human resource inventory is accounted for.

The supply of human resources may be less because of layoffs, dismissals, voluntary retirements, deaths etc. If the supply is less than the demand for or is inadequate to meet the requirements for human resources then it can be fulfilled through external sources. The graduates from educational institutions serve the purpose. Also the existing manpower be asked to work extra and overtime wages may be paid to them. This is purely ad hoc arrangement. After some time the organization has to hire the required number and kind of people to meet the need.

(5) Make Comparison

The HRD manager must make a comparison between personnel requirement and personnel supply to find out whether the required personnel is available or not.

(6) If No Differences

The comparison between personnel requirements and personnel supply would indicate whether there are any differences. If human resource requirements are equal to human resource supply, then there are no differences and as such no action need to be taken.

(7) If There Are Differences

The comparison may reveal differences between the human resource requirements and human resource supply. There may be:

(a)Personnel surplus, or (b) Personnel shortage. So, necessary actions need to be taken.

(a) If there is Personnel Surplus

The management needs to take proper action:

- Voluntary retirement,
- Lay-off,
- Termination, etc.

(b) If there is Personnel Shortage

The management needs to take proper action:

- Hire
- Promotion
- Overtime
- Training to improve quality, etc.

(8) Motivating the Manpower

An important aspect of human resource planning is to motivate the personnel by providing monetary and non-monetary incentives.

(9) Monitoring Personnel Requirements

The organization needs to monitor the requirement of personnel. This is because there is constant need for additional personnel, as some of the existing personnel do leave the organization due to resignation, retirement, and so on.

Factors Affecting Human Resource Plan

Several factors affect HRP. These factors can be classified into external factors and internal factors.

Factors Affecting HRP

- External Factors
  - Government's Policies
  - Level of Economic Development including future supply of HRS
  - Business Environment
  - Level of Technology
  - Natural Factors
  - International Factors
- Internal Factors
  - Policies and Strategies
  - Human Resource Policy of the company.
  - Formal and Informal Groups
  - Job Analysis
  - Time Hunting
  - Company's Productional operations policy
  - Trade Unions

Exhibit 2.2:Factors Affecting Human Resource Planning

External Factors

(i) Government Policies. Policies of the government like labour policy, industrial relations policy, policy towards reserving certain jobs for different communities and sons of the soil etc affect the HRP.

(ii) Level of Economic Development. Level of economic development determines the level of HRD in the country and thereby the supply of human resources in the future in the country.

(iii) Business Environment. External business environmental factors influences the volume and mix of production and thereby the future demand for human resources.

(iv) Level of Technology. Level of technology determines the kind of human resources required.

(v) International Factors. International factors like the demand for then resources and supply of human resources in various countries.

Internal Factors

(i) Company Policies and Strategies. Company's policies and strategies relating to expansion, diversification, alliances etc determines the human resource demand in terms of quality and quantity.

(ii) Human Resource Policies. Human resource policies of the company regarding quality of human resources, compensation level, quality of work life etc influences human resources plan.

(iii) Job Analysis. Fundamentally, human resource plan is based on job analysis. Job description and job specification determines the kind of employees required.

(iv) Time Horizons. Companies with stable competitive environment can plan for the long run whereas the firms with unstable competitive environment can plan for only short-term range.

(v) Type and Quality of Information. Any planning process needs qualitative and accurate information. This is more so with human resource plan, strategic, organization and specific information .

(vi) Company's Production Operations Policy. Company's policy regarding how much to produce and how much to buy from outside to prepare a final product influence the number and kind of people required.

(vii) Trade Unions. Influence of trade unions regarding number of working hours per week, recruitment sources etc affect the HRP.

Organizing Human Resource Planning

Every line manager is responsible for planning manpower of the respective department and the top management is responsible for the planning of resources for the entire organization. The personnel department supplies relevant information and data to all the line managers and helps them regarding interdepartmental transfers, promotions, demotions etc. Personnel department also helps in using the techniques and forecasting the manpower. Personnel department forecasts internal mobility surplus or deficit of human resources for the entire organization, prepare action plans regarding redeployment, redundancy, employment, development and internal mobility and submits plans to the management at the top which either by its own or by appointing a committee reviews departmental plans and overall plans, make necessary adjustments and finalizes the plans. Personnel department in its turn prepares modified plans for the departments basing on finalized overall plan and communicates them to respective heads of department.

Personnel department may coordinate the control activity of human resource plan and it has sent coordinated reports to the management reports at the top for actual review, control and monitor the human resource system. The management at the top may appoint a committee consisting of heads of department and external identification of deviations, reasons therefore and steps to be taken to correct the deviations. The committee further helps the management in executing the programmes of corrections.

Merits of Human Resource Planning

HRP anticipates not only the required kind and number of employees but also determines the action plan for all the functions of personnel management. The major benefits of human resource planning are:

(i) It checks the corporate plan of the organization.

(ii) It offsets uncertainty and change. But the HRP offsets uncertainties and changes to the maximum extent possible and enables the organization to have right men at right time and in the right place.

(iii) It provides scope for advancement and development of employees through training, development etc

(iv) It helps to anticipate the cost of salary enhancement, better benefits etc.

(v) It helps to anticipate the cost of salary, benefits and all the cost of human resources facilitating the formulation of budgets in an organization.

(vi) To foresee the need for redundancy and plan to check it or provide alternative employment in consultation with trade unions, other organizations and government through remodeling organizational, industrial and economic plans.

(vii) To foresee the changes in values, aptitude and attitude of human resources and to change the techniques of interpersonal, management etc

(viii) To plan for physical facilities, working conditions and the volume of fringe benefits like canteen, hospitals, conveyance, child care centers, quarters, company stores etc.

(ix) It gives an idea of type of tests to be used and interview techniques in selection based in the level of skills, qualifications, intelligence values etc., in the human resource.

(x) It causes the development of various sources of human resources to meet the organizational needs.

(xi) It helps to take steps to improve human resource contributions in the form of increased productivity, sales, turnover etc.

(xii) It facilitates the control of all the functions, operations, contribution and cost of human resources.

Limitations of Human Resource Planning

HRP suffers from the following drawbacks or limitations:

1. Future is uncertain

Forecasting of changes in technological, social, economic, and political conditions cannot be made with accuracy. HRP is based on certain assumptions, which may prove to be dangerous. However, it is better to try and plan for human resources, rather than leaving actions to chance.

2. Conservative attitude of management

In India there is a high rate of unemployment. As such conservative managements feel that there is no need for HRP as there is abundance of labor in our country. The lack of interest on the part of top management is vital limitation to the success of HRP.

3. Problem of discarding surplus staff

In India, management often finds problem in discarding surplus employees due to various labor laws and trade union activities. Even the voluntary retirement schemes often do not get a favorable response from the surplus staff even when attractive packages are offered.

4. Time Consuming and Paper Work

HRP requires considerable time and effort on the part of human resource planners. Also, a good deal of reports and other paper work is required in order to undertake HRP process.

5. Problem of recognizing change

In India, companies fail to recognize the changes in the environment. This is truer in case of those companies, which are traditionally managed. As a result of this, they do not give much importance to HRP. They consider HRP is just a time consuming and non-productive activity. To make HRP more effective, there is a need for professional attitude on the part of the management of Indian companies.

6. Shortages of highly skilled personnel

Although India is having the second largest pool of scientific and technical personnel in the world, yet there is shortage of highly skilled personnel of the right type. For instance, there is the irony of doctors without patients and patients without doctors. Thus, HRP may be able to recognize the shortages and plan accordingly to get the right type of personnel, yet an organization may find it difficult to identify and recruit the selective personnel.

7. Expensive

HRP is expensive process. This is because, HRP experts may be required and they do charge a good amount of fees. Again, a good amount of money is spent in collecting of data relating to future objectives of the organization, listing out various activities, determining manpower requirements, etc. Again, a lot of money is spent in recruiting and selecting the people and also in providing training.

Conclusion

Human resource planning is a vital sub-activity of employment function. In fact, employment process begins with human resources planning. But it never ends with this function. It pervades through a number of activities after the process of human resources planning. Those activities include searching for prospective human resources, attracting them to the work and organization, finding out their suitability to the job and organizational requirements and finally taking steps to absorb those human resources as organs of the company.

Recruitment

Introduction

Once the required number and kind of human resources are determined, the management has to find the places where the required human resources are/will be available and also find the means of attracting them towards the organization before selecting suitable candidates for jobs. All this process is generally known as recruitment. Some people use the term 'recruitment' for employment. These two terms are not one and the same either. Technically speaking the function of recruitment precedes the selection function and it includes only finding, developing the sources of prospective employees and attracting them to apply for jobs in an organization, whereas the selection is the process of finding out the most suitable candidate to the job out of the candidates attracted (i.e., recruited).

Definition

Recruitment is defined as, "as a process to discover the sources of manpower to meet the requirements of the staffing schedule and to employ effective measures for attracting that manpower in adequate numbers to facilitate effective selection of an efficient workforce."

Edwin B Flippo defined recruitment as "the process of searching for prospective employees and stimulating them to apply for jobs in the organization." In addition to filling job needs, the recruitment activity should be concerned with satisfying the needs of the job candidates. Consequently, recruitment not only attracts individuals to organizations but also increases the chance of retaining the individuals once they are hired.

Objectives of Recruitment

(i) To attract people with multi-dimensional skills and experiences those suit the present and future organizational strategies.

(ii) To induct outsiders with a new perspective to lead the company.

(iii) To infuse fresh blood at all levels of the organization.

(iv) To develop an organizational culture that attracts competent people to the company.

(v) To search or head hunt/head pouch people whose skills fit the company values.

(vi) To devise methodologies for assessing psychological traits.

(vii) To seek out non-conventional development grounds of talent.

(viii) To search for talent globally and not just within the company.

(ix) To design entry pay that competes on quality but not on quantum.

(x) To anticipate and find people for positions that does not exist yet.

Importance of Recruitment

Important activities that are part of recruitment include:

1. Determining the organization's long and short-range needs by job title and level in the organization.

2. Staying informed of job market conditions.

3. Developing effective recruiting materials.

4. Developing a systematic and integrated programme of recruitment in conjunction with other human resource activities and with the cooperation of the line managers.

5. Obtaining a pool of qualified job applicants.

6. Recording the number and quality of job applicants produced by the various sources and methods of recruiting.

7. Following up on applicants- those hired and not hired- in order to evaluate the effectiveness of the recruiting effort.

Recruitment Planning

Recruitment is a form of business competition, and it is a fiercely competitive. Just as corporations compete to develop, manufacture and market the best product or service, so they must also compete to identify, attract, and hire the most qualified people. Recruitment is a business, and it is a big business. It depends serious attention from management, for any business strategy will falter without the talent to execute it.

Recruitment begins with a clear specification of:

(1) The number of people needed (e.g., through workforce, forecasts and utilization analysis).

(2) When they are needed. Implicit in the latter is the time frame- the duration between the receipt of a resume and the time a new hire starts work. This time frame is sometimes refereed to as the "Recruitment Pipeline". The "flow" of events through the pipeline is represented below:

AVERAGE TIME SPAN FOR EVENTS IN A RECRUITMEN

Sequence of events		
From	*To*	*Average number of days*
Resume	Invitation	5
Invitation	Interview	6
Interview	Offer	4
Offer	Acceptance	7
Acceptance	Report to work	21
Total Length Of The Pipeline		**43**

Exhibit 3.1:Average Time Span For Events in a Recruitment Pipeline

The table shows that if an operating manager sends a requisition for a new hire to the HR department today, it will take almost a month and a half, 43 days on average, before an employee fulfilling that requisition actually starts work. Among organizations with between 1 and 500 employees, one survey found that, in practice the average length of the pipeline is 41 days. A recent study by Fortune 500 firms found that average firm cut about 6 days off its hiring cycle by posting jobs online instead of paper ones, and more than a week by screening and processing applications electronically. The HR department must make sure that operating and staff managers realize and understand information such as represented in the pipeline.

One of the ways that operating and staff managers can be sure that their recruitment needs will fit the length of the recruitment pipeline is by examining the segments of the overall by job group (e.g., clerical, sales, production, engineering, managers). For each of these job groups, the HR department with the cooperation of operating managers who represent each job group should examine what has occurred over the past several years in terms of new hires, promotions, transfers and turnover. This will help provide an index of what to expect in the coming years, other things remaining equal.

Sub-systems of Recruitment

(a) Finding out and developing the sources where the required number and kind of employees are/will be available.

(b) Developing suitable techniques to attract the desirable candidates.

(c) Employing the techniques to attract candidates.

(d) Stimulating as many candidates as possible and making them to apply for jobs irrespective of number of candidates required. Management has to attract more candidates in order to increase selection ratio (i.e., number of applications per one job vacancy) in order to select the most suitable candidates available and due to lower yield ratio. Recruitment is positive as it aims at increasing the number of applicants and selection is somewhat negative as it selects the suitable candidates in which process the unsuitable candidates are automatically eliminated. Though, the function of recruitment seems to be easy, a number of factors make performance of recruitment a complex one.

Recruitment Policy

Recruitment policy of any organization is derived from the personnel policy of the same organization. In other words, the former is a part of the latter. However, recruitment policy by itself should take into consideration the government's reservation policy, policy regarding sons of soil etc, personnel policies of other organizations regarding merit, internal sources, social responsibility in absorbing minority sections, women etc. Recruitment policy should commit itself to the organization's personnel policy like enriching the organization's human resources or serving the community by absorbing the weaker sections and disadvantaged people of the society, motivating the employees through internal promotions, improving the employee loyalty to the organization by absorbing the retrenched or laid-off employees or casual/temporary employees or dependents of present/formal employees etc.

The following factors should be taken into consideration in formulating recruitment policy. They are:

(a) Government policies

(b) Personnel policies of other competing organizations

(c) Organization's personnel policies

(d) Recruitment sources

(e) Recruitment needs

(f) Recruitment costs.

(g) Selection criteria and preference etc.

Process Of Recruitment

Sources Of Recruitment

The sources of recruitment are broadly divided into internal sources and external sources. Internal sources are the sources within an organizational pursuit. External sources are the sources outside organizational pursuits.

Internal Sources

(a) Present Permanent Employees. Organizations consider

the candidates from this source for higher-level jobs due to:

(i) Availability of most suitable candidates for jobs relatively or equally to the external source,

(ii) To meet the trade union demands,

(iii) To the policy of the organization to motivate the present employees.

(b) Present Temporary or Casual Employees. Organizations find this source to fill the vacancies relatively at the lower level owing to the availability of suitable candidates or trade and pressures or in order to motivate them on the present job.

(c) Retrenched or Retired Employees. Generally a particular organization retrenches the employees due to lay-off. The organization takes the candidates for employment from the retrenched employees due to obligation, trade union pressure and the like. Sometimes, the organizations prefer to reemploy their retired employees as a token of their loyalty to the organization or to postpone some interpersonal conflicts for promotion etc.

(d) Dependents of Deceased, Disabled, Retired and Present Employees: Some organizations with a view to developing the commitment and loyalty of not only the employee but also his family members and to build up image provide employment to the dependent(s) of deceased, disabled and present employees. Such organizations find this source as an effective source of recruitment.

External Sources

(a) Campus Recruitment: Companies realize that campus recruitment is one of the best sources for recruiting the cream of the new blood. The techniques of campus recruitment include:

(i) Short listing the institutes based on quality of students' intake, faculty facilities and past track record.

(ii) Selecting the recruiting team carefully.

(iii) Offering the smart pay rather than high pay package.

(iv) Presenting a clear image of the company and the corporate culture.

(v) Present the company but do not over sell the company

(vi) Getting in early. Make an early bird offer.

(vii) Focusing on career growth opportunities that the company offers to the recruits.

(viii) Include young line-managers and business school (B-school) and engineering School (E- school) alumni in the recruiting team.

(ix) Build the relationships with the faculty, administrators and students to grab them before the rivals do.

The figures below present the process and techniques of campus recruitment.

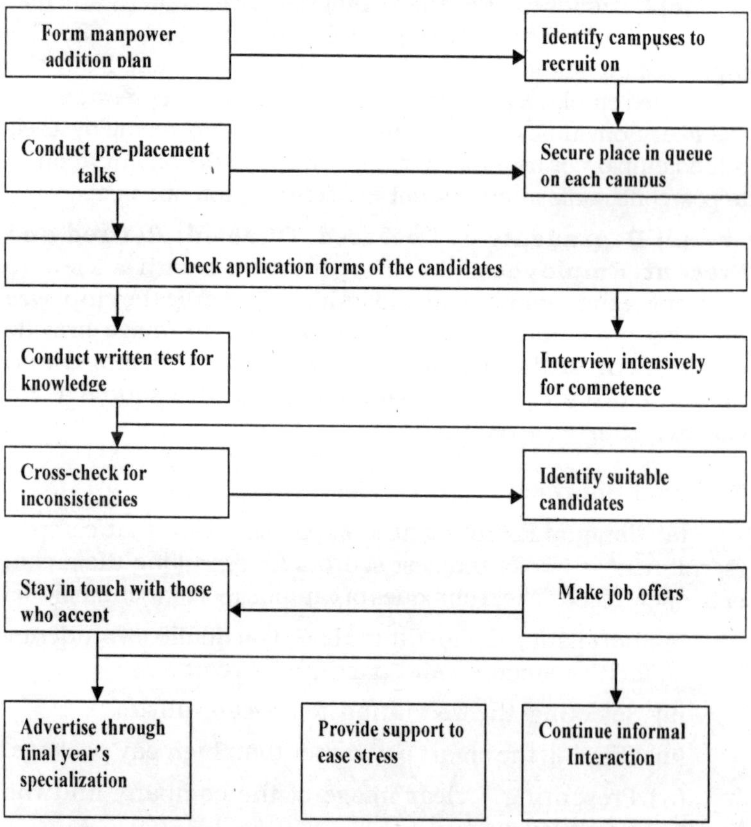

EXHIBIT 3.3: PROCESS OF CAMPUS RECRUITMENT

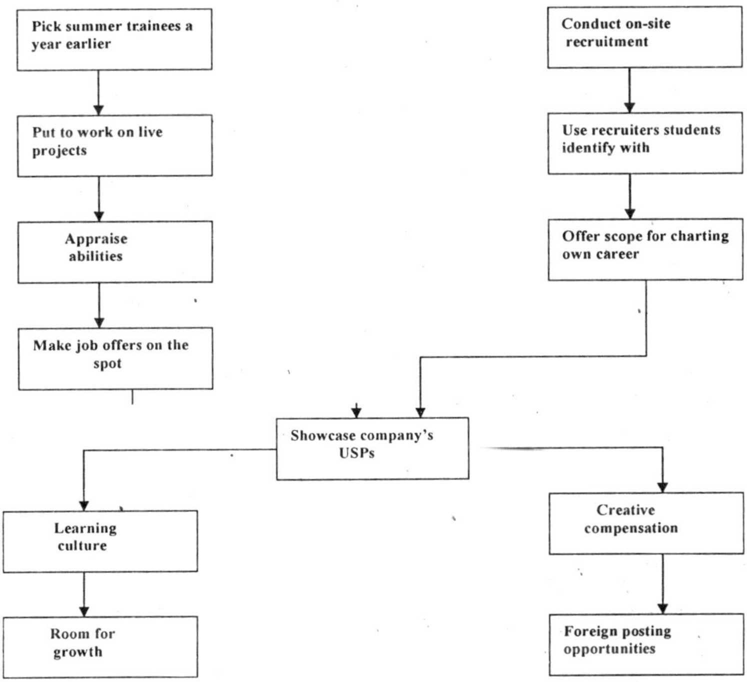

EXHIBIT 3.4: TECHNIQUES TO WIN ON CAMPUS

(b) Private Employment Agencies/Consultants. Consultants in India perform the recruitment functions on behalf of a client company by charging fee. Line managers are relieved from recruitment functions so that they can concentrate on their operational activities and recruitment functions is entrusted to a private agency or consultants. Most of the organizations depend on this source for highly specialized positions and executive positions.

(c) Public Employment Exchanges. The Government set-up Public Employment Exchanges in the country to provide information about vacancies to the candidates and to help the organizations in finding out suitable candidates.

The employment Exchange (Compulsory Notification or Vacancies) Act, 1959 makes it obligatory for public sector enterprises in India to fill certain types of vacancies through public employment exchanges. These industries have to depend on public employment exchanges for the specified vacancies.

(d) Professional Organizations. Professional organizations or associations maintain complete bio-data of their members and provide the same to various organizations on requisition. They also act as an exchange between their members and recruiting firms in exchanging information, clarifying doubts etc. Organizations find this source more useful to recruit the experienced and professional employees like executive, managers, engineers.

(e) Data Banks: The management can collect the bio-data of the candidates from different sources like Employment Exchange, Educational Training Institutes, candidates etc., and feed them in the computer. It will become another source and the company can get the particulars as and when it needs to recruit.

(f) Casual Applicants. Depending upon the image of the organization, its prompt response, participation of the organization in the local activities, level of unemployment, candidates apply casually for jobs through mail or hand over the applications in Personnel Department. This would be a suitable source for temporary or lower level jobs.

(g) Similar Organizations. Generally, experienced candidates are available in organizations producing similar products or are engaged in similar business. The management can get most suitable candidates from this source for executive positions and for newly established organization or diversified or expanded organizations.

(h) Trade Unions. Generally, unemployed or underemployed persons or employees seeking change in employment put a word to the trade union leaders with a view to getting suitable employment due to latter's intimacy with the management. As such the trade union leaders are aware of the availability of candidates. In view of this fact and in order to satisfy the trade union leaders, management enquire trade unions for suitable candidates.

Merits of Internal Sources

(1) It is time saving and economical as there is no need to advertise the 'jobs' in external media and also no need to conduct interviews of several candidates.

(2) There is no need for induction training, especially in respect of company-related information.

(3) It reduces executive turnover.

(4) It develops loyalty and a sense of responsibility.

(5) The internal candidate is well versed with company's policies, rules and regulations.

(6) It improves morale of the company personnel.

Demerits of Internal Sources

(1) It prevents candidates from outside with innovative ideas, fresh thinking and dynamism from entering the company.

(2) It offers limited scope for selection and there is a possibility of not finding the required executive within the company.

(3) The position of the person so promoted or transferred falls vacant.

(4) There may be bias or partiality in promoting or transferring personnel from within the company.

(5) It may be generate a feeling of discontent among those who are not promoted.

(6) It requires well-maintained confidential reports of employees so that the right executive is promoted or transferred.

Merits of External Sources

(1) It encourages new talent with innovative ideas, fresh thinking, drive and dynamism to enter the company.

(2) It offers wider scope in selection, as there is a possibility of a large number of candidates with the requisite

qualifications and experience appearing for the selection process.

(3) There are less chances of partiality, as outsiders have less chance in influencing selection decisions.

(4) It does not require well-maintained confidential records.

Demerits of External Sources

(1) There are chances of existing executive turnover, as outsiders are given a chance.

(2) It may develop loyalty among the existing executives.

(3) It is time consuming, as lengthy selection process is required.

(4) It is also expensive as advertisements, and various tests need to be conducted.

Techniques and Modern Sources of Recruitment

Recruitment techniques are the means or media by which management contracts prospective employees or provide necessary information or exchange ideas or stimulate them to apply for jobs. Management uses different types of techniques to stimulate internal or external candidates. Techniques useful to stimulate internal candidates are:

(i) Promotions. Most of the internal candidates would be stimulated to take up higher responsibilities and express their willingness to be engaged in the higher level jobs if management gives them the assurance that they will be promoted to the next higher level.

(ii) Transfers. Employees will be stimulated to work in the new sections or places if management wishes to transfer them to the places of their choice.

(iii) Recommendations of the Present Employees. Management can contact, persuade the outsiders to apply for job in the organization through the recommendations to the candidates by the present employees, trade union leaders etc.

(iv) Scouting. Scouting means sending the representation of the organizations to various sources of recruitment with a view to persuading or stimulating the candidates to apply for jobs. The representatives provide information about the company and exchange information and ideas and clarify the doubts of the candidates.

(v) Advertising. Advertising is widely accepted technique of recruitment, though it mostly provides one-way communication. It provides the candidates in different sources, the information about the job and company and stimulates them to apply for jobs. It includes advertising through different media like newspapers, magazines of all kinds, radio, television etc.

A number of modern recruitment sources and techniques are being used by the corporate sector in addition to traditional sources and techniques. These sources and techniques include:

(i) Walk-In. The busy organizations and the rapid changing companies do not find time to perform various functions of recruitment. Therefore, they advise the potential candidates to attend for an interview directly and without a prior application on a specified date, time and a specified place. The suitable candidates from among the interviewees will be selected for appointment after screening the candidates through tests and interviews.

(ii) Consult-In. The busy and dynamic companies encourage the potential job seekers to approach them personally and consult them regarding the jobs. The companies select the suitable candidates from among such candidates through the selection process.

(iii) Head-Hunting. The companies request the professional organizations to search for the best candidates particularly for the senior executive positions. The professional organizations search for the most suitable candidates and advise the company regarding the filling up of the positions. Headhunters are also called search consultants.

(iv) Body Shopping. Professional organizations and the hi-tech training institutes develop the pool of human resources for the possible employment. The prospective employers contact these organizations to recruit the candidates. Otherwise, the organizations themselves approach the prospective employees to place their human resources. These professional and training institutions are called body shoppers and these activities are known as body shopping. The body shopping is used mostly for computer professionals.

(v) Business Alliances. Business alliances like acquisitions, mergers, and takeovers help in getting human resources. In addition, the companies do also have alliances in sharing their human resources on ad-hoc basis.

(vi) Tele-Recruitment. The technological revolution in telecommunication helped he organizations to use Internet as a source of recruitment. Organizations advertise the job vacancies through the World Wide Web (www) Internet. The job seekers send their applications through email or Internet. Alternatively, job seekers place their CVs in the world wide web/internet, which can be drawn by the prospective employees depending upon their requirements.

Types of Recruitment Appeal

The recruiter should know what his organization can offer and what the potential candidate wants. Different candidates – like young, old, women, and men – have different needs. Effectiveness of an appeal depends upon applicant's fundamental and immediate needs and those needs, which are not met by his present job. Recruiters' should have the talents of an advertising expert, the skills of a salesman and a market research specialist. They should also know that an organization's appeal might be effective in hiring employees but not in retaining them.

To sum up the employees desire the following features in the given order of importance:

Order of Importance	Area
1.	Opportunity for growth and advancement
2.	Identification with the company

3.	Decent salary
4.	Status and recognition
5.	Technical competence of the supervisors
6.	Confidence in management
7.	Inter-personal relations with superiors
8.	Job security
9.	Employee benefits
10.	Effectiveness of administration
11.	Communication
12.	Friendliness and co-operation of colleagues
13.	Job pressures and demands
14.	Physical and working conditions

Exhibit 3.5: Types Of Recruitment Appeal

Managing Recruitment Operations

Administratively, recruitment is one of the easiest activities to foul up – with potentially long-term negative publicity for the firm. Traditionally recruitment was intensively paper based. It proceeded as shown in figure below. A traditional employment department receives paper resumes, date-stamps them, and distributes them to individual recruiters. The recruiters then manually code, categorize and file each individual resume, frequently repeating this manual process hundreds of times a day.

Finding and matching candidates to open requisitions entails more manual paper processing. Paper must then be copied and forwarded to hiring managers for review, tracked manually with notes and comments, and refiled manually. Individuals are identified as future candidates or as employees, if they have been hired. The process is cumbersome and time-consuming.

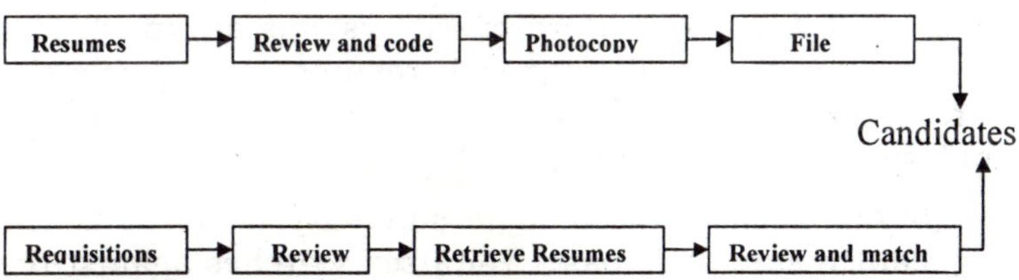

Exhibit 4.1: Traditional Approach To Resume Processing

Recruitment in the Information Age

The modern system employs automation process with the help of latest knowledge-based software in recruitment of the employees as compared to previous system of manual methods and procedures as reflected below:

Resume ⟶ • Scan • Fax • Email ⟶ • Optimum Character recognition • Information / skill Extraction • Automatic Categorization ⟶ Database candidates

Exhibit 4.2:Modern Approaches To Resume Processing

• Employs advanced scamming optical character recognition (OCR), and imaging technologies to capture an exact on-line image of the original resume (for resumes that are faxed or mailed in hard-copy form).

• The Knowledge Base software contains 25,000 skills that combine into 10 million practical combinations of search terms to extract key resume information into an applicant resume database.

• Provides instant on-line access to resume and skills information in the database.

After a resume is processed, the loaded software creates a summary, containing the key information extracted from the resume, including name, addresses, telephone numbers; degrees, schools, grade-point average; work history, including dates, companies, job titles; and up to 80 skills. The Knowledgebase software recognizes the contextual meanings of words within the resume. For example, it can distinguish between John Harvard, a candidate; 140 Harvard Street, an address; Harvard University, a school, and Harvard ID, a town. Simply keyword-based systems are much less efficient, for they will return all resumes containing the word "Harvard", those resumes will then require subsequent analysis and classification.

Information in the resume summary is stored in the applicant resume database. The user searches against the database by building requisitions containing specific skill and experience criteria, and clicking on the search button. The Knowledgebase software then provides a prioritized list of qualified applicants for review. It can also integrate to applicant kiosks, Interactive Voice Response (IVR) systems and corporate Intranets.

This process has cut cost of hire by up to 50 percent, and shortened their hiring cycles by an average of 48 percent.

Evaluation and Control of Recruitment Operations

The reason for evaluating past and current recruitment operations is simple: to improve the efficiency of future recruitment efforts. To do this, it is necessary to analyze systematically the performance of the various recruitment sources. Consider collecting the following kinds of information.

- Cost of operations, that is, labor costs of company recruitment staff, operational costs (e.g., recruiting staff's travel and living expenses, agency fees, advertising expenses, brochures, supplies, and postage), and overhead expenses (e.g., rental of temporary facilities and equipment).
- Cost per hire, by source.
- Number and quality of resumes by source.
- Acceptance/offer ratio.
- Analysis of post-visit and rejection questionnaires.
- Salary offered – acceptances versus rejections.

Which recruitment sources are most effective? Over the past 30 years, this is one of the most intensely researched areas in recruitment. However, a recent review of that literature found that alternative sources did not consistently explain differences in subsequent performance, job attitudes, or turnover (Barber). However, research with a national sample did reveal that the types of recruitment sources used vary by income and education (higher for applicants identified by recruiters, lower for walk-ins). It also revealed differences by gender (relatively more men were hired via recruiters and more women were hired via newspaper advertisements), and race (relatively more nonwhites were hired via recruiters and relatively more whites were hired via walk-ins and employment agencies). (Vecchio, R.P. (1995). The impact of referral sources in employee attitude: Evidence from a national sample. Journal of Management, 21,953-965).

However, regardless of the recruitment sources used to generate applicants, once a final applicant pool, has been assembled, organizations can maximize the economic returns of selection by ignoring recruitment sources and using a top-down (i.e., rank order from best to least qualifies) selection strategy. (Williams, C R., Labig, C.E., Jr., & Stone, T.H. (1993). Recruitment sources and posthire outcomes for job applicants and new hires: A test of two hypotheses. Journal of Applied Psychology, 78, 163-172).

Several studies have examined the recruitment process from the perspective of applicants – how applicants regarded the various sources of information (on-campus interviewer-recruiter, friend, job incumbent, professor) about a job opportunity. (Rynes, S.L. Bretz. R.D., Jr., & Gerhart, (1991). Personnel Psychology, 44, 487-521). The studies have investigated whether applicants regarded the information source as credible or not, which sources provided favorable or unfavorable job information, and which sources led to greater acceptances of job offers.

Timing issues in recruitment delays, are important factors in the job choice decision of applicants. Research indicates that (1) long delays between recruitment phases are not uncommon; (2) applicants react to such delays very negatively, often perceiving that 'something is wrong' with the organization; (3) regardless of their inferences, the most marketable candidates accept other offers of delays become extended. What are the implications of these findings? In a competitive marketplace, top talent disappears quickly. If you want to compete for it, streamline the decision-making process so that you can move fast.

Factors Affecting Recruitment

Internal Factors	**External Factors**
• Company's Pay Package	• Socio-economic Factors
• Quality of work life	• Supply and Demand Factors
• Organizational Culture	• Employment Rate
• Career Planning and Growth	• Labor Market Conditions
• Company's Size	• Political, Legal and Governmental Factors like Reservations for SC/ST/BC and Sons-of-soil.
• Company'sProducts/Services	• Information System like Employment Exchanges/ Tele-recruitment like Internet
• Geographical Spread of the Operations	
• Company's Growth Rate	
• Role of Trade Unions	
• Cost of Recruitment	
• Company's Name and Fame	

Exhibit 4.3:Factors Affecting Recruitment

Impact of Recruitment on Productivity

"People are not fixed assets." It is emphasized that they are treated in a dignified manner. The recruitment is the foundation stone in the selection and hiring of employees in an organization. The quality of recruitment policies, processes devised etc and adopted by the companies has an impeccable impact on the productivity of an organization with regard to the following parameters:

(1) It improves the image of the organization in the corporate world and general public.

(2) It is possible to achieve the company's short-term and long-term targets and objectives in an effective manner.

(3) The motivation and morale of the employees is very high and they put their dedicated efforts to complete the assigned task.

(4) There is a matching of employees and organization goals.

(5) There is a sense of job satisfaction among the employees.

(6) There is a conducive environment on the work spot to carry out the given jobs.

(7) Quality of work life gets improved.

(8) The turnover of the employees is minimized leading to reduction in hiring costs.

(9) The employees are more willing to serve the organization and their retention rate is quite high in the company.

(10) Sincerity and loyalty towards organization rises.

(11) The cost of recruitment per employee reduces significantly.

(12) The relation between the management and employees are more cordial leading to peaceful atmosphere.

(13) Customer relations improve significantly.

(14) The profits and growth of the company is assured.

(15) The ethical standards of the organization are quite high.

(16) The company can effectively meet the competition in the market place.

(17) The employees become more creative and result-oriented.

(18) The jobs are carried out in a planned and organized manner and chaos are reduced.

(19) Training costs are reduced.

(20) Change can be introduced in the organization due to more co-operative attitude of the employees.

(21) Conflict and resentment attitude is avoided.

(22) There is reduction in litigation costs.

(23) Mental and physical health of employees and their capabilities increases and they realize their full potential.

Summary

Recruitment is a major activity in an organization's program to manage its human resources. After human resource needs have been established and job requirements have been identified through job analysis, a recruiting program can be established to produce a pool of job applicants. These applicants can be obtained from internal or external sources.

For recruitment to be effective, it must address not only the needs of the organization but also those of society and the individual. Society's needs are most explicitly defined by various federal and state regulations in the name of equal employment opportunity. Individuals' needs figure prominently in two aspects of recruiting: attracting and retaining desirable employees.

Keeping legal considerations firmly in mind, the organization must recruit sufficient numbers of potentially qualified applicants so that the individuals selected are adequately matched to jobs. This matching will help ensure that the individuals will perform effectively and not leave the organization. An organization can attract and retain these job applicants by numerous methods and through various sources. Although some methods and sources are more effective than others, the ones chosen are often necessarily determined by the type of applicant sought.

As with other human resource activities, recruitment assessment is essential. Evaluating the associated benefit and cost criteria can assess recruitment. For example, the benefits of reduced turnover or enhanced performance can be assessed and compared with the costs of the program to recruit job applicants. Costs of sources and methods can also be assessed and weighed against the benefits, such as the ease of recruiting or the number of qualified applicants obtained. After these assessments are made, recruiting methods and sources can be revised as appropriate.

Bibliography

(1) Cascio. F. Wayne. (2003). *Managing Human Resources: Productivity, Quality of Life, and Profits.* (6th Ed). McGraw- Hill Publishing Company. Pg 199-234.

(2) Dwivedi R S. (1997). *Managing Human Resources: Personnel Management in Indian Enterprises.* Galgotia Publishing Company. Pg 5-18, 48-79.

(3) Rao Subha P. (1999). *Essentials of Human Resource Management & Industrial Relations.* (2nd revised Ed). Himalaya Publishing House. Pg 105-133,135-154.

(4) Schuler S Randall & Huber L Vandra (1993). *Personnel & Human Resource Management.* (5th Ed). West Publishing Company. Pg 127-153, 189-229.

(5) Sharma A M (2000). *Personnel and Human Resource Management.* (3rd revised Ed). Himalaya Publishing House. Pg 33-38,86-92.

(6) Sheikh A M. (1999). Human Resource Development *and Management.* (1st Ed). S Chand & Company Ltd. Pg 17-24.

(7) Singh P N. (1993). *Developing and Managing Human Resources.* (2nd Ed). Suchandra Publications. Pg 78-94, 95-117.

(8) Vaz Michael & Paralikar Vinayak. (2002). *Management & Human Resource Development.* (14th Ed). Manan Prakashan. Pg- 278-284, 293- 296.

7

Performance Appraisal

- Introduction
- Nature and Meaning of Performance Appraisal
- Objectives for Performance Appraisal
- The Evaluation Process
- What not to appraise
- Requirements of Effective Appraisal System
- Performance Appraisal and Total Quality Management (TQM)
- Legalities of Performance Appraisal
- Components of Performance Appraisal
  What to evaluate
  When to conduct appraisals
  Who should conduct appraisals
- Sources of Performance Appraisal Information
  Objective Data
  Personnel Data
  Judgmental Data
- Factors Deterring Objective Evaluation
  Ratee Characteristics
  Rating Errors
- Communicating Appraisal Results To Employees
- Secrets of effective performance feedback interviews
- Summary

Introduction

Today's working climate demands a great deal of commitment and effort from employees, who in their turn naturally expect a great deal more from their employers. Psychologically, performance appraisal is a powerful organizational tool with tremendous impact on the minds of employees and, through them, on the organization.

Performance appraisal is designed to maximize effectiveness by bringing participation to a more individual level in that it provides a forum for consultation about standards of work, potential, aspirations and concerns. It is an opportunity for employees to have a significantly greater influence upon the quality of their working lives.

Appraisal therefore acts as an information-processing system by which progress towards objectives can be monitored and errors spotted, including the identification of under-achievers whose weakness can be corrected efficiently and rationally.

In simple terms performance appraisal may be understood as the assessment of an individual's performance in a systematic way, the performance measured against such factors as job knowledge, quality and quantity of output, initiative, leadership abilities, supervision, dependability, co-operation, judgment, versatility, health and the like. Assessment should not be confined to past performance alone. Potential of the employees for future performance must also be assessed.

In other words, performance appraisal is the step where the management finds out how effective it has been at hiring and placing employees. If any problems are identified, steps are taken to communicate with the employee and to remedy them.

Nature and Meaning of Performance Appraisal

Performance Appraisal is also known as employee appraisal, employee evaluation, employee performance evaluation, merit rating, personnel rating, personnel performance evaluation, performance review, confidential report etc. among others. The common purpose of all these is a systematic and periodic, evaluation of the performance by their superiors and or others who are familiar with the performance and or even by the employee himself.

Performance appraisal or merit rating is a technique which endeavors to assess, as impartially as possible, the attributes of the individual employee, his strengths and weaknesses. It is a system of measuring both qualitatively and quantitatively an individual's' capacity and attitudes in relation to his job. The system usually involves use of forms and procedures that are developed for the purpose. The recorded evaluations usually become a part of the personnel record of the individual employees.

A simple definition of performance appraisal is that "it is a systematic means of ensuring that managers and their staff meet regularly to discuss past and present performance issues, and to agree what future action is appropriate on both sides". The meeting should be based on a clear and mutual understanding of the job in question, and the standards and outcomes which are a part of it.

Performance appraisal is defined "as a formal structured system of measuring, evaluating and influencing an employee's job-related attributes, behaviors, and outcomes as well as level of absenteeism, to discover how productive the employee is and whether he or she can perform as more effectively in the future, so that the employee, the organization and society all benefit".

According to Flippo performance appraisal "is the systematic, periodic and an impartial rating of an employees' excellence in matters pertaining to his present job and his potential to his present job and his potential for a better job".

According to Gary performance appraisal "is a process of estimating or judging the value, excellence, qualities or status of some object, person or thing".

According to Heyel performance appraisal "is the process of evaluating the performance and qualifications of the employees in terms of the requirements of the job for which he is employed, for purposes of administration including placement, selection for promotions, providing financial rewards and other actions which require differential treatment among the members of a group as distinguished from actions affecting all members equally".

Relevant Objectives for Performance Appraisal

Organizations need to consider their objectives long before they design their schemes. To establish the relevance of objectives in performance appraisal they have to be considered in the light of organizational objectives. Objectives must also be considered in the much wider context of people management and how they relate to organizational priorities in maximizing human resources. Following are the objectives of performance appraisal

1. Personnel Training. One of the main objectives of performance appraisal information is employee feedback. Feedback highlights employees' strengths and weaknesses. The appraisal should pertain to job-related characteristics only. Deficiencies or weaknesses then become targets for training. Training should involve only those areas where poor performance can be attributed to the individual and not to aspects of the work environment. The supervisor plays a key role in helping to develop the employees' skills. Performance appraisal according to definition is evaluative but in this context it serves as diagnostic aids. Since most employees will not acknowledge their weaknesses, supportive supervisor is more effective than one who is threatening or critical.

2. Wage and Salary Administration. Performance appraisal is used to determine raises. Pay increases are often made on the basis of job performance. Appraisal programs can be designed so that there is a direct relationship between the evaluation and the size of the raise. For example, an employee who is judged to be performing in the top 10% of the workforce might get a 12% raise. Conversely, an employee who performs in the bottom 10% might get only a 2% raise. Unfortunately, the "personnel development" and "salary administration" aspects of appraisal are often uncomfortable partners. Many employees attach far more meaning to raises because they are more immediate and real than revelations about weaknesses on the job. If two functions are combined in the same appraisal, employees can become defensive. When admitting weaknesses means getting a smaller raise, personnel development may take a back seat.

3. Placements. Performance appraisal information is vital for placement decisions. New employees (e.g. management trainees) are often exposed to many tasks or jobs at first. Over a 12-month period, a trainee might have jobs in marketing, finance and accounting. After being appraised in each, the trainee might be permanently assigned to that area where he / she performed best. By identifying the employees' strengths, performance appraisal indicates where the person's talents might be used.

4. Promotion. Promotions may be based on how well an employee performs on his/her current job. Appraisals identify the better-performing employees, and an employee who cannot perform well on his/her current job will not be considered for promotion. However, performance is not the sole determinant of promotion. Promotions are usually granted based on a combination of seniority and merit. If based strictly on seniority, there is nothing to ensure that competent people get promoted. Promotions based strictly on performance are more defensible, but most experts agree that experience in a job is also worth considering. Promotions have often served as the criterion in validating assessment centre ratings.

5. Discharge. Termination of employment must be predicted on just cause. A typical just cause is inadequate job performance, as determined through performance appraisal. It is also highly advisable for organizations to document the efforts made to enhance the employees' performance and that the decision to terminate employment was the organizations' last resort. Many lawsuits stemming from performance appraisals allege the fired employee was the victim of a "wrongful discharge". In such cases the organization must demonstrate the fairness, job-relatedness and accuracy of the performance appraisal process that led to the termination decision.

6. Personnel Research. In many criterion-validity studies, assessments of the criterion are derived from performance appraisals. Criterion is a measure of job-performance, and that is what performance appraisals are supposed to measure. When I /O psychologists want to validate a new predictor test, they correlate scores with criterion measures, which are often exhumed from a company's performance appraisal files. Any selection device is only as good as the criterion it tries to predict, so the appraisal must be a relevant measure of job success. Research has found that for the purpose of personnel research, specifically constructed performance appraisal instruments yielded more useful and less biased information than evaluations originally collected from administrative purposes.

- **The Evaluation Process**

Stolz proposes that "the process of performance appraisal follows a set pattern namely, a man's performance is periodically appraised by his superiors." Next sometimes in consultation with the man himself, tentative decisions are made on what might be done to advance his development.

Usually the resulting plan is then reviewed at a higher echelon of management, where it may be challenged, changed or added to. Broadly speaking, the process of evaluation begins with the establishment of 'performance standards'. At the time of designing a job and formulating a job-description, performance standards are usually developed for the position. These standards should be clear and not vague and objective enough to be understood and measured. These standards should be discussed with the supervisors to find out which different factors are to be incorporated, weights and points to be given to each factor and these then should be indicated o the appraisal form, and later on used for appraising the performance of the employees.

The next step is to communicate these standards to the employees, for the employees left to themselves, would find it difficult to guess what is expected of them. To make communication effective, "feedback" is necessary from the subordinate to the manager. Satisfactory feedback ensures that the information communicated by the manager has been received and understood in the way that was intended. The third step is the 'measurement of performance'. To determine what actual performance is, it is necessary to acquire information about it. We should be concerned with how we measure and what we measure. Four sources of information are frequently used to measure actual performance: personal observation, statistical reports, oral reports and written reports.

The fourth step is the comparison of actual performance with standards. The employee is apprised and judged of his potential for growth and advancement. Attempts are made to note deviations between 'standard performances' and 'actual performance' At the next stage, the results of appraisal are discussed periodically with the employees, where good points, weak points and difficulties are indicated and discussed so that performance is improved. The information that the subordinate receives about his assessment has a great impact on his self-esteem and on his subsequent performance. Conveying good news is considerably difficult for both managers and subordinate than when performance has been below expectations.

The final step is the initiation of corrective action when necessary; immediate corrective action can be two types. One is immediate and deals predominantly with symptoms. The other is basic and delves into causes. Immediate corrective action is often described as "putting out fires", whereas basic corrective action gets to the source of deviation and seeks to adjust the difference permanently. Coaching and counseling may be done or special assignments and projects may be set; persons may be deputed for formal training courses and decision-making responsibilities and authority may be delegated to the subordinates. Attempts may also be made to recommend for salary increases or promotions, if these decisions become plausible in the light of appraisals.

What not to appraise

(1) Disciplinary Issues

The inclusion of disciplinary matters in appraisal by some organizations almost certainly contributes to some negative about the process. Strictly speaking, in carrying out performance appraisal, items which belong in the disciplinary arena such as time-keeping or appearance are not up for discussion. Problems relating to these points of conduct would normally be dealt with as and when they arose, and persistent offenders would ultimately go through the prescribed sequence of disciplinary warnings. The stage at which points of conduct might be discussed in appraisal is when they affect performance.

One of the benefits of continuous appraisal, is that performance problems can be nipped in the bud, but if they do reach the disciplinary stage it may be better to postpone an appraisal meeting, if one is due, until a more positive climate is established. If the appraisal were to go ahead, it would be essential to indicate what matters are under review in the disciplinary procedure in a written summary and record that the meeting had considered the positive aspects of performance.

The appraisal should never ignore problems and employees must not be confused about where they stand.

(2) Personality

Appraising performance should be held to mean literally that, and not appraising personality and personal characteristics. The subjectivity of such an approach makes it impossible for it to be particularly meaningful, and it is also difficult to produce an action plan for the future based on restructuring personality. Additionally, this approach is too personal and emotive to be well received by appraisers or appraises.

(3) Agreement

Performance appraisal should be seen by those involved as an opportunity for honest discussion. In this discussion the appraiser does not judge but promotes agreement about how the future might be approached. The record of the appraisal interview should in fact be an agreed summary of the discussion, from which a description of current performance and future action plans must be discernible.

(4) Future

Considering the future in performance appraisal can be a matter of aiming towards improving performance in the exiting job to bring up to minimum required standards. It can also be about developing a good performer with the object of enhancing job satisfaction and ensuring that maximum potential is being reached both by the job holder and by the job itself. Additionally, it can be about assisting individuals to progress towards different or more responsible positions within the organization or profession.

When looking to the future in performance appraisal, a great deal of objectivity and realism must be applied. The term future will have different relevance in different circumstances. For example there are certain individuals who do a perfectly good job and the future to them is a desire to be left alone, within reason, to carry on doing so. Another possibility might be the necessity to deal with those who have burning ambitions and who, at least for the time being, do not have the ability to realize them.

When communicating the intentions of appraisal to potential appraisers and appraises alike it is necessary to emphasize that "future" does not necessarily imply promotions or developments. It may simply mean planning towards a better performance in the existing job. It may also mean acknowledgment that the job is being done well and encouragement to carry on doing so.

Requirements of Effective Appraisal System

(1) Relevance

This requirement implies that there are clear links (1) between the performance standards for a particular job and an organizations' goal and (2) between the critical job elements identified through a job analysis and the dimensions to be rated on an appraisal form. In short, relevance is determined by answering the question "what really makes a difference between success and failure on a particular job, and according to whom?" The answer to the latter question is : 'customer'. Customers may be internal (e.g. immediate boss, workers in another department) or external (e.g. those who but your company's products). In all cases, it is important to pay attention to the things that the customer believes are important (e.g. on-time delivery, zero defects etc.).

Performance standards translate job requirements

into levels of acceptable or unacceptable employee behavior. They play critical role in job analysis – performance appraisal linkage. Job analysis implies what is to be done. Performance standards specify how well work is done. Such standards may be quantitative or qualitative. Relevance also implies the periodic maintenance and updating of job analysis, performance standards and appraisal systems.

(2) Sensitivity

This requirement implies that a performance appraisal system is capable of distinguishing effective from ineffective performers. If it is not, and the best employees are rated no differently from the worst employees, then the appraisal system cannot be used for any administrative purposes, it certainly will not help employees develop, and it will undermine the motivation of both supervisors and subordinates.

A major concern here is the purpose of the rating. One study found that raters process identical sets of performance appraisal information differently, depending upon whether a merit pay rise, a recommendation for further development, or the retention of a probability employee is involved. These results highlight the conflict between appraisals made or administrative purposes and those made for employee development. Appraisal systems designed for administrative purposes demand performance information about differences between individuals, while systems designed to promote employee growth demand information about differences within individuals.

(3) Reliability

A third requirement of sound appraisal systems is reliability. In this context, reliability refers to consistence of judgments. For any given employee, appraisals made by raters working independently of one another should agree closely. In practice, ratings made by supervisors tend to be more reliable than those made by peers. To provide reliable data, each rater must have an adequate opportunity to observe what the employees have done and the conditions under which they have done it; otherwise, unreliability may be confused with unfamiliarity.

(4) Acceptability

In practice, acceptability is the most important requirement of all, for it is true that human resource programs must have the support of those who will use them, or else human ingenuity will be used to thwart them. Unfortunately, many organizations have not put much effort into garnering the front-end support and participation of those who will use the appraisal system. How much simpler it is to enlist the active support and cooperation of subordinates or teams by making explicit exactly what aspects of job performance they will be evaluated on.

(5) Practicality

This requirement implies that appraisal instruments are easy for managers and employees to understand and use.

Performance Appraisal and Total Quality Management (TQM)

TQM emphasizes the continuous improvement of products and processes to ensure long term customer satisfaction. Its group problem–solving focus encourages employee empowerment by using the job-related expertise and ingenuity of the work force. Cross-functional teams develop solutions to complex problems, often shortening the time taken to design, develop or produce products and services. Since a team may not include a representative of management, the dividing line between labor and management often becomes blurred in practice, as workers themselves begin to solve organizational problems. Thus adoption of TQM generally requires cultural change within the organization as management reexamines its past methods and practices in light of the demands of the new philosophy.

The father of TQM, "W. Edwards Deming", proposes that appraisal systems that tie individual performance to salary adjustments should be eliminated. In his view, such systems hinder team work, create fear and mistrust, and discourage risk-taking behavior, thereby stifling innovation. Deming argues that most appraisal systems are based on the faulty assumption that individuals have significant control over their own performance i.e. that most individuals can improve if they choose to do so by putting forth the necessary effort.

The basis for the argument is that everything done in an organization is done within a framework of systems that provide limits on the activities of machines, processes etc. In a well designed system, it will be nearly impossible to do a job improperly. Conversely, a poor system can thwart the best efforts of the best employees. If the system itself prevents good work, performance appraisal cannot serve its intended purpose of differentiating among individuals for purposes of salary adjustments.

The bottom line is that as a basis for implementing a "pay-for-performance" philosophy, performance appraisal is a meaningful tool only if workers have significant control over the variables that affect their individual performance. If not then that appraisal measure only random statistical variation within a particular system.

Three suggestions for harmonizing these two processes are

(1) Let Customer Expectations Generate Individual or Team Performance EExpectations. Identification of customers by product or service is very important. Customer may be internal or external. Then individuals or teams can begin to assess their performance against those expectations. Using this baseline of achievement individuals or teams can develop continuous improvement targets. Comparing actual performance against expected performance helps avoid detrimental intra-team competition, because individuals or teams are compared against their won benchmarks, rather than against the accomplishments of others.

(2) Include Results-Expectations That Identify Actions to Meet or Exceed Those Expectations. Employee or Team and supervisor together consider these customer expectations in conjunction with the business plan and begin to establish priorities for improvement opportunities.

(3) Include Behavioural Skills that Make a Real Difference in Achieving Quality Performance and Total Customer Satisfaction Effective customers require "attention to detail", "initiative", and "listening skills". These continuous-improvement skills are as important to total quality as are results-oriented targets.

• Legalities of Performance Appraisal

There is a rich body of case law on performance appraisal, and three reviews of it reach similar conclusions. To avoid legal difficulties, one must take the following steps

(1)Conduct a job analysis to determine the characteristics necessary for successful job performance.

(2) Incorporate these characteristics into a rating instrument. This may be done by trying rating instruments to specific job behaviors (e.g. BARS), but the courts routinely accept less sophisticated approaches, such as simple graphic rating scale. Regardless of the method used, provide written standards to all raters.

(3) Train supervisors to use the rating instrument properly, including how to apply performance standards when making judgments. The uniform application of standards is very important. The vast majority of cases lost by organizations have involved evidence that subjective standards were applied unevenly to members of protected groups versus all other employees.

(4) Include formal appeal mechanisms, coupled with higher-level review of appraisals.

(5) Document the appraisals and the reason for any termination decisions. This information may prove decisive in court. Credibility is enhanced by documented appraisal ratings that describe instances of poor performance.

(6) Provide some form of performance counseling or corrective guidance to assist poor performers.

The type of evidence required to defend performance ratings is linked to the purposes for which the ratings are made. For example, if appraisal of past performance is to be used as a predictor of future performance, evidence must be presented to show (1) that the rating of past performance are valid (2) that the ratings of past performance are statistically related to future performance in another job. Finally, to assess adverse impact, organizations should keep accurate records of who is eligible for and interested in promotion. These two factors, eligibility and interest, define the "applicant group".

In summary, it is not difficult to offer prescriptions for scientifically sound, court-proof appraisal systems, but implementing them requires diligent attention by organizations, plus a commitment to making them work. In the development of a performance appraisal system, the most basic requirement is to determine what one wants the system to accomplish.

• Components of Performance Appraisal

Performance appraisal or management system involves

- Determining the needs of the business, particularly its strategic objectives.
- Linking performance appraisal planning with organizational planning.
- Conducting a job analysis to identify job duties and responsibilities for which criteria needs to be developed.
- Choosing an appropriate and valid performance appraisal method to assess job behaviors or outcomes.
- Developing a process for conveying job expectations to incumbents prior to the appraisal period.
- Establishing a feedback system relating to job performance.
- Evaluating how well the performance appraisal system is doing in relation to its stated objectives.

How well the system works depends on the organization's culture, its strategic objectives, and the characteristics of the rater and the incumbent.

To develop a performance management system, deciding (1) what to evaluate, (2) when to conduct appraisals and (3) who should evaluate performance is important.

What to Evaluate

A valid performance appraisal system grows out of a

comprehensive job analysis that identifies important job duties and tasks. Once these are delineated, performance criteria can be developed. Criteria are evaluative dimensions against which an incumbent's, a team's or a work unit's behaviour or performance are measured.

Types of Performance Criteria. One of the most important decisions relating to performance appraisal centers is the type of performance criteria. There are three basic categories of performance criteria.

Trait-based criteria focus on the personal characteristics of an employee. Such factors as loyalty, dependability, communication ability, and leadership skill exemplify traits that are often assessed during the appraisal process. This type of performance criteria asks a lot about what a person is, but fails to focus on what a person accomplishes or does not accomplish on the job. While trait-based appraisal instruments can be constructed easily, they are not generally valid. Unfortunately, the link between traits and performance is often weak. This is due to the influence of situational factors. Traits also are difficult to accurately define. To one person dependability may mean showing up to work on time every day; to another person it may mean to stay up late when the boss requests to; it may also mean not using sick days when one is genuinely sick. Because of these concerns, trait-based criteria are not generally defendable in the courts.

Behaviour-based Criteria. Focus on how work is performed. Such criteria are particularly important for jobs which involve interpersonal contact. For example, how a counselor opens a discussion with a marital couple experiencing interpersonal trauma is critical to success of the counseling session. Behavioral criteria are particularly useful for employee development. With behaviors clearly identified, an employee is more likely to exhibit those acts that lead to peak performance. Behavioral criteria are less appropriate for jobs in which effective performance can be achieved using many different behaviors.

With the increased emphasis on productivity and international competitiveness, *outcome-based criteria* have risen in popularity. This type of criteria focuses on what was accomplished or produced rather than how it was produced. Outcome criteria are appropriate when it is not important how results are achieved, but they are not appropriate for every job. For example, the number of cases handled annually by a lawyer can be easily counted. However such a performance indicator would not indicate the quality of legal counsel given or the resolution of the cases. Second, it may be impossible to indicate in advance how many cases can be handled or how much time a given case may take.

Another concern is that the easy-to-measure aspects of a job are often assessed rather than the more important but more evasive aspects of the job. A results-at-all-costs mentality may also plague outcome-based appraisals.

Closeness to organizational goals. Depending on the organization's strategy and its ability to measure performance, criteria can be developed that relate either to the individual or group job behavior or outcomes or to overall organizational effectiveness. Organizational effectiveness involves an inferential leap; it entails aggregating individual and group outcomes in order to determine how well the organization is functioning.

Single or Multiple Criteria. If coordinating market activities is the only job duty, then only criteria that relate to this single duty are needed. More often, however, jobs are multidimensional, composed of many different duties and related tasks. For the assistant vice-president job, the primary duty of "coordinating market activities" is accompanied by other duties, such as "staying abreast of current events" etc. If job analysis identifies all these duties as important, all should be measured by the performance appraisal instrument.

If the form used to appraise employee performance lacks the job behaviors and results important and relevant to the job, the form is said to be deficient. If the form appraises anything either unimportant or irrelevant to the job, it is contaminated. Many performance appraisal forms actually used in organizations measure some employee attributes and behaviors that are unrelated to the employee's job. These forms are contaminated and are in many cases also deficient.

When to Conduct Appraisals

In addition to identifying appropriate criteria, we must identify the time period for which performance is to be assessed and the timing of appraisal.

Cycle length. On average, most organizations require formal performance review sessions at six-month to one year intervals. This makes some sense since it fits with the natural rhythm of the organization. However, there are reasons to believe that performance of some jobs should be evaluated more or less frequently. Some writers contend that evaluation period should correspond to the time span of the job, the length of time it takes to recognize the performance level of someone who is doing a job. In the case of some simple, lower-level jobs, the time span may e be as short as a few minutes; in the case of a senior level management job, the appropriate time period may be as long as several years.

Assessing performance on a cycle that roughly approximates the characteristics of the job can be advantageous. If performance is to be assessed before it can be reasonably measured, mis-assessment is likely. If the time span is too long, motivation and performance may suffer significantly. This is particularly detrimental in the case of a poor performer. If the time period is too long then the employee will not come to know what needs to be done to improve his performance until it's too late.

The evaluation period may also depend on the purpose of the appraisal. To meet communication and evaluate purposes, the focus should be on current employee performance during a single performance period. For promotion and training decisions, an examination of performance across multiple appraisal periods may be of use. If performance is steadily increasing or is consistently high, a promotion may be justified. If performance remains consistently low, training may be necessary.

Timing of appraisal In many organizations performance appraisal are conducted according to when the individual joined the organization. This approach is referred to as "the anniversary model". This approach spreads the workload throughout the year, so the appraisal task is not overwhelming. However, it typically does not tie individual or team performance to the overall performance of the organization. Consequently, the strategic benefits of the appraisal process are compromised. Research also indicates that ratings given to employees early in the year are higher or more lenient than ratings given later. This is particularly so when appraiser / raters are allocated a specific number of high and specific number of low ratings. A third drawback is that the organization does not know how the supervisor is appraising performance and subsequently can't determine how well the total organization is performing until the year is over and all evaluations have been completed.

The other approach is called a *focal-point system* in which every employee is appraised at approximately the same time in the year. The major advantage of the focal point system is that comparisons between employees can be made. Supervisors can look at all individuals, report to them, and get a sense of how their performance compares during the same period. Similarly, top management can compare the performance of different strategic business units to assess how well corporate objectives are being met. Such comparative information is particularly important if performance information is to be used in evaluation decisions. The major dis-advantage of focal-point reviews is that they produce a tremendous workload at one time. This burden can, however, be reduced in two ways : first, by having clear criteria against which performance to evaluate, second, by ensuring that subordinates share the responsibility with their supervisor for defining performance criteria and documenting accomplishments relative to performance standards.

Why of Appraisal

- Creating and maintaining a satisfactory level of performance of employees in their present job.
- Highlighting employee needs and opportunities for personal growth and development.

- Aiding in decision-making for promotions, transfers, lay-offs, and discharges
- Promoting understanding between the supervisor and his subordinates.
- Providing a useful criterion for determining the validity of selection and training methods and techniques and forming concrete measures for attracting individuals of higher caliber to the enterprise.

Where of Appraisal

The where indicates the location where an employee may be evaluated. It is usually done at the place of work or supervisor's office. Informal appraisals may take place anywhere and everywhere, both on the job and off the job.

How of the Appraisal

Under how the company must decide what different methods are available and which of these may be used for performance appraisal.

Who of the Appraisal

Critical in determining who should conduct the appraisal is the amount and the type of work contact the evaluator has with the person being evaluated. The quantity and quality of task acquaintance may vary with organizational level as well as with the proximity of the rater the worker.

Appraisal by Superiors. The superior is the immediate boss of the subordinate being evaluated. The assumption is that the superior knows the subordinate's job and performance better than anyone else. However, appraisal by the superior has drawbacks. First, because the superior may have rewards and punishment power, the subordinate may feel threatened. Second, evaluation is often a one-way process that makes the subordinate feel defensive. Thus, little coaching takes place; justification of actions prevails. Third, the superior may not have the necessary interpersonal skills to give good feedback. Fourth, the superior, by giving punishments, may alienate the subordinate.

Because of the potential liabilities, organizations often

invite other people to share in the appraisal process. Allowing other people who have knowledge of job performance to gather performance data increases the reliability and perceived fairness of the appraisal process. Additionally, it creates a greater openness in the performance appraisal system, thus helping enhance the superior-subordinate relationship.

Peers. In some jobs, such as outside sales, the immediate supervisor may observe a subordinate's actual job performance only rarely. Thus, peer evaluation under such circumstances is considered as one of the most reliable sources of appraisal data. Peers can provide a perspective on performance that is different from that of immediate supervisor. Thus a member of a cross-functional team may be in a better position to rate another team member than that team member's immediate supervisor. Also peer appraisal is considered effective because, first, peers are close to the action. Daily interactions provide them with a comprehensive view of an employee's job performance. Second, using peers as raters results in a number of independent judgments. A boss can offer only a single evaluation, but peers can provide multiple appraisals. And the average of several ratings is often more reliable than a single evaluation. But on the downside, peer evaluations can suffer from co-workers' unwillingness to evaluate one another and from biases based on friendship or animosity.

Self – Evaluation. Having employees evaluate their won performance is consistent with values such as self-management and empowerment. Self-evaluations get high marks from employees themselves; they tend to lessen employees' defensiveness about the appraisal process; and they make excellent vehicles for stimulating job performance discussion between employees and their supervisor. However, they suffer from over-inflated assessment and self-serving bias. Moreover, self-evaluations are often low in agreement with supervisors' ratings. Because of these serious drawbacks, self-evaluations are probably better suited to developmental uses than for evaluative purposes.

Immediate Subordinates . A fourth judgment source is an employee's immediate subordinates. Its proponents argue that it's consistent with recent trends toward enhancing honesty, openness and empowerment in the workplace. Immediate subordinates' evaluation can provide accurate and detailed information about a manager's behavior because the evaluators typically have frequent contact with the person being evaluated. The problem with this form of rating is fear of reprisal from bosses who are given unfavorable evaluations. Therefore, respondent anonymity is crucial if these evaluations are to be accurate.

360-Degree Evaluations. The latest approach to performance evaluations is the use of 360-degree evaluations. It provides for performance feedback from the full circle of daily contacts that an employee might have, ranging from mailroom personnel to customers to bosses to peers. The number of appraisals can be as few as three or four evaluations or as many as 25. The appealing factor is that such evaluation fits well into organizations that have introduced teams, employee involvement, and quality-management programs. By relying on feedback from co-workers, customers, and subordinates, these organizations give everyone more a sense of participation in the review process and gain more accurate readings on employee performance.

- ***Reasons Why 360- degree fails***
  - ambiguous objectives
  - changing the ground rules after the process has begun.
  - Inadequate attention to identifying what each rater should do
  - Failing to develop an action plan following feedback
  - Lack of follow-through.

Ways in which the above potential problems can be solved

- Employee and manager should identify key customers for each of employee's goals and commitments.
- Contract with each customer regarding his or her expectations. The objective should be to pay attention to the same things that the customer thinks are important.

- Meeting regularly with each customer to assess progress, planning plan for future performance, and to receive feedback during the performance period is important.

Sources of Performance Appraisal Information

(1) *Objective Production Data*

Using objective production data as an index of how well an employee is performing on the job is limited in its frequency and value. For a person in the job of a machine operator, job performance may be measured by counting the number of objects produced per day, per week, and so forth. Although each of these objective production measures has some degree of intuitive appeal, none is usually a complete measure of job performance. Two problems in particular affect each of these measures. First, it is assumed that differences in performance across people reflect true differences in how well these people perform their jobs. Unfortunately, variability in performance can be due to factors beyond the individuals' control. One machine operator may produce more because he / she work with a better machine. This problem of variation in performance stemming from external factors represents a form of criterion contamination.

The second problem is that they rarely tell the whole story. A machine operator who produces more objects per day but who also produces more defective objects should not be described as the 'best'. Quality may be as important as quantity, but this cannot be recorded in a simple count of objects produced.

Relevance of Objective Production Data. Objective production data has some relevance which differs in degree. It is a mistake to give more too much importance to objective production data in performance appraisal. This is sometimes a great temptation because these data are usually very accessible, but the meaning of those clear – cut numbers is not always evident. Finally, for many jobs, objective production data does not exist or if they do, they have little relevance to actual performance. Criterion relevance is the question of judgment.

(2) ***Personnel Data***

The second type of appraisal information is personnel data, retained by a company's personnel office. The three most common indices of performance are absenteeism, turnover and accidents. The critical issue with these variables is criterion relevance.

Absenteeism is probably the most sensitive measure of performance. In almost all jobs, employees who are often absent are often judged as performing worst than others, all the factors being equal. Most organizations have policies for dealing with absenteeism, which attests to its importance as a variable in judging overall performance. However, the measurement and interpretation of absenteeism are not clear-cut. Absences can be "excused" or "unexcused" depending on many factors pertaining to both the individual and the job. An employee who has ten days of excused absence may still be apprised as performing better than an employee with five days of unexcused absence. Whether the absence was allowed must be determined before performance judgments are made. Measuring absenteeism is a thorny problem, but it is seen as a highly relevant criterion variable in most organizations.

Turnover is also used to measure performance. It too has some measurement problems. Some turnover is voluntary (the employee quits), some is involuntary (employee is fired). An employee who quits is probably apprised "better" than an employee who is fired. Some organizations also allow employees to resign in order to improve her/his chances of getting another job. This clouds the value of turnover as a measure of performance. The attitude towards a chronic job-hopper has also changed over the years. Earlier, job-hoppers were viewed with some suspicion at the management level, they seemed unstable and unable to hold a job for long. Today, however, job-hoppers are regarded more positively. Exposure to different jobs is taken to mean that they have more breadth of experience.

Accidents can be used as a measure of job-performance but only for a limited number of jobs. Frequency and severity of accidents are both used as variables, as are accidents resulting in injury or property damage. Accidents are a more relevant criterion variable for blue-collar than for white-collar jobs. People who drive delivery trucks may be evaluated in part on the number of accidents they have. This variable can be contaminated by many sources like road conditions, miles driven, time of the day etc. while relevance is limited to certain jobs, accidents can contribute greatly to appraisal.

Relevance of Personnel Data. Factors like absenteeism, turnover and accidents are meaningful measures of job performance. Employees may be discharged for excessive absences or accidents, and they may be rewarded for perfect attendance or a perfect safety record. However, personnel data rarely gives a comprehensive picture of the employees' performance. Other highly relevant aspects of job performance often are not revealed by personnel data.

(3) Judgmental Appraisal. Judgmental data are commonly used for performance appraisal because finding relevant objective measures is difficult. A wide variety of measures have been developed, all intended to provide accurate assessments of how people are performing.

Norm- Referenced Appraisals

For decisions like "who should be retained or who is the best performer", norm-referenced performance standards are used.

Straight Ranking. It is the oldest and simple method of performance appraisal, by which the man and his performance are considered as an entity by the rater. No attempt is made to fractionalize the rate or his performance; the whole man is compared with the whole man. The relative position of each man in a work group is done against that of another. The relative position of each man is tested in terms of his numerical rank. It may also be done by ranking a person on his job performance against that of another member of a competitive group by placing him as number one or two or three in total group. This method is rather easy to develop and use and is the simplest method to differentiate between most efficient and least efficient.

However, this method in practice is very difficult to compare a single individual with human beings having varying behavior traits. Secondly, the method only tells us how a man stands in relation to others in a group but does not indicate how much better or worse he is than another. Thirdly, the task of ranking individuals is difficult when a large number of persons are rated. Fourth, the ranking system does not eliminate snap judgments, nor does it provide us with a systematic procedure for determining the relative ranks of subordinates.

Alternative Ranking. The first step is to put the best subordinate at the head of the list and the worst subordinate at the bottom. The superior then selects the best and worst from the remaining subordinates; the best is placed second on the list, the worst next to last. The superior continues to choose the best and worst until all subordinates are ranked. The middle position on the list is the last to be filed by this method.

Paired Comparison. This approach involves comparing each incumbent to every other incumbent, two at a time, on a single standard to determine who is "better". A rank order of the individual can be obtained by counting the number of times each individual is selected as the better of the pair. An advantage of this approach is that it overcomes the problem of "evaluation set". That is, it forces the rater to compare the performance of each incumbent to all other incumbents, one by one. Several potential problems exist with paired-comparison method. If the number of incumbents is large, the number of comparisons may be unmanageable. (There are N [N-1] / 2) total comparisons, where N is the number of individuals. Intra-sensitivity in judgment is another problem. It occurs if incumbent A is rated better than B, and B is rated better than C, but C is rated better than A.

A problem with all three methods is that each person is assigned a unique rank. This suggests that no two subordinates perform exactly alike. Although this may be true, many supervisors believe that some incumbents perform so similarly that individual differences cannot be discerned.

Forced Distribution Method. This method was evolved by Joseph Tiffin after statistical work. This system is used to eliminate or minimize raters' bias, so that all personnel may not be placed at the higher end or at the lower end of the scale. It requires the rater to appraise am employee according to a pre-determined distribution scale. Under this system, it is assumed that it is possible and desirable to rate only two factors viz., job performance and promotability. For this purpose, a five-point performance scale is used without any descriptive statement. Employees are placed between the two extremes of good and bad job performances; for example 10 percent placed at the top end of the scale, given superior or outstanding merit; 20 percent given good rating; 40 percent satisfactory rating ; 20 percent fair and 10 percent unsatisfactory. This method assumes that, of the total personnel, 10 percent must go to top grade, 20 percent second grade , 40 percent middle grade, 20 percent grade next to the lowest end of the scale and 10 percent to lowest grade.

In addition to job performance, employees are rated for promotability. A three-point scale is often used for this purpose:

(a) very likely promotional material

(b) may or may not be promotional material

(c) very unlikely to be promotional material.

The good point is that by forcing the distribution in this manner, the problem of different appraisers using different parts of the scale is avoided. Second, this method tends to eliminate or reduce bias; third, the method is highly simple to understand and very easy to apply in organizations.

Grading Method. Under this system, the rater considers certain features and marks them accordingly to a scale. Certain categories of worth are first established and carefully defined. The selected features may be analytical ability, co-cooperativeness, dependability, self-expression, job knowledge, leadership etc. they may be: A – outstanding , B- very good , C-good , D- fair , E- poor, and -B – very poor.

Man – To – Man Comparison. In this method, certain factors are selected for the purpose of analysis and a scale is designed by the rater for each factor. A scale of man is also created for each selected factor. The each man to be rated is compared with the man in the scale, and certain scores for each factor are awarded to him. This method is used in job evaluations and is known as the "factor comparison method".

Field Review Method . Under this method, a trainer employee from the personnel department interviews line supervisors to evaluate their respective subordinates the appraiser is fully equipped with definite test questions, usually memorized in advance, which he puts to the supervisor. The supervisor is required to give his opinion about the progress of his subordinates, the level of the performance each subordinate, his weaknesses, good points, outstanding ability, promotability and the possible plans of action in cases requiring further consideration. The questions are asked and answered verbally. The appraiser takes detailed notes of the answers, which are then approved by the supervisor and placed in the employee's personal folder. The success of this system depends upon the competence of the interview. This system minimizes bias and prejudice on the part of the supervisor. The over-all ratings are obtained by largely using a three-way categorization : outstanding, satisfactory and unsatisfactory. It relieves the supervisor of the need for filling out appraisal forms. The main defect is that it keeps two management representatives busy with the appraisal.

Group Appraisal Method. Under this method, employees are rated by an appraisal group, consisting of their supervisor and three or four other supervisors who have some knowledge of their performance. The supervisor explains to the group the nature of his subordinates' duties. The group then discusses the standards of performance for that job, the actual performance of the job-holder, and then the causes of their particular level of performance and offers suggestions for future improvement. The advantage of this method is that it is thorough, very simple and is devoid of any bias, for it involves multiple judges. But it is very time consuming.

Free Essay Method. Under this method, the supervisor makes a free form, open-ended appraisal of an employee in his own words and puts down his impressions about the employee. He takes note of these factors :

- Relations with fellow supervisors and personnel assigned to him.
- General organization and planning ability
- Job knowledge and potential
- Employee characteristics and attitudes
- Understanding and application of company policies and procedures
- Production, quality and cost control
- Physical conditions
- Development needs for future

There are several advantages of this method. An essay can provide a good deal of information, especially if the supervisor is asked to give two or three examples of each judgment he makes. The explanations will give specific information about the employee, and can reveal even more about the supervisor. However, there are certain drawbacks too.

- It contains a subjective evaluation of the reported behavior of an individual and may affect such employment decisions as promotion, lay-of etc.

- Some appraisers may be good at narrative appraisal, while others may not have the facility to write a descriptive report.

- The appraisal may be loaded with a flowery language about the quality of the rate than with the actual evaluation of performance.

- Under this system, the supervisor is required to devote considerable time and thought to the procedure. He has to be critical. The appraisal depends on the appraiser's literary skills than on the employees' abilities and performance.

- Rater bias is easily introduced into such ratings, since the essay is in the supervisor's own words.

Comments on Norm- Referenced Appraisals. Regardless of the approach, all methods are based on the assumption that performance is best captured or measured by one criterion- overall performance. Because this single criterion is a global measure and is not anchored in any objective index, such as units sold, the results can be influenced by rate subjectivity. As a consequence, the rankings lack behavioral specificity and may be subject to legal challenge.

Absolute Standards Formats

This format allows the evaluator to assess performance in relation to trait or behavioral criteria. Consequently, it is possible for ratees to receive identical ratings.

Graphic Rating Scale. This is the most commonly used method of performance appraisal. Under it , a printed form, one for each person to be rated. According, to Jucius, these factors are : employee characteristics (initiative, leadership, co-cooperativeness, dependability, loyalty, creative ability etc.) and employee contribution (quantity and quality of work, leadership offered, regularity of attendance, attitude towards supervisors, versatility etc.). These traits are then evaluated on a continuous scale, wherein the rater places a mark somewhere along a continuum. Sometimes a discontinuous or multiple type of scale is used, wherein one factor is used along a discontinuous scale, consisting of appropriate boxes or squares which are to be ticked off. The scale may be represented by or broken down into 3,7,10, or more parts.

The rating scale is easy to understand and easy to use, and permits a statistical tabulation of scores. A ready comparison of scores among the employees is possible. These scores indicate the worth of every individual. Besides, when ratings are objectively given, they can provide useful feed back. However, this method suffers a serious disadvantage, for it is arbitrary, and the rating is generally subjective. Often, the rating clusters on the high side when this method is used. Another limitation is that it assumes that each characteristic is equally important for all jobs. Perhaps, it assumes everyone's definition of dependable is the same.

Critical Incidents. Critical Incident are behaviors that result in good or poor job performance. Anderson and Wilson (1997) noted that the critical-incident technique is flexible and can be used for performance appraisal and job analysis. Supervisors record behaviors of employees that greatly influence their job performance. They keep a running tally of these critical incidents as they occur on the job or recall them at a later time. Critical incidents are usually grouped by aspects of performance: job knowledge, decision-making ability, leadership and so on. The end result is a list of behaviors that constitute effective and ineffective job performance. The critical-incidents method is used to guide employees in the specifics of their job performance. Each employees' performance can be described in terms of the occurrence of these critical behaviors. The supervisor can then counsel the employee to avoid the bad and continue the good behaviors.

Behaviourally Anchored Rating Scale. This is a new appraisal technique which has recently been developed. Its supports claim that it provides better, more equitable appraisals as compared to other techniques. The procedure for BARS is usually five stepped.

(a) **Generate Critical Incidents** : Persons with knowledge of the job to be appraised are asked to describe specific illustrations (critical incidents) of effective and ineffective performance behavior.

(b) **Develop Performance Dimensions** : These people then cluster the incidents into a smaller set of performance dimensions. Each cluster is then defined.

(c) **Reallocate Incidents** : Any group of people who also know the job then reallocate the original critical incidents. They are given the cluster's definition and critical accidents and asked to redesign each incident to the dimension it best describes. Typically, a critical incident is retained if some percentages of this group assign it to the same cluster as the previous group did.

(d) **Scale of Incidents** : This second group is generally asked to rate (7 or 9 point rating scale) the behavior described in the incidents as to how effectively or ineffectively it represents performance on the appropriate dimension.

(e) **Develop Final Instrument** : A subset of incidents (usually 6 or 7 per cluster) are used as "behavior anchors" for the performance dimensions.

Though BARS technique is more time – consuming and expensive than other appraisal tools, yet it has got certain advantages, such as :

(a) A more accurate gauge, since BARS is done by persons expert in the technique, the results are sufficiently accurate.

(b) Clear standards. The critical incidents along the scale help to clarify what is meant by "extremely good" performance, "average" performance and so on.

(c) Feedback. The use of critical incidents may be more useful in providing feedback to the people being appraised.

(d) Independent dimensions. Systematically clustering the critical incidents into 5 or 6 performance dimensions, helps in making the dimensions more independent of one another.

(e) Rater – independence. The technique is not biased by the experience and evaluation of the rater.

Checklists Method . In its simplest form, a checklist presents a rater with a list of items that describe a variety of possible work behaviors and or personality traits, and asks the rater to indicate (check) those items that are applicable to the worker being evaluated. Overall, evaluations can then be determined by summing the number of positive items checked. Sometimes the total number of negative or undesirable items that have been checked is subtracted from the number of positive items checked. Summated checklists are a variation on this format. The rater is typically instructed to use a five-item scale to indicate his or her level of (dis) agreement concerning the extent to which each of a series of items accurately describes the job performance of the worker being rated. Unlike simple checklist, these require the rater to respond to each item. Once again, overall evaluations are determined by summing the number of positive or desirable items that the rater agreed were descriptive of the rate, as well as the number of negative or undesirable items that the rater believed were not descriptive.

Mixed Standards Scales. Mixed standards rating cales were developed to eliminate some of the problems associated with BARS. Like BARS, critical incidents underscore the development of these scales. The format consists of sets of three statements that describe high, medium, and low levels of performance for a specific performance dimension. These items have been scaled using a process similar to that employed in the development of the BARS scales. The behavioral examples for each dimension are arranged randomly on the rating sheet. Unlike BARS, in which scale values are known, no values are attached to the behavioral incidents. Instead, the rater makes one of three responses to each example. A score on each performance dimension is calculated on the basis of the pattern of the results. Once gathered, these ratings are then transcribed by the human resource department into numerical ratings, with more points given for "+" than for "0"or "-" respectively. The advantage of MSS format is that the rater is not dealing with numbers. Consequently, some of the most common errors associated with rating are overcome. Additionally, analysis of rater response patterns can identify raters whose use of the scales is haphazard. A drawback of MSS is that scale values are not known. Consequently, developmental information is lost. Still, once developed, MSSs are relatively easy to use.

Behavioural Observation Scales. A more recent development in behavioral scales is called the Behavioral Observation Scales (BOS). These scales are derived from critical incidents of job behavior. BOS scales differ, however, in that job experts are not asked what level of performance they illustrate. Instead, job experts are asked to indicate the frequency with which job incumbents engage in the behaviors. Scores are obtained for each behavior by assigning a numerical value to the frequency judgments. These scores can then be summed to get an overall rating. The advantages of BOS include :

(a) It is based on a systematic job analysis.

(b) Its items and behavior anchors are clearly stated.

(c) It allows participation of employees in the development of the dimensions, which facilitates understanding and acceptance.

(d) It is useful for performance feedback and improvement because specific goals can be tied to numerical scores on the relevant behavioral anchor for the relevant performance criterion or dimension.

(e) BOS appears to satisfy the uniform guidelines in terms of validity and reliability.

The limitations of BOS are the cost and time for its development. While the behavioral orientation of these scales appears, on the surface, to be a advantage, there is evidence that raters do not respond to these scales in terms of behaviors. Rather they use their overall, subjective evaluations to guide their behavior ratings. Thee is also evidence that most raters do not have sufficient time or ability to accurately assess the frequency with which behaviors are observed. The accuracy demanded for accurate BOS ratings may best be achieved through computer monitoring.

Comments on Absolute Standards Formats

The utilization of these formats is expected to increase for two reasons. First, the service sector of the economy is growing rapidly. Second, employee development is increasing in importance. Behavioral formats provide useful information for modifying the behavior of employees. On the other hand, absolute standards format are difficult and time-consuming to develop.

Output based Formats

Output Based Formats focus on job products as the primary criteria. These approaches to performance evaluation rely upon job analysis to identify critical job duties and tasks. Once duties are identified, the level of proficiency that an employee must attain is determined.

Management By Objectives (MBO) . Peter F. Drucker gave the concept of MBO in 1954. The MBO reflects a management philosophy which values and utilizes employee contributions. MBO is a widely used management system in both private and public sector settings. MBO is a method of appraisal that begins with the establishment of goals or objectives. After appropriate goals have been established for the upcoming performance period, the superior and subordinate need to delineate an appropriate strategy for goal attainment. Experienced and high-performing managers can develop their strategies on their own; the freedom to perform the job in the way they think best is reinforcing in and of itself. However, for less experienced or low-performing incumbents, the supervisor may need to intervene. Clearly, delineating how the goal is to be attained reduces ambiguity and makes goal attainment more likely. Strategy development includes outlining the steps necessary to attain the objective. Additionally, it is important to identify any constraints that may block the attainment of the objective. Finally, it is important to specify the responsibilities of the incumbent and those of the supervisor.

At the conclusion of the performance period, actually performance is evaluated relative to the agreed-on objectives. Here, it is important to develop an appropriate scoring algorithm. Because people do not synthesize multi dimensional data well, each objective should be scored separately. Scoring algorithms can be either simple (indicating whether the objective was or was not met) or complex (signaling how far above or below the objective actual performance was). After evaluation the superior and subordinates jointly explore the reasons goals were not attained or were exceeded. This step helps determine training needs and development potential. The final step is to decide a new goal and possible new strategies for goals not previously attained. At this point, subordinate and superior involvement in goal setting may change. Subordinates who successfully reach the established goals may be allowed to participate more in the goal setting process the next time.

Management must clearly be committed to the process if the MBO system is to be effective. Management should recognize that, MBO systems do not lead to immediate increases in productivity. On average, it takes about two years after implementation for MBO systems to work efficiently.

Finally, the objectives are only guidelines that facilitate two-way communication. They can and should be changed if the job changes or situation changes. In some organization, the superiors and subordinates work together to establish goals, in others, superiors establish goals for work groups or individuals, in still others, the goals are derived from time and motion studies. Goals can refer to desired outcomes to be achieved, means for achieving the outcomes or both.

MBO has its own set of criticisms. One comment made against the approach is that it is not applicable to all jobs in all organizations. Jobs with little or no flexibility , such as assembly – line work, are not compatible with MBO. The MBO process seems to be most useful with managerial personnel and employees who have a fairly wide range of flexibility and self-control in their jobs. Besides, when the results of an MBO system are to be used to allocate organizational rewards, employees may be less likely to establish challenging goals – goals they are confident that they can accomplish.

Psychological Appraisals . Large organizations employ full-time industrial psychologists. When psychologists are used for evaluations. They assess individuals' future potentials and not past performance. The appraisal normally consists of in-depth interviews, psychological tests, discussions with supervisor and a review of other evaluations. The psychologists' then write an evaluation of the employees' intellectual, motivational, emotional and other work related characteristics that suggest individual potential and may predict future performance. The evaluation by the psychologists' may be for a specific job opening for which the person is being considered, or it may be a global assessment of his future potential. From these evaluations, placement and development decisions may be made to shape the person's career. Because this approach is slow and costly, it is usually required for bright young members, who think may have considerable potential in the organization. Since the quality of the appraisal depends largely on the skills of the psychologists, some employees object to this type of evaluation, especially if cross-functional differences exist.

Performance Standards Approach. The Performance Standards Approach uses more direct measures of performance and is usually applied to non-managerial employees. Standards, like objectives, need to be specific, time-bound, conditional, prioritized and congruent with organizational objectives. Compared with objectives, there are generally more standards, and each is more detailed. This format specifies the average expected behavior as well as the level of performance that would be considered exceptional.

Direct Index Approach. The Direct Index Approach differs from other approaches primarily in how performance is measured. This approach measures performance by objective, impersonal criteria, such as productivity, absenteeism, and turnover. For example, a managers' performance may be evaluated by the number of manager's employees who quit or by the employees' absenteeism rate. For non-managers, measures of productivity may be more appropriate. These measures of productivity can be broken into measures of quality (scrap rates, customer complaints, parts produced) and measures of quantity (units of output per hour, new customer orders, sales volume etc.).

Human Asset Accounting Method . The Human Asset Accounting Method refers to activity devoted to attaching money estimates to the value of a firm's internal human organization and its external customers goodwill. If able, well-trained personnel leave a firm, the human organization is worthless, if they join it, its human assets are increased. If distrustful and conflict prevail, the human enterprise is devalued. If teamwork and high morale prevail, the human organization is a very valuable asset. The current value of a firm's human organization can be appraised by developed procedures, by undertaking periodic measurements of "key causal" and "intervening enterprise" variables. The key causal includes the structure of an organization's management policies, decision, business leadership, skills. Behavior etc. the intervening enterprise include internal stateand health of an organization i.e. loyalties, attitudes, motivations etc.

Assessment Centre Method. This concept was initially applied to military situations by Simoniet in the German Army in the 1930. The purpose of this method is to test candidates in a social situation, using a number of assessors and a variety of procedures. The most important feature of this method is job-related simulations. These simulations involve characteristics that managers feel are important to the job success. The evaluators observe and evaluate participants as they perform activities commonly found in these higher level jobs. Under this method, many evaluators join together to judge employee performance in several situations with the use of a variety of criteria. It is used mostly to help select employees for the first level supervisory positions. Assessments are made to determine employee potential for purposes of promotion. The assessment is usually done with the help of a couple of employees and involves a paper and pencil test, interviews and situational exercises.

Assessments centers are used for

- To measure potential for first level supervisors, sales and upper management positions and also for higher levels of management for development purposes.
- To determine individual training and development needs of employees
- To select recent college students for entry level positions
- To provide more accurate H.R. planning information
- To make an early determination of potential
- To assist in implementing affirmative action goals.

The assessment centers generally measure interpersonal skills and other aspects such as : organizing and planning, interpersonal competence, quality of thinking, resistance to stress, orientation to work etc. However, the problems with this method are : it is strongly influenced by the participants' interpersonal skills. Judges tend to evaluate the quality of the individual's social skills rather than the quality of the decisions themselves. Further, organizing and decision-making abilities are measured by in-basket exercises, verbal ability and personal traits. Another problem is that of exam-taking. Another drawback is the potential bad effects on those who are not selected to participate in the exercises. Thus, the relatively inexpensive paper and pencil tests for measuring potential may be as accurate as the high cost high stress assessment center.

To make assessment center programs successful, it is necessary that heavy emphasis must be placed on clear statement of goals, the obtaining of top management commitment, job analysis, assessor training and program audit and evaluation.

Comments on output based formats With the increased emphasis on performance enhancements, the use of output based appraisals continues to increase. The major advantage of these formats when done correctly is that they provide clear, unambiguous direction to employees regarding desired job outcomes. When exceptional performance is also specified these scales can motivate the average as well as exceptional performers. However, the disadvantage is that these formats require time, money and cooperation to develop. Second, essence of job performance may not be captured completely by output based criteria. Consequently important job behaviors may be ignored in the evaluation process. The production of desired products or outputs may also induce unintended competition among employees.

Balanced Scorecard

The Balanced scorecard is a conceptual framework for translating an organization's vision into a set of performance indicators distributed among four perspectives: Financial, Customer, Internal Business Processes, and Learning and

Growth. Balanced scorecard indicators are maintained to measure an organization's progress toward achieving its vision; other indicators are maintained to measure the long term drivers of success. Through the Balanced scorecard, an organization monitors both its current performance (finances, customer satisfaction, and business process results) and its efforts to improve processes, motivate and educate employees, and enhance information systems—its ability to learn and improve.

Balanced Scorecard Customer Satisfaction

This Balanced scorecard perspective captures the ability of the organization to provide quality goods and services, effective delivery, and overall customer satisfaction. For purposes of this model, both the recipient of goods and services (the internal customer) and the sponsor/overseer are regarded as customers of the business processes. In a governmental model the principal driver of performance is different than in the strictly commercial environment; namely, customers and stakeholders take preeminence over financial results. Recognizing that budgets are limiting factors, public organizations and the major contractors have a greater stewardship responsibility and focus than do private sector entities.

Balanced Scorecard Financial

In government, the "financial" Balanced scorecard perspective differs from that of the traditional private sector. Private sector financial objectives generally represent clear long-range targets for profit-seeking organizations, operating in a purely commercial environment. Financial considerations for public organizations have an enabling or a constraining role, but will rarely be the primary objective for business systems. Success for such organizations should be measured by how effectively and efficiently these organizations meet the needs of their constituencies. In government this perspective captures cost efficiency, delivering maximum value to the customer for each dollar spent.

Balanced scorecard Internal Business

This Balanced scorecard perspective provides data regarding the internal business results against measures that lead to financial success and satisfied customers. To meet the organizational objectives and customers expectations, organizations must identify the key business processes at which they must excel. Key processes are monitored to ensure that outcomes are satisfactory. Internal business processes are the mechanisms through which performance expectations are achieved.

Balanced scorecard Learning and Growth

This Balanced scorecard perspective captures the ability of employees, information systems, and organizational alignment to manage the business and adapt to change. Processes will only succeed if adequately skilled and motivated employees, supplied with accurate and timely information, are driving them. This perspective takes on increased importance in organizations that are undergoing radical change. In order to meet changing requirements and customer expectations, employees may be asked to take on dramatically new responsibilities, and may require skills, capabilities, technologies, and organizational designs that were not available before.

The Balanced Scorecard:

- Translates vision and strategy
- Defines the strategic linkages to integrate performance across organizations.
- Communicates objectives and measures to a business unit, joint venture, or shared service.
- Aligns strategic initiatives
- Aligns everyone within an organization so that all employees understand how what they do supports the strategy
- Provides a basis for compensation
- Provides feedback to senior management if the strategy is working

The Balanced Scorecard thus, is part of a Performance Management system to enable organizations to achieve their goals.

Balanced Scorecard Benefits

Balanced Scorecard benefits according to Kaplan and Norton, 1992:

- Make strategy operational by translating strategy into performance measures and targets.
- Helps focus entire organization on what must be done to create breakthrough performance.
- Integrates and acts as an umbrella for a variety of often disconnected corporate programs, such as quality, re-engineering, process redesign, and customer service.
- Breaks down corporate level measures so local managers, operators, and employees can see what they must do well in order to improve organizational effectiveness.

People Capability Maturity Model

The motivation for the P-CMM is to radically improve the ability of software organizations to attract, develop, motivate, organize, and retain the talent needed to steadily improve software development capability.

The strategic objectives pursued in the P-CMM are to

- Improve the capability of software organizations by increasing the capability of their staff,
- Ensure that software development capability is an attribute of the organization rather than of a few individuals,
- Align the motivation of the staff with those of the organization, and
- Retain assets (i.e., people with extensive skills and capabilities) within the organization.

THE P-CMM INCLUDES PRACTICES IN THE AREAS OF

- Staffing (includes recruiting, selection and planning)
- Managing performance
- Training
- Compensation
- Work environment
- Career development
- Organizational and individual competence
- Mentoring and coaching
- Team and culture development

Need For PCMM

In order to improve their performance, organizations must focus on three interrelated components-people, process, and technology. With the help of the Capability Maturity Model for Software many software organizations have made cost-effective, lasting improvements in their software processes and practices [Herbsleb94]. Yet many of these organizations have discovered that their continued improvement requires significant changes in the way they manage, develop, and use their people for developing and maintaining software and information systems-changes that are not fully accounted for in the CMM. To date, improvement programs for software organizations have often emphasize process or technology, not people.

The P-CMM is a maturity framework, patterned after the structure of the CMM that focuses on continuously improving the management and development of the human assets of a software or information systems organization. The P-CMM provides guidance on how to continuously improve the ability of software organizations to attract, develop, motivate, organize, and retain the talent needed to steadily improve their software development capability. The strategic objectives of the P-CMM are to improve the capability of software organizations by increasing the capability of their workforce

- Ensure that software development capability is an attribute of the organization rather than of a few individuals the motivation of individuals with that of the organization
- Retain human assets (i.e., people with critical knowledge and skills) within the organization

Factors Deterring Objective Evaluation

The ideal approach to performance evaluation is that in which the evaluator is free from personal biases, prejudices, and idiosyncrasies. This is because when an evaluation is objective, it minimizes the potential capricious and dysfunctional behavior of the evaluator which may be detrimental to the achievement of the organizational goals. However, a single foolproof evaluation method is not available. Inequities in evaluation often destroy the usefulness of the performance system – resulting in inaccurate, invalid appraisals.

There are many significant factors which deter objective evaluation. These factors are

(A) Ratee Characteristics. Ratee Characteristics directly influence performance ratings particularly when performance criteria are not precise. The gender of the rate and the "gender" of the job interact, hence males receive a higher ratings as compared to females. Due to perceptual congruence, ratees tend to receive higher ratings from same-race raters. Also, managers often associate job tenure with job competency. As a result they tend to give higher ratings to senior employees.

(B) Rater Characteristics . Characteristics of the rater exert a more subtle and indirect influence on performance judgments. Limited data suggest that female raters are more lenient than male raters. When performance standards are used, female raters also tend to give more extreme ratings to high and low performers than do male raters. Younger and less experienced raters and raters who have received low evaluations themselves rate more strictly than older, more experienced, and or high- performing raters do. The personality of the rater may also affect judgment accuracy.

Finally, the quality and not quantity of interaction between a rater and a rate affects ratings positively.

(C) Halo Errors. The Halo error is a tendency to let the assessment of an individual's one trait influence the evaluation of that person on other specific traits. There is this effect in appraisal when the appraiser assigns the same rating to all traits regardless of an employee's actual performance on these traits. The halo effect refers to the tendency to rate an individual consistently high or low or average on the various traits, depending upon whether the rater's overall impression of the individual is favorable or not. This means that the halo effect allows one characteristic, observation or occurrence to influence the rating of all performance factors. The halo effect arises when traits are unfamiliar, ill-defined and involve personal relations. This often occurs when an employee tends to be more conscientious and dependable, that the appraiser might become biased toward that individual to the extent that the appraiser rates him high on many desirable attributes : or when the employee is more friendly or unfriendly toward the appraiser. In such cases, a very high rate may be given to a favored employee, whereas a low rating may be given to an unfriendly employee so that he may be bypassed even though he is a very capable one, when the question of a promotion arises. The halo effect problem can be alleviated by : (1) providing a five to ten minutes training program to the evaluators (2) restructuring the questions by requiring the evaluator to consider each question independently and (3) having the evaluator appraise all rates on each dimension before going to the next dimension.

The opposite of a halo error is a "horn error", when negative performance on one dimension supercedes any positive performance.

(D) Leniency and Severity. Some raters consistently give ratees evaluations that are better or worse than the ratees' actual job performance warrants. These tendencies are known as "leniency" and "severity errors" respectively (Sall, Downey, and Lahey, 1980). Although raters are not always aware of these biases, some of the reasons for their existence are not hard to understand.

A rater may exaggerate the quality of ratees' performance because of :

- a desire to be liked
- a desire to avoid hostility on the part of ratees, particularly during any subsequent performance-feedback sessions.
- A fear that other raters will exaggerate the performance of their raters, who will then have an unfair advantage when promotions or pay raises become available
- A perception that it will reflect positively on the rater's own capabilities
- Abnormally low standards of excellence

On the other hand, a rater may consistently underestimate the quality of others' performance for a variety of reasons, including :

- A perception that employees who receive high ratings may eventually compete for the rater's job.
- A wish to 'motivate' employees by giving them "room for improvement"
- Unusually high, and perhaps unreasonable, standards of excellence.

Whatever the dynamics that underlie leniency or severity errors, the implications for the purposes of performance appraisal are unfortunate. If all or most ratees are rated high or low, that restriction in the range of ratings makes it very difficult for anyone who must discriminate among employees for the purposes of promotion, training, or pay raises. And, because lenient or severe ratings are , by definition, higher or lower than they should be, any subsequent performance feedback based on those ratings will be inaccurate. Overly lenient feedback may result in complacent ratees, whereas overly severe feedback can be extremely discouraging.

(E) Central Tendency. This is another instance where the rater restricts the range of assigned ratings. Instead of uniformly rating people too high or too low, however, the rater in this case rates all or most of the ratees somewhere "in the middle" of the rating scale or "above average". Sometimes raters are unwilling to "stick their neck out" and commit themselves to very high or very low ratings because they haven't been able to carefully observe ratees' job performance. This may be due to either to the rater's own inadequacies (poor observation skills , not much time at his disposal) or to the nature of the ratees' jobs. Such tendencies seriously distorts the evaluations making them most useless for promotion, salary or counseling. Regardless of the causes, central tendency errors undermine a performance appraisal system in the same way that lenient or severity errors do.

(F) Reliability. Although not a rating error in the same sense as severity or halo, lack of reliability can also undermine the quality and usefulness of rating data. Reliability refers to the consistence with which something is measured. Reliability of ratings is typically assessed by asking two or more individuals who are familiar with a given worker's performance to provide independent ratings of that performance. To the extent that these raters tend to agree with each other, we can have more confidence in the reliability of those ratings. This is usually referred to as inter-rater reliability . if the raters do not agree in their assessments of a given ratee's or more commonly, a given group of ratee's performance, then those ratings lack reliability.

(G) Perceptual Set . This occurs when the rater's assessment is influenced by previously held beliefs. If the supervisor, for example, has a belief that employees hailing from one particular region are intelligent and hard working, his subsequent rating of an employee hailing from that region tends to be favorably high.

(H) Performance Dimension Order. Two or more dimensions on a performance instrument follow or closely follow each other and both describe or rotate to a similar quality. The rater rates the first dimension accurately and then rates the second dimension similar to the first because of their proximity. If the dimensions had not been arranged in a significantly different order, the ratings might have been different.

(I) Spillover Effect. This refers to allowing past performance appraisal ratings to unjustifiably influence current ratings. Past records, good or bad, result in similar rating for the current period although the demonstrated behavior does not deserve the rating, good or bad.

(J) Status Effect. It refers to over-rating of employees in higher-level jobs or jobs held in high esteem, and underrating employees in lower-job or jobs held in low esteem.

(K) Similarity Error. This type of error occurs when the evaluator rates other people in the same way he perceives himself. For example, the evaluator who perceives himself as aggressive may evaluate others by looking for aggressiveness. Those who show this characteristic may be benefited while others may suffer. This error also washes out if the same evaluator appraises all the people in the organization.

(L) Miscellaneous Biases. Bias against employees on grounds of sex, race, religion or position is also common error in rating. For example, a higher rating may be assigned to a senior employee. The rater may also be influenced by organizational influence and give higher ratings to those holding higher positions. Besides these, there may be opportunity bias, group characteristics bias and knowledge-of-predictor bias. Beach observes that "supervisors will rate their people near the middle of the spectrum if their bosses put pressure on them to correct the sub-par performers and if they are called upon to really justify an outstanding rating.

(M) Social Differentiation. Rating is sometimes impeded by the evaluator's style of rating behavior. Pigou has classified raters as "high differentiators"– i.e. using all or most of the scale or "low differentiators" – i.e. using a limited range of the scale. They tend to suppress or ignore differences, perceiving the universe as more uniform than it really is while high differentiator tend to utilize all available information to the utmost and thus, are better able to perceptually deny anomalies and contradictions.

(N) Personal Bias. The most important error of all arises when supervisors carry out objective judgments entirely independent of their values, prejudices and stereotypes. All kinds of inappropriate criteria and standards may be introduced into the evaluation process, with the result that, on occasion, ratings relate not so much to company goals as to the personal goals of a particular manager. Thus, evaluations can be influenced by factors like manner of dress, social standing, attractiveness etc. Biases of this kind can operate without the rater being aware of what is happening or the biases may be conscious and intentional.

(O) Primacy and Recency Effects. The typical appraisal period is far too long for any rater to adequately retain in memory all performance relevant information. As a cognitive shortcut, raters may fall prey to primacy and recency effects. Raters may use initial information to categorize a rate as either good or bad performer. Subsequently, information that supports the initial judgment is amassed and un-confirming information is ignored. Because special attention is given to information initially collected, this bias is called as primacy bias. Conversely, a rater may not pay attention to employee performance throughout the appraisal period. As the appraisal interviews draws near, the rater searches for information cues about the value of performance. Unfortunately only recent behavior or outputs are salient. Thus, recent events are weighed more heavily than they should be. This is called recency error.

(P) Contrast Error. If criteria are not clear or if ranking systems are not used, contrast effects will occur. When compared to weak employees, an average employee would appear outstanding, when evaluated against outstanding performer , will be perceived as low performer. The solution is to have specific performance criteria established prior to the evaluation period.

(Q) Escalation of Commitment. This costly error occurs when managers are unable to cut their losses. Research indicates that if one has made the initial hiring decisions, then he is likely to escalate his commitment and invest in the person a bit longer. One may even go as far as to provide the individual with additional training so that she can succeed. On the other hand, if one did not make the initial decision, and there are no investments, then one is more likely to immediately recommend termination.

(R) Anchoring and Adjustment Bias. When ratings are used for performance or pay decision, they should be based on current performance. Unfortunately, prior performance information often anchors judgments about current performance and adjustments away from that value will be insufficient. The tendency to use prior information inappropriately to make current judgments is referred to as anchoring and adjustment bias. This bias can be controlled by limiting access to prior rating information and having clear, concise performance standards and data available to judge performance.

Communicating Appraisal Results To Employees

The most important use of performance-evaluation data is to provide feedback to the employees and assess his strengths and weaknesses so that further training can be implemented. Although this training and feedback should be an ongoing process, the semiannual evaluation might be the best time to formally discuss employee performance.

Normally, in most organizations a supervisor gives feedback to employees every 6 months to tell them about the scores they received during the most recent evaluation period. Furthermore, seldom does evaluating employees benefit the supervisor. There seems to be at least three reasons. First, managers are often uncomfortable discussing performance weaknesses directly with employees. Given that almost every employee could stand to improve in some areas, managers fear a confrontation when presenting negative feedback. Second many employees tend to become defensive when their weaknesses are pointed out. Instead of accepting the feedback as constructive and a basis fir improving performance, some employees challenge the evaluation by criticizing the manager or redirecting blame to someone else. Finally, employees tend to have an inflated assessment of their own performance.

The solution to the performance feedback problem is

not to ignore it, but to train managers in how to conduct constructive feedback sessions. In addition, the performance review should be designed more as a counseling activity than a judgment process. This can best be accomplished by allowing the review to evolve out of the employee's own self-evaluations.

Research suggests that certain techniques can be used to make the performance appraisal interview more effective: time, scheduling and preparation.

Before the interview

Allocating Time Both the supervisor and the employee must have time to prepare for the review interview. Both should be allowed at least 1 hour to prepare before an interview and at least 1 hour for the interview itself.

Scheduling the interview The interview location should be in a neutral place that ensures privacy and allows the supervisor and employee to face one another without a desk between them as a communication barrier. Performance appraisal reviews should be scheduled at least once every 6 months.

Preparing for the interview While preparing for the interview, the supervisor should review the ratings she has assigned to the employee and the reasons for those ratings. This step is important because the quality of feedback given to employees will affect their satisfaction with the entire performance appraisal process. Furthermore, employees perceive and react to the amount of time that a supervisor prepares for the interview.

Meanwhile, the employee should rate her own performance, using the same format as the supervisor. The employee also must write down specific reasons and examples that support the ratings she gives herself.

During the interview

At the outset of the interview, the supervisor should communicate the following :

(1) The role of performance appraisal- that making decisions about salary increase and terminations

is not its only purpose.

(2) How the performance appraisal was conducted

(3) How the evaluation process was accomplished.

It is also advisable that the supervisor communicates his feelings about the performance appraisal process. The review process is probably best begun with the employee communicating her own ratings and her justifications for those ratings. Research indicates that employees who are actively involved in the interview from the start will be more satisfied with the results.

The supervisor then communicates her rating and the reasons for them. The supervisor should limit this communication to statements about behavior and performance rather than traits that are or are not possessed by the employee. It is always nice to communicate positive feedback because employees are more satisfied with their reviews and often develop negative attitudes towards management if feedback is negative. Thus positive feedback should be given first because employees are likely to avoid negative feedback in order to maintain their self-image.

Next, because few employees receive perfect evaluations, it is essential to discuss the reasons why an employee's performance is not considered to be perfect. The employee may lack some knowledge as to how to perform the job properly, may have been assigned too many duties etc.

The supervisor's acknowledgement that there may be external reasons for an employee's poor performance can increase the employees' satisfaction with the review and allow her to perceive the feedback and evaluation as accurate and helpful. In addition, it will also help the employee understand and appreciate the supervisor's perceptions. Feedback should be candid, specific and behavioral rather than personal. Awareness and acknowledgement of external factors for performance are especially important because we have a tendency called "the fundamental attribution error", to others' failure or poor performance to rather than situational factors.

Once the problems are identified, the next step is to find the solutions to those problems. The idea here is that solutions to the problems results from joint-efforts. At the conclusion of the interview, goals should be mutually set for future performance and behavior, and both supervisor and employee should understand how these goals are met.

Secrets of Effective Performance Feedback Interviews

(1) Communicate Frequently Research on the appraisal interview clearly indicates that once-a-year performance appraisals are of questionable value and that coaching should be an everyday activity-particularly with poor or new employees. Feedback has maximum impact when it is given as close as possible to the action.

(2) Get Training in Performance Feedback and Appraising Interview Training allows raters to observe behavior more accurately and fairly. Rater training should focus on managerial characteristics that are difficult to rate and on characteristics that people think are easy to rate but which generally result in disagreements. Such factors include risk taking and development of subordinates.

(3) Encourage Subordinates to Prepare Research indicates that subordinates who spend more time prior to performance feedback interviews analyzing their job responsibilities and duties, problems they encounter on the job, and the quality of their performance are more likely to be satisfied with the performance management process.

(4) Encourage Participation A perception of ownership- a feeling by the subordinate that his or her ideas are genuinely welcomed by the manager-is related strongly to subordinates' satisfaction with the appraisal interview. Participation encourages the belief that the interview was a constructive activity, that some current job problems were cleared up and that future goals were set.

(5) Judge Performance, Not Personality In addition to the potential legal liability of dwelling on personality rather than on job performance, supervisors are far less likely to change a subordinates' personality that they are his performance.

(6) Be Specific , and Be an Active Listener By being candid and specific, the supervisor offers clear feedback to the subordinate concerning past actions. She should demonstrate knowledge of the subordinates' level of performance and job duties. By being an active listener, the supervisor demonstrates genuine interest in the subordinates' ideas. Active listening requires (1) take time to listen – hold all phone calls and do not allow interruptions. (2) communicate verbally and non verbally. (3) as the subordinate begins to tell his side of the story, interruption or any sort of argument should be avoided. (4) summarizing what was said and what was agreed to is very important.

(7) Set Mutually Agreeable Goals Goals direct attention to the specific performance in question. They mobilize effort to accomplish higher level of performance and they foster persistence for higher levels of performance. By setting specific, challenging goals with the subordinate, he precisely knows what is expected of him which in turn leads to higher performance.

(8) Continue to Communicate, and Assess Progress Towards Goals Regularly. Periodic tracking of progress towards goals has three advantages : (1) it helps keep behavior on target (2) it provides a better understanding of the reasons behind a given level of performance and (3) it enhances the subordinates' commitment to perform effectively.

(9) Make Organizational Rewards Contingent on Performance. If subordinates' see a link between appraisal results and employment decisions regarding issues like merit pay and promotion, they are more likely to prepare for performance feedback interviews, to participate actively in them and to be satisfied with the overall performance management.

Summary

Performance appraisal is not a single act or a particular form to evaluate job behavior. Rather, it is a system that evolves overtime. A performance appraisal system is premised on the beliefs that individuals will vary in performance over time and that individuals can exert some influence over their performance. Thus, an effective performance appraisal system must generally serve two purposes : (1) an evaluative role to let people know where they stand and (2) a developmental role to provide specific information and direction so that individuals can change or improve their performance. Performance appraisal is therefore, linked to other important human resource activities such as compensation, promotion decisions, human resource planning, development and training, and validation of selection systems for legal compliance. Increasingly, it is also linked to the strategy and plans of the business.

Because performance appraisal is linked to so many other H.R. Activities, it is important to understand why performance appraisal data are gathered, as well as how this information is used. Legal considerations have also heightened the need for organizations to review this process. Special emphasis is placed on the need for job analysis as a means of developing job-related performance criteria. In general the more subjective the performance appraisal approach, the more vulnerable the performance appraisal system to legal challenge. Although various approaches to performance appraisal exists, they can be classified into three broad based categories : norm – based, absolute standards and output based. The choice of the best approach is really a function of several criteria : the purpose of the performance appraisal system, the costs of developing and implementing of the system, the degree to which rater errors are minimized etc.

A number of obstacles can contribute to rater resistance to a performance appraisal system : raters may not have the opportunity to observe subordinates performance, raters may not have performance standards, raters as human judges are prone to errors, and raters may view performance appraisal as a conflict-producing activities and therefore avoid it. For these reasons and others, it is important to examine why and how performance appraisal data are gathered.

REFERENCES

1. Aswathappa, K. (1980). *Human Resource and Personnel Management.* (4th edition). Himalaya Publications, Bombay. 485-557.
2. Bernardian, J.H. and Jyoce, E. A. (1993). *Human Resource Management : An Experimental Approach.* (2nd Edition). McGraw Hill Publications. New York. 393-410.
3. Blazer, W. K and Sulsky . L.M. (1992). *Halo and Performance Appraisal Research : A critical Examination. Journal of Applied Psychology.* Prentice Hall Publications., New Jersey. 77, 975-985.
4. Bratton, J. and Gold, J. (1994). *Human Resource Management : Theory and Practice.* (1st Edition). Macmillan Press Ltd. London. 169- 180.
5. Casio, W. F. (1998). *Applied Psychology in Human Resource Management.* (5th Edition). Upper Saddle River, New Jersey. Prentice Hall Publications.
6. Cowling, A. and Mailer, C. (1990). *Managing Human Resources.* (3rd Edition). Arnold Publishers. Great Britain. 197-205.
7. Das Gupta ,A. (1974). *Personnel Management and Human Resource Management.* (2nd edition). Vikas Publications, New Delhi. 112-140.
8. Edwin, B.F. (1975). *Personnel Management.* (1st edition). Collier Macmillan Publishing Co., New York. 567-634.
9. Henderson , R. I. (1984). *Performance Appraisal.* (4th Edition). Prentice Hall Publications. 134-400.
10. Mamoria, C.B. (1980). *Personnel Management.* (2nd edition). Personnel Management. (2nd Edition). Himalaya Publishing, Bombay. 403-448.
11. Miner, J.B. (1992). *Industrial Organizational Psychology.* (International Edition). McGraw Hill Inc. New York, London, New Delhi, Tokyo. 377-408.
12. Muchinsky, P.M. (2000). *Psychology : Applied To Work.* (6th Edition). Wardsworth Publications.

Thomas Learning. 205-223.

13. Murphy, K. R. and Cleveland, J.N. (1991). *Performance Appraisal : An organizational Perspective.* Boston : Allyn and Bacon. 811-826.
14. Myland, L. (1992). *Managing Performance Appraisal.* (1st Edition). Croner Publication Limited, London. 1-30.
15. Robbins, S.P. (2004). *Organizational Behavior.* (10th Edition). Pearson Education. 498-508.
16. Saal, E. F. and Knight. P.A. (1987). *Industrial and Organizational Psychology : Science and Practice.* (1st Edition). Brooks and Cole Publication Company, California. 98-130.
17. Schular, R.S. and Huber, V.L. (1993). *Personnel and Human Resource Management.* (2nd Edition). West Publication Company, New York, Los Angeles, San Francisco. 280-315.
18. Sikula, A.F. and McKenna, J.F. (1984). *The Management of Human Resource.* (1st Edition). Joh Wilay and Sons. New York, Brisbane, Toronto. 250-270.

8

Developing the Human Resource

1. **Training and Development**
- *Define*
- *Purpose*
- *Benefits*
- *The Strategic value of training & development*
- *The Pre Training Environment*
- *The Training Cycle*
2. **Conducting a Training Needs Assessment**
- *Purpose*
- *Organizational Analysis*
- *Task Analysis*
- *Individual/Person Analysis*
3. **Designing Training and Development Program**
4. **Techniques/Methods of Training and Development**
- *On-the-Job Technique*
- *Off-the-Job Technique*
5. **Training the Trainers**
6. **Evaluation of the Training Program**
- *Need for Evaluation*
- *Principles of Evaluation*
- *Importance of Evaluation*
- *Models of Evaluation*
- *Current Trends in Training Evaluation*
7. **Post Training Environment**
8. **Conclusion & Suggestions**
9. **References**

Training and Development

Management development is an attempt at improving an individual's managerial effectiveness through a planned and deliberate process of Learning. All development is Self-Development. It must be generated within the man itself. Development is highly individual. The development of the individual is due to his day-to-day experience on the job. Hence, emphasis should be on experiences from day-to-day work. Any activity designed to improve the performance of existing managers and to provide for a planned growth of managers to meet future organizational needs is Management Development.

Training is the most important activity and plays an important role in the development of human resources. To put the right man at the right place with the trained personnel has now become essential in today's globalized market. No organization has a choice on whether or not to develop employees. Therefore training has nowadays become an important and required factor for maintaining and improving interpersonal and inter-group collaboration.

Human resources are the lifeblood of any organization. Only through well-trained personnel, can an organization achieve its goals. There are many ways to define training:

- Training is defined as "the systematic acquisition of attitudes, concepts, knowledge, roles, or skills that result in improved performance at work." - **Goldstein (1991)**
- It is teaching specific skills in a structured way.
- It is a short-term process utilizing a systematic and organized procedure by which non-managerial personnel learns technical knowledge and skills for a definite purpose.
- Training facilitates the implementation of strategy by providing employees with the capability to perform their jobs in the manner dictated by the strategy.
- Training is often defined as the activity when an expert and learner work together to effectively transfer information from the expert to the learner (to enhance a learner's knowledge, attitudes or skills) so that the learner can better perform a current task or job.

To sum it up, Training is a process of enhancing employee skills. Training and Development are two words that often go hand-in-hand. Development is often viewed as a broad, ongoing multi-faceted set of activities (training activities among them) to bring someone or an organization up to another threshold of performance. This development often includes a wide variety of methods, e.g., orienting about a role, training in a wide variety of areas, ongoing training on the job, coaching, mentoring and forms of self-development. Some view development as a life-long goal and experience. It is a process of learning continuously to help one grow within the organization. Typically, learning is viewed as enhancing one's knowledge, understanding or skills. Some professionals view learning as enhancing one's capacity to perform. It's important to note that learning is more than collecting information - knowledge is converted to skills, that is, the learner knows how to apply the knowledge to get something done. Ideally, the skills are applied to the most appropriate tasks and practices in the organization, thereby producing performance- results needed by the organization.

Purpose for Employee Training and Development

- Creating a pool of readily available and adequate replacements for personnel who may leave or move up in the organization.
- Enhancing the company's ability to adopt and use advances in technology because of a sufficiently knowledgeable staff.
- Building a more efficient, effective and highly motivated team, which enhances the company's comp etitive position and improves employee morale.
- Ensuring adequate human resources for expansion into new programs.
- To "benchmark" the status of improvement so far in a performance improvement effort.
- As a part of succession planning to help an employee be eligible for a planned change in role in the organization.

General Benefits from Employee Training and Development

- Increased job satisfaction and morale among employees
- Increased employee motivation
- Increased efficiencies in processes, resulting in financial gain
- Increased capacity to adopt new technologies and methods
- Increased innovation in strategies and products
- Reduced employee turnover
- Enhanced company image, e.g., conducting ethics training
- Risk management, e.g., training about sexual harassment, diversity training
- Increased productivity.
- Decreased need for supervision.

Employees frequently develop a greater sense of self-worth, dignity and well being as they become more valuable to the firm and to society. Generally they will receive a greater share of the material gains that result from their increased productivity. These factors give them a sense of satisfaction through the achievement of personal and company goals.

The Strategic Value of Training and Development

Organizations do not train their employees for the sheer sake of doing so. The competitive strategy an organization uses is the means by which it competes for business for business in the marketplace. There is a linkage between the type of competitive strategy an organization uses and its training and development practices. (Jackson & Schuler, 1990).

- *Speed Strategy:* is designed to offer the customer a competitive value in terms of reduced time for products or services.
- *Innovation Strategy:* is used to develop products

or services that differ from the competition. Its primary business objective is to offer something new and different. The focus of training in this context is to develop new products, services and technologies.

- *Quality-Enhancement Strategy:* is designed to provide value by offering a product or service of higher quality than that offered by competitors.
- *Cost-reduction Strategy:* is to gain a competitive advantage by a low-cost provider of services.

In reality most organizations adopt a mix of competitive business strategy. Accordingly, training and development activities are directed to meeting multiple objectives.

The Pre-Training Environment

Tannenbaum and Yukl (1992) reviewed evidence suggesting that events that take place prior to training can influence the effectiveness of training. Management actions and decisions provide cues that signal employee motivation for training. Employees start to learn about the way training is viewed in the organization early in the socialization process. Cohen found that employees with more supportive supervisors entered training with a stronger belief that training will be useful. Supportive supervisors discuss an upcoming training program with the employees, establish training goals, provide them release time to prepare and generally encourage the employees.

Another factor that finds importance in pre-training is trainee input and choice in training. Allowing trainees to specify what training they wanted increased their motivation to learn provided they were given the training of their choice. However, trainees who are allowed to choose and then assigned another course are less motivated to learn from the program. Similarly Quinones (1995) concluded that one way employee motivation in training can be enhanced is by giving individuals the chance to choose their own training programs and ensuring that these preferences are honored. Factors that strengthen the linkage between training and relevant outcomes can be as critical as training itself.

The Training Cycle

Training is seen as pivotal in implementing organization-wide culture-change efforts, such as developing a commitment to customer service, adopting total quality management or making a transition to self-directed work teams. Because the objective of HRD is to contribute to the organization's overall goals, training programs should be developed systematically and with the organization's true needs in mind. Hence it is important to develop an Instructional Systems Design model as follows:

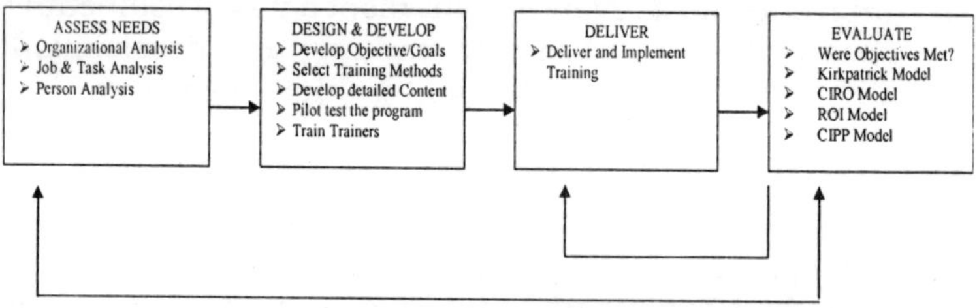

Modify and Improve Program

The model shows four phases of the Training cycle:

1. Needs assessment.
2. Design and Development.
3. Delivery of training.
4. Evaluation of training.

If each step is carefully implemented, effective and relevant training is likely to be the results.

Conducting a Training Needs Assessment

Successful training begins with a thorough Needs Assessment to determine which employees need to be trained and what they need to be trained to do. A need is not a want or desire. It is a gap between "what is" and "what ought to be". The need assessment serves to identify the gaps, and considers if training can solve the problem. The assessment is part of a planning process focusing on identifying and solving performance problems. Allison Rossett and Joseph Arwady state: "The question is not whether you will solicit this kind of information through needs assessment. It's how much of it you will do and using which kind of tools." The culmination of the assessment phase is a set of objectives specifying the purpose of the training and the competencies required in trainees after they complete the program. Conducting an assessment is a way to collect information that can be used to decide what type of development will be perceived as useful and relevant.

Purpose of Needs Assessment

- To determine what training is relevant to your employees' jobs.
- To determine what training will improve performance.
- To determine if training will make a difference.
- To distinguish training needs from organizational problems, and
- To link improved job performance with the organization's goals and bottom line.

The terms *need assessment* and *need analysis* are interchangeable, but they have the same meaning and purpose, to assess and analyze. The primary purpose of the training needs assessment - analysis process is to ensure that there is a need for training and to identify the nature of the content of the training program. Conducting an assessment is a way to collect information that can be used to decide what type of development will be perceived as relevant and useful. An assessment enables a conversation to take place that questions what skills and knowledge is required to be more effective. Efforts to improve one part of the organizational system will affect other jobs in the workplace environment. The needs assessment process is an important first step in the development of a training program or performance improvement initiatives.

A needs assessment provides an opportunity to consult with a variety of people in the organization. The information collected, ideas generated, and the conversations that take place when people discuss their work lives lend enthusiasm to the process. The data collected - whether obtained through interviews, observations, focus groups, performance data, questionnaires or tests - can clarify issues and provide a focus on performance.

The assessment of training needs consists of a classic three-step process: Organizational Analysis; Task Analysis; Person Analysis.

Organizational Analysis

In the evolution of thinking on training and development, the early focus of organizational analysis was on factors that provided information about where and when training could be used in an organization. More contemporary thinking has transformed organizational analysis into an examination of system wide components that determine whether the training program can produce behaviour that will transfer to the organization. Goldstein (1991) observed that persons who participate in training are faced with a problem: they are required to learn something in one environment, the training situation and to use it in another i.e. on the job. Corporate culture compatibility is especially important for management training and executive development. Efforts to train managers to lead, make decisions, or communicate in ways that are not valued or expected by powerful others in the work environment are doomed to failure.

Rouillier and Goldstein proposed the concept of an organizational transfer climate to explain why training can differ in its effectiveness. They determined that trainees demonstrated more transfer of skills from training to the job in organizational units where they were encouraged to use what they had learned and were rewarded for doing so.

The impact that the training of one unit has on other related units must also be considered in an organizational analysis. For instance, if the accounting group is trained to produce different measures of financial performance, then the other groups that either provide input or use the reports produced by the accounting groups may also need some orientation.

If training needs to be provided to a large number of employees across the organization, the organizational analysis may ask which unit may receive the training first. One may decide to begin with units known to be especially receptive to training in order to develop a record of success and a positive image about the training program. When a cultural or value change is the aim of the program it is usually a good idea to train from top down, so that individuals who have already learned about and accepted the change manage each group of trainees.

The organization's future plans must also be considered. Finally, the availability of trainers, facilities, and financial resources and the priorities of competing training programs must be considered as part of the organizational analysis.

In summary, organizational analysis examines system wide factors that facilitate the transfer of skills from training to the job. Whatever factors facilitate development of new skills in training should also be present on the job to facilitate maintenance of those skills.

Task Analysis

A task/job analysis typically produces a job description and the context in which the work activities are performed. The duties and responsibilities of the job, together with the knowledge, skills and abilities needed to perform them, are the focus of the second stage of needs analysis. A Task Analysis is used to determine the training objectives that are related to the performance of particular activities and job operations. The task analysis results in a statement of activities or work operations performed on the job and the conditions under which the job is performed.

Task analysis is used to provide realistic information about what jobs will be like. This information helps reduce applicants' unrealistically high expectations about the jobs and reduce employee dissatisfaction and turnover. It also helps in developing training programs and performance appraisal systems. Task analysis procedures have been used to design jobs for maximum efficiency. The effectiveness of the Japanese industries has often been attributed to task analysis.

Task Analysis Involves the Following Four Steps

(a) Development of Task Statements. The first step is to completely specify the tasks performed on the job i.e. a written narrative of the activities performed on the job as well as information of the equipments used and the working conditions and environment in which the job is performed. Creating task inventories can help pinpoint specific tasks performed on the job. The goal is to write a sentence that conveys what the worker does, how the worker does it, whom or what and why the worker does it. It would not be unusual to have as many as 100 tasks statements written to describe the tasks performed on the job. The more varied the job, the greater the number of task statements.

(b) Development of Task Clusters. In this step task statements are grouped into homogeneous clusters to make them more usable and manageable. Subject matter experts (SMEs) are responsible for sorting the task statements into meaningful categories that reflect important dimensions of work. For example, for the job of a secretary one cluster might pertain to tasks involving maintenance of records.

(c) Knowledge, Skill, and Ability Analysis. A useful way for specifying the human capabilities needed to perform tasks is through knowledge, skills, and abilities (KSA's). Knowledge (K) refer to a body of information, that, if applied makes adequate job performance possible. Skill (S) refers to the capability to perform job operations with ease and precision and typically refers to psychomotor abilities. Ability (A) refers to cognitive capabilities necessary to perform a job function. The purpose of this analysis is to establish KSA's needed to perform particular tasks. Most often, persons who directly supervise the job being analyzed serve as SMEs to provide this information because they often think about what a job incumbent needs to know or what skills and abilities the incumbent needs in order to perform the tasks.

(d) Development of Training Programs from the KSA-Task Links. The linkage between the KSAs and tasks provides the basis for directing training to enhance those KSAs that are critical to job performance. While the relevance of the training for KSA enhancement is established through the linkage, it may actually be quite difficult to disentangle what may be K, S or A. one can generally train people to acquire new knowledge, but it is more difficult to train them in the ability to use that knowledge wisely.

- **Individual/Person Analysis**

The final level of analysis looks at the individuals' to be trained. The individual analysis attempts to determine which employees should receive training and what their current levels of skill and knowledge are. The trainer mat single out individuals on the basis of their past performance or select an entire work group or all incumbents with a specified job title. Then the trainer assesses, or at least estimates, the skill and knowledge levels of the chosen trainees so that the training is neither too simple nor too complex.

Attention must focus on prerequisite basic skills as well as on existing job related skills and knowledge. For instance, Hewlett-Packard Company conducted a training program on statistical quality control for a number of employees. Later the company found that the employees were unable to use the techniques that they were taught. Careful investigation revealed that many of the employees were unable to do basic mathematics and were too embarrassed to reveal it. To resolve this problem the company offered a remedial program in basic math to 500 the employees. If a better individual analysis had been conducted before the quality control program was initiated, the trainer could have included basic math at the start of the course and the employees could have been better prepared to benefit from the program.

In summary, Ostroff and Ford (1989) concluded that the classic tripartite approach of needs analysis is entrenched in the literature as the basis upon which all subsequent training issues are based. While we still regard these three perspectives as a useful framework for determining training needs, the specific content of each continues to evolve over time. The most recent advances in training have demonstrated the critical importance of cues and consequences that promote the transfer of skills from training to the job.

Designing Training and Development Program

Earl (1987) defines design as: "The plan, structure and strategy of instructions used, conceived so as to produce learning experiences that lead to pre- specified learning goals". The preparation of precise behavioral objectives is considered to be very important. This stage is also concerned with the administrative aspects of the training program like when to hold the training program, where to hold it-in the organization premises or outside, whether to have an internal trainer or an external trainer. The advantage of an internal trainer is that he is familiar to the people and also he can see things from the organization perspective. The advantage of an external trainer is that he can bring new and different views and people may not be afraid to ask questions (which could be a handicap with an internal trainer where people may refrain from asking questions due to hierarchy etc).

The stages of designing a training program can be explained as follows:

1. First Stages of Design

At this stage there are two important decisions to be made-who is to be trained and what should be the nature of learning. The HR person normally decides who should be trained in consultation with the superiors of the trainees. The mix of the group is also decided whether to have a similar group or a cross-functional group, which may give the employee an all, round view. At this stage the HR person also decides as to what methods are to be used in consultation with the trainer. The various methods of training are lecture, conferences, seminars, workshops, role-play, case studies etc.

2. Scheduling

The fixed elements of the program are taken care of

in this step like meals, normal working hours, etc. These considerations are especially important if there is little chance of changing them. The program is usually started with what needs to be learnt first. The small units are started, followed by more complex activities. Later on the elements are consolidated in a cohesive way.

3. Balance

The aims and objectives should be used to determine how much time ought to be devoted to each topic. In part, the trainee will perceive time spent on each topic as an indication of the topic's importance. There should also be a mixture and balance of training methods.

4. Facilitating group formation

Unless a course consists of an existing, fully coherent group, a process of group formation will occur. The longer the course, the more important this is. Even on short courses the group will develop. Its capacity to tackle exercises increases, as does confidence to challenge and question. Activities should help people to identify with each other rather than cause conflict or embarrassment.

5. Timings

The design has to be modified as the material is developed. Training is often a compromise between three factors. The *range* of learning, which will be covered, the *depth* to which the coverage will go, and the *time*, which will be taken. This maybe considered as a balance. If more range is required, then either the time must be increased or depth reduced. Similarly, if more depth is required then either the range of coverage must be decreased or the time must increase.

6. Finally

After the design has been produced, modified and refined, think again to filter through ideas. Once the course has been run, revise it and amend further with the help of feedback from participants. Most of the experienced trainers found that it usually took about two to three courses before they could attain an accurate training program.

Techniques/Methods of Training and Development

On–The–Job Techniques

Where the object of managers' development is improving on-the-job behaviour, this method of training and education has its own value. It is inexpensive and saves productive hours. But the main drawback is that neither the trainer nor the trainee is free from daily chores and the pressure of their respective routine jobs. A senior has seldom the time and patience to impart training to the person.

Most popular techniques under this type are:

1. The Coaching or Guided Method.
2. Job Rotation Method.
3. Understudy assignment or attachment Method.
4. Participation deliberations of the Boards and Committee.

(1) The Coaching or Guided Method

Coaching is a method that is used in developing managerial thinking processes as well as operative skills. In coaching, the superior plays the role of the guide and the instructor. The coach sets some mutually agreed upon goals and tells the trainee what he wants to be done, suggests how it might be done, follows up suggestions and correct errors. He helps the trainee live up to those goals through periodic reviews of the trainee's progress and by suggesting modifications in his behaviour where needed. The objective of coaching is not only to teach and guide a subordinate in the performance of his immediate assignments but also provide him with diversified work so that he may grow and progress.

Advandages

- It requires the least centralized staff co-ordination, for every executive can coach his men even if no management development programme exists.

- Periodic feedback and evaluations are also a part of coaching, which yields immediate benefits to an organization, to the coach and to the subordinate. *It is Learning by Doing*

Disadvantages

- The coaching technique is authoritarian, for an executive tends to familiarize his subordinates with his own work habits and beliefs, even though these maybe faulty. In other words, it has tendencies to perpetuate the current managerial styles and practices in the organization.
- It heavily on the coach's ability to be a good teacher, which he may not necessarily be.
- The training atmosphere, free from worries of the daily duties, is not available.

To be effective, coaching demands that the superior should render assistance when the subordinate seeks or needs it. The superior should have the ability to communicate and to stimulatc and should have patience to help his subordinates. He should have the ability to communicate and to stimulate and should have patience to help his subordinates. He should also set aside time for scheduling sessions. He should avoid being too dominant in the performance process, so that the trainee can experience things for himself and does not become completely dependent upon the coach for decisions.

Coaching can work well only if the coach provides a good model with whom the trainee can identify, if both can be open with each other, if the coach accepts his responsibility fully; and if he provides the trainee with recognition of his improvement and suitable rewards.

(2) Job Rotation or Channel Method of Development

Job Rotation represents an excellent method for broadening the manager or potential manger, for turning specialists onto generalists. It refers to the transfer or movement of executives from one job to another and from one plan to another on some planned basis for educational learning purposes. Job Rotation is often designed for beginning level managers while planned progression is more likely to occur higher managerial levels. Such rotations may continue for a period ranging from 6 months to 24 months. This method provides a great deal of job experience for those who are potential executives who need broadening of outlook and an increased understanding of the various aspects of management. The emphasis is on diversified instead of specialized skills and knowledge.

Under this method, the trainees are rotated over various routine jobs in a department, division or unit before they are due for promotions as mangers. The idea is to impart an overall knowledge and familiarity with the different sectional jobs before they are posted as managers in the department. This secures a compromise between over-specialization even from the lowest most routine level, and a minimum of special skills and expertise necessary for middle level managers. These persons are moved from one job to another according to a schedule of rotation. It also includes moving people between lines and staff positions.

Job Rotations are mostly horizontal or lateral. Such rotations can be instituted (i) on a planned basis; i.e. by means of a training program whereby the worker spends 2 or 3 months in an activity and is then moved on; or (ii) on a situational basis, i.e. by moving the person to another activity when the first is no longer challenging to him, or to meet the needs of work scheduling.

Advantages

- It breaks down departmental provincialism for everyone is moved from one to another. It rather develops inter-departmental co-operation.
- Boredom, monotony are reduced and since job rotation permits a greater understanding of other activities within the organization people are prepared more rapidly to assume greater responsibility especially at the upper echelons.
- Job Rotation injects new ideas into the older departmental personnel who may otherwise fall in a rut. New ideas are infused in them and they are diffused through out an enterprise.
- Through this system, a man does not end up in just one place. He gets a chance to step into a higher position. In this way, an organization gains management strength in depth.

- Job Rotation ensures the avoidance of the problem that arises when a newly promoted manager is required to supervise his former peers.
- It makes it possible for the management to compare one man with another, and gives everyone an equal chance for advancement.
- It does not develop specialists but produces generalists, i.e. men who take a broad, company-wide point of view, men whose chief ability is to handle people and make decisions.
- Awareness of what is happening elsewhere and familiarity with other task-centers helps a balanced and informed attitude to enterprise goals and activities.
- Each manager's abilities and talents are best used tested in a variety of jobs so the enterprise can secure his best utilization in the ultimate assignment.

Disadvantages

- It upsets family and home life because many a time transfers are affected to different geographical areas.
- It undermines organizational morale, efficiency since executives may have little inducement to sink their teeth deeply into an assignment. Established operations are disturbed and the manager is prone to error in a new seat.
- It becomes difficult for a subordinate to adjust himself to new bosses. Interpersonal relationships take time for adjustment, and employees with frequent moves are apt to feel insecure.
- The new incumbent is likely to bring a zeal for a change; while sound changes are good, ill conceived and hasty innovations may lead to costly experimen-tations.
- Job Rotation can demotivate intelligent and aggressive trainees who seek specific responsibility in their chosen specialty.

- It develops sharp cleavages, friction, jealousy and other non-co-operative and dysfunctional forms of human behaviour.
- The system is like a highly competitive game of "musical chains". Whenever there are promotions and transfers, some people are left behind. Therefore, smart, young people avoid taking risks.
- Rotation sometimes leads to subtle class distinctions. Men who are not rotated tend to develop defensive reactions. This leads to misunderstandings and poor communication.
- The system may eventually become over- centralized, inflexible and "closed".

(3) Understudy Assignment or Attachment Method

An "Understudy" is a person who is under training to assume, at a future time, the full duties and responsibilities of the positions currently held by his superior. In this way, it is ensured that a fully trained person is available to replace a manager during his long absence or illness, or on his retirement, transfer or promotion.

This technique is also known as "*Apprentice Training*". An understudy maybe picked up by a manager from amongst a large number of subordinates, or several individuals. Such an understudy learns the complexities of the problems and how to solve them, learns also the process of decision-making and investigation and making written recommendations to his superior. He is generally assigned a project, which is closely related to the work in his selection. He is deputed to attend executive meetings as a representative of his superior, at which he makes a presentation and proposals. The essence is that the senior routes much of the departmental work through the junior, discusses problems with him and allows him to participate in the decision-making process as often as possible.

Advantages

- It is practical and quick in training persons for greater responsibility for it lays emphasis on learning by doing.

- The learners' interest and motivation are high and the superior is relieved of his heavy workload.
- The trainee manager is also not overburdened with work and responsibility; at the same time he secures full participation in the running of the function and insight into the job-content.
- The trainee is able to continuously obtain guidance of the superior. The work that passes through him opens up windows for him to appreciate different angles and viewpoints related to job. He receives an opportunity to see the job in total.
- It ensures continuity of management facilities even when the superior leaves his position.
- The chances of costly mistakes or upsetting relationship within the group are eliminated.

Disadvantages

- Since the superior often on the basis of favoritism picks up the understudy, he tends to perpetuate the existing practices of in breeding.
- The motivation of all the employees in the unit may decrease since the incentive to get ahead is partially destroyed when one particular subordinate is identified in advance as one who will be the next occupant of a higher managerial position.
- Under a competent senior, the junior trainee might lose his independence and his critical appraisal of the way the job is performed.
- The subordinate employees might ignore him and withhold cooperation; they might tend to treat him as an intruding appendage to the function without authority and accountability.

(4) Participation in Deliberations of The Board and Committees / Multiple-Management Technique: -

It is a technique whereby juniors are assigned to Board and committees, by the chief executive. They are asked to participate in deliberations of these Board and committees.

In these problems, real life and actual problems are discussed and decisions are taken. The juniors get an opportunity to share in managerial decision-making, to learn by watching others and to delve into specific organizational problems. When committees are of 'ad hoc' or temporary nature, they often take a task force activities designed to delve into a particular problem, ascertain alternative solutions, and make a recommendation for implementing a solution. These temporary assignments can be both interesting and rewarding to the employees' growth. On the other hand, appointment to permanent committees increases the employees' exposure to other members of the organization, broadens his understanding, and gives him an opportunity to grow and make recommendations under the scrutiny of other committee members.

Advantages

- It gives Board members an opportunity to gain knowledge on various issues.
- It helps identify those who have executive talent. Multiple judgments are obtained on each individual through the Board rating system.
- The members gain practical experience of group decision-making and of teamwork. As a result of the interaction process, they develop respect for the rights and view of their associates.
- It is relatively inexpensive method of development.
- It permits a considerable number of managersto participate in certain activities within a reasonable period of time. Besides, the Boards do make important contributions to efficiency, productivity and a better human relations climate. In fact, they assist in a better administration in the organization.

Disadvantages

- It is only suitable for middle and senior level managers.
- It does not permit any specific attention to the

training needs of the managers.

- The debates in these committees often tend to be lacking purpose or authority. They often degenerate into academic discussions without the participants feeling committed to the conclusions.

The above are the various methods/ techniques for On-the-Job training. Let us conclude by looking at some limitations of this method.

Limitations

- The management program has become complex, but on-the-job training does not allow adequate facilities, environment and teaching expertise.
- Though the main objective of the management development is to improve behaviour of the managers in different environment, in actual practice, this objective is not well achieved.
- Technological developments demand that managers need to be placed in highly maneuvered and stimulated atmosphere to derive maximum from training techniques. This is not possible through on the job training.
- In a group of participants drawn from different spheres of management and different enterprise cultures, the participants are exposed to new ideas, new ways of analysis and divergent experiences of members of the group. This provokes introspection and generates impulses to behaviour change.

Off – The – Job Techniques

Although a number of on the job programs are in vogue, they are still considered inadequate for a number of reasons. Hence, there is a need for off-the-job techniques. There is a wealth of management development techniques that mangers can partake in off-the-job techniques.

Most popular techniques under this type are:

(1) The Case Study Method.

(2) The Incident Method.

(3) Role Playing.

(4) Simulation.

(5) Grid Training.

(6) Lectures.

(7) Audio Visual Material.

(8) Conferences.

(9) Programmed Instructions.

(10) Business and Management Games.

(11) Computer-Assisted Instructions (CAI).

(1) The Case Study

Case method is an excellent medium for developing analytical skill. It was started by Harvard Business School. A 'case' is a written description of an actual situation in business which provokes in the reader the need to decide which is going on, what the situation really is, what the problems are and what the solutions should be. A case is an objective description of a real life business situation in which executives are required to take action and are responsible for the results.

In this method, an actual business situation is described in writing and in a comprehensive manner. The trainees are asked to appraise and analyze the problem-situation and suggest solutions. The actual decision taken in the subject case is known only to the executive and is disclosed only at the end of the session when it is compared with other solutions offered by the group.

Case Study can provide stimulating discussions among participants as well as excellent opportunities for individuals to defend their analytical and judgmental abilities. It is rather an effective method for improving decision-making abilities within the constraints of limited information.

This method represents a dynamic and powerful approach to learning. Sometime the case discussion, takes place in a small syndicate before they are called upon to discuss before the whole class.

The case study method accomplishes several objectives

of the management development programs; (i) It distributes knowledge and facts; (ii) It improves participants' skills in problem analysis.

(2) The Incident Method

This method was developed by Paul and Faith Pigors. The central aim of this method is to stimulate self-development in a blend of understanding that is essential for productive interaction. This blend combines *intellectual ability* (power to think clearly, incisively and reasonably about specific facts); *practical judgment* (capacity to modify conclusions arrived at intellectually to meet the test of common sense); *social awareness* (Being able to appreciate the force of other peoples' feelings and willing to adjust or implement a decision so that it can be more acceptable persons who are affected by it). Group work of each of these cases begins when a group meets. Each member, working along for a couple of minutes, studies a written incident. Appended to each incident is an invitation to make short-term decisions in the role of a person who had to cope with the incident when it actually happens.

Under this method, group members address questions to the discussion leader. The general trend of questioning is to find out about the what, when, where and how of the situation in which an incident developed, and who was present at the time. Clues are also tracked down if they seem to offer reliable insight into the why behaviour. After the collection of data, it is necessary to isolate the most important items for decision-making.

(3) Role Playing

Role Playing is a training method often aimed at enhancing either human relations skills or sales techniques. It originally evolved out of Clinical Psychology, in which problems involving human interaction are presented ad then spontaneously acted out. The enactment is normally followed by a discussion to determine what happened and why.

The role assumes a real life situation and enhances the participants' growth, sensitivity and development.

The value of role-playing is:

- It requires the person to carry out a thought or decision he may have reached.
- It permits the practice of carrying out an action and makes it clear that good human relations require skills.
- Attitudinal changes are effectively accomplished by placing persons in specified roles. It becomes clear in Role-play that a person's behaviour is not only a function of his personality but also of the situation in which he finds himself.
- It makes a person aware of others' feelings.
- It helps in developing a fuller appreciation of the important part played by feelings.
- Each person gets an opportunity to discover his own personal faults.
- Three types of learning take place through Role-playing: (i) Learning by practice of deserted skills; (ii) Learning through imitation of desirable behaviour; (iii) Learning through analysis and conceptualization.

Thus, Role Playing is especially useful in providing new insight and in presenting the trainee with opportunities to develop interaction skills. Unless the trainer engages in coaching or unless someone states the criteria for behaviour, role-playing may not adhere to the objectives of the training program and the reinforcement of the desired behaviour maybe somewhat lacking.

(4) Simulation

A Simulation is technique that duplicates as nearly as possible the actual conditions encountered on the job. Simulation then, is an attempt to create a realistic decision-making environment for the trainee. Simulations present likely problem situations and decision alternatives to the trainee. For example, activities of an organization maybe simulated and the trainee maybe asked to make a decision in support to these activities. The results of those decisions are reported back to the trainee with an explanation of what would have happened had they actually been made in the work place. The trainee learns from this feedback and makes appropriate corrections thus improving decisions.

The advantages of this method are the opportunities to attempt to create an environment similar to real situations the managers incur, without high costs involved should the action prove undesirable. The disadvantages are that it is difficult to duplicate the pressures and realities of actual decision-making on the jobs, and the individuals often act differently in real life situations when they do in acting out a simulated exercise.

(5) Grid Training

The 'Managerial Grid' is an organizational development technique, developed by Robert Blake and Jane Mouton. The grid represents several possible leadership styles. Each style represents a different combination of two basic orientations-concern for people and concern for organization.

The management training program is built around this managerial grid. It aims at developing open confrontation of organizational problems and high-people-production leaders.

Such a program lasts for 3 to 5 years and involves the following steps:

- Phase I involves a weekend conference, where trainees are taught the fundamental of grid training.
- Phase II comprises the discussion, analysis and solution of the units' problems and practices by the management and the subordinates.
- Phase III involves meeting with various groups with the aim of working out company-wide problems and setting some developmental targets for the company as a whole.
- Phase IV involves outlining specific procedures for accomplishing the company's development targets.
- Phase V includes evaluation of the units' accomplishments and beginning work on any remaining or new problems.

(6) Lectures

This method is a popular form of instruction. Large numbers of people can be taught all at the same time, thus it is quite cost effective. However, the more diversified the audience, the more general the content usually becomes. Hence, its utility for imparting specialized knowledge is more limited. But with a homogeneous audience, a trainer can direct the lecture to specific topics and techniques, which is often more beneficial than using some broad-based material. Thus, lectures are an effective way of training a large group of people at once particularly if they have a common training need.

On the negative side, lectures are usually one-way communication. There is a little chance for dialogue, questions and discussions of individual problems and special interests. Although popular, Lectures are not the best method for skill acquisition.

(7) Audiovisual Material

This method includes television slides, overheads, video-types and films. It allows participants to see as well as hear, and it usually is quite good at capturing individual attention. This underscores the importance of motivation and interest as necessary conditions for learning. This method is useful in training people in a work process or a sequence. People can more readily trace the pattern of workflow when it is laid out graphically. After the initial expense, the cost of repeated use is usually minimal.

On the negative side, it is difficult to modify the material. If the content changes, a whole new film has to be made. Also, like the Lecture method this technique follows one-way communication.

Overall, if the task is very important to the company, then the film is cost effective, with the aid of close-up images, stop action, slow motion, and instant replay, delicate and complex tasks can be broken down into discrete and understandable units.

(8) Conferences

This method uses two-way communication. It is

effective when the ratio of trainees to trainers is not very large. This method is useful when the material needs clarification and elaboration or when a lively discussion facilitates understanding. The success of this method depends heavily on the skills and personality of the discussion leader/trainer. A dogmatic leader can stifle discussion. A good leader knows when to lead the discussion and when to allow others to lead. Perhaps because this method does not usually involve any tangible assets other than people, the attitudes, enthusiasm and verbal communication skills of the participants affect the outcome more than in any other training method.

(9) Programmed Instructions

PI is a method of training originated by B.F. Skinner. PI may include an actual piece of equipment or a specially constructed paper booklet. This method has three characteristics. First, the participants are active in the training process, infact; they determine their own learning pace. Second, the subject to be learned involves many discrete pieces of material and participants get immediate feedback whether they have learned each piece. Thirdly, the material is divided into an organized sequence.

The common features of PI are:

- A single piece of information is presented at each stage or frame. All the frames put together are called a program. The first frame deals with the first step in some procedure in industry training.
- The participant gives an answer to the question in the first frame. If the answer is correct the participant proceeds to the next frame. If the answer is incorrect, the right answer is given along with an explanation as to why it is correct.
- The frames are arranged in the exact sequence that occurs in the work process. This step-by-step sequence in learning matches the step-by-step sequence followed in performing the task on the job.
- Emphasis is placed on the participants' correct

answers rather than work speed. At the end of the program the number of correct answers is tabulated. If the participants reach above the cut-off scores, the training program has ended. If the scores are below the cut-off points, the participants repeat the program.

Although this method gives participants immediate feedback and the material is presented in a systematic and precise manner, it is rather time consuming. Some work materials are hard to break down into exact sequence as they may have several correct ways to perform tasks. On the other hand, participants work at a pace of their own and suffer no embarrassments when they make mistakes while learning.

(10) Business or Management Game

Business games are classroom simulation exercises in which teams of individuals compete against one another or against an environment in order to achieve a given objective. These games are designed to be representative of real life conditions. Under these, an atmosphere is created in which the participants play a dynamic role, and enrich their skills through involvement and simulated experience. Most business games are expressed in the form of a mathematical model controlled and manipulated by an electric computer; while the others can be played manually. In the former case, quicker feedback is available, clerical work is avoided and time is controlled. These games consist of several teams, which represent competing companies. Each team consists of 2 to 6 players. Teams take decisions regarding production, prices, research expenditure, marketing, advertising, and attempt to maximize hypothetical profit in this simulated environment. The decisions of a team are fed into a computer, which has been programmed according to a particular model of the market.

These games are intended to teach trainees how to make management decisions in an integrated manner. The participants learn by analyzing problems and by making trial and error decisions. Such games illustrate the existence of various group processes, including planning, problem solving, communication, resolution of conflicts, emergence of leadership, and development of ties of friendship.

A major problem with games is that they can be very expensive to develop and implement particularly when the game itself is computerized. Though games maybe accurate simulations, they are never totally realistic, for no evidence is available which may indicate that those who are successful in business games will also be successful in a real job.

(11) Computer- Assisted Instruction (CAI)

CAI is the most recently developed training method. CAI has been used to teach a wide range of skills, ranging from how to speak a foreign language to how to fly a :

The advantage of CAI includes individualized instruction, reduced training time, and elimination of travel for training. Some advantages to the trainee are being able to work at his or her own pace, to begin and end a lesson when convenient and to enter a program at his or her current level of achievement. Goldstein (1991), however cautioned that CAI requires careful needs assessment, careful design of training based on the needs and evaluation efforts to fine-tune the program. Although much more work needs to be directed toward meeting the potential promise of this method, CAI appears to be a very promising and viable technique for enhancing complex skills.

Training the Trainers

One of the most important aspects of training is the Trainer itself. A lot can be learnt from the program if the trainer is motivating and eager to share knowledge with the participants.

Given below are some training strategies for an effective trainer:

- **Be enthusiastic.** Your success as a trainer depends as much on your attitude as your expertise. You must believe what you are teaching. Be excited about the topic and share that excitement in your training - it will rub off on your training participants.

• **Always be positive.** It is easy to be condescending, negative, or even rude when people don't see the need or importance of the training topic. Inspire your training participants to learn because they want to, not just because they're supposed to.

• **Do not apologize.** Making your learners feel that you are not prepared or not fully qualified is a cardinal sin of teaching. The first words out of the presenter's mouth are an apology for not being prepared, not having the right resources, or for forcing you to listen to them. Immediately the trainees' expectations go out the window. Even if you are not prepared, feel unqualified, or don't believe you know everything there is to know about the topic, don't let your audience know. A good trainer is confident (not cocky) and appears knowledgeable at all times

• **You don't know everything.** Even though you should appear knowledgeable at all times, you don't know everything, and don't be afraid to say it. When faced with questions or problems that you don't know or can't solve. Don't fake it. It's better to say, "I don't know, but will find out and get back to you," than to provide incorrect or incomplete information. When you express your own opinion or idea, be sure to let your audience know it.

• **Be yourself.** Training a group of people can be nerve racking. Relax and be yourself. Don't be afraid to share personal experiences and stories - these are often what training participants remember most.

• **Get to know your training participants.** In small or medium sized groups, ask people to introduce themselves. Even in large groups, you can invite the audience respond to questions by raising their hands (e.g., How many of you are comfortable with HTML?). Call them by name. If you're terrible with remembering names, then name badges or papers are helpful. The relationships participants form can be as valuable as the content you give them.

• **Give an overview and a review.** Always tell your learners what you're going to teach them, teach them what you're going to teach them, then tell them what you just taught them.

• **Involve the audience.** A training session is going

well when the audience is talking as much as the trainer. Let them get their hands dirty. Keep them busy. Your training participants should be saying, "Is it over already?" rather than, "Is this ever going to end?"

• **Build on content they already know.** Ask them questions and use their experiences, situations, and knowledge to teach..Use analogies and stories they can relate to.

• **Find a good balance between depth and breadth.** This is one of the hardest things for a trainer - deciding how much content to cover in a training versus how in depth to cover it. You must often choose between training a little bit about a lot of topics or a lot about a few topics.

• **Be careful with jargon.** As trainer, you are intimately familiar with the content you are teaching. Sometimes we forget that others don't understand 'techno speak' or some of the technical words, terms, and acronyms that we use.

• **Use the tools at your disposal.** If your training participants have computers, make sure they use them. If you have access to an overhead or LCD projector, use it to demonstrate and present techniques and information. Invite individuals to share their experiences or insights. This especially applies to individuals with disabilities. Provide plenty of examples and resources. If your training participants leave empty handed, they're probably leaving empty headed to. Give them handouts, notes, URL's, examples, contact information, and anything else that they could use in the future. Chances are they will forget most of what you will tell them, but if they have a resource they can turn to when they need it, you have done your job well.

• **Give thorough instructions before starting activities**. If your training involves small group or hands-on activities, give them all of the instructions they need, before allowing them to begin. Once your learners are engaged in a task or conversation, they are less likely to hear additional instructions. Avoid giving the same instructions multiple times by giving detailed instructions the first time around.

• **Give them a break.** One and a half hours is usually

the longest you want to go without a break (especially right after lunch). If training participants are off-task or dozing off, give them a chance to stretch and get a drink of water.

- **Be prepared.** Show up on time and have everything ready. Know the training setup. Test technology beforehand. Know the content you are going to present inside and out.

- **Have a backup plan.** Some of the wisest words of wisdom are these: *Never, never, never trust technology.* What will you do if the bulb burns out on your LCD projector or if your Internet connection goes down? What if that dot-com Web site you were going to demonstrate suddenly disappears into the abyss of the Internet, never to be found again? For on-site training, I always try to plan for the worst-case scenario. In my case, it would be to have my laptop computer die on me. Does your backup plan cover all possible situations or does it simply contain the word, "hide"?

- **Ask for and apply feedback and evaluations.** Whenever possible, ask for feedback. You'll never become a more effective trainer if you don't get feedback as to what you can do better. Ask the specific questions on your evaluation that will give you specific feedback. Encourage your training participants to honestly complete them. Use the feedback you are given.

- **We're all on the same team.** There are many accessibility trainers, information resources, service providers, projects, businesses, and individuals who are working on making the organization more competant. They may have different motivations than your own. Many do not provide useful or even beneficial information. Despite this, we're all working toward the same important goal. Never criticize or degrade one's efforts. Establishing positive relationships and partnerships with others in the field can be a positive move that will help each of us improve.

Evaluation of the Training Program

The last stage in the training and development process is the evaluation of results. Since huge sums of money are spent on training and development, how far the program has been effective must be judged. Evaluation is the determination of the extent to which the training activities have met their goals. Planning for the evaluation should start at the same time that planning for the training program begins. If the goals of the program are clearly stated as specific objectives, the appropriate evaluation method can be implemented at the same time as the program.

Need for Evaluation. The main objective of evaluating a training program is to determine if they are accomplishing specific training objectives, that is, correcting performance deficiencies. A second reason is to ensue that any changes in trainee capabilities are due to the training program and not due to any other conditions. Training programs should be evaluated to determine their cost effectiveness. Evaluation is useful to explain program failure, should it occur. Finally, credibility of training and development is greatly enhanced when it is proved that the organization has benefited tangibly from it.

Principles of Evaluation. Evaluation of the training program must be based on the following principles:

(i) Evaluation specialist must be clear about the goals and purposes of evaluation.

(ii) Evaluation must be continuous.

(iii) Evaluation must be Specific.

(iv) Evaluation must provide the means and focus for trainers to be able to appraise themselves, their practices, and their products.

(v) Evaluation must be based on objective methods and standards.

(vi) Realistic target dates must be set for each phase of the evaluation process. A sense of urgency must be developed, but deadlines that are unreasonably high will result in poor evaluation.

Importance of Evaluation. Although for many years trainers have attempted to evaluate their programs, until quite recently, there has not been a bona fide effort to use valid and reliable methods to conduct such evaluations. Furthermore, some trainers gather data for evaluation but do not analyze those data for trends or use them to improve existing training programs. Such an oversight can be costly, especially in light of the billions of rupees that have been spent and will continue to be spent annually on training efforts as a result of the demographic, economic, and technological changes just discussed. It is important to remember that effective evaluation is multifaceted. All of the literature recognizes the importance of evaluation in terms of client orientation and economic return. In other words, most researchers in the field understand that clients, whether they are those who have hired the trainer or those who have participated in the training, must be satisfied with that training. If clients do not perceive a return on their investment, whether measured in terms of time or rupees, they may not be willing to continue to invest in training.

Models of Evaluation

There are several models for effective evaluation of the training program. Let us consider some:

1. The Kirkpatrick Model of Training Evaluation

A Brief Historical Perspective: Donald Kirkpatrick set forth his four-level approach to the evaluation of training in a series of articles appearing in the journal of what was then known as the American Society of Training Directors. The first of these four seminal articles was published in November of 1959. The remaining three articles were published in the succeeding three months, with the fourth and final article appearing in February of 1960. These articles can be found in *Evaluating Training Programs*, a collection of articles compiled by Kirkpatrick from the pages of the ASTD Journal and published by ASTD in 1975.

Kirkpatrick's model includes four levels or steps of outcome evaluation:

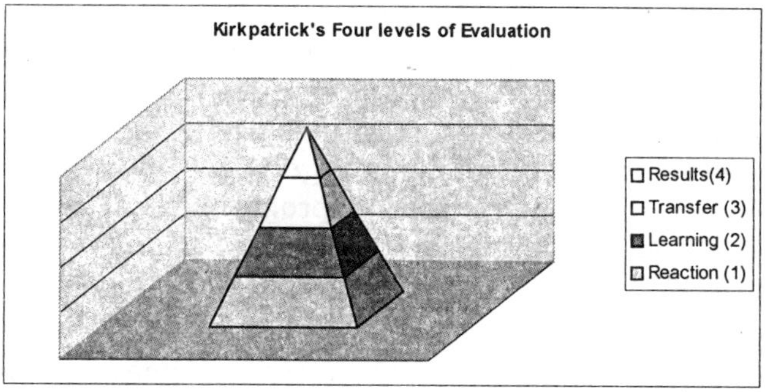

- Level 1 Evaluation—Reaction
- Level 2 Evaluation—Learning
- Level 3 Evaluation—Behavior
- Level 4 Evaluation—Results

According to Donald Kirkpatrick, evaluators should establish performance standards on the outcomes, when possible, so that the four steps in the logic of evaluation can be utilized and evaluative judgments can be made. Also, the results must be communicated because utilization of evaluation results will not happen without dissemination and communication.

- **Level 1—Reaction**

Here your goal is to measure participants' reactions to the training program. You should measure their reactions immediately after the program. Level one evaluation should not just include reactions toward the overall programme (e.g., Did you like the programme?); it should also include measurement of participants' reactions or attitudes toward specific components of the programme, such as the instructor, the topics, the presentation style, the schedule, audiovisuals, etc. Furthermore, each of these components can be further broken down into sub-components for evaluation (e.g., you can ask participants to evaluate specific characteristics of the instructor, the presentation, etc.). In short, level one evaluation is far more than just the measurement of overall satisfaction.

Learning (Level two outcomes) and transfer of learning (Level three outcomes) are unlikely to occur unless participants have positive attitudes toward the training program. Therefore, it is important to determine participants' reactions to the training program. Also, positive reactions are important because managers are more likely to eliminate unpopular training programmes. Finally, the measurement of specific aspects of the training programme can provide important information about what aspects of the training program can be improved in the future.

Level 1 evaluation relies on the measurement of attitudes, usually through the use of a questionnaire. It is important to include closed-ended items (including rating scales) as well as open-ended items on your questionnaire. Here are two open-ended items that I like: In your view, what were the three most important weaknesses of the programme? Or In your view, what were the three most important strengths of the programme? It is important to learn the weaknesses, as well as the strengths, in order to improve a program.

Advantages of Level one Evaluation

- Trainers will know how the participants felt about the training event.
- It may point out content areas that trainees felt were missing from the training event.
- It will tell trainers how engaged the participants felt by the training event.
- It can provide information about overall participant reaction as well as participant feedback and evaluation of specific aspects of the training event.
- Detailed level one evaluation can provide formative evaluation information that can be used to improve future versions of the training program.

• Level 2—Learning

Here your goal is to determine what the training program participants learned during the training event.

Because the training instructor should have specific learning objectives, one hopes to find clear learning outcomes. Learning outcomes can include changes in knowledge, skills, or attitudes. The evaluation should focus on measuring what was covered in the training event (i.e., the learning objectives).

Level two evaluation should be done immediately after the training event to determine if participants gained the knowledge, skills, or attitudes. A couple of issues here are (a) how shall one measure knowledge, skills, and attitudes, and (b) what research design should be use to demonstrate improvement in level two outcomes?

First, let's talk about the measurement of level two outcomes. Knowledge is typically measured using already available or instructor constructed ***achievement tests*** (i.e., tests designed to measure the degree of learning that has taken place). In the training environment, these tests are usually criterion-referenced. These tests are constructed to determine whether learners have mastered one or more learning objectives and these tests include a cutoff point (pass/fail). The results of criterion-referenced tests often take the form of a negatively skewed curve, where the vast majority of the learners have reached or surpassed the criterion or cut-off point (i.e., the point at which one must reach in order to pass the test) and only a few learners have lower scores. In constructing a criterion-referenced test, you should develop a pool of items potentially measuring the content, have a panel of experts examine the items, pilot test the selected items, and analyze each item for item difficulty (i.e., the percentage of people who answer the item correctly), item discrimination (i.e., the high performers should be more likely to get the item correct than low performers if it is a good item), and distracter effectiveness (are the distracters working well?). Eliminate items with poor performance on difficulty, discrimination, and items whose distracters do not work well.

Skills typically require some kind of motor or manual response on the examinee's part, or some kind of manipulation; therefore, a ***performance test*** is used. A performance test is just a test that requires the test taker scales), and you should include some open-ended items to allow participants to respond in their own words

Second, Kirkpatrick also briefly discusses the issue of research design. He suggests that you include a control group in your design when possible, and he briefly mentions using a pretest measure when possible.

Advantage of Level two Evaluation

- Demonstrating participant learning should help trainers in promoting their training program.
- Knowledge of level two evaluation can help in interpreting the results of level three evaluation (e.g., if level three results do not occur, it may because of workplace factors and not because of any flaw in the training program).
- Detailed level two evaluation can provide formative evaluation information that can be used to improve future versions of the training program (e.g., you may find certain learning objectives that are not being met).

- **Level 3—Behaviour**

Here your goal is to find out if training program participants change their on-the-job-behavior (OJB) as a result of their having attended and participated in the training program. If the behavior change does not occur, you also want to find out why the change did not occur. The level three question is, did the training have a positive effect on job performance? Level three evaluation specifically involves measuring the *transfer* of knowledge, skills, and attitudes from the training context to the workplace.

Remember that level one and level two outcomes are still important because participants generally need to react positively to the training program (level 1 outcome) and they need to learn the material (level 2 outcome) if they are going to be motivated and able to apply what they have learned when they return to their jobs.

Learning is likely to transfer only if the conditions in the work setting are favorable for transfer. In addition, there on job performance? Level three evaluation specifically involves measuring the *transfer* of knowledge, skills, and attitudes from the training context to the workplace.

Remember that level one and level two outcomes are still important because participants generally need to react positively to the training program (level 1 outcome) and they need to learn the material (level 2 outcome) if they are going to be motivated and able to apply what they have learned when they return to their jobs.

Learning is likely to transfer only if the conditions in the work setting are favorable for transfer. In addition, there are obviously many things that trainers can do to increase the likelihood of transfer. In other words, transfer is affected by "training factors" before trainees go back to their workplace as well as "workplace factors" that operate in their workplace when they return.

A. These are some factors in the training program or event that can help facilitate transfer of learning:

- The training or learning environment or context or culture is made to be similar to the actual work environment or context or culture of the organization (this is called *situated learning*). Learning that takes place in "authentic" contexts is more likely to by used later.
- Provide real world examples and actual experience performing and practicing the behaviors.
- Make sure trainees understand the general principles behind the behaviors (called "transfer through principles").
- Explain the importance and applicability of the future on-the-job behaviors (i.e., motivate the trainees).

B. These are some factors in the receiving organization that can help facilitate transfer of learning:

- The organizational culture and climate support change.
- The participant's direct supervisor and others with whom he or she works support and/or facilitate the participant's new behaviors through direct extrinsic

rewards such as help, encouragement, praise, increased freedom and responsibility, pay increases, and recognition.

- The participant gains intrinsic reinforcement from applying his or her new knowledge, skills, or attitudes (i.e., he or she likes what was learned and enjoys performing the new related behaviors).
- The participant has the opportunity to use his or her new knowledge or skills on the job.

Level three is often harder than level one and level two evaluation because behavior changes at the workplace are often harder to measure than reaction and learning directly after the training event. You must give the behavior time to transfer and collect data at the workplace.

Probably the most common design used for level three evaluation is the one-group pretest-posttest design (i.e., get a baseline measure of the behavior you plan on training, train the participants, and then measure the participants' behavior again after the training). If you are able to include a control group, you will be able to use the pretest-posttest nonequivalent control group design (i.e., in addition to measuring the training participants before and after the training, you also find a set of similar people, who do not undergo training for the control group, and you measure these control group participants' behavior before and after the training program).

Advantages of Level three Evaluation

- Provides measurement of actual behavior on the job, rather than only measuring or demonstrating positive reaction and/or learning. This is important because you want to have actual on-the-jobresults from the training program.
- Level three outcomes are required for level four outcomes (i.e., they are the intervening variables or factors that lead to level four outcomes); therefore, it is good news when level three outcomes are found.

- Most level three outcomes are intrinsically useful, even if level four outcomes (i.e., final organizational or business results) are never fully demonstrated (e.g., it is useful to have managers who are effective listeners and supportive, or employees who know how to do basic work on their computers, or employees who act respectfully toward employees from different ethnic or cultural groups).
- In many situations, evidence of level one outcomes, level two outcomes, and level three outcomes will be sufficient evidence of the merit and usefulness of a training program. This is especially true when all of these provide evidence of positive results of the training program.

- **Level 4—Results**

Frequently thought of as the bottom line, this level measures the success of the program in terms that managers and executives can understand. From a business and organizational perspective, this is the overall reason for a training program.

Examples of different kinds of level four outcomes:

- Improved quality of work.
- Higher productivity.
- Reduction in turnover.
- Reduction in scrap rate (i.e., less wasted resources).
- Improved quality of work life.
- Improved human relations (e.g., improved vertical and horizontal communication).
- Increased sales.
- Fewer grievances.
- Lower absenteeism.
- Higher worker morale.
- Fewer accidents.
- Greater job satisfaction.

- Increased profits.

2. CIRO Model for Evaluating Training Effectiveness

Warr, Bird and Rackham (1970) developed a four level different approach for evaluation. This model (CIRO) proposes four categories for evaluation as follows:

(a) Context Evaluation

Context evaluation involves reviewing and assessing the operational requirements for the training event and determining the individual training needs and objectives applied at three levels; Ultimate objectives, Intermediate objectives, Immediate objectives.

(b) Input Evaluation

Input evaluation involves an evaluation of the training event. This includes assessing whether or not the chosen methodology is the most appropriate means of meeting the training need and/ or whether alternative means or resources could be used to equal effect.

(c) Reaction Evaluation

The level of reaction is similar to Kirkpatrick's and Hamblin's Level 1 evaluation; it involves measuring the reactions of trainee's both during and immediately after the training event. Evaluation of participants' reactions consists of measuring their feelings; it does not include a measure of actual learning.

(d) Outcome EEvaluation

The outcome evaluation level comprises four stages; defining the training objectives, selecting or constructing the evaluation tools and measures, using the evaluation tools and instruments, assessing and reviewing the results.

3. The Philips five Level ROI Model

With the requirement to identify the financial benefits derived from training in mind, Jack Philips (1995, 1996, and 1997) extended Kirkpatrick's model by adding a fifth, cost/ benefit stage. Philips model is summarized below:

(a) Reaction

This level measures participant's reactions to the

programme and outlines specific plans for implementation. Reaction means to gather data on participant's reactions during and at the end of a training program. Participant reaction is a measure of "customer satisfaction" indicating the level of effectiveness and usefulness of the training program at the time the participants are experiencing it and sometimes weeks or even months afterward.

(b) Learning

Learning measures skills, knowledge or attitude change. A pre test and posttest are usually administered so that any learning can be attributed to the training program. The measurement tools used to evaluate learning should reflect each training program's particular objectives.

(c) Behavioural Changes

This step measures the change in behavior on the job and specific application of training material. A statistical analysis is made to compare before and after performance and to relate changes to the training program. This level of evaluation not only assesses the performance of the Person who receives the training, but also provides valuable feed - back to those involved in redesigning existing training programs or in designing programs to meet future needs of the organization.

(d) Business Results

This step measures business impact of the program. This evaluation requires significant resources and budgets. Because of the importance placed on bottom-line profitability, the trend appears to be leading toward some form of monetary measures of training, including Return on Investment (ROI), Benefit Cost Analysis (BCA), and Return on Expectation (ROE).

(e) Return On Investment

This step measures the monetary values of the results and costs for the programme, usually expressed as a percentage. Phillips places particular importance on the up-front planning required to utilize any monetary measurement and the significance of focusing on the primary goals of any ROI, i.e. to convince the Human

Resource staff that the process works and to show senior management that training can make a difference.

ROI (%) = Net Program Benefits x 100

Program Costs

4. CIPP Model for Evaluating Training Effectiveness

The CIPP Model is a comprehensive framework for guiding formative and summative evaluations of projects, programs, personnel, products, institutions, and systems. The model is configured for use in internal evaluations conducted by an organization's evaluators; self-evaluations conducted by project teams or individual service providers, and contracted or mandated external evaluations.

(a) Context Evaluations

This step assesses needs, problems, assets, and opportunities to help decision makers define goals and priorities and help the broader group of users judge goals, priorities, and outcomes.

(b) Input Evaluations

This step assesses alternative approaches, competing action plans, staffing plans, and budgets for their feasibility and potential cost-effectiveness to meet targeted needs and achieve goals. Decision makers use input evaluations in choosing among competing plans, writing funding proposals, allocating resources, assigning staff, scheduling work, and ultimately in helping others judge an effort's plans and budget.

(c) Process Evaluations

This step assesses the implementation of plans to help staff carry out activities and later help the broad group of users to judge program performance and interpret outcomes.

(d) Product Evaluations

This step identifies and assess outcomes—intended and unintended, short term and long term—both to help a staff keep an enterprise focused on achieving important outcomes and ultimately to help the broader group of users to gauge the effort's success in meeting targeted needs.

Current Trends In Training Evaluation

Changing Times and Changing Methods of Evaluating Training

Changing Expectations of Training

Organizational expectations for training have shifted dramatically. The most pronounced change is a new and vigorous justification of the cost of training based on return on investment (ROI) and organizational impact. This transition has been driven by the competitive nature of the international economy and resulting changes in organizational structure, which produce flat, thinner, and fewer administrative cost centers.

In addition, training professionals are being asked to do more and play an important role in the strategy of the organization. The ability to generate and apply knowledge is a competitive advantage and source of new products, services, and revenue.

The nature of training itself is undergoing a transformation. Trainers no longer hold the privileged position of "all knowing" content expert. Groups being trained often contain individuals with more depth of knowledge about, more experience applying, or more time to access current knowledge on the subject of the training. The training professionals thus become facilitators of learning and guides to available knowledge instead of content experts who bring "the info" into the training room with them. Trainers no longer "own" the knowledge. Instead, they synthesize and provide resources to clients who also have access to the knowledge.

As training has moved from satisfying trainees to improving organizational performance, the definition of customer has broadened. Trainees themselves are still among the "customers" of training — and the trainee's evaluations are important sources of feedback for continuous improvement and quality — but the trainee's organizational unit and the organization as a whole are now part of the client system. Training is performed to solve the business problems of the unit and have a positive impact on the organization.

Evaluating Training — Recent Models

Business changes have resulted in increased pressure on training professionals to demonstrate their worth. Do they do a good job? What is their impact on our work? Is there a cheaper way to do this? What is the value added? What is the effect on our profitability — that is, will we have a return on our investment in training?

The literature of training evaluation provides a framework to answer these questions and has addressed many of the current issues for trainers. Some time ago Donald Kirkpatrick (1975) provided a framework of four levels of evaluation:

Level I — the effectiveness as perceived by the trainee

Level II — measured evaluation of learning

Level III — observed performance

Level IV — business impact.

More recently, Jack Phillips (1991) has written that evaluation must go beyond Level IV and focus on real measurement of ROI. Dana Gaines Robinson, whose writing (1989) redirected the attention of trainers to business impact, now (1995) exhorts trainers to become "performance consultants" and de-emphasizes training as an intervention. Robert Brinkerhoff (1988) uses data gathering and evaluation to make the training function more customer-focused and practice continuous improvement.

A New Way of Looking at Evaluating Training

However, these approaches do not represent choice. Kirkpatrick's Level I data is still needed to get feedback on the trainee's perceptions of the experience. Level II evaluation has probably become less important in today's business environment. Level III evaluation is all-important to both trainees and their business units. Individual performance (Kirkpatrick's Level III) is not a level in itself; it is a focus only when individual performance is the solution of a business problem or is integral to customer satisfaction.

Level IV evaluation — the impact on the business problem—probably provides the most important data to the unit and organization.

Evaluators must respond to the new requirements by implementing all these concepts and evaluating at multiple levels. These levels will measure training's success at completing its business tasks.

1. Customer Satisfaction. The evaluation of customer satisfaction may be multi-dimensional for two reasons. First, the definition of training has expanded to include the trainee's unit manager, the unit, and the organization — not just the trainee in the classroom. Second, we are measuring perception of quality, convenience, and value. This information is crucial to continuous improvement.

2. Impact on the Business Problem. This level is usually the most important to the business unit manager. It answers the question, "Did the training make a positive difference in the business problem I have?" You work with the business unit manager to identify the business problem up front, not what needs to be taught, delivery or trainees to be serviced. This level of evaluation also makes trainers think of training as one problem-solving intervention among many.

3. Return on Investment. Training professionals have no choice but to demonstrate the effects of their work on corporate profitability in today's organization. This is true of every unit in the organization. Whereas it was once considered impossible to measure the ROI of training, many organizations now are doing so. The knowledge to achieve this goal is readily available to the practitioner, although the goal is still difficult, complex, and dependent on a long-term perspective. Discussions with cost accounting experts are helpful. However, the goal is reachable, and once you begin to measure ROI your process will improve.

The challenges to justifying investments in training are significant, and more meaningful methods of evaluation will provide solutions. Training professionals are being asked to do more, to meet an expanded definition of "customer." But these changes and the changing organizational context have created new roles and opportunities for training.

Post Training Environment

Tannenbaum and Yukl noted that the effectiveness of a training program could be influenced by events that occur after a trainee returns to the job. Some employees leave training with new skills and with strong intentions to apply those skills to their job, but limitations in the post training environment interferes with the actual transfer of training. Ford et al. studied technical trainees after they completed training and found significant differences in opportunities to apply the training and wide variations in the lengths of time before trainees first performed the tasks for which they had been trained. Thus researchers concluded that post training knowledge and behaviour are more likely to perseverate in organizations that have strong social support systems.

Conclusion and Suggestions

Training is a planned effort by an organization to facilitate employees' learning of job-related knowledge and skills for the purpose of improving performance. The approach to training involves four phases: Needs Assessment, Design and Development, Delivery of Programs and Evaluation of training.

Management development of the Human resource is intended to improve the present and future performance of the managers. Many millions are spent each year on formal management training, although managers probably do most of their learning from on- the- job experiences. This suggests that a complete management development system must include both training courses and challenging job assignments. Action learning programs should be a combination of on-the-job and off-the-job learning for managers.

To conclude, the utility of a training program can be calculated by assessing its costs and putting a monetary value on its benefits to the organization.

References

1. Fisher C.; Shaw J. (2004). Human Resource Management. (5th Edition). New Delhi: Biztantra, pp.- 372 – 416.
2. Kirkpatrick D. L. (1959). Techniques for evaluating training programs. Journal of the American Society of Training Directors, 13, pp. - 3-26.
3. Tannenbaum, S. I.; & Yukl, G. (1992). Training and development in work organizations. Annual Review of Psychology, 43, pp.-399–441.
4. Aswathappa. K. (2003). Human Resources and Personnel Management. (3rd Edition). New Delhi: Tata Mc Graw – Hill Publishing Company Ltd. pp. 177-192.
5. Bramley, P. (1996). Evaluating training effectiveness. New Delhi: Maidenhead: McGraw Hill.
6. Goldstein, I. (1993). Training and Development Organizations. (3rd Edition). California: Brooks/Cole), Chapter 3.
7. Hamblin, A. C. (1974). Evaluation and control of training. New Delhi: Maidenhead: McGraw-Hill.
8. Hinrichs J. (1976). Handbook of Industrial and Organizational Psychology. Chicago: Rand McNally, pp. 830.
9. Muchinsky P. (2001). Psychology Applied at Work.(6th Edition) Bangalore: Wadsworth, pp.173-186.

9
Employee Counseling

- Introduction to Employee Counseling
- Need for Counseling
- Functions of Employee Counseling
- The Managers Counseling Role
- Types of Employee Counseling
    - Directive Counseling
    - Nondirective Counseling
    - Participative Counseling
    - A Contingency View
- Selection of Safe Skills
- Nondirective Skills
- Accomplishments of Employee Counseling
- Some Practical Considerations in Employee Counseling
- Location of Counseling Services
- Articles on Employee Counseling
- Conclusion
- References

Introduction to Employee Counseling

Counseling is discussion with an employee of a problem that usually has emotional content in order to help the employee to cope with it better. Counseling seeks to improve employee mental health. *Good mental health* means that people feel comfortable about themselves, right about other people, and able to meet the demands of life.

The definition of counseling implies a number of characteristics. It is an exchange of ideas and feelings between two people, a counselor and a counselee, so it is an act of communication. Since it helps employees cope with problems, it should improve organizational performance, because the employee becomes more cooperative worries less about personal problems, or improves in other ways. Counseling also helps the organization become more human and considerate of people's problems.

Counseling may be performed by both professionals and nonprofessionals. For example both a human resource specialist in counseling and a supervisor who is not trained in counseling may counsel employees. Company physicians also counsel employees, and even an employee's friends may provide counseling.

Counseling usually is confidential so that employees feel free to talk openly about their problems. It involves both job and personal problems, since both types of problems may affect an employee's performance on the job. For example, one employee may be experiencing the stress of new job expectations, while other may be distraught with grief following the death of a family member. Both employees are potential candidates for receiving the benefits of counseling at work.

Although a few companies had employee counseling programs at an earlier date, the recognized beginning of employee counseling was in 1936 at Western Electric Company in Chicago. It is believed that this was the first time a company used the term "personnel counseling" for employee counseling services. Employee job satisfaction definitely improved as a result of employee counseling.

Need For Counseling

The need for counseling arises from a variety of employee problems, including stress. When these problems exist, employees benefit from the understanding and guidance that counseling can provide. For example, one employee feels insecure about retirement. Another is hesitant to take the risk required by a promotion and thus ceases growing on the job. A third employee may become unstable on the job. In all cases, counseling is a necessity.

Most problems that require counseling have some emotional content. *Emotions are a normal part of life.* Nature gave people their emotions, and these feelings make people human. On the other hand, emotions can get out of control and cause workers to do things that are harmful to their own best interests and those of the firm. They may leave their jobs because of trifling conflicts that seem large to them, or they may undermine morale in their departments. Mangers want their employees to maintain good mental health and to channel their emotions along constructive lines so that they will work together effectively.

It is regardless of whether we are faced with attitude problems, frustrated employees, or motivation difficulties – any of these would introduce communication problems-the remedy lies in the same direction.

A supervisor who sees difficulties with people as problems to solve and who wants to understand the employee's situation will use the employee as a source of information. This means he must become adept at drawing the other person out. In any conversation the person who talks the most is the person who learns the least about the other fellow. The good supervisor therefore must become a good listener.

Although most of our dealings with people do not involve unpleasantness or misunderstandings, instances that do occur are sufficiently disturbing to cause management personnel to become interested in some of the basic counseling skills. Among groups of supervisors there is general acceptance of the statement that about 10 percent of the employees are problems. Meltzer reports that the adjustment problems found in the industry include almost the whole array of behaviors found in the clinic.

Many so-called "problem employees" are known to higher management, which means that a single problem employee is discussed at several levels of management. This inclusion of higher management in discussions about employees involves the use of expensive time. One president of a large company spent over half an hour describing a problem his company had with an elevator operator. To know all the details, he must have been in close touch with the matter over a period of months.

Certain valuable byproducts brighten the picture in that they help to compensate supervisors for time spent in counseling activities. Ordinarily, misunderstandings come to our attention when they become acute. However, a supervisor who has counseling skills may use them to prevent subsequent problems or prevent minor disturbances that merely depress morale. Anything that can be done to make good conditions better or to reduce the number of temporary dissatisfactions and disappointments represents a gain. In interviewing a cross section of over 100 male and female employees, the writer found that more than 85% indicated that there were times when they would welcome an opportunity to speak their minds and complain about something. However, only a few scattered individuals said they ever spoke their minds to anyone who was their superior, and an even smaller felt free to speak up and criticize at all.

According to Eisenberg and Delaney, the aims of counseling are as Follows:

1. Understanding self
2. Making impersonal decisions
3. Setting achievable goals which enhance growth
4. Planning in the present to bring about desired future
5. Effective solutions to personal and interpersonal problems.
6. Coping with difficult situations
7. Controlling self defeating emotions

8. Acquiring effective transaction skills.
9. Acquiring 'positive self-regard' and a sense of optimism about one's own ability to satisfy one's basic needs.

Functions of Employee Couseling

The general objective of counseling is to help employees develop better mental health so that they will grow in self-confidence, understanding, self-control, and ability to work effectively. This objective is consistent with the supportive and collegial models of organizational behavior, which encourage employee growth and self-satisfaction.

The counseling objective is achieved through one or more of the following *counseling functions*.

ADVICE	Telling a person what you think should be done
REASSURANCE	Giving a person courage and confidence to face a problem
COMMUNICATION	Providing money and understanding
RELEASE OF EMOTIONAL TENSION	Helping a person feel more free of tensions
CLARIFIED THINKING	Encouraging more coherent, rational thought
REORIENTATION	Encouraging an internal change in goals and values

1. Advice. Many people view counseling as primarily an advice-giving activity, but in reality this is only one of the several functions that counseling can perform. The giving of advice requires a counselor to make judgments about a counselee's problems and to lay out a course of action. Herein lays the difficulty, because it is almost impossible to understand another person's complicated problems, much less tell that person what to do about them. Advice giving may breed a relationship in which the counselee feels inferior and dependent on the counselor. In spite of all its ills, advice occurs in routine counseling because workers expect it and managers tend to provide it.

2. Reassurance. Counseling can provide employee with reassurance, which is a way of giving them courage to face a problem or a feeling of confidence that they are pursuing a suitable course of action. Reassurance is represented by such counselor remarks as "You are making good progress, Linda," and "Don't worry; this will come out all right."

One trouble with reassurance is that the counselees do not always accept it. They are smart enough to know that the counselor cannot know that the problem will come out all right. Even if counselees initially accept reassurance, their new self-confidence may fade away as soon as they face their problems again, which means that little real improvement has been made. Their false sense of self-confidence may even lead them to make poor personal decisions.

Though reassurance has its weakness, it is useful in some situations and is possible to prohibit. Reassurance cannot be prohibited just because it is dangerous, anymore than automobiles can be prohibited because they cause accidents; but, like automobiles, reassurance should be handled carefully.

3. Communication. Counseling can improve both upward and downward communication. In an upward direction it is a key way for employees to express their feelings to management. As many people have said, often the top managers in an organization do not know how those at the bottom feel. The act of counseling initiates an upward signal, and if the channels are open, some of these signals will travel higher. Individual names must be kept confidential, but statement of feelings can be grouped and interpreted to management. An important part of any counselor's job is to discover emotional problems related to company policies and to interpret those types of problems to top management. Counseling also achieves downward communication because counselors help interpret company activities to employees as they discuss problems related to them.

4. Release of Emotional Tension. An important function of nearly all counseling is release of emotional tension; this release is sometimes called *emotional catharsis.* People tend to get an emotional release from their frustrations and other problems whenever they have an opportunity to tell someone about them. Counseling history consistently shows that as people begin to explain their problems to as sympathetic listener, their tensions begin to subside. They are more relaxed, and their speech is more coherent and rational. This release of tension does not always solve people's problems, but it does remove mental blocks in the way of solution, enabling them to face their problems again and think constructively about them. In some cases emotional release accomplishes the whole job, dispelling an employee's problems as if they were mental ghosts.

5. Clarified Thinking. Another function of counseling is that of clarified thinking. This thinking tends to be a normal result of emotional release, but a skilled counselor ca aid this process. In order to clarify the counselee's thinking, the counselor serves as an aid only and refrains from telling the counselee what is "right". Further, the clarified thinking may not take place while the counselor and the counselee are talking. Part (or all) of it may take place later as a result of developments the counseling relationship. The result of any clarified thinking is that a person is encouraged to accept responsibility for emotional problems and to be more realistic in solving them.

6. Reorientation. Another function of counseling is reorientation of the counselee. This is more than mere emotional release or clear thinking about a problem. Reorientation involves a change in the employee's psychic self through a change in basic goals and values. For example, it can help people recognize and accept their own limitations. Reorientation is a kind of function needed to help alcoholics return to normalcy or to treat a person with severe mental depression. It is largely a job for professional counselors who know its uses and limitations and who have the necessary training. The manager's job is to recognize those in need of reorientation before their need becomes severe, so that they can be referred to professional help in time for successful treatment.

The Manager's Counseling Role

Excluding reorientation, managers usually can perform the counseling functions successfully. They will at times perform all five counseling functions. On other occasions, if professional counseling services are available, they will refer employees to the professional counselors. The point is that when counseling services are established, *managers must not conclude that all their counseling responsibilities have been transferred to the counseling staff.*

Managers are important counselors because they are the ones in day-to-day interaction with the employees. If managers close their eyes to the emotional problems of employees and refuse to discuss them, it appears that mangers are saying to employees, "I don't care about you, just your work." Managers cannot, when an emotional upset arises, say, "this is not part of my job. Go see a counselor." Emotions are part of the whole employee and must be considered a part of the total employment situation for which the manager is responsible. For this reason all managers, from the lowest to the highest levels, need training to help them understand problems of employees and counsel them effectively.

Since almost all problems brought to a manager have a combination of factual and emotional content, a manager should not spent all day looking for emotional content when a rational answer will solve the problem.

During a reorganization of office space, if an employee asks, "Is my desk going to be moved?" it may be that she is really wondering why anyone would want to move her desk or whether doing so would reduce her status; but it is also possible- just possible- that she only wants to know, "Is my going to be moved?" If you answer, "Yes, over by the window," you have solved the problem she brought you, and there is no need to try to be an amateur psychiatrist

It is said that the father of psychiatry, Sigmund Freud, warned about the dangers of seeing emotional meaning in everything a person says or does. When a friend asked him what was the emotional meaning of the pipe he smoked, he replied, "Sometimes, sir, a pipe is just a pipe," meaning that it had no particular emotional interpretation.

There are seven core techniques given by Rogers, Carkhoff and Patterson, which assist the manager to apply appropriate core counseling conditions. They are as follows:

- Structuring
- Active Listening
- Silence
- Responding
- Reflection
- Questioning
- Interpretation

Types of Counseling

In terms of the amount of direction that a counselor gives a counselee, counseling can be viewed as a continuum from full direction (directive counseling) to no direction (nondirective counseling). Between the two extremes is participative counseling. These three counseling types are discussed in order to show how counselors may vary their direction in a counseling situation.

Directive Counseling

Directive counseling is the process of listening to an employee's problem, deciding with the employee what should be done, and then telling and motivating the employee to do it. Directive counseling mostly accomplishes the counseling function of *advice,* but it also may reassure, communicate, give emotional release, and- to a minor extent- clarify thinking. Reorientation is seldom achieved in directive counseling.

Almost everyone likes to give advice, counselors included, and it is easy to do. But is it effective? Does the counselor really understand the employee's problem? Does the counselor have the knowledge and judgment to make a "right" decision? Even if the decision is right, will the employee follow it? The answer to these questions is usually "No"; hence advice may not be helpful in counseling.

Though advice is of questionable value, some of the other functions are worthwhile. If the directive counselor is a good listener, then the employee should feel some emotional release. As the result of emotional release coupled with ideas that the counselor imparts, the employee also may clarify thinking. Furthermore, useful communication probably takes place. Both advice and reassurance can be worthwhile if they give the employee more courage to take a helpful course of action that the employee supports.

Nondirective Counseling

Nondirective, or client-centered, counseling is at the opposite end of the continuum. It is the process of skillfully listening to and encouraging a counselee to explain troublesome problems, understand them and determine appropriate solutions. It focuses on the counselee rather than the counselor as judge and adviser thus is client-centered. Managers can use their nondirective approach however care should be taken to make sure that managers are not so oversold on it that they neglect their normal directive leadership responsibilities.

One company gave a full two days of training to its managers on the nondirective approach. They went back to their jobs thoroughly sold on the idea and ready to put it into practice. The trouble was that they did not sufficiently understand its limitations. They refrained from stating their own opinions to employees in their day-to-day interaction. They hesitated to issue instructions and directives. Employees became confused, and their frustrations multiplied. The results were harmful rather than helpful, so finally management had to instruct its managers to return to their former ways of working with employees. They were told that if the nondirective approach was to be used to counsel, it should be a supplement along with normal directive approaches.

Two groups developed nondirective counseling concurrently: Elton Mayo, Fritz Roethlisberger, and others at Western Electric Company and Carl R. Rogers and his colleagues. Here is the way nondirective counseling can work:

Harold Pace went to a counselor, Janis Peterson, for assistance. Peterson attempted to build a relationship that encouraged Pace to talk freely. At this point Peterson defined the counseling relationship by explaining that she would not tell Pace how to solve his problem but that she would try to help him understand it and deal it satisfactorily with it.

Pace then explained his feelings, and the counselor encouraged their expression, showed interest in them, and accepted them without blame or praise. Eventually the negative feelings were drained away, giving Pace a chance to express tentatively a positive feeling or two, a fact that marked the beginning of Pace's emotional growth. The counselor encouraged these positive feelings and accepted them without blame or praise just as she did the negative feelings.

Over time, Pace began to get some insight into his problem and to develop alternative solutions to it. As he continued to grow, he was able to grow; he was able to choose a course of positive action and see his way clear to try it. He then felt a decreasing need for help and recognized that the counseling relationship should come to an end.

Throughout the counseling relationship, it is important for the counselor to *accept* feelings- rather than *judge* them, offering blame or praise- because judgment and evaluation may discourage an employee from stating true feelings. The basic idea is to get the employee to discuss feelings, to explore solutions, and to make wise decisions.

Used by Professionals. Professional counselors usually practice some form of nondirective counseling and often accomplish four of the six counseling functions. Communication occurs both upward and downward through the counselor. Emotional release takes place even more effectively than with directive counseling, and clarified thinking tends to follow. The unique advantage of nondirective counseling is its ability to cause the employee's reorientation. It emphasizes *changing the person* instead of *dealing with only the immediate problem*, in the usual manner of directive counseling.

Professional counselors treat each counselee as a social and organizational equal. They primarily listen in a caring and supportive fashion and try to help the counselee discover and follow improved courses of action. They especially "listen between the lines" to learn the full meaning of an employee's feelings. They look for the assumptions underlying the employee's statements and for the events and feelings that are so painful that the employee tends to avoid talking about them. Nondirective counselors follow an iceberg model of counseling, in which they recognize that sometimes more feelings are hidden under the surface of the counselee's communication than are revealed. For this reason they constantly encourage the counselee to open up and reveal deeper feelings that may help solve the employee's problem.

Limitations. With all its advantages, nondirective counseling has several limitations that restrict its use at work. First of all, it is more time-consuming and costly than directive counseling. Since just one employee with just one problem may require many hours of counselor's time, the number of employees the counselor can assist is limited. Professional counselors require professional education and consequently are expensive. Nondirective counseling also depends on a capable, willing employee. It assumes that an employee possesses a drive for mental health, has enough social intelligence to perceive what problems need solution, and has sufficient emotional stability to deal with them. The nondirective counselor needs to be careful not to become a crutch for emotionally dependent employees to lean on while they avoid their work responsibilities.

In some cases counseling itself is a weak solution because it returns the employee to the same environment that caused the problem. What is really needed is a better environment for employee psychological support. In this situation the counselor may step beyond the usual counseling role and give advice to management to take corrective action.

Participative Counseling

Nondirective counseling of employees is limited

because it requires professional counselors and is costly. Modern, independent employees do not accept directive counseling often. The type of counseling typically used in organizations is between the two extremes of directive and nondirective counseling. This middle ground is called participative counseling.

Participative counseling ,(also called cooperative counseling) is a mutual counselor-counselee relationship that establishes a cooperative exchange of ideas to help solve a counselee's problems. It is neither wholly counselor-centered nor wholly counselee-centered. Rather, the counselor and the counselee apply their different knowledge, perspectives, and values to problems. Participative counseling integrates the ideas of both participants in a counseling relationship. It, is therefore, a balanced compromise that combines many advantages of both directive and nondirective counseling while avoiding most of their disadvantages.

Participative counseling starts by using the listening techniques of nondirective counseling; but as the interview progresses, participative counselors may play a more active role than nondirective counselors would. They offer bits of knowledge and insight; they may discuss the situation from their broader knowledge of the organization, thus giving an employee a different view of the problem. In general, participative counselors apply the four counseling functions of reassurance, communication, emotional release, and clarified thinking.

MARY Carlisle was emotionally upset because she was not getting the promotions that she wanted. Although she discussed her problems with her supervisor, she was not wholly satisfied and asked to see a counselor. She and the counselor established open communication early in their discussion because at this point Carlisle was ready to open to her problems.

The counselor did not tell Carlisle what to do (directive approach) and did not merely listen (nondirective approach). Rather, the counselor explored various alternatives with Carlisle, communicated some ideas about training, and provided reassurance that Carlisle could become fully qualified for promotion. The result was that Carlisle saw her problem more clearly (clarified thinking) and chose an appropriate course of action.

A Contingcy View

A manager's decision to use directive, participative, or nondirective counseling with an employee should be based on an analysis of several contingency factors. It should not be made solely on the manager's personal preference or past experience. However, the manager's knowledge and capacity to use a variety of methods are clearly critical factors in choosing how to proceed.

One of the key contingency elements to consider is the degree to which the employee's problems appears to be focusing on *facts* and the need for a timely, logical *solution* (implying the use of a more directive approach) versus focusing on personal feelings and emotions (implying a more nondirective approach). Another consideration is the degree to which the manager is willing to devote time and effort to the growth and development of a more independent employee. There is also evidence to suggest that counselees have different expectations for the behaviors and characteristics of their counselors, so their preferences need to be considered. For example, some counselees prefer the nurturing role provided through participative or nondirective methods. Others seek someone with job-related expertise or problem solving skills, which are more easily shared through the directive approach. Overall, an effective manager requires awareness of the alternatives available, the skills to be comfortable with each method, and the analytical ability to make a choice that fits the situation.

The Selection of Safe Skills

The Set of Skills Required for an Efficient Counselor are:

- Decency skills, i.e., social etiquettes, warm manners.
- Excellent communication skills which also include non-verbal communication and listening skills.
- Objectivity

- Maintaining confidentiality
- Empathy

Through these attitudes and skills the counselor creates a positive feeling in the counselee, and a hope that the counselor will be of some help. The establishment of this rapport marks the start of treatment.

Some of the important skills to deal with emotionally disturbed people have been developed in clinics and counseling centers. Many of these skills may be carried out of the original setting and practiced in industry. Any clinical or therapeutic procedures which are to be practiced or used by laymen must be foolproof. Sometimes alittle knowledge is dangerous; sometimes a little knowledge is a lot better than no knowledge. The principles that are to be practiced by supervisors must be above criticism. Fortunately, the researches of Carl Rogers and his students have supplied us with procedures, which, if practiced by a skilled person, seem to be as good as any known alternatives, and if practiced with minimum skill, at least permits the person to do no worse than he would have done before training.

Nondirective Skill

Active Listening

Philosophers in the past have spoken of the wisdom of listening, but the development and refinement of listening as a clinical tool is relatively recent. Listening is more than refraining from speaking. A listener must show by his behavior that he is trying to understand, that he accepts the person as well as what he says. For a counselor or a listener to indicate doubt, surprise, disagreement, or criticism places him in the role of a judge or critic; for him to express agreement, pity or even sympathy, places him in the role of a supporter. As a judge he stimulates defensive behavior; as a supporter he stimulates dependent behaviour.

The active listener's behaviour includes a posture indicative of attention, a friendly facial expression, patience, and acceptance of pauses. Certain vocal expressions may rightly be included under listening. These include expressions such as "Uh-huh," "I see," "I understand," and

"Do what you want to tell me about that?" even if the counselor is directly asked to express an opinion, he can avoid entering into a discussion by saying, "Would you like to tell me how you feel about it?" or "I think it is best for you to tell me about it."

Sometimes when people ask questions they want an opinion and the benefit of someone's knowledge. No one should deny another this favor when it is sincerely wanted. However, emotionally disturbed people are often afraid of facts and confused by opinions that conflict with their acts. They resent advice given when they have requested it because it is bound to show that the advisor does not understand. Some people ask for helpful suggestions and then proceed to prove that his ideas given are inadequate. They seem they want to have an insoluble problem. Others ask advice about a general problem or principle, but all the same have in mind, a specific instance in which they are emotionally involved. When one is in doubt about a request for advice, it is best to explore what lies behind questions before giving answers. In learning situations and problem solving discussion, questions are less likely to be emotionally loaded and one need not be on guard. The cautions expressed here are limited to emotional problems, discussions of values, and requests for advice about important decisions. Fortunately, people who persistently ask for advice seldom take it; as a consequence, people who give advice freely do little harm.

Reflecting Feelings

Although listening is an easy skill to describe, it is a difficult one to follow. Associating with people is a give-and-take relationship in which one person alternates talking and listening with another person. Now one is expected to give up a well-learned manner of responding to another person and merely listen to him. This new method of relating to people is difficult because it requires one to inhibit the tendency to respond by speaking.

It is easier to give up a habit if a new one was substituted for the old than if the old one was just broken off. This principle of learning suggests that counseling skills should permit one to replace his advice-giving responses with some useful kind of verbal response. The method of responding to feelings by re-stating or reflecting them effectively satisfies this requirement. Since substituting one response for another is easier that withholding a response, training in reflecting another person's feelings should be introduced ay an early stage.

Reflecting feeling seems awkward at first but supplements the benefits of listening and at the same time makes it necessary for the counselor to speak. However, to reflect feelings properly a counselor must listen carefully and selectively. Selective thinking means that one pays attention to and looks for certain things in a speech. In counseling, one pays attention to feelings while factual material is allowed to fall into the background. Inconsistencies are accepted and indicate to the counselor the need for clarification for further expression. What is *meant* by what is said, not the words *used* to say it, becomes important.

The method of reflecting feelings is analogous to the counselor or interviewer serving as a selective mirror. He mirrors or restates some things that are said to him and allows other things to pass. Facts, incidents, justifications, reasons of arguments and reasons, the chronology of events, where a person went, and what he did, are relatively unimportant; but how the person feels about any of these things is important. These feelings must be reflected so that they can be seen and viewed in a different setting. The counselor helps a person get a more objective view of his feelings by restating them in different words.

In learning to reflect feelings the following points should be observed:

1. Re-stating other person's expressed feelings in your own words rather than serve as a mimic or a parrot.

2. Preface reflected remarks, at first, with "You feel.........," " You think........," it seems to you that......," " It sometimes appears to you that........," and so on. Later in the interview you can dispense with such prefatory phrases.

3. Formulate reflected remarks as statements, not as questions. Speak quietly, slowly, and without emotional tone.

4. Wait out pauses. Long pauses often enable a person to say things that are hard to say. Inexperienced interviewers often are embarrassed by pauses and make distracting reflecting remarks to fill them.

5. When many feelings are expressed, as in a long speech, only the last feeling area expressed should be reflected.

6. Only feelings actually expressed should be reflected. It may be reflected unless it is explicitly stated. Counselors who diagnoses or anticipates nay injure the counseling relationship. Skilled counselors sometimes lead, in that they reflect feelings just a little ahead of those expressed, but unless this leading is accurately and skillfully done it breaks the relationship and frightens the client.

7. When a person contradicts himself, saying on one occasion that he can't understand why someone did something, and on another, that he knows why that person acted as he did, one should reflect each opinion when it is expressed and proceed as if no inconsistency were present. Such changes in expression indicate progress and a clarification of feeling.

8. If a person cries during an interview, references to the act may be made in reflecting remarks, provided the person is not attempting to hide the tears.

9. Watch for mixed feelings involving a conflict between (1) what the person wants to do and feels he should do; (2) what others think and what he thins; and (3) his values and those of society. These ambivalent feelings should be reflected.

10. In reflecting another's state of mind, any indication of approval or disapproval must be avoided. It is important to refrain from questioning, probing, blaming, and interpreting, giving advice, persuading, reassuring, and giving sympathy.

11. Diagnoses should be avoided. A diagnosis is a counselor's interpretation of why the disturbed person feels as he does and leads to biased listening.

12. It is almost safe to assume that what initially appears to be the problem is not the real one.

13. Avoid being solution-minded. Remember that the solution must come as a result of the person's own insight.

The method of reflecting feelings helps and supplements listening, but it introduces two additional values. First, it gives the counselor a way to pass the conversation back to the client when he feels he is expected to give some kind of reaction or judgment. Even a direct question, such as "what would you do if you were in my place?" can be reflected by "you feel you would like me to tell you what to do?" second, it stimulates further expression in the general feeling area reflected. Many of the everyday benefits of listening are never realized because the expression stops short of the important and more complete release of feeling.

The Use of Questions

The unskilled counselor should avoid the use of questions as much as possible. The everyday use of questions tends to direct conversation, and it puts a disturbed individual at a disadvantage because he either does not know answers or he does not feel free to give the one he knows. Questions that are in the spirit of nondirective counseling may serve a convenient and helpful function, however.

Questions such as "Would you like to tell me about it?" "Did that bother you a lot?" and "Was anyone there at the time?" stimulate further expression in a feeling area under examination. Such questions neither pry nor direct the course of the discussion. Care must be taken to avoid questions that can be answered by "Yes" or "No".

When the counseling process has reached the stage of exploring various behavior possibilities, questions may be used to explore consequences. Such questions as "What do you think would happen if you did that?" "How would that affect the others?" and "Do you feel you could eventually adjust to that?" cause the person not only to evaluate the actions but also the consequences of actions. Note, however, that none of the questions indicate approval or disapproval; they merely explore whether or not the consequences of various actions have been considered.

Essential Attitudes

The counselor's attitude toward a client will influence the skill with which he practices his methods. If he likes and respects another person he can do a better job of listening and reflecting feelings than if he dislikes or feels superior to this person. In nondirective counseling certain attitudes, beliefs, and values are consistent with and supportive to the methods.

Accomplishments of Counseling

Attitudes and Needs are Discovered

The importance of preventing misunderstandings as well as correcting them has been emphasized. It is apparent that one can have more satisfactory dealings with an employee if one knows why that employee turned down a particular promotion, why he was disturbed because he wasn't offered a job he didn't want, why he refuses to cooperate with another, why he violated a company rule, or why he resists change. Nondirective counseling skills provide a way for recognizing and dealing with misunderstandings caused by differences in attitudes and needs even when the question of therapy is not raised. Not only does the nondirective interviewer better understand an employee but the employee understands himself better. A person's attitudes and needs may be vague and confusing to him until they are expressed. The mere telling of a complex experience clarifies it by showing up hitherto unperceived defects, inconsistencies and gaps in continuity.

Because the nondirective approach to people respects attitudes and needs as well as clarifies them, sincerity and skill in its use becomes an important asset for many interview and face-to-face situations. Furthermore, the basic skills are essential to conference leadership where permissive climates are prerequisites to constructive participation.

Frustrated Condition is Reduced

Any procedure, which permits expression of hostile and regressive behavior without introducing unfavorable experiences, reduces tensions and relieves frustration. The process of obtaining relief from emotional tension through the mere expression of feeling (such as talking out loud about a deeply felt problem) is known as *catharsis*. It is clear that supervisors who understand the process of frustration, and who can furnish a climate in which employees can furnish a climate, in which employees can gain relief from frustration, will be able to deal with many types of emotional behavior problems. Some of the situations may be passing affairs and relief is all that is needed; others may continue and so the relief will be merely temporary. However, even temporary relief may be sufficient to introduce some problem-solving behavior and create opportunities for readjustment.

Many frustrations go back to childhood experiences. Memories of unjust punishment or parental rejection may be vague and seemingly forgotten, but their emotional effects remain strong and color adult reactions to marriage, reprimand, men of superior rank, or failure. If these pockets of feeling are located and the childish hostilities are expressed, marked changes in meanings may occur and behaviors can become more mature. A state of frustration common to a whole group may be released through "gripe sessions." In this instance the discussion leader uses his permissive skills and his ability to reflect feelings in a way that will stimulate further expression in a group discussion.

True Problem is Located and Accepted

In a state of frustration a person is inclined to blame others, insist that there is nothing he can do, doubt the worthwhile ness of life, and generally bemoan his misfortune. But regardless of how unfortunate a person may be, he must come face-to-face with the present. If he is to achieve an adjustment he must ask himself, "What can I do about it?" suppose a young man, through no fault of his own, has lost an arm. Quite naturally he feels that his problem is the loss of an arm and that there is nothing to do about it. An artificial arm, at best, is a poor solution. As he sees it, his problem is insoluble. Before problem-solving behavior can take place, one must be confronted with a soluble problem. Strictly speaking, the loss of an arm is an obstacle rather than a problem. Problem solving is the search for a way to circumvent, remove or overcome an obstacle that is blocking progress toward some goal. This goal must be a part of any description of a true problem. If our young man's goal is to live a happy life, then this problem becomes, "How can I get the most out of life with what limbs and abilities I have?"

Accepting reality- including one's deficiencies, injuries, and bad luck- is the first prerequisite to solving life's problems. As long as a person blames others, hides his weaknesses, or his faults, he has not located the difficulty in a way that permits him to solve his problem. Looking backward, thinking of what might have been, and wishing are important feelings; and they must be expressed so that they do not stand in the way of discovering the soluble problem.

Only as a person obtains relief from frustration is he able to focus on his true problem. Until then he is too preoccupied with his feelings to be able to see a problem. If anyone points out to him how he should constructively view his situation, he is unable to accept the counsel and instead may feel that he is in an unsympathetic world. Until a person is ready to *accept* his problem he is unable to *see* it, and from the good advice given to him he merely learns that no one understands.

Problem-Solving is Stimulated

Problem-solving behaviour is characterized by explanatory or searching activity and a ready recognition of existing realities. Various routes or approaches to goals must be examined and evaluated before the best decision is reached. Listening and reflecting ideas helps this process because it stimulates the movement or flows of ideas. A person will persist in an idea if it is challenged, but when the idea is accepted and reflected he has to go beyond it. Furthermore, the restatement of an idea in other words enriches it, encourages new meanings, and stimulates examination of new approaches.

The following excerpt from an interview between the head of the department and the safety director illustrates how reflecting them influences learning.

SAFETY DIRECTOR: I think our supervisors have been too lax with our employees. If men persist in violating these safety regulations we will just have to step up the penalty.

DEPARTMENT HEAD: you feel the failure to solve our safety problem is due to lack of enforcement and inadequate penalty.

SAFETY DIRECTOR: Yes, I do. I can't do this job alone, and supervisors will have to help. They are too soft and don't like to lay a man off. Then, once they let one fellow get away with something they have to ignore other violations so as not to get charged with discriminatory practices. You just can't get supervisors to see what you can't make exceptions. (Long pause) Maybe the trouble is that our penalties are too severe. It's harder to lat off a guy you know than to make a rule.

Problem-solving behavior is also aided by the effective use of questions. One can increase the range of a person's or a group's thinking by asking good questions. A question can take a person out of a rut in his thinking, cause him to explore various ideas, get him to evaluate good and bad features of various alternatives, and stimulate an interest in or a search for facts without imposing, evaluating, or suggesting. Questions upgrade the quality of thinking, even when they supply no clues or disclose no preferences.

Responsibilty is Developed

A person who has difficulties in coping with life's problems often is a dependent person. He looks to someone to get him out of one difficulty after another. Frequently, his background reveals parents who have always made all the decisions. Such an individual has been denied the opportunity to become emotionally mature; even if a counselor or a friend gave him good advice and even if he took it, his basic problem-that of immaturity- would not have been solved. Nondirective counseling, from the outset, makes no pretense of solving a client's problem. Instead, he is told that he must decide to do what he thinks best. The role of counseling is that of helping a person to help himself.

Nothing creates a sense of responsibility as quickly as having responsibility. The counselor gives the individual responsibility for solving his own problem, even for returning for other visits. If a client asks, "Do you want me to come again?" the counselor may reply, "That is up to you. If you feel you would like to come again the time is yours." Clients who have been requested to visit a counselor and show resentment on their first visit usually return voluntarily.

The Counselor as an Expert

Once a person has rid himself of feelings that interfere with solving problems, he often is in a position to solve them. However, the counselor or the supervisor often has useful knowledge. The very information or the relevant facts that may be avoided because they are threatening to a disturbed person becomes realities that must be faced when the problem-solving stage is reached. The counselor should be willing to assist a client in obtaining information that can help in solving problems and making decisions.

The counselor plays a dual role: on the one hand, he facilitates the client's expression of feeling; on he other hand, he aids in the problem-solving process.

Some Practical Considerations in Employee Counseling

Number and Length of Interviews

If the purpose of counseling interview is to assist a disturbed or confused person to improve his emotional adjustment, it is safe to assume that a number of interviews ma be required. Such interviews should have a time limit- for example half or three quarters of an hour- and the employee should be able to feel that this period is his if he wishes to use it. A prearranged time for terminating an interview makes it unnecessary for the interviewer to find an excuse for breaking off a long and sometimes unprofitable session, and it also avoids making the employee feel he has overstayed his welcome. Then too, the spacing of interviews allows a person time to consolidate gains and grow between visits.

The actual number of visits needed varies with the problem. Surprising improvements have occurred after one interview. However, for personal off-the-job problems involving personality difficulties, a skilled counselor regards 10 to 20 visits as typical. An interviewer must not, however, assume that just because a problem points to a difficulty on the job, its true character has been located. Incidents that set off an emotional reaction must not be mistaken for causes.

Single interviews of the counseling type can do solve complex job problems, prevent others, and clarify still others. Some typical examples are briefly described below to illustrate the opportunities for counseling that present themselves in industry.

An employee had been repeatedly interviewed regarding a job change fro lineman to office work. Over a period of twenty five years he had received training on three different jobs, but was found unable to handle them, he now insisted that he be given another opportunity because of his health. His medical reports did not substantiate his claims. The supervisor responded to certain references he made to off-the-job experiences, and before long he spoke freely about them. His background revealed marital difficulties and adjustment problems going back to his childhood. Although these personal problems were not solved by these interviews, it became apparel to the employee as well as the supervisor that a job change would not help him. In this instance counseling prevented further waste of interview time.

An employee reacted in highly emotional fashion when a supervisor explained why he was unable to give her time off to visit her boyfriend in another town. Assuming that the denial of such a favor was not a sufficient reason for causing so violent a reaction, he responded to the feeling expressed. He finally learned that the girl was pregnant. As a consequence he altered his decision and gave her a leave of absence.

Time and Place

Time and place arrangements should take into account the employees feelings. An interview should be of interest to both parties, and the employee should be invited and given a choice of times convenient to the interviewer. The setting for the interview should be one in which the employee can feel at home. Elegant surroundings, being seated in an open area while a desk, distractions, interruptions - any of these make for a strained atmosphere, protect an interviewer. When suitable surroundings are not available at the plant, it is sometimes best to adjourn to the coffee shop. The president of one company wondered why he learned so much more from his men when he visited them in the field than when they came to his office. He failed to realize that a president's office furnishings often reflect his high position and introduce a barrier to communication. Most supervisors, however, are close enough to the men who report to them so their offices are familiar places. If not, things should be done to make them more familiar.

Keeping Confidences

It goes without saying that confidences should be kept. To use permissive methods to gain information this will be used to the detriment of the employee which will cost more in the long run than the immediate gain or saving warrants. Even so, the method, no matter how skillfully used, will not cause employees to give a supervisor the incriminating evidence that they give to a professional counselor or a priest. The fact that a supervisor is an authority-figure is one of the important limitations of counseling as practices by supervisors. However, not all problems involve this limitation, it is not necessary to confine counseling to supervisors. Rather, counseling skills make men better supervisors. On some occasions a counseling interview may disclose a problem that can be solved by making certain changes or by involving other people. The way this is done should always be worked out in discussions with the employee to avoid any feeling that confidences have been betrayed, even when the change is it the employee's advantage.

Location of Counseling Services

The management of a company might recognize the value of counseling and wish to make services available to its employees. How should this be done? It could hire professional counselors and make them a part of either the medical or the personnel department, or it could train its supervisors and thereby expand the scope of their responsibility.

Perhaps the greatest disadvantage in the use of expert counselors is that the service is not readily used. Only a limited number of employees seek help when the service is available in medical and personnel departments. The experience of Western Electric and the Ohio Bell Telephone Company, who pioneered in counseling programs, showed that it was rather difficult to get employees and supervisors to accept counselors. Supervisors felt threatened by the program because they felt employees could unjustly criticize them. The general experience was that acceptance of the counseling program required from one to two years. Both the pioneering companies abandoned their programs, not because they failed, but because they failed, but because top-management support was lacking after the initial supporters had retired.

The strongest arguments against training supervisors for counseling are limitations of skill and time. However, a limited amount of skill will assist the supervisor in dealing with superficial disturbances and it can do a great deal in helping him prevent problems. Psychopaths, of course, require professional treatment.

Perhaps the ideal method is to combine the two approaches. Training supervisors permits them to deal with some emotionally disturbed employee and at the same time gives them an understanding of the role an expert might play. An understanding supervisor can do a great deal to encourage an employee to visit the counselor.

Today, the trend in management training is in the direction of increasing the amount of time and emphasis devoted to listening and to rudimentary counseling skills. Supervisors welcome this training and see it not only as an increase in their workloads but as an aid in their performance of their jobs. There is also an increase in placement of psychologically trained persons in personnel departments and it is not uncommon to have a trained counselor in the department.

Meltzer describes opportunities for the skilled personnel man to improve the mental health of employees. These occur in various interviews he conducts (induction, appraisal, follow-up, and exit): his daily rounds; his attendance at monthly departmental meetings; his role in supervisory training problems; and his services as a counselor. Dr. Meltzer advocates a projective type of interviewing, in which the specific purpose of the interview is considered, and also creates an opportunity to learn about the employee. Details of his background, attitudes, feelings, history of frustration, and sources of pleasure and tension serve as a useful purpose in providing understanding of some of his reactions that appear to be more irrational than the situation warrants. Skilled personnel in key positions can accomplish a great deal to make supervisory personnel aware of mental health problems and to create an appreciation for the types of counseling skills.

Articles on Employee Counseling

Real Life Disasters

"Animal / Human Bonding Grieving, Coping, Counseling" by: Dave Johnson Cascades Biomedical Consulting Intl. Inc.

This presentation provides a focus on the emotional impact of a disaster to the research animal staff. The devastating loss of animal lives, providing care to the injured and ill animals, ongoing chaos, hardships of the working conditions, uncertainty of the near and long-term future of the institutions solvency, along with personal and family crises issues, places a serious emotional burden upon the staff.

Urgent Actions Staff Effects

An emergency crisis stimulates and energizes many of the animal care providers since they possess the skills required for intervention. This adrenalin rush and call to duty activates the staff to extraordinary efforts of productivity. The chaos and urgent problem solving stirs creativity and problem solving. It also leads to exhaustion, frustration, and a sense of being overwhelmed. The psychological well being of the research animal staff is clearly stretched.

Grief: Dead and Dying Animals

The shock of reality rapidly sets in as the staff witnesses the delay of being allowed entrance back into the animal facility until safety officials deem it safe. This is followed by the shock of seeing many dead and injured animals. The psychological trauma of mass death and then coping with surviving animals can lead to serious emotional consequences for the staff.

Grief: Surviving Animals

After triaging the animals, the staff then carries out the difficult tasks of providing intensive care treatment to the animals. Witnessing the non response of certain animals to treatment leads to frustration. An additional emotional factor is having to euthanasia clinically normal animals whose exposure to the effects of the disaster no longer qualifies them for future research. Examples include inhalation exposure to smoke, drenching from water and exposure to unknown environmental chemicals. For animals that do recovery, they need to be re-qualified for new studies. Re-qualification is frequently undefined and thus places further new challenges to the staff. On top of these factors, there is the need for mass euthanasia for animals too injured or ill. Although this is intrinsically ethical, the process of heuthanizing hundreds of animals can take its emotion toll on employees who are also feeling the emotional stress of the surrounding crises as they think of their immediate families, personal health, and future career.

Grief: Post-Disaster

The grief following the aftermath of a disaster, poses challenges to the research animal staff as they must deal with post disaster issues of animals, co-workers, facility destruction, chaotic organizational responses, and for themselves.

Coping

Grieving Cascades of Emotions

–Denial

–Anger

–Bargaining

–Depression

–Acceptance

Staff will demonstrate an array of these emotions

–Adds to the stress for Supervisors and Managers

The cascades of events are denial, anger, bargaining, depression, and finally acceptance. The staff may demonstrate a variety of these emotions and in any order. Even if they are close to acceptance, emotional factors can trigger them back to re-start this process. Depending on the event that they are coping with, they may have a multitude of these feelings whether their focus of event is loss of animals, facility destruction, inner feelings of their own loss, and response to co-workers. Supervisors and managers require the skill to deal with their staff displaying a wide array of emotions. In addition, supervisors and managers are coping with their own grieving feelings.

Personnel Management

Uncertainties facing the staff may be real or perceived. Yet perceived uncertainties trigger feelings that are genuine requiring equivalent coping responses. Personnel management unknowns include future employment, financial stability of the institution, key investigators with major grant awards relocating to a different institution, personal financial hardships, and family members wishing or insisting to relocate to a different geographical location. Meanwhile, there may be a temporary layoff and reduced work hours with a loss of income during the facilities recovery process.

Counseling

A disaster preparation plan can incorporate counseling services to deal with these emotional and coping issues that will arise. These counseling services are readily available and many organizations provide them as part of their Wellness Programs. Fully confidential services are available to employees for emotional issues such as family problems, marriage strains, drug abuse, alcoholism, depression, etc. The counselors can be briefed about the organizational disaster plan so in the event of a catastrophe, the counselors are better prepared to provide professional counseling to the staff. These Wellness Programs are usually fully paid by the organization for multiple initial sessions. If long term counseling is needed, then this care is transferred to the employee's medical insurance program.

Counseling - Post Disaster

Having this post disaster counseling services pre-arranged through the contracted Well Programs, allows readily available counselors to help the staff. Emergency training programs related to disasters can include participation from the Wellness Program counselors. By addressing these emotional and coping issues prior to a disaster, it complements the organizational Disaster Plan and gives excellent resources for the employees.

Pre and post disaster counseling is key to any Disaster Plan. Employees will require comfort, care, conciliation, and companionship. Even arranging for certain employees to bring their own pets to the employee staff lounge following a disaster provides excellent emotional support.

Getting by with a Little Help From Friends - peer helping programme. HR Magazine, Oct, 2000 by Rudy M. Yandrick

Employees with personal problems may respond more readily to a peer-to-peer intervention from a trained co-worker.

Every manager has had to deal with problem employees who resist help: the welder whose heavy drinking has gotten out of control, the emotionally fragile secretary who sabotages projects, the computer technician who fails to show up for three or four days at a time.

Chances are, they have been counseled, been given sub-par performance evaluations and even had their pay docked—everything short of being fired. Still, their behaviors continue to give managers their biggest headaches and pose great risks to the company.

To deal with such behavioral health problems and intervene with them earlier, some employers and occupational groups are turning to peer-to-peer programmes.

"Time and again I've seen situations where an impaired worker will listen less defensively to a colleague than to a supervisor, from whom he is more likely to be hiding the problem. It's a matter of being approached about their problem by a co-worker, with whom they share much in common, instead of an authority figure," says E. Paul Hoover, a Kansas City, Mo.-based health and productivity consultant. "Employers will always use tools like progressive discipline and management confrontation to Ideal with employee personal problems, but often they can be addressed earlier and more effectively with the involvement of a trained peer."

Two That Lead the Way

One company that has produced convincing results using a peer-to-peer program is Weyerhaeuser Corp. Since 1997, the Seattle-based forest products company has been using trained peer referral agents, or "helpers," at its work sites. According to Dr. Jeffery N. Thompson, the company's medical director, the Peer Helping program was designed to prevent or intervene early in issues including work stress, alcohol and drug abuse problems, and other disabilities when impairment becomes noticeable on the shop floor.

"Weyerhaeuser has found that peer helpers can become adjuncts to its team-based management, where peer helpers act as listeners, mentors and coaches, freeing up the time of managers and supervisors," says Thompson. "Their primary role is to identify and intervene with troubled co-workers and, in some cases, refer employees to the corporate employee assistance program (EAP)."

Peer helpers are trained in basic listening skills, peer-to-peer counseling, work stress, return-to-work issues and substance abuse. "While the skills are basic, they are powerful tools to assist employees in both simple and complex problem solving," Thompson adds. Local EAPs assist the helpers by augmenting their training and serving as mentors and referral resources for more difficult problems.

As often happens with successful workplace initiatives, Weyerhaeuser's Peer Helping program has evolved beyond its founding mission. Today, it also functions informally as an organizational development tool and talent mine. Many peer helpers develop a knack for spotting problems that cause work stress. When stress is high due to situational problems like layoffs, work system changes or return-to-work issues following a disability or turmoil at the mills, they help employees to cope. In short, they manage crises.

Peer helpers usually are selected by the workers. "As the helpers gain self-assurance," Thompson adds, "they become more assertive in seeking out people for active intervention. Over time, many of them use their skills in new roles in the company. They become effective and mature team leaders."

Weyerhaeuser's Peer Helping program is being studied under the Workplace Managed Care grant program of the Substance Abuse and Mental Health Services Administration (SAMHSA) of the U.S. Department of Health and Human Services. Outcomes data from SAMHSA suggest the program is cost-effective, especially when used in conjunction with a managed care program. Early results from an in-house study at Weyerhaeuser show that as mental health utilization goes up at Peer Helping sites, costs remain stable. "The findings tell us that we are intervening with employees earlier and more successfully," Thompson notes.

Outplacement Techniques - Counseling of Terminated Employees. Folio: The Magazine for Magazine Management, April, 1990 by Katherine Smith.

For the person in your publishing company who has just been dismissed, regardless of the reason, the termination or exit interview is the beginning of a personal ordeal. Searching for a new job can be one of the most debilitating experiences in life. For many people, this is intensified by their lack of knowledge about the job search process.

Confusing practical problems surface: How do I prepare a resume? How do I get it into the right hands, instead of into the waste basket? How do I find out about the best jobs? How do I answer when a potential employer asks why I was let go? What kind of reference will I get from the company?

Even the simplest mistake made in putting together a resume or in answering an interviewer's question can extend the period of unemployment-and in many cases, the period of time that person is collecting on your unemployment account. in addition, if the person has personal trauma, he or she can be out of work for a long time and grow to resent you and your company for the fate that has befallen him.

One way to help ensure that an employee leaves your company feeling as good as possible about how he has been treated is to provide out-placement counseling.

Outplacement strategies can be very complex or very simple, but should always be designed to meet the specific needs of the individual involved. Many publishing companies offer these services, including Times Mirror Magazines, Hearst, McGraw-Hill, Reader's Digest, CMP Publications, Capital Cities/ABC, New York Times Magazines and Maclean Hunter Media. All realize that the out-placement counseling does not mean the company has assumed responsibility for getting the person a job. Rather, the counseling is intended to provide these people with advice, instruction and a sounding board-all of which should help them organize and execute a job search with effective results.

Whether internal or external specialists are used, the outplacement should be conceived as part of the support package being provided to an exiting employee. Although the company is sponsoring and paying for the outplacement services, the terminated employee is the client throughout the process. The outplacement counselor must have the complete trust of the employee and believe that the advice and suggestions being offered are intended solely for the employee's benefit.

In many cases, employees initially believe that the counselor's job is to be supportive of the company's reasons for letting them go-or that it may be the counselor's role to steer employees away from applying to competitors. Problems of this type can typically be resolved during the initial meeting as long as the counselor is careful to clarify his or her role and answers questions in a straightforward manner. A counselor must be sensitive to the need for establishing a relationship of trust between himself and the terminated employee. However, this does not mean that the counselor needn't abide by the company's rules and policies.

Internal or External?

A company's choice of an internal or external counselor will depend on its unique needs. There are advantages to both. Internal outplacement counselors are readily available to respond to the needs of the company. And because they are part of the company, they can often spot problem areas in termination practices. They may also have more impact on events leading up to the decision to let a person go.

External outplacement counselors, on the other hand, are experienced in a wide range of industries and have a level of credibility that is not afforded to an internal counselor. Because of their objectivity, they are often better able to handle sensitive terminations. And it is often easier for them to obtain the confidence of the terminated employee, since they are not employees themselves.

One specific and important advantage of providing such a counseling service is the elimination of pressure on the manager of the terminated employee. The manager will be less likely to offer ill-advised promises of help or to make other mistakes in the termination meeting. Just knowing that the terminated employee will be meeting with an outplacement counselor where he or she will be given ample opportunity to ventilate feelings about the company allows the manager to proceed with the meeting. The terminated employee then proceeds through a structured process that focuses on the future, rather than on the past.

The problems that confront a terminated person are

complex and can be complicated by strong emotions aroused regarding failure, loss of self-esteem, jealousy and so forth. A structured outplacement program goes a long way toward alleviating some of the problems brought on by the loss of a job. It also extends the company's sense of obligation to its employees and protects its position with those who remain behind.

Preventing Work Place Violence: Dealing with an Angry Employee. Drew W. Edwards, MS Violence in the workplace is an increasingly common yet poorly understood problem. But experts agree that workplace tensions reflect what is happening in the society at large. Stress, personal problems and the uncertainty of modern life have left many workers feeling alone, vulnerable and ill-cquipped to cope with conflict—now more than ever. When anger is unresolved, the chances of violence increase.

Recognizing the early sign of a problem before it becomes a disaster is the key to preventing workplace violence. Although there are no clear-cut indicators that tell us when anger will turn to violence, there are signs that tell us when anger is unresolved and becoming destructive.

Anger is a normal emotional response to stress, a perceived threat or conflict. Reasonable people can disagree, sometimes vehemently, without ever threatening or intimidating another person. In fact, research shows that expressing anger appropriately is healthy—like releasing the pressure in a tire that has been over inflated. But if the pressure remains too high and the tire is driven at high speeds, a blowout is inevitable.

Stressors

Rarely does a single event send a happy, cooperative worker over the edge into violence. And while we seldom know all that is going on in our co-workers' lives, stress is the common denominator for workplace violence. It usually comes from:

- a serious personal problem that has made its way to the workplace

• changes or threats to job status, such as a new assignment or supervisor

• a personality conflict with a manager or another employee

Stages of Anger

Whatever the cause, angry workers generally progress through predictable and sequential stages of increasingly negative attitudes and behaviors. The four stages of anger are:

• negative attitude

• power struggle, excessive arguing

• cutting criticism, malicious gossip and sarcasm

• revenge, vandalism and violence

For Example

Let's say you have just been promoted as the new manager in a new department. After several weeks, you observe that one of your employees frequently challenges your decisions. You are aware that this employee was expecting to get the promotion that you received. This individual is hurt, angry and choosing to deal with it by arguing and power struggling with you (stage 2). Consequently, one of two things may happen:

• It will get worse—he will progress into stage 3 and become more covert with his anger via gossip and sarcasm, which will escalate the situation.

• It will get better—he will quit power struggling, and slide back into stage 1. This is a sign that things are improving.

By understanding the stages of anger, you can assess if the strategies you choose to implement are making the situation better or worse.

What You Can Do

If you are concerned about an employee's anger, try to place him in one of the stages of anger. That will give you a baseline of understanding the present situation—so that you can create appropriate intervention strategies—and a way to measure if strategies to remedy the situation are working or not. Second, try to pinpoint a time when things weren't so tense. This may offer a clue as to what may be contributing to the present situation. For example, a recent divorce or an expected promotion that did not happen may be contributing factors.

Remember, whenever there is a potential for violence, talk with an employee assistance program (EAP) professional. They are trained in counseling, conflict resolution and communications, and can discuss options to help you develop a strategy to effectively handle the situation.

Employee Counseling – Are We Ready For It? Prof. Gowri Joshi

A primary research was carried out in the year 2002 at a manufacturing company based in Mumbai, India. This public limited company has five manufacturing sites across the country and four sales divisions. This research aimed at investigating the (felt) need for employee counseling in the organization. The design of this research study was exploratory in nature. The primary source of data collection was structured interviews, the sample being one hundred and ten (110) employees which is 20 % of the employee strength – five hundred and fifty three (553) of the corporate office of the company. The interview schedule comprised of both closed and open ended questions. A random sampling technique was used. The employee sample was 20 % of each of the divisions operating from the corporate office and was a perfect mix of managerial level employees, staff level employees and worker level employees.

Some important conclusions that were derived from the research study are:

- Majority of the employees of the company (61% of the sample) were unaware of the concept of Employee Counseling. Those employees who had a partially correct idea (25 % of the sample) about employee counseling knew that it was related to helping an employee in distress, advising, creating self-awareness and personality development. The remaining 14 % had an incorrect understanding about the concept.

- After the researcher had explained what employee counseling was all about, 69 % of the sample agreed that there was a (perceived) need for employee counseling in the company. The reasons were many, most common ones being to assist employees solve their personal and/or work related problems and to improve the employee relationships and overall culture of the workplace. Among the 31 % who were of the viewpoint that employee counseling as an institutionalized process was not needed in the company, 57 % of this group felt that the company had a family culture and the informal relationships between the employees could be leveraged upon.

- Only 22 % /of the sample disagreed on the importance of employee counseling as a part of HR –systems while 78 % of the employees felt that counseling is an important HR function.

- 83 % of the employees were unaware of the companies practicing Employee Counseling in India (this could also be because the sample was a mix of managerial employees, staff level and workers)

The research results indicate that majority of the sample under study responded positively to the hypothesis i.e. a need for Employee Counseling was felt and that it would benefit the organization. However, the awareness about the concept of counseling and employee counseling, particularly so was found to be exceptionally low. Psychological counseling is of various types. Rational Emotive Behavior Therapy by Dr Albert Ellis popularly known as REBT is most widely applied. Rational Emotive Behavior Therapy (Source: Albert Ellis Institute, NewYork) REBT is a practical, action-oriented approach to coping with problems and enhancing personal growth. REBT places a good deal of its focus on the present: on currently-held attitudes, painful emotions and maladaptive behaviors that can sabotage a fuller experience of life. REBT then provides a variety of methods to help people reformulate their dysfunctional beliefs into more sensible, realistic and helpful ones by employing the powerful REBT technique called "disputing." Ultimately, REBT helps people to develop a philosophy and approach to living that can increase their effectiveness and happiness at work, in living successfully with others, in parenting and educational settings, in making our community and environment healthier, and in enhancing their own health and personal welfare. REBT is based on a few simple principles having profound implications:

1. You are responsible for your own emotions and actions.

2. Your harmful emotions and dysfunctional behaviors are the product of your irrational thinking,

3. You can learn more realistic views and, with practice, make them a part of you,

4. You'll experience a deeper acceptance of yourself and greater satisfactions in life by developing a reality-based perspective.REBT distinguishes clearly between two very different types of difficulties: practical problems and emotional problems. Your flawed behavior, unfair treatment by others, and undesirable situations, represent practical problems. Regrettably, your human tendency is to upset yourself about these practical problems, thereby unnecessarily creating a second order of problems—emotional suffering.

Some other types of counseling processes are Sigmund Freud's Psychoanalytic Therapy; Carl Roger's Client Centered Therapy; Carkhoff Model of Personal Counseling; Gestalt approach to counseling; Rational Emotive Behavior Therapy by Albert Ellis. Freud's Psychoanalytic Therapy is based on the power of the unconscious mind. According to Freud, who is the Father of Psychology the human mind is like an iceberg. As only the tip of the iceberg is seen by the naked eye so is only one tenth of the human mind known to us. Psychoanalytic therapy taps this semi and unconscious mind through different techniques like dream analysis, etc. It was Carl Roger who supported a view that counselees should be addressed as 'clients' and unlike Freud's psychoanalytic therapy where a counselee plays a passive role, in Client centered therapy the client plays a more active role as compared to the counselor. Hence the name Client Centered Therapy." Carkhoff model of personal counseling is an offshoot of Roger's Client Centered Therapy. It focuses on attending, responding, personalizing and initiating action as indispensable counselor skills. Gestalt approach to counseling focuses on looking at human beings from a 'holistic' perspective. The word 'gestalt' means "a whole being".

Whatever type of therapy the counselor has expertise in, whether it be Client Centered Therapy or REBT or any other, institutionalizing an employee counseling system in an organization is a different ball game all together. Right from getting top management approvals and budgetary sanctions to getting trained counselors on the rolls or on part time basis all are equally challenging. Preparing the employees for counseling is another yet important area. One of the biggest fears that prevent employees from using the services of a counselor is the social and professional stigma attached to counseling.

Conclusion

Many firms today realize the importance of attracting and retaining highly skilled, quality employees as a necessary component of their competitive advantage. One of the reasons that a quality workforce along with innovative tools for attracting and retaining has become so important is because previous sources of competitive advantage have become less important overtime.

Today, HR practitioners are busy developing new and innovative tools to attract and retain quality workforce. Employee counseling is a service offered by companies to their employees. Organizations that care for their employees are perceived as more meaningful and purposeful. Every organization has economic and social goals. Here, it is worthwhile to note some observations made by the Chairman of Infosys in this regard. He states, "The task of leadership is to make people believe in themselves, the organization, in the aggressive targets the organization sets. Belief comes from trust: the trust that this organization isn't about making one set of stakeholders better off; it is about making every one of us better off...."

A firm may gain competitive advantages from Employee Counseling activities especially if its reputation and image is valuable, rare and not easily imitated. Employee counseling therefore is a very powerful tool in the hands of companies in attracting and retaining quality workforce. Employee counseling has shown some effectiveness over the years, as a process of helping people come through with their troubles.

Preparing the employees for counseling is another yet important area. One of the biggest fears that prevent employees from using the services of a counselor is the social and professional stigma attached to counseling.

Counseling is a process of helping people to learn how to solve certain interpersonal, emotional and decision problems. Counselors help their counselees to 'learn'. Largely, employee counseling has been a 'remedial approach'. But recently there has been a slight change in emphasis, from remedial to 'preventive'.

References

(1) Norman R F Maier. (1976). Psychology in Industry. (Third Edition). New Delhi: Oxford & IBH Publishing Co., pg. no.- 652-673.

(2) John.W.Newstrom and Keith Davis. (2001). Organizational Behavior- Human Behavior at Work. (Tenth Edition). New Delhi: Tata Mc Graw Hill Edition, pg. no. –429-458.

(3) K.M.Phadke and Rita Khear (1998). Psychology in Industry: A Rational Approach. (First Edition). Mumbai: Himalaya Publishing House.

(4) Internet Information: www.google.com Articles related to Employee Counseling:

REAL LIFE DISASTERS: "Animal / Human Bonding Grieving, Coping, Counseling" by: Dave Johnson, Cascades Biomedical Consulting Intl. Inc.

GETTING BY WITH A LITTLE HELP FROM FRIENDS -

peer helping program. HR Magazine, Oct, 2000 by Rudy M. Yandrick.

OUTPLACEMENT TECHNIQUES - counseling of terminated employees. Folio: The Magazine for Magazine Management, April, 1990 by Katherine Smith.

PREVENTING WORK PLACE VIOLENCE: Dealing With an Angry Employee. By Drew W. Edwards, MS.

EMPLOYEE COUNSELING – ARE WE READY FOR IT ? Prof. Gowri Joshi.

INDUSTRIAL AND ORGANIZATIONAL PSYCHOLOGY

INDUSTRIAL AND ORGANIZATIONAL PSYCHOLOGY

(In Two Volume)

(Volume - 2)

Dr. H.L. Kaila

PUBLICATIONS

KALPAZ PUBLICATION

Delhi - 110052

Industrial and Organizational Psychology

Rs. 1500 (Set)

ISBN : 81-7835-525-6 (set)
ISBN : 81-7835-526-4 (vol. 2)

Published in 2006 in India by
Kalpaz Publications.
C, 30 Satyawati Nagar,
Delhi-110052
email : kalpaz@hotmail.com

Laser Type Setting by: Mega Graphics, Delhi
Printed at: Salasar Imaging System, Delhi

Contents

10

Perspectives Of Workplace Counselling

- Introduction to Workplace Counselling
- History of Workplace Counselling
- History of Workplace Counselling in India
- Models of Workplace Counselling
- An Integrative Model of Workplace Counselling
- Performance Counselling
- Career Counselling And Planning

"The role of the organization is to support the process of employee empowerment through promoting mental health education, counseling and other information services to the workforce".

N.Tehrani, Counseling psychology Quarterly

The modern workplace seems to demand more employee time than ever before, there are fewer resources with which to do the work and more and more employees are suffering from "presenteeism". Levels of stress seem to be at an all-time high. Statististics bombard us daily on how stressful the workplace has become. Not only have learned journals published their research studies, but stress has become a constant feature in the popular press and glossy magazines. There is a constant reminder that the changes in the organizations are putting extra stress on those employees and that employers are becoming worried by the legal implications. **O'Leary (1993)** and **Cartwright and Cooper (1994)** have documented some statistics around mental illness in the workplace:

- One in five of the working population suffers some form of mental illness each year (approximately 6 million people)

• Approxim ately 20 percent of any workforce are affected by personal problems that impact on their work performance

• When asked about the 'true' reasons for absence from work, over half the employers felt that emotional/ personal problems and stress were to blame

But as a new era dawns many firms have realized the importance of attracting and retaining highly skilled, productive and quality employees as a necessary component of their competitive advantage. Previously, a firm's success was attributed to an emphasis on product and process technology, access to financial markets, developing economies of scale & learning curves, patents, protected and regulated markets & individual attractiveness. Recently, however, some scholars have noted that these traditional sources of success are less important than in the past and emphasize that the selection and management of a quality workforce has become an increasingly critical factor to organizational success. Today, HR practitioners are busy developing new and innovative tools to attract and retain quality workforce, as they are concerned of having healthy and a high performing employees. As a result, many employers are providing facilities to help employees increase their level of physical fitness and reduce instances of physical illness. These may be either in-house facilities or the use of other facilities in the locality (O'Leary, 1994).

Among others provisions that are being made for the well being of the employees by the organization, there is a growing awareness amongst the organizations that it makes practical, humane and economic sense to provide **workplace counseling** to the employees which can help them to deal with their personal and professional problems. Organizations that care for their employees are perceived as more meaningful and purposeful. Here, it is worthwhile to note some observations made by the Chairman of Infosys in this regard. He states, "The task of leadership is to make people believe in themselves, the organization, in the aggressive targets the organization sets. Belief comes from trust: the trust that this organization isn't about making one set of stakeholders better off; it is about making every one of us better off...."What is workplace counseling?

Despite recent literature on workplace counseling, and despite the length of time counseling has been a part of the workplace, there is still a great deal of uncertainty about what it entails. But largely workplace counseling can be defined as a discussion between the counselor and the employee about the real or perceived performance deficiency or job-related behavior, the employee's perception of the identified behavior, the supervisor's involvement in helping the employee correct these behaviors, and the employee's attempt to reduce or eliminate the misconduct or incompetence. Egan (1994) has noted the financial cost to organizations due to psychological and social problems, and has listed the kind of everyday problems that can be costly to the organization: a poor relationship between two key members of a production team, a middle manager who is becoming dependent on alcohol, a secretary grieving for a dead relative who misplaces an important letter. When these individual problems are seen in the context of a large workforce, and when they go unnoticed and undealt with, then, collectively the cost can be immeasurable. As a result employee counseling is deemed necessary in the workplace.

There are various reasons why employers are turning to counseling as one method, among the others, of caring for their workforce.

Employer's responsibility for the welfare of their employees is one reason. More and more employers realize that illness and productivity do not go well together. Counseling also highlights the value of people as organizational assets. Pfeiffer's (1994) research into successful organizations showed clearly that the most important factor was the way they cared for their employees.

Secondly, employers are turning to counseling as one way of helping to manage the mammoth changes taking place in organizations. Change is never easy: it disrupts, disorientates, causes grieving and takes time. Support is needed for individuals and teams as transitions in organizations are managed. Counseling is one way of supporting employees as they cope with organizational change.

Thirdly, counseling can itself be a source of organizational change. Rather than being just an appendage to a company, counseling can bring the values, the energy of change, the vitality of acceptance to the very dynamics of workplace life. Counseling can influence organizational culture to work towards the ideal strong and adaptive culture that serves the company.

Fourthly, a firm may gain competitive advantages from employee counseling activities especially if its reputation and image is valuable, rare and not easily imitated. Employee counseling therefore is a very powerful tool in the hands of companies in attracting and retaining quality workforce. Counseling services within the workplace are being viewed not just as 'crisis' points or for severely disturbed individuals, but also as a preventive service. Counselors are in a unique position within the organizational setting to offer the kind of training and education that prevents mental illness. In the long run, preventive measures are more cost effectiveThus, these are some of the reasons why employers introduce counseling into the workplace. Cooper (Magnus, 1995) has divided the reason into three categories: according to his research, 76 percent of employers see counseling as a caring facility; 70 percent expect counseling to help employees deal with workplace change; and 57 percent view counseling as a means of managing stress. Thus, having counseling available in the workplace means that problems can be dealt with fairly quickly and can be worked through in the very environment from which they often emerge.

The History of Workplace Counseling

The historical development of employee counseling gives an insight into various reasons for establishing counseling provision. In brief there have been three phases in workplace counseling

The history of workplace counseling began in the U.S and was intertwined with the arrival in industry of medical, psychiatric and social work provision

The Human Relationship Era

Counseling in the workplace, specifically, has existed since the 1900s but in quite different formats.

The first era in employee counseling emphasized human resources and human relations as the key factors in effective management. It focused on the link between the working problem of the employees and organizational behavior. Tehrani (1995) has traced the roots of British employee counseling to the late nineteenth century with the introduction of welfare officers whose job it was to monitor the physical and mental well being of employees. The lull in mental health provision seems to have taken place between the 1940s. Mayo was a keen figure in rescarching employee needs, criticizing industry for not paying adequate attention to psychological needs of employees and himself establishing a counseling service in 1936.

When a new phase of interest emerged directed at employee health, the earlier emphasis on 'attendance production, health and disciplinary problems' gave way to issues of alcoholism, accident, psychosomatic accidents, the ageing worker, executives' emotional problems, techniques of management and structuring of the work environment". Alcohol concerns dominated much of the counseling provision fro this stage until the 1960s. The term Employee Assistance Programme (EAP) was coined by the National Institute of Alcohol Abuse and Alcoholism as a way of widening provision to include problems other than alcohol. The 1940s witnessed the beginning of the EAP era of workplace counseling with such provision centered principally on alcohol issues in industry.

Era of Employee Growth

The second era in workplace counscling put in place services for helping employee growth. There was still emphasis on "unhealthy" employees and how to help them to return effective work and the main providers of help tended to emerge from medical backgrounds with the "medical model" uppermost in their minds. Presnall saw 'persistent' and 'pervasive' work place needs which gave rise to employee assistance programs as fourfold:

1. To do more about problems in the workplace

2. To act upon the realization that the workplace is both a human problem breeder, and a problem resolver

3. To humanize the workplace

4. To develop new work practices based on the awareness that areas are interrelated in the workplace etc, i.e. health, wholeness, work and relationships.

Internal And External Counseling Provision

The third phase in employee counseling was ushered in with the Employee Assistance Programs, which moved beyond solely dealing with alcoholic issues. Still with an emphasis on drink and drug problems, they moved swiftly in the 1960s, 1970s and 1980s to provide a range of services, legal and financial help, stress management, telephone counseling and face-to-face counseling. Counselors and counseling psychologists were now part of mental health teams and individual counseling became a major part of EAP services. Throughout the history of workplace counseling, EAPs have been the most visible form of counseling provision. They were set up as internal or external services, the former as part of an organization and the latter usually as a service specializing in providing EAPs to a number of organizations. What has existed, in the third era of workplace counseling alongside EAP provision, both internal and external, has been the "in-house" counselor. Here, rather than opt for a range of services, presently in the pioneering stage of this and the first generation of in-house counselors has laid the foundation for counseling in organizations.

The present day practice of counseling in the workplace places emphasis on an array of services for the employee, on confidential settings and particularly a holistic approach to emotional well being at work.

Thus, the history of workplace counseling unveils a progressive movement towards greater employee care on the part of the employers. Today, those companies who utilize counseling provision, either internal or external, tend to combine counseling with a broad range of other helping facilities. Perhaps the next stage in workplace counseling is to see it as a helpful mode of organizational change and not just as an aid to individuals within the organizations.

History of Workplace Counseling in India

Although we have traced the history of workplace counseling, it still has to become prominent in India. Counseling is still considered a taboo and a person who avails of counseling facilities is looked down upon. But this may not be the case everywhere. There are a few companies, especially BPO's who hire counseling services for their employees.

According to Bhooma Dand, Assistant Manager, CETC, counseling in the workplace has yet to be a permanent feature in companies. Organizations are unwilling to spend money on the well being of their employees understanding fully well the pressures that their employees work under. She has stated that in India counseling in workplace has emerged in three trends.

The first trend was seen when innumerable training programs made their way in organizations. These training programs along with enhancing the productivity of workers, to a large extent also resolved a lot of problems of the employees. The training programs cover a lot of issues such as stress management, assertiveness programs, communications skills and the like. Since most of the problems of the employees revolved around these issues, knowing how to handle such issues made employees better equipped at handling their own problems. It also increased the self-esteem of the employees because they were more equipped at handling issues that bothered them rather then seeking help from a third party.

But a lot of times, problems become unmanageable and employees need to take advise from a third party. This is where the second trend in counseling emerged. At such times when employees need the support of someone else, managers/superiors in the organization lent a ear to the employee's problems. Although mangers were not skilled at counseling, they could still ask their employee to "talk it out", if they realized that an employee was having a bad day at work. Similarly, they also supported and advised employees who came to them with their problems.

Although many managers advised and supported their employees when in need, many employees were uncomfortable and scared of talking about their personal problems to their managers for the fear of being negatively evaluated and being sacked. At this point of time many of them turned to someone outside their organization, namely counselor who could understand the issues bothering them and resolve the issues. This is where the third trend comes into the forefront. But although people have started meeting counselors, very few organizations have realized the importance of hiring an in-house counselor. Thus, it can be seen that at various levels the problems of employees have been addressed but there yet has to be a huge change in the mindset of the organizations as far as hiring an in-house counselor is considered or providing counseling services outside the organizations.

Professor Gauri Joshi carried out a primary research at a manufacturing company based in Mumbai in 2002.This public limited company has five manufacturing sites across the country and four sales divisions. This research aimed at investigating the (felt) need for employee counseling in the organization. The design of this research study was exploratory in nature. The primary source of data collection was structured interviews, the sample being one hundred and ten (110) employees that is 20 % of the employee strength – five hundred and fifty three (553) of the corporate office of the company. The interview schedule comprised of both closed and open ended questions. A random sampling technique was used. The employee sample was 20 % of each of the divisions operating from the corporate office and was a perfect mix of managerial level employees, staff level employees and worker level employees.

Some important conclusions that were derived from the research study are:

• Majority of the employees of the company (61% of the sample) were unaware of the concept of Employee Counseling. Those employees who had a partially correct idea (25 % of the sample) about employee counseling knew that it was related to helping an employee in distress, advising, creating self-awareness and personality development. The remaining 14 % had an incorrect understanding about the concept.

• After the researcher had explained what employee counseling was all about, 69 % of the sample agreed that there was a (perceived) need for employee counseling in the company. The reasons were many, most common ones being to assist employees solve their personal and/or work related problems and to improve the employee relationships and overall culture of the workplace. Among the 31 % who were of the viewpoint that employee counseling as an institutionalized process was not needed in the company, 57 % of this group felt that the company had a family culture and the informal relationships between the employees could be leveraged upon.

• Only 22 % of the sample disagreed on the importance of employee counseling as a part of HR –systems while 78 % of the employees felt that counseling is an important HR function.

• 83 % of the employees were unaware of the companies practicing Employee Counseling in India (this could also be because the sample was a mix of managerial employees, staff level and workers)

The research results indicate that majority of the sample under study responded positively to the hypothesis i.e. a need for Employee Counseling was felt and that it would benefit the organization. However, the awareness about the concept of counseling and employee counseling, particularly so was found to be exceptionally low.

The way the corporate sector has opened up to the world economy, it is now high time for organizations to open up for employee-orientated HR processes like counseling, coaching and mentoring. The corporate world is changing and so are the Human Resource Management practices. It is imperative that we adapt the changing styles to manage our people better. It is not just for the benefit of the employees but in the interest of the organization to show that 'we care' about this important segment of our stakeholders.

MODELS OF WORKPLACE COUNSELING

Various models portray the roles and tasks of counselors in the workplace. There are altogether seven models of workplace counseling. A number of these models can also be combined; in fact, it could be said that the effective employee counselor has access to a range of models applicable to different clients and different situations. The eight models of counseling are as follows

1. Counseling Orientation Models
2. Problem Focused Models
3. Manager Based Models
4. Work Oriented Models
5. Welfare based Models
6. Externally based Models
7. Internally based models

1. Counseling-Orientation Models

The Counseling-Orientation model is characterized by its use of a counseling approach as the key factor in what is offered to as employee clients. Counselors by and large, subscribe to or are affiliated to, and often trained in, a particular therapeutic approach, which they use when working with organizational clients. Historically, this has been the common way of engaging in employee counseling. Subscribing to a particular counseling orientation means accepting a specific view of human nature and an explanation of why individuals behave the way they do. This in turn leads logically to an assessment congruent with the counseling approach and interventions designed to bring about change.

Several authors have taken particular counseling orientations and reviewed how they might apply in the workplace counseling; for example, cognitive behavioral therapy (Webb, 1990), neuro-linguistic programming (NLP) (Sanders, 1990); Psychodynamic (Gray 1984).

Most Counselors who use particular counseling approaches apply their counseling theory within organizations in the same way as they do when practicing independently. There is some understanding of how organizations are assessed using a particular counseling model. For example, *Kets de Vries* and *Miller (1984)* have used a psychoanalytic approach to designate different types of organizations, where *Morris (1993)* has adopted a rational-emotive therapy as a paradigm for organizations. However most counseling orientations do not have such a typology. The main interest is still focused almost exclusively on individuals and the organizational dimensions of counseling work are largely ignored.

2. The Problem Focused Models

The problem-focused model of counseling sees the counselor's role as helping individuals to work with the immediate problems they bring.

There are several other problem-focused models available. *Nelson-Jones (1995)* developed DASIE, a five-stage model in what he calls "life skills counseling". The five stages comprise a very helpful problem solving methodology:

D Develop the relationship, identify and clarify problems

A Assess problems and redefine in skills terms

S State working goals and plan interventions

I Intervene to develop self-helping skills

E End and consolidate self helping skills

The above model is practical and applicable. It is based on the theoretical position that "most problems brought to helpers are educational in nature" but it can also be used without such belief.

Problem focused counseling emerges for a number of reasons: the limited amount of time counselors can provide to clients, the number of counselors available to service company, the theoretical background from which the counselors emerge and organizational constraints, e.g. finance.

3. Manager Based Models

There is a tendency in some organizations to view managers as quasi counselors for their staff. Since much managerial time and many of their tasks involve working with and managing people, it is a short step to propel them into the counseling role. *Reddy (1993a)* has suggested that, when managers are using counseling skills they ought to be recognized as counselors. *Nixon and Carol (1994)* however argue against the managers taking on a formal counseling role. According to them, not only does it cross boundaries but also puts employees in an impossible situation: asking, on one hand, that they share personal issues with their manager, and, on the other hand, that they be ready for appraisal vis-à-vis their career with the same manager. In short, asking managers to be counselors creates role conflicts for them and confusing responsibilities for their employees.

With the advent of counseling training for personnel officers, human resource officers, managers, there is a tendency for people to combine a number of roles with employees. But important differences have to be drawn between counseling professionally, the use of counseling skills and the employment of counseling skills as one role among many. This distinction will indicate what managers can and cannot do with respect of their "Counseling" with employees.

4. Work Oriented Models

The work-oriented model of counseling is so named, because it is centered solely on issues blocking an individual in his or her work. Work oriented models of counseling pinpoint the immediate problem as a workplace issue and work with it. They do not spend time on the underlying areas of why problems exist, nor are they interested in issues that are not related to the workplace. Their aim is to facilitate the individual to the workplace problems and move back to work as quickly as possible.

This is an attractive counseling model for managers who want value for money and want to think that the time spent in counseling is for the welfare of the organization through the individual. However, it is not always easy, in practice, to differentiate between what is a workplace problem and what is a personal problem not related to work.

5. Welfare Based Models

Welfare based models of counseling combine a number of roles with employees, one of which is counseling. Welfare officers have traditionally been employed in a number of organizations to fulfill several tasks depending on client needs: befriending, information giving, counseling etc.

Welfare based models of counseling have been the predecessors of counseling provision in the workplace. Such models were more social work based, seeing counseling as one of the many roles enacted with employees. Their strength is their ability to provide a range of interventions, one of which may be counseling. Their limitations depend on the abilities of the welfare officer to work across roles.

6. Externally Based Models

Externally based models are those brought in from outside the organization. Usually in the form of an EAP, they are administered and organized from outside. The format used can be any of the above models, or indeed mixtures of them, since EAP providers generally do not employ counselors on the basis of their counseling orientation.

There are several formats of external counseling provision used by organizations: some employ established EAPs, others set up an internal EAP, others again opt for employing individuals to work on a sessional basis with employees. *Jones (1985)* has outlined the characteristics of several EAP programmes:

(A) Full Service Programmes

Employees and dependent

Retirees and dependent

Disabled and dependents

Any kind of problems

Voluntary

Confidential

Follow up and outcare

Outreach

Employee orientation

(B) Limited Utilization Programmes

Provide approximately five to eight free sessions but charge the individual or third person carrier for anything beyond that this can be a fee-for-service arrangement

(C) Information and Referral only Programmes

- No face-to-face counseling
- Referrals made by telephone
- Little or no follow-up

Externally based models of workplace counseling have increased over past decade and it is anticipated that they will continue to increase over the next few years.

7. Internally Based Models

In house counseling provision is the norm in a number of companies. A part or full time counselor, or in some instances a team of counselors, is employed to work with employees. The counseling service can be a part of an already- existing department or an independent unit in its own right.

In-house counseling provision can be set up in a variety of ways: an in-house EAP, with a team of counselors, with an individual counselor, as within a particular departments, as outside all departments, as a part time or full-time. Internal and external counseling provision can be combined within one organization.

An Integrative Model Of Workplace Place Counselling

Counseling in an organization is more of a triadic relationship with the client counselor and organization in a three-way relationship. Models that involve more than two people in counseling are the closest models to counseling in the workplace.

Workplace counseling is divided into five stages. The five stages of the integrative model are:

Stage 1: Preparation for Workplace Counseling

Stage 2: Assessment

Stage 3: Contracting/Referring

Stage 4: Engaging in Workplace Counseling

Stage 5: Terminating in Workplace Counseling

The above stages do not have to be followed rigorously. They are meant to be flexible and simply act as a guide. Workplace counselors are flexible and adapt their time and therapeutic relationships to particular situations. The five-stage model needs drastic adaptation at times: often there is a crisis or an emergency that bypasses stages in the model and focuses immediately on the presenting problem.

Stage 1: Preparation for workplace counselling

Preparation for counseling allows the counselors to operationalize and think through before they begin to see clients. By doing so they can have a system in place that can be further adapted in the light of their experience.

The counselor prepares for workplace counseling by organizing:

- Clear policies regarding the roles and responsibilities of the counseling service to clients and to the organization. This policy indicates the interactions between all the three systems: clients, counselors, and organization.
- A clear structure for managing the counseling process.
- A focused counseling location set up ready for counseling.
- An understanding of the objectives of workplace counseling; the counselor should be clear about workplace counseling and what aims are being achieved.
- Information they want from the clients to help with (a) assessment, (b) counseling, and (c) evaluation of counseling.
- A network of referral.
- Appropriate insurance by the counselor.
- Information to be given to the clients before counseling and during it.
- An understanding of what model is being used.
- Personal supervision for client work.

- Methods of advertising the counseling service.
- A method for keeping the statistics and presenting reports.
- Clarity around what information will be given to the employing organization.

Clients also Prepare for the Counseling by Knowing

- About the counselor: name, phone number, place of counseling service.
- What is counseling is about.
- The parameters of confidentiality.
- The roles and responsibilities of each person in the counseling system: counselor, organization, client

Careful organizing and planning for counseling means extra safety and containment for the clients.

Stage 2: Assessment

Assessment is the means by which; (a) clients decide if they wish to continue to see this counselor; (b) counselors make an initial formulation of why the client has come for counseling; (c) counselors/clients can decide to work together or an appropriate referral is made

The Stages of Assessment Cover The Following Areas:

1. **Understanding the Clients and their Issues**
2. **Methods of Assessment**
3. **Agreeing an Assessment**
4. **Considering Interventions**
5. **Agreeing Counseling**
6. **Sharing Information**

1. Understanding The Clients and Their Issues

The 'judgments' formulates and defines what counselors consider to be the problem, whether or not counseling is the appropriate intervention for the client, and whether or not the is the best person to work with the client.

2. Methods of assessment

There are several formats available for assessing clients in the workplace. The choice of which of these to use will depend on several factors such as the belief of the counselors, the needs of the workplace, the setting of the counseling service, etc. Methods of assessment can be divided into two areas; those that assess the individuals and those that assess taking an organizational aspect.

(A) Formal Assessment using an Existing Formula. The Diagnostic and Statistical Manual of Mental Illness (DSM) is the most commonly used method of diagnosis.

(B) Psychometric Assessment. Some counselors use psychometrics as a way of understanding clients. For instance the Myers-Briggs Inventory. Other tests for personality, depression, decision-making and stress can also be utilized to assess the clients.

(C) Interpersonal Assessment. Many counselors rely on the relationship between themselves and their clients and the use of transference and counter-transference as their guide in assessing clients. Monitoring what is happening in the therapeutic relationship gives insights into the client's personality, interpersonal style, characteristics and way of handling conflict.

(D) Assessment of presenting problems and underlying psychological needs: Crouch (1992). Provides a helpful distinction in clarifying what is happening to the clients. He draws the distinction between particular problems and psychological concerns. The former usually present difficulties with which the client needs help: a financial difficulty, etc. Psychological concerns are underlying patterns in a person's life that give rise to present problems: the inability to hold down a close relationship, not being able to get on with people of authority. Psychological concerns generate problems.

There are also two assessment models where the emphasis is on the organizational aspect of assessment.

(A) Workplace Assessment. Because counseling is in the workplaces there are further aspects of client problems that deserve consideration. Many a times poor performance in the workplace is due to factors outside work for instance, an unhappy marriage, problems with children, medical illness etc. At other times the poor performance may be due to the organization itself, for instance, difficult manager, poor management overall, etc. In such cases it is very important for the workplace counselor to discover the actual problem and then work out a way to enhance the performance of the employee by reducing or eliminating the problem.

(B) Assessment of client within the organization. Torjman (1985). Offers a five step approach to assessment which combines individual and organizational assessment issues:

- Obtain a clear description of the situation troubling the employee
- Determine who sees the situation as problematic
- Why has the situation become problematic
- How often has the situation occurred and for how long
- What efforts have been made to deal with the situation
- What solutions are possible and what helping resources may be required

In summary, it is essential that workplace counselors have clear methods by which they articulate how they understand what is happening to their clients. It is equally important that those methods take the workplace into consideration in assessing clients and do not presume that all problems arise from within the individuals.

3. Agreeing an Assessment

Although it seems obvious that the counselor and the client will work towards a common agreement on what is happening to the client, this does not always happen. Sometimes counselors formulate an assessment and never share it with clients thus leading to a conflict between both the participants. By and large, clients are relieved when some definition of what is happening to them is offered. This gives the clients more say in the discussion, it helps them to understand that they too have resources and are not totally dependent on an 'expert' who understands them more than they understand themselves.

If a formulation of the issue, problem or difficulty can be agreed between counselor and client, then this goes a long way in setting up appropriate interventions.

4. Considering Interventions

Counselors tend to err in seeing most issues in "counseling' terms and do not always consider other interventions as well as they might. There are many forms of interventions, all of which have valuable contributions to make: medicine, psychiatry, social work, etc. As suggested by *Malan (1976)*, it is worthwhile to think:

Medically: does the client need medical help?

Psychiatrically: does the client need psychiatric help? There can be a tendency for counselors to be vary of psychiatrists and not utilize their services

Psychodynamically: are there any underlying issues for this client?

Practically: what does the client need to help him or her just now?

Matching intervention to client is a key skill for workplace counselors. Getting it wrong can result in Wasted time and strong feelings on the part of the client. As a result, there must be an adequate evaluation of clients, of methods of intervention, of goals, and a rational method for aligning candidates, interventions, therapists and goals.

5. Agreeing Counselling

Presuming that, as a result of assessment, data intakes and reviewing possible interventions, both counselor and client agree that counseling is the preferred intervention, then counselor and client should agree on which counselor is the best suited for this individual. In many instances, it will be the workplace counselor, the person who did the initial assessment. But within a counseling service there may be a choice of counselors and allocation can be made, with the agreement of the client, on a number of factors:

- **Gender:** Sometimes clients will choose a same sex counselor in the hope that it will facilitate understanding.
- **Race and Culture:** Like gender, race and culture can be difficult issues to work with and giving clients the choice of similar race counselors is a great sign of respect for individual needs.
- **Sexuality:** It is essential in the workplace, where homophobia can be rife- among individuals; groups and institutionally gay individuals have the freedom to have counselors who can work with them effectively.

Referral to counselors outside the company can also be made possible. Specialized counselors may be available through them or through other resources.

6. Sharing Information

Once agreement has been made to engage in a counseling relationship, then counselor will share information on the service and answer questions from the client. This may have taken place at an earlier stage. However, once they have decided to meet, there will probably be other issues that need clarifications. Counselors may need to explain:

What counseling is about?

How counseling works

What information is needed from both counselors and clients?

In conclusion, the assessment stage of workplace counseling is a key element in its overall success. It demands particular skills in diagnosis, in formulating problems, in understanding workplace, in negotiating with clients. From the employee counselors perspective, it demands a clear understanding of what workplace counseling is about, how to utilize assessment effectively, and how to get the best help possible for this client with this problem.

Stage 3: Contracting/Referring

The third stage of counseling in organizations is the contracting phase. The counselor and client agree to work together or agree that client needs referral to another counselor or agency.

This stage of counseling contains several components:

1. **Agreeing to work together**
2. **Contracting on**
   - **practicalities**
   - **roles of client and counselor**
   - **roles of the organization**
3. **Referring, if appropriate**

1. *Agreeing to work together*

This is a formal agreement whereby the counselor and client agree to work together within a counseling relationship:

2. *Contracting*

The contract or agreement outlines the issues which have been negotiated and agreed, and include

- Confidentiality
- When information would go back to the organization, with or without permission of the client
- What information will be kept on file by the counselor
- Who will have access to notes
- Who will own counselor notes
- What is counseling and what is expected from the clients
- How to contact the counselor
- What to do if a session needs to be cancelled
- Supervision arrangements by the counselor
- Where to meet
- How often to meet

- What to do if either cannot keep an appointment
- What to do if either wishes to terminate counseling before the agreed date
- Number of counseling sessions

3. Refering to Clients when Appropriate

Instead of working together, counselor and client will agree that a referral is required. This conclusion will have implications for action in the following areas:

One area pertains to the question of who, whether the client contacts the appropriate agent or will the counselor set up the referral. Sometimes counselor will contact the referral agency and make a formal referral, possibly a written letter. The client will then telephone to arrange a meeting time. At other times, clients simply need knowledge of the referral group and can set up help for themselves.

Another area that needs to be clarified is the contact between the referral agency and the workplace counseling service. In such cases it is appropriate that referral agency write a report., for example, referral for a psychiatric assessment which is shared with the counseling service. At other times, there will be no contact between referral agency workplace counselor unless finance is involved, in which case it may be sufficient to have a letter indicating services rendered.

Thus, contracting in workplace counseling helps all parties involved- counselor, client, and clients department, the organization, the referral agency- to be clear about the rules, roles, responsibilities involved in engaging in counseling.

Stage 4: Engaging in workplace counseling

Engaging in workplace counseling, besides the actual contact with the individual clients, contains a number of other elements: identifying clients who need counseling, assessing clients for counseling, working with clients as counselors, working with employees and the organization in other capacities. This fourth stage is when the actual counseling sessions together occur. The following four issues are given importance here:

1. **Managing with personal dimension**
2. **Working with the administrative side of counseling**
3. **Working with the organization**
4. **Fulfilling other roles within the organization**

By and large counseling is a private affair between consenting adults behind closed doors. Two individuals meet, form a working relationship, and combine efforts towards helping the client deal more effectively with his/her life. This can be regarded as the interpersonal part of counseling process: what takes place when the counselor and the client are together.

Besides the above given dimension, there are two other dimensions that do not get quite as much attention: the administrative and organizational aspects. Effective counseling takes all three areas into consideration in setting up, maintaining and terminating counseling.

1. The Personal side of Counseling

Essential to counseling in general, and to workplace counseling in particular, is the value of personal/ interpersonal dimensions of counseling. Setting up a counseling relationship and establishing rapport with clients is crucial to effective counseling. The personal side of counseling takes place in the counseling room where the right kind of therapeutic relationship is forged by counselors who are able to engage in the kind of relationship that best serves the client at the time.

2. The Administrative side of Counseling

The face-to-face encounter between the counselor and the client needs to be administered so that his professional relationship remains professional and safe for both parties. The administrative side of counseling (the arrangements around the counseling work) is about good house keeping, involving a number of areas before, during and after actual counseling contact.

First Contact Between Client and Counselor

1. How do clients contact the counselor?

2. What information is given to the client at this first contact?

3. What happens in the intervening time between first contact and first meeting? Does the client receive any further information?

4. Where do counselors and client meet? How is this setting arranged, organized and made safe for both clients and counselors?

5. Are counselors covered by the insurance of the organization or do they need to have their own indemnity arrangement?

First Meeting

1. Do clients have clear directions on how to get to the locations of their counseling session?

2. Who meets them? What is said to them? Where do they wait before seeing the counselor? What arrangements are in order should they come early?

3. What information is needed at this first meeting: by the client, counselor?

After The First Meeting

1. How are notes written?

2. Where are they kept?

3. Who has access to these notes

4. How are referrals handled, if needed?

5. How do clients pay for counseling, if that is appropriate?

During counseling

1. How are emergencies dealt with?

After termination

1. What happens to notes? For how long are they kept before being destroyed?

2. Are there other types of relationships formed with clients after they have terminated counseling? What are the guidelines for this?

3. If a referral is made, what information is given to the new counselor? Is there any contact made between the two counselors?

4. How is referral handled?

5. How is counseling evaluated?

Answers to the above questions will depend on a number of factors: the counseling orientation will often dictate how arrangements are handled; the freedom counselors actually have. However, a lot of times these issues are not thought before they happen. The administrative aspects of counseling create a safe system where information flows throughout and at any given moment in the whole process there is safety for both participants.

3. The Organizational side of Counseling

Besides personal and administrative dimensions of counseling there is the organizational side. The organizational aspect of counseling provision has to be considered carefully by counselors. The organization plays a significant part in the counseling provision offered to the clients. A number of organizational questions need to be considered carefully before counseling begins so that they can be dealt with in a prepared way when they intrude into the counseling work:

- What kind of organization is this and how does it understand counseling?
- Where do the loyalties of the counselor reside and whom: company or client
- What happens when the values of the organization conflict with those of the counselor

There are a very few counseling situations where an organizational context does not enter and influence the work being done, even in private practice. Individuals do not live in isolation, they belong to families, learning communities, work organizations, etc. And these systems not only have an effect on their lives and are a part problems but often need to be involved in their treatment. Therefore social support is seen as a crucial element in the efficacy of counseling. Thus, the more support an employee has in the workplace the more effective will be their counseling be.

4. Fulfilling other Roles Within The Organization

Re-entry of Employee into the Workplace

An organizational issue affecting workplace counseling, and one rarely dealt with, is that of helping individual employees who have been out of workplace dealing with personal problems, on return to workplace. By and large, individuals are left to find their own way back into the system they left. Their fellow workers are anxious about the re-entry, how they deal with their colleague, whether they talk what has happened, or do not mention it. And how does the individual employee re-enter the system they left to deal with mental illness? A format needs to be set up formally whereby the group is helped to deal with the individual's return, and where the individual is able formally to re-establish his/her place in the community. This can be best done in the following way, and the counselor is often the best person to do it:

1. Meet with the individual client and assess what has happened. Establish why he/she was off work. In such cases the workplace counselor ideally will have contact with the specialist who worked with the individual, know about the medication and possible side effects, and know on what basis the employee is coming back to work. In many companies it will be important for the employee counselor to work in close liaison with the occupational health department, particularly doctors since it is often they who monitor the return of employees and direct their working hours.

2. With the client's mission, meet with the department to which he/she belongs to. The counselor may give explanation on why the employee has been on sick leave, what the main issue was, and the development of the employee. This is an opportunity for the team members to ask questions, for information to be given, and advise and guidance received on how best to re-establish relationships.

3. A formal meeting where the individual meets the department, with the counselor present At this meeting there is an opportunity to welcome the individual back, to talk openly about how he/she is, and to establish any guidelines for re-entry.

It is essential to recognize any individual preferences and the team's ability to deal with issues in this whole operation. Forcing individuals to go through a process that would stress them unreasonably, even for good intentions, is not helpful. Employee counselors will judge the situation carefully before implementing procedures for re-entry of employees.

In summary, it is important to take into consideration not only the personal dimension of counseling, but also the administrative as well as the organizational dimension of counseling in order to having a fruitful relationship with the client.

STAGE 5: Terminating in Workplace Counseling

Terminating the counseling relationship is viewed as an essential part of the whole counseling process. Termination is not just about the ending phase of counseling: it is built into the very contract itself. Where a client is seen for one or two sessions, it may not be very formal. Where employees continue to work in the same company as the counselor, it is always possible that they will return at a later date for further counseling. Still termination needs to be considered even though it may be different from termination in other settings where counselors have choices (in the workplace counselors cannot refuse to see clients because they have worked with them previously).

Termination Can Be Seen Through A Number Of Issues

1. **Agreeing a termination date**
2. **Working towards termination**
3. **The process of termination**
4. **The final session**
5. **After termination**

1. Agreeing A Termination Date

Workplace counselors will agree a termination date at the beginning of counseling, perhaps six or eight sessions. This date will be clear to both counselors and clients. The termination date will be flexible in that, as it approaches, more time is negotiated to help clients continue to work on their issues. Reminding clients about the number of sessions left can motivate them towards work and can help them rehearse terminating counseling. In some instance counseling can continue by default: both parties are anxious about mentioning in case it hurts or offends the other. Whatever the decision about how counseling will be terminated, leaving sufficient time aside to deal with termination issues is essential. Termination in counseling should never take place during session in which the issue is raised. Some counselors build "termination contracts" into their work: that is, should either party (counselor or client) decide that counseling will finish, then it is agreed that a certain number of sessions be continued before the contract is terminated. This allows time to deal with unfinished business and to terminate the relationship in a clear, negotiated way. Clients will sometimes try to avoid the pain of ending by terminating abruptly, or simply not coming back. Termination contracts attempts to forestall all this.

2. Working Towards Termination

In longer term counseling work, counselors keep an eye towards the time when clients might be ready to end counseling. In assessing readiness, counselors sometimes look for the following cues on the part of the clients:

- Initial problems or symptoms have reduced
- Initial stress has dissipated
- Coping has increased
- Understanding and value of self and others is greater
- Levels of relating to others and loving and being loved have increased
- Ability to plan and work productively is better
- Ability to play and enjoy life has increased

Clients sometimes give hints of their readiness to finish counseling by lateness for appointments or not coming to their session. Decrease in the intensity of the work, and even apathy on the part of the clients can indicate that they are beginning to withdraw from counseling.

3. The Process of Termination

There are various ways in which termination can take place. In the termination phase of counseling, time can be valuably spent on:

- Reviewing the counseling time together and summarizing from the experience.
- Looking to the future and ways of consolidating what has been gained.
- Any further areas for consideration should the client move to other counseling.
- A formal ending.

4. The Final Session

The final session ought to be structured so that formal goodbyes are said. The final session of terminating counseling may not be satisfactory conclusion for all participants. Clients may be unhappy in the end because their needs were not met. The counselor may be unhappy because they were not allowed to intervene, or because they have been used by the client. The organization may be unhappy with the ending because no change is apparent, or because a change has occurred that it did not want.

Thus, the final session can be concluded peacefully in the following ways:

- Agreeing any future contract
- Resolving any unfinished business
- An appreciation of the time together where both can recount what they have valued about counseling and the counseling relationship
- A goodbye gesture, e.g., a handshake, a hug.

5. After Termination

What is more contentious than the possibility of meeting after counseling has ended is the possibility that counselors/clients can create a new form of relationship after counseling one. If the relationship between *the counselor and former client does continue in whatever form it takes, it needs to be talked through carefully so that it is not a way of avoiding ending the counseling relationship*

So far we saw workplace counseling in a nutshell, namely its history, the various models of workplace counseling and an integrative model of workplace counseling. But workplace counseling covers many other areas that equally contribute towards the success of an organization namely Performance Counseling and Career Counseling.

Performance Counseling

A subordinate should know what standards of performance are expected of him. He also deserves a clear cut understanding of how he is performing with emphasis upon his strong areas as well as his weak points, showing to what extent he meets the managers standards. In order to convey the above information to the subordinates, managers carry out performance counseling.

Performance counseling is defined as a regular although not necessarily formal contact between the manager or the supervisor and the individual employees for the purpose of discussing successes and failures in completing assignments and duties in a particular organization. Performance counseling offers the organization a valuable communication tool that, if properly used, can significantly enhance relations between the superiors and subordinates and improve the organization's chances of obtaining its goals. Performance counseling is also known as "coaching" mainly because the purpose of counseling is to improve the performance of the employee.

Performance counseling mainly aims at the development of the employee. It involves the following:

Inter-personal effectiveness by giving him feedback about his behavior and assisting him in analyzing his inter-personal competence

- Encouraging him to set goals for further improvement
- Encouraging him to generate alternatives for dealing with various problems

- Providing him empathetic atmosphere for sharing and discussing his tensions, conflicts, concerns and problems
- Helping him to develop various action plans for further improvement
- Helping him to review in a non-threatening way his progress in achieving his objectives.

Performance counseling is a person-specific activity because in a particular organization all employees are not seeking to achieve the same goals nor are they motivated by the same rewards. Further, not all employees have the same job responsibilities and, therefore, individual achievement cannot be measured by the same criteria. It is also unlikely that all individuals will be at the same stage of their careers. Senior and experienced employees must be approached differently from less experienced employees in tenure-track appointments. Thus, in order to conduct performance counseling, superiors turn to job-description. Job descriptions accurately outline the duties and responsibilities assigned of each employee and become the standard against which performance can be assessed during performance appraisal.

In almost every organization, performance counseling is carried out by the managers after the employees are appraised, but ideally performance counseling should be conducted frequently depending upon the needs of each employee and the availability of time for the manager. The purpose behind this is that firstly, the more attention a manager pays to counseling his subordinates, the more time he is likely to gain in the long run as a result of improved capabilities of his subordinates. Secondly, when employees perform well, continuous performance counseling serves to acknowledge good performance and encourage more of the same whereas in instances of unsatisfactory performance, continuous performance counseling serves to remedy problematic performance and motivate the individual to invest the effort needed to improve. Although time consuming, ongoing performance counseling is more effective than a program of annual review because the evaluative comments are more timely and, therefore, more beneficial. Both positive and negative evaluative statements carry more meaning when they are delivered in relation to a specific event and not tucked in a file for discussion at some future review.

As said before the aim of performance counseling is to help the employee grow and develop in his organization. Therefore every manager counsels his employee knowingly or unknowingly in his day-today work life. But effective counseling requires the use of skills, which few managers are likely to acquire in the normal course of their work. It is essential; therefore, that training should be given to appraisers on how to counsel during formal and informal discussions. Counseling skills are best developed by practice under guidance and such guidance is a requisite part of any performance counseling workshop or a performance appraisal scheme. Thus a part of performance counseling also involves teaching the managers on how to counsel their subordinates effectively so that their subordinates perform efficiently at work. According to the *IPD (Statement on Counseling in the Workplace),* managers can be effective as counselors when they are trained to develop to following skills to counsel their subordinates:

- **Problem Identification.** Recognizing that the problem exists.
- **Open Questioning.** Probing by open ended, non-directive questions to identify the real focus of the problem rather than concentrating on its symptoms.
- **Listening.** The ability to listen actively to obtain the full story by probing, evaluating, interpreting and supporting.
- **Sensitivity.** To individual beliefs and values, some of which may be based on culture or religion.
- **Reflecting Being.** Able to restate the problem from the individual's point of view.
- **Empathy.** Having regard for the feelings and anxieties of the individual.
- **Impartiality.** The ability to remain non-judgmental and to refrain from prescribing solutions.
- **Sincerity.** Having a genuine attitude of interest and openness to the individual's problems.

• **Belief.** Having the belief that individuals have the resources to solve their own problems, albeit with passive or active help.

Having stated the above requisite skills, managers may also have their own approaches or styles of the way they counsel their subordinates. Norman Maier described one of the best-known methods of counseling some time ago (The appraisal Interview, Wiley, 1958). He suggested that there are three approaches available in a performance appraisal meeting, which can be adopted by managers in order to have an effective counseling session with their employees. They are as follows:

• **The Tell And Sell Approach**

In this appraisers first let the appraisees know how they are doing, then gain their acceptance of the evaluation and, finally get them follow a plan outlined for their improvement. The problem with this method is that considerable skill is required to get people to accept criticisms delivered in this way and to change in the required manner. There are occasions when people have to be told what to do, but it may not always be possible to provide the motivation for change, unless resort is made to crude inducements or threats

• **The Tell And Listen Approach**

In this approach, the evaluation is communicated to appraisee who is then allowed to respond to it. Instead of appraisers dominating the discussion they sit back and become non-directive counselors during the second part of the meeting. Appraisees are encouraged to think things out for themselves and to decide on what needs to be done. The assumption is made that they are more likely to change in these circumstances than if they had been told what to do. An advantage of this approach is that appraisers can profit more from the discussion by receiving feedback from appraisers on how improvements can be achieved with regard to management, work methods, the provision of resources, dealing with problems outside the control of appraisees and job assignments. However, this method also requires skill on the part of appraisers in listening, reflecting feelings and summarizing opinions.

- **The Problem-Solving Approach**

This approach requires appraisers to start by encouraging appraisees to identify problem areas and then starts to exchange ideas about solutions. Appraisees therefore play an active part in reviewing problem areas and in deciding what should be done about them. The evaluation of performance emerges from this discussion rather than being imposed on appraisees. In this approach the emphasis is less on what went wrong or right with performance in the past and more on ensuring that steps are taken to improve performance in the future. According to Maier, this method motivates original thinking and provides the intrinsic motivation that can be derived from the work itself and the process of overcoming work problems. Job satisfaction can be improved by reorganizing or enriching the job, by changing the appraisee's perception of their role and by increasing the appraisers ability to provide guidance and help in the for needed. This approach needs skill but it is the most fruitful method and Maier recommends that appraisers should adopt it and abandon the "tell and sell" and the "tell listen" approach.

Once the manager has the required skills for effective counseling, he can adopt hose skills and integrate it with the formal counseling stages that have been suggested by *G.Egan* in the book *In The Skilled helper: A Systematic Guide to Effective Helping* (Brooks Cole, 1990). G.Egan has proposed the following stages for performance counseling:

- **Listening, Understanding And Communicating**

This focuses on understanding the perspective of the other person and communicating that understanding. It is non-judgmental and concentrates on ensuring that both parties have the same understanding of the situation.

- **Changing the Picture**

Talking through an issue can help to change appraisee's perspectives and indicate a solution to the problem. But this does not always happen and as a counselor, you may have to use the "tougher "tougher skills" of challenging and confronting, sharing with appraisees their different perceptions and providing a different framework.

The initial listening phase should have established an atmosphere of acceptance and openness, which enables this tougher stage to take the process forward into action

- **Implementing Action**

In this stage the manager resources the individual to take action. He/she becomes a facilitator, helping the individual to formulate action plans and providing expertise and guidance as necessary.

However, it is not the manager's role as a counselor to tell the individual what action to take. The individual must be helped to work out for himself or herself what needs to be done, although the manager should provide the resources required in the shape of coaching, training or the provision of better working facilities or systems. He/she can be also available to provide any additional guidance or help if the individual; requires

In summary performance counseling is a key ingredient in building an effective organization. When employees perform at optimal levels in behavior that supports the department mission and objectives, they contribute to the organizational goals. Performance counseling also serves, as a vehicle for organizations to make sure that every individual employee understands how their job contributes to the welfare and success of the entire organization. Through performance counseling, managers or superiors can clarify the mission of the organization and individual job responsibilities. This helps individual employees perceive themselves as members of a team with responsibility to the total organization and not merely independent agents who happen to be housed in particular units. Managers will also reap important benefits from their consistent pursuit of ongoing performance evaluation.

Career Counseling

A career is a sequence of positions or jobs held by a person during the course of his working life. According to *Flippo, "a career is a sequence of separate but related work activities that provide continuity, order and meaning to a person's life"*. A persons choice of career is shaped by many factors e.g., heredity, parents, culture, age level, job experience etc. But in today's modern world different kinds of occupations are emerging. Most young men and women are handicapped by inadequate information about the opportunities available to them, the requirements, which they have to fulfill to enter those occupations, and the places where specialized training facilities are available. Young men and women should know all about the opportunities open to them so that they can make the best use of them. Educational institutions as well as governmental agencies are realizing their potentialities largely owing to their ignorance concerning how people put their potential to use. Career counseling thus largely concerns itself with providing occupational information. It may be defined as *a process which enables people to recognize and utilize their resources to make career-related decisions and manage career-related problems.* The career counselor provides time, support, attention, skill and a structure, which enables clients to become more aware of their own resources in order to lead a more satisfying life. He also counsels students in schools and colleges and tries to resolve their problems regarding studies or any other problems they might be affecting them.

Career counseling is conducted not only for students but also for employees at all levels. For employees career counseling entails giving advise and guiding employees in their possible career paths and the direction in which they ought to be heading. The need for career counseling arises when employees have to plan their own careers and develop themselves for career progression in the organization.

Most career counselors offer the following services to clients:

- ***One-to-one career counseling***

A series of one-to-one meeting without assessments.

A series of one-to-one meetings with test administration, feedback and counseling.

A series of career counseling meetings with written assignments.

A series of career counseling meetings with tests and written assignments.

- ***Group career counseling***

Career development workshops (also known by other titles, such as career planning or reviewing workshops, or self development groups).

- Access to libraries.
- Access to computerized *occupational* information and self-help career *guidance* tools.
- Coaching in job-hunting, CV writing and interviews practice: this may be one-to-one or group based.

A typical career counseling session encompasses the following stages:

1. Assessments. Assessment procedures help individual to understand themselves not only in terms of their interests, values, and personality characteristics. The greater the self understanding an individual has, it is assumed more likely the person is to make realistic and satisfying educational and career choices. Assessment devises such as aptitude tests, self-report techniques, personality tests are used for career exploration as well as employment. Aptitude tests like The General Aptitude Test Battery (GATB), Differential Aptitude Test as well as specialized tests such as Bennett's Mechanical Comprehension Test are commonly used. With regards to personality tests, The Myers-Briggs Type Indicator (MBTI) is generally used.

2. Explore and Narrow Career Options. Using given guidelines and resources, the counselee identifies and explores innovative career alternatives and match these to his/her personal qualities, aspirations, and desired work and lifestyle.

3. Clarify and Achieve Ones Desired Career and Lifestyle Goals. The career counselor helps the counselee to outline a workable plan that gets the counselee from where he/she is now to where he/she wants to go. The counselee acquires innovative problem solving techniques that enable the counselee to clarify the desired goal and overcome barriers to living ones desired life. Innovative strategies enable one to cultivate and use ones intuition, enhance ones optimism, strengthen ones will to risk, conquer fears, and keep motivated as one works towards ones goals.

Theories of Career Development

Each counselor has a set of assumptions that guide his actions in the pursuit of his role as a career counselor. The set of assumptions, which guide his actions, comprise his 'theory' of vocational development. Several theories of career development exist and were systematically classified as Trait-and-factor theory, decision theory, psychological theory, sociological theory and developmental theory.

Herr and Cramer (1972) have suggested a working classification of vocational development theories.

Trait-and-factor or actuarial theory. This theory emphasizes the individual's innate abilities and acquired interests and their relations to the demands of the different work situations.

Parsons, Darley, Paterson and Williamson (1920). Were one of the few who developed the trait-and-factor theory at Minnesota. The underlying thesis of this approach is that individuals have different innate capacities, abilities, and aptitudes for different kinds of work. In vocational guidance, the purpose is to match the individuals and occupations optimally for mutual benefit. This view is based on the psychometric tradition. Further this theory takes the static and somewhat rigid point of view that individuals fit into specific jobs and would be like fish out of water if they found themselves in different kinds of jobs. It is thus increasingly being realized from the experiences of several people that an individual, on taking up a job which is not to his liking is helpless to get out it and would in the course of time adjust himself and not remain frustrated for the rest of his life.

Decision Theory. This theory holds that individuals consider various alternatives and decide on the one, which promises satisfaction. This does not however mean that the alternatives are rationally or dispassionately considered. They also hypothesize that there are critical points in our lives when choices are made that greatly influence our career development. These decision-making points are such events as educational choices, entry-level job positions, changing jobs, etc.

Sociological Theory. This theory emphasizes sociological factors, which influence individual development and vocational choice. For example, one's social status, social group, conventions, etc., exert an influence on ones vocational choice.

Psychological theory. This theory holds that's vocational choice is affected by the individual's personality structure, his early experiences, motivations and needs.

Developmental Theory. This theory emphasizes that vocational choice is not a static decision, but that it is a process subject to continuous pressures for modification for individual's life experience. Environmental factors affect young people by providing or denying them opportunities for their growth. *Flanagan, Critics, Gibbons, Lohnes,* also hold developmental points of view. *Anne Roe, Holland, Hoppock* and other stress psychological needs to be of paramount importance in determining choice. Psychoanalytically oriented thinkers like *Bordin, Segal* explain vocational development in terms of personality dynamics. *Miller, Hollingshead* and others emphasize sociological factors, such as influence of the home, school, community, etc in vocational choice. *Donald Super's* as well as *John Holland's* theory are often used as examples of developmental theories

According to *Donald Super* career patterns are determined by socioeconomic factors, mental and physical abilities, personal characteristics and the opportunities to which persons are exposed. People seek career satisfaction through work roles in which they can express themselves and implement and develop their self-concepts. Self-concept is an underlying factor in Super's model. Vocational self-concept develops through physical and mental growth, observations of work, and identification with working adults, general environment, and general experiences. As experiences become broader in relation to awareness of world of work, the more sophisticated vocational self-concept is formed Career maturity, a main concept in Super's theory, is manifested in the successful accomplishment of age and stage developmental tasks across the life span. *Super and*

Thompson (1979) identified six factors in vocational maturity:

(1) Awareness of the need to plan ahead,

(2) Decision-making skills,

(3) Knowledge and use of information resources,

(4) General career information,

(5) General world of work information, and

(6) Detailed information about occupations of preference.

Holland's theory places emphasis on the accuracy of self-knowledge and career information necessary for career decision- making (Zunker, 1994, p. 49). Holland suggests "people can function and develop best and find job satisfaction in work environments that are compatible with their personalities" (ICDM, 1991). Holland based his theory of personality types on several assumptions. People tend to choose a career that is reflective of their personality. Because they tend to be attracted to certain jobs, the environment reflects this personality. He classified these personality types and work environments into six types that he labeled realistic, investigative, artistic, social, enterprising and conventional. He suggests that the closer the match of personality to job, the greater the satisfaction.

Thus, in conclusion career development involves the making of increasingly responsible choices. The choice of a career is based on:

1. Subjective factors, namely values.

2. Occupational opportunities.

3. The degree of expectation the individual has of being accepted.

4. The expectation of satisfaction.

As said earlier students and employees alike need career counseling but their needs may differ. The need of the employees is to advance and grow in his career. Most individuals develop quite early in life with an idea or a mental image of what career they want to pursue. An individual with managerial position joins an organization not for a job but for a career. Unless an organization meets these desires and aspirations of its employees it cannot make optimum use of its human resources. But organizations have their own requirements and constraints, which limit their capacity to meet the employee expectations. Changing expectations of the employees and organization's inability to meet these expectations creates conflict. If this conflict is not resolved properly, the organization cannot attain higher levels of efficiency and effectiveness. *Career planning* is an important technique for productive resolution of this conflict between the individual and the organization.

What Is Career Planning?

Career planning is the systematic process by which one selects career goals and the path to these goals. From the organization's viewpoint it means helping employees to plan their career in terms of their capacities within the context of organization's needs. It involves designing an organizational system of career movement and growth opportunities for employees from the employment stage to the retirement stage. Individuals who can fill planned positions are identified and prepared to take up these positions. It is managerial technique for mapping out the entire career of young employees. It requires the discovery, development, planned employment and reemployment of talents.

The Objectives of Career Planning are as Follows.

- To attract and retain the right type of persons in the organization.
- To map out careers of their employees suitable to their ability, and their willingness to be trained and developed for higher positions.
- To ensure better use of human resources through more satisfied and productive employees.
- To have a more suitable workforces by reducing labour turnover and absenteeism.
- To increasingly utilize managerial talent available at all levels within the organization.

• To improve employee morale and motivation by matching skills and job requirements and by providing opportunities for promotions.

• To ensure that promising persons get experiences that will equip them to reach responsibility for which they are able.

• To provide guidance and encouragement to employees need to fulfill their potentials.

• To achieve higher productivity and organizational development.

The Process Of Career Planning

A career planning process generally involves the following steps:

1. Identifying Individual Needs and Aspirations. Firstly a.n objective analysis of the hopes and aspirations of different categories of employees is done. Further, a Personnel Inventory of the organization and employee potential are ascertained. Personnel Inventory reveals the age, qualifications, experience and aptitude of present employees. It is important to develop a Personnel Inventory so that the career goals, aspirations and career anchors are communicated to the respective employees. Appràisal of employees is then carried out to identify the employees having the necessary potential for climbing up the ladder and are willing to get promoted and to take up higher responsibilities.

2. Analyzing Career Options. The organizational set up, future plans and career system of the employees are analyzed to identify the career opportunities available within it. Career paths can be determined for each position. It is also necessary to analyze career demand in terms of knowledge, skills, experience, aptitude, etc. Long term and short term career goals can be defined after relating specific jobs to different career opportunities.

3. Identifying Match and Mismatch. A mechanism for identifying congruence between individual current aspirations and organizational career system is developed to identify and compare specific areas of match and mismatch for different categories of employees. For this purpose specific jobs are related to different career opportunities. Such matching helps to develop realistic career goals for both long term and short term.

4. Formulating and Implementing Strategies. Alternative strategies and action plans for dealing with mismatch are formulated and implemented. Some of the strategies are as follows:

- Changing employee needs and aspirations by helping them to scale down unrealistic goals and aspirations or by creating new aspirations.

- Training and development of suitable people, so as to meet the needs both individuals and the organizations.

- Seeking new basis for integration through problem solving, negotiation and compromises.

5. Reviewing Career Plans. A periodic review of career plans is necessary to know whether the plans are contributing to effective utilization of human resources by matching employee objectives to job needs. Review will indicate to employee organization is moving, what changes are likely to take place and what skills are needed to adapt to changing needs of the organization.

Thus, it can be seen how both career planning as well as career counseling can help an individual to choose the right career and head in the right direction. It is very important for an individual to know where he is heading in order to block the uncertainties in his life. If an individual does not have a clear plan as to where his career is taking him he may suffer from a serious career problem, which is known as the *Career Depression Syndrome.*

The following is the description of Career Depression Syndrome:

Career depression Syndrome (CDS). Is a problem consisting of career unhappiness leading to discouragement, self-doubt, and feelings of inadequacy, hopelessness, and depression. People with CDS may seem clinically depressed, but CDS differs from true clinical depression because the source of CDS is a lack of fit with one's career or job. Still,

CDS can take a disastrous toll in lower levels of motivation, productivity, commitment, and bottom-line success. This, in turn, can affect the company. Because the employee will often hide career dissatisfaction from the employer, by the time the employee with CDS seeks career counseling, it may be too late for the company to salvage that employee's commitment and motivation.

With the help of career counseling, over 10,000 people have been clinically interviewed and tested (personality and aptitude testing) and it is believed that certainly there's an increase in CDS.

Expected among those whose careers are disrupted by current trends such as downsizing, restructuring, and constant technological changes.

However, it is seen that there is depression in people from their mid-20 through retirement age, and many are making a good living in a wide variety of career areas. Twenty-five years ago, perhaps one out of ten career counseling clients had career depression. Today, we believe that it is more than half.

Individuals with CDS are:

• Clearly are not happy in their work (yet they may not express this to their company).

• Have career depression no matter what their occupation.

• Have higher than average levels of self-criticism.

• Experience lower levels of motivation and competitiveness.

• Have lower self-confidence.

• Have unclear goals.

The three stages of career depression syndrome are as follows:

Without taking action and getting appropriate help, the person with CDS will go through 3 stages:

-Stage 1: Career Dissatisfaction.

-Stage 2: Career Demotivation.

-Stage 3: Career Paralysis.

Those in Stages 1 and 2 are unhappy, feel "stuck" in their careers, and often are not proactive in doing something about the problem (such as an active job search or obtaining career and job search counseling). They lack self-esteem in their professional role, but not in their basic self-concept as a person. The typical solutions to Stage 1 are job enrichment, job change, or planned career change with the help of a counselor with combined expertise in career and clinical areas. In Stage 2, additional help is needed to remove motivational problems or roadblocks.

By the time a person reaches Stage 3, other areas of life (such as family or social life) are affected. The level of depression and impact on these other areas of life may be so intense that the original career issue can become masked, and the person may be treated as clinically depressed (e.g., take medication, enter intensive psychotherapy). While these measures are certainly appropriate and often necessary, they are not designed to directly address the career and job search issues. Career and job search counseling incorporating expertise in clinical issues is necessary along with these other professional measures.

In summary, career means differently to different people. For some career means initial start of employment. For others, it may mean how one advances, in his job, to different higher positions. For others it may mean choosing one profession out of alternative professional opportunities available. Yet for some other person, it may involve following a career path during his lifetime employment, whether in one organization or in many. For the above reasons individuals turn to *career counseling* as it provides them a direction and well as helps them achieve their goals in terms of their career keeping in mind their interests, values and aspirations. Similarly, *career planning* has become one of the major functions of the HR practioners in today's times. Organizations have realized that they can support and encourage the career management of their employees by providing honest feedback, realistic career grids and opportunities for individual career exploration and planning.

References

Carroll, M. (2002). *Workplace Counseling: A Systematic* Approach to Employee Care. New Delhi: Sage Publications

Cartwright, S. and Cooper, C. (1994). *No Hassle: Taking the Stress out of Work.* London: Century Business Book.

D.E Super. (1953). *'A theory of Vocational Development'*, American Psychologist, 8(1): 189-190.

Egan, G. (1994). *Working the Shadow-side: A guide to Positive Behind the Scenes Management.* San Francisco: Jossey-Bass.

Herr, E.L, and S.H.Cramer. (1972). *Vocational guidance and Career Development in the Schools: Towards a Systems Approach.* Boston: Houghton Mifflin.

Hoppock, R. (1976). *Occupational Information.* United States of America: McGraw-Hill Books.

Kets de Vries, F.R. and Miller, D. (1984). *The Neurotic Organization.* San Francisco: Jossey-Bass.

Malan, D. (1976). *The Frontier of Brief Psychotheraphy.* New York: Plenum.

Magnus, S.M. (1995). *'Taking the agony'*. Guardian, 1 July, p.2.

Morris. G.B. (1993). *'A rational-emotive paradigm for organizations'*, Journal of Rational Emotive and Cognitive Behavior Therapy, 11(1):33-49.

Nelson-Jones, R. (1995). *The Theory and Practice of Counseling*, 2nd edn. London: Cassell.

Nixon, J. and Carroll, M. (1994). *'Can a line manager also be a counselor?'* Employee Counseling Today, 6(1): 10-15.

O'Leary, L. (1993). *'Mental health at work'*, Occupational Health Review, September/October: 1993:14-16

Pfeiffer, J. (1994). *Competitive Advantage through People.* Boston: Harvard Business Press.

Presnall, L.F. (1985). *'Foreword: historical perspective of EAP's*, in S.H.Klarreich, J.L.Francek and C.E.Moore (eds), The Human Resource Management Handbook: Principles and Practice of Employee Assistance Program. New York: Praeger.pp.ix-xvi.

Reddy, M. (1993a).The *counseling firmament short trip round the galaxy'.*Counselling, 4(1): 47-50.

Rao, V & Pareekh,U.(1984). Performance Appraisal and Review. New Delhi: Learning Systems.

Torrington, D & Hall, L.(1998). *Human Resource Manangement.*Europe: Prentice Hall.

Torjaman, S.R. (1985). '*Training referral agents for* EAP's: knowledge, skills and attitudes', in S.H.Klarreich, J.L.Francek and C.E Moore (eds), The Human Resources Management Handbook: Principles and Practice of Employee Assistance Program. New York: Praeger.pp.188-200.

11
Quality Of Work Life

- Introduction
- What is Quality Of Work Life (QWL)
- Definition Of QWL
- Criteria for QWL
- Specific Issues in QWL
- How to measure QWL
- Obstacles to QWL programmes
- Strategies for improvement on QWL
- Development of QWL programmes
- Types of QWL programmes
- Conclusion
- References

Introduction

In recent years the phrase "quality of life" 'has been used with increasing frequency to describe certain environmental and humanistic values neglected by industrialized societies in favor of technological advancement, industrial productivity, and economic growth. Within business organizations, attention has been focused on the "quality of human experience in the work place." At the same time many firms have questioned their viability in increasingly competitive world markets. These dual concerns have created a growing interest in the possibilities of redesigning the nature of work. Many current organizational experiments seek to improve both productivity for the organization and the quality of working life for its members.

What is Quality of Work Life (QWL)

The term Quality of Working Life has different

meanings to different people. Some label it as a happiness programme, others especially trade unions name it as a subtle employee incentive or just another productivity device. Quality of Working Life (QWL) has assumed increasing interest and importance in both industrialized as well as developing countries of the world. In India, its scope seems more broader than many labour legislations enacted to protect the workers. It is more than a sheer work organization movement which focuses on job security and economic growth to the employees.

Quality of Work Life improvements are defined as any activity which takes place at every level of an organization, which seeks greater organizational effectiveness through the enhancement of human dignity and growth... a process through which the stockholders in the organization management, unions and employees -learn how to work together better to determine for themselves what actions, changes and improvements are desirable and workable in order to achieve the twin and simultaneous goals of an improved quality of life at work for all members of the organization and greater effectiveness for both the company and the unions.

Defining The Term Quality of Work Life (QWL)

There are no generally acceptable definition about this term. However, some attempts were made to describe the term Quality Of Work Life (QWL). The American Society of Training and Development established a task force on the QWL in 1979. This task force defined QWL as *"a process of work organizations which enables its members at all levels to actively participate in shaping the organizations environment, methods and outcomes. This value based process is aimed towards meeting the twin goals of enhanced effectiveness of organization and improved quality of life at work for employees"* (Skrovan,1980).

A more specific definition by *Cohen and Rosenthal (1980)* describes it as an

" intercooperation to jointly solve the problem of improving organizational performance and employee satisfaction".

According to Llyod Suttle, "*Quality Of Work Life is the degree to which members of a work organization are able to satisfy important personal needs through their experiences in the organization*". It focuses on the problem of creating a human working environment where employees work cooperatively and achieve results collectively. QWL, as it is understood today, includes four essential elements:

- The programme seeks to promote human dignity and growth.
- Employees work collaboratively.
- They determine work changes participatively.
- The programme assumes compatibility of people and organizational goals.

Criteria For The Quality of Work Life

Richard E. Walton (1975) proposes eight conceptual categories that make up the quality of working life. These are briefly mentioned below.

(1) **Adequate and Fair Compensation**

The typical impetus for employment is earning a living. How well that aim is achieved fundamentally affects the quality of working life. More than any of the other criteria, adequacy of compensation is a relative concept. There simply is no consensus on objective or subjective standards for judging the adequ acy of compensation. Fairness in compensation, on the other hand, has various operational meanings. Job evaluation specifies relationships between pay and factors such as training required, job responsibility, and noxiousness of working conditions. By other approaches, supply and demand for particular skills or community averages determine the fair level of compensation. Another standard of fairness relates to ability to pay more profitable firms should pay more A variant of this standard is that when changes in work rules increase productivity of employees, it is only fair that the economic fruits of productivity be shared with the employees involved. Occasionally the application of one standard of fairness produces a pattern of compensation that is judged unfair by another standard.

The adequacy and fairness of pay are partly ideological questions. For example a twenty-to-one ratio between the pay of the top executive and the hourly worker of a firm may have been accepted in the recent past, but it may be regarded as too large in the future.

Although accepted operational measures are not available to judge the adequacy and the fairness of work compensation, both factors are important determinants of the quality of working life.

Adequate income. Does the income from fulltime work meet socially determined standards of sufficiency or the subjective standard of the recipient?

Fair compensation. Does the pay received for certain work bear an appropriate relationship to the pay received for the other work?

It may be useful to point out here that in India such labour legislations as Payment of Wages Act, 1936 and Minimum Wages Act, 1948 ensure adequate and fair compensation to the employees.

(2) Safe and Healthy Working Condition

In order to improve QWL the work environment should be free from hazards or other factors detrimental to health and safety to the employees. Walton (1975) specifically refers to reasonable hours enforced by a standardized normal work period beyond which premium pay is required; physical working conditions that minimize risk of illness and injury; age limits imposed when work is potentially descriptive to the welfare of persons below (or above) a certain age. Once again, concern for safety in the work place in India is enshrined in the Factories Act, 1949 which lays down minimum standards of protection from machine and other hazards (noise, pollution, fume, gases, etc) at the work place.

(3) Immediate Opportunity to Use and Develop Human Capacities

The industrial revolution and a simplistic extension of its underlying logic have taken much of the meaning out of work.Work has tended to be fractionated, deskilled, and tightly controlled. The planning of work has been separated from its implementation. These tendencies have progressed in varying degrees from one job to the next; therefore jobs differ in how much they enable employees to use and develop their skills and knowledge. Some of the job qualities necessary for this development follow:

Autonomy. Does the work permit substantial autonomy and self-control relative to external controls?

Multiple skills. Does the work allow one to exercise a wide range of skills and abilities rather than merely repeat the same narrow skill?

Information and perspective. Is one allowed to obtain meaningful information about the total work process and the results of his own action, so that he can appreciate the relevance and consequences of his actions?

Whole tasks. Does one's work embrace a whole task or is it some fragment of a meaningful task

Planning. Does one's work include planning as well as implementation of activities?

These aspects of the job affect the ego involvement, self-esteem, and challenge obtained from the work itself.

(4) Future Opportunity for Continued Growth and Security

Here the focus shifts from the job to career opportunities. The typical industrial job can now be completely learned within a few weeks or a few years, after which the blue- collar worker has reached nearly the peak of his earnings and can look forward to only minor improvements. Promotion of blue-collar workers to supervisory and managerial positions is often foreclosed by formal educational prerequisites. Engineers and other professionals tend to peak somewhat later, but they often confront an additional source of discouragement, the obsolescence of their knowledge and skills. When these professionals reach their middle thirties, their earnings begin to level off. Frequently by this time their knowledge has been exploited and their specialties deepened, but no provision for continued education or broadened capabilities has been made. There is little prospect for advancement in salaries and promotions. This period coincides with a stage of life where professionals are likely to be reevaluating their commitments to careers, families, and avocations. The result is that many lose interest in their professional work, no longer invest in their career pursuits, and increase the sterility of their work lives. Thus attention needs to be given to the following aspects of working life:

Development. The extent to which one's current activities (work assignments and educational pursuits) contribute to maintaining and expanding one's capabilities rather than leading to obsolescence.

Prospective application. The expectation to use expanded or newly acquired knowledge and skills in future work assignments.

Advancement opportunities. The availability of opportunities to advance in organizational or career terms recognized by peers, family members, or associates.

Security. Employment or income security associated with one's work.

(5) Social Integration in the Work Organization

The preceding categories relate to the worker's immediate and long-range opportunities of expressing and developing individual abilities. Since work and career are typically pursued within the framework of social organizations, the nature of personal relationships becomes another important dimension of the quality of working life. Whether the worker has a satisfying identity and experiences self-esteem will be influenced by the following attributes in the climate of his work place:

Freedom from prejudice. Acceptance of the worker for work-related traits, skills, abilities, and potential without regard to race, sex, creed, and national origin, or to life styles and physical appearance.

Egalitarianism. The absence of stratification in work organizations in terms of status symbols and/or steep hierarchical structures.

Mobility. The existence of upward mobility as

reflected, for example, by the percentage of employees at any level who potentially could qualify for higher levels.

Supportive primary groups. Membership in face-to-face work groups marked by patterns of reciprocal help, socio-emotional support and affirmation uniqueness of each individual.

Community. The sense of community in work organizations that extends beyond face-to- face work groups.

Interpersonal openness. The way members of the work organization relate to one another their ideas and feelings.

(6) Constitutionalism in the Work Organization

A member of a work organization is affected by many decisions that are made on his behalf or about this status in the organization. What rights does he have, and how can he protect his rights? The labor unions have brought constitutionalism to the work place to protect employees from arbitrary or capricious actions by employers. In a few unions workers now enjoy some of these same rights vis-a-vis the union authority structure itself; mechanisms exist whereby a member may appeal, ultimately to an impartial judge, certain union actions that affect the member. In unorganized employment, there are wide variations in the extent to which the organizational culture respects personal privacy, tolerates dissent, adheres to high standards of equity in distributing organizational rewards, and provides for due process in work-related matters. The following aspects of constitutionalism are key elements in providing higher quality to working life:

Privacy. The right to personal privacy; for example, withholding from the employer information about the worker's off-the-job behavior or about actions of members of his family

Free speech. The right to dissent openly from the views of superiors in the organization without fear of reprisal.

Equity. The right to equitable treatment in all matters including the employ compensation scheme, symbolic rewards, and job security.

Due process. Governance by the "rule of law" rather

than the rule of men in such matters as equal opportunity in all aspects of the job, privacy, and dissent, including procedures for due process and access to appeals.

(7) Work and the Total Life Space

An individual's work experience can have positive or negative effects on other spheres of his life, such as his relations with his family. Prolonged periods of working overtime can have a serious effect on family life. If frequent transfers are required, there are psychological and social costs when families are uprooted from their networks of friends, acquaintances, and local affiliations. The relationship of work to the total life space is best expressed by the concept of balance. The balanced role of work is defined by work schedules, career demands, and travel requirements that do not take up leisure and family time on a regular basis. Likewise balance refers to advancement and promotion that do not require repeated geographical moves. The application of this criterion is often debatable. When a person invests enormous time and energy in work at the expense of family, it is unclear whether this pattern is a cause or symptom of deficiencies in the family situation. Sometimes the employing organization is imposing demands that seriously affect the employee's ability to perform other life roles, such as spouse or parent. In other cases, however, these demands are largely self-imposed to escape the responsibilities and strains of family roles. If work did not absorb this time and energy, the person would shift his attention to other pursuits outside the family, such as hobbies or civic activities.

(8) The Social Relevance of Work Life

The organizations lack of concern for social causes, like waste disposal, low quality product, overaggressive marketing, employment practices make employees depreciate the value of their work and careers, which in turn affects their self-esteem. The social responsibility of the organization is an important determinant of QWL.

Specific Issues in Quality of Work Life

Trade unions claim that they are responsible for the improvement in various facilities to workers whereas management takes credit for improved salaries, benefits and facilities. However, P/HR manager has (identified) specific issues in QWL besides normal wages, salaries, fringe benefits etc., and takes lead in providing them so as to maintain higher order QWL. Klott, Mundick and Schuster suggested 11 major QWI issues." They are:

(1) Pay and Stability of Employment

Good pay still dominates most of the other factors in employee satisfaction. Various alternative means for providing wages should be developed in view of increase in cost of living index, increase in levels and rates of income tax and profession tax. Stability to a greater extent can be provided by enhancing the facilities for human resource development.

(2) Occupational Stress

Occupational mental-health programmes dealing with stress are beginning to emerge as a new and important aspect of QWL programmes in recent years. Obviously, an individual suffering from an uncomfortable amount of job-related stress cannot enjoy a high quality of work life. To this end, the personnel manager have to look into the working conditions, nature of work, workers abilities, etc. There must be a conscious attempt to put employees on jobs that are best suited to their talents. All avenues must be kept open so that employees not only use their talents in the service of organizational goals, but also use such contributions for their career advancement. In other words, to reduce job-related stress, the organization must ensure the best fir between employees capabilities and organizational requirements and thereby ensure continued development of people at all levels.

(3) Organizational Health Programmes

Organizational health programmes aim at educating employees about health problems, means of maintaining and improving of health etc. These programmes cover drinking and smoking cessation, hypertension control, other forms of cardiovascular risk reduction, family planning etc.

Effective implementation of these programmes result in reduction in absenteeism, hospitalisation, disability, excessive job turnover and premature death. This programme should also cover relaxation, physical exercise, diet control etc.

(4) Alternative Work Schedules.

Employees demand more freedom at the workplace, especially in scheduling their work. Among the alternative work schedules capable of enhancing the equality of work life for some employees are

(a) ***Flexitime.*** A system of flexible working hours.

(b) ***Staggered Hours.*** Here groups of employees begin and end work at different intervals.

(c) ***Compressed Workweek.*** It involves more hours of - work per day for fewer days per week.

(d) ***Job Enrichment.*** It attempts to increase a person's level of output by providing that persons with exciting, interesting, stimulating or challenging work. Such work, in turn, gives a person a chance to satisfy higher level needs and is therefore a motivational influence.

(e) ***Autonomous Workgroup.*** Here a group of workers will be given some control of decision-making on production methods, distribution of tasks, recruitment of team members, selection of team Leaders, work schedules and so on.

(5) Participative Management and Control of Work

Trade unions and workers believe that workers' participation in management and decision-making improves QWL. Workers also feel that they have control over their work, use their skills and make a real contribution to the job if they are allowed to participate in creative and decision-making process.

(6) Recognition

Recognising the employee as a human being rather than as a labourer increases the QWL. Participative management, awarding the rewarding systems, congratulating the employees for their achievement, job enrichment, offering prestigious designations to the jobs, providing well furnished and decent work places,offering membership in clubs or association, providing vehicles, offering vacation trips are some means to recognize the employees.

(7) Congenial Worker-Supervisor Relations

Harmonious supervisor-worker relations gives the worker a sense of social association, belongingness, achievement of work results etc. This in turn leads to better QWL.

(8) Grievance Procedure

Workers have a sense of fair treatment when the company gives them the opportunity to ventilate their grievances and represent their case succinctly rather than settling the problems arbitrarily.

(9) Adequacy of Resources

Resources should match with stated objectives, otherwise, employees will not be able to attain the objectives. This results in employee dissatisfaction and lower QWL.

(10) Seniority and Merit in Promotions

Seniority is generally taken as the basis for promotion in case of operating employees. Merit is considered as the basis for advancement for managerial people whereas seniority cumerit is preferred for promotion of ministerial employees. The promotional policies and activities should be fair and just in order to ensure higher QWL.

(11) Employment on Permanent Basis

Employment of workers on casual, temporary, probationary basis gives them a sense of insecurity On the other hand, employment on permanent basis gives them security and leads to higher order QWL.

How To Measure QWL

Several tools have been developed by social scientists to measure and evaluate the QWL programmes in organizations. These include:

(i) Turnover data

(ii) Absenteeism data

(iii) Morale surveys

(iv) Number of grievances handled.

(v) Personal interviews carried out from time to time.

(vi) Performance criteria etc.

An organization interested in evaluating the effectiveness of QWL, may resort to more than one method cited above.

Obstacles to QWL Programs

(1) Managerial Attitudes. QWL demands democratization in the workplace. Managers must be willing to share their decision-making powers with employees. They must allow employees to speak up and participate actively in organizational matters. However, this is easier said than done. Managers may consider the whole affair a threat to their existence. They may be reluctant to give a part of the 'decision making power', which traditionally belongs to them.

(2) Union's Attitudes. Unions may have a genuine feeling that WQL programmes speed up work performance and achieve productivity improvements without paying adequate returns to workers. QWL may be another ingenious device to extract more work from employees. It may be a productivity play. To allay such fears, managers need to sell the QWL programme, explaining the purposes and the benefits that are likely to be given to employees in the long run.

(3) Cost Considerations. The capital costs and the day-to-day operational expenses of QWL programmes seen to be quite phenomenal beyond the reach of an organization. Moreover, there is no quarantee that the programme will yield positive results. As a justification it may, however, be added that the programme needs to be implemented cautiously, keeping a close watch on the budget.

Strategies for Improvement on Qwl

(1) Self-managed work teams. These are also called

autonomous work groups or integrated work teams. These work teams are formed with 10 to 20 employees who plan, co-ordinate and control the activities of the team with the help of a team leader who is one among them. Each team performs all activities including selecting their people. Each team has authority to make decisions and regulate the activities. The group as a whole is accountable for the success or failure. Salaries are fixed on the basis of individual and group achievement.

(2) Job redesign and enrichment. Narrow jobs can be combined into larger units of accomplishment. Jobs are redesigned with a view to enriching them to satisfy higher order human needs.

(3) Effective leadership and supervisory behaviour. For effective leadership and supervisory behaviour '9-9' style of managerial grid is suitable.

(4) Career Development. Provision for career planning, communication and counseling the employees about the career opportunities, career path, education and development and for second careers should be made.

(5)_Alternative work schedules. Provision for flexible working hours, part-time employments, job-sharing and reduced work week should be made.

(6) Job security. This tops the employees list of priorities list of priorities. It should be adequately taken care of.

(7) Administrative or organizational justice. The principle of justice, fair and equity should be taken care of in disciplinary procedure, grievance procedures, promotions, transfers, demotion, work assignment, leave, etc.

Employees should be allowed to participate in management participative schemes which may be several types.The most sophisticated among them is quality circle. Implementation of these strategies ensures higher level of Quality of Work Life.

QWL Programming

QWL programmes are concerned with better

communications and interactions among various groups in the organization; improvement of decision-making by soliciting inputs from all levels of the organization; developing higher morale and solidarity in work departments; and establishing higher productivity and quality levels in work performance. In QWL programmes, the level of concern is the work department or some functional work group. The outcome to be expected is a group measure (productivity, quality improvement, or morale). The QWL programme may be restricted initially to a pilot program or a limited number of departments, but in the long run the programme is designed to encompass everyone in the organization. The concern in this programme is with organizational change in the broadest scale possible. The technology to achieve results in QWL programs is a combination of group process, work redesign, organizational development, and training activities.

QWL programmes are concerned with many different social and technical relationships in the workplace. It seeks to alter relationships between supervisors and employees and among co-workers in the same or related departments. The intention is to develop a more human work environment and also to provide a structure to involve the employees in decision-making matters and in problem-solving. The QWL programme's focus on the employee is not clinical or problemme-focused. Instead, the emphasis is on employee capabilities or skills to communicate, interact, and solve problemmes. Consequently, QWL programmes concern themselves with a more diffuse view of employee behaviour.

The staff of the QWL programmes tends to be small, with a reliance in many instances on outside consultants for specialized expertise. Typically staff members are administrators of facilitators, rather than practitioners, with little specialized expertise. It is not unusual for such staff members to come from the ranks of the local union, the labor relations office, the personnel department, or even from the floor of the shop. Their knowledge centers on an in-depth understanding of the organization, how it operates and how to expedite group contributions to problem identification problem solving and decision-making.

The essence of QWL programmes is that they represent an attempt to change employee behavior from one of responding solely to management initiatives to some kind of participation in decisions and problem-solving which will affect what happens in the workplace. The concern in QWL programmes is with long-term fundamental changes in employee behaviour and the organization, not with a short-term, quick fix. The success of QWL programmes is not measured by immediate changes in employee behaviour but in long-term changes in group productivity, job satisfaction, morale, grievance rates, quality, and absenteeism. While short-term gains are possible, most of the returns from QWL programs will take time to develop.

Finally, in a generic QWL programme there is a central group or plant steering committee coordinating the efforts of the programme. In unionized facilities, this group is usually a blend of management and union leadership. It may include the chief executive officer, plant manager, personnel director, union president and/or bargaining chairman, or the international representative. It can add to this committee any management or union staff person to follow-up and implement policies determined by this assembly. This committee is a resource to the multitude of groups in the plant, not simply a controlling authority. The activities of the committee may include: developing and maintaining communication systems in the union and company to make members aware of QWL program activities and progress; assisting the groups when called upon; making available information and technical help when needed; evaluating the effectiveness of groups working on a problem; and providing training to improve group capabilities. The committee will often receive and evaluate suggestions from employees who wish to see particular problems worked on or who want departmental solving teams set up in their areas. The major contribution of this central committee is to provide the resources and know-how to facilitate the work and to implement the decision of the groups.

Development of QWL Programmes

The first step in the development of a QWL programme is to create a conducive climate of mutual respect and trust between the workers and management. The QWL programme basically aims at establishing proper conditions of work for the overall human development of the workers so that human dignity of workers can be elevated, a sense of self-fulfilment developed, and a mutual co-operative effort promoted. Trade unions, workers and the management must make constant efforts to make the programme successful.

While the quality of work-life programme is basically meant to improve the workers' lot, improvement of production quality and cost reduction are also achieved. Obviously both workers and the management must give whole hearted support to the programme. Unions are also to be involved in the programme. The programme is truly voluntary. In case the actual objectives are not served, both the parties are at liberty to withdraw from the programme. It means that all the concerned parties must be convinced to the benefit of the programme.

Generally a meeting takes place between the top management and the representatives of all people concerned before the QWL programme is envisaged. The trade unions are closely involved in initiating and implementing the programme, while the aims and objects of the programme must be made clear to both management and the trade unions as well as their members. A close co-operation of the trade unions and the managements is the basic requirement for any QWL programme to be successful. By any means QWL programme is not an alternative to collective bargaining.

Any contribution made by the workers result in appropriate reward and improvement in the quality of work life of the workers in the programme.There is a constant endeavour on the part of management to implement many such programmes one after another in which workers are directly involved. Lay-offs or retrenchments are generally avoided during the QWL programmes so that the workers can fully involve themselves in the programme. A "speed-up" in the work pace or any direct action like strike from the trade unions should also be avoided for the programme to be successful.

As in any workers' participation programme, middle management may have some sort of reservation against such programmes since they fear that their authority may be jeopardised. Hence it is necessary to involve them in the programme. Supervisors and lower management people may face some sort of role conflict unless they are property involved in the programme.

If the QWL programme is properly implemented, it is bound to improve morale and job satisfaction on the part of the workers and the overall communication system on the part of the company. Resultantly a good industrial climate can be established leading to improvement in production and productivity as well as cost reduction. American experience has proved that such programmes have reduced the grievances and improved the job satisfaction and involvment. Development of internal unions, good public relations, correction of management mistakes, workers access to information, reducing dispute and strife, better relations between workers and management, mutual trust and co-operation, and improvement of industrial climate and productivity are the results of these programmes.

Types of QWL Programmes

Recent trends in management practices, particularly in developed countries like the United States, are dominated by Quality of Work Life programme. More than one fourth of the U.S. labour force is directly involved in it. Companies introduce various types of programmes to improve the quality of life of their people and use their ability to solve the various production problems.

Some of these programmes are: humanisation of work, quality circles, work-place participation, orgánisational development, work improvement programme, flextime, suggestion system, job redesign, relations by objective, etc. These quality of work-life programmes have started making results from early 1970's. Many unions have already signed national agreements committing themselves to QWL schemes. These programmes give the worker a right to some sort of determination of his conditions of employment. Some of the programmes of QWL is mentioned below briefly:

(1) **Humanization of Work**

The basic concept underlying the QWL is what has come to be known as "humanisation of work". It involves basically the development of an environment of work that stimulates the creative abilities of the workers, generates cooperation, and interest in self-growth. Herrick and Maceoby (1975) have identified four basic principles summarise the humanisation of work. These principles are briefly discussed below.

1. ***The principle of security***. Humanisation of work implies freedom from anxiety, fear, and the loss of future employment. The working conditions should be safe and there should be no fear of economic want preconditions will guarantee utmost development of skills and ideas.

2. ***The principle of equity***. Hostility is generated if there are substantial differences between efforts and rewards. The equity principle requires that there is a just way of evaluating the conditions employee. Another aspect of equity refers to paying for knowledge and skill to carry out the task and not for the task alone. If work has to be humanised, equity would also require sharing in the profits of the organisation according to the individual or group contribution.

3. ***The principle of individuation***. Individuation refers to the work environment in which employees are encouraged to develop themselves to their utmost competence, a system of work that facilitates blossoming of individual potential. A basic precondition for this is the availability of freedom and autonomy in deciding their own pace of activity and design of operations.

4. ***The principle of democracy***. Akin to the principle of individuation, this also implies greater authority and responsibility vested into the work force. Increasing controls, close supervision, and a general institutionalisation inhibit humanisation of work. Meaningful participation in decision-making also guarantees the "right of citizenship"

(2) **Workers Participation**

The concept of participation is generally seen as a way of reducing power differences between the workers and the management. According to Strauss (1963) equity is stressed. While more precise conceptual properties of participation are hardly clear, Golembiewski (1965) suggests that participation involves the following.

1. The amount of verbal interaction between supervisor and subordinate.

2. The degree to which a supervisor performs his role in a group centered way.

3. The degree to which a supervisor is active in making decisions and setting goals for his work units.

Though many authors have defined the concept of participation differently, there seems to be a general agreement that participation means sharing, in an appropriate way the decision–making powers with the lower levels in the organization. Mhetras (1966) has suggested the following five levels of participation.

Informative participation. Refers to sharing the information on production, expansion, balance sheet, etc, without the right to have a closer scrutiny by the employees.

Consultative participation. Entails consultations with employees on such matters as welfare, safety, work methods, etc, but the management retains the prerogative of taking final decisions.

Associative participation. The management is under some obligation to accept and implement the unanimous decisions of the council.

Administrative participation. A decision already taken comes to the council for choosing an alternative to implement.

Decisive participation. Involves joint decision-making on matters relating to production, welfare, etc.

Interest in workers participation in management stems from three basic problems of work organizations.

1. Power sharing between managers and those that they manage.

2. Reduction of conflict by encouraging effective cooperation between workers and managers.

3. The personal involvement of workers in their tasks and work situations.

Participative management is essentially a style of managing human resources which deals with the process rather than the structure (Alexander, 1972). The basic objective is to provide workers a sense of importance, pride, freedom, and opportunity for self expression, a feeling of belongingness so as to create positive conditions for industrial relations and an atmosphere of industrial peace.

(3) **Quality Circles (Qc)**

A Quality Circle (QC) is a small group of staff that meets regularly to solve problems relating to their job scope or workplace. QC works on the basis of a continuous and on-going process in an organisation.

The philosophy is that everyone will take more interest and pride in their work if they have a share in the decision-making process or have a say in how their work should be conducted. QC gives employees greater satisfaction and motivation.

The concept of quality circles is basically built around the principle of participative management. It consists of a group of people who meet together on a regular basis to identify, analyze, and solve quality and other problems in their area. Members from the same work area form into such circles generally. The emphasis is on improving the quality of work. One of the popular QWL programmes is the QC programme in the United States. A quality control circle is an autonomous group of a few workers led by a foreman/ supervisor or a senior worker at the grass root level. It is a study group which is involved in solving job-related quality problems. It enables to improve methods of production. It is also focused on self- development of workers including development of the leadership abilities, skill development among workers, improvement of worker morale and motivation, and promoting team spirit and ream work within the work group. The total work life of the people at work improves if the programme is sincerely implemented.

Quality control circle is composed of members ranging

from 3 to 8, which is able to solve many of the worker's and workshop problems. Job- related quality problems or problems of improving methods of production are the main concern of quality circles. The circle meets regularly to discuss and solve many of the quality problems. The meetings can be held even during working hours with the permission of the management. Many such circles function within one factory unit, and such circles are formally independent. Any circle is at liberty to have common meetings with any other circle for discussing common problems. Generally, circles jointly work on common problems. All members are given specific problems and assignments which are expected to be completed by them before the next meeting.

Definition of Quality Circle (QC)

A quality circle has been defined as a "self-governing group of workers with or without their supervisors who voluntarily meet regularly to identify, analyse and solve problems of their work field. But there is a misconception that quality circle and task force are one and the same. However, a quality circle is not a task force. The former is broader than the latter.

A task force is group of skilled employees, selected and appointed by management, engaged various functions, with the orientation to problem-solving. The QC is a voluntary association of workers engaged in similar work with an orientation of human relations. QCs are formed to attain specific objectives.

Objectives

The important objectives of quality circles are

1. To develop, enhance and utilize human resources effectively.

2. To improve quality of products/services, productivity and reduce cost of production per unit of output.

3. To satisfy the workers' psychological needs for self urge, participation, recognition etc., with a view to motivate them. Accomplishment of this objective will ensure enhancement of employee morale and commitment.

4.To improve various supervisory skills like leadership, problem solving, inter-personnel and conflict resolution.

5.To utilize individual imaginative, creative and innovative skills through participation, creating and developing work interest, inculcating problem solving techniques etc. Achievement of these objectives effectively requires the use of certain techniques.

Benefits of Forming Quality Circles

QCs aim to inculcate effective team dynamics through communication, trust, shared vision, commitment, involvement, empowerment, and a learning culture among the staff. The benefits are that QCs:

- Promote individual self-development
- Promote teamwork and fellowship
- Improve overall company performance and corporate image

Techniques Used in Quality Circles

Mainly three techniques are used in discussing various problems within the quality circles. They are 1. Brain storming processes, 2. Cause and effect or Fishbone diagrams and 3. Sampling and charting methods.

1. ***Brainstorming Processes***. Under this techniques, a free environment is created with a view to stimulate creativity. In this free environment, employees' ideas are free from criticism. Hence, employees voice all their (worthy as well as stupid) ideas. All these ideas are recorded seriously. This techniques is useful to generate as many ideas as possible. Later, the plus and minus points of each idea are discussed, before taking a final decision.

2. ***Cause and effect Diagrams***. Members are asked to find out the causes for the identified problem. In this process members identify one important effect of this cause on the problem. Then, they identify other causes and their effects. Charting out of those causes and effects resembles a fish bone diagram. Hence this technique is also called 'fish bone diagram'.

3. ***Sampling and Charting Methods***. Members of the quality circles observe the events and their consequences in the form of positive or negative results. They chart out all their observations either in sequence or in some other relationship, which gives a clear idea of the problem. These techniques will work effectively in attaining the objectives only when the organizational structure of QCs is sound and systematic.

Many organisations in India are now using this method and some of them have already found success. TISCO, TELCO, and BHEL are examples. At TELCO, Jamshedpur over 800 quality circles are successfully functioning. Several problems are solved with the help of QCs. Participation, team spirit and creativity are ensured among the work force which improve the quality of work-life of the people at work. While self respect, confidence and value are inculcated into the minds of people, productivity is improved. Suggestions of the organisation's own people are valued with expectation, and acceptable suggestions are implemented. Creativity of the work-force is always encouraged. While leaders get the co-operation of the people, leaders help the members to develop themselves. Proper training is also provided for all concerned to participate better in the circle meeting and programmes. In fact QCs bring about a new organizational culture.

4. **Job Redesign**

A number of exercises broadly called job redesign, can be introduced depending upon the diagnosis of the system. They are as follow:

Job Enlargement. Job enlargement as a concept deals with expansion of the job contents by allowing employees to inspect their work, affect minor repairs on the work and equipment and to select their own work methods or "set-ups". These refer to "vertical enlargement" and are designed to involve the employees much more in their work by control on the pace of their activity and greater responsibility. Another kind of job enlargement is horizontal in nature. Under this scheme one simply adds number of somewhat similar tasks to the present job. The basic difference between vertical and horizontal involvement is that in the first case the additional inputs demand greater involvement while in the latter case, they convert a non-attention job to a surface attention job. On other words, it requires relatively more attention because the job becomes less mechanical.

Job Rotation. It refers to systematically moving employees from one job to another. It reduces boredom and provides an employee a chance to learn additional skills. An employee can get out from a narrow specialist position to a generalist cadre and become a more broad-based versatile worker. From the point of view of an organization, job rotation helps develop a common culture because of wide and common exposure and at the same time infuses :fresh-blood: in tasks. This is particularly useful to "plateau employees" (those who are not growing) as it gives them a fresh challenge and opportunity to prove themselves. However, it also has two distinct disadvantages. Firstly, it counteracts the establishment of a long range perspective in the same job as the tenure may not be long enough. Secondly, in some cases the learning time may be high leading to reduced output for larger duration.

Job Enrichment . It refers to the process of making jobs more interesting and satisfying, adding to that a sense of achievement, increasing responsibility and providing opportunities for advancement and growth. It refers to the change in the contents of the job. Basic to job enrichment is content/direction/variety hypothesis. By content is meant additions in job contents. These additions are not more of the same kind as in enlargement. But these are "new contents". Discretion refers to increasing responsibility and providing opportunity. Increase in content and discretion lead to variety making repetitive jobs less monotonous and more satisfying. The effectiveness of job enrichment programme is enhanced if changes are seen as opportunities rather than demands. Opportunities may elicit much favourable acceptable demands.

Conclusion

Quality of work life has gained a lot of importance in industries today. To be successful, QWL must be planned be examined closely before launching the programme. The work must be studied carefully, and a congenial work atmosphere must be provided where the work is interesting and workers genuinely want to progress on their own. Above all Supervisors and Line managers must be adequately trained to interact with employees in a friendly and democratic manner.

References

1. Essentials Of Human Resource Management And Industrial Relations- Dr P. Subba Rao......pp., 472-479.

2. Human Behaviour At Work- M.G. Rao.......pp., 48 to 50.

3. Human Resource Management-Mirza SSaiyadain.......Page 310 to 324.

4. HRM Concepts- Fedrick E. Schuster......pp., 39-40.

5. Human Resources Management And Human Relations- V.P Michael......pp., 265 to 268.

12
Training And Development

"Training and development professionals sometimes equate learning with mastering content whereas most business leaders equate learning with improved job performance" - DAVID VAN ADELSBERG (1999).

Learning is a key factor in the development and modification of behaviour, including those activities related to job performance. Behaviour is learned as a consequence of certain kinds of experiences. Training refers to industrial efforts to provide those experiences calculated to facilitate the development of attitudes, skills and knowledge most germane to satisfactory job performance. The value of both of management and employees of training for job-related behaviour is self-evident. An effective training programme may increase productivity; generate increased job satisfaction decrease turnover and accidents and so on. All these desirable ends improve the quality of the product or services and reduce operating costs. Job training and employee development are becoming generally accepted activities in industry. Many companies have facilities and training aids that would make the college classroom out of data. In addition, employee training has become a concern of great social importance. Educationally and socially deprived opportunities for productive citizenship. Wexley and Latham (1986) defined training as a "planned effort by an organization to facilitate the learning of job related behavior on the part of the employees", while Goldstein's (1986) definition focused on "the systematic acquisition of skills, rules, concepts or attitudes that results in improved performance in another environment."

Training consists of planned programmes designed to improve performance at the individual, group, and/or organizational levels. Improved performance, in turn, implies that there have been measurable changes in knowledge, skills, attitudes, and/or social behaviour. Training also decreases breakage. The replacement of abrasive cutting wheels declined progressively over a period of 12 weeks of job training. Some accident reduction has been accomplished through job training. The fact that training also reduces absenteeism and turnover suggests that training has a favorable effect on moral and job satisfaction. These effects also may improve production and reduce accidents. Regardless of the dearth of evidence and measurements of saving produced by training, industry is moving in the direction in the direction of more and more specialized instructions. If training is accepted as worthwhile activity the serious problem becomes one of selecting the proper method and the optimum to devote to it.

Determining Training Needs and Objective

(Assessing training needs)

There are 3 levels of analysis for determining the needs training can fulfill:

- Organizational analysis focuses on identifying where within the organization training is needed.
- Operational analysis attempts to identify the content of training-what an employee must do in order to perform competently.
- Individual analysis determines how well each employee is performing the task that makes up his or her job.

Training needs might surface in any one of these 3 broad areas, but in asking productive questions regarding training needs managers often find that an "integrative model" is helpful. Preemployement training programmes (PET) are prime examples of close alignment between organizational needs and training curricula. PET programmes is industrial-specific, community-based coalitions, member companies contributes time, money and expertise to designing training, and they also contribute employees to teach courses. Such programmes can be found in the aviation industry (Clarksburg, West Virginia), in manufacturing technology (Licking Country, Ohio), in polymer chemistry (Parkerburg, Ohio), and in customer service (Knox Country, Ohio).

Training Objectives

A training programme properly conceived permeates all levels and actives of an industrial organization. Workers with varying amounts of experience and various levels or classification feel its impact.

- Orientation and Indoctrination. This type of training is designed for newly hired personnel regardless of whether these workers have had prior experience. It service primarily to explain the company's policies and practices. Secondarily, it may seek to develop attitudes of prides in the company and personal identification of the employees with it.

- Job related skills and knowledges. Such training is mandatory when a company is compelled to hire relatively inexperienced employees either because of the condition of the labor market or because of the job to be fulfilled is novel or unique to the particular company. Training for in-service personnel may be necessary also to upgrade present levels of employee performance.

- Personal Improvement and Enrichment. It is based on the assumption that more broadly educated employees handle their work more efficiently. Programmes with more general educational objectives lay the groundwork for teaching new skills and knowledge demanded for workers by an ever-expanding technocracy. Thus, an organization like the National Secretaries Association has considered it desirable to sponsors courses for its members in such areas such as art appreciation and human relations. Individual companies, likewise, provide opportunities for employees at various levels to take such courses such as speed-reading, blueprint reading, speech, and written communication.

- Management and Development. The executive, administrative, and human relations skills required for effective leadership are not acquired by virtue of seniority or demonstrated job performance. As men progress to increasingly higher positions, their responsibilities shift from the specific to the general; they must decisions having broad impact and affective many other people.

- Technology and Scientific information. Rapid technological and scientific advances have necessitated special program designs to keep employees abreast of the most recent developments. In a competitive society it is imperative that industrial organizations avail themselves of all pertinent technology advances. To do so requires that scientific and professional employees be provided the opportunity and incentive to learn about such advances.

Learning Principles Underlying Industial Training

Industrial training is a learning situation fundamentally similar to formal kinds of schoolroom learning. To be conducted successfully, a training programme must take into account certain basic psychology principles of learning and forgetting. Four steps are essential for training or learning to occur, these are:-

1. A stimulus
2. A response
3. A motivation or drive
4. A reward or incentive

There must be present a stimulus that is clear to the learner. The industrial interest in communication is largely recognition of the fact that the stimulus or message has to be clear for communication to occur. Unless a reader understands a message on the paper, he can't be expected to be influenced in the direction that the communicator intends. Although training stimuli are usually words, whether spoken or written, there are other kinds of stimuli as well. There may be a machine, or a picture, or a demonstration by a person. It is necessary to have a stimulus known and understood by the learner before training can be effective.

The learner responds in ways calculated to attain these goals. However, his initial responses are limited by the "givens" which he brings with him into the learning situation. These initial givens include:

(a) The sum total of his past learning and abilities.

(b) The way in which he interprets the goal.

The learner is motivated only when he wants to be so to attain his goals. The importance of motivation as a

13
Stress in Organizations

"Stress has become the emotional toothache of the workplace. It leads to serious impairment that can cause big mistakes and serious injuries. As the economy worsens, we need the equivalent of a root canal – employers need to help educate their people on how to fight the infection and ease the pain."

- Frank Kenna III, President of The Marlin Company

Stress is as an adaptive response to an external situation that results in physical, psychological and/or behavioral deviations for organizational participants.

Occupational stress is a growing problem that results in substantial cost to individual employees and work organizations around the globe. The changing nature of work has placed unprecedented demands on employees, and fuelled concerns about the effect this change is having on the well being and health of employees and their work organizations.

Although these changes have led to greater mobility and more flexible work arrangements for some employees, for others they have raised concerns about employment security, increased work demands, and loss of "connectedness" that can result from the move toward less secure forms of employment. In many organizations, these changes have also been coupled with rapid technological change, and a strong push for greater efficiency, increased competitiveness and improved customer service. Conventional wisdom suggests that it is this climate of continual change that is placing many employees under pressure and creating the types of work organizations that will produce high levels of occupational stress. This places a premium on being able to understand the causes and consequences of occupational stress, so that appropriate policies and practices can be developed to ameliorate these concerns.

Stress can manifest itself in both a positive and

of criteria that can be used to evaluate training programme effectively. These are usually referred as "reaction, learning, behavior and result" criteria.

- **Reaction Criteria.** These are nothing more than the opinions concerning the perceived effectiveness of a training program. That is, they are the reactions of the trainee to the question "what do you think of the training just completed?" The value of these measures is extremely limited. Trainees may react favorably to a program for any number of irrelevant reasons, perhaps because it was fun or entertaining or perhaps they believe it will lead to faster promotion or greater pay increase. Reaction criteria do not logically require any "before vs. after" comparisons. Without such comparisons there is no way to answer the first important question about whether or not a change has occurred. The relative convenience of reaction criteria undoubtedly accounts to their popularity, In spite of the fact that they are useless for evaluation purpose. Eden's (1985) study of team development within the Israeli army confirmed that reaction can be very favorable, even when every other piece of evaluative information suggests that a training program produce no useful changes in employees or the organization.

- **Learning Criteria.** It is an improvement over the reaction criteria. These data are immediately collected following the completion of training, and are intended to reflect whatever trainees learned during the program. Final written or performance examination immediately at the completion of training is most common forms of learning criteria. Unfortunately, systematic difference between trainee's pre and post test scores may emerge that has absolutely nothing to do with the training program. Conditions or factors capable of producing such changes will be examined in our discussion of "threats" or internal validity.

- **Behaviour Criteria.** This specifically addresses the issue of transfer of training to the job setting. The most common e.g. of behavior criteria of training effectiveness are measures of job performance that are collected after the trainee have returned to their jobs.

• **Result Criteria.** This directly addresses the organizational needs identified during needs assessment. This level of criteria transcends mere measurement of job performance, and speaks to the question of whether any emergent changes in work behavior are translated into the kind of broad changes in the organization that prompted training in the first place. Because result criteria reflect changes at the level of the organization, you can see that they also imply a comparison of conditions before and after the training has taken place.

Evaluation of Training Methods

1. The lecture method. Lecturing is an economical training method because it permits coverage of a considerable amount of information for a number of people. Many people learn more from hearing lectures than from reading. Good lecture aid understanding and selective learning, but no lecture is efficient in helping people make simple associations unless it is conducted in a drill session. Lectures are of little value in changing attitudes, developing job skills, or training in human relations skills. Lectures can be boring. Even the best lecturers have a difficulty in holding attention for more than 45 minutes without a break. The aspect of training program that lends themselves to lectures is those involving principles and presentations of background information. Some companies have their officials talk to their new employees and present their companies history and their policies to them. Such talks give the employee an impression of the company and their officials. Subject matter that require the learning of speech sound, intonations, phrasing and so on, is better taught by lectures and voice sound than by printed words.

2. Booklets and circulars. The number of people that select material from a bookrack sometimes impresses companies that distribute booklets to tell their story. However, taking a pamphlet and reading it are quite different activities. Many of the booklets, are taken because they are free and many instances. Serious reading is confined to 20% of the population. Even many collage graduates discontinue reading upon graduation. Usually, therefore, reading matter appearing in company bookracks is prepared for the average person, who is not a reader. The hope is to make him one. One unique advantage of reading material is that it permits repetition. That is, a person can reread as often as often as he wishes. The problem is to motivate him to reread. Booklets, pictures and other reading material have little value for human relational training. One merit in their favor, however, is that they constitute something tangible that can be purchased over a counter; hence the distribution of such materials by a company does indicate a first step in the direction of improving supervision.

3. Sound Motion Picture. The original cost of the sound motion picture is high, but since it can be used with many audience it is a relatively in experience investment for large companies. Many companies make their own films and also purchase films made by other companies. As a result, a randomly selected film library is likely to teach philosophies or values that are inconsistent with a particular company's point of view may be assembled, but it will not be a complete resource for training. A film has its greater value in visual learning.

4. Demonstrations, visual aids, and sound film strip. Direct demonstration, visual aids for slap-on boards, and sound film strips are less expensive ways of accomplishing what is achieved by a movie. Like the movies, their main value is in aiding visual learning and associating sounds with visual descriptions. Demonstrations and visual aids permit somewhat greater flexibility, since they can be adapted to the interest and level of the audience. However this may also be a disadvantage in that the trainer is given a certain amount of leeway. One of the advantages of this so called "canned" training material is that the prearrangement of materials prevents trainers from introducing their own pet notion.

5. On the job training. Supervised training on the job is ideal when the job requirements permit low initial performance. If a certain level of proficiency is needed before work in the actual situation is feasible, off the job training in which the actual job s are set up for the use of trainees is often used. In other cases, facsimiles of the job are set up, with hazard removed and opportunities for drill increased. In these improved situations men ca learn to climb utility poles without going high enough to injure themselves in case of failure; girls can operate telephone equipments with coaches servings as customers, and not disrupt service. A unique feature of on the job training and its equivalent in the vestibulc school is that it is training through doing. Another feature is that it is primarily individual instruction. Even if several persons are trained simultaneously, each receives opportunities to practice and each should receive help on his particular difficulty or weakness. Because of the individual nature of instruction, this type of training is somewhat costly and should be reserved for those aspects of training that requires skills and a personal touch.

6. The case method. The case method was developed at the Harvard School of Business and is one of the first deviations from the standard teaching method in that the teacher or trainer is not the source of knowledge. Instead, learning occurs through participation in discussion and problem analysis. The idea of using case discussion evolved from legal training methods where cases are used as a basis for argumentation. The objective of finding the correct solution is replaced by the objectives of using facts effectively and of developing convincing rationale for a position or decision. Executive training programs frequently use the case method. A complex situation typically of a real life problem is presented to a small group. The case becomes the theme for discussion "What to do?" "How the problem could have been prevented?" and "What are some of the policies issues involved?" .The case method gives the trainees practice in problem solving, and utilize the benefit of discussion. One important insight gained form case discussion is discovering that there is no one correct answer or solution and the best solution are often the matter of opinion or personal preference. The procedure should develop interest and skills in group problem solving.

7. Discussion method. Insofar as participation is a motivating force, the use of discussion introduces motivation and involvement. It stimulates understanding and upgrades attitudes, and gives practice in problem solving. Because considerable time is consumed by a limited subject matter, the coverage is through, but there is a sacrifice of systematic organization and of wide coverage of content. Discussion method are used to deal with content for which acceptance is limited and situations in which emotions and attitudes confuse the problem, both coverage and acceptance can be effectively and economically be accomplished.

8. The incident process. Instead presenting a group of trainees with a rather detailed account of the case situation that requires the reporting of the background information, the procedure in the incident process is to describe an event that requires action. This method offers training in getting vital facts and becomes a game in detective work. It is not skill training in ways to obtain information from a person because the leader is willing and ready to answer any questions; rather the skill requirement is in asking the relevant questions. The next stage of the discussion requires the participants to make the decision and supply a rationale for it. These may be individual reports which become the subject of discussion in the third stage. Finally, the leader tells what actually happened and why. This report may reveal background acts and considerations the participants failed to elicit during the first period. The values of this part of the process are similar to those in the case discussion.

9. Business games. The most elaborate training procedure is known as the business game. Like war games, business games simulate a complex realistic solution in which groups compete with one another and the effects of decision made by one group has an effect on the others. Business games create a good deal of emotional involvement, similar to that encountered in playing monopoly. The learning gained perhaps is the development of a better appreciation of the range of factors that must be considered in making wise decisions, dangers involved both in risk taking and conservativeness, and the value of cooperative discussions. Business or economical principles are not taught; the emphasis is on gaining intellectual sophistication.

10. The in-basket. The in basket refers to a series of matters or decisions an executive finds on his desk. How will he dispose them? A trainee is confronted with a rush situation, limited information, and a list of action demanding items an executive may find in his basket. He disposes of the matters by delegating, replying to mails, setting up meetings, delaying action, deciding who should do some of the urgent things, or takes any action that seems practical under the circumstances. This technique reveals the kinds of decisions executives make under pressure and could serve a useful purpose in the selection of personnel, which, incidentally, was its original purpose.

11. Role play. The role play method requires the trainees to project themselves into a simulated interpersonal situation and play the part of the persons and situation assigned to them. Role play can be limited to practice in the skills of human relations and of conference leader. The benefits of the case method are combined with the benefits of role play. Role play can be used to develop self insight and therapy.

12. T-group training. The T-group had its origin at the National Training Laboratories in Bethel, Maine, and is a product of a school of social psychology called group dynamics. The basic objective of the training is to improve group interaction and communication by having participants develop an understanding of the impact they have on others. The procedure is to organize groups of about 12 persons and have them meet daily for 2 or 3 hours for a period of 2 or more weeks. T-group training and some of the role-play methods have similar objectives- to facilitate interpersonal and group interaction.

Evaluting Training Programs

To evaluate training, we must systematically document the outcomes of the training in terms of how trainees actually behave on the job and in terms of the relevance of that behavior to the objective of the organization. The most crucial yet very often-neglected questions related to industrial training is the effectiveness of the training Programmes devised in industry. The effectiveness of a Programme depends upon many factors, like motivation, stress, practice, feedback, method of training and practice, and transfer effects, which may together make a Programme effective or in effective. To assess the utility or value of training, we seek answers to questions such as the following:

1. Have trainee's achieved a specific level of skill, knowledge, or performance?
2. Did change occur?
3. Is the change due to training?
4. Is the change positively related to the achievement of the organizational goals?
5. Will similar changes occur with new participants in the same training programme?

In evaluating training programmes, it is possible to measure changes in terms of 4 levels of rigor:

- Reaction
- Learning
- Behavior
- Result (as discussed above)

Since measurement of reaction and learning are concerned with outcomes of the training program per se, they are referred to as internal criteria. Measurement of behavior and result indicate the impact of training on the job environment; they are referred to as external criteria.

Training Trends

Both economic and demographic trends suggest radical changes in the composition of workforce in the 20th century. Other factors that effect the number, types and requirements of available jobs includes automation; continuing worker displacement as a function of mergers, acquisition, and downsizing; and the shift from manufacturing to service jobs. In 2001, for e.g., 87 percent of U.S employees worked in service based industries. These issues suggest 5 reasons why the time and money budgeted for training will increase during the next decade.

1. The number of unskilled and undereducated youth who will be needed for entry-level jobs, and the need to train currently underutilized groups of racial and ethnic minorities, women, and older workers. This is the social challenge.

2. Increasingly sophisticated technological systems that will impose training and retraining requirements on the existing workforce. This is the high performance work systems challenge.

3. Ongoing need to meet the product and service need of customers. This is the quality challenge.

4. The need, as more firms move to employee involvement and teams in the workplace, for team members to learn behaviors such as asking for ideas, offering help without being asked, listening and feedback skills, and recognizing and considering the ideas of others. This is the interpersonal challenge.

5. Training needs stimulated by the expansion of many firms into global market. Such needs involve the training of local nationals, as well as preparing employees from the home country to work in foreign markets. This is called the global challenge.

Former Labor Secretary ROBERT REICH described the challenge clearly: "If we have an adequately educated and trained workforce and a state of the art infrastructure linking the together and with the rest of the world, then global capital will come here to create good jobs. If we don't, the only way global capital will be invested here is if we promise low wages."

The Center for Workforce Development estimates that the U.S companies spend between $30 billion and $50 billion per year on formal training, but that 70 per cent of all workplace learning is informal. Indeed, since 1995 the time spent in training by the average large-company employee has risen about 25 per cent. At the individual-firm level, Merck, one of the world's largest pharmaceutical companies, is exemplary.

Team Training

Today there is an increasing emphasis on team

performance. Cross-functional teams, intact or virtual, are common features of many organizations. A team is a group of individuals who are working together towards a common goal. It is this common goal that defines a team, and if team members have opposite or conflicting goals, the efficiency of the total unit is likely to suffer. There is a core set of skills that characterizes effective teamwork. These include adaptability, shared awareness of situations, performance monitoring and feedback, leadership or team management, interpersonal skills, coordination, communication, and decision-making skills. When teams work effectively, there is more stability in their performance than that of individuals, at least over the short term. In fact, high performance teams include the following components:

- A clear sense of direction.
- Talented members.
- Clear and enticing responsibilities.
- Reasonable and efficient operational procedures.
- Constructive interpersonal relationships.
- Active reinforcement systems.
- Constructive relationships with other teams and key organizational players who are not members.

Training can modify and enhance each of these. Moreover, research has revealed 2 broad principles regarding the composition and management of teams. One, the overall performance of the team depends on the individual expertise of its members. Thus individual training and development are still important. Two, managers of effective work groups tend to monitor the performance of their team members regularly, and they provide frequent feedback to them. In fact, as much as 35 per cent of variability in team performance can be explained by the frequency of use of monitors and consequences. Incorporating these findings into the training of team members and their managers should lead to better overall team performance.

Concluding Remarks

In the preceding pages, we have outlined the importance of industrial training, its vast scope, and how the task of developing a sound training Programme by paying due attention to the principles of learning and training have evolved through psychological research and live experience, in these matters, in the industry over a long period of time. To make our discussion more fruitful, we consider the various needs of training that are available today and also the various techniques that have come up as a result of greater emphasis in modern industry on human relations and management training. we also noted that no training Programme can be taken as good or bad, sound or effective on its face value, or because it is lauded by those who have developed it. The crux of the problem of developing a good training Programme always depends on its constant evaluation and refinement by using appropriate scientific research methods, though this aspect is most neglected today.

The pace of change in our society is forcing both employment and displaced workers continually to acquire new knowledge and skills. In most organizations, therefore, lifelong training is essential. To be maximally effective, training programmes should follow a 3-phase sequence: needs assessment, implementation, and evaluation. One of the most neglected areas of training is new employee orientation. Clearly, a new employee's initial experience with a firm can have a major effect on his or her later career. To maximize the impact of orientation, it is important to recognize that new employees need specific information in three major areas:

1. Company standards, traditions, and policies;
2. Social behaviour; and
3. Technical aspects of the job.

This suggests two levels of orientation: company, conducted by an HR representative, and departmental, conducted by the immediate supervisor. An orientation follow-up is essential to ensure proper quality control plus continual improvement.

Reference

- DR.P.K.Ghosh, PROF.M.B Ghorpade, Industrial and Organizational Psychology, Himalaya Publication House.
- Knight. A. Patrick, Saal.E.Franke, Industrial/Organizational Psychology Science and Practice, Brook/Cole Publication Company.
- Lane.M. Irving, Irwining.D.Richard, Siegel Laurance, Psychology in Industrial Organizations, 1962, 1969, 1974.
- Viteles.S. Morris, Industrial Psychology,W.W. Norton and Company, Inc. Publishers, NewYork.
- Anderson Nell, Ones.Deniz, Sinangil, Handankepir, Hand Book of Industrial, Work and Organizational Psychology, Volume1, Sage Publication, 2001.
- Maier.R.F.Norman, Psychology in Industry, Oxford and IBH Publication Co.
- Robbins.P.Stephen, 8th ED, Organizational Behaviour, Prentice Hall of India.
- Kolb, McIntyre, Rubin, 4th ED, Organizational Psychology, Peterson Publication.
- Sudha.G.S, Management Approaches and Theorists, Pointer Publication.
- Narayanan.P.S, Rao.V.S.P, Organizational Theory and Behaviour, Konark R.K. Publication.

13
Stress in Organizations

"Stress has become the emotional toothache of the workplace. It leads to serious impairment that can cause big mistakes and serious injuries. As the economy worsens, we need the equivalent of a root canal – employers need to help educate their people on how to fight the infection and ease the pain."

- Frank Kenna III, President of The Marlin Company

Stress is as an adaptive response to an external situation that results in physical, psychological and/or behavioral deviations for organizational participants.

Occupational stress is a growing problem that results in substantial cost to individual employees and work organizations around the globe. The changing nature of work has placed unprecedented demands on employees, and fuelled concerns about the effect this change is having on the well being and health of employees and their work organizations.

Although these changes have led to greater mobility and more flexible work arrangements for some employees, for others they have raised concerns about employment security, increased work demands, and loss of "connectedness" that can result from the move toward less secure forms of employment. In many organizations, these changes have also been coupled with rapid technological change, and a strong push for greater efficiency, increased competitiveness and improved customer service. Conventional wisdom suggests that it is this climate of continual change that is placing many employees under pressure and creating the types of work organizations that will produce high levels of occupational stress. This places a premium on being able to understand the causes and consequences of occupational stress, so that appropriate policies and practices can be developed to ameliorate these concerns.

Stress can manifest itself in both a positive and

negative way. It is positive, when the situation offers an opportunity for one to gain something, also known as "Eustress". It is often viewed as a motivator since in its absence the individual lacks that 'edge' necessary for peak performance. It is negative when stress is associated with heart disease, alcoholism, drug abuse, marital breakdowns, absenteeism, child abuse, and a host of other social, physical, organizational and emotional problems.

Stress is associated with constraints and demands. The former prevents presents an individual from doing what s/he desires. The latter refers to the loss of something desired. Aspiring to own a new Maruti car and not be able to mobilize the necessary cash is a constraint. A desire to attend a social function but unable to do so because of pressing official work, amounts to a demand.

Constraints and demands can lead to potential stress. When they are coupled with uncertainty of the outcome and importance of the outcome, potential stress becomes actual stress. Stress is high when there is uncertainty of outcome and outcome is significant.

Nature of Stress

Our emotional life and behaviour are closely linked with our mental and physical health. Hans Seyle, an endocrinologist, revealed how human beings adapt themselves to emotional stresses and strains in their lives. According to him, emotional stress occurs in 3 important stages:

- Alarm reaction
- Resistance
- Exhaustion

An *alarm or emergency reaction* may occur in response to any stress, which may be physical or psychological. Such alarm reactions bring about complicated physiological changes and when they become sufficiently intense, give rise to symptoms like fatigue, headache, run-down condition and various other conditions. When such physiological changes continue for a long time, they are followed by a stage of resistance in which the organism develops resistance to the particular stressors, which bring unwanted physiological changes. When sufficient resistance results, the symptoms generally disappear.

Hormones in the human body known as adrinocorticotrophic, ATCH, bring about *resistance.* These hormones work to restore the internal equilibrium of the body, as a result of which the symptoms disappear. Younger people have a greater capacity to withstand stress because they have ample energy to face stressful situations. But as we grow older, the supply of energy diminishes and vulnerability to stress increases. Stress is tolerated adequately only when the body has ample resources to face it. People do not face stressful situations all the time, so during the intervening periods, the body replenishes its resources. For those who are continually exposed to stressful situations, there is always the possibility of exhausting its stored energy.

When stress continues beyond the resistance stage, the limited ACTH and cortin resources of the body soon get exhausted because of their increased utilization. When this happens it leads to the stage of *exhaustion* in which the symptoms reappear with greater intensity. Exhaustion may lead to serious illness and even death. The concept of GAS has helped in understanding many emotion-produced disorders. Since Seyle's discovery of the GAS, many researches have followed his line of investigation and today we have a large volume of literature on stress. A new field known as psychosomatic medicine has come into being as a result of this research on stress.

Stressful situations always bring about dramatic physiological changes. The release of adrenalin hormone in such states in the blood stream usually results in the acceleration of bodily functions such as heart rate and blood pressure. Similarly, extra sugar released in blood brings additional energy to the muscles and brain, making the organism more alert and stronger so that he can cope with the emergency situation. Thus, the body functions at an accelerated pace and when such a state is experienced continually, the reservoir of body energy is depleted which leads to a state of exhaustion.

Measurement of Stress

The major problem before the stress researchers was to develop a tool that could measure the amount of impact of stress on human beings. The Social Readjustment scale developed by Dr. T.H Holmes, at the university of Washington served the purpose of understanding the possible role of stress caused by various life events as in individuals adjust to them.

Dr. Holmes et. al. devised a system to simplify the prediction and recognition of stress related illness. The Social readjustment rating scale is a list of 43 life events that associated with varying amounts of disruption in the average person's life.

The scale was constructed by having hundreds of persons of different ages, cultures and walks of life rank the relative amount of adjustment necessitated by the various life events.

In studies going back to the 1940's, Holmes found that a clustering of life events often precedes the onset of psychological and physical ailments. His studies indicate that an accumulation of 200 or more life-change units in a single year may cause disruption than a single individual can stand.

Work Stress

Stress and Strain are integral feature of our lives. The stress at work appears to be increasing, as a result of cutthroat competition, changing global economy, inflation, rapidly changing job roles and corporate culture. Stress at work has been recognized as one of the most important occupational health hazards. Occupational stress jeopardizes the physical and mental health of the employees leading to many psychosomatic illnesses. The effects of stress on individuals, eventually have a collective impact on the organization - leading to organizational problems of job dissatisfaction, poor working relationships, low morale and productivity, high absenteeism and lateness, job alienation, work sabotage, early retirement and high rates of job turnover. The view of the dysfunctional impact of stress, there is an urgent need to tackle it. Occupational Stress has been viewed as resulting from an imbalance between environmental demands and individual capabilities.

Psychological disorders in the workplace have been identified among the 10 leading work-related diseases and injuries in the United States (National Institute for Occupational Safety and Health, 1988). Ilgen (1990) stated, *"The health of the work force is one of the most significant issues of our time"*. Recognition of the psychological risk of work has prompted research on medical, psychological and behavioral stress. Pelletier (1977) reported that stress and psychosocial factors play a far more central role in chronic disorders than they do in acute and infectious diseases. As a consequence, both employees and organizations have become increasingly aware of the negative effects of work-related stress. A nationwide survey by Northwestern National Life insurance Company (1991) showed that nearly 46% of American workers felt that their jobs were very or somewhat stressful, whereas nearly 27% reported that their jobs were the single greatest source of stress in their lives. Almost 72% of those surveyed experienced frequent stress-related physical and mental problems.

Stress not only produces psychological distress but it is also the prime cause of such physical disorders as ulcers and colitis, heart disease, skin disease, diabetes, allergies, headaches and maybe even cancer! Thus, the body loses its internal balance due to continuous stress; it becomes all the more vulnerable to the diseases to which an individual is prone because of the hereditary or acquired predisposition of the body.

A greater recognition of stress as an all-pervading threat and a devastating factor in human life comes from the practical implications it has in our lives. It saps the rots of human motivation, ability to work efficiently and diligently. The result is usually decreased productivity, increased absenteeism, and accidents, mounting insurance costs and industrial strife and tensions. According to the American statistics, stress-related disorders claim over $ 200 billion annually or about $ 4 billion every year. If we add to these figures, the human suffering caused to the victims of stress has gained such a priority of attention in the industrial problems of today.

Sources of Stress

Conditions that tend to cause stress are called 'Stressors.' Although even a single stressor may cause major stress, usually stressors combine to pressure an employee in a variety of ways until stress develops.

The experience of Walter Mathis, an automobile mechanic, illustrates how various conditions combine to cause stress. Mathis felt that he was doing well, but he did not receive the increment, which he expected. At the same time, his wife filed for a divorce and two weeks later he underwent a detailed audit by the U.S Internal Revenue Service. All these problems conglomerated and Mathis was experiencing a great deal of stress.

The above illustrates a common phenomenon- the major sources of employee stress are generated from individual, group and organizational sources. These sources are illustrated in Fig. 1.

Fig.1: Sources of Stress.

(*Source*: Adapted from Organizational Behavior by Fred Luthans, *op.cit.* p.197).

Organizational Stressors: In organizations frequent causes of stress are task demands, role demands, interpersonal demands, organization structure, leadership and life cycle.

Task Demands. Are factors related to a person's job.

They include the design of the individual's job, working conditions, and the physical work layout. Assembly lines can put pressure when their speed is perceived as excessive. The more interdependence between a person's tasks and task's of others, the more potential stress there is, the more potential stress there is. Jobs where temperatures, noise or other working conditions are dangerous or undesirable can increase anxiety. Even working in an overcrowded room or a visible location where interruptions are constant.

Security is another task demand that can cause stress. Someone in a relatively secure job is not likely to worry unduly about losing that position. On the other hand, if job security is threatened stress can increase dramatically.

The final task demand stressor is overload. Overload occurs when a person simply has more work to do than s/he can handle. The overload can be either quantitative (the individual has too many tasks to perform or too little time in which to perform them) or qualitative (the person may believe that s/he lacks the ability to do the job). The opposite of overload is also undesirable. The Fig. 2 shows low task demands can result in boredom and apathy just as overload can cause tension and anxiety. Thus, a moderate degree of workload-related stress is optimal leading to high levels of energy and motivation.

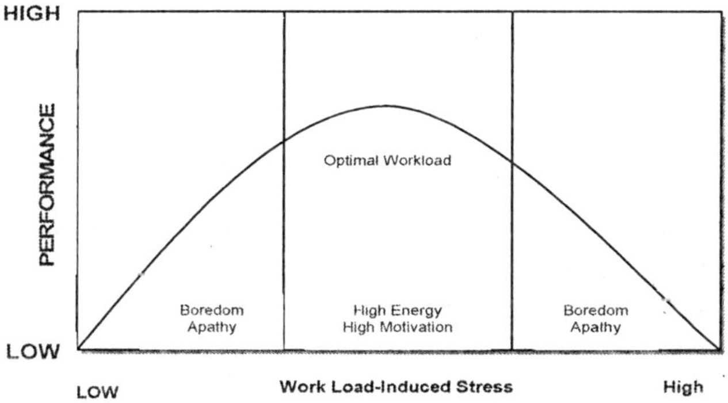

Fig.2: Workload Stress and Performance.

(*Source:* Moorhead and Griffin, Organizational Behavior)

(*Source:* Richard M. Hodgetts, op.cit, p. 338).

CONSEQUENCES OF WORKLOAD		
Under-load	*Optimal Level*	*Overload*
Bored	Highly motivated	Irritable
Overqualified	Mentally alert	Absent
Irritable	Calm under pressure	Accidents
Absent	High level of energy	Indecisive
Lethargic	Exhilarated	Withdrawn
Negative attitude	Excellent perception	Lack of memory
	Keen memory	Poor judgment

Role Demands. Include role conflict, role ambiguity, role erosion and role overload. It occurs when an individual receives competing and conflicting expectations from others. *Role ambiguity* results from having unclear expectations. *Role erosion* arises when someone else performs the functions of one incumbent. *Role overload* occurs hen there are too many expectations than one is able to fulfill. All these role demands are stressors.

Inter-Personal Demands. Conflicting personalities and behaviors may cause stress. Conflict can occur when two or more people work together even though their personalities, attitudes and behaviors differ. For instance, a smoker and a non-smoker who are assigned adjacent work places obviously experience stress. Similarly, a person with an internal locus of control, who always wants to control how things turn out, will get frustrated while working with an external person who likes to wait for things to happen.

Organization structure defines the level of differentiation, the degree of rules and regulations, and where decisions are made. Excessive rules and lack of participation in decisions that affect an employee are examples of structural variables that might be potential stressors.

Organizational leadership represents the managerial style of the organization's senior executives. Some chief executive officers create a culture characterized by tension, fear and anxiety. The established unrealistic pressures to perform in the short run, impose excessively tight controls, and routinely fire employees who fail to measure up.

Organization's Life Cycle: The life cycle of an organization comprises of eight stages:

- Birth
- Growth
- Policy
- Procedure
- Theory
- Religion
- Ritual
- Last rites.

In this cycle, the organization is born and then grows. Policies are developed to guide decisions, which are carried out through procedures. These procedures are refined and made more efficient with theories about efficiency. In time, organizations may develop characteristics of a religion worshipping the way it does things. Performance is ritual; things are done through habit without question. The death and last rites ordinarily follow. Each stage of the life cycle poses its own challenges and problems. While the early stages are exciting, the latter ones create anxiety and tension.

Group Stressors. The group can also be a potential source of stress. There are 4 ways in which the functions of the group can lead to stress:

- *Lack of group cohesiveness.* Starting with historically famous Howthrone Studies, it has become very clear that cohesiveness is essential to employees, particularly at the lower levels of organizations.

- *Lack of social support.* Employees are greatly affected by the support of one or more members of a cohesive group. By sharing their problems and joys with others, they are better adjusted.

- *Interpersonal and inter-group conflict.* Conflict between individuals or groups at a personal or professional level lead to tension manifesting itself in stress.

- *Sexual Harassment.* Is unwanted contact or

communication of a sexual nature. Sexual harassment is increasingly becoming a source of stress in many of today's workplaces. The stressful effects stem from either the direct affront to the victim's personal dignity or the harasser's interference with the victim's capacity to do the job. Thus, leading many to experience symptoms of illness, physical or mental and voluntary turnover.

Individual Stressors. Individual differences among employees may cause some to extract positive stress, which stimulates them, while others experience negative effects causing them to detract from their efforts. Resulting in either constructive or destructive consequences for both the organization and employee. These effects may be short-term and diminish quickly or may be long-term sapping the energy from the individual.

There are also behavior patterns that determine how an individual responds to stress- *Type A* and *Type B* personality. The achievement orientation, impatience, aggressiveness and perfectionism of individuals with Type A personalities may create stress in work circumstances that other people are relatively stress-free. Thus, they bring stress onto themselves.

Type B personalities, by contrast, are less stress-prone. They relax and focus more on the quality of life. They are patient, play for fun, are mild-mannered and never in a hurry.

Stress Consequences

"*Nearly 10,000 Japanese die each year from Karoshi (heart attack) of stroke triggered by overwork.*"- Stephen P. Robbins

Stress can have serious effects for both health and job performance. According to medical practioners, 50-70% of all physical illnesses are related to stress. The link between stress and heart disease is well known. High levels of stress are also associated with diabetes, ulcers, high blood pressure and arteriosclerosis. Stress can cause depression, irritation, anxiety, fatigue, and lowered self-esteem and reduced job satisfaction. Sustained over a long period, stress can lead to attempts to escape through the use of drugs or alcohol. It may also lead to *burn out* which is a state of mind resulting from prolonged exposure to intense emotional stress and involving physical, emotional and mental exhaustion.

The most serious consequence of stress relates to performance. Moderate levels of stress stimulate the body and increase its ability to react; individuals then perform better on the other hand, too much stress places unattainable demands or constraints on a person, which in lower performance.

Stress Vulnerability

Worker vulnerability to stress is a function of both internal (organizational) and external (non-work) stressors. One internal factor is an employee's *stress threshold*- the level of stressors (frequency and magnitude) that the person can tolerate before negative feelings of stress occur and adversely affect performance. Some people have a low threshold, and the stress of even relatively small changes or disruptions in their work routines causes a reduction in performance. This response may stem partly from their experience and confidence in their ability to cope. A higher stress threshold helps prevent lowered performance unless a stressor is major or prolonged.

The amount of *perceived control* people have over their work and working conditions also account for the amount of stress that can be endured. Employees who have a substantial degree of independence, autonomy and freedom to make decisions seem to handle work pressures better. Since two employees may have the same actual control and flexibility, it is clearly their relative perception of that freedom that counts. Managers can respond to this need for control through a variety of measures such as allowing flexible work schedules, enriching jobs, placing individuals on self-managing teams or empowering employees by using participative leadership styles.

Stress vulnerability is also related to the Type A or B behaviour patterns discussed earlier. Research on these behaviour patterns is ongoing. For instance, some of the type A behavior patterns, like competitiveness and a drive for career success, appear to be consistent with society's values. At the same time, the hostility and aggression these people exhibit may make it difficult for many employees to work with them. Some studies also suggest that there may be different forms of type A personalities. As a result, the type A's who are more expressive and less hostile may be less prone to heart disease. Other type A's apparently enjoy their success so much that they disregard the surrounding stress and do not suffer heart attacks or other physical consequences.

Model of Stress

Kahn and Byosiere (1992) developed a model of stress, which conceptualizes stress in organizations in terms of 7 major categories There are complex associations among the antecedents of stress, individual differences in how people respond to stress and the consequences of stress. A casual sequence is hypothesized to exist among these categories.

Organizational Antecedents to Stress. Research on organizational antecedents to stress is generally directed toward understanding how broad based and abstract factors induce stress. Brenner and Mooney (1983), examined the relationship between economic conditions and social indicators of health. The variables were examined in what are referred as to as "lagged relationships"; that is, changes in economic conditions produce changes in health several years later. The authors examined the relationship between economic change and morality in 9 countries: Australia, Canada, England, Denmark, Finland, France, Germany, Sweden and United States. Unemployment and business failures predicted death from heart disease in 8 of the 9 countries with a one-year to four-year lag and controls for such variables as alcohol consumption. Kivimaki et. al. (1997) reported on the work lives of employees in Finland when the national unemployment rate reached 18%. The loss of control in their lives (caused by the economy) added to psychosocial illnesses, which resulted in marked increases in absence.

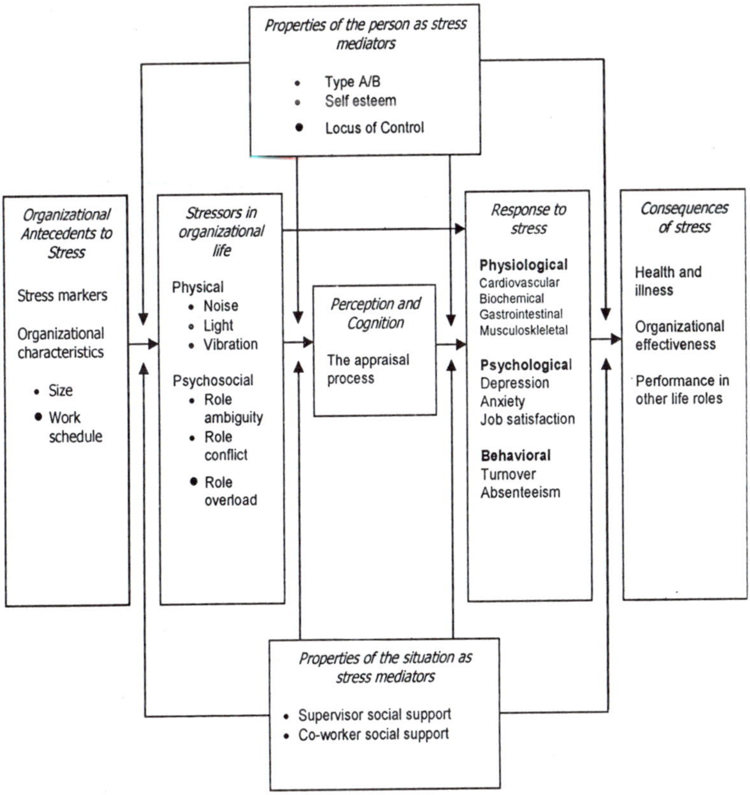

Fig. 3: Theoretical Framework for the study of stress in organizations.

(Source: adapted from "stress in organizations" by Kahn and Byosiere, 1992, in handbook of industrial organizational psychology (p.592), edited by Dunnette and Hough, Palo, C.A consulting psychologists press.

Cobb and Kasl (1977) conducted a longitudinal study on U.S plant closings for the purpose of understanding the relationship between impending job loss and health. Workers in plants that did not close were compared to those in plants that were marked for closing. Five waves of data were collected over a 2-year period, spanning the sequencing of events from rumor to actual job loss and reemployment. Psychological measures of health were collected along with self-reported information. The results showed that the threat of unemployment triggered some physiological changes long before actual job loss occurred tainted. For most people involuntary job loss was an event that generated stress, both directly and indirectly.

Stressors in Organizational Life: The term 'Stressors' designates stimuli that are generated on the job and have negative consequences, physical or psychological, for significant proportions of people exposed to them. Kahn and Byosiere (1992) reduced the stressors to 2 major types:

1. Task Content includes such dimensions as simplicity-complexity and monotony-variety.

2. Role Properties, which refers to the social aspects of the job and includes supervisory relationships and role conflict.

Research findings have demonstrated relationships between ill health and jobs that are characterized by highly repetitive, monotonous work and sustained vigilance. Shift work and physical stressors also produce stress. Ill health has also been associated with working in air-conditioned offices, a phenomenon referred to as the "sick building syndrome." Hedge, Erickson and Rubin (1992) reported that sick building syndrome produces the following symptoms: sensory irritation, skin irritation, neurotoxic effects such as runny nose and asthma-like symptoms. Research has demonstrated that sick building syndrome is not caused solely by indoor pollutants but may be related to the electromagnetic fields from video display terminals, which attract irritating fibers and particles to the screens. The syndrome may be related to respiratory ailments associated with re-circulated air. There is a growing body of research (e.g. Soine, 1995; Stenberg & Wall, 1995) that suggests women are more susceptible than men to sick building syndrome. Other research (Hoffman, 1997) has examined the workplace stress associated with HIV disease on infected individuals, coworkers and members of the care giving occupations (e.g.: medical personnel and counselors).

However, it is with role properties that most organizations stressors have been identified. Role conflict refers to perceptual differences regarding the content of a person's role r the relative importance of its elements. Such differences occur between the individual and other people in a work group who do not hold the same role expectations. Role conflict generates negative affect, tension and physical symptoms on the part of the focal person. Conflict among the demands of different roles filled by the same individual can also occur. Such conflicts have been reported most often in occupations such as military service, police work and teaching, where the compartmentalization of time between work and family cannot easily or dependably arranged. Role overload is a variant of role conflict in which conflict is experienced as a necessity to compromise quantity, time schedule or quality. Findings from many studies reveal that overloaded individuals describe their work demands as excessive and their reactions as negative.

Perception and Cognition: The Appraisal Process: the appraisal process seeks to explain that different people react differently to stressors that are objectively the same. The stressors encountered within organizations are often embedded in complex situation. Successful coping requires one to analyze both positive and negative features and decide upon a course of action. Researchers have examined the stages through which individuals perceive and evaluate situations in assessing stress. Lazarus and Folkman (1984) proposed primary and secondary appraisal processes based on a temporal sequence.

Primary appraisal consists of the initial determination that a stimulus (person, event, situation) is positive (benign), negative (stressful), or negative (irrelevant) in its implications for well-being.

Secondary appraisal is a judgment about what can be done to minimize damage or maximize gain. The appraisal process may be cyclical as the individual takes into account a previous coping strategy or some new information.

The importance of the appraisal process as a predictor of stress outcomes is illustrated by a study of patients who had undergone surgery for breast cancer (Vinokar, Threatt, Vinokur-Caplan & Satariano, 1990). Neither the objective stage of the disease nor the extent of surgery predicted the person's appraisal of threat but that appraisal was a major predictor of subsequent anxiety and depression. Other studies as well have indicated that appraisal plays a similar important role in predicting the outcome of job-generated stress.

Response to Stress. Researchers have identified 3 major categories of possible responses to tress- physiological, psychological and behavioral.

Physiological response includes cardiovascular symptoms such as increased blood pressure and cholesterol level, biochemical measures such as catecholamines and uric acid and gastrointestinal symptoms like peptic ulcers. Faster heart rates have been reported under conditions of role conflict, ambiguity regarding future developments on the job and overall reported stress at work. Levels f catecholamines change rapidly and respond to a variety of stimuli. Unpredictability at work, loss of control over pace and method and distracting noise have all been associated with increased levels of catecholamines. Air traffic controllers, for example, show significant associations between daily levels of cortisol secretion and work variables such as load and pace. Research on gastrointestinal symptoms has shown less consistent results compared to the other types of physiological responses.

Psychological responses to stress at work involve affective variables with job dissatisfaction being the most common. Stress has also been found to influence more intense and aroused affective states such as anger, frustration, hostility and irritation. More passive but perhaps no less negative responses include boredom, burnout, fatigue and depressed mood. The psychological effects of work related stress have been found to produce lowered self-confidence and self-esteem.

Behavioral responses to stress have not been studied as frequently as psychological responses. However, 5 broad categories of behavioral responses have been examined-work role, oppressive behavior at work, flight from job, degradation of other life roles and self-damage. Dompierre and Lavoie (1994) reflected on the methodological and ethical difficulties of conducting research on work stress and family violence. Nevertheless, the research results indicate that work-generated stressors have behavioral effects tat are manifested both on the job and away from it thus imposing substantial costs on organizations.

Consequences of Stress. The consequences of stress typically affect the performance of the individual on the job and in other life roles. Other ramifications involve the heath of the individual, as affected by prolonged exposure to physical stressors and through responses to recurrent psychological stressors. Alfredsson & Theorell (1983), in Sweden developed standardized measures of job characteristics for 118 occupational groups on a nationwide basis. Men in jobs characterized by high demand and low control were at twice the risk for heart attacks compared with men in the same age range (40-54) employed in all other occupations. The authors concluded that the next step is to conduct field experiments and interventions to discover ways of reducing such sources of stress.

Non-work stresses can also affect attitude and behavior at work. Research suggest such relationships are particularly evident for single parent families and families in which both parents are employed. Frankenhaeser (19988), showed that the characteristic elevation of catecholamine levels as the stresses of the workday for men, but for married, employed women the elevation persists until the household responsibilities are also fulfilled. Lowman (1996) presented a classification of mental disorders that are specifically work related. The classification includes patterns of under-commitment, over-commitment, anxiety in the work role, and work related depression.

Properties of the Person as Stress Mediators. Individual differences in resistance to stress have long been recognized. Type A and type B behavior play a role here. As mentioned earlier, *Type A* personality type intensifies the effects of various job stressors. They walk, talk and eat rapidly. They are aggressive and competitive. *Type B* are less concerned about time, play for fun and relax without guilt. Barling and Boswell (1995) identified an irritability dimension to Type A behavior that adversely affects health and concentration. Wright (1988) concluded that Type A have a high need for achievement, experience early success, which seems to breed a greater than usual sense of hope that striving efforts will eventually pay off. In assessing the proclivity of Type A individuals to feel stress from work, Wright said, " what is needed are ways of training ourselves and others to maintain diligence with pacing- i.e. to run the race of life like a marathon and not a series of 100-yard dashes,".

Another personality characteristic that mediates stress is *locus of control (LOC)*. LOC differentiates people who believe that they themselves are primarily responsible for what happens to them from those who believe that major events in their lives are determined mainly by other people or forces beyond themselves. People, who have an internal LOC, are more likely to take action against the source of the stress itself or to mitigate its effects in other ways. Externally oriented are more likely to see effective actions as beyond their powers and thus endure rather than act.

Properties of Situation as Stress Mediators. In addition to certain characteristics of individuals, certain properties of situations can mediate the effects of a stressor. The buffering effect reduces the tendency of organizational properties to generate specific stressors, alter the perceptions and cognitions evoked by stressors, mediate the responses that follow the appraisal process or reduce the health-damaging consequences of such responses. The primary variable hypothesized to provide this buffering effect is *social support.* Social support reduces the relationship between various job stressors and indicators of mental and physical health. Thus, social support has been found to have a positive effect on occupational stress (Shaw, et al. 1993). According to research, there are essentially two ways in which social support may influence stress. The first viewpoint is that social support has a main effect on outcomes or strains. This suggests that possessing a strong social support network in fact directly enhances an individual's well being. In effect, this viewpoint proposes that receiving social support simply makes one happier and healthier from the very beginning (Ganster, Fusilier, & Mayes, 1986; House, 1981; and Beehr, 1985). The second approach proposes that social support functions as a buffer. In this approach, the more social support a person receives, the less impact job stressors will have on that person. It follows that if a person experiencing stressors receives little or no social support, he or she should then experience more of the negative outcomes commonly associated with high levels of stress (House, 1981; Leavy, 1983; Cohen & Wills, 1985; Beehr, 1985). The buffering hypothesis is similar in concept to Karasek's (1989) job demands-control model. This model indicates that worker control or social support, (or both) interacts with stressors in a manner that reduces the effects of the stressors on the individual's well being. It is proposed that the worker's control over social support provides a means by which stressors can be changed, in order to lessen their potential impact.

Kahn and Sutton (1987) proposed 3 other situational variables as potential buffers against stress:

- The extent to which the onset of a stressor is predictable
- The extent to which it is understandable
- The extent to which aspects of the stressor are controllable by the person who must experience it.

Of these 3, the strongest support emerged for the predictability the stressor if the occurrence of a stressful event can be predicted, its absence can also be predicted. Thus, the individual knows when it is safe to relax and need not maintain a constant state of vigilance or anxiety.

Coping With Stress

From the organization's standpoint, management may not be concerned when employees experience low to moderate levels of stress. The reason is that such levels of stress may be functional and lead to higher employee performance. But high levels of stress or even low levels sustained over a long period of time, can lead to reduced employee performance and thus require action by management.

While a limited amount of stress may benefit an employee's performance, employees may not see it that way. From the individuals standpoint even low levels of stress are likely to be perceived as undesirable. It's not unlikely therefore for employees and management to have different notions of what constitutes an acceptable level of stress on the job. What management may consider as a "positive stimulus that keeps the adrenalin running" is very likely to be seen as "excessive pressure" by the employee.

Coping strategies can thus be categorized into individual and organizational strategies.

Individual Strategies

An employee can take personal responsibility for reducing his or her stress level. Individual strategies that have proven effective include implementing time management techniques, increasing physical exercise, relaxation training and expanding the social support network.

• ***Time Management.*** Many people manage their time poorly. The result is feeling work overload, skipped schedules, and attendant tension. If one can manage time effectively he can accomplish twice as much as the person who is poorly organized. So an understanding and utilization of basic time management principles can help individuals better cope with tension created by job demands. The table below includes a some strategies:

TAKING TIME TO MANAGE TIME

One of the major causes of stress for managers comes from time pressures. No matter how fast some managers work and how much time they put in; they are still unable to get all their work done. Today many organizations are training their managers how to get more done in less time. Some of the most helpful guidelines for effective time management are:

1. Make a to-do list that identifies things that must be done during the day. Helps keep track of work progress.
2. Delegate work to subordinates.

3. Set time aside when no interruptions are allowed.
4. Have a secretary screen calls to turn away those that do not require personal attention
5. Eat lunch in the office at least once a week so you can catch up on backlog.
6. Discourage drop-in visitors by turning desk to avoid eye contact with door or hallway.
7. Read standing up. The average person reads faster and better when in a slightly uncomfortable position.
8. Make calls between 4:30-5:00pm. People tend to keep their conversations brief so they can go home.
9. Do not feel guilty about those things that have not been

(**Source**: Fred Luthans, Organizational Behavior, p.310)

Research has reported that effective time management has resulted in reduction in blood pressure, clarity in thinking, steep decrease in consumption of tranquillizers and relaxed feeling in action.

- ***Physical exercise.*** Noncompetitive physical exercise like aerobics, walking, jogging, swimming and riding a bicycle have long been recommended by physicians as ways to deal with excessive stress levels. These forms of activity increase stamina, provide mental diversion from work pressures and offer means to "let off steam".

- ***Relaxation:*** Some employees have turned to various means of mental relaxation to adjust to the stresses in their lives. Patterned after the practice of meditation, the relaxation response involves quiet, concentrated inner thought in order to rest the body physically and emotionally. It helps remove people temporarily from the stressful world and reduce their symptoms of stress. The ideal ingredients of this relaxation effort involve:

- A comfortable position in a relatively quiet location.
- Closed eyes and deep, comfortable breathes.
- Repetition of a peaceful word, or focus on a pleasant mental image.

- Avoidance of distracting thoughts and negative events.
- Soothing background music.
- ***Biofeedback.*** In this technique, people under medical guidance learn from instrument feedback to influence symptoms to stress, such as increased heart rate or severe headaches. Earlier, it was thought that people could not control their involuntary nervous system, which, in turn controls internal processes such as heartbeat, oxygen consumtion, stomach acid flow, and brain waves. There now is evidence that people can exercise some control over these internal processes; thus biofeedback may be helpful in reducing undesirable effects of stress.
- ***Yoga*** is probably the most effective remedy for stress. Yoga has been used all over India for centuries. There are several yoga asanas but the following are some useful ones to cope with stress.
- Annamaya Kosha Kriyas- Traditional voluntary internal cleansing techniques, yogasanas and shavasana.
- Praanamaa Kosha-Praanaama- 5 types of systematic regulated slow deep respiration with or without breath holding.
- Manomaya Kosha- meditation and devotional session.
- Vijnanamya Kosha- Analysis and understanding the nature of one's problems.
- Anandamaa Kosha- Practicising joy under all circumstances.

Studies have reveled that Yoga has cured several stress-related diseases. Datey et. Al. (1973) and Patel (1973) showed that the practice of Shavasana effectively reduced the blood pressure. Yoga therapy has been found to be effective in controlling Asthma (Bhole, 1967; Anadananda and Varandani, 1975; Melkote, 1973; Varandani et al., 1973), and neuriticism (Kochan and Pratap, 1971 and Fochar, 1971).

- ***Social Support.*** Some people experience stress because they are detached from the world around them. They lack warm interpersonal relationships. Individuals with a driving ambition and strong need for independence may fail to develop close attachments to friends and colleagues. To achieve their success, they often sacrifice fulfillment of their social needs. Their lack of social attachments may result in anger, anxiety and loneliness-all producing stress in their lives.

A powerful anecdote to this problem lies in the presence of social support at work. Social support is a network of helpful activities, interactions and relationships that provide an employee with the satisfaction of important needs. There are 4 types of support in a total network: instrumental (task assistant), informational, evaluative and emotional. Research suggests that when employees have at least one person from whom they can receive social support, they experience lower stress. Women in particular, feel more comfortable in providing it to others. Supervisors need to develop the capacity to play this role for their employees when support is needed. An alternative action is to simply provide opportunities for social support and encourage it to develop among a group of workers. Managers may need to allow time for employees to develop and nurture their social support networks at work.

- ***Control the Situation.*** Unrealistic deadlines must be avoided but at the same time, should be aware of limits. It is impossible to please everyone.

- ***Open up to Others.*** Venting emotions, frustrations, fears and feelings in a comfortable surrounding helps in freedom of stress and brings on a feeling of relaxation.

Organizational Strategies

Individuals are capable of increasing their own resistance to stress, but find it almost impossible to eliminate work related stresses. While they may be able to help minimize its effects, they may not be able to prevent stress in the first place. For this reason, organizations play a key role in stress management. Fig. 4 below demonstrates the individual versus organizational tactics of stress management.

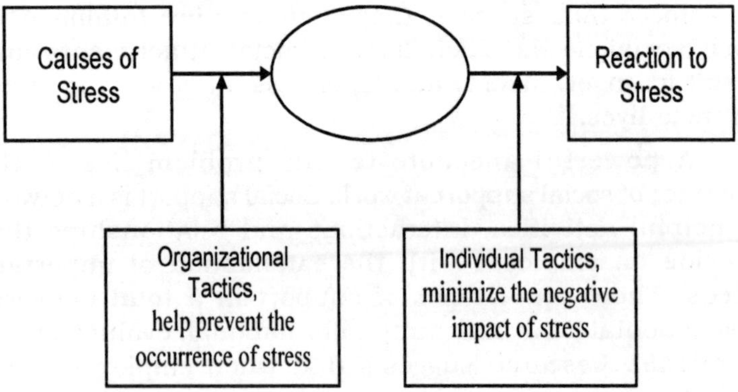

Fig. 4: **Individual versus Organizational Tactics of Stress Management**

(**Source**: Greenberg and Baron, Behavior in Organizations, p.271).

Some of the techniques in which organizations can use to reduce stress are descried below:

• ***Participative decision Making.*** Role stress is detrimental to a large extent because employees feel uncertain about goals, expectations and how they will be evaluated. By giving employees a voice in decisions, which directly affect their job performances, management can increase employee control and reduce the role stress. So managers should consider increasing employee participation in decision-making.

• ***Redesigning jobs.*** Involves enriching jobs either by improving job content factor or improving core job characteristics. Give employees more responsibility; meaningful work, greater autonomy and increased feedback can reduce stress, as enriched tasks will eliminate the stress found in more routine and structured jobs. Although employees with a low need for growth might need less responsibility and increased specialization. If individuals prefer structure and routine, reducing skill variety should also reduce uncertainties and stress levels.

• ***Organizational Communication.*** Increased formal communication with employees reduces uncertainty by lessening role ambiguity and role conflict. Given the importance that perceptions play in moderating the stress-response relationship management can also use effective communications as a means to shape employee perceptions.

• ***Selection and Placement.*** While jobs differ in the amount of stress, as we discussed earlier, individuals also differ in their response to stress. Individuals with little experience or an external locus of control, tend to be more stress-prone.

• ***Goal Setting.*** Based on an extensive amount of research, individuals perform better when they have specific, challenging goals and receive feedback on how well they are progressing toward these goals. The use of goals can reduce stress as well as provide motivation. Specific goals that are perceived as attainable clarify performance expectations. Additionally, goal feedback reduces uncertainties as to actual job performance. The result is less employee frustration, role ambiguity and stress.

• ***Wellness Programmes.*** There is an increasing trend towards in-house programmes of preventive maintenance, which focuses on the employee's total physical and mental condition. Corporate wellness centers may include disease screening, health education and fitness centers. Health care practioners encourage changes in lifestyle like breathing regulation, muscle relaxation, positive imagery, nutrition management and exercise enabling employees to use more of their full potential. The assumption underlying most wellness programs is that employees need to take personal responsibility for their physical and mental health. The organization is merely a vehicle to facilitate this end.

Organizations, of course, aren't altruistic. They expect payoff from their investment in wellness programs. And most of those firms that have introduced wellness programs have found significant benefits. For instance, Johnson & Johnson calculated the following annual savings in insurance premiums when an employee exchanges bad habits for healthy ones: quitting smoking ($1,110); starting to exercise ($260); lowering cholesterol from 240 to 190 milligrams ($1,200); and slimming down from obese to normal weight ($117).

• ***Changing Cognitive Reactions; Emotive Therapy .-*** Rational emotive therapy is based on the idea that people chose to appraise the situation as involving demands which are beyond their abilities. The solution involves teaching individuals to become more aware of their belief system so that they can modify 'irrational' beliefs as a means of reducing stress. The therapy thus involves encouraging individuals to modify their negative perception of a situation.

This idea is clearly based on an interactive, cognitive model of stress. When individuals perceive situations as threatening, dangerous or out of control, the stress they experience rises. Some people take this further and when exposed to such a perceived situation, they start to engage in negative 'self-talk'. They tell themselves how horrible and unbearable it will be if they fail, if they are not perfect or if they cannot get others to agree with their point of view. The aim of cognitive therapy is to make people aware of this irrational and self-defeating quest for perfection. The assumption is that once the person is aware of how irrational he is being, he will be able to modify his appraisal of potentially threatening situations and think about things in a more 'rational' way.

The problem with this approach is that it focuses the blame on the individual. The stress is the result of their irrationality. This alleviates any need for the organization to consider ways in which the job and organization could be changed to reduce the likelihood that the likelihood that employees will find certain situations threatening and therefore stressful.

• ***Changing Behaviors: Employee Assistance Programmes.-*** In the 1960's and 70's many companies, especially in the USA, introduced programmes concentrating on alcohol and drug related problems. These programmes were generically called Employee Assistance Programmes (EAPs). Today EAP's cover a wide variety of personal problems, including marital, financial, parent-child difficulties (Wrich, 1980). The programmes vary in detail but are generally consistent in the method used, which has been termed 'constructive confrontation.' The confrontation is between the supervisor and employee, with the focus on deterioration in work performance. The employee is offered the opportunity of assistance to help her deal with the problem under EAP. If the work doesn't improve, the confrontation may need to be repeated with more serious consequences attached to failing to improve, with ultimate sanction being loss of job.

Research by Macleod, (1985) suggests that EAP's can be successful if introduced and managed sensitively. For example, Wrich (1984), of United Airlines estimated that for every dollar spent on the company's EAP programme, the company gets back $16.35 in the form of reduced absenteeism alone.

Nevertheless, EAP's deal only with reducing the negative behavior impact of stress. EAP's do not attempt to treat the environmental factors, which were causing the stress.

- ***Counseling.*** Industrial counseling programmes are usually traced back to the classic Hawthrone studies conducted at Western Electric Company in Chicago, in 1936. One aspect of the research involved interviews with approximately 20,000 employees and the main conclusions from this were:

- The complaint was often not the real source of the individual's difficulty. Consequently, taking action to deal with this stated source did not ensure that the difficulty was resolved.

- Giving employees the opportunity to talk about problems gave many employees a 'new enthusiasm' for their work.

On the basis of these conclusions, Western Electric developed a counseling service, which could be used by any of its employees. This is seen as a pre-cursor to development of other counseling services provided in the context of employment. However, most services offered to employees focus on treating troubled employees rather than counseling 'normal' employees, as the latter tends to be seen as outdated paternalism.

Counseling is more broadly based than rational-emotive therapy, which is a specific form of therapeutic, counseling, based on changing cognitions. Counseling as a generic method can be introduced to help employees cope with stress of all kinds. A counseling session may lead an individual to reappraise a situation, but it may also encourage the person to think through other strategies, which she can use actually to cope with the problems, which she perceives.

Several organizations, recognizing the costs of stress, both to the individual and the organization, have introduced counseling services. The aim is to help the individual cope more effectively with the stress that is being experienced so that the costs to the organization are reduced. The aim is not to reduce the source of stress. The Post Office was one of the first organizations in the U.K to introduce a counseling service for employees. Any employee could make use of the service and there were guarantees given that the problems discussed in the counseling sessions would be kept confidential. While the service had some success, there was also an unexpected side effect. In the course of talking through their problems employees became aware of how it was their job, which was largely to rather than returning to their employment happier and more content, some employees who had used the counseling service actually became more discontent and even left the organization. This emphasizes the point that although we need to take into consideration an individual's appraisal of the situation if we are going to understand the experience of stress, it is nevertheless the case that some jobs and environments do place pressures on people such that almost of counseling will eradicate it. The Post Office has now abandoned its counseling service.

Other companies are also experimenting with introducing counseling services, but not necessarily by employing their own counselors. Some companies have arrangements with independent counseling providers. Employees can use the counseling services free of charge and can access them through picking up the phone and dialing a particular number. An advantage of this form of counseling is that there is more likelihood that confidentiality will not be breached. In the Post Office, the issue of confidentiality was a perceived problem even though employees were told that is was guaranteed. Nevertheless, the same fundamental problem exists with this external provision of counseling in that it does not actually change the fact of a job that continually places the incumbent under pressure.

Stress reduction programmes may always be necessary, as not all stress is induced directly from work environment. The person who is experiencing stress because of marital or financial difficulties may still suffer from impaired work. The provision of some kind of stress reduction service may well be beneficial to the organization if it helps the person to cope more effectively with the stress being experienced. The individual's work may improve in consequence. Also, some would argue that it is never going to be possible to remove all the potential sources of stress from the work environment, so that the provision of stress reduction programmes will always be needed.

Epilogue

Thus, work stress not only is a frequent problem for employees but also appears to be more and more accepted as part of the price individuals' pay for employment. The fact that stress management programs are directed not at making work less stressful but at increasing our capacity to deal with stress suggest that few people believe stress can be eliminated or drastically reduced from work. One of the consequences of organizational downsizing is that fewer employees have to do the work that was once performed by a greater number of employees. The prevailing sentiment is that organizations are expected to do more work with less resource. Technological advances have also accelerated the speed at which work is performed. Those changes have the potential to diminish overall mental health by reducing autonomy or control and thus worker self-esteem (Locke, McClear and Knight, 1996). In the evolution of work design, employees are becoming increasingly controlled by situational factors, as opposed to exerting control over their own work environments. As research on mental health and stress has revealed, the reduction in self-regulation (i.e., feeling "out of control") impairs psychological well being

(Murphy, Hurrell and Quick, 1992). Rather than denying the reality of work stress or assuming no responsibility for it, organizations are becoming increasingly committed to addressing it.

A Lasting Thought...

Scientists at the Rocket launching station in Thumba, were in the habit of working for nearly 12 to 18 hours a day. There were about seventy such scientists working on a project. All the scientists were really frustrated due to the pressure of work and the demands of their boss but everyone was loyal to him and did not think of quitting the job. One day, one scientist came to his boss and told him – "Sir, I have promised to my children that I will take them to the exhibition going on in our township. So I want to leave the office at 5 30 pm." His boss replied – "O K, You are permitted to leave the office early today."

The Scientist started working. He continued his work after lunch. As usual he got involved to such an extent that he looked at his watch when he felt he was close to completion. The time was 8.30 p.m Suddenly he remembered of the promise he had given to his children. He looked for his boss he was not there. Having told him in the morning itself, he closed everything and left for home. Deep within himself, he was feeling guilty for having disappointed his children. He reached home. Children were not there. His wife alone was sitting in the hall and reading magazines. The situation was explosive; any talk would boomerang on him. His wife asked him - Would you like to have coffee or shall I straight away serve dinner if you are hungry. The man replied - If you would like to have coffee, I too would have but what about Children?

Wife replied- "You don't now - Your manager came at 5 15 p.m and has taken the children to the exhibition."

What had really happened was the boss who granted him permission was observing him working seriously at 5.00 p.m. He thought to himself, this person will not leave the work, but if he has promised his children they should enjoy the visit to exhibition. So he took the lead in taking them to exhibition. The boss does not have to do it every time. But once it is done, loyalty is established.

That is why all the scientists at Thumba continued to work under their boss even though the stress was tremendous.

The boss was no other than Dr. A P J Abdul Kalam.

Aspiring to be like Dr. Kalam, preventing stress and helping the employee maintain a fine balance between personal and professional life.

References

K. Aswathappa, Organizational Behaviour, Himalya Publishing House, 2001.p. 516-530.

Fred Luthans, Organizational Behaviour, New York, Mc Graw-Hill, 1989, p. 195.

Stephen p. Robbins, Organizational Behaviour, New Delhi, PHI, 1991, 1991 p. 602

Richard M. Hodgetts, Organizational Behaviour, Macmillan, 1991, p.347

Dr. P.K Ghosh and Prof. M.B Ghorpade, Industrial and Organizational psychology, Himalaya Publishing House, 1991, p.575.

Neil Anderson, Deniz Ones, Handan Sinangil, , C Viswesvaran, Handbook of Industrial, Work and Organizational Psychology, vol. 2-organizational psychology, sage publications, 2002, p.93.

Stephen P. Robbins, Organizational behaviour, 8th ed., Prentice Hal of India, 1998.

C. Ratnam, B. Srivastav, Personnel Management and Human Resource, Tata Mc Grawhill Publishing Company Ltd., New Delhi, 1991

Udai Parekh, Organizational Behaviour Processes, Rawt Publishing, 1996.

Susan Newell, The healthy Organization, Routledge, 1995.

M.G Rao, Human Behaviour at Work, vol. 2, Discovery Publishing House, 1993.

J. Newstrom, K. Davis Organizational Behaviour, 10th ed. Tata Mc Graw Hill Publishing Company Ltd., Delhi, 1998.

Websites

http://www.usasbe.org/knowledge/proceedings/2001/045.pdf

http://jam.sagepub.com/cgi/reprint/32/1/49

http://www.usasbe.org/knowledge/proceedings/2001/045.pdf

http://jam.sagepub.com/cgi/reprint/32/1/49

file:///C:/Documents%20and%20Settings/Kainaz/Local%20Settings/Temporary%20Internet%20Files/Content.IE5/WHYVKDQF/306 Chapter15% 5B1%5D.ppt #326, 1, Stress at Work

http://www.midwestacademy.org/Proceedings/2005/papers/Teague_ob108.doc

http://www.leaonline.com/doi/abs/10.1207/S15327043HUP1604_2;jsessionid=ifXjSC_TrFL-?cookieSet=1&journalCode=hup

http://www.leaonline.com/doi/pdfplus/10.1207/S15327043HUP1604_2

http://www.iaapsy.org/25icap/common/OP145.htm

http://www.ncbi.nlm.nih.gov/entrez/query.fcgi?cmd=Retrieve& db=PubMed&list_uids =3585696 &dopt=Abstract

http://medind.nic.in/iay/t03/i2/iayt03i2p6.pdf

http://www.stress.org/job.htm

http://www.megantough.com/articles-others-5.html

http://www.findarticles.com/p/articles/mi_m3495/is_n6_v43/ai_20817109

http://www.topten.org/public/AE/AE29.html

http://www.megantough.com/index.html

http://www.gov.sk.ca/psc/hrmanual/appendices/ps804-ga.pdf

http://www.workhealth.org/strain/jsfinded.html

http://www.workhealth.org/strain/jsaltpe.html

http://www.workhealth.org/OSI%20Index/OSI%20Home%20Page.html

http://www.msnbc.msn.com/id/3072410/

http://www.canville.net/malone/jobstress.html

14
Core Competences

Competences

"No letters after your name are ever going to be a total guarantee of competence any more than they are a guarantee against fraud. Improving competence involves continuing professional development ... That is the really crucial thing, not just passing an examination." – Colette Bowe, American Business Executive.

Competencies can be thought of as the inner tolls for motivating employees, directing systems and processes, and guiding the business towards common goals that will allow the organization to increase its value. Competency is the state or quality of being adequately or well qualified to perform a task. It is synonymous with ability. A person gains competency through education, training, experience, or natural abilities. While there are many definitions of competency, most of them have two common components:

The competencies are observable or measurable Knowledge, Skills, Abilities and Personal characteristics (KSAP).

These KSAPs must distinguish between superior and other performers.

Definition

The New Oxford Shorter Dictionary defines competence as the "*power, ability, capacity to do, for a, task.*" whereas Merriam Webster defines competence as "*a sufficiency of means for the necessities and conveniences of life.*"

Boyatzis (1982) defines competency as "*a job competency is an underlying characteristic of an employee - i.e., motive, trait, skill, aspects of one's self image, social role, or a body of knowledge - which results in effective and/or superior performance in a job.*"

Dubios (1993), a leading expert in the applied competency filed, defines competence as "*the employee's capacity to meet (or exceed) a job's requirements by producing the job outputs at an expected level of quality within the constraints of the organization's internal and external environments."*

Spencer and Spencer (1993) in their work 'Competence at Work: Models for Superior Performance' have defined competency as *"an underlying characteristic of an individual that is casually related to criterion-referenced effective and/or superior performance in a job or situation."*

Parry (1996) defines competency as *"a cluster of related knowledge, skills and attitudes that affects a major part of one's job (a role or responsibility) that correlates with performance on the job, that can be measured against well accepted standards and that can be improved via training and development."*

In 1982, Zamke interviewed several experts in the field of Human Resource Management to determine "precisely what makes a competency" and he captured his findings thusly – *"Competency, competencies, competency models and competency-based training are all Humpty Dumpty words meaning only what the definer wants them to mean. The problem comes not from malice, stupidity or marketing avarice, but instead from some basic procedural and philosophical differences among those racing to define the concept and to set the model for the way the rest of us will use competencies."*

Thus we can see that defining competency fully is not as simple as addressing the individual application alone. It is much broader a concept than that. With competency emerge terms such as organizational competence and core competency, which potentially permits, improved strategic human resource management. Organizational competence and core competency are the components, which link an organization's essential values and business to those of its employees.

Historical Origin

For 3000 years, the Chinese empire recognized differences in individual abilities by employing civil service exams in selection for government jobs. In medieval times, apprentices were expected to develop the specific skills they would need for effective job performance by working with a master craftsman. For hundreds of years, educators have defined the knowledge and skills to be covered in their curricula. The English biologist, Sir Francis Galton, and American psychologist James McKeen Cattell, pioneered the development of objective techniques to measure human intellectual capabilities in the late 19th and early 20th centuries.

In the 1940's and 1950's, Ernest Fleishman and John Flanagan systematically analyzed the work behaviour of supervisors and identified broad performance factors. Beginning in the 1960's, many psychologists attempted to identify individual variables that would effectively predict job performance without inherent bias against subgroups. By then numerous research studies had demonstrated that's assessments of academic aptitude, tests of knowledge, grades and credentials were not good predictors of either job performance or success in life.

Competency Profiling

Furnham (1990) states, "the term competence is new and fashionable, but the concept is old. Psychologists interested in personality and individual differences, organizational behaviour and psychometrics have long debated these questions of personality traits, intelligence and other abilities."

Competency – based methodology was pioneered by Hay – McBer Company founder David McClelland, a Harvard University psychologist in the late 1960's and early 1970's. McClelland set out to define competency variables that could be used in predicting job performance and that were not biased by race, gender, or socioeconomic factors. His research helped identify performance aspects not attributable to a worker's intelligence or degree of knowledge and skill. McClelland's article, in American Psychologists in 1973, entitled "Testing for Competence Rather Than for Intelligence," was a key point of development of the competency movement as an alternative to the intelligence testing movement.

A competency profile is generally composed of five to ten competences but can include as many or as few as are required to accurately reflect performance variations in the position. Competency – based models are used to recruit, select, train, and develop employees.

Competency profile development can be handled in a number of ways, two of which are the top – down and bottom – up approaches. The top – down approach generally involves picking, based on a strategic analysis of the organization's performance objectives, an array of competences from a dictionary of competences and assessing those for a particular position or a class of positions. The shortcoming associated with this approach is that the competences survey becomes an additional step separate from the creation of the profile. This process has the potential to reduce the applied face validity of the profile and can thereby reduce employee buy – in.

The bottom – up approach on the other hand involves exploratory checklist surveys and subsequent confirmatory interviews to derive the competencies from employees, thereby increasing the face – validity and simultaneously developing the assessment questions to tap into them. These approaches may result in employees being directly involved in the development of competency profiles that will describe behaviours that are relevant to their tasks. This is useful for gaining employee understanding of, input to, buy – in, and loyalty to the process.

Behavioural Competences

Competences that define behaviours (or attitudes) can often be covered by shorter lists, because many jobs often require the same, or similar, approaches. For example, being concerned with customer care is a behavioural competency and this is an increasingly important aspect of an increasing number of jobs. It may be possible to create one definition of the competency of customer care that applies to many different jobs or roles.

In a survey of 49 employers core frameworks involving 553 competences in total, it was found that competencies like team orientation; communication, people management etc. topped the list of employers' most popular competences while those like leadership, decision making, interpersonal skills, self confidence and assertiveness were found in the middle order. Competences like responsibility, anticipation, behaving ethically were found to be least common in this framework.

One important group of behavioural competencies addresses how individuals manage their emotions. This subset of competencies is known collectively as "emotional intelligence". It covers such skills as being able to have the empathy to understand other people (and, therefore, work more productively with them), and someone being able to control their own reactions when put under pressure.

The approach of defining performance at work was developed in the USA by a Harvard psychologist, David McClelland and taken further by Richard Boyatzis. Their work primarily involved defining the behaviours that successful managers demonstrated.

The approach developed by McClelland and Boyatzis emphasized superior performance and looked for behaviours that average or under-performing managers did not have. They were most interested in differentiating behaviours.

The work that David McClelland and his colleagues at the McBer consultancy had undertaken was pushed a decisive step further in 1981 when the American Management Association commissioned McBer consultant Richard Boyatzis, to examine whether a generic model of managerial competency could be derived from various individual competency models.

Boyatzis re-analyzed studies of more than 2000 people in 41 management jobs in 12 organizations. He set down an explicit definition of "competency" that had underpinned the McBer work. A competency, according to him, was an underlying characteristic of an individual, which is casually related to effective or superior performance in a job. Competencies can be motives, traits, skills, aspects of one's self-image or social role, or a body of knowledge that one uses.

Boyatzis placed the concept of competency firmly in the context of effective performance. “Effective performance is the attainment of specific results (outcomes) through specific actions while maintaining policies, procedures and conditions of the organization environment”. And a person’s competencies allow him or her to perform these actions. A competency is ability: “A person’s set of competencies reflect his or her capability. They are describing what he or she can do, not necessarily what he or she does, nor does all the time, regardless of the situation and setting”.

Boyatzis defines competencies as those characteristics that differentiate superior performance from average and poor performance, but he had to deal with the question of how to define those characteristics that are essential to performing a job, but do not lead to superior performance. His solution was to define these as threshold competencies.

Boyatzis says that motives, traits, self-image and social role, skills and knowledge all count as competencies, they form a hierarchy. Each competency may exist in an individual at various levels: motives and traits can be found at the unconscious level; self-image and social role at the conscious level, and skills are the behavioural level. Knowledge, he says, has pervasive effect on all the other competencies.

Boyatzis then analyzed various studies and picked out those characteristics that distinguished effective performance in a job but were not unique to a specific product or service. This resulted in a list of 19 generic management competencies that he included in his 1982 landmark publication, The competent manager. Of this set of 19, 12 were defined as competencies (that is, differentiating competencies) and 7 as threshold competencies.

In 1989, Lyle Spencer and Signe Spencer began to analyze all the competency studies completed by the Mcber consultancy to date. These covered not just managers but also entrepreneurs, and technical and professional, sales and “human service” workers from a wide range of organizations.

The Spencers compared all the models of competencies

and translated the findings into a common language. Next, the behavioural indicators were analyzed to identify the lowest common denominator or smallest unit of observation directly comparable across all models. Then they listed all the behavioural indicators mentioned in any of the models. Around 760 different types of behaviour were identified. Of these, 360 indicators defining 21 competencies were found to account for 80% to 98% of behaviours reported in each model, and these were compiled into a preliminary dictionary of behavioural indicators.

The work of McClelland and the McBer consultancy has spawned an enormous industry. Organizations – both consultancies and individual employees – in the USA, the UK and worldwide have used the methodology to develop their own competency models and apply them to the whole range of human resource management processes.

Though McClelland's approach has been very influential, it has been largely ignored by the publicly funded competence movement in the United Kingdom. Occupational standards are primarily lists of technical, job-specific competences.

Unlike the US approach, where competencies are often defined from the bottom up i.e.; by individual employers or by particular firms of consultants, the UK's occupational standards were intended to be cascaded from the top – the national level, led by government – down to individual employers and training companies.

These standards define minimum, acceptable performance levels instead of differentiating or superlative levels like those of McClelland. In addition, they produce their definitions by studying jobs, while US/the McClelland approach studies people.

Traditional job related qualifications in the UK usually attempted to list all the knowledge and skills required for an occupation, and then decided whether or not candidates merited a qualification by setting an examination. The idea developed of creating an alternative approach, where activities that could be observed would be listed, and then candidates would be assessed by watching their performance.

These lists of activities became known as standards of competence, and the qualifications that are based on them are known as National Vocational Qualifications.

Core Competency

A company's core competency is the one thing that it can do better than its competitors. It can be anything from product development to employee dedication. Modern theorists suggest that those activities that are not in company's core competencies should be outsourced. But this can't be done when one concentrated on individuals core competencies in the company. Since individual core competencies cannot be outsourced they need to be identified, roles should be defined better and essential training should be imparted.

Definition

The concept of core competence was developed in the field of management. C. K. Prahalad and Gary Hamel (1990) introduced this concept in Harvard Business Review article. They defined core competency as *"an area of specialized expertise that is the result of harmonizing streams of technology and work activity."*

Leonard-Barton, D; say *"capabilities are considered core if they differentiate a company strategically."*

Galunic and Rodon (1998) argue that *"core competencies differentiates not only between firms but also inside a firm it differentiates amongst several competencies and thereby guides a firm recombining its competencies in response to demands from the environment"*.

It is important to distinguish between individual competencies or capabilities and core competencies. Individual capabilities stand alone and are generally considered in isolation. Gallon, Stillman, and Coates (1995) are of the opinion that core competencies are more than the traits of individuals. They defined core competencies as *"aggregates of capabilities, where synergy is created that has sustainable value and broad applicability."* That synergy needs to be sustained in the face of potential competition.

So according to this definition, core competencies are harmonized, intentional constructions.

Coyne, Hall, and Clifford (1997) proposed that *"a core competence is a combination of complementary skills and knowledge bases embedded in a group or team that results in the ability to execute one or more critical processes to a world class standard. The skills or knowledge must be complementary, and taken together they should make it possible to provide a superior product."*

These definitons concentrate more on holistic aspect of competency which benefits the organization as a whole from the perspective of marketing and sales.

Core competency can refer to either an organization or an individual and resource based analysis. Lado and Wilson (1994) suggest that a tight link between individual and organization core competencies is a good way to achieve the sustained and desired competitive advantage.

Dubios (1993) says, *"employee core competency is principal or critically essential competency for successful job performance for a given job at a given level in an organizational hierarchy."*

Fogg (1994) defines organization core competency as *"those few internal competencies at which you are very, very good, better than your competition, and that you will build on and use to beat the competition and to achieve your strategic objectives"*.

Core competencies are a bundle of knowledge and skills that create sustained competitive advantage for a company. A core competency represents an organization – wide capability, which is created, based on the combined skills of individuals and teams.

The concept of 'core competences' was the brainchild of the Harvard professors C.K Prahalad and Gary Hamel, through the series of articles in the Harvard Business Review followed by the best-seller – Competing for the Future. The success of this book gave the term core competencies a long due recognition. Their central idea is that over time companies may develop key areas of expertise, which are distinctive to that company and critical to the company's long term growth.

Prahalad and Hamel (1990) say, *"In the 1990s managers will be judged by their ability to identify, cultivate and exploit the core competencies that make the growth possible – indeed they will have to rethink the concept of the corporation itself."*

These areas of expertise many be in any area but are most likely to develop in the critical, central areas of the company where the most value is added to its products.

Like for a manufacturer of electronic equipment, key areas of expertise could be in the design of the electronic components and circuits. For a software company, the key skills may be in the overall simplicity and utility of the program for the users. Hamel and Prahalad go on to quote of their favourite examples of Honda's expertise in engines. Honda was able to exploit this core competency to develop a variety of quality products from lawn mowers and snow blowers to trucks and automobiles.

While Honda's development is apparently based on the overt exploitation of its position in engines and transmissions, its ultimately successful entry into the American motor – cycle market was a saga of learning from trial and error. Honda simply had a product, the lightweight Super – Cub bike, which they wanted to sell in an America dominated by Harley Davidson.

The idea resulted from studies of the way successful firms, mainly Japanese, appeared systematically to acquire and exploit combinations of fundamental technologies in order to develop generic or core products with which to dominate global markets. Thus many of the quoted examples of the exploitation of core competences relate to manufacturing technology and to global business. However, the concept also has validity for non-manufacturing and for non-global businesses. Core competence is not simply the possession of a particular technological or managerial capability. Core competence is a combination of such capabilities that provide the firm with a leadership position in the development of certain generic or core products. This is what gives the business a sustainable competitive advantage.

Core competences are the basis of competitive

advantage in achieving strategic intent. Acquiring and nurturing competences that are not core is simply a waste of resources and effort and serves only to dissipate concentration.

Core competencies are not seen as being fixed. Infact they should change in response to the change's in the company's environment. They are flexible and evolve over a period of time. As the business will evolve and adopt to new circumstances and opportunities, the core competencies will have to change too.

The two categories of core competencies are identified as: domain and enabling

Domain Competencies are Described as

1. Required for success in a particular job family; and.

2. Typically involving demonstrated knowledge in a technical, professional, Moccupational, vocational, or process area.

In other words, if one wants to be an accountant one must possess accounting knowledge, skills and behaviours.

Enabling competencies, on the other hand, are:

1. Essential to the realization of business strategy or organizational values;

2. Typically critical behaviours and skills; and

3. Generally relevant to all employees.

For example, for the competency communication, a chancellor as well as a custodian needs communication skills, perhaps different skills, but each must be able to communicate.

In most cases, they are invisible assets, which are very difficult for other companies to copy or imitate. Unlike technology and financial resources, core competencies represent skills and capabilities that are extremely difficult for competitors to acquire or develop quickly.

Some commonly used core competencies include strategic thinking, problem solving, relationship management, team building, decision-making, customer focus, innovation/creativity and communication. Some of the factors that make up a competency definition include personality, knowledge, ability, motivation and interest.

The most commonly known core competencies, which are considered essential, are as follows:

1. Creativity – applies news of thinking; creates new ideas.

2. Vision – understand the context of the organization within the outside world; is aware of organization's critical success factors; anticipates and influences the future.

3. Influence – having an impact on others; convincing them to perform certain activities; garners respect; inspiring them to work towards organizational objectives.

4. Entrepreneurship – understands customers; builds organizational credibility; develops new revenue sources.

5. Organizational Design and Development – organizes for success; understands how to facilitate functional needs and structure to achieve strategic plans.

6. Building teamwork – co-operates to achieve common goals; values and encourages diversity of opinions; creates synergies across the workgroup.

7. Communication – clear expression of ideas and thoughts as well as active and empathetic listening.

8. Understanding Self and Others – healthy, trusting, interpersonal relating; accurate self-assessment; understands that people process information differently; takes initiative to build relationships; understands cultural differences.

9. Development of people – enhances one's own ability and the ability of others to contribute.

10. Performance Management – motivates; delegates; clarity and specificity of expectations; win-win agreements.

11. Programme/Process Management – resource utilization and maximization; time, financial, and human resource management.

12. Staffing – identifies and defines needs; attracts

appropriate candidates; determines fit; selects the most qualified.

13. Compliance/ Ethics – personal compass composed of clear principles and the flexibility to balance between literal adherence to rules and the use of policy as a guide.

Identification of Core Competences

A firm's existing core competences can be identified by analyzing its product or service. What are the fundamental skills and knowledge on which successful products are based? They may relate to straightforward world leadership in specific technologies or they may be more related to particular organizational or managerial skills.

Companies that successfully build global leadership in more than one core competence are few and far between; those that have done so in several are extremely rare. Every management team needs to know what competences form the foundation of its most successful products, so that they can develop those competences and nurture the people on whom they depend.

For many businesses, the acquisition and development of core competences is somewhat haphazard. As Mintzberg (1987) noted, even the clearest strategic positions may emerge from a process of repeated trial and error, or even as a result of simple good luck. The extent, to which strategic positions emerge, as opposed to being deliberately planned, can never be unknown – many emergent strategies are post rationalized to give the impression of careful and sophisticated planning.

Prahalad and Hamel suggest three factors to identify core competencies in any business.

They are:

1. The key core competencies are those that enable the creation of new products and services.

2. Core competencies are the skills that enable a business to deliver a fundamental customer benefit – i.e.; what core competency about a certain product makes a customer chose it over other products.

3. The core competencies should be competitively unique. To qualify as a core, a competence should be something that other competitors wish they had within their own business.

As far as when establishing appropriate competencies in human resources are concerned, it may still be helpful to break down the competency areas. The following may be a helpful model:

· 'Natural' competencies – personality traits and characteristics

· 'Acquired' competencies – those that the individual has attained or developed such as qualifications and experience

· 'Adapting' competencies – how the individuals has applied themselves during their career.

It is necessary to identify the actual competencies and this can be achieved through a number of techniques such as inventories and questionnaires, interviews, observation, repertory grids and testing.

Inventories and Questionnaires

This approach involves using an inventory (or questionnaire or checklist) to break down the job requirements into key tasks, which are then subdivided into day-to-day activities. The inventory information is obtained by talking to the jobholder and manager, as well as through observing the jobholder in action. Following the initial identification of activities, the jobholder is asked to give a score for elements such as the time taken to undertake the work, its complexity and the consequences of error. The greater the score, the greater the criticality of the tasks. Following this, each competency is rated to provide an indication of the importance of each competency.

This approach is helpful where jobs are well defined and predictable and it can be a cost-effective way of gauging the views of a large number of jobholders and managers.

However, it is essential that adequate time and resources are provided to enable effective analysis of the inventory/ questionnaire results.

Interviews

This involves interviewing jobholders and /or managers in order to identify the specific events that form a critical part of the job. Interviewees are usually asked to describe particular experiences in their work and the interviewer will then probe to determine the actions taken and the outcome. From this, the interviewer can infer the competencies, required particularly when dealing with critical ideas.

This approach tends to be most helpful to identify competencies, which are critical when dealing with demanding situations, rather than standard competencies, so determining the difference between average and superior performance. This approach is helpful as it focuses directly on the competencies required. It is essential that the interviewer is experienced in a competency approach and has the necessary interview skills.

Repertory Grid

This approach attempts to identify competences, which differentiate between poor, average and superior performance. The manager is interviewed and asked to place people in various categories of performance. The interviewer then prompts the manager to describe some of the examples of performance and then attempts to break these examples down to certain elements that can isolate and identify the behaviors that accompany performance at different levels.

This approach only takes into account the views of the manager and not the jobholder. It is also necessary to ensure confidentiality during the process. The process requires a suitably experienced and skilled interviewer and can be time consuming.

Observation

This approach involves the observation of jobholders

undertaking their normal day-to-day activities. The observer will normally develop a record from that lists possible behaviour indicators and then records when these behaviors are displayed during the observation process, which might focus on a particular time period.

This approach enables the observer to see the work at first hand and prevents disruption to the manager or jobholder. However, the jobholder may have concerns about being observed for long periods of time and may need reassurance of the purpose of the exercise.

Testing

Ability and psychometric test are undertaken by a cross section of jobholders. The results are correlated against levels of job performance in order to identify differentiating characteristics and key competencies.

This approach can provide differentiators between performance levels and also some benchmark data on the current workforce, which can then be used as a measure for the future employees.

Building Core Competences

Two tools helps the firms identify and build core competences. The first tool consists of four specific criteria that firms use to determine which of their resources and capabilities are core competencies. The second tool is the value chain analysis. Firms use this tool to select the value – creating competences that should be maintained, upgraded, or developed and those that should be outsourced.

Capabilities that are valuable, rare, costly to imitate, and non-substitutable are strategic capabilities. Strategic capabilities are also known as core competences and hence serve as a source of competitive advantage for the firm over its rivals. Capabilities failing to satisfy the four criteria of sustainable competitive advantage are not core competences.

1. Valuable - Valuable capabilities are those that create value for a firm by exploiting opportunities or neutralizing threats in the firm's external environment. Valuable

capabilities enable a firm to formulate and implement strategies that create value for specific customers.

2. Rare – Rare capabilities are those possessed by few, if any, current or potential competition. A key question managers seek to answer when evaluating this criterion is "How many rival firms possess these valuable capabilities?" Capabilities possessed by many rival firms are unlikely to be source of competitive advantage for any one of them. Instead, valuable, but common (i.e., not rare), resources and capabilities are sources of competitive parity. Competitive advantage results only when firms develop and exploit capabilities that differ from those they share with competition.

3. Costly to Imitate – Costly-to-imitate capabilities are those that other firms cannot develop easily. Capabilities that are costly to imitate can occur because of one or a combination of three reasons.

First, a firm sometimes is able to develop capabilities because of unique historical condition. As firms evolve, they pick up skills, abilities and resources that are unique to them, reflecting their particular path through history. Another way of saying this is that firms sometimes are able to develop capabilities because they were in the right place at the right time.

A second condition of being costly to imitate occurs when the link between the firm's competences and its competitive advantage is causally ambiguous. In these instances, competitors are unable to understand clearly how a firm uses its competences as the foundation for competitive advantage. As a result, competitors are uncertain about the competences they should develop to duplicate the benefits of a competitor's value – creating strategy.

Social complexity is the third reason that capabilities can be costly to imitate. Social complexity means that at least some, and frequently many, of the firm's capabilities are a product of complex social phenomena. Examples of socially complex capabilities include interpersonal relationships, trust, and friendships among managers and between managers and employees and firm's reputation with suppliers and customers.

4. Non-substitutable – No substitutable capabilities are those that do not have strategic equivalents. This final requirement for a capability to be a source of competitive advantage "is that there must be no strategically equivalent valuable resources that are themselves either not rare or imitable. Two valuable firm resources are strategically equivalent when they each can be exploited separately to implement the same strategies. In general, the strategic value of capabilities increases the more difficult they are to substitute for. The more invisible capabilities are, the more difficult it is for the firms to find substitutes and the greater challenge is to competitors trying to imitate a firm's value – creating strategy. Firm – specific knowledge and trust – based working relationships between managers and nonmangerial personnel are examples of capabilities that are difficult to identify and for which finding a substitute is challenging.

Value Chain Analysis.

Values Chain Analysis describes the activities that take place in a business and relates them to an analysis of the competitive strength of the business. Influential work by Michael Porter suggested that the activities of the business could be grouped under two headings:

- Primary Activities – those that are directly concerned with creating and delivering a product.
- Secondary Activities – which whilst they are not directly involved in production, may increase effectiveness or efficiency (e.g., Human Resource Management).

Value Chain Analysis is one way of identifying, which activities are, best undertaken by a business and which are best provided by others.

Linking Value Chain Analysis to Competitive Management.

What activity a business undertakes is directly linked to achievement competitive achievement. For example, a business, which wishes to outperform its competitors through differentiating itself through higher quality, will have to perform its value chain analysis better than the opposition. By contrast, a strategy based on seeking cost leadership will require a reduction in its costs associated with the value chain activities, or a reduction in the total amount of resources used.

Steps in Value Chain Analysis

Value chain analysis can be broken down into a three sequential steps:

1. Break down a market/organizational into its key activities under each of the major headings in the model;

2. Assess the potential of adding value via cost advantage or differentiation, or identify current activities where a business appears to be at a competitive disadvantage;

3. Determine strategies built around focusing on activities where competitive advantage can be sustained.

Acquiring Core Competences

A firm's capacity for competitive innovation is based on its ability to acquire relevant core competences and to apply them effectively in the development of core products. Capability is infinite. It is not constrained by the competences one already has, or even the resources at ones disposal, but can be extended by careful definition of the competences required and the means of their acquisition and development.

Missing competences can be painstakingly developed internally through focused investment in R&D or acquired externally through various forms of collaborative arrangements. Internal development is extremely expensive and beyond the means of all but the largest organizations. So, for a variety of reasons, the acquisitions of core competences through collaboration have become an attractive proposition. It is a way of reducing costs and eliminating wasteful competition, especially in R&D.

The potential benefits from collaborations are tremendous, but the risks are also considerable. Many firms seem to enter such arrangements for reasons, which are not very apparent, possibly even because they are fashionable, and as a result they lose out to their collaborative partner, sometimes disastrously. The overriding principle in engaging in any collaboration is to make sure you know exactly what you are trying to achieve when you enter a collaborative arrangement and then to make sure you achieve it. Some firms have adopted forms of alliance and mutual collaboration in order to close the competence gap.

Competency Mapping

Competency – based HR is considered the best HR. The questions that arises is – Is the underlying principle of competency mapping just about finding the right people for the right job? The issue is much more complex than it appears, and most HR departments have been struggling to formulate the right framework for their organization.

Competency mapping is a process of identifying key competences for a particular position in an organization, and then using it for job – evaluation, recruitment, training and development, performance management, succession planning, etc. " The competency framework serves as the bedrock for all HR applications. As a result of competency mapping, all the HR processes like talent induction, management development, appraisals and training yield much better results," states well-known HR consultant Ulhas Pagey.

Experts agree that the competency mapping process does not fit the one-size-fits all formula. It has to be specific to the user organization. One can develop models that draw from but are not defined by existing research, using behavioural interview methods so that the organization creates a model that reflects its own strategy, its own market, its own customers, and the competencies that bring success in that specific context.

Stephen Martin, an international authority in the field who is also the president of ITAP Europe says competency mapping can be rather good at providing organizational pain relief when applied effectively – and so making the case for extending it. Martin suggests the following methodology for designing and developing competency frameworks. The most effective route is to employ recognized best – practice internal research methodology using behavioural event interview (BEI) techniques to selectively sample the target population and so build up the models from the data that emerges.

He adds that once the behavioural data is collected, it should be sorted, categorized and leveled carefully to create models that are concise and comprehensive, simple and sophisticated. Developing BEI skills within the organization has the added benefit that once the model is complete, it can be used more effectively by transferring these skills to selection interviewing, development assessments, and so on.

Martin cautions that international organizations must ensure that the methodology does not screen-out those competencies that do not match the culturally – influenced pre – conceptions of what high – performance competencies are.

Competency mapping can play a significant role in recruiting and retaining people as it gives a more accurate analysis of the job requirements, the candidate's capability, of the difference between the two, and the development and training needs to bridge the gaps. Competencies enable individuals to identify and articulate what they offer – regardless of the job they happen to have at the time – so that their organization can see, value and utilize what capability is actually available.

Lynette D'Silva, manager, learning and development, HR, Zensar Technologies, points out that competency mapping helps identify the success criteria (i.e.; behavioural standards of performance excellence) required for individuals to be successful in their roles. It helps to:

- Support specific and objective assessment of their strengths, and specify target and areas for professional development.
- Provide development tools and methods for enhancing their skills.
- Provide the basis for a more objective dialogue with

their manager or team about performance, development, and career related issues.

"If an individual is able to discuss the above with his manager, it will help him to chalk out his growth perspectives in the company", states D'Silva.

Zensar has a behavioural competency model, which is based on various job roles in the organization. D'Silva describes the process of implementation:

- Having defined the various job roles, a focused study was initiated where job role holders were interviewed on the critical incident method and the data of success – critical factors was collated.

- The job roles and deliverables were finalized on the basis of the competencies, derived from the data. This data was further analyzed, and on the basis of these competencies that had an impact on the job roles and deliverables were finalized.

- After identifying the competencies, a job analysis exercise was carried out where the importance level of every competency was ascertained before freezing the competency model.

L&T Infotech, has a successful competency – based HR system. Recruitment, training, job –rotation, succession planning and promotions – all are defined by competency mapping. Says Dr. Devendra Nath, executive vice – president of the company, "Nearly all our HR interventions are linked to competency. Competencies are enhanced through training and job – rotations." He adds that all people who have gone through job – rotation undergo a transformation and get a broader perspective of the company.

Dhananjay Savarkar, head of the training department, L&T Infotech, asserts that in no two organizations can competency frameworks be the same; it will vary over the time even in one organization. It is not timeless, it is contextual. "We call it the DNA of success... it is what makes star performers work in a particular way. Isolate the DNA and make it available to ten other." says Savarkar. He acknowledges that there was resistance from the line people, but when the numbers started flowing they sat up.

Competency Management

"In hierarchy, every employee tends to rise to his level of incompetence. Therefore, in time, every post tends to be occupied by an employee who id incompetent to carry out his duties, and work is accomplished by those employees who have not reached their level of incompetence – The Peter Principle.

Competency Management takes guesswork out of predicting future on-the-job performance and behaviour and give hiring managers the need to make an informed hiring decisions or recommendation.

The Competency Management module focuses not only on competencies but also on tools designed for managing competencies. Competency Management is a pivotal element of aligning corporate core values with individual goals and career plans.

Competencies are baseline measurements for skill development. They are categories for assessment of an individual's expertise; know – how, mastery, or qualifications for a particular job.

Competency Management module includes:

- Competency categories
- Competency definitions
- Behaviours associated with specific competencies.
- Coaching tips linked to competencies and/or behaviour.
- Coaching tips for employees and for managers.
- Definitions of employee roles and job descriptions.
- Assessment tools to identify and rate competencies and preferences.
- Tailored feedback for improvement.

The Competency Management is useful in the following ways:

- Facilitates skill tracking by department, job family, or position.
- Provides skill and competency profiles for training and development.

- Provides candidate job – to – competency rating analysis.
- Facilitates career path planning by providing individual skill comparisons to job requirements.
- Ensures managers make job placements.
- Ensures employee career plans are realistic and available.
- Measures success factors associated with competencies.

Competency Development

There are 3 steps to competency development:

Step 1: Defining and Mapping Out

The first step in this process is to define 'what you need' to get where you want to be.

Defining 'what you need' is best answered through a comprehensive discussion with senior management as well as organization research via a range of information sources on core corporate values, future business scenarios and implications, strategic business objectives and 'employee behaviour' requirements and prevailing/desired work culture.

Following which, one needs to design a core competency frame work that is aligned with the organization's strategic business objective, develop the behaviours underlying the competencies in a simple and clear manner, validate the competency model with a cross section of employees, communicate the competency model through change sponsors and agents and educate employees at all levels on 'what, why and how' and finally use the competency model as a foundation for multiple human resource applications.

Step 2: Assessing and Understanding.

This is about assessing and understanding 'where you are' currently.

- First, identify and develop appropriate assessment tools that create opportunities to measure the competencies in a consistent, reliable and valid manner.
- Then use multiple assessment tools for different

levels including in – tray exercise, presentation exercise, group exercise, role play exercise, competency based interview, multi – source feedback, aptitude tests, personality questionnaire and the likes.

- Validate and constantly review assessment tools. Train the line managers to conduct assessments in a self – sufficiency mode.
- Conduct assessments, which require discussion and deliberation of what was observed against an absolute standard rather than based in relativity.
- Provide individual and team/organizational reports of strengths and development needs.

Step 3: Developing and ManagingKnowing the diagnosis is really the beginning or merely a means to an end. Like most diagnosis, no positive change will occur without managing and implementing a course of action.

Hence how do organizations provide and facilitate meaningful developmental opportunities?

Meaningful development occurs when the experience is viewed by the employee as relevant to his/her work, requiring him/her to exercise 'behaviours' that have not received much attention and reinforced and supported by superiors who actively participate in the developmental process.

Core competences: Cautions and Reminder

Evidence and company experiences show that the value of core competences as sources of competitive advantage should never be taken for granted. Moreover, the ability of any particular core competence to provide competitive advantage on a permanent basis should not be assumed. The reason for these cautions is the central dilemma that is associated with the use of core competences as sources of competitive advantage; namely, that all core capabilities simultaneously have the potential to be core rigidities. This reality is captured by the following comment from Leslie Wexner, CEO of The Limited, Inc.: "Success doesn't beget success. Success begets failure because the more that you know a thing works, the less likely you are to think that it won't work. When you've had a long string of victories, it's harder to foresee your own vulnerabilities." Thus, each capability is both a strength and a weakness – a strength because it is the source of competitive advantage and, hence, strategic competitiveness – and a weakness because, if emphasized when it is no longer competitively relevant, it can be a seed of organizational inertia.

Events occurring in the firm's external environment create conditions through which core competences can become core rigidities, generate inertia, and stifle innovation. "Often flip side, the dark side, of core capabilities is revealed due to external events when new competitors figure out a better way to serve the firm's customers, when new technologies emerge, or when political or social events shift the ground underneath. It really isn't changes in the external environment that cause core capabilities to become core rigidities; rather, it is strategic myopia and inflexibility on the part of firm's managers that results in core competences being emphasized to the point that strategic inertia strangles the firm's ability to grow and to adapt to environmental changes through innovations.

References

1. Pearson, Gordon. The Competitive Organization – Managing for organizational excellence. England: McGraw Hill Book Company, 1st Edition; pages 99-109.

2. Hilt, Michael; Duane, R; Hoskisson, Robert E. Strategic Management Competitiveness and Globalization – Core and Cases. South Western Thomas Learning, 2001 ed; pages 113 –131.

3. Hamel, Gary; Prahalad, C.K. Competing for the_Future. Harvard Business School Press.

4. http://www.tutor2u.net/business/strategy/core_competencies.htm

5. http://en.wikipedia.org/wiki/Core_competency

6. http://humanresources.ucr.edu/Static/HRUnits Competencies/GuideToCompetencies.htm.

15
Assessment Centre

Assessment Centre refers to a method or approach, aims to give information about the participants current or potential competence.

Thus an important defining characteristic of assessment centre is their objective to obtain best possible indication of people's actual or potential competence to perform at the target job or job level. This objective is achieved by combining a range of assessment techniques so that the fullest and clearest indication of competence is achieved.

One of the advantages of the assessment centre method is that it is flexible: the centre should be designed to meet the needs of the organization, be they development, selection or some combination of the two.

Features of Assessment Centre

The main feature of assessment centre is that they are a multiple assessment process. There are 5 main ways in which that is so. A *group* of participants takes part in a *variety* of exercises observed by a *team* of trained assessors who evaluate each participant against *number* of predetermined, job related behaviours. Decisions are then made by pooling *shared data.*

1. Multiple Participants

Several people participate in the centre at the same time. Although there are no absolute rules, six is the usual number in each batch of people, but there might me more than one batch running parallel. At batches of beyond 12 participants the logistics can get out of hand very easily.

2. Combination of Methods

The focal point of most assessment centres is the use of work sample tests or simulations. The principle of their design is to replicate, so far as in possible, the kind of tasks that a participant would be required to do in the job for which they are being considered. To gain full nderstanding of a person's range of capabilities one simulation is not enough to develop anything like a complete picture. Thus in order to achieve the objective more than one assessment techniques are used.

3. Team of Assessors

To escape the difficulties associated with the one-to-one interview used either as a means of selection or in some aspect of performance measurement, it is important to use a team of assessors. A ratio that worked well is one assessor for each pair of participants. The team of assessor should include a balance between exerts-that is psychologists and human resource mangers- and line managers, all of whom need appropriate training.

4. Behaviourally Based, Founded on Job Analysis

The staring point of assessment centre has to be some analysis of the job to determine what it is that discriminates between the performance of successful job incumbents and those that perform less successfully in the same job. Successful performance in any job is likely to be founded on a combination of factors, some of which may be to do with disposition, some to do with attitude, some with particular skills that have developed over time, some to do with energy levels, some to do with particular ways of thinking or problem solving and some may be to do with knowing about particular things. The objective of job analysis is to determine which of these things are more important.

5. Shared Data

From the earliest days an essential feature of the design of assessment centres was that data about participants is shared between the assessors. This process of conferring together is variously known as consensus meeting, the wash-up or assessors discussion.

A History of Assessment Centres

The use of Assessment Centres in the UK

We can trace the existence of assessment centres back to 1942 when they were used by War Office Selection Boards (Anstey, 1989). Their introduction stemmed from the fact that the existing system was resulting in a large proportion of those officers it had predicted would be successful being 'returned to unit' as unsuitable. This is hardly surprising when one considers that the system as it was relied on interviewing to select officers and had as selection criteria things like social and educational background. Even the criteria of 'achievement in the ranks' which one might imagine as being more job relevant included things like 'exceptional smartness'. No wonder unsuitable people were chosen as officers and potentially excellent officers overlooked. The assessment centre approach subsequently adopted was an attempt to accurately elicit the types of behaviour that an officer was required to display in order to be successful in their job. The tasks included leaderless group exercises, selection tests and individual interviews by a senior officer, junior officer and psychiatrist respectively. This new system resulted in a substantial drop in the proportion of officers being 'returned to unit' as unfit for duty. During the post war years this system was so successful that it was introduced for selection to the Civil Service and a variation of it is still used for officer selection in the armed forces to this day.

The use of Assessment Centres in the US

In the United States assessment centres were initially used by the Office of Strategic Studies to select spies during the Second World War. Subsequently the use of assessment centres was taken up by the private sector especially the giant American Telephone and Telegraph Company (AT&T) which began using assessment centres for management selection in 1956 as well as Standard Oil Ohio, IBM, Sears and General Electric. There were differences between the US and UK approaches which largely stemmed from the original background to their introduction. In the UK a greater emphasis was placed on group exercises with an appointed leader, group discussions and long written exercises whereas in the US more emphasis was placed on in-tray exercises, leaderless group exercises with assigned roles and two person role plays (Woodruffe, 1993).

The use of Assessment Centres in Industry

Modern assessment centres in the UK tend now to follow the American format although there are still some which have their roots in the public sector Civil Service model. The growth of the use of assessment centres in the UK has been rapid. In 1986 Robertson and Makin reported that slightly more than one quarter of organisations who employed 500 people or more used assessment centres, in 1989 Mabey reported that more than one third of companies employing over 1000 people used them while most recently Boyle et al (1993) reported that 45% of organisations who responded used assessment centres and that their use was more prevalent in the private sector and by larger organisations. We have also seen a rise in the use of what we could term 'pure' development centres. The main reasons behind this have been the realisation that centres that have an element of selection decision making to them can have a demoralising effect on those individuals who have been deemed unsuccessful. Organizations have also come to realize that to be competitive they must constantly invest in the development of their staff in order to enable them to respond effectively to an increasingly uncertain marketplace. This has meant that rather than selecting new employees organizations are now investing more in their existing workforce. Traditionally companies who wished to train their staff would send them on a training course external to the organization, indeed many still do, but there has been an increasing emphasis placed on delivering training that is relevant to the organization's needs and business objectives. A development centre run as part of an integrated training strategy is an excellent way of ensuring that training is carried out in a context of organizational relevance. A final reason for the growth in use of development centres has been the widespread adoption of the idea of behavioral competencies in the human resource field, because development centres are designed around the job simulation format which requires the participant to actively do something they are a naturally effective way of assessing competencies in individuals.

Uses of Assessment Centres

The use of assessment centres has increased despite the cost of installation and the on-going cost of operating them. One of the reasons all this investment is seen as worthwhile is the belief in the quality of the assessment that is obtained. The assessor see how people behave in the centre and can be confident that this is a good indication of how they would behave in the job.

1. Recruitment and Promotion

Where particular positions need to be filled exist, both internal and external candidates can be assessed for suitability to those specific posts. It allows the organization to place its new recruits wisely according to their strengths and interests. Assessment centres can also be used to sell the organization. Candidates see them as a sign that the organization is thoroughly professional in its personnel practices (Robertson at al, 1991). Successful applicants will also be subject to psychological effect of felling committed to an organization that puts them through a rigorous selection process before letting them in (Fletcher, 1989). Applicants also get a taste for the job. A realistic preview boosts people's overall opinion of the organization (Meglino et al, 1988).

2. Analysis of Competencies

The disciplined approach to assessment forces the organization to analyze its jobs properly. It also results in the common language of the competency dimensions that differentiate successful from the average performer. Through assessor training these dimensions can become part of the folklore of the organization.

3. Performance Appraisal

The competencies can become part of an appraisal system. This will contribute to a rational and integrated overall system of human resource assessment and development, and will specifically improve the appraisal process because competencies will be well understood.

4. Motivation

Participants at internal centres can gain a sense of being valued by the organization through being chosen to attend the centre. Attendance implies a vote of confidence and is a clear sign of the organization devoting resources to their development.

5. Diagnsing Training and Developing Needs

Assessment centre offer the chance to establish individual training and development requirements, while proving candidates with a greater appreciation for their needs. It emphasize self-assessment and the diagnosis by participants of their own and each other's strengths and limitations during the centre.

6. Organizational Planning

Assessment centres can be used to identify areas where widespread skill deficiencies exist within organizations, so that training can be developed in these areas. Results can also be integrated with human resource planning data to provide additional information concerning the number of people with particular skills needed to meet future needs.

7. Development

Assessment centres when extended can be used as development centre which can help in incorporating specific skills like team building, leadership etc. Coaching and counseling can also be a part of these centers.

8 Assessor Benefit

The process of being trained as an assessor carries the general benefit of imparting the skills of assessing people and of giving feedback. These skills will be useful in the assessor's normal job of managing people (Glaze, 1989). People from different parts of the organization work together and build a network, which extends his interaction.

Stages in Assessment Centre

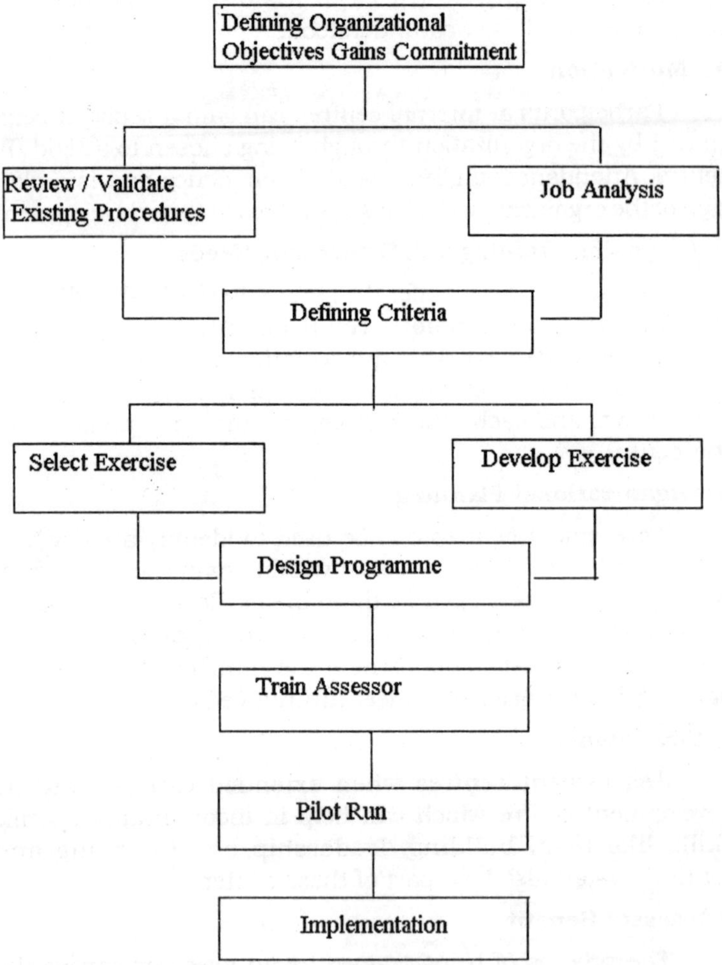

ORGANIZATIONAL OBJECTIVE

Assessment centres need to be an integral part of human resource strategy. Defining of the objective of the centre is also important. This should be done as per the need of the organization. Next in the process comes the drafting of the policy. This policy statement is of utmost important is arrangement of a brief meeting with the key individuals in the organization to gain commitment to the procedure.

Job Analysis

In the context of designing an assessment centre, the start point is a clear and accurate picture of what the centre is measuring. If it is wrong, people are likely to be judged against inappropriate criteria, the exercises will be difficult to design and evaluating behaviour accurately will be a problem. Job analysis is nothing more than a systematic analysis of a job that is used to develop class specifications, pay, selection standards, tests, performance evaluation standards, training programs, and similar functions. In the case of selection activities, it is an absolute mandate according to professional standards.

Structure of Job Analysis

Following are the steps required for job analysis.

Direct Observation

Direct observation gives analysts an opportunity to take an overview of the context in which a person works and the tasks that they do, at the start of research program. Direct observation means watch people work. There are varying levels of directness and precision, ranging from observing someone through a one-way mirror taking fairly precise notes and measurements of whole body movement, to sitting with or going along with a manger as they go through their daily routine. Since this analysis in only restricted to observation there are several issues hidden from this - like thinking, problem solving approach or setting priorities. Thus the next step is to interview the job incumbent to find out why they do what they do.

Incumbent Interview

The best way to understand what counts in a particular job is to go and ask the person who is currently doing the job is to go and ask the person who is currently doing the job. For this purpose a semi-structured approach is preferred which has some fairly precise and detailed questions, particularly task related questions, mixed with a number of open questions which may need discussion and further probing before a summary answer is recorded.

Manager Interview

Interviews with mangers of job incumbents are conducted to unearth performance characteristic of the job, particularly to identify what makes people relatively successful or relatively unsuccessful in the job being studied. Following are the two likely approach used -*Critical Incident Interviews.*

The technique can be used either individually in an interview or collectively as a group discussion. Managers are asked to identify incidents that clearly demonstrate both effective and non effective job-related behavior. The data obtained are in the form of anecdotes or stories about the way a number of individuals behaved on particular occasions.

Repertory Grid Interview

This technique is developed from the personal construct theory of George Kelly, who used it in clinical setting to understand the world of psychologically ill people. In the context of job analysis a manager is asked to delineate those constructs that differentiate between the good performers and those who are less good. This technique is well used in revealing hidden criteria such as decision making approaches, the style of relationship with other people and so on.

Coding and Classifying Behaviour

After gathering information on what incumbents do (task analysis) and how they behave when they perform well or less well (performance), the important concern is regarding the classification of behavior. Although this is somewhat a subjective process. The basic approach is to identify the behaviour, skill, competency, attitude or whatever that underpins the performance of a task. The next step in the analysis is to generate more quantitative data for selection of the final criteria.

Questionnaire

There are two types of questionnaire that can be developed to give further detail in a job analysis.

1. Job Activity Questionnaire.

These are used when one cannot interview enough incumbents to obtain a representative sample of their views. The objective is not to gather new information but to expand, validate and quantify what you already have. Here the respondents are asked to rate a list of activities on a number of different scales. The outcome of the interview is to identify those aspects of the job task that are sufficiently frequent and sufficiently important to warrant inclusion in the assessment centre.

2. Behavioural Criteria Questionnaire

Due to organizational constraints it is not possible to interview all managers who are subject experts when critical incident or repertory grid interviews are being conducted. Thus behavioral criteria questionnaire is used with the objective of quantifying data rather than collecting new data. In these the criteria that have been identified by classifying and coding interview transcripts are listed together with their definition. Respondents are then asked to rate on a scale.

Defining Criteria

On the basis of the available information and evidences from the job analysis, relevant criteria are included in different parts of selection process and different simulations are used in an assessment centre.

Gaugler and Thornton (1989) demonstrated that the accuracy of rating or classifying declines when the number of categories is increased. They go on to recommend no more than six as the maximum number that assessor can actually make use of. The practical rules of thumb are -

- Include a criterion if at least half of the expert see it as important
- Include a criterion if it is amenable to observation in a specific context or simulation, but not otherwise.
- Consider excluding criteria that can easily be learned.

Another issue is ensuring that sufficient emphasis is given to those criteria which emerged as most important for success in the target job. An appropriate mix of exercises should be selected to give due weighting to the most important criteria.

Exercise

All assessment center exercises are either individual, in which the participant completes the exercise without interacting with other participants, or they are group exercises, in which participants interact with one or more other participants in order to accomplish the exercise objectives.

Within these two broad categories, there are a number of specific assessment center exercises. While the format for the exercises is basically the same for any position, the content changes, depending on the job, level, and organization.

Group Discussion Exercise

Group discussion exercises can take several forms but there are two main parameters by which they can be classified. Firstly, there is the purpose/ type of meeting, which usually means choosing between a co-operative or competitive setting. Co-operative group discussion meetings usually have a problem-solving flavor about them, in that the participants are required to analyze a set of information and to come up with recommendations within an allotted timeframe. These are often referred to as "non-assigned roles" because participants are all given the same information and no one is assigned any particular role.

A competitive group discussion is the alternative type of meeting in which participants are required to persuade and negotiate in order to achieve the best deal they can. In this type of exercise the participant receive some common information as well as some information that is exclusive to them. They need to sell a particular viewpoint to the other team members. This type of exercise is often referred to as an "assigned role", since each participant has been tasked with an individual assignment.

The second parameter to consider when selecting group discussion exercises, is whether or not to assign the role of leader. The decision is usually influenced by whether you are wishing to assess the quality of leadership or not.

Another factor to be considered is the size of the group. This will be affected by the number of participants but in general group sizes are best when kept between 4 to 6.

This allows each participant a reasonable amount of 'air time', that is, an average of 10-15 minutes each, for a session of 45-60 minutes' duration.

It is possible to include more than one group discussion in an assessment centre, which enables a mix of assigned and non-assigned role. This mix provides the opportunity to observe participants in different group discussion situations.

Finally group discussion exercises are seen as the most popular and most influential exercise included in the assessment centre.

Oral Presentation

An oral presentation might also be viewed as a form of group process, but one where the participant has a specific and highly visible role. It is also possible for the oral presentation to be run as one-to-one session.

In this exercise the participant is asked to prepare for and make a presentation. The level of formality and the nature of the presentation will be determined by the demands of the target job. It is not uncommon therefore to include such a presentaion in assessment centre where participants are assessed in relation to jobs in sales, marketing or training. The exercise can also elicit other important criteria, depending on the topic of presentation.

Interview Simulation Exercises

These exercises simulate one-to-one interactions between a role-player in the guise of a customer, customer, colleague, boss or subordinate and the participant in the target job-role. It should be emphasized that although the participant is asked to presume that they are in the target job-role, they are not asked to role-play. Indeed it is essential that the participant appreciate the need to be themselves and act as he or she would, if they were put in that role, otherwise assessors will not be able to assess their true behaviour.

The usual format of this type of exercise is to give the participant a detailed brief with general background information, a description of particular situation and some notes about the person they are about to meet. They then have a period of time to understand and prepare for their meeting. The range of situations to which an interview simulation can be applied is quite varied.

Indeed the interview simulation is a rich and powerful exercise, which is often viewed by assessors as providing a significant input to a participant's overall performance on an assessment centre.

Fact-Find and Decision-Making Exercises

This is also a one-to-one exercise. In this type of exercise the role-player is often referred to as a resource-person, because they are in possession of a large amount of data and it is participant's task to gather relevant information in order to make a decision and recommendation about a particular situation.

In this exercise the participant is given a very brief outline description about an incident and is told to prepare questions to put to the resource person. They are then allowed to question the resource person for a fixed period of time, at the end of which they must make a decision and appropriate recommendation. Once they have declared their decision, the resource person questions them to test the soundness of their arguments and their level of resolve.

This provides an excellent opportunity to observe an individual's judgement, decisiveness and tenacity.

This type of exercise is very good at establishing how effectively a participant can think and reason with words and such as is particularly good at assessing sills in the area of problem solving and decision-making.

In-Basket Exercises

The in-basket or in-tray exercise is one of the best types of written exercise. The participant is asked to handle a typical pile of papers that simulate what would be encountered by someone in the target job. These papers might include letters, internal memos, reports, junk mails and so on. The task of the participant is to sort through the items, determining priorities, deciding what can be delegated and to whom and deciding how to action items. In basket exercise can vary in length and duration. In baskets range from 10-40 items and last from one to three hours. The size and scope of this exercise should reflect the demands of the target job, for it is quite possible to have a large number of relatively simple items or a small number of more complex items.

The main skill areas measured by in basket exercise are planning and organizing, prioritizing, decision making and delegating. It is also possible to measure written communication skills as well as the level of interpersonal sensitivity employed. This is particularly important in jobs that necessitate handling difficult matters in writing.

Analysis Exercises

Analysis exercises require the participant to review a certain amount of information which may be presented in a verbal and / or numerical form and to reach logical conclusions. Once again the content and duration of the exercise should reflect the likely demands of the target job. Participants may receive two or three pages of text, possibly accompanied by tables and / or graphs and could be allowed one of two hours to assimilate the information and write a report with recommendations.

Such exercises reveal a participant's analytical skills, namely problem solving and decision-making. They also act as a good indicator of written communication skill and the ability to organize and structure their work. It is possible to link an analysis exercise to a group discussion exercise and / or oral presentation if it is felt useful to do so.

Additional Assessment Methods

In addition to exercise simulations, many assessment centres include the use of some other form of assessment method. These usually enable them to create a complete and clear picture of the participants. It helps them in the feedback process. And it also aid to the scheduling of the centre, for it is often helpful to be able to give the participants a test of some sort, so as to relieve the pressure on assessors. The additional assessment method that can be used include the following:

Interview

It is quite common to include one or more interviews with an assessment centre. Interview must be directed at gathering evidence in relation to some of the criteria being assessed on the centre. This type of interview is often referred to as a 'Criteria Based Interview' (CBI) and it entails preparing specific questions before the interview which will elicit behavioral evidence of the criteria in question. Once the behavioral evidence has been collected, it is recorded and evaluated systematically, using the same rating scale that is applied to the simulation exercises.

Psychometric Tests

The purpose of an assessment centre should always influence the decision about whether to include psychometric tests or not. If the event is more of a development centre, then psychometrics facilitate feedback process and enables the participant to gain a comprehensive picture of themselves. If the purpose of the centre is selection then these tests help assessors reach a valid decision.

Generally speaking aptitude tests of verbal and numerical reasoning are most popular and valid predictors of potential. These are timed tests, taken under exam conditions, designed to measure your intellectual capacity for thinking and reasoning, particularly your logical/ analytical ability. The tests are designed for specific roles and are meant to be challenging but you won't be expected to have prior knowledge or experience of the role for which you are applying. Accuracy is more important than speed. Most tests are multiple choice and designed so that very few candidates both finish and get the correct answers.

The other types of tests used are personality inventories. These assess your personality and how you might react in different situations. They are not usually timed, have no right or wrong answers and are often used to see if you would fit into the company culture and can identify a working situation that would suit you.

Designing the Assessment Centre Programme

Once the job analysis is carried out and criteria are well defined, the next step is to select a set of exercises which will adequately measure the criteria required for effective job performance. A useful document at this stage is one which shows the criteria that will apply to each exercise. This document is often referred to as a criteria-exercise matrix.

In terms of activities that occur during as assessment centre, the elements that need to be combined are: participants, exercises, assessors, equipment, rooms and, according to needs, role-players and resource people. All the people concern will need to know at any one time where they are supposed to be, what they are meant to be doing, with whom and, in case of assessors who they are observing. Thus the planning issues to consider are:

- The variety of people to be bought together.
- The number of people involved.
- Scheduling exercises.
- The master schedule.
- Room allocation.
- Equipment needs.
- Service at the facility.
- Briefing procedures.
- Checklists.

Assessor Training

The essential aspects of assessment centre are the exercises and the criteria against which participants are assessed, but the ultimate success of the centre will be determined by the efforts of the assessors. Thus the assessor must be carefully selected and thoroughly trained in the requisite skills.

The key issue when selecting assessor is ensuring that they are familiar with the demands of the target job. It is beneficial to have assessors who are two levels above the participants in the organization.

Assessor characteristics will vary in terms of job function, work experience, age, race, sex, length and service, and so on.

Assessor-training content can be arranged sequentially as below-

- Introduction (personal introduction, objectives and timetables).
- Introduction to assessment centre (background, purpose and key features).
- The criteria (the job analysis research, criteria definitions, and so on).
- The behavioral assessment processes (observe, record, classify and evaluate).

- Practicing the assessment process on the exercises.
- Non-exercise components of the assessment centre.
- The assessor discussion
- How to give feedback.

Pilot Run

A trial run need to be set up using real assessors and participants who come most close as real participants. The purpose of running this is to collect feedback and accordingly make amendments as per the requirements.

Implementation

Starting the Event

Following events should be checked before morning of the centre

- Check the facilities.
- Label the rooms to be used.
- Finalize the timetable.
- Lay out the assessors' room.
- Arrange for participants' photographs.

Briefing

Assessors

Briefing assessor serves various functions. It provides an opportunity to recap on several points covered in the training program, as well as dealing with the logistics of the event.

The issues to be covered under logistics include-

- The timetable
- The facility
- Assessor-Participant-Exercise Matrix
- Issue and talk through Assessor Manuals.
- Demonstrate the lay out of room and explain what is kept where
- Indicate how work completed by participants should be handled.

- Issue job application forms and any previous notes on participants.

Additional points to be covered while briefing:

- A reminder of criteria and their definitions.
- A reminder of each of the exercise and corresponding criteria.
- Reminder of skills of observing and recording.
- A reminder of behaviorally specified observations.
- A reminder of the integrity of the process and avoid interchange of views about particular participants.
- A reminder of their duty to help the centre run to time.

Participants

The need to brief participants will vary according to the amount of detail that has been previously available to them. For most in-company events, such as promotion board or development centre, it is probably that prior briefing will have been extensive. With selection events, participants may arrive with no real idea about what is expected of them except that they have been asked to give up 1 or 2 days of their time. For all it is beneficial to brief participants before the event proper on the following:

- The nature of exercises.
- The role of assessors.
- Expectations of them.

Finally emphasize that many exercises are conducted under time pressure. It is important that participants listen carefully to their briefing and respond immediately if they have any doubts.

Administering Exercises

It is essential to ensure that participants get a consistent briefing. For most exercises the administrator's role is mainly to invigilate to ensure that, for example, participants do not discuss any briefing material they have during preparatory period. In general the administrator like the assessor should not intervene in the process with the following exception:

- Timing announcements.
- Clear misinterpretation of the rules.
- Answering questions as the exercise proceeds.

Most exercises, once completed will require participants to complete a Participant Report Form. Administers should make it their business to read all Participant Report Form quickly with a view of noting any information which may be useful in the evaluation of the participant.

Feedback

Feedback should be a part of every assessment centre, even if the event is being run purely to help make a Yes/No hiring decision, for it would be a missed opportunity not to provide feedback to the successful job applicants.

Review and Validate

The validity of an assessment centres in general is very good. Following questions underlie the themes that are at the heart of any attempt to validate an assessment centre, whether a particular event or the process in general.

- Does your assessment centre do what it is supposed to do?
- Does your assessment centre work as well as it could?

Qualitative Validation

Qualitative validation is essentially asking for reactions to the process from all the people involved. This will always include participants and assessors. And will include managers in case of promotional board or a development centre.

This can be done either by talking directly to people or with the help of questionnaire. Since both the techniques as a sole have certain advantages and disadvantages. And to maintain the balance between an appropriate degree of focus and totally free comment, a good format is to have a number of open questions and a number of questions that have multiple choice responses indicating varying degree of satisfaction. The issue will vary with the audience, but the point of focus should be the experience of assessing or being assessed.

Participant Reactions

It is assumed that the survey would take place shortly after initial feedback has been given.

Assessor Reactions

There are two broad themes to consider in understanding the reactions of assessors: their reaction to the process and any view of potential spin-off benefits.

Managers' Reactions

Managers may or mat not have acted as assessors, but they play an important role in nominating participants and in sponsoring any development action plan.

The issues discussed and reactions obtained from the above sources should enable an organization to get a good grip on any perceived deficiencies and to consider what, if any, remedial action is required.

Quantitative Research

The main method of validating assessment centre is to assess their predictive validity, which is a long-term process. However there are ways to examine the structure of an assessment centre, which can give an indication of potential weaknesses from the outset. If the data analysis is set up with the first use of the centre, the procedure should become semi-automatic as each subsequent centre proceeds. The entire statistic should be rerun periodically and concentrate on analyzing the relationship among the assessment ratings.

The Evolution of Assessment Centre

The type of centre can vary between the traditional assessment centre used purely for selection to the more modern development centre which involves self-assessment and whose primary purpose is development. One might ask the question 'Why group assessment and development centres together if they have different purposes?' The answer to that question is threefold. Firstly, they both involve assessment and it is only the end use of the information obtained which is different i.e. one for selection and one for development; secondly, it is impossible to draw a line between assessment and development centres because all centres, be they for assessment or development naturally lie somewhere on a continuum somewhere between the two extremes; thirdly most assessment centres involve at least some development and most development centres involve at least some assessment. This means that it is very rare to find a centre devoted to pure assessment or pure development. The issue is further confused by the political considerations one must take into account when running such a centre, it is common practice for an assessment centre with internal candidates to be referred to as a development centre because of the negative implications associated with assessment.

It is easier to think about assessment centres as being equally to do with selection and development because a degree of assessment goes on in both. Development centres grew out a liberalisation of thinking about assessment centres and it is a historical quirk that while assessment centres were once used purely for selection and have evolved to have a more developmental flavour the language used to describe them has not. Another problem with using the assessment - development dichotomy is that at the very least it causes us to infer that little or no assessment goes in development centres. While you will hear centres being called assessment or development centres remember that assessment goes on in both and so to some extent at least they are both assessment centres. The end result of this is that it is not possible to talk about assessment or development centres in any but the most general terms. It is more useful to talk about the constituent parts and general processes involved in each. In these terms we can identify a number of differences between assessment and development centres that one might typically find:

Assessment centres usually : -

- have a pass/fail criteria
- are geared towards filing a job vacancy
- address an immediate organisational need
- have fewer assessors and more participants
- involve line managers as assessors
- have less emphasis placed on self-assessment
- focus on what the candidate can do now
- are geared to meet the needs of the organisation
- assign the role of judge to assessors
- place emphasis on selection with little or no develop mental feedback and follow up
- give feedback at a later date
- involve the organisation having control over the information obtained
- have very little pre-centre briefing
- tend to be used with external candidates

Development centres usually -

- do not have a pass/fail criteria
- are geared towards developing the individual
- address a longer term need
- have a 1:1 ratio of assessor to participant
- do not have line managers as assessors
- have a greater emphasis placed on self-assessment
- focus on potential
- are geared to meet needs of the individual as well as the organisation
- place emphasis on developmental feedback and follow up with little or no selection function
- give feedback immediately
- involve the individual having control over the information obtained

- have a substantial pre-centre briefing
- tend to be used with internal candidates

A Final Word

While there is strong evidence that multiple assessment procedures generally provide sound, objective data on which to base selection and development decisions, it is important to consider carefully the applicability of the process and, more importantly, the specific program to a situation. Information arising from an Assessment or Development Centre should always be interpreted in context by appropriately trained individuals and treated as confidential information. Results are normally considered valid for a period of two to three years, but this would depends on the pace at which individuals, jobs and organizations change.

References and Further Reading

Ballantyne, I & Povah, N (1995) Assessment Centres. England: Gower Publishing House.

http://www.careerpsychologycentre.com/ac.htm

http://pass-prep.com/overview/overview.html

http://www.prospects.ac.uk/cms/ShowPage/

Home_page/Applications_and_interviews/Interviews/

Assessment_centres/p!egFlLd

http://www.psychometrics.co.uk/adc.htm

Kaila H.L. (2006). Human Resource Management (Two volumes). Delhi: Kalpaz Publications.

Woodruffe, C (19993) Assessment Centres: Identifying and Developing Competence (2nd Edition) London: Institute of Personal Management.

16
Performance Management

What is Performance Management?

Performance management is a relatively new concept to the field of management. Simply put, performance management includes activities to ensure that goals are consistently being met in an effective and efficient manner. Performance management focuses on performance of the organization, a department, processes to build a product, or service, employees.

Some of the definitions of performance management are as follows:

* According to an Institute of Manpower Studies Report in 1992 performance management ' is a management system whereby the organization's objectives are set and met by means of a process of objective setting for individual employees. Performance improvement can be obtained by identifying a 'shared vision' of where the organization want to be and clarifying the role of each employee in that process. Thus, the achievement of an organization's strategic objectives is assumed to equate with the sum of the achieve-ment of each individual's objectives'.
* Lockett, 1992 has defined performance management 'as a continuous process in which organizations clarify the level of performance required to meet their strategic objectives, convert them into unit andindividual objectives and manage them continually so that they remain relevant consistent with overall strategic objectives'.
* According to Myers, 1992 has defined performance management as all those processes led by managers that help employees perform as effectively as possible.
* Performance management is a set of ongoing processes needed to define and plan performance, to develop the skills, knowledge and abilities to perform as planned, to facilitate self assessment, to reviewand record performance, and to reward performance.

* Performance management is an ongoing communication process that involves both the performance manager and the employee in - identifying and describing essential job functions and relating them to the mission and goals of the organization, developing realistic an appropriate performance standards, giving and receiving feedback aboutperformance, writing and communicating constructive performance appraisals, planning education and development opportunities to sustain, improve or built on employee work performance.

Performance management is critical to key human resources transactions. The compensation programme of many employers includes performance based pay, in which past performance, has documented in performance appraisal, is a key determinant of the size of an employee's pay increase. Promotion decisions are often based in part on past performance as documented in a performance appraisal. And performance appraisal often served as a critical tool in validating an employer's selection process.

But more importantly, performance management can serve as a key transformation tool for the employer. It can help transform the employer's stated mission, vision, and values in to specifics for employees – specific results expected or specific behaviours required. In fact, an organizational initiative must eventually become the responsibility of an individual or individuals. Any program or process created to accomplish the initiatives must be somehow communicated to individuals, action plans developed and implemented, and progress monitored.

Performance management is driven by vision, corporate goals and business strategies of the organization. The first essential, therefore is that top management produces and communicates a powerful and cohering vision of the organization, and ensures that goals and strategies to achieve it are relevant are understood by all employees.

Principal Goals of Performance Management

The major goals of performance management are a follows:

* **Improve Employee Performance.** Most employers adopt performance management processes primarily to help employees perform more effectively in their current positions and to be more successful in accomplishing organizational goals. Performance management processes includes a future orientation designed to paint a clear picture of what is expected from employees and how the employer will support them in their efforts.

* **Develop People for Promotional Opportunities.** Identifying candidates for promotion or new organizational assignments is a selection decision that requires a through look at the extent to which a candidate possesses the necessary competencies to perform well in the new job. Past performance may provide a good indication of likely success where the required competencies are very similar, but will likely provide little guidance if different competencies are necessary. For example, the promotion into a supervisory assignment may require new competencies like team – building, interpersonal communications, conflict resolution, planning, and decision making, which may not have been so essential in the previous non supervisory assignment. Performance management processes can serve to help develop people for new assignments and promotional opportunities.

* **Meet Employees' Need for Feedback.** Most agree that the majority of employees want to know how they are doing on the job. They would like positive feedback from their employer about their accomplishments and suggestions on how they can improve. It is clear, however, that most employees do not look forward to performance review sessions, nor do most managers look forward to conducting them. While the reasons for this disconnect are numerous and varied, the principal answer seems to be that employees want regular feedback on their job performance, not a once – a – year review. A well – designed and well – implemented performance management process helps accomplish this goal, by providing the tools with which employees can monitor their own performance and engage in self-feedback.

* **Ensure That Employees are Working Toward Organizational Goals.** Some traditional performance appraisal programs ask the question, "Are you performing well?" More effective performance management approaches rephrase it as "Are you performing well on the right things?" Performance management programs can serve to link the organization's strategic planning process to individual efforts. nd objectives is meaningless without individuals being held accountable for their accomplishment. Employees must have a sense of the relative importance or priority of the many duties and projects to which they are assigned. Similarly, organizational values are meaningless without those values being made real to employees and translated into behavioral expectations. Performance management serves this function.nd objectives is meaningless without individuals being held accountable for their accomplishment. Employees must have a sense of the relative importance or priority of the many duties and projects to which they are assigned. Similarly, organizational values are meaningless without those values being made real to employees and translated into behavioral expectations. Performance management serves this function.

Responsibilities of Performance Manager

Assessment

Help your employees to set career goals that are consistent with their skills, knowledge, experience and interests by providing feedback based on your observations and assessment of their abilities, readiness and potential. The assessment should be based on your actual experience and observation of employee performance and behavior rather than on assumptions and personal biases.

Providing Information

Performance managers support career development when they inform an employee about options for and possible barriers to career movement. For example, you may tell your employees about upcoming positions or openings for which they may be qualified, or about budgetary constraints which may inhibit career options or development opportunities in the unit or department. Make sure that all of your employees have access to the electronic or printed versions of the Job Bulletin which is updated weekly.

Referral

Refer your employees to others who can assist them in achieving development goals. As a performance manager, it is your responsibility to be aware of the appropriate referral sources both within and outside of your department.

You may refer employees to books, journals, professional associations or other sources of information. You may also put them in touch with people who might be willing to serve as mentors or with those who might provide an information interview in which employees can learn more about a field or position from someone who is currently working in that area or capacity.

Guidance

Encourage your employees to focus on clear, specific and attainable career goals. Share your knowledge and experience with your employees. Typical questions employees have are: (1) what is required to move to the next logical position, (2) what are the chances for advancement in this department, (3) what is the difference between a promotion and an upward reclassification, (4) how to qualify for training and development opportunities,) who to contact for further information or career counseling. Provide guidance to your employees about steps they might take to improve existing skills and knowledge or develop in new functional areas.

Develop

Performance managers support employee development when they assign employees roles or tasks which challenge them and provide the opportunity to grow. Base the decisions about development options and opportunities on a careful assessment of the employee's readiness to accept additional or new responsibilities or challenges. Consider delegating a responsibility that is currently your own which is appropriate to the employee's classification and development.

Provide on-the-job training and refer employees to classes, workshops, and other learning and development opportunities, and recommend employees to serve on committees, task forces or cross-functional teams.Provide on-the-job training and refer employees to classes, workshops, and other learning and development opportunities, and recommend employees to serve on committees, task forces or cross-functional teams.

The Performance Management Model

The performance management model comprises of seven elements. The elements are as follows:

(1) Strategy and objectives.

(2) Performance measurement.

(3) Performance appraisal.

(4) Performance-related skills training.

(5) Coaching and counselling.

(6) Performance-related pay.

(7) Succession planning.

The constituent elements or parts of performance management system should never be viewed in isolation. The constituent parts are necessarily interlinked. There is often a feedback loop from one facet to the other.

The elements of performance management and the feedback loop is discussed further in detail

The Performance Management Model

Strategy and Objectives

The words 'performance management' have over the recent past become some of the most overworked in the lexicon of personnel management. But what is performance management and how will it help your business. When operated successfully performance management will give the means for evaluating and improving both individual and company performance against pre-defined business strategies and objectives.

A clear corporate strategy with defined objectives is necessary on which to base performance management. Objectives must be defined in terms of clear standards and with individual key skill requirements through competency profiling and succession planning.

The setting of objectives is the management process which ensures that every individual employee knows what role they need to play and what results they need to achieve to maximize their contribution to the overall business. In essence it enables employees to know in advance what is required of them and on what basis their performance and contribution will be assessed.

This requires that mechanisms are established which ensure the objectives :

(1) Are jointly agreed in advance between the manager and the individual employee as both realistic and challenging and, as such, that they are 'owned'

(2) Measure the actual level of achievement so that the basis on which performance is assessed can be understood in advance and is as clear as possible.

(3) Support the overall business strategies of the company so that the objectives, taken together, are mutually supportive and consistent throughout the organization.

To achieve these three key principles the system uses a cascade process down the organization from the very top through the four or five management levels. Typically it will take a month to complete the whole exercise for every single person in the company. Every manager, starting with the

MD, holds and individual meeting with each of their 'direct reports' at which they discuss their objectives and jointly agree on their content and realism.

At these face-to-face meetings the rationale for the objectives in supporting the overall company business strategies is agreed as are the specific measures that will be used to assess the actual level of achievement. Typically each person agrees with their manager six to eight ongoing objectives for the year. These are recorded and used as a working document by both the manager and the direct report at regular informal reviews throughout the year. Where appropriate, objectives are amended, deleted or added to as business requirements change. In this way objectives are not seen as rigid but dynamic, and as the means by which ongoing achievement is reviewed and controlled.

At the end of a 12-month period performance against objectives is reviewed as part of the formal appraisal process. Using this approach there should be no real surprises at the formal appraisal, as both the manager and the individual will have been regularly reviewing what has been achieved as part of the normal working process.

Effective performance management relies on effective objectives being determined. The acronym SMART is a useful guide in that objectives should be: Specific Measurable Agreed Realistic Time-related. There are three types of objectives:

(1) Objectives which contribute to the achievement of the business objectives of the unit – key result areas.

(2) Objectives which contribute to an improvement in the performance of the individual job – performance standards.

(3) Objectives which contribute to the development of the individual – Performance development.

The emphasis on the three different areas will typically vary according to the level and nature of the job and the individual's career development. A newly recruited graduate may well have a heavier emphasis on personal development objectives. An administrator or secretary who is operating processes may well have a predominant emphasis on job-related performance standards. A senior manager may well set objectives where almost all the emphasis is on the achievement in key result areas.

Objective setting is a vital part of performance management but in reality not a difficult process provided managers know what they are trying to achieve.

Measurement-The Foundation of Performance Management

The measurement of performance in an organization is at the core of any system of performance management. This is because, in order to evaluate and improve anything in life, we have to know from where we are starting, and how we are progressing as time passes. It would be inconceivable to think of financial management without the foundations of management accounts; or of production management without output statistics. Equally, the management of people's performance can be effective only if it is founded on relevant and reliable information – which can only be derived from the measurement of their performance.

The importance of good performance measurement is illustrated by the logical model which states that:

(1) Success depends on achievement of performance targets,

(2) Targets are set against established performance standards and

(3) Standards are defined on the basis of measured performance.

The measurement of performance is, therefore, the foundation upon which performance management is built. If the foundation is flawed, the whole structure is suspect. Precisely what should be measured in any individual organization depends upon the nature of that organization's business, and on the jobs of the people within it. What is important is to identify the considerations that should guide management in deciding what should be measured, how it should be measured and how standards of performance and targets for achievement should be assessed.

To identify the important guidelines for performance measurement, it is necessary to consider those aspects of an organization's business which will have a great impact on its performance measurement system. These are:

(1) The market in which the organization operates.

(2) Specific corporate challenges for the individual organization.

(3) Identification of the right population for consistent measurement systems.

(4) The involvement of people as a key business asset.

The performance of a machine can be measured clinically, but there is risk that too clinical a measurement of people's performance can be dehumanizing. The challenge is for performance measurement, and the associated appraisal of performance, to be established as part of employees' personal development, and not as an annual test or a judgment. There are some principles that can be observed that will make the performance measurement system work better which are as follows:

(1) Distinguish between precisely measured standards and more subjective ones.

(2) Measure only what is relevant to each employee and target what can realistically be influenced.

(3) Include standards for personal as well as corporate development.

Performance Indicators

The fundamental principle upon which professional performance management depends is continuous communication about performance. Whatever is being measured, and however targets are set, the employee will feel ownership of the system only if involved thoroughly in it on a continuous basis.

It is in this context – the continuity of communication – that performance indicators are important. Performance indicators for a job can be different from the standards of performance which are defined for it. Their purpose is to produce quick, simple and non confrontational measures of how things are going, so that the employee and manager can have a basis for reviewing progress. Performance indicators form a basis for communication, not for appraisal. Their purpose defines their key characteristics, so they need to be:

(1) **Quick to produce and present.** They describe how the job is going. Producing them should not be a job in itself.

(2) **Simple.** They are headlines of performance measurement system. They do not require perfectly rounded commentaries with them. They are only the basis for discussion.

(3) **Non-confrontational.** Both parties should agree on their relevance to the job, but agreement is not paramount if their separation from performance standards is understood.

Once established, performance indicators can also prove useful in other areas such as job evaluation. This is a valuable addition to the job evaluation system as well as for goal-setting.

Performance Appraisal

Performance appraisal is a systematic, periodic, and so far as humanly possible, an impartial rating of an employee's excellence in matters pertaining to his present job and his potential for a future job in the organization. Performance appraisal systems are basically designed to help the individual, the group, and the organization to convert its core competency into competitive advantage on the one hand and indicate the appropriate HR intervention desired for it, on the other. In addition, there are specific purposes which are as follows:

(1) Performance appraisal provides feedback to the employees to know where they stand.

(2) Performance appraisal information may be used to determine whether an employee or a group of employees requires additional training and development.

(3) Performance appraisal gives management a means of identifying employees for promotion.

(4) Performance appraisal is useful in effecting transfer decisions.

(6) Performance appraisal assists the employees in their self-improvement and development.

(7) Performance appraisal is beneficial for the introduction of sound personnel policies.

(8) Appraisal improves morale of the employees as they are aware that their services are recognized and rewarded by the management.

(9) Performance appraisal enables managers to coach, counsel and assist employees in their career development.

Appraisal – in Context of Performance Management

An organization intending to set up or overhaul an appraisal scheme, in the context of performance management, should consider following the process which is discussed below:

(1) **Set up a Working Group.** Commitment to the (new) scheme is vital. It must be seen seen as being for, and belonging to, the population group intended. Whereas the personnel/management development function should involved, they should from the outset work with other functions. The working group probably 6 to 8 people) should be representative vertically as well as horizontally.

(2) **Define the Objectives.** Be precise as to the outcomes wished for. Do not just say that performance improvement is desired, but state how it will be measured. How will the scheme link with pay, and how with personal development?

(3) **Design Methods and Procedure:** Be creative in thinking about how best the objectives can be met. Who will be asked to appraise whom, when and how?

(4) **Draft Documentation.** Keep things as simple as possible, but still be reasonably explicit. Who is going

to have access to the documentation? Can appraisees use the same form as appraisers for their preparation?

(5) **Communication.** Although communication is vital at the stage when draft documentation of the scheme is available, this is far too late to start communicating about it. There is a risk that the consultative spirit implicit in setting up the working group (step 1) stops there, that this group becomes the 'in group' and keeps information and ideas to itself. What is needed instead is frequent, broad communication, at all levels, and using a variety of methods – written communication certainly, but backed up by meetings andcommunication should betwo-way.

(6) **Pilot Project.** It is advisable to pilot the scheme in one smallish department, division or other group, for various reasons. A pilot project can be a useful communication and participation device. It also enables the working group to modify some aspects, without loss of credibility, as a result of experience from the pilot. The group to choose for the pilot should be one which will act as an effective ambassador for it.

(7) **Training.** Everyone involved in appraisal, needs training in order to derive maximum benefit from the scheme. Training in appraisal can include briefing on the aims and procedures, but active participative discussion is also needed in order to influence attitudes. Skills training is invaluable, with case studies to increase awareness of problems such as the halo effect and central tendency, and role-playing interviews for development and increased self-aware-ness of appraisal style.

(8) **Full Implementation.** The timetable for implementationrequires careful thought. During the first cycle, additional specialist resources may be needed to monitor progress and iron out problems as they arise. The timing planned for subsequent years may not be ideal for the first full run-through.

(9) **Individual Follow-up.** Particularly during the first

year's implementation, but also subsequently, sufficient resources have to be put aside for making sure that the scheme is working at the individual level, and that action plans are being put into action.

(10) **Validation.** Validation is also necessary at an organizational level. Did the working group get it right first time? What further improvements could be made? Continue to rely on participation and communication, and make selective use of surveys, meetings and briefings about how it is going and how it can be made to work better.

Performance-Related Skills Training

Sometimes some skills training for the managers and professional people can be very little related to required performance. The prime reason why skills training may on occasions not be related to performance is that it is quite possible to design and implement a programme which develops skills, but for those skills to have no direct link to what is either desirable or achievable within the organization in which the learner works. The skill may not in fact be needed because the person does not currently have (and has little chance in the future of having) a need for the skill developed.

An even more frequently encountered problem, felt particularly strongly by participants, arises when the skills developed on a programme have no chance of implementation within the reality of the organization. Clearly, the appropriate way of avoiding such problems is to ensure that any training undertaken is derived from a large-scale and effective review of business needs. This strategy is known as the diagnostic strategy. There is however, an alternative strategy, which can be described as the opportunistic strategy. The two strategies can be summarized as follows:

The Diagnostic Strategy. This involves a review of organization's purpose and plans. The skills, knowledge and attitudes necessary for the effective pursuit of organizational goals are identified. An audit of the extent to which staff currently met the requirements is carried out. Priorities are identified and skill-focused training is set up.

The Opportunistic Strategy. This strategy takes the reality of managerial life as the starting point. Managerial life tends to revolve around a dynamic of fluctuating and changing managerial priorities and incidents. This strategy accepts that managers are often driven by pressing immediate circumstances and priorities to develop their own skills, and to propose the enhancement of the skills of others. It accepts the reality of the often repeated managerial claim that most learning is learning from experience.

While the emphasis of most trainers to date has been on the more effective development of diagnostic processes, the two strategies need not be held in opposition to each other. Indeed, they ought to be designed as an integrated total process for development.

Skills, Competences, Behaviours

Traditionally, trainers and educators have distinguished between skills, knowledge and attitudes. This distinction has been helpful in the past because it contributed to clarification of the problems trainers were attempting to resolve. More recently, the training and education lexicon has been supplemented by a focus on 'behaviours'- those things which people do and which, of course, represent a wide range of skills. So the disciplines of behaviour analysis have evolved, and subsequent processes of behaviour modification, and the requirement to spell out behavioural objectives on training courses. Of course, knowledge, attitudes and skills all contribute to exhibited behaviours.

In the world of management training, the newest word is 'competences'. There are a number of issues about competences in relation to performance-related skills training. The most important is that there is likely to be an inherent conflict between the attempt to set nationally agreed standards of management competence, and the actual requirements of managers in particular organizations. Secondly, there are issues of what competences are supposed to mean and cover – embracing, as they often seem to, a combination of skills, knowledge and attitudes.

Integrating Performance and Development

The enhancement of performance through training is most likely to be achieved when the training itself is focused on performing real tasks of significance to those involved. The second proposition is that such activities can be designed effectively through the adoption of the principles of learning which include the learning cycle and individual learning styles. The third proposition is that if we are concerned with performance skills, as distinct from knowledge or attitudes, it is necessary to enhance the relationship between – in fact to integrate – the different kinds of learning offered through course 'training' and by direct experience. The primary reason for this is that unless we attempt to achieve this, skills training will still be seen as an isolated event which, however brilliantly managed at the time, will cease to have a continuing impact on the manager as learner. If we want to make sense of the principles of continuous learning and development, we must provide for continuity of thoughtfulness about both the managing process and the learning associated with it.

Counselling and Coaching

The terms 'coaching' and 'counselling' are constantly bandied about in organizations when problems and stresses occur. As organizations become more competitive, additional pressures are heaped on all employees at all levels. Managers are under pressure not only to achieve results but also to become more sophisticated in the way they handle their staff. As the incidence of stress-related conditions escalates, a manager has to know how to respond to problems such as anxiety, depression and alcohol abuse, which may all contribute towards poor performance.

Managers who normally cope well with their own stress at work may themselves unwittingly be the instigators of stress in others, by imposing unreasonable deadlines or requiring staff to undertake tasks for which they have either not been adequately trained or they lack the necessary expertise. In such circumstances an member of staff may experience the same feelings of impotence and inability to cope as some managers experience. In both associated with feeling of being unable to control, contain or remedy the situations.

There are certain basic principles which the organization must accept which can help to reduce the impact of stress. These are as follows:

(1) Some employee problems are caused by the company itself.

(2) Managers need to be taught a range of skills to cope with such problems.

(3) If these problems are ignored, the company will bear the cost in terms of absence, inefficiency, poor performance, high accident levels, early retirement and increased recruitment and training.

Counselling or Coaching

Counselling is about helping people to manage their lives effectively. It is a process of helping them find and achieve what they want in life. In coaching, the manager is heavily involved in the definition of objectives and needs, in counselling it is for the individual to determine these. Coaching is work-related and problem-centered, while counselling is more about the person and the person's feelings. Coaching is often a more public affair than counselling, which has strong boundaries of confidentiality. The coaching role has no limitations, the counselling role does.

Coaching

Although formal training is appropriate for the acquisition of specific theoretical, technical or conceptual knowledge, individuals learn most from day-to-day applications of skills, by trying things out in practice. If these learning experiences are controlled and feedback is provided by managers who understand the job and can identify needs, then quality and speed of learning are enhanced. The results are greater job satisfaction, greater enthusiasm and improved and performance on the part of the employee.

This, in essence, is coaching using every day work, together with discussion and planned activity, as a learning experience for people. The basic components of coaching have been described as:

- Dealing essentially with the development of skill through practice.
- Analyzing the components of particular skills, techniques and the environment in order to assist the learners.
- Setting increasingly challenging exercises.
- Seeking to identify problems or weaknesses to be remedied.
- Spotting potential, building on strengths and taking advantage of talent and opportunity.

It thus aims at improving both current and future performance. It requires joint commitment to mutually accepted goals coupled with a plan of action for achieving them. Good coaching requires a supportive, consultative approach and well developed listening skills. The listening process is assisted by creating an environment which encourages the learner to open up: by talking where one will not be interrupted, by using good eye contact, by using prompting words and nods and by adopting a posture which conveys full attention. Key to the coaching process is the effective use of a range of question styles. For example, probing questions aid the understanding of the learner's thinking and reasoning; checking questions allow the person to expand on a topic; challenging questions encourage a second look at ideas and methods, perhaps allowing for change; prompting questions allow the learner to explore a number of options before deciding upon a particular course of action; and open questions (what, when, where, how and why?) place the onus on the learner to think issues through, rather than simply being able to answer 'yes' or 'no'.

Coaching is a long-term strategy. The opportunities for coaching are numerous. They may arise as the result of promotion, job restructuring, job rotation, system changes, secondment. Creating a special project assignment also opens up avenues.

The first step in the process is to identify need. What evidence is there of current job performance as a result of the performance appraisal procedure? What aspects cause difficulty? What objectives are not met? Can he / she also identify what changes need to take place, what the areas are for improvement? Thus target can be agreed, ground rules and time scales set. How often will progress be reviewed and how long will reviews take? Once these decisions have been reached, there is responsibility on the part of the managers to ensure that all necessary information is available to the learner and that potential problems have been considered. Learning can be completed only with effective, objective feedback from the coach. Concentration should be on action and behaviour and, whether feedback involves commendation or criticism, it must always be positive, constructive and sensitive. The skills used in effective coaching are communication, motivation, delegation, planning and monitoring.

Counselling

The task of counselling is to assist others to make changes in their work or life, or to accept or to adjust to the change which they are experiencing in a way that, without counselling, they are finding difficult or impossible. The purpose is not to advice, but to provide the vehicle for individuals to achieve their own solutions to their problems.

Good managers are always been alive to the impact of personal problems and emotional conflicts on job performance and satisfaction, and have sought to offer an appropriate ear. The extensive use of counselling skills and the provision of counselling facilities for employees, can have great impact on reduction of stress, thereby helping employees to remain to effective and productive. It also represents an organizational investment in health and wellbeing. The dividends in return are commitment, motivation, good performance, loyalty and staff retention.

It is widely accepted that 20% of any workforce at any given time is troubled, so most of us at some time or another would gain from counselling opportunity. However, when making an assessment as to who might be in need of counselling, there are certain indicators which may assist in deciding to offer it. One of the soundest clues to an individual being under severe stress is change in behaviour. People are fairly predictable in their day-to-day behaviour. Any disruption to this general pattern may be significant. Equally, changes in health, habits and work performance may be a key. Some examples of changes which may occur are: increased irritability, loss of concentration, decrease in output, withdrawal from social interaction, increased absence, failure to meet performance targets, failure to meet deadlines, inability to make decisions, inability to handle situations which normally present no difficulty, lack of energy and enthusiasm, displays of anxiety and tension.

The Skills of Counselling

There are many different styles of counselling, but research suggest that style is not of great importance, so long as the relationship between the counsellor and the individual being counselled is one which is appropriate for producing change. However, the style most generally used to train people in counselling skills is that of client-centred counselling, based on the work of Carl Rogers (1951).

The counselling relationship is the main vehicle for growth and change, but there are three basic conditions which need to be establish before development can occur :

- The first is acceptance : complete acceptance of individuals as they are, in non-judgmental way which makes them feel valued. The first step is trying to do so is to attempt to see the world through the eyes of the individuals.

- Second, the counsellor must genuinely be him or herself. There must be no hiding behind a role. Straightforwardness and sensitivity are crucial.

- The third condition be empathy : being empathetic means engaging in a sharing with the person, thus creating a trusting environment in which they feel secure enough to talk about things which they dare not talk about to anybody else.

Employee Counselling Services

Employee counselling services are in-house or external. They may focus on specific problems (alcohol and other substance abuse), or they may be 'broad brush'. Gaining and maintaining confidentiality is the basis of any counselling service. When the nature of counselling service is determined the quality of its launch is important. Successful introduction of such venture will involve education and training within the company, and adequate publicity in the shape of brochures, posters and newsletters. It is important to ensure the appropriate awareness levels are reached for the service to succeed.

Performance-Related Pay

Performance-related pay is probably the most controversial element of performance management. Many human resource managers, and their line colleagues, feel profoundly uncomfortable about linking pay to performance; several unions have policies that oppose it. But there are some who believe that without performance-related pay no organization can hope to construct a reward system appropriate to the turbulent, competitive world of today.

However, the most ardent supporters of performance-related pay recognize that it is extraordinarily difficult to manage well. Most organizations which have performance-related pay arrangements are still trying to perfect this element of performance management; it is a part of managing people which requires constant attention and improvement.

There is also evidence that in performance-oriented cultures performance-related pay is seen by employees as a more equitable reward system than systems that offer no relationship to performance.

Definition

'Performance-related pay' is a term used to cover a variety of reward arrangements. Within organizations performance-related pay (or its abbreviation 'PRP') can be used to designate a particular scheme – for example, the merit pay or bonus system. It can be defined as that part of financial, or financially measurable, reward to an individual which is linked directly to individual, team or company performance.

The principal types of performance-related pay are merit pay, individual incentive bonuses, individual discretionary bonuses, team/company performance bonuses, skill-based payments and any other payments which employees may earn or receive related to individual, team or organization performance improvement. This definition also includes performance-related arrangements that pay out in shares or gifts. Excluded from consideration are those payments which are made in the form which are made in the form of bonuses but are not performance-related, for example Christmas and Diwali bonuses.

Reasons Advocating Performance-Related Pay

In practice, organizations that introduce performance-related pay do so for a number of reasons. The most commonly quoted are:

(1) Focusing attention and harnessing effort where the organization wants it.

(2) Supporting a performance-oriented culture.

(3) Strengthening the performance-planning process.

(4) Rewarding the right people.

(5) Sharing in the success and increasing employee identification with the business.

(6) Motivating all the people.

The Pitfalls and Cautions

If the argument for introducing performance-related pay sounds compelling, those who operate such arrangements know that the gap between the promise of theory and the reality of what can be achieved is often very large indeed. The most obvious pitfalls are:

(1) **Inadequate performance management systems.** Many performance-related pay systems are not backed up by a high-quality performance manage-

ment system. If performance management is not working, and not trusted by employees, then pay arrangements that depend on it are ot going to be regarded as fair.

(2) **Short terminism and inflexibility.** The focus of many schemes has been criticized for being far too heavily biased towards the short term, with little emphasis on longer-term measures of performance, or support for innovations and investments which have delayed paybacks. Similarly, many schemes are not flexible enough to reflect changes in job demands that emerge during the year.

(3) **Costs.** Like most changes to payment systems, the introduction of performance-related pay can cost money. This can result in substantially increased costs. If performance-related pay forms part of base salary, drift of 1 or 2% is not unusual. Bonus schemes introduced on top can result in additional costs of anything from nothing to 50% or more. The question here is whether the costs are under control, properly planned and justified on a cost benefit basis.

(4) **Corruption of the Performance Appraisal Process.** It is inevitable that performance-related pay will have an impact on performance appraisal; the pitfalls not making allowances for it at the time schemes are introduced and taking action to avoid obvious problems.

Essential Ingredients for Making Performance-Related Pay Schemes Work

Although performance-related pay schemes may sound easy to implement and run, many schemes fail because the environment in which they are introduced is not favourable. Preliminary groundwork is essential for success; there are particularly five areas to cover prior to design which are as follows:

(1) **Understanding of What Performance-Related Pay is and what it involves.** It is a management tool, it gives management discretion and requires good

sound judgment. It involves planning, managing, assessing and rewarding performance. It requires time, effort, and resourcefulness. It will put pressure on the organization's performance planning and budgeting processes, on style management and ability, and may highlight existing eaknesses.

(2) **Making sure it is introduced for the right reasons.** Performance-based reward is all about raising company performance through individual performance improvement. It cannot be a substitute for inadequate base pay. If employees see performance-related pay is only a façade they lose confidence in the process and it is extremely difficult to in them back.

(3) **Gaining Management Commitment and Trust in Management.** As with most other aspects of pay, management must be committed to performance-related pay. Without this, any arrangements will not be implemented and maintained properly and will be unlikely to succeed. Similarly, performance-based rewards need to be introduced into an environment here employees have trust in their management.

(4) **Integrating the new scheme into the Company's Total reward system.** The total pay and benefits package must 'hang together' to provide a balanced system of rewards. Performance-related pay must fit in with this package. In choosing and determining the elements of performance-related pay, consideration needs to be given to the balance of variable and non-variable pay; rewards for individual, team and organization contributions; discretionary rewards and rewards triggered automatically; and current and deferred pay.

(5) **Tailoring it to the specific needs of the Organization.** Performance-related pay should be specific to an organization: schemes can seldom be bought 'off the shelf'. It should reflect the business and how it is managed, its corporate culture and the people

working within it. In light of these factors, choices need to be made about the types and levels of performance pay.

Succession Management

There has been a wholly justified resurgence of interest in succession planning in recent years. Organizations have realized that they need to make the best use of their internal human resources and that talented individuals wish to be involved in their own career planning. Constant change means that skills can rapidly become redundant and that if planned development of individuals does not take place both they and their employers will suffer. These activities are a central plank of effective performance management.

Succession Planning

Succession planning is the business of identifying particular individuals as possible successors for specific posts and suitable posts for particular individuals. The need for succession planning may arise when the organization grows creating new opportunities at the top level. Succession planning may be from within the organization or people from outside can be recruited and selected to fill up the vacancies at the top level. Succession planning is just part of the succession management process.

Succession Management

Succession management is a long-term HR strategy based on the human resource and business plan requirements. Succession management extends beyond the focus of filling future vacancies/skill gaps through individual development, but utilizes other HR strategies such as retention, restructuring, etc. to meet the business needs. Many progressive organizations are adopting succession management. This encompasses all activities aimed at ensuring a suitable supply of successors for senior or key posts and, in this sense, subsumes traditional succession planning within it. Effective succession management is a key element of good performance management. The activities which form the core of succession management are as follows:

(1) Analysis of the demand for managers and professionals by level, function, skill.

(2) Audit of existing executives and projection of likely future supply from internal and external sources.

(3) Planning individual career paths based on objective estimates of future needs and drawing on reliable appraisals and assessments of potential.

(4) Career planning undertaken in the context of a realistic understanding of the future needs of the firm as well as those of the individual.

(5) Accelerated promotion schemes with development targeted against the future needs of the business.

(6) Performance-related training and development to prepare individuals for future roles as well as their current responsibilities.

(7) Planned recruitment not only to fill short-term vacancies but also to provide people for development to meet future needs.

Succession management is one of the main strategic activities of the personnel function-it is business driven and concerned with the longer-term success of the organization. Succession management provides processes and tools that encourage and facilitate individual advancement at the same time it addresses the need for critical backups (replacement planning) on any job category, including key people in the professional, technical, clerical, and production ranks.

Succession Management as a Part of the Performance Management Process

Any planning activity will be worthwhile only if it is incorporated in the continuing management processes of an organization. Otherwise it is a one-off exercise which, although extremely useful, will rapidly become out of date and therefore irrelevant. Computers allow for the maintenance of up-to-date succession plans without the chore of having to retype the whole exercise. Computers are ideal for internal search enquiries to list, for example, all staff with certain experience, qualifications, languages and managerial competencies.

A succession plan should be much more than an organization chart showing who will succeed whom. It should first of all set the business scene against which future succession will take place. It should indicate the likely shape and size of the organization and the content of future management jobs. It should be a flexible network which can be adjusted to cope with changes in business plans, unexpected resignations, or the emergence of new talent by recruitment or, for example, from an acquisition.

The Benefits of Succession Management

Succession management is fundamental to organizational learning as it is aimed at preserving institutional memory and continuous improvement in individual and organizational effectiveness. The benefits of succession management are as follows:

(1) Advance job filling. This really amounts to making appointments ahead of requirement.

(2) Candidate listing. This seems to be the major objective of short-term succession planning for senior posts and has a number of purposes: reassuring top management, broadening fields of candidates, speeding up appointments and aiding career planning.

(3) Planned development. Moving people with potential through the organization in a planned way to offer broadening experiences, exposure to a range of top managers and hence their commitment to later promotions.

(4) Improved career counselling. The use of objective succession information where career counselling is offered can make the process more relevant to the organization's future needs.

(5) Planned training and development. the selection of training and development opportunities with

succession in mind as opposed to the needs of current job.

(6) Help individuals realize their career plans within the organization.

(7) Provide increased opportunities for high potential employees.

(8) Contribute to implementing the organization's strategic business policies.

Succession Management Programme

A good succession management program is identified through its:

(1) Frequent opportunities for employees to accept new challenges.

(2) Recognition that employees have a stake in the organization and share in its success.

(3) Systematic approach to identifying succession candidates.

(4) Managers and professional employees all having a career development plan.

(5) Cross-divisional/cross-departmental sharing of people and information.

(6) Career paths that don't just move up a specialized ladder, but across the organization.

The Feedback Loop

The constituent parts of performance management system should never be viewed in isolation and the outcomes should be fed back to those planning the future of the organization. The constituent parts are necessarily interlinked. There is often a feedback loop from one facet to the other. It is the role of the human resource specialist to facilitate the capture of this information so that it is fed back into the strategic and business planning process.

Consolidation of all individual outputs forms the basis for a review of the total organizational capacity of each part of the company – in terms of succession, career development, training and level of skills and knowledge. This information is then formally linked to the business review.

Performance management is not simply for the benefit of the organization. It is designed positively to encourage people to reach their full potential. Appraisal, coaching and counselling are part of the performance management process. In terms of the organization, considerable information is generated during the formal appraisal which should be captured and fed back into other parts of the performance management system.

Other outputs from the appraisal process which should be fed back to the business-unit level include training needs and career development plans. Career development outcomes from appraisal must be fed back into a central process. Training programmes are also an integral part of the feedback loop.

So we can see that there are interrelationships between all the elements of the performance management process and that each can produce information which needs to be fed directly back into future business plans. But what is the role of the human resource specialist in all this? The most significant roles must be those of catalyst and facilitator: a catalyst in terms of gaining the commitment of those at the top and in actually defining the process; and a facilitator in terms of providing the appropriate training and in communicating the benefits to every employee of the organization.

The Performance Management Process

The performance management process begins with analysis and description of the job. The performance manager identifies essential functions in the job description and the strategic mission and goals of the department or organizational unit. Standards of minimum acceptable performance are developed for the position with the employee. Additionally, standards for performance which exceeds expectations may be set to encourage the employee to strive for even better results.

Throughout the appraisal period (typically one year),

the performance manager observes and provides behavioural feedback on the performance of the employee, focusing on helping the employee to achieve successful performance. At the end of the appraisal period, and in collaboration with the employee, the performance manager prepares, writes, delivers and then produces a final copy of the written performance appraisal.

At any time in the process, the employee and the performance manager may identify needs and create a plan for employee education, training or development in job – or career-related areas.

The issues related to performance management of teams and team members arise out of the variety of reporting relationships and degree of independent responsibility that teams exercise, as well as the need to reinforce team values and efforts without undercutting individual responsibility. Adaptations of the performance management process with teams in mind may be made which are consistent with company policy and procedures.

Thus the performance management process foster improved communication with the employees and it will lead to increased level of productivity for the organization.

Benefits of Performance Management

The benefits of performance management are:

(1) Performance manageme are forced to be accountable, to "put a stake in the ground".

(2) Performance management identifies organizational goals, results needed to achieve those goals, measures of effectiveness (outcomes) toward the goals, and means (drives) to achieve the goals. This chain of measurements is examined to ensure alignment with overall results of the organization.

(3) In today's age of high expectations when organizations are striving to transform themselves and society, having measurable results can verify whether grand visions are realistic or not.

(4) Performance management helps ensure equitable

treatment of employees because appraisals are based on results.

(5) It cultivates a change in perspective from activities to results.

(6) Performance is seen as an ongoing process, rather than a one-time event.

(7) It supports ongoing communication, feedback and dialogue about organizational goals. It also supports communication between employee and supervisor.

(8) Performance management produces specificity in commitments and resources.

(9) It provides specificity for comparisons, direction and planning.

(10) Performance management cultivates a systems perspective, that is, focus on the relationships and exchanges between subsystems, e.g., departments, processes, teams and employees. Accordingly, personnel focus is on patterns and themes in the organization, rather than specific events.

(11) Performance management redirects attention from bottom-up approaches (e.g., doing job descriptions, performance reviews, etc., first and then "rolling up" results to the top of the organization) to top-down approaches (e.g., ensuring all subsystem goals and results are aligned first with the organization's overall goals and results.

(12) Continuing focus and analysis on results helps to correct several myths, e.g., "learning means results".

Legal Issues In Performance Management

In our increasingly litigious society, employer human resources decisions are more frequently challenged. The many exceptions to the employment-at-will doctrine and the explosion of fair employment practices statues (Title VII of the Civil Rights Act, the Age Discrimination in Employment Act, etc.) have forced employers into court to defend their decisions. "Because performance appraisals are often the only tangible evidence by which a jury can determine the employee's worth, appraisals potentially provide either a devastating weapon for the employee or an impenetrable shield for the employer " (Davidson 1995). The design of the performance management and appraisal process as well as its implementation and use provide critical indicators as to whether the performance appraisal will be an employee weapon or employer shield supporting the performance-based decisions of the employers. To develop a defensive performance management and appraisal program, an employer must consider the following factors:

Job Related or Valid. The factors being assessed should be relevant, given the tasks and duties expected of the employee. An employer attempting to use the same set of performance criteria for vastly different jobs might have difficulty proving that an individual performance appraisal is an accurate reflection of his or her performance. As a result, some employers identify not only core performance factors, perhaps reflecting identified organizational values that are required of all its employees, but also individual performance factors unique to each position and/or employee. Examples of core organizational performance factors could include behaving ethically, having a customer focus, or being a good team player. The same employer may also identify other performance factors or expectations that are specific to the job of the individual employee, such as "increase market penetration by 5 percent by the end of the year."

Minimum Subjectivity. Defensibility of performance-based decisions is enhanced when performance expectations are clear and unambiguous. Objective standards of performance that are specific, measurable and with clear timelines help minimize subjectivity and the possibility of misunderstanding. An example is "reduce the time required to fill employment requisitions by five days by the end of the third quarter." Similarly, clearly provided examples of expected behaviours give much better guidance than general statements like "be a good team player." Such a clear behaviour example of team-work could include- (a) treats all team members with respect, (b) supports team decisions even when the decision may not entirely reflect one's own position, (c) tries different approaches to work with people that will create better results and working relationships.

Consistent Application/Procedural Fairness. The essence a of discrimination charge is that one was treated inconsistently because of race, sex, age, disability, or some other prohibited characteristic. Unjust dismissal claims in state courts often require establishing that there was an implied employment contract created through an employer handbook or oral promise and that the contract was breached when the employer did not do what it promised. Employers must be diligent, therefore, in ensuring that the procedures it enunciates in policies and handbooks are scrupulously followed by all appraisers. If required, employees must be notified of performance standards or expectations, must receive feedback about their performance, and must have an improvement plan if their performance is substandard. Required signatures must be provided. Consistency in the administration of the process is critical to employee perceptions of a fair process, which is critical to the process having the desired impact.

Instructions and Training for Appraisers. For a system to be administered consistently and in line with its stated objectives, those required to appraise must, at a minimum, receive training on the process. Such training should include not only the mechanics of the particular system, but also performance planning, problem solving, coaching, and feedback skills. Perceptions of fairness are maximized when the employer trains not only appraisers, but also those whose performance is being appraised on the process and their role in it.

Forewarning. Perhaps the most important requirement for developing a defensible performance management process is that those whose performance is to be appraised receive forewarning. Forewarning includes prior knowledge of the results and behaviours expected of them, and of the process and their role in it. Forewarning also includes communication of performance or behaviour problems early, while there is time for correction. And finally, it includes a clear message that adverse employment consequences (e.g., dismissal, repudiate, discharge) can result if the employee does not improve within a set time frame.

Tips for Improving Performance

Some of the valuable tips for improving performance useful both for employees and managers are as follows:

(1) Ask your people how you can help them achieve their career goals and work objectives. If an employe perform better.

(2) Have detailed job descriptions, they provide job clarity to the employee, clarity of expectation to the employer or manager and improve performance in the bargain as well.

(3) If your employees are not functioning properly, then assess the root causes for the lack of performance and analyze the circumstances that lead to it. Rectify both for improving performance.

(4) If you have an employee who possesses a positive attitude towards his work, but is weak in skills then spruce up his skills through adequate training.

(5) For optimum performance a manager must know what is expected from the employees and by when it should be delivered.

(6) Ask your employees what they expect from the organization and how they compare their own career development with the growth of the organization.

(7) People perform most effectively when they are clear about the job, they know what is expected from them, they have the right tools, skills, knowledge and information.

(8) It is always better to help an employee understand his strengths and weaknesses on a day-to-day basis, rather than waiting to point them out during a performance appraisal.

(9) Use motivation techniques where you find that an employee has the right skills but is not inclined to be productive.

(10) You must prevent generation of negative energy. Anger, avoiding people, attacking individuals, taking punitive action etc. are some examples of negative energy.

(11) Develop a positive atmosphere by encouraging subordinates to express their concerns, doubts and feelings.

(12) Always set high but realistic standards of performance.

(13) Recognize performance and compliment your employees whenever you see them perform well.

(14) Keep your communication channels open with the employees.

(15) Counsel and help your employees train and develop themselves for career growth.

(16) The primary objective of the appraisal process is to helpemployees identify the areas of improvement and to then develop the plan to improve upon them.

(17) How you treat your subordinates will on most occasions decide how they perform. Treat them like successful individuals and they will be successful in whatever they do.

(18) Weed out the people who are chronic complainers, bad team players, skeptics etc., they are a bad influence upon the performers.

(19) If you are carrying out an exercise of setting targets and goals, involve employees of all levels in the process. Don't just let decisions flow down from the top.

(20) Performance standards can be set in any area through mutual agreement, on the measurement, between the manager and the subordinate.

References

(1) Brennan, E. James (1989). Performance Management Workbook; Prentice Hall, Englewood Cliffs, NJ.

(2) Harrison, R.(2000). Employee Development; University Press (India) Ltd., pp. 223 – 312.

(3) Kossek E., Block R.(2000) Managing Human Resources in the 21st Century; South Western College Publishing, pp., 15.4 – 15.19.

(4) Neale, F. (1995). Hand book of Performance Management; Jaico Publishing House.

(5) Sadri S., Jayshree S., Ajgaonkar M. (2002). Geometry of HR; Himalaya Publishing House, pp., 346–400.

(6) Sethi, R.(1996). Tips for Improving Performance; Beacon Books.

(7) Weightman, J.(2002). Managing Human Resources; Jaico Publishing House, pp., 132–142.

www.successfactors.com/performance
www.quickmanagement.com
www.commerce-database.com
www.businessranks.com
www.pm-news.com
www.bambooweb.com

17
Ergonomics

Introduction

Ergonomics is derived from the Greek word *ergon*, meaning work, and *nomos*, meaning natural laws. Historically, Ergonomics was another name for Human Factors. Today, Ergonomics refers to designing work environments for maximizing safety and efficiency. In conjunction with engineers, engineering psychologists apply their knowledge of psychology to the formulation of natural laws of work. Thus, ergonomics is an approach which puts human needs and capabilities at the focus of designing technological systems. The aim is to ensure that humans and technology work in complete harmony, with the equipment and tasks aligned to human characteristics.

Until the 1940s, the design of machinery, equipment, and industrial plants was solely the responsibility of engineers. They made design decisions on the basis of mechanical, electrical, space and size considerations. Little attention was paid to the workers who would have to operate the machines. The machine was a constant factor, incapable of change and it was only the employee who would have to adapt no matter how uncomfortable, tiring, or unsafe the equipment was.

Adapting the worker to the machine was accomplished through the time-and-motion study, in which jobs were analyzed to determine how they could be simplified. It was during the Second World War that development of engineering psychology was spurred. Authorities recognized that human abilities and limitations would have to be taken into account when designing machines if the overall system was to operate efficiently. The immediate impetus for its emergence came from the increasing complexity of the machines that men were called upon to operate. High-speed aircraft, rockets and radar were among the many new instruments whose operation taxed human capacities to unprecedented degrees. It soon became apparent that selection and training were inadequate to provide a sufficient number of operators who could function at the required level of proficiency. The solution was to redesign the equipment so as to make the operator's job simpler, less confusing, less demanding, or in other ways more manageable. This was accomplished by improving the displays through which information is received, by making controls easier to operate, or by having the machine to take over some of the complicated intervening processes formerly carried out by the human operator.

Present day engineering psychology differs in a number of ways from earlier work. The most conspicuous difference is in its magnitude. Since its formal beginnings in World War II, it has been expanding at a prodigious rate. Companies once thought that there was a bottom-line tradeoff between safety and efficiency. Now they embrace ergonomics because it has been proven and learnt that designing a safe work environment can also result in greater efficiency and productivity. The easier it is to do a job, the more likely it is to see gains in productivity due to greater efficiency. Analogously, the safer it is to do a job, the more likely it is to see gains in productivity due to reduced time off for injury. Workplace ergonomics addresses both of these issues concurrently by maximizing the workspace and equipment needed to do a job.

Time-and-Motion Study

Time-and-motion study was an early attempt to redesign work tools and to reshape the way workers performed their jobs. It was developed from the effort of three pioneers who tried to make work more efficient. The first systematic attempt to study the way work was performed began in 1898 when Frederick W.Taylor, the promoter of scientific management, undertook an investigation for Bethlehem Steel of the task of shoveling. His aim was to increase productivity by improving the performance of the workers. Taylor said that even in the simplest unskilled operation, the way in which the worker carries out the job can make a substantial difference in productivity. He found that workers were using shovels of many sizes and shapes and lifted loads which varied from 3 ½ to 38 pounds. He found out through empirical study that the optimal load for the workers to be most efficient was 21 ½ pounds. When they tried heavier or lighter loads, their total daily output declined. So, he designed different sizes of shovels for different materials, so that it would lead to approximately this load. Thus, a small spade-shovel was provided for handling heavy iron ore and a large scoop for shoveling ashes. Therefore, a hundred and forty men could accomplish the same amount of work that previously required five hundred men. Taylor's work saved the company more than $78,000 a year. The workers of the company too could increase their wages by 60% as the company offered an incentive of higher pay for greater productivity. Taylor's work was the first empirical demonstration of the relationship between work tools and worker efficiency. Time study was essentially a process of analyzing an operation into its component parts and noting the time required by the best workers to perform each part. Taylor defined time study to include elimination of useless movements and the selection of the best way to perform the remaining movements but nothing much was done along these lines because he was primarily concerned with tool design and incentive wage systems.

The next pioneers in the field were Frank Gilbreth, an engineer, and his wife Lillian Gilbreth, a psychologist, who did more than anyone else to promote the time-and-motion study. The Gilbreths were interested in the mechanics of job performance and their goal was to eliminate all unnecessary motion.

Frank Gilbreth was an apprentice brick layer and he noticed that bricklayers made many unnecessary motions in their work. He thought he could redesign the job to make it faster and easier and within a year he was the fastest bricklayer on the job. He persuaded his co-workers to try his method and within no time the entire crew was accomplishing far more work without becoming exhausted. He designed a scaffold that could be raised or lowered so that the worker would always be at a height convenient to the work. He brought about an increase in their productivity from laying 120 bricks to laying 350 bricks per hour by reducing the number of motions for laying each brick from eighteen to four and a half.

Frank and Lillian Gilbreth's lives and household were organized around the principles of time-and-motion economy. Every activity was scrutinized for wasted motion. For example, Gilbreth always buttoned his vest from the bottom up because it took four seconds less than buttoning it from the top down. The efforts to schedule the activities of the twelve Gilbreth children were recounted in the popular book and movie, Cheaper by the Dozen. Lillian Gilbreth carried on the work even after the death of her husband. She applied her ideas to problems of efficient work in the home as well as the factory. The shelves inside a refrigerator, the foot-pedal to open the lid of a dust-bin were all her ideas to make life simpler.

Time-and-motion engineers, sometimes called efficiency experts, have applied the Gilbreths' technique to many types of jobs, with the goal of reducing the number of motions required. Previously, surgeons sought out tools themselves, which increased operating time, but with the advent of the time-and-motion study, this time was cut-short by having nurses place each tool in the surgeon's hand.

In motion study, movements are broken down into much smaller elements that was done in the earlier time study of Taylor. The time and motion analyst eliminates unnecessary movements and rearranges the remaining movements in the quickest and easiest pattern. In a typical motion study the worker's movements are recorded on film or videotape and analyzed frame by frame with a view toward modifying or eliminating inefficient and wasteful motions.

The following are the guidelines to increase the ease, speed, and accuracy of manual jobs:

- Minimize the distance workers must reach to get tools and supplies or to operate machines.
- Begin and end the movement of both hands at the same time.
- Never keep the hands idle except for authorized rest breaks.
- The hands should never do tasks that can be performed by other parts of the body, particularly legs and feet.
- Whenever possible, instead of holding working materials by hand, a mechanical device must be used.
- The work bench or table should be of sufficient height so that the job can be performed while standing or sitting on a high stool which helps relieve fatigue.

A fundamental weakness in the approach of the early time and motion analysts was their failure to recognize individual differences in work methods. There is no "one best way" for performing a job which suits all people. Due to differences in physical or psychological characteristics among workers, no one method can be universally good for all the workers. Hence, it has been proposed by Likert (1961) that workers and supervisors should be trained in the basic techniques of work simplification so that it would allow flexibility for each person to select and apply one method that best suits them. Time and motion analysis is most applicable to routine tasks.

Person-Machine Systems

A person-machine system is one in which both components work together to accomplish a task. A person driving a car, for example is a person-machine system.

Neither part is of value without the other. If either the human or the mechanical part fails, then all other parts of the system will be affected. In all person-machine systems, the human operator receives input on the status of the machine from the displays. The person-machine systems vary in the extent to which the human operator is actively and continuously involved. Even in case of automated machine, although it can operate itself, humans remain important components of such systems even when they are not directly or continuously operating the equipment. Infact, automation complicated the task of engineering psychologists because it is found that people required to monitor automated equipment find the job to be more fatiguing and boring than the job of actually running a machine. A machine that can design, build and maintain other machines is yet to be developed.

The initial step while designing a person-machine system is to decide about the division of labor between the human operator and the machine. Although machines have certain advantages like, greater physical force, greater storage capacity, ability to engage in repetitive tasks for long with no performance deterioration, ability to detect stimuli that are beyond human sensory capacities, and ability to do large, rapid and accurate calculations, they have several limitations too that have to be kept in mind. For example, they are not very flexible, they cannot learn from errors or modify their behavior based on past experiences nor can they improvise as they are unable to reason. Hence, humans remain necessary to the operation of the system.

It has been seen time and again that fully automated systems can fail with disastrous results. Humans supervising automated equipments also find the job boring as they have little to do or wait for something to malfunction. It lacks challenge and responsibility and rarely requires the humans to use their skills. As the operators become more dependent on computer controlled equipment, they become less capable of making crucial decisions in emergencies no matter how well they have been trained because skills that are rarely used tend to deteriorate.

Person machine systems' operators receive inputs from the machine though the physical senses. The most important decision to be made about the presentation of information in the design of a person-machine system is to select the most effective means of communication. Visual presentation of information is most frequently used when the message is long, difficult and abstract or when the environment is too noisy for auditory messages. It is also used when the auditory channels of communication are overloaded or the message consists of many different kinds of information that must be presented simultaneously. Auditory presentation of information is used when the information is short, simple and straightforward, or when the message is urgent and if the environment is too dark or if the operator's job requires movement to different location. Here, auditory presentation is more helpful as it typically attracts attention more readily that visual ones and ears can receive messages from all direction, whereas the eyes must be focused on the display to receive messages.

There are three types of visual displays which are commonly used in person-machine systems. They are qualitative, quantitative and check reading. Quantitative displays present a precise numeric value. It is used in situations dealing with speed, altitude, or temperature where the operator must know the precise numerical value of a condition of the system as in an aircraft pilot.

Qualitative displays on the other hand, can be used when a precise numerical reading is not necessary and the operators only need to know if the system is in the safe operating range. They are often coded in different colors. Such a display permits quick, accurate verification of the system's status and reduces the amount of technical information thc opcrator must absorb.

Check reading visual displays are the simplest kind of visual display which tells the operator whether the system is on or off, safe or unsafe, or operating normally or abnormally. The most common check reading display is the warning light. There are simple visual displays also which are common and are used by millions everyday like the push/

pull door signs in stores, factories and office buildings. In this, the most effective sign was that which used a combination of the drawing of a hand with an arrow and the word push or pull displayed on it.

Auditory displays however, are more compelling than visual displays because of three primary reasons: our ears are always open, but our eyes are not, we can receive auditory information from all directions, and our visual sense is often taxed to capacity. Humans can receive and interpret a variety of information through the auditory sense and are capable to responding to formal signaling procedure like warning horns or buzzers as well as to informal cues like the wail of a mis-wound audiotape or the sound from a car tyre puncture.

Once human operators receive input through the displays and mentally process that information, they must communicate some control action to the machine. The control decisions are transmitted through such devices such as switches, pushbuttons, levers, mouse, foot pedals etc. Human factors decisions must be made about the choice, location and shape of the controls which are in turn based on the task's requirements. Some broad guidelines regarding the controls are that they must operate with the least amount of force possible and must be within reach for the operator. Also, the following points must be kept in mind:

- No one limb should be given too many tasks to perform.
- A control action should imitate the movements it produces. For example: pulling a control column to the right in a plane should pull the plane to the right.
- The controls for similar or related operations should be combined. For example, on and off controls.
- Controls must be clearly marked or coded to assure their correct and rapid identification.
- Shape coding allows rapid visual identification of the correct control by touch even in low-lighting condit-conditions or when the eyes must focus elsewhere.
- Location of controls should be consistent or uniform to avoid confusion and prevent accidents. For exam-

ple, the gas pedal is expected to be to the right of the brake pedal.

- Emergency control functions must be placed in the normal line of sight where they can be distinguished from other controls. They must be within reach and protected with a cover or shield from accidental operation.
- Controls on consumer products should be easy to operate even by people who have physical limitations. They should be modified for use by people who are deficient in strength or in the ability to make precise movements.

The Components of Ergonomics

Ergonomics deals with the interaction of technological and work situations with the human being. The basic human sciences involved are anatomy, physiology and psychology; these sciences are applied by the ergonomist to realize two main objectives" the most productive use of human capabilities, and the maintenance of human health and well-being. In a phrase, the job must 'fit the person' in all respects, the work situation should not compromise human capabilities and limitations.

The contribution of basic *anatomy* lies in improving physical 'fit' between people and the things they use, ranging from hand tools to aircraft cockpit design. Achieving good physical fit is not an easy task when one considers the range in human body sizes across the population. The science of anthropometrics provides data on dimensions of the human body, in various postures. Biomechanics considers the operation of the muscles and limbs, and ensures that working postures are beneficial, and that excessive forces are avoided.

The knowledge of human *physiology* supports two main technical areas. Work physiology addresses the energy requirements of the body and sets standards for acceptable physical work rate and workload, and for nutrition requirements. Environmental physiology analyses the impact of physical working conditions – thermal, noise and vibration, and lighting – and sets the optimum requirements for these.

Psychology is concerned with human information processing and decision-making capabilities. In simple terms, this can be seen as aiding the cognitive 'fit' between people and the things they use. There is also a strong thread of organizational psychology.

The importance of psychological dimensions of ergonomics should not be underestimated in today's 'high-tech' world. The ergonomist advises on the design of interfaces between people and computers (Human Computer Interaction or HCI), information displays for industrial processes, the planning of training materials, and the design of human tasks and jobs. The concept of 'information overload' is familiar in many current jobs. Paradoxically, increasing automation, while dispensing with human involvement in routine operations, frequently increases the mental demands in terms of monitoring, supervision and maintenance.

Hence, it is seen that Ergonomics is of a multidisciplinary nature. Ergonomists work in teams which may involve a variety of other professions like design engineers, production engineers, industrial designers, computer specialists, industrial physicians, health and safety practitioners, and specialists in human resources. The overall aim of ergonomists is to ensure that the knowledge of human characteristics is applied to the practical problems of people at work and in leisure because although humans can adapt to unsuitable conditions, such adaptation usually leads to inefficiency, errors, unacceptable stress and physical or mental stress.

Application of Egronomics

Ergonomics deals with the interaction of technological and work situations with the human being. Ergonomics focuses on designing workstations, tools and work tasks for safety, efficiency and comfort. Effective ergonomic design reduces discomfort, and injuries and increases job satisfaction and productivity. Some of the common ergonomic risk factors are awkward body postures, excessive repetition, excessive force, contact stress and vibration. Also, common job injuries affecting muscles, tendons, ligaments, joints, nerves and discs can be reduced or eliminated using ergonomics. These injuries are frequently called Musculoskeletal disorders, Repetitive Strain Injuries, and Cumulative Trauma Disorders. Ergonomics has a wide application to everyday domestic situations, but there are even more significant implications for efficiency, productivity, safety and health in work settings. For example:

- Designing equipment and systems including computers, so that they are easier to use and less likely to lead to errors in operation in high stress and safety- criticaloperations such as control rooms.

- Designing tasks and jobs so that they are effective and take account of human needs such as rest breaks and sensible shift patterns, as well as other factors such as intrinsic rewards of work itself.
- Designing equipment and work arrangements to improve working posture and ease the load on the body, thus reducing instances of Repetitive Strain injury or Work Related Upper Limb Disorder.

- Information design, to make the interpretation and use of handbooks, signs, and displays easier and less error-prone.
- Design of training arrangements to cover all significant aspects of the job concerned and to take account of human learning requirements.
- The design of military and space equipment and systems.
- Designing working environments, including lighting and heating, to suit the needs of the users and the tasks performed.
- Design of personal protective equipment for work and hostile environments.

An Ergonomic evaluation would involve the following:

- Workstation setup, relative to a person's posture, length of time in a position or doing a particular task, types of movements, or repetition of movements.
- Job surrounding, including the work surface, lighting, noise level, temperature, and humidity.
- Job tools which includes any device used to per form your job duties, such as a computer mouse or scanning machines.

To have an effective design of human operator's workspace, the following guidelines are important:

- All materials, tools and supplies needed by the workers should be placed in the order in which they are to be used to ensure continuous movements which would saves time from searching.
- Tools should be pre-positioned and should be ready for use.
- All parts and tools should be within comfortable reaching distance.
- Heights of all working surfaces to be fully adjust able to suit people of different heights and people who are overweight or women who are pregnant.

- Size and shape of individual hand tools should be such that one should be able to use them without bending their wrists.

Proper design of hand tools affects productivity, satisfaction and physical health. Continuous use of tools that require bending the wrist while working can lead to nerve injuries like carpal tunnel syndrome which is very painful. It is also prevalent among people who spend a great deal of time playing the piano, knitting, or playing video games. Even at work, if the seats that we use are improperly designed, it can cause back and neck pain and lead to fatigue, thus reducing efficiency.

A lot of research has been done in ergonomics on every conceivable aspect of the design of workplace seating and various other kinds of jobs. For the millions of people who work at a desk or work bench, improperly designed seats can cause back and neck pain and lead to fatigue, which, in turn, reduces productive efficiency. Extensive effort is also devoted to the problems of industrial safety and accident prevention. The procedures employed in industrial safety programs vary widely, from the development of safety devices and protective clothing to safety campaigns and competitions. Studies of fatigue, rest periods, length of workweek, and shift work have frequently employed accident rate as a criterion. Also, a significant part of training programs is training the employees to follow safe operating procedures. Characteristics of the working environment and equipment design have been investigated with reference to safety.

Ergonomists also study accident proneness with regard to task variables and situational variables. It is found that any condition that increases the complexity or the difficulty of the operator's task will lengthen the response time and increase the likelihood of error. Interest has been shifted to the application of ergonomics to the design of highways and equipment, placement of controls, displays, seats, and windows in buses and trucks. Situational variables relating to accidents are also being studied like the relation between accident rate and physical discomfort, as from excessive heat, noise, vibration or dust. Thus, a lot of research in ergonomics has been done to make the process of work easier and comfortable for the employee as well as profitable for the employer and ergonomics is also applied in the industrial sector to ensure safety and prevent accidents.

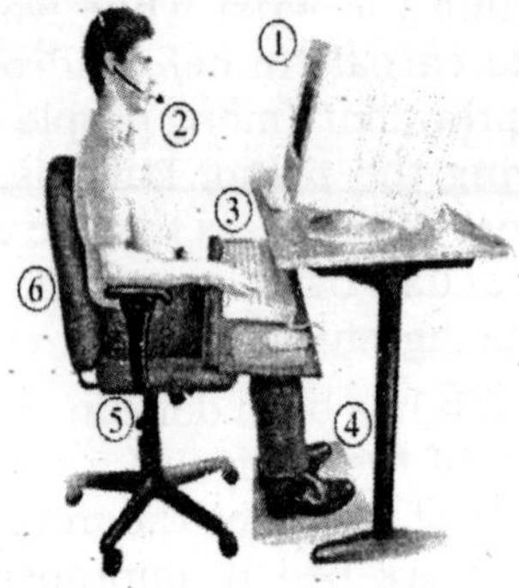

Above is an example of an ergonomically correct work station. The first pointer shows the top of the monitor screen which should be at the eye level. The second pointer shows a telephone headset which helps avoid awkward positions while talking and doing other tasks such as typing. The third pointer shows a wrist pad at the bottom of the keyboard which helps keep the wrists in a neutral, almost straight position. The fourth pointer shows a footrest that raises the feet to reduce the pressure on the lower back. Pointer number five shows armrests that are adjusted so that the elbows are close to the side of the body and bent at an angle between ninety and hundred degrees. The sixth pointer shows an adjustable chair that has a height adjustment to allow the feet to rest on the floor or a footrest and the back of the chair also adjusts for different positions. To prevent backs strain, it is desirable to sit with ears directly above our shoulders, which in turn are over the hips. Placing a lumbar pillow or a roll against the small of the back provides additional support.

Ergonomics may prevent musculoskeletal injuries such as back strain or carpal tunnel syndrome by reducing physical and mental strain caused by the workstation setup. It is also important to evaluate the work process, including job organization, worker rotation, task variety, demands for speed and quality, and the social aspects of work structure and supervision.

Working intensely over long periods of time without taking proper breaks increases the risk for musculoskeletal injuries. Hence, taking regular breaks from work and doing stretching exercises reduces the risk of repetitive motion injuries.

Workstation can be improved by keeping in mind the following things:

- Arranging work so that one can sit or stand comfortably in a position that does not put stress on any specific area of the body. We should be able to keep our neck in a neutral position and minimize the need to look up or to the sides continuously while we are working.
- Eliminating any movement from the waist. Keeping the workstation and workstation tools within reach without having to lean, bend, or twist at the waist frequently.
- Varying postures if possible.
- Taking 10- to 15-second breaks frequently throughout the task. For example, looking away from the computer monitor, standing up, or stretching the arms. Short breaks help reduce eyestrain and buildup of muscle tension.
- Stretching the body by getting up out of the chair and stretching the arms, shoulders, back, and legs. When sitting, shrugging and relaxing our shoulders.
- Maintaining good health through regular exercise, proper nutrition, not smoking, and following prescribed treatment for any other health conditions one may have. Exercise has been proven to be an effective method of preventing back and neck pain.

To improve a workstation, one must choose workstation tools that fit their personal physical and comfort needs, such as:

- A desk or work surface that is:

  o Large enough to accommodate papers, reference manuals, and other workstation tools, but arranged properly to access items easily with the forearm.

KEEP WORK CLOSE!

  o At a height that allows enough space for the knees and thighs to comfortably fit under the desk.

- A computer monitor that is:

  o Clear and easy to see without leaning forward or looking up.

  o At a height where the top of the screen is at eye level, or within 15 degrees below eye level.

  o Less than an arm's length away from the operator.

  o Protective against eyestrain, which may lead to vision problems and headaches. For example, glare guards that are available either as part of the monitor or to be placed over the monitor screen.

- A chair that maintains normal spinal curvature. A supportive chair:

- o Is adjustable, so that one can set the height to rest their feet flat on the floor. Keeping one's feet supported on the floor or on a footrest to reduce pressure on lower back. Some people like to sit in a slightly reclined position because it puts less stress on the back, although this may increase stress on the shoulders and neck when reaching for items.
- o Supporting the lower back.
- o Having adjustable armrests that allow the elbows to stay close to the sides. It is important to keep the arms close to our sides even if we choose not to use armrests.
- o Has a breathable, padded seat.
- o Rolls on five wheels for easy movement without tipping.

- A computer keyboard at a height that allows the elbows to be open and close to the sides. Various recommendations for keyboard placement include positions with elbows open to a 90-degree angle, or a 100-degree angle with the keyboard slanted downward at the top.

- A computer mouse or pointing device that does not require a lot of forearm movement or force, such as a trackball mouse or touch pad.

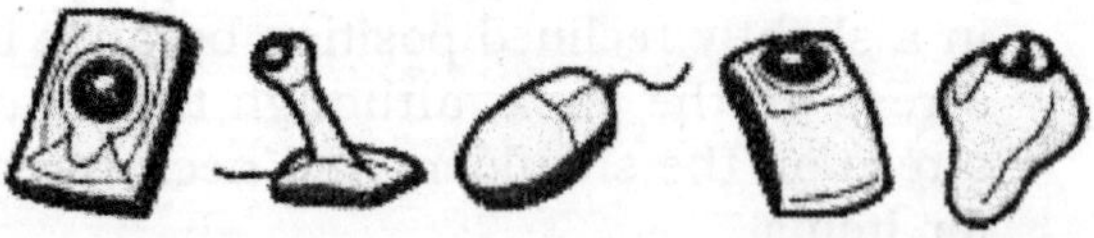

- A document holder that holds papers level with the computer monitor, so that as we look back and forth between paper and monitor, our eyes do not need to continually refocus.

- A comfortable room temperature, a relatively quiet area, and sufficient lighting without glare from of fice lights, sunlight, or the computer screen.
- A telephone headset, to avoid awkward positions while talking and doing other tasks, such as typing.

- A location for any reference manuals that is close to the center of the workstation, for easy access.

Laptop computers are also largely at use today but they must never be used as the primary computer because it does not provide an adjustable keyboard. Incase one must use laptops for long periods of time then proper care must be taken to avoid injuries by taking breaks every 20 to 30 minutes, keeping the head in a neutral position 18 to 30 inches away from the monitor, positioning the wrists relatively straight and by using and external mouse instead of the small touch pad or track ball.

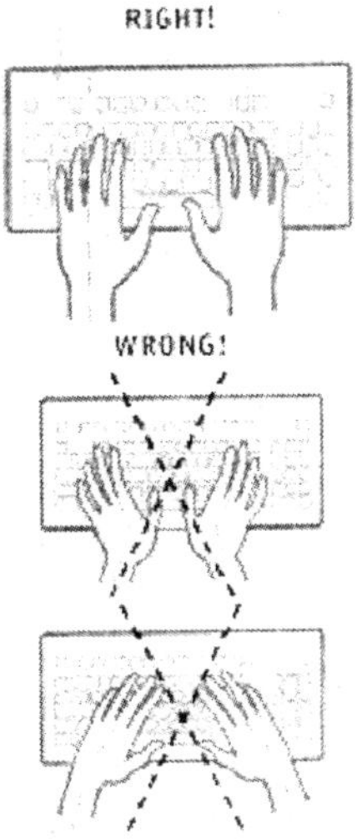

Another important aspect is the lighting at computer workstations. Computer workstations present complex visual needs. Glare and monitor screen reflections can produce visual discomfort. Individual differences also affect light requirements. For example, a sixty year old worker may need up to ten times more light than a twenty year old worker. The color of the light affects visual comfort and productivity. Soft white fluorescent bulbs are preferred over bright white bulbs as they are warmer in color and create fewer glares although indirect lighting is the best. Reflections and glare can interfere with visual comfort when working at a computer. They can be reduced by reducing the light from the windows, reducing the ceiling glare, using indirect lighting, using anti-glare screens etc.

Conclusion

Ergonomics deals with designing operating procedures, equipment, and environments to fit human capabilities, limitations, needs and preferences. Ergonomists contribute to this goal through research on human performance. They work closely with specialists from other fields, within the broad area of human factors engineering in developing appropriate procedures, products, and operating systems.

Reducing fatigue, preventing injuries and accidents, making life simpler and increasing the productivity of the workers by fitting the job to the person as well as the person to the job by providing a comfortable working environment are the main goals of ergonomics. In a day and age where stress and tension have become a part and parcel of a person's everyday life, ergonomists seek to reduce the stress atleast at a physical level as it is said 'a healthy mind in a healthy body'. So, if we are comfortable at our workspace, then we could be more relaxed both physically and mentally and thus, increases performance.

References

1. Anastasi, Anne. *Fields of Applied Psychology* New York, McGraw Hill Book Co., 1979. p-169 to 194.
2. Schultz and Schultz. *Psychology and Work Today.* New Jersey; U.S, Prentice Hall Publishers. p-408 to 437.
3. *http://www.ergonomics.ucla.edu*
4. *http://www.ergonomics.org.uk*
5. *http://ergo.human.cornell.edu*

18

Absenteeism and Managers as Counsellors

1 Absenteeism

1.1 Introduction

1.1.1 Abstract

It is a fact of life that from time to time employees become unwell and is unable to attend work for days and sometimes weeks on end. Many awards and industrial instruments make provision for such an occurrence by providing a paid sick leave entitlement for employees when they find themselves in this unfortunate position.

Where an employee is genuinely ill, these provisions ensure that employees and their families do not miss out on wages they would otherwise be entitled to if they were working.

In some businesses however, a percentage of employees advise managers they are unwell or unable to attend work for days or extended periods of time, in circumstances, which suggest that the absence was avoidable. This is often referred to as absenteeism, and the costs to business can be enormous.

1.1.2 Definition

Absenteeism is the chronic or continued failure of employees to attend for duty, especially when the pattern of absenteeism suggests either that the absence was avoidable or that the employee failed in their duty to the employer in accordance with their employment contract. Taking sickies and malingering also form part of absenteeism.

Employers can address the problem of absenteeism by identifying the problem in the first instance and putting in place various measures to address such behaviour.

1.1.3 Types of Absenteeism

1.1.3.1 Innocent Absenteeism

Innocent absenteeism refers to employees who are absent for reasons beyond their control; like sickness and injury. Innocent absenteeism is not culpable which means that it is blameless. In a labour relations context this means that it cannot be remedied or treated by disciplinary measures.

1.1.3.2 Culpable Absenteeism

Culpable absenteeism refers to employees who are absent without authorization for reasons, which are within their control. For instance, an employee who is on sick leave even though he/she is not sick, and it can be proven that the employee was not sick, is guilty of culpable absenteeism. To be culpable is to be blameworthy. In a labour relations context this means that progressive discipline can be applied.

For the large majority of employees, absenteeism is legitimate, innocent absenteeism, which occurs infrequently. Procedures for disciplinary action apply only to culpable absenteeism. Many organizations take the view that through the process of individual absentee counselling and treatment, the majority of employees will overcome their problems and return to an acceptable level of regular attendance.

1.1.4 Tackling Absenteeism

1.1.4.1 Identifying Excessive Absenteeism

Attendance records should be reviewed regularly to be sure that an employee's sick-leave days are excessive compared to other employees. If a supervisor suspects that an employee is excessively absent, this can be confirmed through reviewing the attendance records.

If all indications show that an employee is excessively absent, the next step is to gather as much information as possible in order to get a clearer picture of the situation. The employees' files should be reviewed and the employees' immediate supervisor should document all available information on the particular employee's history.

1.1.4.2 Individual Communication

After all available information has been gathered, the administrator or supervisor should individually meet with each employee whom has been identified as having higher than average or questionable (or pattern) absences. This first meeting should be used to bring concerns regarding attendance to the employee's attention. It is also an opportunity to discuss with the employee, in some depth, the causes of his or her attendance problem and possible steps he or she can take to remedy or control the absences. Listen carefully to the employee's responses.

The tone of the meeting should not be adversarial, but a major purpose of the interview is to let the employee know that management treats attendance as a very important component of overall work performance. Keep your comments non-threatening and work-oriented. Stick to the facts (i.e. patters, profiles, rates etc.). The employee should be given a copy of their attendance report with absences highlighted for discussion.

This interview will give you the opportunity to explore in depth with the employee the reasons for his or her absence. Gather facts - do not make any assumptions. Provide support and counselling and offer guidance as the occasion demands to assist the employee to deal with the specific cause of the absence.

Often, after the initial meeting employees reduce their absenteeism. The meeting shows that you are concerned and that absenteeism is taken seriously. The employee's attendance should be closely monitored until it has been reduced to acceptable levels. Appropriate counselling should take place as is thought necessary. If a marked improvement has been shown, commend the employee. The meeting should be documented and a copy placed in the employee's file.

1.1.4.3 Proof of Illness

Sometimes it is helpful in counselling employees with excessive innocent or culpable absenteeism to inquire or verify the nature and reasons of their absence.

The extent to which an employer may inquire into the nature of and reasons for an employee's absence from the workplace is a delicate issue. The concepts of an employee's privacy and an employer's need for information affecting the workplace often come into conflict. Seldom is the conflict more difficult to resolve than where personal medical information is involved.

Unions will often strongly object to any efforts by management to inquire more deeply into the nature of an employee's illness. We will need to consider the restraints of any language in collective agreements in relation to this issue.

The following "rules of thumb" can be derived from the existing jurisprudence:

1. There is a prevailing right to privacy on the part of an employee unless the employer can demonstrate that its legitimate business interests necessitate some intrusion into the employee's personal affairs.

2. When such intrusion is justified it should be strictly limited to the degree of intrusion necessitated by the employer's interests.

3. An employee has a duty to notify his employer of an intended absence, the cause of the absence and its expected duration. This information is required by the employer to meet its legitimate concerns to have at its disposal facts, which will enable it to schedule work and organize its operation.

4. An absent employee has an obligation to provide his employer with information regarding any change to his condition or circumstances relating to it which may affect the employer's needs as described in item 3 above. As such, the interests of the employer in having this information outweigh the individual employee's right to privacy.

5. An employer rule requiring proof for every absence is unreasonable if an absenteeism problem does not exist.

6. A mere assertion by the person claiming to be sick is not satisfactory proof.

7. The obligation to prove sickness, where the employer requires proof, rests with the employee.

8. An employer is entitled upon reasonable and probable grounds to refuse to accept a physician's certificate

until it contains sufficient information to satisfy the employer's reservations. (i.e. seen by physician, some indication of return to work, etc.). Non-production of a required medical certificate could result in loss of pay until the certificate is produced.

9. Where a medical certificate is rejected by an employer (as in 8 above) the employer must state the grounds for rejection and must point out to the employee what it requires to satisfy the onus of proof.

10. An employer may require an employee to prove fitness for work where it has reasonable grounds to do so. In a health care setting the nature of the employer's business gives it a reasonably irresistible interest in this personal information for the purpose of assessing fitness.

11. Where any unusual circumstances raise reasonable suspicion that an employee might have committed an abuse of an income protection program an employer may require an employee to explain such circumstances. For example, an employer may require responses as to whether the illness confined an employee to his/her bed or home; whether an employee engaged in any outside activity and the reasons for the activity.

In summary then, any intrusion into the employee's privacy must be shown to be reasonable, based on the individual circumstances and in relation to the operation of the employer's business. If income protection abuse is suspected the extent to which such intrusion is "reasonable" would be far greater than in the case where it is not. If you are not clear on whether an inquiry is legally justified it is advisable to consult your superior.

1.1.4.4 After the Initial Interview

If after the initial interview, enough time and counselling efforts, as appropriate, have passed and the employee's absenteeism has not improved, it may be necessary to take further action. Further action must be handled with extreme caution - a mistake in approach, timing or severity can be crippling from both an administration and labour relation's point of view.

Determining whether counselling or disciplinary action is appropriate depends on whether the employee's absences are innocent or culpable. If the employee's absenteeism is made up of both innocent and culpable absences, then each type must be dealt with as a separate issue. In a labour relation's context innocent absenteeism and culpable absenteeism are mutually exclusive. One in no way affects the other.

1.1.4.5 Counselling Innocent Absenteeism

Innocent absenteeism is not blameworthy and therefore disciplinary action is not justified. It is obviously unfair to punish someone for conduct, which is beyond his/her control. Absenteeism, no matter what the cause, imposes losses on the employer who is also not at fault. The damage suffered by the employer must be weighed against the employee's right to be sick. There is a point at which the employer's right to expect the employee to attend regularly and fulfil the employment contract will outweigh the employee's right to be sick. At such a point the termination of the employee may be justified, as will be discussed.

The procedure an employer may take for innocent absenteeism is as follows:

1. Initial counselling(s)
2. Written counselling(s)
3. Reduction(s) of hours and/or job reclassification
4. Discharge

1.1.4.5.1 Initial Counselling

Presuming you have communicated attendance expectations generally and have already identified an employee as a problem, you will have met with him or her as part of your attendance program and you should now continue to monitor the effect of these efforts on his or her attendance.

If the absences are intermittent, meet with the employee each time he/she returns to work. If absence is prolonged, keep in touch with the employee regularly and stay updated on the status of his/her condition. (Indicate your willingness to assist.)

You may require the employee to provide you with regular medical assessments. This will enable you to judge whether or not there is any likelihood of the employee providing regular attendance in future. Regular medical assessments will also give you an idea of what steps the employee is taking to seek medical or other assistance. Formal meetings in which verbal warnings are given should be given as appropriate and documented. If no improvement occurs written warning may be necessary.

1.1.4.5.2 Written Counselling

If the absences persist, you should meet with the employee formally and provide him/her with a letter of concern. If the absenteeism still continues to persist then the employee should be given a second letter of concern during another formal meeting. This letter would be stronger worded in that it would warn the employee that unless attendance improves, termination might be necessary.

1.1.4.5.3 Reduction of Hours and or JOB RECLASSIFICATION

In between the first and second letters the employee may be given the option to reduce his/her hours to better fit his/her personal circumstances. This option must be voluntarily accepted by the employee and cannot be offered as an ultimatum, as a reduction in hours is a reduction in pay and therefore can be looked upon as discipline.

If the nature of the illness or injury is such that the employee is unable to fulfil the requirements of his/her job, but could for example benefit from modified work, counsel the employee to bid on jobs of such type if they become available. (N.B. It is inadvisable to "build" a job around an employee's incapacitates particularly in a unionized environment. The onus should be on the employee to apply for an existing position within his/her capabilities.)

1.1.4.5.4 Discharge

Only when all the previously noted needs and conditions

have been met and everything has been done to accommodate the employee can termination be considered. An Arbitrator would consider the following in ruling on an innocent absenteeism dismissal case.

1. Has the employee done everything possible to regain their health and return to work?

2. Has the employer provided every assistance possible? (i.e. counselling, support, time off.)

3. Has the employer informed the employee of the unworkable situation resulting from their sickness?

4. Has the employer attempted to accommodate the employee by offering a more suitable position (if available) or a reduction of hours?

5. Has enough time elapsed to allow for every possible chance of recovery?

6. Has the employer treated the employee prejudicially in any way?

As is evident, a great deal of time and effort must elapse before dismissal can take place.

These points would be used to substantiate or disprove the following two-fold test.

1. The absences must be shown to be clearly excessive.

2. It must be proven that the employee will be unable to attend work on a regular basis in the future.

1.1.4.6 Corrective Action for Culpable Absenteeism

As already indicated, culpable absenteeism consists of absences where it can be demonstrated that the employee is not actually ill and is able to improve his/her attendance.

Presuming you have communicated attendance expectations generally, have identified the employee as a problem, have met with him/her as part of your attendance program, made your concerns on his specific absenteeism known and have offered counselling as appropriate, with no improvement despite your positive efforts, disciplinary procedures may be appropriate.

The procedures for corrective/progressive discipline for culpable absenteeism are generally the same as for other progressive discipline problems. The discipline should not be prejudicial in any way. The general procedure is as follows: [Utilizing counselling memorandum]

1. Initial Warning(s)
2. Written Warning(s)
3. Suspension(s)
4. Discharge

1.1.4.6.1 Verbal Warning

Formally meet with the employee and explain that income protection is to be used only when an employee is legitimately ill. Advise the employee that his/her attendance record must improve and be maintained at an improved level or further disciplinary action will result. Offer any counselling or guidance as is appropriate. Give further verbal warnings as required. Review the employee's income protection records at regular intervals. Where a marked improvement has been shown, commend the employee. Where there is no improvement a written warning should be issued.

1.1.4.6.2 Written Warning

Interview the employee again. Show him/her the statistics and point out that there has been no noticeable (or sufficient) improvement. Listen to the employee to see if there is a valid reason and offer any assistance you can. If no satisfactory explanation is given, advise the employee that he/she will be given a written warning. Be specific in your discussion with him/her and in the counselling memorandum as to the type of action to be taken and when it will be taken if the record does not improve. As soon as possible after this meeting provide the employee personally with the written warning and place a copy of his/her file. The written warning should identify any noticeable pattern

If the amount and/or pattern continue, the next step in progressive discipline may be a second, stronger written warning. Your decision to provide a second written warning as an alternative to proceeding to a higher level of discipline (i.e. suspension) will depend on a number of factors. Such factors are, the severity of the problem, the credibility of the employee's explanations, the employee's general work performance and length of service.

1.1.4.6.3 Suspension (Only after Consultation with the Appropriate Superiors)

If the problem of culpable absenteeism persists, following the next interview period and immediately following an absence, the employee should be interviewed and advised that he/she is to be suspended. The length of the suspension will depend again on the severity of the problem, the credibility of the employee's explanation, the employee's general work performance and length of service. Subsequent suspensions are optional depending on the above condition.

1.1.4.6.4 Dismissal (Only after Consultation with the Appropriate Superiors)

Dismissals should only be considered when all of the above conditions and procedures have been met. The employee, upon displaying no satisfactory improvement, would be dismissed on the grounds of his/her unwillingness to correct his/her absence record.

1.2 Case Studies

1.2.1 Case 1: Employment Protection and Absenteeism in the German Public Sector

1.2.1.1 Framework and Hypothesis

The case study evaluates the effect of employment protection on absenteeism looking at employees in the private and public sector in Germany. Overall German workers enjoy a relatively high level of employment protection (cf. Grubb and Wells 1993 or OECD 1999) where e.g. notice periods in case of layoff increase rapidly with tenure: Starting out with a notice period of 4 weeks for all permanent employees it increases to 2 months after 5 years of tenure and in steps up to 7 months after 20 years of tenure. These basic rules can be modified by bilateral agreements between unions and employers. Layoffs are allowed for three general reasons: those related to the individual employee (e.g. ability or health), worker misconduct, or important business requirements (e.g. business cycle related lack of orders or down-sizing).

Within the German institutional framework there are two basic differences in the level of employment protection for employees in the private and the public sector: First, dismissals for important business requirements are almost inconceivable in the public sector, yielding a fundamental difference in employment security between the private and public sector. Second, employees in the public sector enjoy an additional level of job protection: Those employed in the public sector for at least 15 years and of at least 40 years of age cannot be dismissed except in rare cases of severe misconduct. Thus the degree of employment protection for public sector employees generally exceeds that of those in the private sector and after 15 years of tenure and age 40 reaches the almost "un-dismissable" level enjoyed by civil servants. Based on these institutional rules the theoretical framework described above suggests first that public sector employees should have higher absenteeism than private sector workers and second that even higher absenteeism will be observed among those public sector workers who meet the tenure-age condition. These hypotheses are tested below.

1.2.1.2 Data and Approach

To compare the absence behavior of public and private sector workers we utilize data taken from the 2001 wave of the German Socioeconomic Panel (GSOEP). The GSOEP is a panel household survey administered annually since 1984. The 2001 survey covered approximately 22,000 individuals in about 14,000 households. We restrict our sample to fulltime-employed workers between ages 18 and 60. The self-employed and civil servants are dropped from the sample because for both groups' employment protection regulations and their implied incentive mechanisms differ from the institutional setting described above. After dropping observations with missing values on key variables our sample contains 6,737 observations of which 1,330 are employed in the public and 5,407 in the private sector. Of those employed in the public sector 362 meet the conditions for extended employment protection. Our dependent variable describes the absenteeism rate, which is defined as the number of days individuals missed work due to illness in the past calendar year divided by 240 work days for the year. For the full sample we observe a mean value of 10 days (or a rate of 4.3 percent) and a median of 3 days (or a rate of 1.25 percent) indicating the large impact of the top percentile of the distribution of absence days. 43 percent of all observations had no absence days and another 32 percent did not exceed ten days of absence. In the aggregate absenteeism rates of private and public sector workers differ significantly (at the 2 percent level) with a mean of 4.1 percent for the former and 4.9 percent for the latter. Among public sector workers, those with extended employment protection took significantly more days of absence compared to those without this protection: 16.1 vs. 10.3 days yielding 6.7 vs. 4.3 percent, which is significantly different at the 1 percent level.

Below we describe whether these differences can be confirmed in linear regression analyses, which control for potential composition effects.

1.2.1.3 Results and Interpretation

The results of our empirical analyses are presented in Table 1.

The model in column 1 includes merely an indicator of whether the employee is working in the public sector and an indicator of whether the individual is one of those who are working in an "un-dismissible" position in the public sector after having reached 15 years of tenure and age 40. Both indicators yield positive deviations from the private sector absence rate of 4.1 percent, yet only the difference for the high-protection group is statistically significant. Those in highly protected positions on average miss another 2.56 percent of work annually compared to private sector workers. This confirms the hypothesis derived in our theoretical model above. The difference between the average public and private sector employee is surprisingly small and imprecisely estimated.

In column 2 we add control variables for basic demographic indicators such as age, sex, and marital status. With these controls the coefficient of the high protection indicator in row 1 declines in magnitude, now showing a difference of 1.51 percentage points compared to other public sector workers and a total of 1.57 percentage points above the absent rate in the private sector.

In column 3 we control for health measures, where we use the level of a possible disability (an objective measure in the German disability system) and the subjectively indicated degree of health satisfaction. Both variables yield coefficients that are highly significant and suggest that the healthy have fewer days of absence. The effect of adding these controls for the high-protection indicator is small and the overall public sector indicator stays insignificant.

In columns 4 and 5 additional control variables are considered. First we add a set of human capital indicators for school and vocational degrees in column 4, then we control for measures that describe the employment situation with indicators for blue vs. white collar job, tenure, tenure squared, and four categorical indicators of firm size. All of these controls are highly significant, yet they leave our main indicator of the association between high levels of employment protection and annual absence rates almost unaffected. In column 4 it is somewhat less precisely measured, but the sizeable difference in absence rates is constant across specifications. We find that workers in secure employment miss on average about 5.8 percent of work, compared to about 4.2 percent for private sector employees. This amounts to a difference of about 38 percent, even when controlling for all other factors.1 Note that our regression procedure follows the logic of a difference-in-differences analysis and rests on the assumption that the observable difference between absences in the public and the private sector conditional on age and tenure is the result of different employment protection regulations, as all other mechanisms are controlled for. Therefore this case study corroborates the conjecture we described in Section 1.

Table 1: Absenteeism Rates in the German Public and Private Sectors

	1	2	3	4	5
Difference: High employment protection vs. all public sector (in percentage points)	2.41***	1.51*	1.40*	1.17	1.57**
Difference: Public vs. Private sector worker (in percentage points)	0.15	0.06	-0.01	0.21	0.05
Predicted absenteeism rate: Private sector (in percent)	4.14	4.21	4.25	4.20	4.21
Accounting for:					
demographic effects		yes	yes	yes	yes
health effects			yes	yes	yes
human capital effects				yes	yes
effects of the employment situation					yes

Note: ***, **, and * indicate statistical significance at the 1, 5, and 10 percent level of the difference in absenteeism rates across groups. The linear regressions use 6737 observations. The control groups are defined as follows: Demographic effects: age, male sex, living with a partner; health effects: degree of disability, subjective health satisfaction; human capital effects: 4 indicators of schooling degree, 3 indicators of vocational degree, effects of the employment situation: indicator for blue collar status, tenure, tenure squared, 4 indicators of firm size. Standard errors are reported in parentheses (Huber-White robust).

1.2.2 Case 2: Employment Protection and Absenteeism in the Italian Private Sector

1.2.2.1 Framework and Hypothesis

The case study looks at the private sector in Italy,

where, since the approval of the Chart of Workers Rights of 1970 (*Statuto dei Lavoratori),* the degree of employment protection offered to workers varies strongly depending on the firm size. As a result of this law and other related regulations, firms with more than 15 employees can fire an individual worker only if this decision is sustained by "justified reasons concerning the production activity, the organization of labor in the firm and its regular functioning" or "in case of a significantly inadequate fulfillment of the employee's tasks specified by the contract". Given how vague this requirement is for practical purposes, a worker who is fired can file suit against the firm, in which case one judge (or more in case of appeal) decides on whether there exists a justified motive for firing. If the ruling is that such motive does not exist, the firm is forced to take the employee back on payroll and to pay the full wage that the worker has lost during the litigation period (which typically last at least one year and often more) plus social insurance contributions. In addition, the firm has to pay a fine to the social security system for the delayed payment of welfare contributions up to 200 percent of the original amount due. Precisely for this set of regulations the OECD considers Italy as one of the countries with the most stringent protection against firing (Grubb and Wells 1993 and OECD 1999).

This, however, holds only in large firms: Workers in firms with less than 16 employees can be fired at a cost which cannot be higher than six months of wages even if a judge rules that the firing is not sustained by a justified motive. Interestingly, this difference of treatment is the focus of considerable attention in the Italian policy debate, which led to a referendum in June 2003 aiming at extending the extreme protection against firing granted in large firms to all workers. The extension was however not approved mostly because it was clearly felt that it would have significantly damaged small businesses and firms, which constitute the driving force of the most competitive part of the Italian economy. The conjecture that excessive employment protection reduces workers' incentive to exert effort, therefore lowering productivity and increasing labor cost per unit of output, has clearly conditioned the debate at the time of the referendum, although typically only anecdotal evidence was used to prove or disprove the opposing claims. Here we provide some evidence on this issue, based on the comparison of absenteeism rates among workers in small and large firms. Although we cannot claim that the differences we will describe can be solely attributed to different degrees of employment protection, our results suggest that these regulations are likely to play a significant role in raising absenteeism in large firms.

1.2.2.2 Data and Approach

We use data from the 1995 wave of the Italian Survey of Household Incomes and Wealth (SHIW), which collect information on the Italian population once every two years and are administered by the Bank of Italy. In this wave, 8,135 households are interviewed for a total of 23,924 individuals of which 14,699 are income recipients. We restrict the analysis to 3,347 non self-employed full time workers and we calculate their absenteeism rates as the fraction of reported days of absence in a standard 240 workday year. Our goal is to compare average absenteeism rates of workers subject to different regimes of employment protection as a result of the different size of the firm in which they are employed. Unfortunately, the firm size categories in the SHIW do not match those that determine the two firing cost regimes described above. The distinction offered by the data is between firms with more or less than 20 employees. This distinction is however sufficiently close to the one, which is relevant for the employment protection legislation and is therefore informative for the question in which we are interested. Note in particular that if a bias is produced by using the "20 employees" threshold, it goes against showing the existence of a difference, because part of the workers in our "Small firms" category (i.e. less than 20 employees), are actually subject to the same degree of protection offered to workers in "large firms" (i.e. more than 19 employees).

1.2.2.3 Results and Interpretation

Our results are reported in Table 2 where raw averages are compared in the first two columns. The mean absenteeism rate is 1.6 percent in small firms while it is as high as 2.8 percent in large firms. The table reports in brackets under each estimate its 95 percent confidence interval. It is easy to see that the two confidence intervals do not overlap, which shows that the absenteeism rate is considerably higher in larger firms not only in absolute terms but also in terms of statistical significance. It should of course be considered that many different mechanisms may cause a correlation of absenteeism and firm size independent of employment protection, including systematic differences in the age and health of employees in small and large firms as well as different distributions of firm size across occupations, sectors and regions (see Barmby and Stephan 2000 and the literature cited there). Ideally one would like to compare identical workers in identical firms with two regimes of employment protection, but this is of course not possible. What we can do is to perform the comparison controlling for the observable characteristics of the workers and the firms, which are offered in the data. This is done in the third and fourth column of the table where the mean absenteeism rates in the two categories are computed on the basis of regressions which include, in addition to the dummy variable for firm size, also the following list of controls: gender, age, 8 education level dummies, 5 qualification dummies, 9 sector dummies, 3 geographic area dummies and 4 self-declared health status dummies. Sample averages of this variable have been used to compute the controlled absenteeism rates. Even controlling for all these observable characteristics we find that workers in large firms are characterised by an absenteeism rate, which is 75 percent higher, then the one of workers in small firms, and this difference is statistically significant. This evidence is supportive of the conjecture that different regimes of employment protection might affect the propensity of a worker to be absent. As a minimum, it is difficult to think of other systematic differences between small and large firms, in addition to the ones controlled by the observable variables included in our regression, which might account for such a large difference in absenteeism.

To further reinforce the evidence in favour of our conjecture we now move to the analysis of the behaviour of a group of employees working for one single firm, who were entitled to two different employment protection regimes in subsequent periods.

Table 2: Absenteeism Rate in Small and Large Italian Firms (in Percent)

Not controlled		**Controlled**	
Small firms	Large firms	Small firms	Large firms
1.6	2.8	1.6	2.7
[1.3 - 1.8]	[2.4 - 3.0]	[1.3 - 1.9]	[2.4 - 2.9]

Note: The table reports mean absenteeism rates in percentage terms, with 95 percent confidence interval in brackets. Absenteeism rates are calculated as the fraction of days of absence in a standard 240 workday years. Controlled means are computed at sample averages using regressions which include, in addition to the dummy variable for firm size, also the following list of controls: gender, age, 8 education level dummies, 5 qualification dummies, 10 sector dummies, 3 geographic area dummies and 4 self declared health dummies. These regressions use data on 3347 non self-employed full time Italian workers interviewed in the 1995 *Survey of Household Income and Wealth (SHIW)* collected by the Bank of Italy. Firms are defined as "Small" if they have less than 20 employees. Within this group, firms with less than 16 employees face significantly lower firing costs.

1.2.3 Case 3: How Workers React to a Change in Employment Protection. Evidence from an Italian Firm.

1.2.3.1 Framework and Hypothesis

This case study is analyzed in Ichino and Riphahn (2003). In this paper, to which we refer the reader interested in more details, we test the effect of employment protection on absenteeism in a sample of employees who are observed during their first year of tenure at an Italian bank. This bank is one of the largest in Italy, employing 17,971 workers at the time our data were collected (1993) and with branches all over the Italian territory. As we noted in the previous section, Italy provides a particularly suitable institutional framework for a test of our conjecture, as it is one of the countries with the most stringent firing protection among OECD members. Given the size of the bank, all its workers (excluding managers) are fully protected against firing, according to the *Chart of Workers' Rights,* during their entire career except for a probation period of three months at its beginning. During this initial period workers have basically no protection, so that the change of job security implied by the end of probation is equivalent, from the viewpoint of the worker, to the change from a "US style" weak protection system to the most protective of the "European style" systems. In our data we observe newly hired workers for one year and can compare their individual weekly absenteeism during and after probation, i.e. with and without job security. Based on the prediction of our theoretical model we expect an increase in absenteeism after the end of probation.

1.2.3.2 Data and Approach

To test this hypothesis we consider the sample of 858 individuals who were newly hired by the bank between January 1, 1993 and February 28, 1995. For each employee we constructed a panel of weekly observations covering the first full year of tenure. During the first three months these workers were on probation and could be fired at will, while during the remaining nine months they enjoyed full firing protection. Our sample of 545 men and 313 women is a relatively homogeneous group of young individuals at the beginning of their career: Half of them have a college degree and all but 12 have a high school degree. About 70 percent of the degrees are in banking and economics. Also, 98 percent of these workers are hired at the entry level in the bank hierarchy, typically with internal labor market careers ahead of them.

We computed absenteeism rates as the number of days of absence "due to illness" for each calendar week divided by 5 (days in a week). Each worker is observed for 52 weeks of which the first 12 are during and the latter 40 are after the probation period. So the sample consists of 44,616 worker-week observations with an average of 0.065 days of absence per week or an absenteeism rate of 1.3 percent of working time. To investigate whether absence days are more likely during or after probation we apply a linear estimator. However the results do not change when a non-linear model such as a Poisson estimator is applied.

1.2.3.3 Results and Interpretation

The empirical results are summarized in Table 3. The first column indicates the results obtained when we consider a model, which contains only an indicator of whether the worker is observed after the end of probation and a constant. They yield that while during probation the predicted absenteeism rate is as low as 0.68 percent, after the end of probation it increases to 1.50 percent indicating that absenteeism more than doubles when full firing protection is granted. The estimates are very precisely measured, and the difference is statistically significant at the 1 percent level. As absenteeism is a highly seasonal phenomenon the result in the first column could be an artifact simply deriving from an unequal hiring pattern of the firm over the course of the calendar year: If e.g. illness is high in February and the firm hires predominantly in November, then after the first 12 weeks of tenure absenteeism might have increased not because of the end of probation but due to the general onset of illness episodes.

In column 2 we take account of potential seasonal effects. However, the results are almost unaffected. After probation the absenteeism rate is still predicted to be more than twice as large as during probation.

To test whether this result may be due to simple composition effects, we next add control variables for some basic demographic indicators such as age, sex, marital status, and education. As could be expected from the fact that these measures are mostly time invariant for a given individual and orthogonal to the probation indicator, the main result of a doubling of the absenteeism rate after probation remains robust and statistically significant with these controls. The fact that absenteeism increases over the first tenure months may be due to a number of mechanisms different from employment protection which might be related e.g. to the branch where the individual is employed or to the simple passage of time. To investigate whether the effect of the end of probation as described above may be explained by such mechanisms, we included a time trend and a wide set of time varying branch characteristics to the specification. The time trend should capture any tenure related development that is not due to the end of the probation period. The results in column 4 of Table 3 show that the effect of probation remains statistically significant and robust with respect to the inclusion of these controls. Moreover, the time trend is insignificant. Across all four of our specifications we thus find highly significant and robust effects of the end of probation suggesting that newly hired workers are significantly more absent after the end of probation. The change of behavior appears to be solely induced by the firing protection that individual workers receive at the end of probation.

Table 3: Absenteeism rates during and after probation in an Italian Bank (in Percent)

	1	2	3	4
Absenteeism rate after probation	1.50***	1.48***	1.48***	1.52***
Absenteeism rate during probation	0.68	0.67	0.67	0.68
Accounting for:				
seasonal effects	no	yes	yes	yes
personal characteristics			yes	yes
branch characteristics				yes

Note: *** indicates statistical significance at the 1 percent level of the difference between the absenteeism rates before and after probation. The rates are computed as predicted number of days of absence per week divided by 5 (days in a week) using OLS regressions which, depending on columns, include controls defined as follows. Seasonal controls: dummies for month of hiring. Personal characteristics: age, sex, years of schooling, marital status. Branch characteristics measure whether the branch is located in the south, the size of the branch, the percentage of managers and females in the branch, the average age of branch workers, average branch weekly absenteeism, and a linear time trend.

2 Managers as Counsellors

2.1 Introduction

The use of counseling and counseling skills in employment content is growing as companies become increasingly aware of the benefits that can be gained, by both employee and employer, for these interactions. Counseling in one way providing the company, as a whole with the means of alleviating different problems which, if not identified, discussed end resolved, could erode the effectiveness of the person, not only as an asset in the organization, but as an individual.

2.1.1 Definition: Counselling

Counselling may simply be described as a form of communication between two people. Counselling is the creation end maintenance of an environment in which a person can be helpful to help himself to overcome the difficult that let them to seek assistance, for as long as the person seeking help requires that environment.

2.1.2 Model of Counselling

5 Stage model for counselling (in organization)

Stage 1-DESCRIBE. This is concerned with building an alliance with the counsellor and client and identifying the problem areas.

Stage 2-OPERATIONALIZE.In this stage the client is encouraged to acknowledge problems and develop new insights.

Stage 3-SET GOALS. The counsellor and client negotiate goals and the interventions required to achieve them.

Stage 4-INTERVENE. The client works on problem areas and receives support from the counselor.

Stage 5-EXIT. The counselling process is reviewed and advice is given on consolidating self-help skills.

2.1.3 Work Place Counselling

Counselling provided by managers and supervisors is probably the fastest, cheapest and most cost effective way of helping employees to solve performance-impairing problems for themselves.

Counselling skill may be applied in a variety of situations, forming an integral part of manger's one to one interactions with employees.

Helping your staff to solve problems brings several benefits:

- It makes better use of your time.
- It helps you to retain your staff and reduces absenteeism.
- It increases the team support spirit.
- It demonstrates respect for, and loyalty towards, your staff.
- It can increase productivity.
- It increases the standing of the company in the public eye.

2.1.4 Problems

Identifying problems - The early identification of an employee's area of concern may save both the person and the company from the loss of considerable time and effort and resources.

How then managers begin to identify an employee with potential problems? A number of factors arising from the employee's behavior and manifested in inconsistent or poor work performance, irregular time, keeping constant daydreaming and so on may have been observed by the manager, promoting him to innate contact with employee to investigate.

Alternatively, the employee may not display any overt activity that may alert the manger to underline problems.

2.1.5 Some cause and Indicators of Problems

Material separation, or threatened separation

Lack of concentration, irritability

Enforced change of residence

Loss (e.g. material)

Financial difficulty

Reduced social contacts

Role of ambiguity at work

Work overload/ under load

work relationship

Family illness

Problems with parents

Alcohol drugs-related problems

Indecisiveness

Poor memory

Verbal attacks

Pain attacks

Slow in thinking/ speech

Feeling tired Poor

Lack of energy/ apathy

Poor judgment in work

Inadequate time keeping

Unacceptable appearance

Other Problems are:

Alcohol and Drug abuse Problems

Alcoholism is the third leading cause of death in the UNITED STATES behind heart disease and cancer- ahead of traffic fatalities, suicide and murder.

The alcoholic in the work place causes multiple problems; chronic absenteeism, changes in behavior, physical deterioration, spasmodic work place, lower quantity and quality of work, partial absences, lying, avoiding supervisors, on the job drinking, on the job accidents, encouraging others to drink. The alcoholic lives in a constant state of denial. With apparent sincerity he/she assures colleagues that bouts of over-drinking were "because of"- job tensions, domestic problems, financial worries, and nausea. The truth is that any reason will do as an excuse for drinking. Usually everyone knows the alcoholic has a problem. They can see the detrimental changes. But people are reluctant to say anything to the person. This is a sad part. Early direction and intervention could do so much to save lives and prevent accidents and domestic abuse. Remember before tell tale signs shows up at work, the alcoholic has already done damage in home and as well as work place. Action has to be taken on correct time to prevent problems at work.

Stress

Stress is something all Americans live to one degree or other. The main symptoms are depressions, anxiety, and bodily complain. Stress is caused when active coping or readjustment is demanded. Primary life events produce stresses are "separation and loss:" the death of spouse or close family member or marital separation and divorce. "Occupational stress," while usually not as a severe, occurs more frequently. Executives, managers, supervisors, workers, labourers live and work under a great deal of pressure. Deadlines squeeze between higher and lower authority, office politics, rivalries, monetary competitions, and competitive lifestyles, personal and interpersonal conflicts all contribute to stress on job. Two major source of occupational stress are "time pressure"-constant worry over deadlines whether self imposed or set by others- and "role conflict"-when one job related task interferes with another. "Relocation" is another widespread cause of stress. When an employee is transferred, the family faces uncertainty causes problems in personal front. "Stress management", a major concern in industry, is usually approached from several perspectives.

Marital and Family Issues

Marital problems range from verbal arguments over money, in-laws and reaction to infidelity and sex. Marital problem bring pain and distress. Symptoms are not obvious. They may manifest themselves depressions, irritability, and tension or bodily complains. The surest signal that marriage is in trouble is the breakdown of trust. A person going through marital and family problems will reflect on work by being more absent, lack of concentration, not meeting deadlines on time, etc. This overall affects the performance of individual and company. Proper counselling or help is required.

2.1.6 Who is the Most Effective Counsellor in the Work Place?

The director, the manger, the supervisor. They are best equipped to provide counselling at work because they know what it is like to work there. They have been there. They are still there. Observe cause effect of work place of problems as they unfold; you can compare to current behavior to past behaviour, you can detect the subtle changes in working relationship as they happen ; you can monitor changes in performance; you have the information to analyze the persons environment.

2.1.7 Reason Why Manager Should Counsel

- You can witness events, behavior and so on, at first hand
- You know people whom you are counselling
- You have a strong motive for making sure that they solve their problem as quickly and effectively as possible
- You have strong motive for ensuring that they acquire problem solving skill to prevent a repetition
- You can encourage self responsibility in line with work ethic
- You can put pressure on the client to do what is required to solve their problems
- You are in position to take some practical action to help them

- You are in position to monitor agreed changes and behaviour
- You are in day to day position to help with changes and follow up as and when required
- You have inside knowledge of what is it like to work in that environment
- You have direct experience of the subtitles of commercial life
- You have advanced persuasions skills

Looking at the problems managers can hire psychologists who can be help to others by giving therapy and manger can arrange talks on problem related issues. Some of the issues given below are dealt usually at workplace by professionals:-

Anxiety Management Training

The use of imagintive scenes and relaxation techniques. The procedure first arouses anxiety through a combination of methods including visualizing the anxiety-producing situations. Anxiety is then reduced through the use of competing responses such as relaxation or visualization of success outcomes.

Stress Inoculation

The capacity to cope in anxiety states by increasing self-control and adapting skills. This procedure involves three phases: "education"-understanding cognitive and behavioural responses to stressful situations; "rehearsal"-learning to control psychological arousal through direct action techniques (e.g. physical relaxation, arranging "escape routes") and cognitive techniques (e.g., monitoring negative self-statements and replacing them with adjustment statements); and "application"- using, coping skills in imagine as well as real life stress producing situations.

Thought Stoppage

A way to gain control over irrational thinking that increases stress. Here clients are instructed to stop irrational thoughts by yelling "stop, stop, stop", by pinching themselves or by snapping a rubber band around their wrists. Once the interruption takes place the client taught how to relax and turn attention to positive mental imagery.

Mental Imagery

The use of a number of techniques for combating stress is also used with meditation and hypnosis. The exercise releases tension very fast.

Exercises and Nutrition

The benefits of physical exercise have been well documented. A regulated program builds a healthier mental outlook and increased feeling of self-control. A well-conditioned body is better able to cope with stressful situations.

Non-Assertive and Aggerssive Behaviour

Usually such types of behaviors or cases are referred to psychologists by managers. These behaviors bring about poor human relations and low self-esteem. The "non-assertive" person is usually self denying, inhabited, hurt, and anxious. Such people allow others to choose and control. Needs are not met and rights are not protected. The non-assertive doesn't speak up on behalf of self and as a consequence feels guilty, angry, and bad about self. The "aggressive" person is usually self-aggrandizing at expenses of others. These people get the way they have coming but end up hurting others in the process. The aggressive person generates so much hatred and frustration that he/she feels hurt, defensive and lonely. In effect non-assertive people let others walk all over them while aggressive people walk all over others.

2.2 Case Studies

2.2.1 Case Study 1

An employee assistance program

After a confidential survey multinational manufacturing company became concerned about the number of employees reporting drink, drug, financial and other potentially serious problems. Evidence from line managers also confirmed that productivity was being undermined by a range of personal and work related problems, with reports of bullying and victimization being of particular worry. Alarmingly, the survey revealed that 20 percent of employees reported being bullied in previous year. The organization called in a firm, specializing in work place counselling on the provision of a counselling service. After discussions with the consultants, who had direct experiences in dealing with the issues raised, the company decided to create an in-house employee assistance program (EAP). This was to be staffed by counsellors provided by the consultancy and a number of specially trained managers.

The EAP was designed to operate in a face-to-face manner during the working day and to provide telephone services out of hours. It was governed by four key principles: -

- Free. It was free to all employees including their immediate family.
- Confidential. All the information provided during counselling sessions was confidential.
- Voluntary. Use of the services at the employees' discretion.
- Brief intervention. Al employees were entitled to up to ten hours of counselling per year.

The mission was to address the serious mental, emotional and physical distress reported by significant proportion employees. The anti-harassment part of the program was supported by a publicized statement made by the Board of Directors, which emphasized that there would be an immediate investigation of all reports of bullying by the swift use of grievance and disciplinary procedures. On a practical level those who were the subject of bullying were advised to work through four point plan culminating in a report to their manger and the union representative. This involved:

1. Telling the bully to stop.
2. Keeping a diary of bullying incidence.
3. Writing to the bully each time an incident occurred, and keeping copies of al communications.

4. Discussing bullying incidence with colleagues inorder to discover the extent of the bully's activities.

Those reporting bullying incidence also received continuous support through the counselling program. A later survey indicated that the new approach had significantly reduced reports of work place bullying. Counsellors were able to provide assistance to number of employees including two seniors' executives with drink related problems, and to support larger group whose work performance was suffering as a consequence of break down of personal relationships. Other issues addressed included emotional, health and legal programs, as well as matters concerning equal opportunities, productivity and personality 'clashes'.

Note

Experts report that bullying take place in every type of organization and that it is a significant cause of work place stress. If victims are bullied so badly that they become ill- and figures suggest that this may be the case in up to 70 percent of incidence- employee have positive grounds for making personal injury claims

2.2.2 Case Study 2

OSI STRESS REPORT

Rhett O'Hara (male)

Date of birth: 1Oct 1985

Date of testing: 25Oct 1993

General information: Sample report

The OSI is a questionnaire which aims to measure aspects of stress. The interpretative framework has four key factors:

- The effects of stress on Rhett at the moment.
- His individual characteristics which may help or hinder coping.
- The external factors ha perceives as stressful.
- The coping strategies he uses.

The Effects of Stress

Rhett appears to feel an average level of satisfaction with the nature of the work itself and the quality of interpersonal relationships in the organization. However, he seems to have a feeling that his individual development needs are neglected and that opportunities for personal growth are lacking. Rhett also expresses dissatisfaction with the way the organization is structured (the hierarchy and flow of communication) and with the way its internal processes operate (the degree of flexibility and involvement afforded and the dynamics of supervision). Rhett's responses suggest that his emotional well being is within normal limits but there is a suggestion that his physical symptoms of stress are above normal levels. These may exacerbate further negative effects of stress if they are not dealt with. It is important to create time for winding down and replenishing resources for coping. Leisure activities or simply having fun can release tension. Rhett should find that regular physical exercise is a useful way of using surplus energy. Techniques for structured muscular relaxation are widely available on audio tape. Such techniques should allow Rhett to release existing tensions and prevent further build up.

Individual Characteristics

Rhett appears to have high level of commitment to work but this is combined with a heightened pace of living. There could be an underlying tendency toward impatience and feeling of time-urgency. This could increase Rhett's vulnerability to stress-related effects. It is important that Rhett tries to slow down occasionally and gives time to the replenishment of resources by creating opportunities to relax. Rhett indicates a perception that, although in life generally outcome depends on individual effort, this is not the case in work setting. He appears to believe that, at work, effort and ability do not influence outcomes. There is a feeling of being unable to effect the functioning of the organization. Rhett seems to perceive the organization as having a constraining influence on individual effort.

External Sources of Stress

Of the six external sources of stress examined by the OSI, Rhett reported that three affected him:

• Rhett's need to achieve personal and corporate success appears to be frustrated to a high degree.

• Rhett seems to feel a great deal of stress caused by his perception of the structure and process features of the organization and the general climate at work.

• The interface between home and work appear to be an area of concern for Rhett. Further exploration may be useful to highlight the exact nature of this concern.

Coping Strategies

Rhett appears to use social support as a means of enhancing his capacity to cope with life's demand. He probably finds that talking things through with colleagues is a useful way to reduce the feeling of being under stress. Even without talking things through, just the knowledge that colleagues are supportive is likely to help buffer him against the negative effects of high stress situations. Rhett will usually confront problems and stressful situations rather than avoiding. However, it may be that his feelings get mixed up with facts and objectivity may be reduced. It is important for Rhett to acknowledge feelings but this can be most effectively dealt if they are separated from facts. It would appear that Rhett doesn't tend to separate home and work to the same extent as most people. He should guard against losing too many opportunities to relax and unwind. These are important in helping to replenish resources and maintaining capacity for coping with the continuing demands of work. Rhett shows a lower than average tendency to employ time management strategies to cope with his workload. Nevertheless, at present he appears to be managing the task requirements of his job without experiencing them as particularly stressful.

References

1. Absebteeism and Employment Protection:Three Case Studies; Andreo Ichino and Regina T. Riphahn.

2. Problem Employees, how to improve their behavior and their performance; Peter Wylie and Mardy Garothe. Printed and published by MacKay's of Chatham PLC, Chatham, Kent.

3. Handbook Creative and Innovative Managers; Robert L. Kuhn-Editor in Chef. Printed and published by – McGraw Hill Book Company.

4. Using Phycology in Business- a practical guide for managers, Mark Parkinson, Gower; Published by Gower Publishing Limited

5. Handbook of Industrial , Work and Organizational Psychology Vol. 1 & Vol. 2; Edited by Neil Anderson, Teniz S. Ones, Handan Kepir Sinangin and Chockalingan Viswesvaran; Sage publication. London. Thousands Oaks. New Delhi.

6. Employee Assistance Programmes and Workplace Counselling ; John Derridge, Carry 1. Cooper and Carrolyn Highliy Marchington. Published by Jhon Wiley & Sons, Chischester. New York. Brisbane. Toronto. Singapore.

7. Counselling for Managers. Nigel MacLennan. Published by Gower.

8. Handbook of Management Skills Third Edition. Edited by Borethy M. Stewart. Published by Gower.

19

Behaviour Based Safety in Organizations

This chapter shall be useful in understanding and application of the concept and process of behavior based safety (BBS) for safety professionals concerned about correcting unsafe behaviors for reduction of accidents and promoting safe behaviors for developing injury free culture in their organizations.

Introduction

BBS emphasizes that employees need to take an ownership of their safe as well as unsafe behaviors. If they behave unsafe, they are not punished, instead they are repeatedly told to correct; and when they behave safe, they are encouraged. Both unsafe and unsafe behaviors are counted and displayed. BBS also discusses the unsafe conditions that influences unsafe behaviors.

BBS is a data driven decision-making process. BBS believes that what gets measured gets done and each employee can make a difference in organizational safety. Employees are the basic source of expertise of behavioral change (observe and correct). BBS begins by briefing sessions for all work areas and depts. BBS is teamwork; it is company wide, and people driven. BBS purpose is not to enforce safety rules, force change, gossip about others, reporting to boss. Its purpose is to identify safe and at-risk behaviors, identify possibility for injury, communicating the risk, and helping to identify safer solutions. An implementation team or BBS steering committee monitors its progress. Essentially BBS is not a managcment driven tool for safety. It's an employee driven approach with management support.

Highlights of BBS

These highlights include different features of BBS, which will help us understanding the concepts and processes involved in BBS. This section is organized in three aspects of BBS as below:

(a) BBS Concepts
(b) Observation and Feedback process
(c) BBS implementation and Steering committee

BBS Concepts

1. Actively caring of unsafe and unsafe behaviors leads to improved safety behavior.

2. Listening, praising, group problem solving, and celebrating safety achievements can increase actively caring behaviors.

3. Attitude and behavior link is weak. What we teach does not necessarily get converted into behavior.

4. Attitude is internal, refers to thinking and realization; whereas behaviour is external, observable, and an active experience.

5. BBS addresses individual and social dynamics for safety.

6. BBS does not substitute or replace process evaluation, incident analysis, or environmental solutions. When at-risk behaviours are identified, thecomments are made on the environmental factors that reduce or prevent such behaviors.

7. BBS effects can be seen by measuring safety climate or awareness before and after its implementation for understanding change in safety performance.

8. BBS finally needs customized approach as per needs of your organization.

9. BBS follows DO-IT: define, observe, intervene and test.

10. BBS has shown positive results in terms of safe behaviour and reduction in accidents rates across industries and countries.

11. BBS increases safe behaviours and reduces injuries, illnesses and related financial costs.

12. BBS involves a process of observation and feedback, a system of collecting, analyzing and dissemination of data,

and a proactive approach of management support.

13. BBS is 'actively caring': its beyond the call of duty for safety for self and others.

14. BBS is "safety for each other".

15. BBS is a continuous process till you intend to prevent unsafe behaviors at workplace.

16. BBS is a peer-to-peer learning of safe behaviours.

17. BBS is a process of determining progress in reduction of unsafe behaviours.

18. BBS is more than safety regulations.

19. BBS is not magic. It's a gradual process.

20. BBS is not punishment or disciplinary action or focusing on incident rate, or personal prejudice, or top-down implementation. It's a praise, encouragement and reinforcement of safe behaviors.

21. BBS is not a top-driven but bottom-up approach.

22. BBS is one of the best and latest safety approaches that will help you increase safe behaviors and decrease unsafe behaviors in your organization if applied with full commitment of everybody.

23. BBS is to ultimately develop concern for each other's safety at the workplace and developing empathy for each other.

24. Behavior is a transaction of person (attitude, personality) and environment (management systems, organizational climate). Total safety culture requires attention to these three areas; actively caring improves all these three.

25. BBS is by the people, of the people and for the people. It is based on the established principles of behavior theory in Psychology.

26. Principles of BBS are based on research and an established theory.

Observation and Feedback Process

27. BBS is process of repeatedly going to an employee and making random observations till he reaches safe behaviors and learns the concept of self-observation and observing others for safe performance.

28. BBS is to collect observation data on specific safe and unsafe behaviors by department, date, month and time.

29. BBS trained observers monitor safety behaviors on regular basis.

30. Behavior change precedes attitude change. We see tiger, run and then experience emotion of fear. Realization occurs better by doing.

31. Behavioral change brings 'attitudinal change', not necessarily vice-versa, so focus on behavior and feedback process.

32. Critical behaviors can be listed in checklist based on previous accident and injury records and also by brainstorming.

33. Different observers will notice different safe and unsafe behaviors, which is why employees need to observe each other.

34. Establish observation routines and continuously improve safety process.

35. Feedback can be on-the-spot and graphical feedback, and also weekly / monthly briefings are given.

36. Feedback is an interaction based on genuine concern; let us not doubt our own attitude in giving and receiving feedback, it provides insight into our own behaviors.

37. Feedback is to be given one on one, immediate, specific behavior to be reinforced, appreciate safe behavior to set example.

38. In Hindi language, BBS is all about dekho, and bolo with sensitivity and concern.

39. Individual name of an employee is not recorded in the BBS checklist.

40. Observers target observable safe and unsafe behaviors of co-workers.

41. Observation and couching may take some time to be accepted by co-workers.

42. Observation and feedback skills improve with practice and by using checklist.

43. Observation sampling should be undertaken randomly (not on fixed timings) throughout week.

44. Observational comments: wrong tool used, instead say which tool needs to be used and why.

45. Observe both safe and at-risk behaviours and use detailed comments for problem solving, follow up etc.

46. Observe in team of two (new observer with veteran observer).

47. Observers provide feedback on safe and unsafe behaviors to an observee as per completed checklist.

48. Observers provide immediate feedback for correction of behaviors.

49. Safety coaching fosters open communication about safety.

50. Safety coaching serves as constant reminder for workplace safety.

51. Safety observer / coach in every department may use different critical behaviors (use of PPE, body positioning, use of tools) on checklist, and coaching process (problem solving, follow up).

52. Some characteristics of BBS observer are: concern for others, self-initiation for correcting the observee, developing mutual insight on safe behavior, transforming the observee for self-observation on safe behavior.

Reasons on why a BBS Observer may fail in Observation and Feedback Process:

- An aggressive way of responding
- Giving feedback in front of others.
- He himself not following SOP.
- Improper communication.
- Incorrect way to pass feedback.
- Lack of cordial relations.
- Lack of knowledge about the job of an observee.
- Lack of patience to correct an observee.

- Lack of responding skills.
- Mentioning person instead of unsafe behavior.
- No proper follow up.
- Personal grudge.
- Superiority complex.
- Unable to convey that we are concerned about injury free culture.

While taking care of the above points, a BBS observer should not formalize too much on the observation and feedback process; he should not dominate. An observer should be flexible and sensitive enough to interact with an observee.

BBS implementation and Steering Committee

53. BBS Implementation problems include lack of work force buy-in; unsafe behaviors not defined with precision; accident records / near miss injuries not analyzed properly for targeting accident causing behaviors.

54. BBS may start small and build which means that make a beginning in one department. Remember that there is no best approach. BBS can be customized.

55. BBS needs to be integrated as an organizational system. It's a new initiative, new emphasis and new direction on safety.

56. BBS secret of success is that the safety control is in hands of each employee, they feel empowered and responsible.

57. BBS should have pre and post measures of safety awareness levels of employees in all departments through Safety Awareness Survey in order tocompare its effects before and after implementation.

58. BBS speed of success depends upon existing injury/ accident rate and readiness to implement it.

59. BBS success depends upon a strong steering team, which clearly defines its roles and responsibilities.

60. Behavioral safety management support and

leadership of first line and senior managers can be measured quantitatively.

61. Implementation team/steering committee routinely monitor the progress of BBS.

62. In the long run, BBS is cost effective as it reduces accidents, which actually cost huge.

63. Initially BBS can be implemented in one or two departments and then introduce to other departments.

64. It requires a steering committee comprising of a senior manager, a front line manager and about ten of BBS trained safety observers.

65. It's a myth that you need a consultant for BBS.

66. It's an employee movement on behavioral safety with support and commitment of management.

67. Management allows observers time to conduct observation tours, conduct feedback session, and organize data analysis to display, without which BBS will fail.

68. People are asked to volunteer to either become observers or be a part of steering team. These people carry out responsibilities / duties.

69. Researches indicate that BBS has reduced 40-75% accident rates within six to one year of its implementation.

BBS Training

Before BBS is launched in organizations, training exposure to the employees is essentially envisaged. Hence BBS training workshop of two days duration should include the following components or inputs:

- What is Behavioral Safety?
- Myths of behavior-based safety
- How does Behavioral Safety work?
- Why all the interest in behavioral safety?
- Outcomes of a behavioral safety project
- Psychology of Behavioral Safety
- What behavioral safety is NOT?

- Implementation problems in BBS
- Behavioral Safety observation and Feedback process
- Managers' role in developing Behavioral Safety culture

Responses of BBS Training Participants

1. BBS will increase interaction among workers.
2. 'It has added to my knowledge as safety professional' – a safety officer.
3. We can implement BBS on day-to day basis at workplace.
4. Maximum employees must take BBS training.
5. Involving all employees shall benefit.
6. BBS training makes participants as mini counsellor.
7. One-day training for senior manager would help in implementing BBS.

Conclusion

People behave unsafe because it saves their time and effort (taking short cuts or not using PPE). Environmental solutions don't work so effectively as people may remove guards and work in bad housekeeping. Punishment may lead to positive or negative effects. Attitude change does not help much, as it does not really convert into behavior. So BBS can be tried for still better safety results.

BBS underlines that take active responsibility for safety of each other. Target observable behaviour, focus on positive consequence we expect to receive i.e. change unsafe to safe behaviour; monitor behavioral trends of each individual or group everyday / week / month in order to understand percentage of safe and at-risk behaviors across departments during the years.

In case, PPE are not being used by 50-60 percent of employees, it's an unsafe behaviour; but it's also a system failure, as it does not take action against violation of non-use of PPE. Total safety culture encompasses that safety mechanisms are in place and active, and then implementing

BBS gives wonderful results. According to a senior safety professional, "punishment never works for sustainable results for safety in organizations". Another safety professional added, "BBS is going to be one of the best components of safety in the years to come". According to another senior safety professional, " you may have operational controls at the workplace, you may have told employees for safety, human beings still meet with accidents due to unsafe behaviors". BBS believes that psychological change can be achieved with repeated and active care of each other. BBS emphasizes that when 80-90 percent of accidents and injuries are due to unsafe behaviors, let us focus on unsafe as well as safe behaviors more than the unsafe conditions. Behavior is objective, definable, observable, correctable and measurable.

BBS approach needs a visible presence and a clear management adoption and open communication down the line for its launch with full breath, failing which it is difficult to succeed.

References for Further Reading

1. Algera, J. (1990) Feedback Systems in Organisations, International Review of Industrial and Organisational Psychology, 5, John Wiley and Sons, London.

2. Chuck B. Pettinger, Ph.D. People-Based Safety: The Optimal Approach to Behavior-Based Safety Safety Performance Solutions, Inc.

3. Krause, T. (1995) Employee Driven Systems for Safe Behaviour, Van Nostrand Reinhold, New York.

4. Krause, T.R. (1990) The Behavioural-Based Safety Process, Van Nostrand Reinhold.

5. Locke, E et al (1981) Goal-Setting and Task Performance, Psychological Bullctin, 90, pp.125-152.

6. Marsh, T. et al (1998) The Role of Management Commitment in Determining the Success of a Behavioural Intervention, Journal of the Institute of Occupational Safety and Health, Vol. 2 (4).

7. Mosteller, W.G. (1989) Usability Analysis of Messages from a Security System, in Proceedings of the Human Factors Society 33rd Annual Meeting, 399-403.

8. Pearse, A. (1997) Cited in Managing the Risks of Organisational Accidents, Reason, J., Ashgate Publishing, 20.

9. Reason, J. (1990) Human Error, Cambridge University Press.

10. Reason, J. (1997) Managing The Risks of Organisational Accidents, Ashgate Publishing.

11. Skinner, B. (1974) About Behaviourism, Jonathan Cape, London.

12. Stewart, M.G. (1991) Dependence of Human Error Probabilities, in Ergonomics and Human Environments. Proceedings of the 27th Annual Conference of the Ergonomics Society of Australia, Coolum, Australia, 207 -14.

20

Counselling in Indian Organizations

This chapter *is a qualitative study of 160 male managers and 120 female managers interviewed in 54 organizations in order to understand the managerial perspective of employee counselling issues: 1. Problems faced by colleagues/ staff of women and male managers; 2. Ways in which problems affect their colleagues/ employees; 3. Ways in which the managers helped their colleagues and subordinates overcome the problems; 4. Attitudes of male and female managers towards introducing counselling in organizations. In-depth personal interviews were conducted with the help of a structured questionnaire using open-ended questions.*

Introduction

V. Orlans (1989) discussed the need for counselling in the workplace, the recognition of that need, and the requirements for counselling schemes, and concluded that the success of a counselling scheme depends on the commitment of senior management to the values of counselling, the design of the scheme, and on the counselors working effectively in the organizational setting.

A study 'workplace counselling from a personnel proffessional's perspective' (Mike Donne,1992) found that employers are slowly increasing their understanding and awareness of counselling, the services it provides and its professionals. Counselling agencies need to promote not only their services but the principles of good counselling to enable employers to make informed decisions and choices.

Kirk, Andrea; Brown, David, (2003) noticed that Employee Assistance Programs (EAPs) provide counselling and consulting services that focus on the prevention and/ or remediation of personal problems experienced by employees, or members of their families. EAPs are currently considered one of the main vehicles for occupational stress management and are rapidly evolving into providers of holistic wellbeing programs in the workplace. This form of service delivery has, however, been criticised for focusing interventions at the individual rather than at the organisational level. While research evidence is not fully supportive of the effectiveness of EAPs, data suggests that these programs do impact positively on employee mental health, and are perceived by employees as a desirable workplace resource.

Swedish hospital personnel were followed over an 8-year period, characterized by staff redundancies and restructuring processes. Self-rated and administrative data sets from 1994 to 2001 allowed for studying long-term consequences of organizational instability for staff health and work conditions. The aim was to identify, on a work-unit level, trends in work and health conditions and their interdependence. Regression analysis showed a downward trend in mental health and an upward trend in long-term sick leave. Increasing trends of work demands were accompanied by deteriorating mental health, and decreasing time to plan work showed the strongest association with increasing long-term sick leave. Job satisfaction and support were decreasing. A stable short-term sick leave rate over years related to lack of support (Petterson, I; Hertting, A; Hagberg, L; Theorell, T. 2005).

Many firms today realize the importance of attracting and retaining highly skilled, quality employees as a necessary component of their competitive advantage. One of the reasons that a quality workforce along with innovative tools for attracting and retaining has become so important is because previous sources of competitive advantage have become less important overtime. Today, HR practitioners are busy developing new and innovative tools to attract and retain quality workforce. One such tool that soon is likely to gain popularity in the corporate world is Employee Counselling. Employee Counselling is a service offered by companies to their employees. Counselling is a process of helping people to learn how to solve certain interpersonal, emotional and decision problems. Organisations that have instituted formal counselling services have reaped the benefits of higher motivation and morale, better stress management, improved productivity and less likelihood of legal claims for negligence.

Purpose of the Study

Stress in the workplace has become a phrase used to describe anything from petty annoyances to critical incidents. Today stress often not only goes beyond issues of low pay, staff cuts and excessive hours, but also is linked to violent attacks, fatal road accidents, addictions, marital problems, divorces, suicide or injuries. While organizations may not be responsible for trauma that occurs outside the workplace, they will still suffer the consequences of incidents such as the illness of a child, marital problems, and death among others. Employees themselves are also driving the trend towards abolishing stress, as they increasingly demand a wider range of leisure facilities and the provision of a tension-free workplace over and above other perks. Facilities such as gyms, yoga and relaxation provisions at the workplaces are being introduced for improving working lives.

But the way, corporate sector has opened up to the world economy, it is now high time for organizations in India to employ employee-orientated HR processes like counseling, coaching and mentoring. The corporate world is changing and so are the human resource management practices. It is imperative to adapt the changing styles to manage our people better. It is not just for the benefit of the employees but in the interest of the organization to show that 'we care' about this important segment of our stakeholders.

This survey was therefore undertaken in order to gauge the attitudes of male and female managers towards workplace counselling and understand how far they are aware of the problems faced by their subordinates and colleagues in the workplace.

Sample

The sample consisted of 160 male managers and 120 female managers between 26 to 55 years of age in 54 organizations (including private and public sector, and MNCs) from different parts of India such as Mumbai, Bangalore, and Hyderabad, ranging from banks to IT, pharmaceutical companies to call centers. Data were collected from varied work backgrounds, different age groups and different levels of management: upper, middle and lower working in various departments through in-depth personal interviews and e-mails in a few cases with the help of a structured questionnaire using open-ended questions. The present paper is extracted from this large study.

Results and Discussion

The survey results have been presented under the following sections:

1. Problems faced by colleagues/ staff of women and male managers
2. The ways in which problems affect their colleagues/ employees.
3. The ways in which the managers helped their colleagues and subordinates overcome problems.
4. Attitudes of male and female managers towards having counselling in organizations.

1. Problems faced by Colleagues/Subordinates of Male and Female Managers

The first question asked to managers was: have you come across any serious personal/professional problem that your employee faced in the past 12 months? Please describe.

Male Managers Responded

1. My subordinate suffered from the *problem of alcoholism* very recently. He started drinking very heavily because of which his attendance record deteriorated which in turn affected his salary. His drinking also wrecked his family life because he started remaining away from home for days together. He shirked his responsibility towards his family. In the office, he never completed assignments on time leading to high tempers from the top management. He also started asking for small loans from his colleagues

in order to get money for alcohol. His reputation in the company took a blow because of his errant behaviours towards his colleagues and superiors. He had taken a loan and now was unable to repay it back.

2. One of my employees was found to be *HIV positive* in the western blot tests. This was revealed when antibiotics were found to be non-effective. For a long time he was physically ill, which everyone thought was normal illness but as time went by, his health started deteriorating and he became a person with only bones and no flesh. No amount of antibiotics would revert his condition.
3. The problem occurred to my two *subordinates who were married to each other*. During the work hours there was to be a competition between them in who would excel whom. Many times, they used to confront each other in the workplace, in the cafeteria etc thus making a public display of their arguments. They also used to bring their personal grudges into the workplace.
4. The problem my colleague faced was *lack of computer skills/ knowledge*. Since she did not know many computer related programmes, her speed of work suffered. She was unable to handle computer programs like Excel and PowerPoint, due to which she had to manually do the assignments, which could otherwise have been done by the computer.
5. My subordinate and his wife were living happily with a child of 4 yrs. His wife headed a Tupperware company. One fine day when he came home from work, he found her dead in his house. She died of a cardiac arrest. The death was very shocking because she did not suffer from any illness or even heart problems.

Female Managers Responded

6. The problem faced by my subordinate was that of *uncertainty and role conflicts* within the organization

due the recent merger. He was in the dark about what functions will be performed by him in the organization. He was unclear about his responsibilities. Secondly, he was de-motivated because he was working on a project without being properly guided. He didn't even know whether the project would see the light of the day or not.

7. One of my female subordinates' husband was a *drug addict*. Hence, she was under constant stress because she did not know the cause of his addiction. Her behaviour too became erratic and was reflected in her efficiency at work.
8. My colleague in office suffered from an *abusive marriage* for 3 years. She did not receive any support from her in-laws as well as her own parents. Her husband would beat her up every second day. She would turn up in office with bruises and scratches on her face and body and give the pretext of falling off the stairs or banging herself against the door. On many occasions she did try to put up a brave front but did not succeed. She has got a divorce now but she is still recovering from her trauma.
9. One of my colleagues bought a *house on loan,* excecting a promotion in this year. But the promotion never came his way. Now since his income remains the same he is struggling to pay off his loan.
10. The problem my colleague faced in the recent times was that of *getting a housemaid* because she and her husband are both working and hold good jobs. The problem occurred because her husband was transferred from Pune to Mumbai. Previously, they did have a maid to look after their child and ailing mother-in-law, but in Mumbai they were unable to find someone as dependable since they were new in the city.

The responses revealed that majority of the staff and colleagues of the male and female managers faced marital problems such as divorce, abusive marriage and rivalry between spouses. Alcoholism, drug addiction and disease such as AIDS also featured on the problems faced by employees and fellow colleagues. Other main problems included death of a spouse, uncertainty and role conflict in ones job, domestic and financial problems. Additionlly, it was seen that some of the employees also faced problems of grappling with new tecnology such as computers.

Overall, it can be gauged the kind of problems affecting the staff/colleagues of male and female managers were personal in nature. the responses given by the managers reflected the extent to which they were updated about the problems their employees were facing. This only goes to show that there are managers who care for their employees and who are aware about the problems that their employees and colleagues are undergoing. Of course, there were other managers in this survey who were not willing to share any problems their employees were facing. This can be interpreted by saying that either they are really unwilling to share their employees personal information or that they are unware and not willing to understsand the problems that bog down the employees. For many managers, the second interpretation might hold true because the managers themselves are becoming so caught up with their own work problems that they forget that colleagues might be suffering too. "People do get so involved with their own work that they sometimes don't think about helping colleagues," says Azim Premji, CEO of Wipro, India.

2. Effects of the Problems faced by Colleagues/ Subordinates of Male and Female Managers

The second question asked to managers was: Please explain in which ways did the problems faced by your colleagues/subordinates (as described in section 1 above) affect him/her personally or professionally?

Male Managers Responded

1. The problem of alcoholism affected my colleague badly in a personal and professional manner. His alcoholism came in the way of his personal life. Since he started staying away from home, he neglected his family and children. He could not

provide money to his family as he started spending it on alcohol. The situation worsened when his wife threatened him that she will leave him and filed for a divorce. Health-wise, he became anorexic as he hardly ate properly. He also suffered from jaundice for a long time but due to lack of money, did not get himself treated. In a professional manner, his reputation in office deteriorated, his absenteeism increased and he rarely concentrated on his job. The situation worsened when the management wanted him to leave the organization.

2. When the employee came to know about his condition (HIV positive) it affected him psychologically as well as physically. He started becoming thinner and thinner day-by-day. His immune system was down so he would catch any and every infection. Since medicines were not having an effect, he was affected with multiple infections at the same time. When the word spre-spread about his condition, his reputation was spoilt as people started looking down upon him. His family stayed away from him, so he did not have their support. They were kept in the dark about his condition. Psychologically he suffered from depression. He would be stressed and sad all the time and feared death. As far as professional effects were concerned, he could not attend his workplace due to which his earning capacity came to almost zero.

3. The couple went into legal action against each other and filed for a divorce. As they were good performers, their altercations demoralized them and their reputation fell down in front of their colleague's eyes. They slowly started losing interest in their jobs and at least one of them would absent from work to avoid arguments with the other. Their arguments in the cafeter-cafeteria had made them a laughing stock in the company. Eventually, both had turned bitter.

4. As my colleague got a transfer he faced problems of accommodation and finance. He had to spend double the amount of money on his accommodation as well

as food and on traveling. Secondly, getting adjusted to the new place as well as the people was causing him tremendous stress. His job profile in the company also underwent a change following the merger, so he was also battling with role conflict. There was unclear communication to him regarding this functions, which led to high anxiety and frustration in him. He felt homesick for a few months.

5. The death affected his personal as well as his family life. His personal life was in a chaotic state since he has to take care of his child all by himself. He underwent depression for around 6-8 months after his wife's death. He was plagued by stress, anxiety and nervousness. Professionally, his productivity decreased because of less concentration on his job. He seemed tensed in the workplace all the time. His absenteeism was on a rise. All in all his condition was extremely pitiable.

Female Managers Responded

6. The problem affected him by bringing down his morale. He felt that he was not important to the organization, as the top management was not taking any initiative to clear his confusions. He was also experiencing confusion regarding what he was supposed to contribute from his side towards the betterment of the organization. He was extremely stressed.

7. Her behavior changed drastically due to her drug addict husband. She faced financial difficulties because he would whisk all her money into addiction. She was under constant stress and anxiety. Her absenteeism increased, started doing poorly at work and appeared tensed and sad all the time as opposed to her cheerful self. Her communication with others in the workplace was also affected.

8. Personally, my colleague became extremely nervous and would cry at the drop of a hat. She would also lose her patience very quickly. She became pale and stressed out because of constant beating and tens-

ions on her home ground. To add to her woes, she had to repay a big loan that she had taken to buy a house and furnishings. In the workplace, she would try and be cheerful, but couldn't manage all the time. Although she was regular in office, she could not concentrate on her job and made silly mistakes. She would work overtime so that she could stay away from home. She did not share her problem with any-anyone till she was admitted in the hospital for a broken back.

9. He seems much tensed at work since he is struggling to make ends meet. He is no longer the performer that he was and tends to blame the organization for his condition.
10. The problem affected her both ways. Professionally, there was less commitment at work from her side because she would keep contacting different people to get a house. She would neglect her work. Absenteeism was also on a rise because she would get embroiled in an emergency at home every now and then. Her superiors were not satisfied with her work, as she would not put quality in it, which led to many altercations between them. Personally there was a lot of stress and physical strain, as she had to work in office as well as home. She was tensed about her family when she was away from work also. Arguments between the spouses were also a common complaint.

The responses revealed that the problems faced by the employees and colleagues of male and female managers affected them personally as well as professionally.

Majority of employees suffered from some or the other kind of marital problem. It was seen from the responses that an abusive marriage lead employees to become pale and nervous due to constant beatings from their spouse. Additionally, they suffered from many physical ailments such as back pain, headaches and fractures. Employees also became extremely sensitive and cried at the drop of a hat. Losing patience, becoming nervous was also a common phenomenon.

Couple rivalry on the other hand created bitter conflicts between the couples. They constantly argued, be it in the workplace or at home. The death of a spouse also had similar effects on employees. Employees experienced demotivation, felt lonely and frustrated.

It could be clearly seen from the responses of the managers that the above problems also affected the professional lives of the employees very badly and affected the organization indirectly. Absenteeism increased, they became less productive, inefficient and made silly mistakes in their work. Their concentration in their job also decreased.

Alcoholic employees too caused multiple problems for themselves as well as for the organization. Alcoholism caused problems such as chronic absenteeism, changes in behavior, physical deterioration, spasmodic work place, lower quantity and quality of work, partial absences, lying, avoiding supervisors, on the job drinking, on the job accidents, borrowing money and encouraging others to drink. Personally, their family life was affected because of neglect and improper behavior towards family members.

In contrast, employees battling with drugs suffered from depression, health problems, become pale and weak and inefficiency in the workplace. Employees whose spouses suffered from drug addictions caused them significant problems in terms of financial and mental constraints. They suffered from nervous bouts and stress. Problems with keeping up with new technology saw employees being inefficient at work, not being able to meet deadline and being under work pressure. Similarly financial and domestic problems created anxiety.

Overall it can be seen that problems affect the personal and professional lives of employees. Productivity, employee morale, efficiency and profits are the key to any successful organizations. But when the employees suffer from problem, all their anxieties and pressures are reflected on their job thus causing observable decreases in the profits of an organization.

3. The Way in which the Managers Helped their Colleagues/Subordinates Overcome Problems

The third question asked to managers was: could you give a title or a heading to the problem faced by your colleagues/subordinates and how did you help your employee/colleague overcome the problem? Please describe.

Male Managers responded

(1) The heading of this problem is Alcoholism. When the management wanted to sack him from our organization, I intervened because he was my immediate subordinate. I showed them his past records where he had consistently performed well and when they were convinced they aborted the thought of asking him to leave. Next, I directly spoke to his family and him. It was then I realized that he was under a financial debt and was not being able to repay the loan that he had taken. I directed him to the Alcoholic Anonymous where he realized that drinking was making the problem worse. He slowly started recovering from alcoholism and started saving money. Till now he hasn't paid the loan fully but he is making efforts to pay bit by bit. His family too has become supportive of him, as they have alsounderstood the cause behind his errant behavior.

(2) I supported the employee financially as well as mentally. Since he was my employee, it was my duty to support him when he was in need. I directed him to counseling centers for HIV+ves where he was counseled and told about the disease in detail. I also helped to battle it out of depression by showing him the positive side of life. I asked him to do

(3) The problem could be titled as *Couple Rivalry*. I helped my colleagues by advising them to have a one-to-one discussion with each other, seek a family counselor and suggested one of them to shift to another job. I spoke them about how they could team up with each other and better their skills and succeed. Finding the root cause of the grudge against each other was another way they could tackle the problem

(4) I advised my colleague to join a computer class close to his house so that he could do better at the workplace and read some books on computers whenever he had some free time on hand.

(5) The title is *Bereavement.* As his manager I saw to it that he got adequate rest to recuperate from the trauma he suffered so I took care of his leaves. As far as I could and whenever I had the time, I would speak to him, and encourage him by speaking positively. I advised his friends in the workplace to interact with him and support him whenever he needs it. Basically, we saw to it that nobody reminded him of his trauma.

Female Managers Responded

(6) *Uncertainty* is the title. I helped my colleague by encouraging him to do his best in the project assigned to him even if the projects would not fall through. I advised him to constantly keep contacting the top management or his superiors to achieve clarity in the role he was supposed to play in the organization. I also advised him to meditate so that he could keep his mind off the tensions.

(7) The problem is *Drug Addiction.* I was observing my lady subordinate since, her behavior changed. It also brought to my notice her increased absenteeism and inefficiency at work. After probing a lot, she told me her problem. With the help of a few colleagues of mine, I traced down a counselor and asked her to go to the counselor along with her husband where they were counseled about the disease and its causes. Further I got him admitted to a de-addiction centre with the help of the counselor. It was Muktangan at Pune. As for the lady employee, she would confide in me whenever she felt a loss of confidence and nervousness. I gave her a patient listening whenever I found the time.

(8) *Abusive Marriage* is the title. When I came to about my colleague's problem, I started to act on it immediately. Firstly, I spoke to her in-laws and parents

and asked for their support. She is a religious person, so I would go with her to various places where there were astrologers and saintly people. I was with her throughout her divorce proceeding and even after that. I couldn't help her financially, but was her strong moral support whenever she needed me. I used to encourage her and advise her to put up a brave front.

(9) I have provided moral support to him.

(10) *Domestic Problem* is what I would title it as. Since I am a citizen of Mumbai, I knew a place where there was a service agency, which specialized in getting a dependable aid. I gave my colleague the contact number and helped her get a dependable aid thus reducing her problem to a great extent.

The responses revealed that employees who suffered from problems such as death of a spouse or an abusive marriage took time to overcome their problem and had not fully recovered from the trauma.

It was indeed a welcome change to see that many managers of both the genders shared the problem of his/her employee and were actively involved in finding a solution to the employee's problem. It was seen that managers whose employees or friends suffered from grave problems such as an abusive marriage, death of a spouse, diseases like AIDS and other kinds of addictions, cared, advised and supported their subordinates/colleagues. These managers directed their employees to seek advise from various professional and qualified counselors/psychologists to deal with their problems. Managers also reported of helping their employee's spouse in getting admitted to a rehabilitation center.

The managers admitted that they provided financial help to their needy subordinates. They also went to the extent of speaking to the families, friends of the employees, asking them to lend a helping hand and open the channels of communications fully. Managers also took care of the leaves of the employees so that their employees would get adequate rest and become more efficient the next time they joined work. They also reported becoming a mediator between the top management and the concerned employee so that the employee's message could be transferred to the management.

Overall, it was seen that managers provided a moral support and lent a patient ear to the problems of their subordinates and friends. But there was one thing that was most common amongst all these managers. They reported that they listened and supported their employees "whenever we had time". This means that as managers, they tried their best to help an employee recuperate from his/her problems, and also provided a moral support, but they too are humans and have deadlines and targets to meet, therefore they too cannot spend a large amount of time from their busy schedule to deal with the problems of their employees. It also happens many times that employees are not comfortable in speaking about their problems due to which the help that a manager can provide to his subordinate is limited.

A business environment can absorb the usual ups and downs of its employees. But as an employer, however, it is important to address the situation if an employee's personal difficulties start to affect job performance or other employees and this was effectively reflected in the responses given by the managers. The care and support shown by the managers can go a long way in boosting commitment, morale and self esteem of the employees.

The managers and superiors are one of the best persons to take care of the employee in the workplace because the managers can witness events, behavior and so on, at first hand, they have inside knowledge of what is it like to work in that environment, they have direct experience of the subtleties of commercial life, they are in a position to follow up with the progress of their colleagues and staff.

4. Attitudes of Male and Female Managers Towards Introducing Counselling in Organizations

The fourth question asked to managers was: do you think counseling in organizations could help employees? if yes, in which ways? What should organizations do to help employee's over-come personal/professional problems?

Male Managers Responded

(1) Yes, I definitely think that counseling in organizations could help the employees. If we refer to the problem above, it makes us realize that the problem was about a financial debt, which led the employee to take to alcohol. If there was a counselor in the organization, the employee would have recovered earlier and a lot of his problems would be solved. Sometimes the cause to a behavior are different which we as corporate processionals do not realize and it takes a counselor make us understand by going to the roots of the issue. As mangers we can support him to our full capacity but there is a limit to what we as managers can do. But a counselor is equipped with professional skills and is adept at counseling people. I fully support the idea of a counselor in organization. An organization can have a counselor on site, which is available to employees whenever they feel to talk about their problems. The organization can also have a telephone counseling facility so that a person may not need to show his identity and that might go a long way, as confidentiality is the key to a good counseling set up.

(2) Yes I definitely think counseling in organization is a must. It is needed for all kinds of employees from the top management to the worker level. As Superiors we can support and encourage employees but when it it comes to serious problems a counselor is the best person. A counselor can not only counsel the employee in the time of need but also at other times can serve the purpose of an information giver on various issues such as Depression, AIDS, Stress Management etc. Programs are conducted more often for educated corporate people, but if the same are conducted with the uneducated/poorly educated workers it may go a long way to prevent various disorders. Counselors can do these programs as they can adapt to all kinds of people. . It is seen that even small problems can have hazardous effects on the employee's morale and productivity and the

skilled counselor is the best person to deal with the employee's problems. Similarly, there are chances of full recovery when problems are solved early with the help of a skilled professional. Similarly if there is a counselor in the organization, then employees do not need to hunt for another counselor because many a times they are unaware of institutes where they find one. Thus, in an organization a counselor and a medical doctor are two people who can be employed to help people cope with their problems and return efficiently to work. An organization can either have an in-house counselor or at least call a counselor on a periodic basis.

(3) Yes surely, counseling in organization could help employees the right direction as there might be chances that they are lost or demoralized due to events at home, work issues or any other tougher problem. This impacts the output in terms of their performance and their productivity at work is reduced. Organizations can hold offsite workshops for relaxation, give satisfactory leaves to employees when needed and cater to them at their level rather than making more business all the time. It is best to solve a problem at the inception stage rather than when it becomes worse. In counseling, (4) key words are the most important Discretion, Confidentiality, Confidence on Counselor, and Trust on Counselor. Organizations can have an in-house counselor to counsel people.

(4) No, I don't think Counseling in organization can hap people solve problems. According to me friends and family members as well as an employee's boss are the prime people because of whom an employee can get solve his problem. Speaking to a third unknown party can create unnecessary dangers, as the personal problem may no longer remain personal. Employees may not be able to relate to a complete outsider, and his problems will remain unsolved.

(5) No I don't think that having counselling in the organization would prove beneficial. I think employees'

colleagues and family members would be the best remedy to help overcome problems. In the workplace, a manager can provide the much needed support.

Female Managers Responded

(6) Yes, Counselling may help if it is individualized and customized. It may create a healthier work environment and increase productivity of employees. Looking at a bigger picture, it will help the organization also as reduced problems will reduce the absenteeism of the employees, and reduce turnover. Employee commitment will be more, as employees will feel secure in the organization. Additionally, organization should conduct training for managers to deliver counselling since managers work more closely with the employees and know them better. Organizations should take more interest in their employees by providing them various facilities such as appropriate leaves, medical help, counseling and other legal/financial help. I also believe, managers can also help employees overcome their problems provided they have the right skills. Organizations should promote this concept and see to it that there is a workshop for managers where they will be trained to be skillful in handling employee's problems. This will also help to build close relations between employee and superiors.

(7) Yes. Counseling should be conducted in organizations. The Organizations can have a counselor who attends to the employees by interacting on one-to-one basis. To keep it confidential the counselor should be assigned a cabin for himself/herself. Counseling can bring about increasing productivity, increased levels of job satisfaction, and increased levels of job commitment. And reduce absenteeism. Also a counsellor, who is an outsider and a stranger, will make it much more easier for employees to share their problems without feeling insecure. Organization can also form a grievance cell headed by the concerned manager and a counsellor to allow employees to voice the problems. Once a week, a meeting should be held

with the concerned employees as to review the progress. This way, both the organization and the employees can work hand-in-hand. An organization can demonstrate the care for its employees by providing appropriate facilities.

(8) Yes, I surely think that counseling in organization would help the employees. A counselor can help people find the right solution so that people do not blindly follow some wrong path just because it comes from someone they know. It will help employees to go to the roots of their problems. It helps the employee in the day-to-day working with the help of a Personal Touch to boost up the morale so that the employee gets motivated. The top management should take such actions. It also improves the core values of the individuals, which can be an indicator towards a good corporate citizen in the organizational family But before introducing counseling in the organization, the HR should take an initiative to clear the misconception of their people about counseling, so that they can make better use of the service provided to them. Counseling can be useful if and only if, it is given at the right time. Problems should be kept confidential and trust should be evoved by the counselor. Organizations can have either a counselor in-house or can have an online chat session with an experienced professional.

(9) Yes, I think counselling would be helpful to solve an employees' personal and professional problems.

(10) Yes, I think counseling in organization would be of great help to employees to reduce their personal and professional problems. Especially in today's "Fight the time" situation, there is no time left for an employee even to reflect his/her own problem peacefully. The organization can play a great role in having a counselor in the organization who can counsel the employees and support them at the time of need. It is extremely important to have an efficient counselor because personal issues and professional issues can hamper an employee's state

of mind leading to decreased efficiency on his part. A counselor can be a mediator between the organization and the employee so that the real reason for an employees' decreased efficiency can be revealed and the employee can be saved from being fired. At the same time an organization can have systems which can give an employee other kind of information such as legal help/financial help etc.

The response analysis revealed that overall there were positive responses towards the idea of introducing counselling in the organization.

Managers who felt that counseling was the appropriate means of overcoming with ones problems articulated various benefits of having counseling in the organization. According to these managers, introducing counseling in the organization would increase productivity, efficiency of employees, increase job commitment amongst the employees, increase levels of job satisfaction and employee morale, reduce absenteeism and improve psychological well being. They felt that individual counseling in the workplace shows promise for helping employees, especially those with poor health, to become more physically active and fit. It helps the employee in the day-to-day working with the help of a Personal Touch to boost up the morale so that the employee gets motivated.

Additionally, the managers were of the opinion that having workplace counseling would benefit the organization by reducing employee turnover, costs and bring about an organizational change. While some others said that providing workplace counseling to the staff will demonstrate that the organization cares for their employees, knows what the employees endure and share their problems as well, this feeling would further boost loyalty towards the organization. Managers also felt that having a counselor in the organization would help to conduct early intervention in the form of support, advice and information. It will also provide peace of mind and reduce the negative effects of any problem. They also felt that a healthy environment in the organization could be developed if counselling was introduced.

Managers also commented that counseling will bring about an increase in the self esteem of the employees because the counselor will help the employees to come up with various alternatives to solve their own problem, giving the employees a feeling that they are not dependent on anyone to solve their problem. According to many, a counselor could play the role of an information giver who could provide information on various diseases such as AIDS and other kinds of addictions. The managers opined that having a counselor in the organization meant that they did not need to hunt for counselors or professionals to help employees with their problems.

There are numerous studies that articulate the benefits of counseling. In a systematic review published by Professor McLeod in his paper, Counselling in the Workplace: A Systematic Study of the Research Evidence, it was found that Counseling can achieve a reduction in work related stress in more than 50% of people. It showed that levels of work related symptoms and stress returned to the normal range for more than 50% of clients in two thirds of the studies included. Levels of sickness and absence also fell by 25-50% in trials evaluating these factors. Counseling interventions had smaller, but significant, positive effects on levels of job commitment, work functioning, job satisfaction, and substance misuse.

In other studies Professor John McLeod (2000) examined over 80 separate studies, published and unpublished, spanning a period between 1954 and 2000 reflecting the experiences of more than 10,000 clients who have made use of workplace counselling. Some of the results are articulated below:

- Levels of work-related symptoms return to the normal range for more than half of all clients, and levels of sickness and absence also fell by 25-50% (In one 1998 study by Professor Cary Cooper of the University of Manchester Institute of Science and Technology, the rates of sickness/ absence actually fell by an average of 60%).
- Over 90% of the employees who make use of workplace counselling are highly satisfied with the service

they have received, would use it again if necessary, and would recommend it to colleagues.

In articulating the benefits counseling would serve in the organization, managers were of the opinion that counselors would help individuals to articulate their problems better to a counselor because they would be complete strangers, therefore feelings of trust and confidentiality would be strengthened. Further they opined that a counselor would be able to go to the roots of the problem and then suggest appropriate measures to overcome the problem, something that the managers may not be able to do.

Secondly, they felt that as managers they were doing their best to help their employees overcome the problems, but since they too had deadlines and targets to meet, they could not give adequate time to their employees. In this regard, Kaila (2002) found amongst managers in metropolitan Mumbai that 80 per cent of them experienced the most common workplace challenges such as: meeting deadlines, working in a competitive industry, managing finances, exhausting working hours, and rotation work in addition to handling regular tasks (such as sales, marketing, training, research and development, and accounts of core clients). Hence the managers may find it difficult to provide counselling in a professional manner. Lastly, the managers felt that very often employees felt inhibited in sharing their problems with employees because of the fear of being negatively evaluated or being sacked.

Indeed, for many employees visualizing their manager in a dual role may be difficult. Not only sharing problems with their managers cross boundaries but also puts employees in an impossible situation: asking, on one hand, that they share personal issues with their manager, and, on the other hand, that they be ready for appraisal vis-à-vis their career with the same manager. In short, asking managers to be counselors creates role conflicts for them and confusing responsibilities for their employees.

While most of the managers felt that counseling would be beneficial to the employees, there were some male managers who said that counseling would not serve any benefits to the employees. In their opinion, an employees' friends, colleagues, and family members are the people who can support the employee and help him deal with the problems. In the workplace, they felt, a manager was the best person who can provide the much needed care. Secondly, they also felt that employees might not be comfortable in speaking to a counselor, who is a complete stranger to them. Here, it can be seen that managers are unaware or are rather unwilling to accept the benefits provided by availing counseling facilities in the organization. This might be because of the misconceptions, taboo or the stigma that surround counselling.

Thus, it can be concluded by saying overall, the attitudes towards having counselling in the organizations were both more positive as well as negative. Since, there were more positive than negative responses towards counselling, we can say that the trend is clearly changing. Employers as well as employees are slowly realizing the benefits that counselling would serve. It is hoped that even the negative views towards counselling will also change with time.

There are various suggestions given by the managers on how counseling in organization can be introduced and other measures an organization should take to help employees overcome their problems.

It was seen that majority of the managers felt that having an in-house counselor would be the best way in which counseling in the organization could be set up. According to them an in-house counselor would be available to the employees whenever they want to speak about their problems. Additionally, they also felt that counselors in the organizations should be given a special cabin, to create a confidential outlook. A few managers also suggested that along with having a counselor in the organization, facilities such as providing legal and financial assistance, medical help etc. should also be set up within the organization. In a nutshell, these managers were actually pointing towards having EAP in the organization which is basically a work located programme of counseling support and advice to assist employees resolve personal anxieties which may be affecting their performance at work. An EAP includes a variety of facilities such as face-to-face counseling, providing legal, financial, medical and a host of other programmes.

Others suggested having an offsite counseling workshops where programs such as stress management, time management, information regarding various diseases such as AIDS and other kinds of addictions will be delivered by experienced counselors. Some felt having a contract with a counselor who will attend the organization on a periodic basis would also be effective.

Managers seemed extremely enthusiastic while speaking about having counseling in the organization and this was reflected in their responses. They came up with innovative suggestions about how counseling could be made a part of the organization. Amongst these, one of them was having an on-line chat session with an experienced counselor whenever an employee was bogged down by a problem. Others suggested having a telephone counselling with a counselor. It can be clearly seen here that some managers are worried about the fact that their identities or their employees' identities should not be revealed while undergoing counseling. Such worries could be put to rest as one response from a manager says that before introducing counselling, the human resource department should take special efforts to clear the misconceptions about counselling from the minds of people so that they are relieved and are not under any sort of doubts while undergoing counselling. This will not only take care of the confidentiality part but the counselling session will move smoothly because both parties involved will trust each other.

Some managers gave suggestions, which would help to strengthen the bond between the organization and the employees. According to them, a grievance cell should be set up in the organization, which includes a counselor and a superior of the employees. This grievance cell will help employees voice their problems and their concerns and then accordingly, the counselor and the superior will suggest measures to help the employee overcome the problem. Such measure will make employee feel cared for and elevate their commitment towards the organization. Another benefit would be that the employees and employers would come close to each other.

Apart from counselling, managers felt that organizations should give employees appropriate leaves, and hold other kinds of offsite workshops. Training managers to develop counselling skills was also one suggestion given by a manager. Indeed, this suggestion is very valuable because it will help the managers develop a closer bond between themselves and their employees because they will be more adept at empathizing with their staff and suggesting measures to overcome problems.

The attitudes and suggestions of managers towards counselling indicate that they are really concerned about the mental and physical well being of their colleagues and subordinates and believe that they are in some way responsible to see to it that their workforce is productive and healthy.

References

Donne, M. (1990). Workplace counselling from personnel professional's perspective. Journal of Workplace Counselling. 2 (4), 185-196.

Kaila H.L. (2002). Stress is a way of life for Mumbai workers. Psychology International, Vol. 13, No. 3, Fall 2002.

Kirk, Andrea; Brown, David (Jul 2003). Employee assistance programs: a review of the management of stress and wellbeing through workplace counselling and consulting. Australian Psychologist. Volume 38, Number 2, pp. 138 – 143.

McLeod, J. and McLeod, J. (2000). Counselling in the workplace -a systematic study of research evidence. Rugby: British Association for Counselling and Psychotherapy. www.emeraldinsight.com

Orlans, V. (1989). Counselling in the workplace: a review and thoughts for the future. Journal of Workplace Learning. 1(1), 33-49.

Petterson, I; Hertting, A; Hagberg, L; Theorell, T. (2005). Are trends in health conditions interrelated? A study of Swedish hospital employees in the 1990s. Journal of Occupational Health Psychology. Volume 10, Number 2, pp. 110 – 120.

21

Managerial Problems in Indian Organizations

This chapter is a qualitative study of 275 male managers and 140 female managers interviewed in 81 organizations in order to review trend of managerial issues: 1. Problems faced by male and female managers; 2. Ways in which problems affect male and female managers; 3. Coping strategies used by male and female managers to overcome their problems; and 4. comparison between the male and female managers with respect these issues. In-depth personal interviews were conducted with the help of a structured questionnaire using open-ended questions.

Introduction

In a study on stress coping styles among German managers (Kirkcaldy, B.D. and Furnham, A.F. 1999), the abbreviated German version of Occupational Stress Indicator's Coping Scale was completed anonymously by over 160 managers. There was no difference in coping profiles of men and women, but different levels of management and educational status did influence preference for coping styles. More specifically, it was seen that at the most senior levels of management, delegation and maintaining stable relationships are considered the most useful forms of coping with stress. The more academically trained manager with a post graduation degree is more likely to implement such coping methods as effective time-management and planning head.

A comparative study on managerial stress in Hong Kong and Taiwan: (Oi-ling, Luo Lu and Cary L.Cooper, 1999) investigated occupational stress in managers in Hong Kong and Taiwan using the Occupational Stress Indicator-2 (OSI-2). The results showed that there were gender differences in managerial stress in Hong Kong: female managers scored higher in sources of stress and quitting intention; but had lower job satisfaction, worse mental and physical well-being than male managers. These differences could not be found in Taiwanese managers, yet Taiwanese female managers did report more stress related to "managerial role" than their male counterparts.

Kaila H.L. (2002) studied 120 managers in metropolitan Mumbai and found that 80 per cent of them experienced the most common workplace stresses and challenges such as: meeting deadlines, working in a competitive industry, managing finances, exhausting working hours, and rotation work in addition to handling regular tasks (such as sales, marketing, training, research and development, and accounts of core clients).

A Malaysian survey on occupational stress among managers (Taap, A.M; Fontaine, R; Chong Siong Choy, 2003) examined sources of stress among Malaysian managers working in multinational companies. A total of 440 managers participated in this survey. Data was collected through a questionnaire distributed to the managers in 34 multinational companies operating in Malaysia. It was found that workloads, working conditions and relationship at work were main concerns of the managers that lead to stress at the workplace. The results also indicated that certain demographic variables do influence the level of stress among managers.

An explorative analysis on managers dealing with work-family conflict was conducted by Kasper, K; Meyer, M and Schmidt, A. 2005). The sample was drawn largely according to the principles of theoretical sampling; family-work constellations provided the basis of selection. Thirty problem-focused interviews were content analyzed. Results showed three distinct prototypes of dealing with work-family-tension: career as subject of social fascination, family as a factual task, the tradition of two worlds, double burden and the pressure of tasks. One outstanding result was that if both partners were professionally active, the family was increasingly dominated by merely functional requirements.

Armstron-Stassen (2005) compared the reactions of executive-level and middle managers prior to a large-scale downsizing, during initial and final phases, and following the downsizing. Compared with executives, middle managers perceived greater job insecurity, were more likely to use escape coping, and reported lower job performance and higher levels of health symptoms. Over time, both executives and middle managers reported a decline in perceived threat of job loss but an increase in sense of powerlessness, a decrease in the use of control-oriented coping strategies, and reduced job performance in the initial phase of downsizing. Although less so, executive-level managers were also adversely affected by the downsizing, suggesting that this group should be included in stress management interventions.

Purpose of Study

Managers posses a job title that's difficult to define, with a myriad of responsibilities that vary from manager to manager. If there's any consistency in the position, it's that they're typically multitaskers and the "go to" people in the office. Being in a management role is a great privilege - but it can also be a great challenge. The average manager's day is quite chaotic and looks like planning, organizing, staffing, directing and controlling sequence found in the textbooks. As one writer puts it, the new role of a manager is more about making sense out of chaos rather than issuing control. Jokes apart, effective managers manage themselves and the people they work with so that both the organization and the people profit from their presence.

They know what needs to be done, when, and by whom. They understand ones subordinates, know that they are different from each other and therefore he / she tries to optimize the family backround, education, skills, hopes and abilities of everyone. The prime duty of a manager is to see that the subordinates are healthy physically and mentally. They need to build an atmostsphere of trust so that the subordinates can share their problems with their manager. At such times a manager takes the role of a guide and a coach, not a judge.

Indeed, looking at the above description, a job profile for the manager might state that he or she does just about everything and with enthusiasm. The manager is someone who praises employees if they are performing well even if things are not going well for him/her elsewhere. A manager may be annoyed about other things but he/she responds to the subordinates' situation, not according to what's going on elsewhere for him/her.

In the midst of all this we often forget that amongst all this enthusiasm, drive for success and efficiency lies a human being just like any of us who goes through personal problems, stress, frustration, insecurity, delusion, and a lot more. Therefore, this study is undertaken in order to know what are the different types of problems a manager encounters, how do these problems affect him/her and what are the kinds of strategies they use to cope with the problems.

Sample

The sample consisted of 275 male Managers and 140 Female Managers between 26 to 55 years of age in 81 organizations (including private and public sector, and MNCs) from different parts of India such as Mumbai, Bangalore, and Hyderabad, ranging from banks to IT, pharmaceutical companies to call centers. Data were collected from varied work backgrounds, different age groups and different levels of management: upper, middle and lower working in various departments through in-depth personal interviews and e-mails in a few cases with the help of a structured questionnaire using open-ended questions. The present paper is extracted from this large study.

Results and Discussion

The survey results have been presented under the following sections:

1. Problems faced by women managers
2. What are the ways in which the problems affect the women managers
3. The coping strategies used by women managers to overcome their problems
4. Problems faced by male managers

5. What are the ways in which the problems affect the male managers
6. The coping strategies used by male managers to overcome their problems
7. A comparison between the women and male managers with respect to the problems faced by them, ways in which the problems affect them and the coping strategies used by them to overcome the problem

1. Problems Faced by Women Managers

The first question asked to managers was: What do you think was the greatest problem you faced in the past twelve months? Please describe.

The managers responded:

1. The greatest problem I have faced during the last 12 months is Time Constraints to meet deadlines. At a managerial level, I am assigned with a lot of responsibilities and the expectation of the superiors from me is also high. Since I have a family to look after it is even more difficult to attend to my work responsibilities. Many a time it leads to an injustice on my part towards either the home responsibilities or work responsibilities.
2. During the recent times I faced the problem of relocation and shifting of archives because of the merger. Since we relocated from our old office to the current one, we had to physically shift more than 100 cartons of important documents and arrange it in the new location. Since there was very little time and less help I had to manually fill the boxes and arrange them in the new location.
3. The greatest problem I have faced is the time constraint to cope up with multiple activities. Since I am a family woman I have to manage both the home as well as office. My responsibilities in office are also tremendous and I have to do

multitasking but the time is so little that I sometime have difficulty in completing my assignments on time.

4. The greatest problem was related to my upgradation. Despite performing well year after year, I was not promoted to the higher cadre. I neglected a lot of areas of my life in the bid to get promoted but unfortunately I was never noticed when it came to promotion. Despite achieving all the goals on time, I saw that a higher number of males had risen to good posts and were the preferred candidates for promotion, resulting in humiliation.

5. During the recent times I have faced the problem of insecurity and uncertainty in my job. This is due to the recent merger that took place between the two pharmaceutical companies. The merger changed the whole structure of our organization. Many posts were declared unnecessary leading to ouster of many employees from the organization. I was constantly living under the fear of being asked to leave from the organization. With many new colleagues joining in there was uncertainty in what I was supposed to do and whether I was required by the organization or not.

6. The problem I suffered recently is altercation with my boss. He wasn't particularly happy with the way one of our core team members was performing. But instead of reprimanding him, my boss started to blame all the core team members. Since I am the project leader of the team I had a few altercations with my boss. I was aware of the performance deficiency of my teammate and the remaining team was compensating for that person. Instead of appreciating the good contacts and trust we were building with the customers/clients, he was getting upset about it. So in order to overcome this he started to mentally harass a few of us. He started to bad mouth about the team members against each other.

7. Due to bogus stamp papers distributed in the workplace and stolen National Savings Certificate issued through authorized vendors, my employees and I faced serious problems. We were accused of creating a fraud in the organization. The customers of my bank could not repay the amount within the stipulated period of time.
8. The greatest problem I faced in the past 12 months was un-cooperative attitude of my workers due to the interference by the internal union. Some of my workers were a part of the internal union. For silly reasons they used to be instigated by their core members to suspend work at the drop of a hat.
9. The greatest problem I faced was loss of communication with colleagues in my prior organization. The merger brought about a whole lot of changes. One of them being shifting the heads of all departments to the Head Office. This relocation led to loss of communication with my colleagues because a lot many of them were not at higher posts so they remained in the old office.
10. The greatest problem I face is working Night Shifts. Since I am in a call center, night shifts are inevitable.

The responses revealed that majority of the women managers faced the problem of meeting deadlines due to time constraints. Many women managers combine their full time paid work with parenthood or household responsibilities. They tend to remain the primary caretakers on the home turf inspite of being assigned with a job which requires long hours of physically and mentally demanding work. Other main problems included getting work done from subordinates, relocation problems as well as feelings of job insecurity and uncertainity. It was also found that women managers find internal politics between their colleagues/subordinates as well as altercations, lack of communication with colleagues/friends and clashes with their superiors extremely stressful. The "Glass ceiling effect" was also reported by one woman manager who said, "She felt that there was a bias against women who wanted to move up the laddcr." Lastly, night shifts too posed a major hindrance for a woman manager who reported "Nights shifts are inevitable in call centers, but I feel guilty for not spending time with my family". According to a woman manager "The glass-ceiling effect and not being able to handle ones subordinate are problems that are very gender specific. In many organizations, inspite of working so hard many women still face discrimination".

2. Ways in which the Problems affect the Women Managers

The second question asked to managers was: Please explain in which ways did problems faced by you (as described in section 1 above) affect you personally or professionally?

The managers responded:

(1) My problem has affected me positively and negatively. In a negative manner it brought about a lot of work pressure as I was falling short of time and I could not spend appropriate time on the assignments given to me by my superiors. Secondly, I found it difficult to maintain a balance between my home and work responsibilities also. But in a positive manner because of my constant efforts as well as correct planning I have become "immune to stress".

(2) Manually shifting achieves affected me personally and professionally. Personally, it caused physical discomfort and muscle pull due to manual shifting of archives. Professionally it affected because being a qualified professional I did not find it a pleasing task to do the work of shifting files and cartons by myself.

(3) The problem of coping with multiple activities in a limited time has affected me personally because I have to complete many assignments together I have to stay late in office which amounts to a lot of physical strain as well as neglect in my home responsibilities. I also tend to miss important events in my personal life. It affected me professionally as I find it difficult to finish projects on the given deadline because of the limited time available to me

thus causing stress. It also leads to crashed expectation from my superiors as they expect a lot out of me. Therefore I am constantly under pressure to prove myself in front of them.

(4) The problem affected me very badly personally. I started neglecting my personal life in the bargain to do well so that at least in the next appraisal I could get promoted. Similarly, I endured a lot of mental trauma and physical strain as I used to work till long hours in office and remain tensed about my promotion. Communication with my family decreased. My self-esteem took a huge blow as I started doubting myself. Professionally I did not let if affect my work, in fact I started working more so that I could do my best.

(5) Personally I felt lost. I felt stressed as I was constantly thinking about my work. For a short while I began to avoid pleasurable events. Professionally, I was very unclear as to where my job was leading me. For a while I was also contemplating to leave my current job and look for a new one. I was confused as my role in the organization was not defined.

(6) This affected my social as well as professional life. Since my manager could not find any faults with my work he started criticizing me for my behaviour. This made me lose interest in my work and as a result I was not able to give my 100% to my job. It also increased my stress level and I was not able to concentrate on my social life.

(7) Though there was no mistake on our part we as employees underwent serious problems. We were taken to court where enquiries were made. Professionally, it affected me because as a Manager I was under pressure to save the reputation of my organization. Secondly, it was my duty to support my subordinates and participate honestly in the enquiries made by legal authorities. Personally, I was under tremendous pressure and stress. I suffered from a mild heart attack because of the pressure I underwent. My family also underwent massive worries.

(8) The above problem affected me personally and professionally. Personally because I used to be under constant stress because I was unable to understand why

were the workers behaving so erratically and why they were not working. Professionally, it affected me because our daily production was affected because they were suspending work. Secondly, my superiors were under the impression that I was unable to handle the workers under my department.

(9) Loss of communication affected me personally by the way of setting in monotony and boredom. I was not in touch with many of my colleagues due to the merger so I was not aware of what was happening with them. In a way my social support system has broken down because with my job I rarely got the time to give them a call or keep in touch with them. In a professional way, less communication means I was not clearly aware of what was happening in different business areas because of the merger. Since I was new in the current organization and not well acquainted with my new colleague there was ambiguity on the professional front.

(10) Working night shifts affected me personally and professionally. Personally, it becomes very difficult to manage my home and work together because at home I have to attend to my 2 yrs old baby and responsibilities in office are equally pressurizing. I felt guilty since I do not get time to spend with my family. Night shifts disrupt the whole schedule due to which I encountered a lot of health problems such as fatigue, headaches and a lot of stress. There is often a spillover of tensions from home to work and work to home. Professionally, my health problems decreased my productivity at work. though I was unable to handle my team, my appraisal rating from my superiors took a blow.

Women Managers Reported that their problems affected Them Personally as well as Professionally

Women managers who faced the problems of meeting deadlines due to time constraints, working night shifts and insecurity and uncertainty regarding ones job reported that personally overwork was causing a strain on their families and relationships as it robbed them of time, energy and attention needed to maintain healthy relationships with partners and children. They also reported missing out on important social events such as weddings or outings with families. According to one female manager "I have to complete many assignments together so I have to stay late in office which amounts neglect in my home responsibilities". Feelings of insecurity and uncertainty regarding ones job created a lot of anxiousness and stress in women managers because they were constantly bombarded with thoughts about their future in the organization. They also remained tensed, as they were unclear regarding their job function in the organization. Many of these women also reported a spill over of tensions about ones work to home and from home to work. This spill over resulted in conflicts between them and their spouses. Their problems are further compounded because they also tended to suffer from health problems due to long working hours or disruptions in shift hours. They complained of headaches, back pain, fatigue, weakness and other physical ailments. Their problems also brought along professional hazards for them in the form of dissatisfaction of superiors regarding their quality of work and low productivity in their performance in the organization.

Women managers who were concerned of interpersonal conflicts at work felt de-motivated and stressed out seeing the conflicts between their colleagues. According to a woman manager "it's a challenge to remain neutral and listen to both sides of the story". As far clashes with bosses were concerned managers felt de-motivated to work especially when the clash was a result of misunderstandings or feelings of insecurity harbored by the superiors. A woman manager reported "Constant clash with my boss made me lose interest in my work and as a result I was not able to give my 100% to my job". Uncooperative subordinates posed a problem for women managers because the attitude of the subordinates gave an impression to their superiors that the manager was unable to handle the subordinates. This problem also affected the productivity of the organization as the subordinates used to suspend work. Women managers reported a lot of confusion as they were unable to understand the real reason behind their subordinates erratic behaviors. They also reported being under constant work pressure as they felt a need to prove themselves in front of their superiors.

Women managers who faced the problem of discrimination in the workplace reported "feeling humiliated" and left out because of unfair appraisals. Decrease in their self esteem was another apparent effect due to the discrimination in the workplace. They also reported of neglecting their family life in a bid to do well resulting in less communication with their family. Stress, feelings of anxiousness and work pressure were their chief problems.

Complaints of monotony, boredom and lack of social support were stated by women managers who reported the problem of communication. They also complained of feelings of ambiguity as they were unware of the ongoings in different bussiness areas due to restrictive communication. Health problems such as muscle pulls were the chief complaints of women managers who suffered from the problem of relocating from one office to another.

So far we saw the negative effects of problems faced by the women manager. But the results of this survey also revealed a welcome change. According to a few women managers, the stress, tension and anxiety caused to them because of work pressure and deadlines had made them "immune to stress" as a result of which they reported handling work pressure much better than before. This effect is called as eustress as it connotes a positive change in the behaviors with respect to handling of stressful situations.

Thus, it can be seen that the problems faced by women managers affected them personally and professionally and the effects of the problems they faced were positive as well as negative.

3. The Coping Strategies Used By Women Managers to Overcome Their Problems

The third question asked to managers was: Could you give a title or a heading to the problem faced by you and how did you overcome the problem? Please describe.

The managers responded:

1. The title of my problem is *Time Crisis*. I overcame the problem by planning and prioritizing the tasks

based on urgency, discussion with my colleagues and collectively resolving issues leading to lesser burden of work. Since, I cannot take long holidays I take short breaks of 20 minutes from my work and listen to soothing music. I also watch plays in the theatre with my family to keep me in good spirits.

2. The problem can be titled as *Relocation Trauma.* I overcame the first problem of shifting by doing what was required i.e. shifted all the cartons manually with colleagues help and took proper medications for the muscle pull.
3. The title of my problem is *Time constraints to meet deadlines.* I have managed to overcome my problem by prioritizing my work based on urgency of the tasks. I plan and organize my time so that multiple activities can lead to their goals. Sometimes I take a day or two off after hectic work schedules and go to resorts. When I return from there I feel recharged and like a new person altogether.
4. I can name my problem as *Glass Ceiling/ Competition.* I have not completely got over the problem as I am still struggling to understand why there was a bias towards the males and why hardworking deserving women like me were left out. But off late I have stopped thinking about it anymore, as it does not lead me anywhere. I constantly take support or spend time with my friends by going out for movies or dinner. I am doing my best but do not harbor the hopes of promotion any more. Volunteering or buying things for my nieces and nephews also helps me divert my attention from core problems
5. The title of my problem is *Job Insecurity Uncertainty.* I have tried to overcome my problem with the support of my colleagues at work and seniors. Secondly, I started spending more time with my child and being with her itself was extremely de-stressing as for some time I would forget about

my own problems. It's been nine months since the merger so I am now getting acquainted with the new structure and begun to understand my job responsibilities better. There have been constant talks with the Management and I been assured that my job is secure hence I have stopped worrying about that aspect also.

6. The problem could be titled as *Clash with Superior.* This problem can be solved if my boss handles this situation in a more mature and intelligent manner. Instead of harassing us to gain an upper hand he can make use of the good connections and trust that we have built up to get more business. Secondly, he can speak to our team member about his performance deficiency and guide him to perform better. In this way not only will our organization benefit but also all the team members will feel secured by having a good boss around us. I haven't been able to overcome the problem but whenever I feel stressed out I go with my friends for a movie or have a good meal somewhere and then I feel better for sometime.

7. *Honesty is the best policy* is the title of my problem. If people were honest and did not commit such a crime then we would not have undergone such stress. Being an honest person, I participated in all the enquiries made on the organization and me, as I had nothing to fear. I fully supported my subordinates and stood by them. I was constantly in discussion with the top management regarding this scam. We won the court case and the culprits were arrested. Thus, we all stuck together like one family at the time of crisis. During stressful times I would either read books so that I could divert my attention from problematic issues or involve myself in making painting and handicrafts to get away from the problems.

8. The title of my problem is *Unco-operative Subordinates. I* called the workers under my department in groups of 5 and advised them

about the losses incurred because of suspending the work for some silly reason. I asked them the reason for suspending work and 50% said that they didn't know the reason and they were doing it because their fellow workers were doing it, 40% said that they were doing it because their union head had asked them to do so. Whereas the remaining 10% were among the ones who were lazy and liked to drop work at the slightest reason. I looked into the matter with the help of our top management and as far as my workers were concerned I brought in an Industrial/Occupational Counselor who gave them appropriate counseling regarding the disadvantages of being instigated by others to suspend work and generally made them aware of their contribution towards their organization so that they could work sincerely in the future. As far as my personal coping was concerned spending time with my baby was itself quite a stress buster and secondly since I am religious by nature, I would say my prayers and keep full faith in God.

9. With regard to my problem, it can be titled as *Loss of Communication.* I haven't been able to overcome the second problem because I have completely lost touch with my old colleagues due to my hectic routine. I feel as if I have lost a backbone, as now I have no one to share my problems with. In the current organization there is still loss of communication as I am new here and not well acquainted with my new colleagues. So there is still ambiguity with respect to my job role also. In order to get away with tension I spend some time on my own "me time" so that I feel much better and relaxed.
10. The problem can be titled as *Shift Work Problem.* I have been able to over come the problem with the support of my family. When I am not around my husband takes care of our baby. Secondly, I spend some of my times with my friends who are

> not from call centers, which takes some load off. I am a member of an N.G.O named Aakansha and there is no other bigger pleasure than buying gifts for the needy children and seeing a smile on their face. I plan and organize my schedule during night shifts so that I can spend adequate time with my child too.

It was seen that only a few managers were not able to overcome their problems. But overall, the responses towards coping with problems was positive.

Different individuals have different styles of coping with their problems. It was seen that many women managers worked actively towards eliminating their problems by meditating, going on holidays, taking short breaks and having appropriate medications. Other common coping strategies reported by women managers included, discussing problems with colleagues and seeking advise from superiors, spending time with friends by going for movies and holidays, planning and organizing ones schedule.

Many women managers were spritually inclined as a result of which they prticipated in different kinds of religoius activities to relax their minds such as singing bhajans, visiting temples or saying prayers. According to a woman manager "whenever I face a problem I send a small prayer up there so that things go well with me". Other interesting ways of coping with problems included pampering oneself by going for shopping or having a good meal. Many women managers joined N.G.Os where they generously donated gifts. One such manager exclaimed "There is no other pleasure than seeing a smile on children's face. Its very destressing". Many of them indulged in giving gifts to relatives and friends in order to feel better. But the unanimous votes went in the favour of spending time with ones family especially ones children. According to one manager "Its extremely destressing to spend time with my child because for sometime I forget that I have a problem. Other indulged in activities like painting or watching plays in a theatre to keep their minds off work pressure.

4. Problems faced by Male Managers

The first question asked to male managers was: What do you think was the greatest problem you faced in the past twelve months? Please describe below.

The managers responded:

1. The problem I faced was Job insecurity in the form of an unwanted transfer. Because of the recent merger of two companies, I was transferred from my earlier posting to Mumbai. I was facing job insecurity because Mumbai was a new place for me, my colleagues were new therefore getting adjusted to the new environment was a little difficult in the first few months and my role in the new structure was also not articulated to m e properly and there was a constant fear of whether I was wanted by the organization or not.
2. "The major problem that I faced in the past one year was lack of clarity in my job function due to a merger in the organization. This led to the entry of many new co-workers in the organization. Also the merger has changed the entire structure of our organization. Many new posts as well as hierarchies have been created leading to division in job responsibilities. With regard to lack of clarity in my job function I was unsure of the deliverables I was supposed to give and also the resources available to meet my objectives. All these above aspects have led to a lot of confusion in terms of job responsibilities I am supposed to handle. Also since I am not aware of my job function clearly it has become difficult to prioritize my work in terms of urgency. There is lack of planning and therefore sometimes I spend a lot of time in the areas, which require least importance".
3. I think the major problem I faced during the past one year is hypertension. Due to constant stress and aging factor my blood pressure was fluctuating from 160/110 to 110/70. This stress

has been because of the loss of my younger brother a year ago. I lost him to lung cancer. Ever since I am taking the responsibility of his family (child and wife) right from paying the school fees to giving money for household affairs. So practically I am managing two families one mine and the second is my brothers. Even though I am doing it willingly it has taken a toll on my life as I am constantly under the pressure to provide both families a life of comfort.

4. The greatest problem I have faced is Attrition. It's a problem because a lot of people join call centers to make money or when they are doing a small time course. Hence they do not take their job seriously. We as team leaders have to work very hard to train them and bring them on the floor. But all these efforts are wasted because they leave very soon. Sometimes they leave at a time when we are just about to get acquainted with them and with their style of working. Again training new people and getting adjusted is very stressful.

5. The greatest problem I have faced is inability to communicate or lack of communication from my side. Since I am a creator / coordinator of various promotional activities for my organization, my job is dependent on my communication with my colleagues. They are dependent on my resources. Because of lack of communication, many events that were to happen could not materialize leading to stress and subsequent delusion.

6. The greatest problem I have faced is the process of Integration. Last year there was a merger between two companies. Firstly it took time for the new structure to establish. I took time to comprehend what was happening in the new structure as new people were joining, hierarchies were changing and job responsibilities were changing. There was a lack of clarity on what roles each person was supposed to play in the

new structure. The roles of different functions were not established.

7. The greatest problem I faced was during the 26th of July 2005. I had to forward an Inter-Office memo to my Head Office, which was to be tabled at the Board meeting of my organization on the 26th of July. But with the telephone lines being disrupted I could not e-mail the memo nor was I able to send the hardcopy with our office peon.

8. The greatest problem I have faced is the process of Integration. It was very difficult to adapt to the new systems, policies and structure after the merger because a lot of changes took place.

9. The problems I have faced in the recent times are Performance Evaluation of the Field Force (Sales People). I face problems because many sales executives are extremely resistant towards criticism even if it is going to do them good. Therefore they do not take the procedure seriously. Many of them agree to the evaluation but are not motivated to change, therefore year after year they are reprimanded for the same problems. I find it extremely stressful to convince each one of them to agree to the goal plan laid out for them and ask them to follow it accordingly. I also feel that quarterly and yearly evaluations do not hold any ground because when the evaluations are conveyed months after an event they become meaningless.

10. "The problem I have faced is that, although my performance has always been the best, all the regional managers only look into their interest i.e. our performance and sales numbers. Nobody looks into our aspirations (not even discuss the same); nobody identifies our strengths & weaknesses in our current job function or for taking up higher responsibilities. Hence we are pushed back, as nobody works on our development areas—related to career progression. Appraisals are done

hurriedly, and not in true spirits and appears only for giving scores and to impress us."

Many male managers reported job insecurity and uncertainty while reporting lack of clarity as the greatest problem they faced. These managers attributed the cause of the above problems to the recent merger that took place in the organization. Other main problems for male managers included communication problems, performance evaluation problems and attrition. Another interesting problem was the lack of mentorship by his superiors. It is an interesting problem because it shed light on the fact that even at a managerial level, mentorship is important. A manager too requires adequate feedback as well as guidance from his superiors without which a manager may feel de-motivated to work or may be unclear with respect to his performance in the organization. A male manager also reported, "I am suffering from hypertension, blood pressure and stress due to overload of work".

5. Ways in which the Problems affect the Male Managers

The second question asked to male managers was: Please explain in which ways did the problems that you faced affect you personally or professionally?

The managers responded:

1. Professionally the first problem affected me in the following way: Since my role in the new structure of the merged entity of two companies was not clear, there was a lot of confusion in the responsibilities I was supposed to handle. For months together I was battling with the lack of communication from the top management about my new profile. Also since it was a new structure there was a constant fear of being asked to leave as the merger had brought a lot of new people into the organization. All these aspects led to a lot of stress and mental confusion. I was constantly living in fear, which took a toll on my physical health as I became a bit weak. It personally affected me by coming in the way of me and my family in the form of lack of communication. I

did not want to burden my family with my problems because of which I started calling up less frequently. Therefore I was constantly worrying about their well-being.

2. The problem of lack of clarity of my job function has affected me both personally and professionally. It has led to frustration because I am not clear about my functions of my post. This lack of clarity doesn't allow me to prioritize and many important work areas are neglected. Personally I am neglecting my personal life as sometimes I am engrossed with thoughts about my workplace and feel tensed about my future.
3. The problem has firstly occurred due to stress and for my blood pressure. It has affected me personally and professionally, as I cannot take more stress and pressure as I used to before and due to stress, diet control and medications I am not able to concentrate on my personal and professional side. I am constantly under pressure so that my family is happy.
4. As far as attrition is concerned, I find it is very difficult to adjust to new people time and again. It is also frustrating because each time I have to put in the same efforts for each new candidate to train him to get him on the floor with an insecurity that he shall leave soon.
5. The lack of communication leads to a high level of stress, anxiety, frustration, confusion, high tempers and chaos professionally. Many superiors had expectation from me and since events couldmaterialize and many were not executed properly, the expectations crashed.
6. The problem of Integration affected me both ways. Professionally, the sales portfolio, which I handle, suffered for the first three months because I was not clearly told my role in handling sales function. My responsibilities were not clearly outlined. Personally, I had to put in a lot of efforts to achieve clarity about my role. Also there were new brands

of sales that were introduced so getting to each one of them took a lot of my time. A new Product Executive joined during this time, it took a while to adjust and get acquainted with the new colleague.

7. The problem led to tremendous pressure, as I did not know the outcome of the meeting since the memo was very important as it contained vital information intrinsic to the deliberations to take place at the Board Meeting.
8. It affected me professionally, but in a positive manner. During the integration new systems, policies, job roles and hierarchies were formulated. It takes a while to comprehend all this as one is acquainted to the old system. It is a challenge to accept changes. This merger allowed me to exploit my strengths and competencies to the full extent.
9. The problem of performance evaluation affects me professionally. Inspite of involving the sales executives in the performance evaluation discussion they do not seem to be motivated and all this indirectly affects my morale as I feel it is my job to develop them personally and professionally. At other times they feel that I have rated them according to a personal bias or favoritisms. All this causes a lot of stress and disturbs my mental peace.
10. Professionally I feel left back (as equivalent managers have climbed up the ladder), and hence demotivated as time is running out, and I was also aware that as time goes by, there would be further-newer challenges and competition to take up higher responsibilities. Currently it is becoming difficult to decide whether to continue with the same company in the same job function or join some other company with a higher job responsibility.

The responses revealed that the problems of male managers affected them personally as well as professionally.

Male managers, whose problems originated due to mergers in the organization, lack of clarity in job function and insecurity and uncertainty regarding their job reported that they felt anxiety and stress about what the future held for them. They also expressed concern over possible loss of their job, loss of effective and close team members, as well as the uncertainty about the new team members and supervisors to be employed. They expressed confusion over the new policies, structure and functions of the organization after the merger. They reported being disorganized because of unclear communication about their role in the new structure. For many, the mergers brought along unwanted transfer due to which relocation and getting adjusted to the new surrounding became an additional burden. Their personal life was also under an upheaval. Communication with their families reduced since they were constantly under tension. They also reported neglecting their personal life to a very large extent.

For managers who reported that their health was causing them the greatest problems reported that they couldn't take as much stress as they used to. They also felt that their health problem was causing them to be less productive on the professional as well as personal front.

Problems such as attrition, lack of communication and lack of mentorship affected the professional lives of the managers. Managers who complained of inefficient mentorship reported being confused with regard to their performance in the organization. Lack of guidance from their superiors was setting demotivation in them. Managers with communication problems reported their problem has caused dissatisfaction and anger amongst superiors with regard to their quality of work. They further stressed that this had brought about large amounts of anxiety, chaos and frustration in their professional lives since they couldn't get the work done due to restrictive communication on their part. As far as the effects of the problem of attrition were concerned, managers reported that they faced adjustment problems with their new teammates, as the team would change every now and then. They also reported being under lot of stress since they had to put in the same amount of hard work for each new candidate without the security that the candidate will remain in the organization for a long time.

The male mangers also felt positive effects because of their problems. A few male managers who reported the problem of insecurity regarding their job because of the recent merger reported that the merger allowed them to explore their competencies and strengths and gave them an opportunity to face challenges..

6. The Coping Strategies Used By Male Managers to Overcome their Problems

The third question asked to male managers was: Could you give a title or a heading to the problem below and how did you overcome the problem? Please describe.

The managers responded:

1. I am trying to overcome the first problem titled as *Job insecurity and role conflict* by constantly being in touch with the Top Management. Confirming and reconfirming my role and responsibilities in the new structure. I am also seeking advise from my senior colleagues in case of confusion and difficulties. Another thing I have learnt is to laugh at myself or crack jokes to lighten my mind. I try and keep a positive mindset.
2. I would title the problem as *Lack of Clarity.* I am trying to overcome the problem by confirming my job function with my superiors. I also do take advise from my colleagues and superiors in case of any problem I face. It's been a couple of months since the mergers so I am now beginning to get quite familiar with the whole structure and also with my new colleagues. Similarly, I have started meditating and exercising so that I remain calm and fresh throughout my working hours.
3. I would name the problem as *Health Problems.* "I believe that with the right health one can comfortably solve life's problems so I have tried to overcome the problem by yoga, meditation, diet and proper medication. Doing something for myself is also very relaxing. It can be spending some time with my friends, or it could be reading a book or just lounging around the house. It just helps me be myself and forget my problems"

4. The title of my problem is *Attrition.* As far as attrition is concerned I try to be patient with each new candidate and train him to my full capacity and do not bring the thoughts of him leaving the team. I have also learnt to accept that the problem of attrition is always going to be there in call centers. There is also a lot of support from my fellow co-workers as they too are at the same post so they understand the problem well. On my off days I exercise, go on short trips holidays with my family Meeting new people and living in a new atmosphere helps to take a load off my mind

5. The title given to my problem is *Communication Problem - Fear of Communication.* I have tried to overcome the problem by straightforward approach (trying to communicate to the point), honest appraisal of the situation and quiet thinking for understanding why things are going wrong and resolving them. I do not resort to pointing fingers at others for things that go wrong. I love sports so I try to divert my mind by watching sports on television or playing tennis with my friends.

6. The title of the problem could be *Chaos during Mergers.* The problem has been overcome over a period of time with the support of the Top management. I constantly clarified my responsibilities and role towards the sales portfolio from superiors. I also share my problems with my family as they understand and support me. It makes me feel a lot lighter Laughter is also incredible. It makes all the difference.

7. *Mail Interrupted* is the title of my problem. I could not overcome the problem, however fortunately the meeting was adjourned for the weekend as some Directors could not make it to the meeting and till that time I was able to forward the memo before the meeting was convened. At other times when I am stressed out I mediate whenever my mind wanders over problematic issues. Meditation helps a great deal in diverting my mind.

8. The title of the problem could be *"Mergers bring Challenges"*. Since I have mentioned that the merger brought about positive changes, it only readied me to face challenges in the face of adversities, which I did with the help of my colleagues and superiors. My positive mindset has also helped me to a great extent. I am spiritually inclined and positivity is something that spirituality enforces.
9. The title of my problem in *Performance Evaluation Problems.* I am trying to overcome this problem by spending some more time with my team in order to motivate them to do better. Constantly I am thinking of new ways to deliver my feedback so that my team can appreciate it by acting on the feedback. I have also stopped thinking about what they feel about my evaluations as I consider it a waste of time. I fully believe that one of my responsibilities is to develop my team and I will try to make thei performance reach to optimum levels. Secondly, I am in constant touch with the Top Management so that they can revise the performance appraisal/evaluation period to make it more often rather than quarterly or yearly. Personally, many things work for me to cope with my problems such as spending time with my son by playing cricket with him, going on holidays etc.
10. With regard to the problem, it can be titled *Lack of Mentorship,* I haven't overcome the problem as yet as there is no consensus about this problem between the superiors and subordinates but what I can suggest to them is that superiors must sit one to one with subordinates and regularly discuss with us (preferably quarterly) to rightly identify our strengths & weaknesses, and work & plan on our areas of development (if need be with the help of HR). This should not be like appraisals and there should be no scoring system in this. Only subjective discussions on developmental fronts must take place.

Different managers used different kinds of coping strategies in order to overcome the problems faced by them.

The most common coping strategies included yoga, meditation, diet, taking appropriate medications, discussing problems with colleagues or superiors. It was seen that many male managers also went on holidays with their family, socialized with friends to feel relaxed. Some of them also used strategies such as diverting their minds from the core problem to other issues to relax their mind. The managers who were spiritually inclined said that their spirituality helped them to keep a positive mind. Unique coping strategies were found among male managers which included cracking jokes or creating humor to lighten the tensions in their mind. According to one male manager "I have learnt to laugh at myself or crack jokes to lighten my mind. It makes all the difference". Another male manager reported "I love sports so I try to divert my mind by watching sports on television or playing tennis with my friends".

7. Comparison between the Women and Male Managers with respect to the problems faced by Them, Ways in which the Problems affect Them and the Coping Strategies used by them to overcome the Problems

This part of analysis will help us to track down the similarities as well as the difference between the male and female managers.

As far as the problems faced by the managers of both genders was concerned, it was found that majority of the managers faced the problems such as insecurity and uncertainity regarding their jobs, lack of clarity regarding their job functions or role responsibilities. They attributed the cause of the above problems to a recent merger that had taken place in the organization. Indeed, a merger represents a significant and a potentially emotional and stressful life event because they can change an individuals working life significantly but fail to provide an individual with any control over the event. As rightly pointed out by the managers, it affects both the personal and professional lives of the employess. Some common merger stressors include job insecurity, fears and concerns regarding job loss, role conflicts, compensation changes, and changes in power, status and prestige. Employees may experience life / career

/ job dissatisfaction, lowered self esteem, depression and anxiety. All these effects were reported by the managers. In many cases there is also a possibility of turnover because of uncertain future in the organization. According to one woman manager "I was contemplating to leave my job and look for a new one". Mergers which bring about feeligs of insecurity and uncertainty affect the personal lives of employees also leading to neglect and loss of communication with family members. According to one male manager "I am neglecting my personal life as sometimes I am engrossed with thoughts about my workplace and feel tensed about my future". For many mergers also bring additional problems in the form of unwanted transfers which only adds to their stress and anxiety. With time, of course, these managers overcame the initial anxiety of mergers by getting themselves more acquainted with the new structure of the organization. In a study, Hunsaker and Coombs (1988), have provided a nine-stage sequential model of employees' emotional reactions during a merger or acquisition, which describes what has come to be known as the 'merger syndrome':

- **Denial**. At first employees feel that the merger will not really happen or that it will not change their work or their organization.

- **Fear**. As plans for the merger begin to unfold, employees begin to fear the unknown and to imagine the worst. Workers become preoccupied with job loss as rumors of mass layoffs and terminations circulate throughout the company. This typically leads to substandard performance and a decline in productivity.

- **Anger**. Once employees feel that they have no control over the situation and that the merger is inevitable, they begin to express anger towards those responsible for the deal. They may feel that they have been sold out after providing the company with many years of quality service.

- **Sadness**. Employees begin to grieve the loss of their corporate identity; they focus on the differences in the way the two companies operate and are managed and adopt a 'we' versus 'they' mindset.

• **Acceptance**. After a sufficient mourning period has elapsed, employees begin to realize that resisting the situation would be futile, and they start to accept reality. This may imply behavioral compliance but not necessarily renewed organizational commitment.

• **Relief.** After much of the integration is completed, employees begin to feel more settled in the new organization and become more accustomed to working with employees from the other company. At this stage, they feel that things are actually better than they had expected.

• **Interest**. As people become more secure in their new positions, they begin to consider the benefits of the new organization. They perceive their situation as a challenge and try to prove their abilities and worth in the new company.

• **Liking**. Employees recognize new opportunities and begin to like their work.

• **Enjoyment.** Employees become committed to their new organization.

Amongst the other problems that were similar between female and male managers were communication problems but the nature of the problem and the way it affected both the genders was different. As far as the male manager was concerned, the problem arose because of fear or lack of communication from his side whereas for the female manager it was loss of communication between her and her colleagues due to relocation from one office to another. Here it can be seen that managers still grapple with the fear of communication. This problem is even graver at a managerial level because a manager has the responsibility of handling people who are primarily dependent on his resources and when the manager is unable to communicate and get the work done, it affects his productivity as well as of the entire team. As the male managers rightly pointed out, because of this problem, the superiors were dissatisfied with the manager's performance and resulted in lowered expectations from the manager. Another aspect, which the issue of communication has shed light on is the fact that the social support gained by communicating ones problems with ones colleagues goes a long way in serving like an antidote to stress and cutting down the stressors of employees. If there is lack of social support it can be extremely depressing because problems remain within the individual and result in frustration. This was experience of a woman manager, who lost touch with her colleagues. She reported" I feel as if I have lost a backbone as now I have no one to share my problems with". The loss of communication may pose a bigger problem for women because sharing or communicating about their problems to friends and colleagues is one of the prime ways in which they overcome their stress.

Another very interesting aspect that was found with respect to problems of managers was that many women managers reported that meeting deadlines to complete assignments due to time constraints, discrimination in the workplace (glass-ceiling effect) and handling uncooperative subordinates was a problem for them. But it was found that none of the male managers reported having the above problems.

Women managers encountering the problem of time constraints in completing assignments may be explained by the fact that women are the primary care takers at home inspite of the fact that their job in office requires a high degree of commitment having a continuous developmental character. Oakley (1974) estimated that mothers with young children work on an average of 77 hours per week at home. Adding a career to that workload can create extraordinary pressures on women to have fulfilling work and home lives.

In contrast males appear to have the expected privilege or option of not taking on household responsibilities, which allows them, time to concentrate solely on their career. Women who try to combine a career and a family is soon reminded that she is flaunting the socially accepted norms. She finds herself in a no win situation. The qualities associated with the role of a wife-mother (nurturance, emotionality, responsiveness to people rather than ideas) are seen to be incompatible with those qualities associated with success in the occupational field (independence, rationality and assertiveness). The result of trying to juggle a home and a career is that she is less competitive in one of the areas. The women managers rightly pointed out this fact. One of them commented "I have to complete many assignments so I have to stay late in office which amounts to neglect in my home responsibilities". Thus, in all one can say that it is a big challenge for women who are trying to build a home and a family life together. Kaila H.L. (2004) pointed out that for women to be working as manager is really a challenge to them in India.

As far as the problem of discrimination in the workplace was concerned, it can be clearly seen that inspite of comprising a large proportion of workforce today, women have, and continue to have diificulties achieving their goals in the corporate world. A woman (assistant) manager in this study reported "Despite performing well year after year, I was not promoted to the higher cadre, instead male candidates had risen to higher posts". Many false beliefs or stereotypes contribute to the failure to include women in the upper level management. Firstly, characteristics considered to be 'masculine' (being forceful, aggressive, objective or competitive) are generally regarded as traits required for upper level management, rather than so called feminine characteristics (such as being cooperative, flexible, subjective, emotional etc), which can be viewed as ineffective management traits.

Ragins et al (1998) reported that 96 percent of female executives surveyed felt that when they embraced a "male oriented" style where direct and aggressive behavior is the norm; they were frequently labeled as 'pushy' or 'bossy'. Secondly, men are viewed as the leaders in the organizations, whereas women are viewed as supportive followers. This perception of women as followers is further strengthened by a lack of strong female role models. In an environment where the number of women as followers in key executive positions is minimal, it is difficult to develop a mental model of women as leaders. This inhibits self-perception and evaluation of a women's potential to be a leader. Having spoken about the false perception about women garnered by many, sometimes there are other obstructions that hinder promotions. They may be the difficulties experienced by women in combining both management and family responsibilities, inability to work for long hours due to lack of back up or family support structures or at other time the difficulty to promote themselves in a male dominated environment.

The results of present study also revealed that women managers experienced a considerable amount of stress due to handling uncooperative subordinates and coping with internal politics in the workplace. A woman manager who reported that handling uncooperative subordinates was a problem said "I used to be extremely confused because I was unable to understand why were the workers behaving so erratically". Women managers may be experiencing difficulties in handling subordinates because, employees do not envision women as a leader since they are perceived as adorable or likeable superiors, whereas men may not encounter the problems of uncooperative subordinates.

Many women managers also found handling office politics stressful. Organizational politics definitely plague men and women alike but may be the female managers are more stressed. Davidson et al (1987) in a study, he found that women may find organizational politics more stressful than men because political exchanges and game playing in the work environment are better handled by men who are integrated in the organizational political networks.

But while reporting the above problems of women managers, there is some good news with respect to women in management, which strengthens the fact that women have managed to break the glass ceiling, and now command the same respect from co-workers, and stand on the same pedestal as that of the men. The good news is that recently many women have reached the top management tier, the invisible barrier not withstanding. In June 2001, Lalita.D.Gupte was made the head of ICICI's global operations. She also ranked 31 in the Fortunes Power Fifty, 2001. Other examples included Gayartri Parathasarthy, Head, development Integration Services, a SBU for IT services division at I-Flex Solutions; and Indra Nooyi, promoted as the CFO and President of PepsiCo. These changing trends in business offer many positive opportunities for both women and men. Instead of undervaluing the power of women, there needs to be a greater focus on the ways in which men and women may work together to bring different but complementary skills. Not underestimating the difficulties of challenging the status quo, nor how deeply entrenched "male" organizational norms and values may be, there are growing indications that the climate is now right for women managers to emerge from the organizational glasshouses within which they have been contained so that they may flourish and develop their considerable skills alongside their male colleagues. The onus is surely on men and women, traditionally the innovators and communicators within the organization, to work together to welcome the challenges that lie ahead.

Now we shall see the similarities and differences in the coping styles of male and female managers. As far as coping with problems was concerned some definite trends can be seen. Amongst both the genders of managers the most common stress-coping themes involved socialization and developing a network of social support through interactions. For example, spending time with family members and friends. This included talking to their spouse, being with friends (e.g., chatting or dining out with friends), and spending time with their children. One female manager noted, "whenever I feel stressed out I go with my friends for a movie or have a good meal somewhere and then I feel better for sometime. Whereas another female manager indicated "Being with my daughter itself was extremely de-stressing as for some time I would forget about my own problems". According to a male manager "I also share my problems with my family as they understand and support me. It makes me feel a lot more lighter". These findings are consistent with the theory of "leisure companionship or "leisure friendship" in the leisure research literature (Coleman & Iso-Ahola, 1993) which says that having a social network of friends and family to share ones problems or to spend ones time with friends helps to reduce stress levels.

Female and male managers shared that engaging in a positive alternative also helped them to reflect thinking about stress in their daily lives. In describing this notion, a female manager noted, "I read a lot of books whenever I am stressed out, it helps me to divert my attention from problematic issues.". Similarly, one male manager noted "I mediate whenever my mind wanders over problematic issues. Mediatation helps a great deal in diverting my mind. This theme is in line with the palliative coping (a form of taking time out from stressful everyday lives). Palliative coping is a self protective function of leisure which buffers against the negative impact of stress by being distracting or generating hope.

Both female and male managers viewed travel, taking holidays as a coping strategy to overcome problems. In speaking of this, one female manager noted, "I take a day or two off after hectic work schedules and go to resorts. When I return from there I feel recharged and like a new person altogether". According to a male manager "On my off days I go for short trips with my friends or family". Meeting new people and living in a new atmosphere helps to take a load off my mind". Female and male managers indicated that travel provided a variety of benefits such as being away from daily routines or stressors. These managers noted that taking holidays or short trips was important to feel rested, relaxed, get recharged and meet new people.

Another important theme common to male and female manager was the importance of taking time out for himself or herself, regardless of the type of activity. One male manager mentioned "Doing something for myself is very relaxing. It can be spending some time with my friends, or it could be reading a book or just lounging around the house. It just helps me be myself and forget my problems". Female managers who emphasized the importance of creating space for themselves exclaimed, "In order to get away with tension I spend some time on my own "me time" so that I feel much better and relaxed.

Another theme was the use of various problem focused coping strategies to directly tackle the root problem. It also included setting boundaries/compartmentalizing, organizing, setting priorities/planning. One women manager described, ""Sometimes at work stress, it takes just ten minutes to sit down, take a break, think about what you are doing, get a little plan, organize things a little better and that relieves stress a lot". Other problem solving strategies, which directly tacked the root problem included appointing a counselor to tackle uncooperative subordinates. "Getting to know ones products better by doing some research work on them" was mentioned by a male manager to describe the way he tackled the unfamiliarity about new products.

Male and female managers also mentioned being spiritually inclined as a result of which they participated in various religious programmes such as singing bhajans. Others mentioned worshipping God or saying a prayer during extremely stressful times. On this note, a woman manager said "I would say my prayers and keep full faith in God". Male managers who were religious by nature claimed that "spirituality enforces positivity". Mediatation, yoga were among the other things that male and female managers indulged in, in order to de-stress them. Thus, it was seen with the help of sprituality, managers learnt to turn negatives into positives, being optimistic and having hope about life.

So far we looked at the coping strategies which were common to both male and female managers.Now we will look at the coping strategies that were geneder specific. Some women managers consiously involved themselves in volunteering activities such as joining N.G.Os, which affirmed their altrustic values, and, through this process reduced their problems. Helping others or buying gifts for ones child or nieces, nephews was highly valued by women managers as it seemed to provide oppurtunities for altruistic need/value as a way of overcoming stress.

Another coping strategy common to women was participating in arts and cultural activities as a means of dealing with their problems. A woman manager claimed that she liked to go to the theatres to watch plays or make paintings whenever she was feeling low. Arts and culture may be used as a problem coping strategy because they provide individuals with an oppurtunity to escape from their routine, everyday world and transport them to a fantasy world. Artistically and culturally stimulating experiences could facilitate psychological enrichment and spiritual renewal.

As far as male managers were concerned again two gender specific coping strategies were indicated. Some male maangers enjoyed watching sports on television or participating in some sports activity such as table tennis. Onc rationale may be that sports, through the media, tend to reinforce cultural hegemony (Dworkin & wachs, 2000). It has been shown that sports broadcasted through the media implicitly define and construe men and masculinity as superior (Duncan & Messner,1998).

Another coping strategy common to men was indulging in humour and laughter. As one male manager explained "I have learnt to laugh at myself or crack jokes to lighten my mind", while another male manager described "Laughter is incredible. It makes all the difference". Laughter provides an oppurtunity to enhance positive mood/emotion and/or reduce negative mood/ emotion. As a result it is also one of the mechanisms to cope with problems one is facing.

This study was conducted in order to gauge at the problems, their effects and coping styles of male and female managers. The results of the study revealed that there was negligible difference between the problems of male and female managers. As far as the coping styles was concerned, both the genders had almost similar coping strategies with some difference. One reason for this negligible difference may be because as the time goes by, the stereotypes regarding the role for women and that for men are merging. Women are no longer taking up traditional occupations and therefore are exposed to the same kind of managerial envoirnment as that of the men. Therefore men and women face similar types of professional problems. Thus, it can be seen that managers, however tough and efficient they appear, they too suffer from various problems, undergo various effects of the problems and sometimes take time to recuperate from the problem. But they emerge with resilience whenever they are needed by their employees and the organization and try to set a good example for their subordinates and colleagues.

References

Armstrong-Stassen, Marjorie (2005). *Coping With Downsizing: A Comparison of Executive-Level and Middle Managers.* International Journal of Stress Management. 12(2), 117-141.

Coleman, D., & Iso-Ahola, S. E. (1993). *Leisure and health: The role of social support and self-determination.* Journal of Leisure Research. 25, 111-128.

Davidson, M.J. & Cooper, C.L. (1987). Female managers in Britain-a comparative review. Human Resource Management. 26, 217-242.

Duncan, M., & Messner, M. (1998). *The media image of sport and gender.* Media Sport, 1(1), 21-35.

Dworkin, S. L., & Wachs, F. L. (2000). *The morality/ manhood paradox: Masculinity, sport, and the media.* London: Kogan Page.

Hunsaker, Philip L., and Michael W. Coombs. (1988). Mergers and acquisitions: Managing the emotional issues. Personnel. 6 (1), 56-63.

Kaila H.L. (2002). *Stress Is A Way of Life for Mumbai Workers.* Psychology International, Vol. 13, No. 3, Fall 2002.

Kaila H.L. (2004). *Indian Women Managers: Their Stresses, Health and Coping Behaviour—A Survey in Mumbai.* Journal of Health Management, Vol. 6, No. 2, 147-161.

Kasper, K; Meyer, M. and Schmidt, A(2005). *Managers dealing with work-family-conflict:an explorative analysis.* Journal of Managerial Psychology. 20 (5),440-461.

Kirkcaldy, B.D. and Furnham, A.F. (1999). *Stress coping styles among German managers.* Journal of Workplace Learning. 11(1), 22-26.

Oakeley,A. (1974). *The sociology of housework.* New York: Pantheon.

Oi-ling,S; Luo,L and Cary, C.(1999). *Managerial Stress in Taiwan: a comparative study.*Journal of Managerial Psychology. 14 (1), 6-25.

Taap, A.M; Fontaine, R; Chong Siong Choy (2003). *Occupational Stress among managers: a Malaysian Survey.* Journal of Managerial Psychology. 18 (6), 622-628.

Index

B

C

D

T